Microsoft® Office 2010

ILLUSTRATED

Third Course

Microsoft® Office 2010
ILLUSTRATED

Third Course

Cram • Friedrichsen • Wermers

COURSE TECHNOLOGY
CENGAGE Learning

Australia • Brazil • Japan • Korea • Mexico • Singapore • Spain • United Kingdom • United States

MT

COURSE TECHNOLOGY
CENGAGE Learning™

Microsoft® Office 2010—Illustrated Third Course
Cram/Friedrichsen/Wermers

Vice President, Publisher: Nicole Jones Pinard

Executive Editor: Marjorie Hunt

Associate Acquisitions Editor: Amanda Lyons

Senior Product Manager: Christina Kling Garrett

Associate Product Manager: Kim Klasner

Editorial Assistant: Brandelynn Perry

Director of Marketing: Cheryl Costantini

Senior Marketing Manager: Ryan DeGrote

Marketing Coordinator: Kristen Panciocco

Developmental Editors: Barbara Clemens, Pamela
   Conrad, Lisa Ruffolo

Content Project Managers: Danielle Chouhan,
   Heather Hopkins, Melissa Panagos

Copy Editors: John Bosco and Mark Goodin

Proofreaders: Harold Johnson and Vicki Zimmer

Indexers: BIM Indexing and Proofreading Services

QA Manuscript Reviewers: John Bosco, John Frietas,
   Serge Palladino, Susan Pedicini, Jeff Schwartz,
   Danielle Shaw, Marianne Snow, Susan Whalen

Print Buyer: Fola Orekoya

Cover Designer: GEX Publishing Services

Cover Artist: Mark Hunt

Composition: GEX Publishing Services

For product information and technology assistance, contact us at
Cengage Learning Customer & Sales Support, 1-800-354-9706
For permission to use material from this text or product, submit all requests online at **www.cengage.com/permissions**
Further permissions questions can be emailed to
permissionrequest@cengage.com

Trademarks:

Some of the product names and company names used in this book have been used for identification purposes only and may be trademarks or registered trademarks of their respective manufacturers and sellers.

Microsoft and the Office logo are either registered trademarks or trademarks of Microsoft Corporation in the United States and/or other countries. Course Technology, Cengage Learning is an independent entity from Microsoft Corporation, and not affiliated with Microsoft in any manner.

Library of Congress Control Number: 2010936993

ISBN-13: 978-0-538-74815-5
ISBN-10: 0-538-74815-X

Course Technology
20 Channel Center Street
Boston, MA 02210
USA

Cengage Learning is a leading provider of customized learning solutions with office locations around the globe, including Singapore, the United Kingdom, Australia, Mexico, Brazil, and Japan. Locate your local office at:
international.cengage.com/region

Cengage Learning products are represented in Canada by Nelson Education, Ltd.

To learn more about Course Technology, visit **www.cengage.com/coursetechnology**

To learn more about Cengage Learning, visit **www.cengage.com**

Purchase any of our products at your local college store or at our preferred online store **www.cengagebrain.com**

Printed in the United States of America
1 2 3 4 5 6 7 8 9 19 18 17 16 15 14 13 12 11

3/17/14

Brief Contents

Contents

Excel 2010

Access 2010

Web Apps

Preface

Welcome to *Microsoft Office 2010—Illustrated Third Course*. This book provides continued coverage from *Microsoft Office 2010 Illustrated Second Course*, featuring advanced skills training on Word, Excel, and Access.
If this is your first experience with the Illustrated series, you'll see that this book has a unique design: each skill is presented on two facing pages, with steps on the left and screens on the right. The layout makes it easy to learn a skill without having to read a lot of text and flip pages to see an illustration.

This book is an ideal learning tool for a wide range of learners—the "rookies" will find the clean design easy to follow and focused with only essential information presented, and the "hotshots" will appreciate being able to move quickly through the lessons to find the information they need without reading a lot of text. The design also makes this a great reference after the course is over! See the illustration on the right to learn more about the pedagogical and design elements of a typical lesson.

About This Book

- **Complete Coverage.** This book covers advanced skills for using Word 2010, Excel 2010, and Access 2010. Use this book in a sequence with our Office First Course book (9780538747158) and Office Second Course book (9780538748131) to provide comprehensive training on Microsoft Office 2010.

- **Maps to SAM 2010.** This book is designed to work with SAM (Skills Assessment Manager) 2010. **SAM Assessment** contains performance-based, hands-on SAM exams for each unit of this book, and **SAM Training** provides hands-on training for skills covered in the book. (SAM sold separately.) See page xviii for more information on SAM.

Each two-page spread focuses on a single skill.

A case scenario motivates the the steps and puts learning in context.

Introduction briefly explains why the lesson skill is important.

UNIT
I
Word 2010

Building a Document in Outline View

You work in Outline view to organize the headings and subheadings that identify topics and subtopics in multipage documents. In Outline view, each heading is assigned a level from 1 to 9, with Level 1 being the highest level and Level 9 being the lowest level. In addition, you can assign the Body Text level to each paragraph of text that appears below a document heading. Each level is formatted with one of Word's predefined styles. For example, Level 1 is formatted with the Heading 1 style, and the Body Text level is formatted with the Normal style. You work in Outline view to develop the structure of the Tour Presentation Guidelines.

STEPS

1. **Start Word, click the View tab, then click the Outline button in the Document Views group**
   The document appears in Outline view. Notice that the Outlining tab is now active. Table I-1 describes the buttons on the Outlining tab.

2. **Type Tour Presentation**
   Figure I-1 shows the text in Outline view. By default, the text appears at the left margin and is designated as Level 1. By default, Level 1 text is formatted with the Heading 1 style. You will work more with styles in the next unit.

   TROUBLE
   If the headings do not appear blue and bold, click the Show Text Formatting check box in the Outline Tools group to select it.

3. **Press [Enter], click the Demote button ⟶ in the Outline Tools group to move to Level 2, then type Presentation Structure**
   The text is indented, designated as Level 2, and formatted with the Heading 2 style.

4. **Press [Enter], then click the Demote to Body Text button ⟶ in the Outline Tools group**

5. **Type the following text: Three activities relate to the organization and running of a QST Tour Presentation: gather personnel, advertise the event, and arrange the physical space. This manual covers each of these activities., then press [Enter]**
   The text is indented, designated as Body Text level, and formatted with the Normal style. Notice that both the Level 1 and Level 2 text are preceded by a plus symbol ⊕. This symbol indicates that the heading includes subtext, which could be another subheading or a paragraph of body text.

6. **Click the Promote to Heading 1 button ⟵ in the Outline Tools group**
   The insertion point returns to the left margin and the Level 1 position.

7. **Type Personnel, press [Enter], then save the document as WD I-Tour Presentation Outline to the drive and folder where you store your Data Files**
   When you create a long document, you often enter all the headings and subheadings first to establish the overall structure of your document.

   QUICK TIP
   You can press [Tab] to move from a higher level to a lower level, and you can press [Shift][Tab] to move from a lower level to a higher level.

8. **Use the Promote ⟵, Demote ⟶, and Promote to Heading 1 ⟵ buttons to complete the outline shown in Figure I-2**

9. **Place the insertion point after Tour Presentation at the top of the page, press [Enter], click ⟶, type Prepared by Your Name, save the document, submit it to your instructor, then close it**

Word 202   Developing Multipage Documents

Tips and troubleshooting advice, right where you need it—next to the step itself.

Assignments

The lessons use Quest Specialty Travel, a fictional adventure travel company, as the case study. The assignments on the light yellow pages at the end of each unit increase in difficulty. Assignments include:

- **Concepts Review** consist of multiple choice, matching, and screen identification questions.

- **Skills Reviews** are hands-on, step-by-step exercises that review the skills covered in each lesson in the unit.

- **Independent Challenges** are case projects requiring critical thinking and application of the unit skills. The Independent Challenges increase in difficulty, with the first one in each unit being the easiest. Independent Challenges 2 and 3 become increasingly open-ended, requiring more independent problem solving.

- **Real Life Independent Challenges** are practical exercises in which students create documents to help them with their every day lives.

- **Advanced Challenge Exercises** set within the Independent Challenges provide optional steps for more advanced students.

- **Visual Workshops** are practical, self-graded capstone projects that require independent problem solving.

Large screen shots keep students on track as they complete steps.

Brightly colored tabs indicate which section of the book you are in.

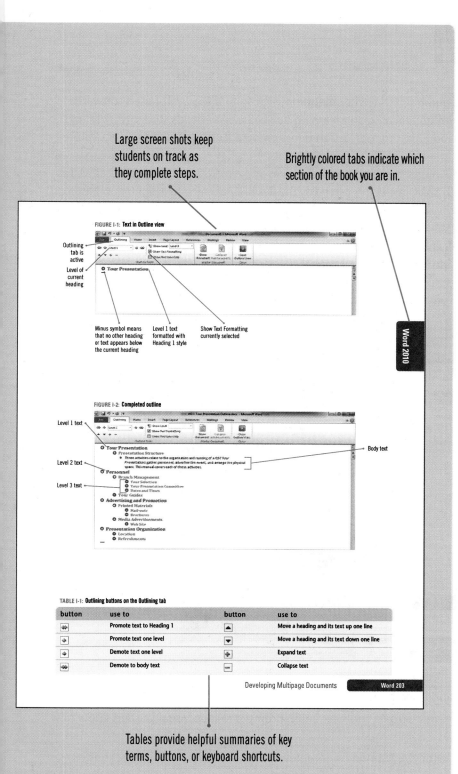

Tables provide helpful summaries of key terms, buttons, or keyboard shortcuts.

About SAM

SAM is the premier proficiency-based assessment and training environment for Microsoft Office. Web-based software along with an inviting user interface provide maximum teaching and learning flexibility. SAM builds students' skills and confidence with a variety of real-life simulations, and SAM Projects' assignments prepare students for today's workplace.

The SAM system includes Assessment, Training, and Projects, featuring page references and remediation for this book as well as Course Technology's Microsoft Office textbooks. With SAM, instructors can enjoy the flexibility of creating assignments based on content from their favorite Microsoft Office books or based on specific course objectives. Instructors appreciate the scheduling and reporting options that have made SAM the market-leading online testing and training software for over a decade. Over 2,000 performance-based questions and matching Training simulations, as well as tens of thousands of objective-based questions from many Course Technology texts, provide instructors with a variety of choices across multiple applications from the introductory level through the comprehensive level. The inclusion of hands-on Projects guarantee that student knowledge will skyrocket from the practice of solving real-world situations using Microsoft Office software. (SAM sold separately)

SAM Assessment
- Content for these hands-on, performance-based tasks includes Word, Excel, Access, PowerPoint, Internet Explorer, Outlook, and Windows. Includes tens of thousands of objective-based questions from many Course Technology texts.

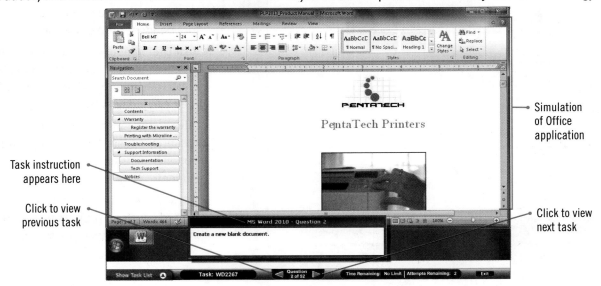

SAM Training
- Observe mode allows the student to watch and listen to a task as it is being completed.
- Practice mode allows the student to follow guided arrows and hear audio prompts to help visual learners know how to complete a task.
- Apply mode allows the student to prove what they've learned by completing a task using helpful instructions.

SAM Projects
- Live-in-the-application assignments in Word, Excel, Access and PowerPoint that help students be sure they know how to effectively communicate, solve a problem or make a decision.
- Students receive detailed feedback on their project within minutes.
- Additionally, teaches proper file management techniques.
- Unique anti-cheating detection feature is encrypted into the data files to ensure learners complete their own assignments. (*Note*: The exercises in this book are not available in SAM Projects at the time of this book's first printing.)

Other Illustrated Titles

 Office Introductory
0-538-74715-3

 Office Second Course
0-538-74813-3

 Office Third Course
0-538-74815-X

 Word Brief
0-538-74482-2

 Word Introductory
0-538-74821-4

 Word Complete
0-538-74714-5

 Excel Brief
0-538-74928-8

 Excel Introductory
0-538-74929-6

 Excel Complete
0-538-74713-7

 Access Brief
0-538-744827-3

 Access Introductory
0-538-74826-5

 Access Complete
0-538-74717-X

 PowerPoint Brief
0-538-74830-3

 PowerPoint Introductory
0-538-74716-1

Illustrated Video Companions: Learning Brought to Life

Experience the rich benefits of teaching and learning with videos using the Illustrated Video Companions, which are available for most of our Office 2010 titles. Students can watch the videos before or after class, or before or after they perform the steps, day or night! Using the videos as a learning tool can deepen the learning experience and help ensure skills are retained longer.

- Each four to five-minute video maps to a two-page lesson in the text and provides a visually dynamic overview of the key concepts and steps in that lesson.
- Videos provide instructional support for distance learning students, and students who need help outside of the classroom.
- Combined with the book, the video companion provides a rich learning experience to keep all students engaged and help them learn and retain skills.
- All videos contain closed captioning to meet accessibility standards.
- Video Companions are sold separately and are available on DVD-ROM for most Office 2010 Illustrated titles. Ask your sales rep for more information or search for a Video Companion on www.cengagebrain.com.

Instructor Resources

The Instructor Resources CD is Course Technology's way of putting the resources and information needed to teach and learn effectively into your hands. With an integrated array of teaching and learning tools that offer you and your students a broad range of technology-based instructional options, we believe this CD represents the highest quality and most cutting edge resources available to instructors today. The resources available with this book are:

- **Instructor's Manual**—Available as an electronic file, the Instructor's Manual includes detailed lecture topics with teaching tips for each unit.

- **Sample Syllabus**—Prepare and customize your course easily using this sample course outline.

- **PowerPoint Presentations**—Each unit has a corresponding PowerPoint presentation that you can use in lecture, distribute to your students, or customize to suit your course.

- **Figure Files**—The figures in the text are provided on the Instructor Resources CD to help you illustrate key topics or concepts. You can create traditional overhead transparencies by printing the figure files. Or you can create electronic slide shows by using the figures in a presentation program such as PowerPoint.

- **Solutions to Exercises**—Solutions to Exercises contains every file students are asked to create or modify in the lessons and end-of-unit material. Also provided in this section, there is a document outlining the solutions for the end-of-unit Concepts Review, Skills Review, and Independent Challenges. An Annotated Solution File and Grading Rubric accompany each file and can be used together for quick and easy grading.

- **Data Files for Students**—To complete most of the units in this book, your students will need Data Files. You can post the Data Files on a file server for students to copy. The Data Files are available on the Instructor Resources CD-ROM, the Review Pack, and can also be downloaded from cengagebrain.com. For more information on how to download the Data Files, see page xxiii.

Instruct students to use the Data Files List included on the Review Pack and the Instructor Resources CD. This list gives instructions on copying and organizing files.

- **ExamView**—ExamView is a powerful testing software package that allows you to create and administer printed, computer (LAN-based), and Internet exams. ExamView includes hundreds of questions that correspond to the topics covered in this text, enabling students to generate detailed study guides that include page references for further review. The computer-based and Internet testing components allow students to take exams at their computers, and also saves you time by grading each exam automatically.

Content for Online Learning.

Course Technology has partnered with the leading distance learning solution providers and class-management platforms today. To access this material, visit www.cengage.com/webtutor and search for your title. Instructor resources include the following: additional case projects, sample syllabi, PowerPoint presentations, and more. For additional information, please contact your sales representative. For students to access this material, they must have purchased a WebTutor PIN-code specific to this title and your campus platform. The resources for students might include (based on instructor preferences): topic reviews, review questions, practice tests, and more.

Acknowledgements

Instructor Advisory Board

We thank our Instructor Advisory Board who gave us their opinions and guided our decisions as we developed our Microsoft Office 2010 texts. They are as follows:

Terri Helfand, Chaffey Community College

Barbara Comfort, J. Sargeant Reynolds Community College

Brenda Nielsen, Mesa Community College

Sharon Cotman, Thomas Nelson Community College

Marian Meyer, Central New Mexico Community College

Audrey Styer, Morton College

Richard Alexander, Heald College

Xiaodong Qiao, Heald College

Student Advisory Board

We also thank our Student Advisory Board members, who shared their experiences using the book and offered suggestions to make it better: **Latasha Jefferson**, Thomas Nelson Community College, **Gary Williams**, Thomas Nelson Community College, **Stephanie Miller**, J. Sargeant Reynolds Community College, **Sarah Styer**, Morton Community College, **Missy Marino**, Chaffey College

Author Acknowledgements

Carol Cram A big thank you to my development editor Barbara Clemens for her patience, good humor, and insight! And, as always, everything I do is made possible by Gregg and Julia. They make everything worthwhile.

Lisa Friedrichsen The Access portion is dedicated to my students, and all who are using this book to teach and learn about Access. Thank you. Also, thank you to all of the professionals who helped me create this book.

Lynn Wermers Thanks to Barbara Clemens for her insightful contributions, invaluable feedback, great humor, and patience. Thanks also to Christina Kling Garrett for her encouragement and support in guiding and managing this project.

Read This Before You Begin

Frequently Asked Questions

What are Data Files?

A Data File is a partially completed Word document, Excel workbook, Access database, or another type of file that you use to complete the steps in the units and exercises to create the final document that you submit to your instructor. Each unit opener page lists the Data Files that you need for that unit. The Access data files are set to automatically compact when they are closed. This requires extra free space on the drive that stores your databases. We recommend that your storage device (flash drive, memory stick, hard drive) always have at least 30 MB of free space to handle these processes.

Where are the Data Files?

Your instructor will provide the Data Files to you or direct you to a location on a network drive from which you can download them. For information on how to download the Data Files from cengagebrain.com, see the next page. **Note:** The Access data files are set to automatically compact when they are closed. This requires extra free space on the drive that stores your databases. We recommend that your storage device (flash drive, memory stick, hard drive) always have at least 30 MB of free space to handle these processes.

What software was used to write and test this book?

This book was written and tested using a typical installation of Microsoft Office 2010 Professional Plus on a computer with a typical installation of Microsoft Windows 7 Ultimate.

The browser used for any Web-dependent steps is Internet Explorer 8.

Do I need to be connected to the Internet to complete the steps and exercises in this book?

Some of the exercises in this book require that your computer be connected to the Internet. If you are not connected to the Internet, see your instructor for information on how to complete the exercises.

What do I do if my screen is different from the figures shown in this book?

This book was written and tested on computers with monitors set at a resolution of 1024 × 768. If your screen shows more or less information than the figures in the book, your monitor is probably set at a higher or lower resolution. If you don't see something on your screen, you might have to scroll down or up to see the object identified in the figures.

The Ribbon—the blue area at the top of the screen—in Microsoft Office 2010 adapts to different resolutions. If your monitor is set at a lower resolution than 1024 × 768, you might not see all of the buttons shown in the figures. The groups of buttons will always appear, but the entire group might be condensed into a single button that you need to click to access the buttons described in the instructions.

COURSECASTS **Learning on the Go. Always Available...Always Relevant.**

Our fast-paced world is driven by technology. You know because you are an active participant—always on the go, always keeping up with technological trends, and always learning new ways to embrace technology to power your life. Let CourseCasts, hosted by Ken Baldauf of Florida State University, be your guide into weekly updates in this ever-changing space. These timely, relevant podcasts are produced weekly and are available for download at http://coursecasts.course.com or directly from iTunes (search by CourseCasts). CourseCasts are a perfect solution to getting students (and even instructors) to learn on the go!

CENGAGEbrain.com

Buy. Rent. Access.

Access Student Data Files and other study tools on **cengagebrain.com**.

For detailed instructions visit **www.cengage.com/ct/studentdownload**.

Store your Data Files on a USB drive for maximum efficiency in organizing and working with the files.

Macintosh users should use a program to expand WinZip or PKZip archives. Ask your instructor or lab coordinator for assistance.

Developing Multipage Documents

Word includes many features designed to help you develop and format multipage documents, such as reports and manuals. Multipage documents can include cross-references, a table of contents, and even an index. You often create multipage documents in Outline view, where you can use headings and subheadings to organize the content. Once the document content is organized under headings and subheadings, you can use the Navigation pane to navigate to specific content to make changes and add new content. Finally, you can divide a multipage document into sections so that you can apply different formatting, such as headers, footers, and page numbers, to each section. You work for Ron Dawson, the marketing manager at the head office of Quest Specialty Travel in San Diego. Ron has asked you to edit and format a set of guidelines to help QST branch managers sponsor tour presentations, tour information sessions, and travel clubs. You start by working in Outline view to revise the structure for the guidelines, and then you use several advanced Word features to format the document for publication.

OBJECTIVES

Build a document in Outline view

Work in Outline view

Navigate a document

Generate a table of contents

Mark entries for an index

Generate an index

Insert footers in multiple sections

Insert headers in multiple sections

Finalize a multipage document

Building a Document in Outline View

You work in Outline view to organize the headings and subheadings that identify topics and subtopics in multipage documents. In Outline view, each heading is assigned a level from 1 to 9, with Level 1 being the highest level and Level 9 being the lowest level. In addition, you can assign the Body Text level to each paragraph of text that appears below a document heading. Each level is formatted with one of Word's predefined styles. For example, Level 1 is formatted with the Heading 1 style, and the Body Text level is formatted with the Normal style.  You work in Outline view to develop the structure of the Tour Presentation Guidelines.

1. **Start Word, click the View tab, then click the Outline button in the Document Views group**
   The document appears in Outline view. Notice that the Outlining tab is now active. Table I-1 describes the buttons on the Outlining tab.

2. **Type Tour Presentation**
   Figure I-1 shows the text in Outline view. By default, the text appears at the left margin and is designated as Level 1. By default, Level 1 text is formatted with the Heading 1 style. You will work more with styles in the next unit.

3. **Press [Enter], click the Demote button ⮕ in the Outline Tools group to move to Level 2, then type Presentation Structure**
   The text is indented, designated as Level 2, and formatted with the Heading 2 style.

4. **Press [Enter], then click the Demote to Body Text button ⮞⮞ in the Outline Tools group**

5. **Type the following text: Three activities relate to the organization and running of a QST Tour Presentation: gather personnel, advertise the event, and arrange the physical space. This manual covers each of these activities., then press [Enter]**
   The text is indented, designated as Body Text level, and formatted with the Normal style. Notice that both the Level 1 and Level 2 text are preceded by a plus symbol ➕. This symbol indicates that the heading includes subtext, which could be another subheading or a paragraph of body text.

6. **Click the Promote to Heading 1 button ⬅⬅ in the Outline Tools group**
   The insertion point returns to the left margin and the Level 1 position.

7. **Type Personnel, press [Enter], then save the document as WD I-Tour Presentation Outline to the drive and folder where you store your Data Files**
   When you create a long document, you often enter all the headings and subheadings first to establish the overall structure of your document.

8. **Use the Promote ⬅, Demote ⮕, and Promote to Heading 1 ⬅⬅ buttons to complete the outline shown in Figure I-2**

9. **Place the insertion point after Tour Presentation at the top of the page, press [Enter], click ⮞⮞, type Prepared by Your Name, save the document, submit it to your instructor, then close it**

FIGURE I-1: Text in Outline view

Outlining tab is active

Level of current heading

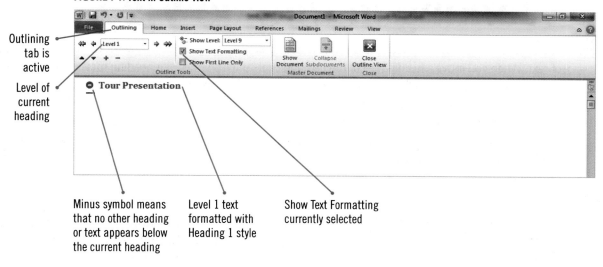

Minus symbol means that no other heading or text appears below the current heading

Level 1 text formatted with Heading 1 style

Show Text Formatting currently selected

FIGURE I-2: Completed outline

Level 1 text

Level 2 text

Level 3 text

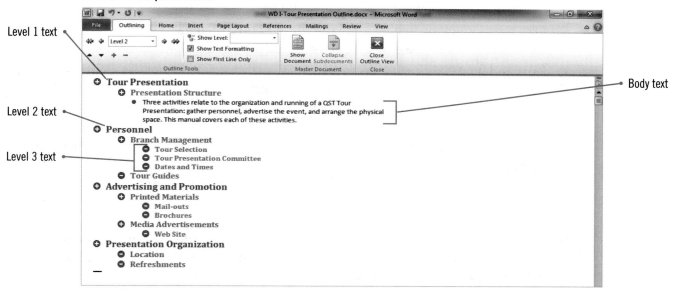

Body text

TABLE I-1: Outlining buttons on the Outlining tab

button	use to	button	use to
⇤	Promote text to Heading 1	▲	Move a heading and its text up one line
←	Promote text one level	▼	Move a heading and its text down one line
→	Demote text one level	＋	Expand text
⇥	Demote to body text	－	Collapse text

Working in Outline View

In Outline view, you can promote and demote headings and subheadings and move or delete whole blocks of text. When you move a heading, all of the text and subheadings under that heading move with the heading. You also can use the Collapse, Expand, and Show Level commands on the Outlining tab to view all or just some of the headings and subheadings. For example, you can choose to view just the headings assigned to Level 1 so that you can quickly evaluate the main topics of your document.  Ron has written a draft of the guidelines for running a tour presentation. He created the document in Outline view so each heading is formatted with a heading style based on its corresponding level. You work with his document to reorganize the structure of the document.

STEPS

QUICK TIP
You can access the Outlining tab from the View tab or from the Outline button on the status bar.

1. **Open the file WD I-1.docx from the drive and folder where you store your Data Files, save the document as WD I-Tour Presentation Guidelines, scroll through the document to get a sense of its content, then click the Outline button ▤ on the status bar**
   The document changes to Outline view, and the Outlining tab opens. The image at the end of the document is not visible in Outline view.

2. **Click the Show Level list arrow in the Outline Tools group, then click Level 1**
   Only the headings assigned to Level 1 appear. All the headings assigned to Level 1 are formatted with the Heading 1 style. Notice that the title of the document Tour Presentation Guidelines does not appear in Outline view because the title text is not formatted as Level 1.

3. **Click the plus outline symbol ⊕ to the left of Printed Materials**
   The heading and all its subtext (which is hidden because the topic is collapsed) are selected.

TROUBLE
You can use [Ctrl] to select multiple non-adjacent headings.

4. **Press and hold [Shift], click the heading Media Advertisements, release [Shift], then click the Demote button ⮕ in the Outline Tools group**
   You use [Shift] to select several adjacent headings at once. The selected headings are demoted one level to Level 2, as shown in Figure I-3.

5. **Press [Ctrl][A] to select all the headings, then click the Expand button ➕ in the Outline Tools group**
   The outline expands to show all the subheadings and body text associated with each of the selected headings along with the document title. You can also expand a single heading by selecting only that heading and then clicking the Expand button.

6. **Click the plus sign ⊕ next to Advertising and Promotion, click the Collapse button ➖ in the Outline Tools group two times to collapse all the subheadings and text associated with the heading, then double-click ⊕ next to Personnel to collapse it**
   You can double-click headings to expand or collapse them, or you can use the Expand or Collapse buttons.

QUICK TIP
You can also use your pointer to drag a heading up or down to a new location in the outline. A horizontal line appears as you drag to indicate the placement.

7. **Click the Move Up button ▲ in the Outline Tools group once, then double-click ⊕ next to Personnel**
   When you move a heading in Outline view, all subtext and text associated with the heading also move.

8. **Click the Show Level list arrow, select Level 3, double-click the plus sign ⊕ next to Printed Materials under the Advertising and Promotion heading, click ⊕ next to Counter Items, then press [Delete]**
   The Counter Items heading and its associated subtext are deleted from the document. The revised outline is shown in Figure I-4.

9. **Click the Show Level list arrow, click All Levels, click the View tab, click the Print Layout button in the Document Views group, then save the document**

Developing Multipage Documents

FIGURE I-3: **Completed outline**

Move Up button

Move Down button

Expand button

Collapse button

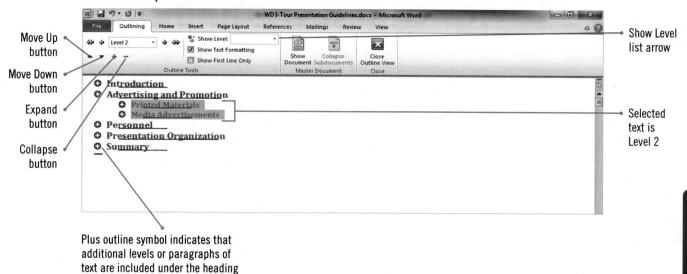

Show Level list arrow

Selected text is Level 2

Plus outline symbol indicates that additional levels or paragraphs of text are included under the heading

FIGURE I-4: **Revised outline**

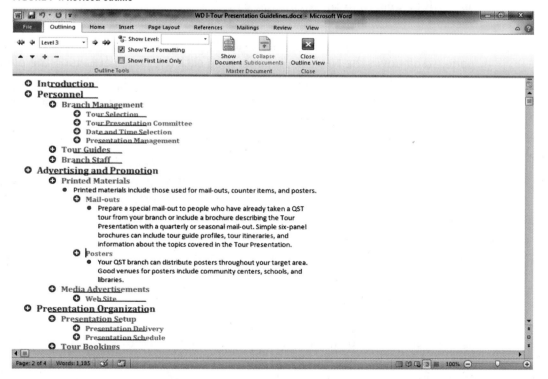

Navigating a Document

You develop the headings and subheadings that make up the structure of your document in Outline view and then work in Print Layout view to add more text. You can also open the Navigation pane in Print Layout view and make adjustments to the document structure. The **Navigation pane** opens along the left side of the document window and shows all the headings and subheadings in the document. You can click a heading in the Navigation pane to move directly to it, and you can drag and drop headings to change their order just like you do in Outline view. You can also view thumbnails in the Navigation pane. A **thumbnail** is a smaller version of a page. In addition to using the Navigation pane to navigate a document, you can create cross-references in your document. A **cross-reference** is text that electronically refers the reader to another part of the document, such as a numbered paragraph, a heading, or a figure.  You work in the Navigation pane to make further changes to the document and then add a cross-reference.

STEPS

1. **Press [Ctrl][Home], click the Navigation Pane check box in the Show group on the View tab to open the Navigation pane, then click Tour Guides in the Navigation pane**
   The Tour Guides subheading is selected in the Navigation pane, and the insertion point moves to the Tour Guides subheading in the document.

2. **Select that in the last sentence in the phrase You should select tour guides that ..., then type who**

3. **Click Branch Staff in the Navigation pane, then drag Branch Staff up so that it appears above Tour Guides, as shown in Figure I-5**
   The order of the headings in the Navigation pane and in the document change.

4. **Click the Browse the pages in your document button ⊞ at the top of the Navigation pane, scroll down the Navigation pane, then click the page containing the pie chart**

5. **Close the Navigation pane, click the pie chart to select it, click the References tab, click the Insert Caption button in the Captions group, click OK in the Caption dialog box, then scroll down to view the default caption text Figure 1**
   The caption **Figure 1** appears below the pie chart and is the element you want to cross-reference.

6. **Press [Ctrl][F] to open the Navigation pane with the Browse the results tab active, type not available in the Search Document text box, click after the period in the phrase not available. in the document (the phrase is highlighted in yellow), press [Spacebar] once, type the text See Figure 1 as the beginning of a new sentence, then press [Spacebar] once**

7. **Click Cross-reference in the Captions group, click the Reference type list arrow, scroll to and select Figure, click the Insert reference to list arrow, then select Above/below as shown in Figure I-6**

8. **Click Insert, then click Close**
   The word **below** is inserted because the figure appears below the cross-reference.

9. **Type a period after below, move the pointer over below to show the Click message, press and hold [Ctrl] to show ⊕, click below to move directly to the pie chart caption, scroll up to see the figure, close the Navigation pane, then save the document**

FIGURE I-5: **Changing the order of a subheading in the Navigation pane**

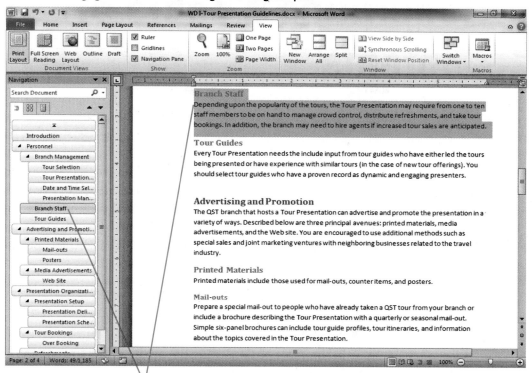

Branch Staff is moved above
Tour Guides in the Navigation
pane and in the document

FIGURE I-6: **Cross-reference dialog box**

Reference type
list arrow

Figure 1
selected

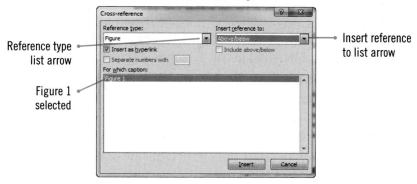

Insert reference
to list arrow

Using bookmarks

A **bookmark** identifies a location or a selection of text in a document. To create a bookmark, you first move the insertion point to the location in the text that you want to reference. This location can be a word, the beginning of a paragraph, or a heading. Click the Insert tab, then click Bookmark in the Links group to open the Bookmark dialog box. In this dialog box, you type a name (which cannot contain spaces) for the bookmark, then click Add. To find a bookmark, press [Ctrl][G] to open the Find and Replace dialog box with the Go To tab active, click Bookmark in the Go to what list box, click the Enter bookmark name list arrow to see the list of bookmarks in the document, select the bookmark you require, click Go To, then close the Find and Replace dialog box.

Generating a Table of Contents

Readers refer to a table of contents to obtain an overview of the topics and subtopics covered in a multipage document. When you generate a table of contents, Word searches for headings, sorts them by heading levels, and then displays the completed table of contents in the document. By default, a table of contents lists the top three heading levels in a document. Consequently, before you create a table of contents, you must ensure that all headings and subheadings are formatted with the heading styles such as Heading 1, Heading 2, and Heading 3. When you work in Outline view, the correct heading styles are assigned automatically to text based on the outline level of the text. For example, the Heading 1 style is applied to Level 1 text, the Heading 2 style to Level 2 text, and so on. You are pleased with the content of the document and are now ready to create a new page that includes a table of contents. You use commands on the References tab to generate a table of contents.

STEPS

1. **Click the Home tab, press [Ctrl][Home], press [Ctrl][Enter], press the [↑] once, type Table of Contents, select the title, then center it and enhance it with bold and the 18 pt font size**

2. **Click after Contents in the Table of Contents title, press [Enter] once, then click the Clear Formatting button ⧉ in the Font group**
    The insertion point is positioned at the left margin where the table of contents will begin.

3. **Click the References tab, then click the Table of Contents button in the Table of Contents group**
    A gallery of predefined, built-in styles for a table of contents opens.

4. **Click Insert Table of Contents to open the Table of Contents dialog box, click the Formats list arrow, click Formal, compare the dialog box to Figure I-7, then click OK**
    A table of contents that includes all the Level 1, 2, and 3 headings appears.

5. **Click the View tab, click the Navigation Pane check box to open the Navigation pane, click the Browse the headings in your document button ▤ at the top of the Navigation pane, right-click the Presentation Management subheading below the Branch Management subheading in the Personnel section, then click Delete**
    The Presentation Management subheading and its related subtext are deleted from the document.

6. **Close the Navigation pane, press [Ctrl][Home], then note that the Presentation Management subheading still appears in the table of contents below the Branch Management subheading in the Personnel section**

7. **Click Introduction to select the entire table of contents at once**
    When the table of contents is selected, you can update it to show changes.

8. **Right-click the table of contents, click Update Field, click Table in the Table of Contents title to deselect the table of contents, then scroll down so you can see the entire table of contents in the document window**
    The Presentation Management subheading is removed, and the completed table of contents appears, as shown in Figure I-8. Each entry in the table of contents is a hyperlink to the entry's corresponding heading in the document.

9. **Move the pointer over the heading Media Advertisements, press [Ctrl], click Media Advertisements, then save the document**
    The insertion point moves to the Media Advertisements heading in the document.

FIGURE I-7: Table of Contents dialog box

Preview of Formal format

Formats list arrow

Formal format selected

Number of heading levels that will be included in the table of contents

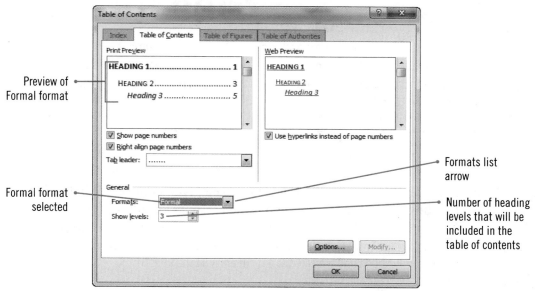

FIGURE I-8: Updated table of contents

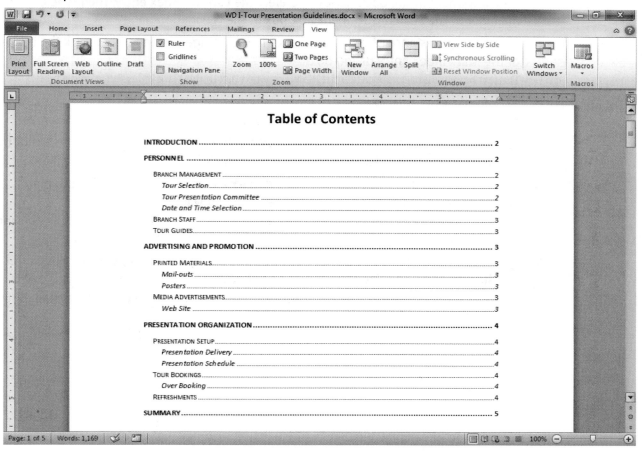

Marking Entries for an Index

An **index** lists many of the terms and topics included in a document, along with the pages on which they appear. An index can include main entries, subentries, and cross-references. ▓▓ To help readers quickly find main concepts in the document, you decide to generate an index. You get started by marking the terms that you want to include as main entries in the index.

STEPS

QUICK TIP

If the dialog box blocks text that you want to see, use the dialog box title bar to drag the dialog box to a new location.

1. **Press [Ctrl][Home], press [Ctrl], then click Introduction in the table of contents**

   The insertion point moves to the Introduction heading in the document.

2. **Press [Ctrl][F] to open the Navigation pane, type branch staff in the Search Document text box, select branch staff under the Personnel heading in the document, click the References tab, then click the Mark Entry button in the Index group**

   The Mark Index Entry dialog box opens, as shown in Figure I-9. By default, the selected text is entered in the Main entry text box and is treated as a main entry in the index.

QUICK TIP

Because you clicked Mark All, all instances of the term branch staff are marked as index entries.

3. **Click Mark All**

   Notice the term branch staff is marked with the XE field code. **XE** stands for **Index Entry**. When you mark an entry for the index, the paragraph marks are turned on automatically so that you can see hidden codes such as paragraph marks, field codes, page breaks, and section breaks. These codes do not appear in the printed document. The Mark Index Entry dialog box remains open so that you can continue to mark text for inclusion in the index.

4. **Click anywhere in the document to deselect the current index entry, then type branch manager in the Search Document text box in the Navigation pane**

5. **Click the first instance of branch manager in the Navigation pane, then click the title bar of the Mark Index Entry dialog box**

   The text branch manager appears in the Main entry text box in the Mark Index Entry dialog box.

6. **Click Mark All**

   All instances of branch manager in the document are marked for inclusion in the index.

7. **Click anywhere in the document, type theme in the Search Document text box, click the title bar of the Mark Index Entry dialog box, then click Mark All**

TROUBLE

Make sure you click in the document to deselect the currently selected text before you enter another search term.

8. **Follow the procedure in Step 7 to find and mark all instances of the following main entries: tour guides, venues, target market, and Ron Dawson**

   Notice that even though avenues is included in the search results for venues, only the one instance of venues is marked as an index entry.

9. **Close the Mark Index Entry dialog box, close the Navigation pane, then scroll up until you see the document title (Tour Presentation Guidelines) at the top of the page**

   You see three entries marked for the index, as shown in Figure I-10. The other entries you marked are further down the document.

FIGURE I-9: **Mark Index Entry dialog box**

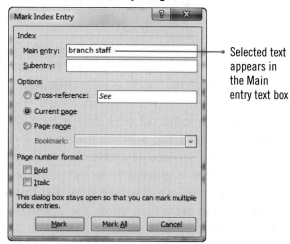

Selected text appears in the Main entry text box

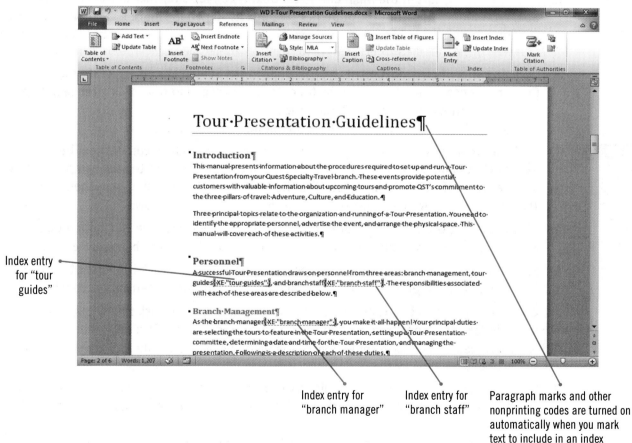

Index entry for "tour guides"

Index entry for "branch manager"

Index entry for "branch staff"

Paragraph marks and other nonprinting codes are turned on automatically when you mark text to include in an index

Word 2010

Generating an Index

In addition to main entries, an index often includes subentries and cross-references. A **subentry** is text included under a main entry. For example, you could mark the text "shopping cart" as a subentry to appear under the main entry "Web site." A **cross-reference** in an index refers the reader to another entry in the index. For example, a cross-reference in an index might read, "lecture. *See* events." Readers then know to refer to the "events" entry to find out more about lectures. Once you have marked all the index entries, you select a design for the index, and then you generate it. If you make changes to the document, you can update the index just like you update a table of contents when you add or remove content. ▓▓▓▓▓ You mark one subentry and one cross-reference for the index, create a new last page in the document, and then generate the index. You add one new main entry, and then update the index to reflect this change. The completed index contains all the main entries, the subentry, and the cross-reference you marked in this lesson and the previous lesson.

STEPS

1. **Press [Ctrl][F] to open the Navigation pane, type** shopping cart **in the Search Document text box, then click** Mark Entry **in the Index group on the References tab**
   The Mark Index Entry dialog box opens. The search term "shopping cart" is already entered into the Mark Index Entry dialog box.

2. **Select** shopping cart **in the Main entry text box, type** Web site, **click in the Subentry text box, type** shopping cart **in the Subentry text box as shown in Figure I-11, then click** Mark
   The first and only instance of the text "shopping cart" is marked as a subentry to appear following the Main entry, Web site. You use the Mark option when you want to mark just one occurrence of an item in a document.

3. **Click anywhere in the document, type** laptops **in the Search Document text box, click the** Cross-reference option button **in the Mark Index Entry dialog box, click after** See, **type** bookings **as shown in Figure I-12, then click** Mark
   You need to also mark "bookings" so the Index lists the page number for bookings.

QUICK TIP
You can also click the term bookings in the phrase bookings on the spot in the Navigation pane to go directly to the term bookings in the document.

4. **Click anywhere in the document, type** bookings **in the Search Document text box, double-click** bookings **in the phrase** bookings on the spot **(end of the paragraph containing the cross-reference to laptops), click the** Mark Index Entry dialog box, **then click** Mark
   The term laptops is now cross-referenced to the term bookings in the same paragraph.

5. **Click** Close **to close the Mark Index Entry dialog box, then close the Navigation pane**
   Now that you have marked entries for the index, you can generate the index at the end of the document.

6. **Press [Ctrl][End], press [Ctrl][Enter], type** Index, **press [Enter], click the Home tab, select** Index **and apply 18 pt, bold, and center alignment formatting, then click below Index**

7. **Click the** References tab, **click** Insert Index **in the Index group, click the** Formats list arrow **in the Index dialog box, scroll down the list, click** Formal, **then click** OK
   Word has collected all the index entries, sorted them alphabetically, included the appropriate page numbers, and removed duplicate entries.

8. **Press [Ctrl][F], type** refreshments, **click the second instance of refreshments in the search results in the Navigation pane, click the** Mark Entry **button in the Index Group, then click** Mark All
   Each instance of refreshments from the currently selected text to the end of the document is now included in the index. The refreshments entry that appears in the table of contents is not included because it appears before the entry you selected.

9. **Close the dialog box and Navigation pane, scroll to the end of the document, right-click the index, click** Update Field, **click** Index **to deselect the index, then save the document**
   The updated index appears as shown in Figure I-13.

FIGURE I-11: Subentry in the Mark Index Entry dialog box

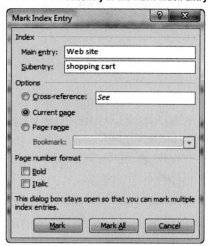

FIGURE I-12: Cross-reference in the Mark Index Entry dialog box

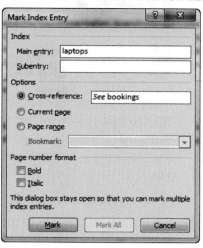

FIGURE I-13: Completed index

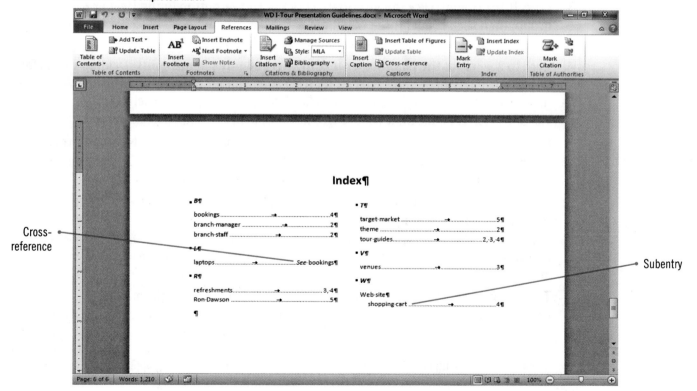

Cross-reference

Subentry

Inserting Footers in Multiple Sections

Multipage documents often consist of two or more sections that you can format differently. For example, you can include different text in the footer for each section, and you can change how page numbers are formatted from section to section. ▓▓▓▓▓ You want to divide the report into two sections, and then format the headers and footers differently in each section. The diagram in Figure I-14 explains how the footer should appear on each of the first three pages in the document.

STEPS

QUICK TIP
You can also turn paragraph marks on or off by clicking the Show/Hide button ¶ in the Paragraph group on the Home tab.

1. **Press [Ctrl][Home] to move to the top of the document, scroll to the page break, click to the left of it, click the Page Layout tab, then click Breaks in the Page Setup group**

   You can see the page break because the paragraph marks were turned on when you marked entries for inclusion in the index. When you work with sections, you should leave paragraph marks showing so you can see the codes that Word inserts for section breaks and page breaks.

2. **Click Next Page under Section Breaks, press [Delete] to remove the original page break, then press [Delete] to remove the extra blank line**

   The document is divided into two sections. Section 1 contains the Table of Contents, and section 2 contains the rest of the document.

3. **Press [Ctrl][Home], click the Insert tab, click the Footer button in the Header & Footer group, then click Blank (Three Columns)**

   The footer area opens showing the Blank (Three Columns) format.

4. **Click to the left of the placeholder text to select all three items, press [Delete], press [Tab] once, type Page, press [Spacebar], click the Page Number button in the Header & Footer group, point to Current Position, then click Plain Number (the top selection)**

   The current footer for the entire document contains the word Page and a page number.

5. **Click the Page Number button, click Format Page Numbers, click the Number format list arrow, click i, ii, iii, then click OK**

   The page number in the footer area of the table of contents page is formatted as i.

6. **Click Next in the Navigation group, then click the Link to Previous button in the Navigation group to deselect it**

   You deselect the Link to Previous button to make sure that the text you type into the footer appears only in the footer in section 2. You must deselect the Link to Previous button each time you want the header or footer in a section to be unique.

7. **Type your name, then press [Tab] once to move Page 2 to the right margin**

   By default, Word continues numbering the pages in section 2 based on the page numbers in section 1. The footer in section 2 starts with Page 2 because section 1 contains just one page. You want section 2 to start with Page 1 because the first page in section 2 is the first page of the report. Note also that the i, ii, iii format is not applied to the page number in section 2. Changes to page number formatting apply only to the section in which the change is made originally (in this case, section 1).

8. **Click the Page Number button, click Format Page Numbers, click the Start at option button, verify that 1 appears, click OK, then compare the footer to Figure I-15**

9. **Click the Close Header and Footer button, then save the document**

Developing Multipage Documents

FIGURE I-14: Diagram of section formatting for footers

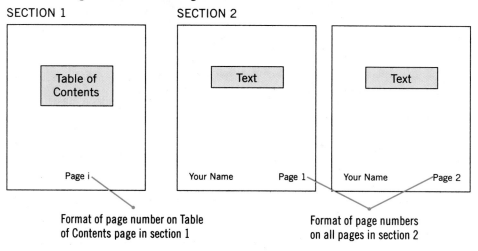

SECTION 1

Table of Contents

Page i

Format of page number on Table of Contents page in section 1

SECTION 2

Text

Your Name   Page 1

Text

Your Name   Page 2

Format of page numbers on all pages in section 2

FIGURE I-15: Completed footer

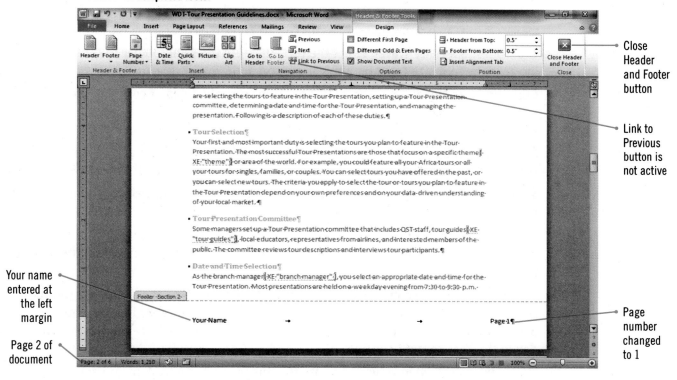

Close Header and Footer button

Link to Previous button is not active

Your name entered at the left margin

Page 2 of document

Page number changed to 1

Using text flow options

You adjust text flow options to control how text in a multipage document breaks across pages. To change text flow options, you use the Paragraph dialog box. To open the Paragraph dialog box, click the dialog box launcher in the Paragraph group on the Home tab, and then select the Line and Page Breaks tab. In the Pagination section, you can choose to select or deselect four text flow options. For example, you select the Widow/Orphan control option to prevent the last line of a paragraph from printing at the top of a page (a widow) or the first line of a paragraph from printing at the bottom of a page (an orphan). By default, Widow/Orphan is active. You can also select the Keep lines together check box to keep a paragraph from breaking across two pages.

Inserting Headers in Multiple Sections

When you divide your document into sections, you can modify the header to be different in each section. As you learned in the previous lesson, you must deselect the Link to Previous button when you want the text of a header (or footer) in a new section to be different from the header (or footer) in the previous section.  The diagram in Figure I-16 shows that text will appear in the header on every page in section 2. You do not want any text to appear in the header on the table of contents page (section 1). You modify the headers in the two sections of the document and then add a cover page.

1. **Press [Ctrl][Home] to move to the top of the document, then double-click in the blank area above Table of Contents**

   The header area opens. The Header -Section 1- identifier appears along with the Header & Footer Tools Design tab. Refer to Figure I-16. Notice that you do not want text in the header in section 1.

2. **Click Next in the Navigation group, then click the Link to Previous button to deselect it**

   The identifier Header -Section 2- appears. You want text to appear on all the pages of section 2. You deselect the Link to Previous button so that the text you type appears only on this page and on subsequent pages.

3. **Type Quest Specialty Travel, select the text, then use the Mini toolbar to center it, increase the font size to 14 pt, apply bold, and apply italic**

4. **Click the Close Header and Footer button, right-click the table of contents, click Update Field, then click OK**

   The page numbers in the table of contents are updated.

5. **Scroll through the document to verify that the header text does not appear on the table of contents page and does appear on the first and subsequent pages of the document text**

6. **Scroll to the Index page, right-click the index, then click Update Field to update the page numbers**

   The page numbers in the index are updated.

7. **Press [Ctrl][Home], click the Insert tab, click Cover Page in the Pages group, then select the Cubicles style**

8. **Scroll to the Subtitle content control (it includes the text Type the document subtitle), click the content control, click the content control handle to select it (the handle turns dark gray and the text in the control turns dark blue), press [Delete], then scroll to and delete the Year content control**

9. **Enter text, as shown in Figure I-17, into the remaining three content controls**

   Some content controls contain placeholder text. If a content control contains placeholder text that you do not want, select the placeholder text and then type the replacement text.

10. **Save the document**

FIGURE I-16: **Diagram of section formatting for headers**

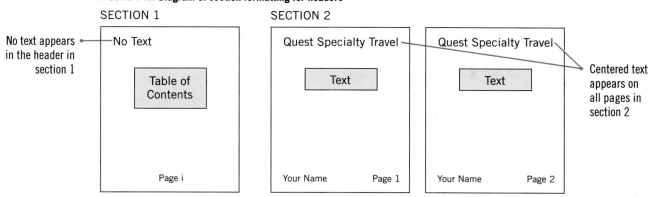

No text appears in the header in section 1

SECTION 1

No Text

Table of Contents

Page i

SECTION 2

Quest Specialty Travel

Text

Your Name   Page 1

Quest Specialty Travel

Text

Your Name   Page 2

Centered text appears on all pages in section 2

FIGURE I-17: **Completed cover page**

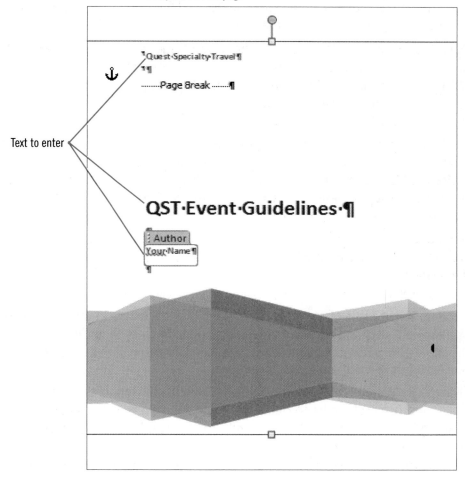

Text to enter

Quest·Specialty·Travel¶
¶
·········Page Break·········¶

QST·Event·Guidelines·¶

Author
Your·Name¶
¶

Understanding headers, footers, and sections

One reason you divide a document into sections is so that you can modify the page layout and the headers and footers differently in different sections. You can even modify the header and footer within a section because each section has two parts. The first part of a section is the first page, and the second part of the section is the remaining subsequent pages. This section structure allows you to omit the header on the first page of section 2, and then include the header on all subsequent pages in section 2. To do this, you place the insertion point in the section you want to modify, then you click the Different First Page check box in the Options group to specify that you wish to include a different header (or no header at all) on the first page of a section. In addition, you can also choose to format odd and even pages in a document in different ways by clicking the Different Odd & Even Pages check box in the Options group. For example, you can choose to left-align the document title on odd-numbered pages and right-align the chapter indicator on even-numbered pages.

Finalizing a Multipage Document

With Word, you can create long documents consisting of multiple sections and then complete the document by customizing the table of contents. By default, a table of contents shows only headings formatted with the Heading 1, Heading 2, or Heading 3 styles (Levels 1, 2, and 3 in Outline view). You can customize a table of contents so it includes headings formatted with other styles, such as the Title style or a style you create yourself. ▓▓▓▓ You copy and paste new text into the current document, and then you modify the headers and footers and customize the table of contents.

STEPS

1. Scroll to see the page break before the index, and following Figure 1, select the **page break**, click the **Page Layout tab**, click **Breaks**, then click **Next Page** in the Section Breaks area

2. Open the file **WD I-2.docx** from the drive and folder where you store your Data Files, press **[Ctrl][A]** to select all the text in the document, press **[Ctrl][C]**, switch to the **WD I-Tour Presentation Guidelines** document, press **[Ctrl][V]**, then save the document as **WD I-Tour Presentation and Information Session Guidelines**

   The three pages of the Information Session Guidelines document appear in their own section.

QUICK TIP

Make sure you click the Link to Previous button before you modify the header text.

3. Scroll to the table of contents page, double-click in the header area for section 1, click **Next**, select **Quest Specialty Travel**, type **Tour Presentation Guidelines**, click **Next** and notice the Header –Section 3- indicator, click the **Link to Previous button** in the Navigation group to deselect it, change the header text to **Information Session Guidelines**, then close the header

4. Scroll to the Index page, insert a **Next Page section break** to the left of Index, double-click in the header area, click the **Link to Previous button**, delete the **header text**, then close the header

   The document now contains four sections, and you have modified the header text in sections 2, 3, and 4.

5. Scroll up to the table of contents page, right-click anywhere in the table of contents, click **Update Field**, click the **Update entire table option button**, then click **OK**

   The title of each document is not included in the table of contents so you cannot easily determine which headings belong to which documents.

6. Click the **References tab**, click the **Table of Contents button**, click **Insert Table of Contents**, click **Options**, select **1** next to Heading 1, type **2**, type **3** next to Heading 2, type **4** next to Heading 3 as shown in Figure I-18, scroll to **Title**, type **1** in the TOC level text box, click **OK**, click **OK**, then click **Yes**

   The Information Session document starts at page 1 and you want page numbering to be consecutive.

7. Press **[Ctrl]**, click **Information Session Guidelines** in the table of contents, scroll to the footer (you'll see Page 1), then double-click in the footer

8. Click the **Page Number button** in the Header & Footer group, click **Format Page Numbers**, click the **Continue from previous section option button**, then click **OK**

9. Click **Next** in the Navigation group, then repeat Step 8

10. Exit the footer area, update the table of contents page, save and close all documents, exit Word, then submit all files to your instructor

    Figure I-19 shows the first page of each of the four sections in the document.

FIGURE I-18: Table of Contents Options dialog box

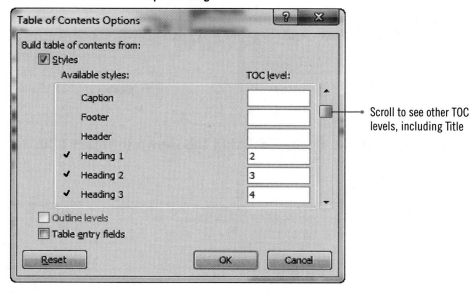

Scroll to see other TOC levels, including Title

FIGURE I-19: Viewing selected pages of the completed document

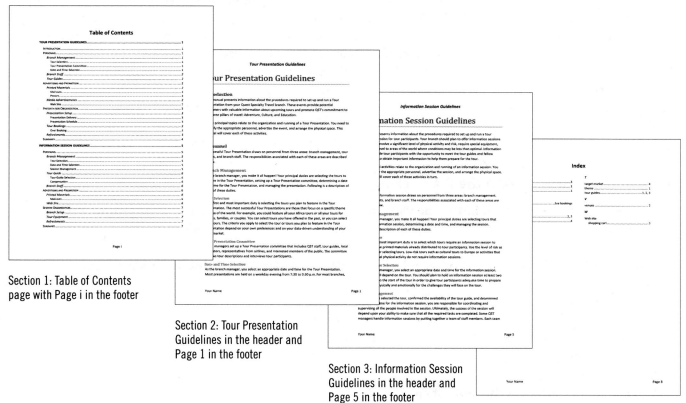

Section 1: Table of Contents page with Page i in the footer

Section 2: Tour Presentation Guidelines in the header and Page 1 in the footer

Section 3: Information Session Guidelines in the header and Page 5 in the footer

Section 4: No header text and Page 8 in the footer

Modifying a table of contents

You can change how Word shows each heading and subheading level included in a table of contents. For example, you can choose to increase the indenting of a level 2 heading, or apply a new leader style to a level 3 heading. You use the Indent buttons in the Paragraph group on the Home tab to change the position of a table of contents entry, and you use the Tabs dialog box to modify the leader style applied to an entry in the table of contents.

Practice

For current SAM information, including versions and content details, visit SAM Central (http://www.cengage.com/samcentral). If you have a SAM user profile, you may have access to hands-on instruction, practice, and assessment of the skills covered in this unit. Since various versions of SAM are supported throughout the life of this text, check with your instructor for the correct instructions and URL/Web site for accessing assignments.

Concepts Review

Label the numbered items on the Outlining tab shown in Figure I-20.

FIGURE I-20

Match each term with the statement that best describes it.

6. Table of contents
7. Demote button
8. Mark Index Entry dialog box
9. Header
10. Cross-reference
11. Link to Previous button
12. Navigation pane

a. Used to enter a lower-level heading in Outline view
b. Text that appears at the top of every page in a document or section
c. Text that electronically refers the reader to another part of the document
d. Open to view the headings and subheadings in a document
e. List of topics and subtopics usually with page numbers, and shown at the beginning of a document
f. Deselect to create a header or footer in one section that is different from the header or footer in a previous section
g. Where you enter text for inclusion in an index

Select the best answer from the list of choices.

13. On the Outlining tab, which button do you click to move directly to Level 1 from any other level?
    a. ➡
    b. ⬅
    c. ⬅⬅
    d. ➕

14. Which symbol in Outline view indicates that a heading includes subtext such as subheadings or paragraphs of text?
    a. ➖
    b. ➕
    c. ▲
    d. ➕

15. Which of the following options is not available in the Navigation pane?
    a. Browse headings
    b. Replace text
    c. Browse pages
    d. Find text

16. Which tab do you access the table of contents feature from?
    a. Page Layout
    b. Insert
    c. References
    d. Review

17. Which index entry appears subordinate to a main entry?
    a. Cross-reference
    b. Next entry
    c. Mark place
    d. Subentry

Developing Multipage Documents

Skills Review

1. Build a document in Outline view.

  a. Start Word, click the Show/Hide ¶ button in the Paragraph group to deselect it and turn off the display of paragraph marks if it is active, increase the zoom to 100%, then switch to Outline view.

  b. Type **Introduction by Your Name** as a Level 1 heading, press [Enter], type **Partnership Requirements** as another Level 1 heading, then press [Enter].

  c. Type **Background Information**, then use the Demote button to demote it to a Level 2 heading.

  d. Type the text shown in Figure I-21 as body text under Background Information.

FIGURE I-21

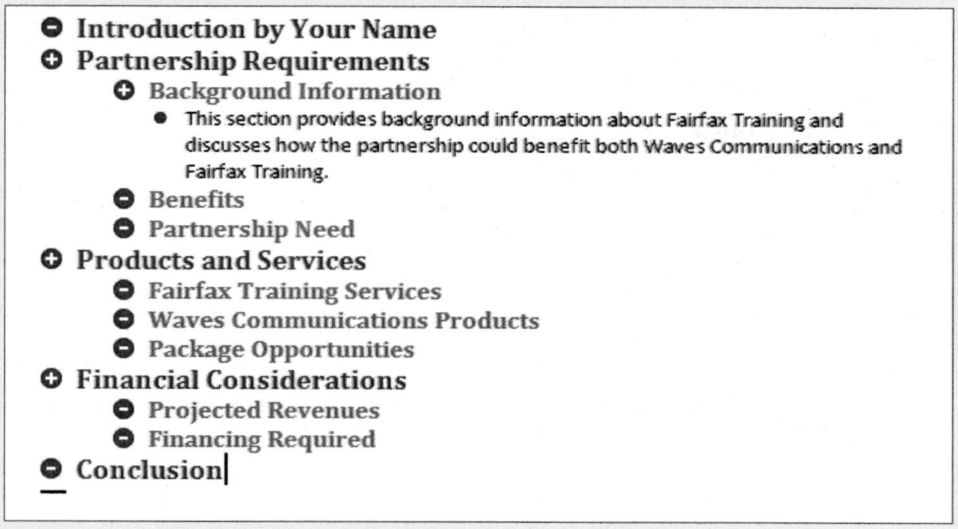

> ⊖ **Introduction by Your Name**
> ⊕ **Partnership Requirements**
>   ⊕ **Background Information**
>   ● This section provides background information about Fairfax Training and discusses how the partnership could benefit both Waves Communications and Fairfax Training.
>   ⊖ **Benefits**
>   ⊖ **Partnership Need**
> ⊕ **Products and Services**
>   ⊖ **Fairfax Training Services**
>   ⊖ **Waves Communications Products**
>   ⊖ **Package Opportunities**
> ⊕ **Financial Considerations**
>   ⊖ **Projected Revenues**
>   ⊖ **Financing Required**
> ⊖ **Conclusion**

  e. Use the Promote button to type the heading **Benefits** as a Level 2 heading, then complete the outline, as shown in Figure I-21.

  f. Save the document as **WD I-Partnership Agreement Outline** to the drive and folder where you store your Data Files, then close the document.

2. Work in Outline view.

  a. Open the file WD I-3.docx from the drive and folder where you store your Data Files, save it as **WD I-Partnership Agreement Proposal**, switch to Outline view, then show all Level 1 headings.

  b. Move the heading Financial Considerations below Products and Services.

  c. Select the Partnership Requirements heading, click the Expand button twice, collapse Benefits, collapse Partnership Need, then move Benefits and its subtext below Partnership Need and its subtext.

  d. Collapse the Partnership Requirements section to show only the Level 1 heading.

  e. Show all levels of the outline, close Outline view, then save the document.

3. Navigate a document.

  a. Open the Navigation pane, show all the headings in the document if they are not displayed, then navigate to Financing Required.

  b. Change **six months** to **year** in the last line of the paragraph below the Financing Required heading.

  c. Navigate to the Package Opportunities heading in the Navigation pane, then use the Navigation pane to delete the heading and its subtext.

  d. View thumbnails of the document pages in the Navigation pane, click the page containing the column chart graphic, close the Navigation pane, select the column chart in the document, then insert **Figure 1** as a caption below the figure.

  e. Find the text **See Figure 1**, then insert a cross-reference to the figure using above/below as the reference text.

  f. Insert a period after the word **below**, test the cross-reference, scroll to see the chart, close the Navigation pane, then save the document.

4. Generate a table of contents.

  a. Press [Ctrl][Home], insert a page break, press [Ctrl][Home], clear the formatting, type **Table of Contents** at the top of the new first page, enhance the text with 18 pt and bold, center it, click after the title, press [Enter], then clear the formatting.

  b. Insert a table of contents using the Distinctive format.

Skills Review (continued)

c. Use [Ctrl][click] to navigate to Partnership Need in the document, open the Navigation pane, view the document headings, then delete the Partnership Need heading from the Navigation pane.

d. Close the Navigation pane, update the table of contents, then save the document.

5. Mark entries for an index.

a. Find the words **computer labs**, and mark all occurrences for inclusion in the index.

b. Find and mark only the first instance of each of the following main entries: **Web page design**, **Networking**, **software training**, and **PowerPoint**. (*Hint:* Click Mark instead of Mark All.)

c. Save the document.

6. Generate an index.

a. Find **online publishing**, click in the Mark Index Entry dialog box, select online publishing in the Main entry text box, type **Waves Communications Products** as the Main entry and **online publishing** as the Subentry, then click Mark All.

b. Repeat the process to insert **writing seminars** as a subentry of Waves Communications Products.

c. Find the text **courses**, then create a cross-reference in the Mark Index Entry dialog box to **software training**. Note that you already have an index entry for software training.

d. Close the Mark Index Entry dialog box and the Navigation pane.

e. Insert a new page at the end of the document, type **Index** at the top of the page, and format it with bold and 18 pt and center alignment.

f. Double-click below the index, and clear any formatting so the insertion point appears at the left margin, then insert an index in the Bulleted format.

g. Find and mark all instances of **Toronto**, scroll to the index page, update the index so it includes the new entry, close the Mark Index Entry dialog box and the Navigation pane, then save the document.

7. Insert footers in multiple sections.

a. At the top of the document, select the page break below the Table of Contents, replace it with a Next Page section break, then remove the page break and the extra blank lines.

b. On the table of contents page, insert a footer using the Blank (Three Columns) format.

c. Delete the placeholders, type your name, press [Tab] twice, type **Page**, press [Spacebar], then insert a page number at the current position using the Plain Number format.

d. Change the format of the page number to i, ii, iii.

e. Go to the next section, then deselect the Link to Previous button.

f. Format the page number to start at 1.

g. Exit the footer area, scroll through the document to verify that the pages are numbered correctly, scroll to and update the pages numbers in the table of contents, then save the document.

8. Insert headers in multiple sections.

a. Move to the top of the document, then position the insertion point in the header area.

b. Go to the next section, then deselect the Link to Previous button.

c. Type **Waves Communications**, center the text, then apply bold and italic.

d. Exit the header area, then scroll through the document to verify that the header text does not appear on the first page of the document and that it does appear on all subsequent pages.

e. Insert a cover page using the Pinstripes style, enter text and delete content controls as shown in Figure I-22, then save the document.

FIGURE I-22

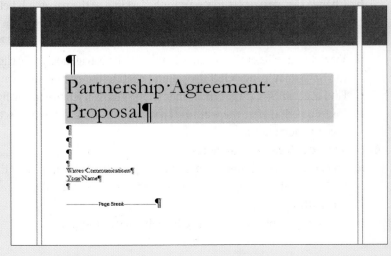

Skills Review (continued)

9. Finalize a multipage document.

a. Insert a section break between the last page of the text and the index page.

b. Open the file WD I-4.docx from the drive and folder where you store your Data Files, copy all the text, paste it into the Partnership Agreement Proposal document, then save the document as **WD I-Partnership Agreements_Fairfax Training and Positive Presenters**.

c. From the table of contents page, access the Header area, move to section 2, replace Waves Communications with Fairfax Training, move to section 3, click the Link to Previous button, then replace Fairfax Training with **Positive Presenters**.

d. Exit the header, insert a Next Page section break before the index and remove the page break, open the header area in section 4 (the index page), then deselect the Link to Previous button and remove the header from the index page.

e. Check that the correct headers appear in each of the four sections, then update the table of contents page (select the Update entire table option).

f. Modify the table of contents options so that Heading 1 corresponds to Level 2 text, Heading 2 corresponds to Level 3 text, Heading 3 corresponds to Level 4 text, and Title text corresponds to Level 1 text.

g. Modify the footers in sections 3 and 4 so that the page numbering is continuous. You should see page 6 on the index page.

h. Update the index and table of contents pages, save the document, submit all files to your instructor, close it, then exit Word.

Independent Challenge 1

You work in the Finance Department of Body Fit, a successful fitness and spa facility in Philadelphia. Recently, the owners of Body Fit began selling franchises. Your supervisor asks you to format a report that details the development of these franchise operations.

a. Start Word, open the file WD I-5.docx from the drive and folder where you store your Data Files, then save it as **WD I-Body Fit Franchises**.

b. In Outline view, organize the document as shown in the following table, starting with Introduction, followed by Scope of the Report, and then moving column by column. Text that you designate as headings will be formatted with the blue font color.

heading	level	heading	level	heading	level
Introduction	1	Marianne Bennett	2	Milwaukee Clientele	3
Scope of the Report	2	Franchise Location	1	Cleveland	2
Owner Information	1	Chicago	2	Cleveland Clientele	3
Gerry Grant	2	Chicago Clientele	3	Opening Schedules	2
Teresa Morales	2	Milwaukee	2		

c. Switch the order of Cleveland and its accompanying subtext so it follows Chicago and its subtext.

Independent Challenge 1 (continued)

d. In Print Layout view and starting from the top of the document, find the text listed in column 1, and mark all instances of that text as Main entry or subentry for an index, based on the information in columns 2 and 3.

find this text	main entry	subentry
Chicago	Location	Chicago
Cleveland	Location	Cleveland
Milwaukee	Location	Milwaukee
Gerry Grant	Owner	Gerry Grant
Teresa Morales	Owner	Teresa Morales
Marianne Bennett	Owner	Marianne Bennett
Marketing Vice President	Marketing Vice President	
Mall	Mall	
Ohio	Ohio	

e. Insert a new page at the end of the document, type **Index** as the page title, format it with bold, a larger font size, and center alignment, then generate an index in the Modern format.

f. At the top of the document, insert a Next Page section break, then on the new first page, type **Table of Contents** as the page title, select the text, click Normal in the Styles group on the Home tab to remove the Heading 1 formatting, then format it with bold, a larger font size, and center alignnment. (*Hint*: If Table of Contents is formatted as Heading 1, it will appear in the Table of Contents, which you do not want.)

g. Generate a table of contents using the Classic format.

h. Add and format a header and footer so that the completed document appears as follows:

location	contents
Table of Contents page (section 1)	Footer containing your name at the left margin and **Page i** at the right margin
Page 1 and the following pages of the report (section 2)	Footer containing your name at the left margin and **Page 1** at the right margin Header containing the text **Body Fit Franchises**, centered, and bold and followed by a blank line (*Hint*: Press [Enter] at the end of the header text)

i. Scroll through the document to ensure the headers and footers are correct.

j. Update the table of contents and index pages.

Advanced Challenge Exercise

- Use the Navigation pane to move directly to the Opening Schedules heading, then create a bookmark called **Dates** using the first of the three dates listed. (*Hint*: Select all or part of the first date—Chicago Franchise: April 22, 2013, click the Insert tab, click Bookmark in the Links group, type **Dates** as the bookmark name, then click Add.)
- Move to the beginning of the document, and go to your bookmark. (*Hint*: Press [Ctrl][G], click Bookmark, click Go To, then click Close.)
- Follow the same process to create a bookmark named **Location** that goes to the Franchise Locations heading, then close the Navigation pane.

k. Save the document, submit your file to your instructor, then close the document and exit Word.

Independent Challenge 2

You work for an author who has just written a series of vignettes about her travels in France and Italy. The author hopes to publish the vignettes and accompanying illustrations in a book called *Eye of an Artist*. She has written a short proposal that she plans to present to publishers. As her assistant, your job is to create a proposal that includes three of the vignettes, each with a unique header.

a. Start Word, open WD I-6.docx, then save it as **WD I-Eye of an Artist Proposal**.

b. Switch to Outline view, then show only text assigned to Level 2 so you can get an overview of the document contents.

c. Show all levels in the outline, switch to Print Layout view, then use the Navigation pane to navigate to the Sample Vignettes heading on page 1.

d. Select Lavender (the first bulleted item), then make Lavender a cross-reference to its corresponding heading as follows: select Lavender, open the Cross-reference dialog box from the References tab, select Heading as the reference type, then select the Lavender heading as the reference text. (*Note*: After pressing Insert and Close, press [Enter] so the titles continue to appear as a list in the document.)

e. Follow the same process to make Ocher and Roman Rain cross-references to their corresponding heading. (*Note*: Click after Rain and press [Enter], then apply the bullet to Roman Rain to place it back in the list of the three vignettes.)

f. Test each cross-reference, using the Navigation pane to navigate back to the Sample Vignettes heading.

g. Close the Navigation pane.

h. Insert a Next Page section break at the beginning of the document, move to the top of the new page 1, clear the formatting, type **Table of Contents** and format the text attractively, then generate a table of contents in the Formal style. (*Hint*: Make sure the text Table of Contents is not formatted as Heading 1.)

i. On the table of contents page, add your name centered in the footer. On the Eye of an Artist Overview page, add your name left-aligned in the footer and the page number 1 right-aligned in the footer. (*Hint:* Make sure you deselect the Link to Previous button before making changes to the footer in section 2.)

j. Exit the footer, then add a Next Page section break before each of the vignettes: before the Lavender document, before the Ocher document, and before the Roman Rain document. The document now consists of five sections. (*Hint*: Double-click in the header area above Roman Rain to confirm that Header -Section 5- appears.)

k. Go to the table of contents page, enter the header area, then add headers to the sections of the document as shown below, formatting the header text with bold, italic, and centering. Make sure you deselect the Link to Previous button before typing new text in a header.
- Section 1: no header
- Section 2: **Overview**
- Section 3: **Lavender**
- Section 4: **Ocher**
- Section 5: **Roman Rain**

l. Update the table of contents, then continue page numbering from the footers in sections 3, 4, and 5.

m. Update the table of contents again, then scroll through the document to verify that the headers and footers are correct in each section.

Advanced Challenge Exercise

- On the table of contents page, increase the font size of each of the four headings associated with Level 1 to 12 pt. (*Hint:* Select Eye of an Artist Overview, increase the font size to 12 pt, then use the Format Painter to apply the formatting to the other three headings associated with Level 1.)
- On the table of contents page, increase the indent of the three headings associated with Level 2 to .5 on the ruler bar. (*Hint:* Show the ruler bar if necessary (View tab, Ruler check box), click Tone (the first Level 2 heading), then drag both of the indent markers on the ruler bar to the .5 mark.)
- Apply the Austin theme to the document. (*Hint:* Click the Page Layout tab, click Themes, then click Austin. The fonts and colors are changed to reflect the formatting associated with the Austin theme.) Scroll through the document to see how the headings and text appear.

n. Save the document, submit your file to your instructor, close the document, then exit Word.

Independent Challenge 3

As the program assistant at Atlantic College in Maine, you are responsible for creating and formatting reports about programs at the college. You work in Outline view to create a report for a college program of your choice.

a. Create a new document and save it as **WD I-Program Information Report**.

b. In Outline view, enter the headings and subheadings for the report as shown in the table starting with **Program Overview**, followed by **Career Opportunities**. You need to substitute appropriate course names for Course 1, Course 2, and so on. For example, courses in the first term of a business studies program could be **Introduction to Business, Marketing Basics**, and so on. You choose the program and courses you want to include in the report.

heading	level	heading	level
Program Overview	1	[Enter name for Course 1]	3
Career Opportunities	2	[Enter name for Course 2]	3
Admission Requirements	2	Second Term	2
Program Content	1	[Enter name for Course 1]	3
First Term	2	[Enter name for Course 2]	3

c. Enter one paragraph of appropriate body text for the following headings: Program Overview, Career Opportunities, and Admission Requirements, then enter short course descriptions for each of the four courses included in the document. For ideas, refer to college Web sites and catalogs.

d. In Print Layout view, add a cover page using the Stacks style: include the name of the program as the title (for example, **Business Program**), the name of the college (**Atlantic College, Maine**) as the subtitle, and your name where indicated.

e. Insert a Next Page section break following the cover page, then insert a page break in the body of the report to spread the report over two pages if it does not already flow to two pages.

f. Format the cover page (section 1) with no header and no footer.

g. Format the section 2 header with a right-aligned page number starting with Page 1 using the 1, 2, 3 format. Make sure you deselect Link to Previous.

h. Format the section 2 footer with the name of the program left-aligned in the footer and your name right-aligned. Make sure you deselect Link to Previous.

i. Insert a next page section break above the Program Overview heading.

j. Scroll up to the new blank page, clear the formatting, type **Table of Contents** as a title, then insert a table of contents in the format of your choice.

k. Customize the table of contents so that it includes only Heading 1 at TOC level 1 and Heading 3 at TOC level 2. None of the Heading 2 headings should appear in the revised table of contents.

l. Double click in the header area on the table of contents page, then delete Page 1.

m. Go to the next section, click the Link to Previous button to deselect it, then insert Page 1 right-aligned. Be sure the page number starts at 1. Verify that the header appears on both pages of the section 3 header and that the footer appears on all pages except the cover page.

n. Update the table of contents.

o. Save the document, close it, then submit your file to your instructor.

Real Life Independent Challenge

Many businesses post job opportunities on their Web sites. You can learn a great deal about opportunities in a wide range of fields just by checking out the job postings on these Web sites. You decide to create a document that describes a selection of jobs available on an employment Web site of your choice.

a. Use your favorite search engine and the search phrase **job search** to find Web sites that post jobs online. Popular sites include jobs.com, workopolis.com, and monster.com.

b. On the Web site you chose, identify two job categories (e.g., Marketing and Web Page Development, or Accounting and Administration) and then find two jobs that appeal to you and that you may even wish to apply for. You can choose to search for jobs in your home town or in another location.

c. Create a new document in Word, then save it as **WD I-Online Job Opportunities**.

d. In Outline view, set up the document starting with the name of the employment Web site (e.g., monster.com), and followed by Job Category 1 as shown in the table. (*Note*: You need to enter specific text for headings such as **Marketing** for Job Category 1 and **Marketing Assistant** for Job Posting.)

heading	level
Name of Web Site	1
Job Category 1	2
Job Name	3
Summary of Job Posting	Body Text
Job Category 2	2
Job Name	3
Summary of Job Posting	Body Text

e. Complete the Word document with information you find on the Web site. Include a short description of each job you select, and list some of the job duties. You do not need to include the entire job posting. If you copy selected text from a Web site, make sure you clear the formatting so that the text in the document is formatted only with the Normal style.

f. Format the document so that a header starts on page 1 and includes the text **Online Job Opportunities for Your Name**. Include a page number on each page of the document in the footer.

g. Save the document and submit the file to your instructor, then close the document.

Visual Workshop

Open the file WD I-7.docx from the drive and folder where you store your Data Files, then save it as **WD I-Term Paper Outline**. Modify the outline so that it appears as shown in Figure I-23. You need to change the order of some sections. In Print Layout view, insert a next section page break at the beginning of the document, clear the formatting, type **Table of Contents** and enhance the title so it appears similar to the title shown in Figure I-24, then generate a table of contents in the Fancy style. Insert a page break before E-Business Challenges in the text, create a footer in section 2 with a page number that starts with 1, then update the table of contents so that it appears as shown in Figure I-24. Be sure your name is on the document, save and close the document, then submit the file to your instructor.

FIGURE I-23

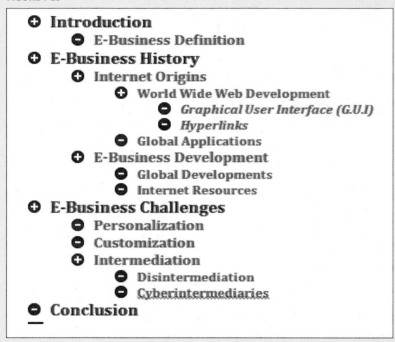

FIGURE I-24

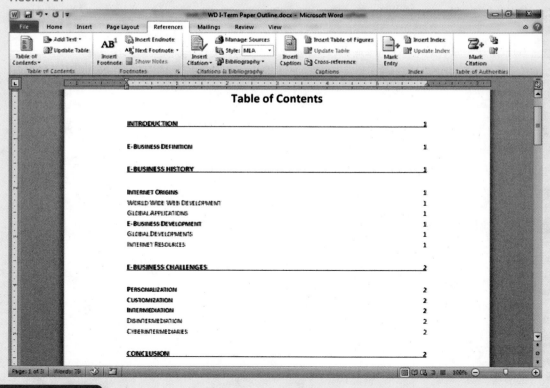

Developing Multipage Documents

Working with Styles and Templates

You can use Word's predesigned Quick Style sets and templates to format your documents quickly, efficiently, and professionally. You can further customize your document-formatting tasks by creating your own Quick Style sets and templates. In this unit, you learn how to create new styles to format paragraphs, characters, lists, and tables, and how to save your newly created styles in a new Quick Style set. You also learn how to manage styles used in a document and how to create, apply, and revise a template.  One of your duties as a special projects assistant at Quest Specialty Travel (QST) in San Diego is to produce profiles of the top QST tour guides for distribution at the company's annual meeting. To save time, you modify styles in an existing profile, create some new styles, and then develop a template on which to base each tour guide profile. This template includes a custom Quick Style set.

OBJECTIVES

Explore styles and templates

Modify predefined styles

Create paragraph styles

Create character and linked styles

Create custom list and table styles

Create a Quick Style set

Manage styles

Create a template

Revise and attach a template

Exploring Styles and Templates

You use styles and templates to automate document-formatting tasks and to ensure consistency among related documents. A **style** consists of various formats such as font, font size, and alignment that you name and then save together as one set. For example, a style called Main Head might contain the following format settings: Arial font, 14-point font size, bold, and a bottom border. Each time you apply the Main Head style to selected text, all format settings included in the style are applied. A **template** is a file that contains the basic structure of a document, such as the page layout, headers and footers, styles, graphic elements, and boilerplate text.  You plan to use styles to format a tour guide profile and then create a template that you will use to develop a series of tour guide profiles. You start by familiarizing yourself with styles and templates.

Information about how you can use styles and templates to help you format documents quickly and efficiently follows:

- Using styles helps you save time in two ways. First, when you apply a style, you apply a set of formats all at once. You do not have to apply each format individually. Second, if you modify a style by changing one or more of the formats associated with that style, then all text formatted with that style is updated automatically. For example, suppose you apply a style named "Section Head" to each section head in a document. If you then modify the formatting associated with the Section Head style, Word automatically updates all the text formatted with the Section Head style to reflect the change. As discussed in Unit I, default heading styles are applied automatically to headings and subheadings when you work in Outline view to create the structure of a document. For example, the Heading 1 style is applied to text associated with Level 1, the Heading 2 style is applied to text associated with Level 2, and so on. You can modify a default heading style or you can create a new heading style.

- In Word, you can choose from 13 predefined Quick Style sets or you can create your own Quick Style set. Each **Quick Style set** contains **Quick Styles**, or simply **styles**, for a wide range of text elements such as headings, titles, subtitles, and lists. All of the styles associated with a Quick Style set are stored in the **Styles gallery**. Figure J-1 shows the list of predefined Quick Style sets, part of the Styles gallery, and styles in the Word 2010 Quick Style set applied to the document.

- Word includes five major style categories. A **paragraph style** includes font formats, such as font and font size, and paragraph formats, such as line spacing or tabs. You use a paragraph style when you want to format all the text in a paragraph at once. A **character style** includes character formats only, such as font, font size, and font color. You use a character style to apply character format settings only to selected text within a paragraph. A **linked style** applies either a character style or a paragraph style, depending on whether you click in a paragraph to select the entire paragraph or you select specific text. A **table style** specifies how you want both the table grid and the text in a table to appear. A **list style** allows you to format a series of lines with numbers or bullets and with selected font and paragraph formats. Figure J-2 shows a document formatted with the five style types. These styles have been saved in a new Quick Style set called QST Profiles.

- Every document you create in Word is based on a template. Most of the time, this template is the **Normal template** because the Normal template is loaded automatically when you start a new document. The styles assigned to the Normal template, such as Normal, Title, Heading 1, Heading 2, and so on, are the styles you see in the Styles gallery when you open a new document.

- Word includes a number of predesigned templates. In addition, you can access a variety of templates online. You can also create a template that includes a custom Quick Style set. Finally, you can attach a template to an existing document and then apply the styles included with the template to text in the document.

Quick Styles gallery

Document formatted with the Word 2010 Quick Style set (the default)

Click to open Quick Styles gallery

Click to access menu of Quick Style sets

List of Quick Style sets; your list may include additional Quick Style sets

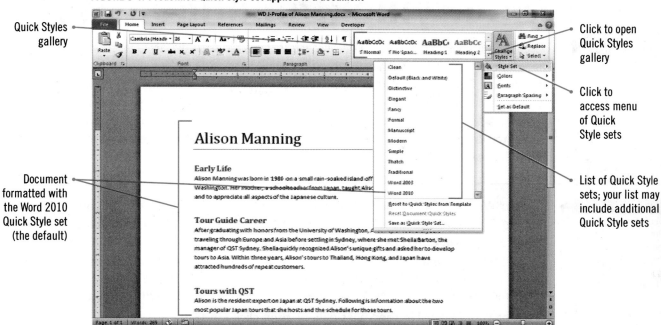

Word 2010

A paragraph style applies formatting to a paragraph, which might be one or more lines of text

A list style adds bullets or numbers to a series of paragraphs

A linked style applies formatting to text within a paragraph or to an entire paragraph depending on how text is selected

A character style applies formatting to text within a paragraph; this character style includes blue and italic

A table style applies formatting to a table grid and table text

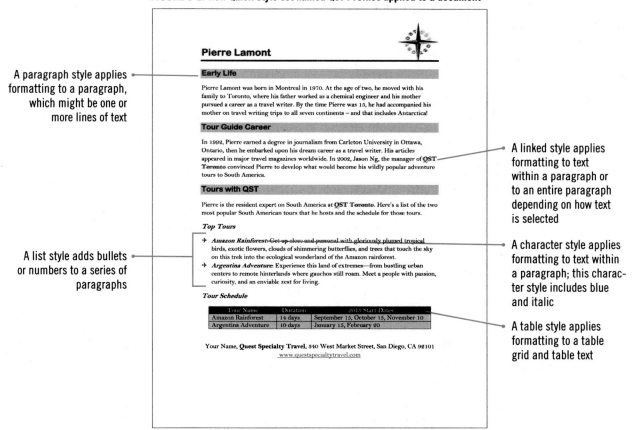

Understanding the Normal style

Text that you type into a blank document is formatted with the Normal style from the Word 2010 Quick Style set until you specify otherwise. By default, text formatted with the Normal style uses the 11-point Calibri font and is left-aligned, with a line spacing of 1.15 within a paragraph and 10 pt After Paragraph spacing. When you select a new Quick Style set, the styles associated with that Quick Style set are applied to the document.

Modifying Predefined Styles

Word 2010 includes 13 predefined Quick Style sets that you can apply directly to text in your document. Each Quick Style set has styles associated with it. Frequently used styles include the Normal, Title, Heading 1, and Heading 2 styles. The Normal style is applied to body text. Heading 1, Heading 2, and so on to Heading 9 styles are applied to headings and subheadings. You can personalize your documents by modifying any style.  Your colleague has written a profile of Alison Manning, a tour guide from the QST Sydney branch. You decide to modify the Normal style currently applied to all body text in the document. You also modify the Heading 1 style.

1. **Start Word, open the file WD J-1.docx from the drive and folder where you store your Data Files, save the file as WD J-Profile of Alison Manning, then click the launcher 🔲 in the Styles group to open the Styles task pane**

   The **Styles task pane** lists all the styles in the Word 2010 Quick Style set and includes options for creating new styles, using the Style Inspector, and managing styles. The Title style is currently selected because the insertion point appears in the text "Alison Manning", which is formatted with the Title style.

2. **Right-click Normal in the Styles gallery, then click Modify**

   The Modify Style dialog box opens, as shown in Figure J-3.

3. **Click the Font list arrow in the Formatting area, scroll to and select Bell MT, click the Font Size list arrow, select 12 pt, then click OK**

   The Modify Style dialog box closes, and all body text in the document is modified automatically to match the new settings for the Normal style. Text formatted with a style other than the Normal style, such as text formatted with the Heading 1 style, does not change.

4. **Select the Early Life heading**

   The Early Life heading is formatted with the Heading 1 style. You want to make formatting changes to the text formatted with the Heading 1 style. In addition to using the Modify Style dialog box, you can apply formatting to text formatted with a style and then update the style to match the new formatting.

5. **Use the commands in the Font group to change the font to Bell MT and the font color to Olive Green, Accent 3, Darker 50%**

   You made changes to the character formatting. You continue by making changes the paragraph formatting.

6. **With the Early Life heading still selected, click the Line and Paragraph Spacing button 🔳 in the Paragraph group, click Remove Space Before Paragraph, click 🔳 again, then click Add Space After Paragraph**

7. **With the Early Life heading still selected, click the Shading list arrow 🔳 in the paragraph group, then click Olive Green, Accent 3, Lighter 60%**

   You have made several changes to the selected text. You can update the style associated with the selected text to include the formatting changes you made.

8. **Right-click Heading 1 in the Styles gallery to open a menu as shown in Figure J-4, then click Update Heading 1 to Match Selection**

   All three of the headings formatted with the Heading 1 style are updated to match the formatting options you applied to the Early Life heading. Notice that the Heading 1 style in the Styles gallery shows a preview of the formatting associated with that style.

9. **Save the document**

   You have used two methods to modify the formatting attached to a style. You can modify the style using the Modify Styles dialog box, or you can make changes to text associated with a style and then update the style to match the selected text. You can use either of these methods to update any predefined style and any style you create yourself.

FIGURE J-3: Modify Style dialog box

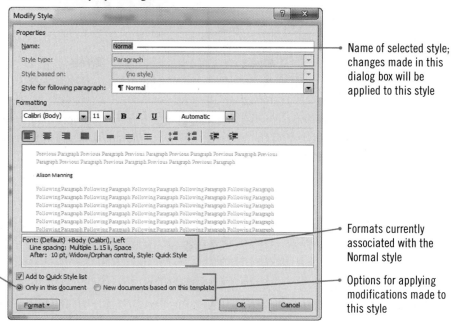

Name of selected style; changes made in this dialog box will be applied to this style

Formats currently associated with the Normal style

Modifications you make to the Normal style apply to text formatted with the Normal style in this document only

Options for applying modifications made to this style

FIGURE J-4: Updating the Heading 1 style with new formats

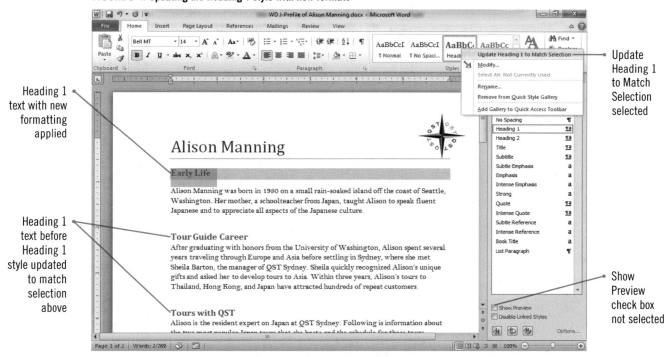

Heading 1 text with new formatting applied

Heading 1 text before Heading 1 style updated to match selection above

Update Heading 1 to Match Selection selected

Show Preview check box not selected

Revealing style formatting

Word includes two ways to quickly determine exactly what styles and formatting are applied to selected text. These methods are useful when you apply a style to text and not all the changes are made. To find out why, use the Style Inspector to open the Reveal Formatting task pane. To open the Style Inspector, click the text formatted with the style, then click the Style Inspector button at the bottom of the Styles task pane. The **Style Inspector** lists the styles applied to the selected text and indicates if any extra formats were applied that are not included in the style. For example, another user could apply formatting such as bold and italic that is not included in the style. You can clear these formats by clicking one of the four buttons along the right side of the Style Inspector or by clicking Clear All to remove all extra formats. If you need to investigate even further, you can click the Reveal Formatting button at the bottom of the Style Inspector to open the Reveal Formatting task pane. The **Reveal Formatting task pane** lists exactly which formats are applied to the character, paragraph, and section of the selected text.

Creating Paragraph Styles

Instead of using the predefined styles, you can create styles. A style you create can be based on an existing style or it can be based on no style. When you base a style on an existing style, all the formatting associated with the existing style is also associated with the new style you create, as well as any new formatting you apply to the new style. One type of style you can create is a paragraph style. A paragraph style is a combination of character and paragraph formats that you name and store as a set. You can create a paragraph style and then apply it to any paragraph.  You decide to create a new paragraph style called Guide Name and apply it to the text formatted with the Title style, and then you create a new paragraph style called Guide Subtitle and apply it to two other headings in the document.

STEPS

1. **Select Alison Manning at the top of the document, then click the New Style button ▦ at the bottom of the Styles task pane**

   The Create New Style from Formatting dialog box opens. You use this dialog box to enter a name for the new style, select a style type, and select the formatting options you want associated with the new style.

QUICK TIP
Any line of text followed by a hard return is considered a paragraph, even if the line consists of only one or two words.

2. **Type Guide Name in the Name text box, press [Tab], then verify that Paragraph appears in the Style type list box**

   The new style you are creating is based on the Title style because the Title style is applied to the currently selected text. When you create a new style, you can base it on the style applied to the selected text if a style has been applied to that text, another style by selecting a style in the Style based on list box, or no preset style. You want the new style to include the formatting associated with the Title style so you leave Title as the Style based on setting.

3. **Select 22 pt, Bold, and the Olive Green, Accent 3, Darker 50% font color, click Format, click Border, click the Color list arrow, select Olive Green, Accent 3, Darker 50%, click the Width list arrow, click 3 pt, click the bottom of the Preview box to apply the updated border style, then click OK**

4. **Click OK, then move your mouse over "Guide Name" in the Styles task pane to show the settings associated with the Guide Name style, as shown in Figure J-5**

   The Guide Name style is applied to the text, "Alison Manning". The Guide Name style appears in the Styles task pane and in the Styles gallery. The Title style is also still available.

5. **Scroll to and select the heading Top Tours, click the New Style button ▦ on the Styles task pane, then type Guide Subtitle in the Name text box**

   The Guide Subtitle style is based on the Normal style because the selected text is formatted with the Normal style.

6. **Select 12 in the font size text box, type 13, select Bold, select Italic, then click OK**

7. **Select the heading Tour Schedule (you may need to scroll down), then click Guide Subtitle in the Styles task pane**

   The new Guide Subtitle style is applied to two headings in the document.

QUICK TIP
You can also use the Format Painter to apply a style to text.

8. **Click the Show Preview check box at the bottom of the Styles task pane, then save the document**

   The Styles task pane and the document appear, as shown in Figure J-6. With the Preview option active, you can quickly see the formatting associated with each of the predefined styles and the new styles you created.

FIGURE J-5: Formatting associated with Guide Name style

Guide Name style applied to text

Formats associated with Guide Name style

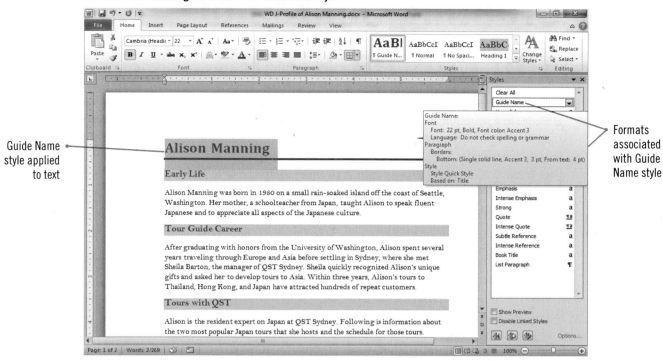

FIGURE J-6: Styles previewed in the Styles task pane

Text formatted with the Guide Subtitle style

Preview of styles

Show Preview check box selected

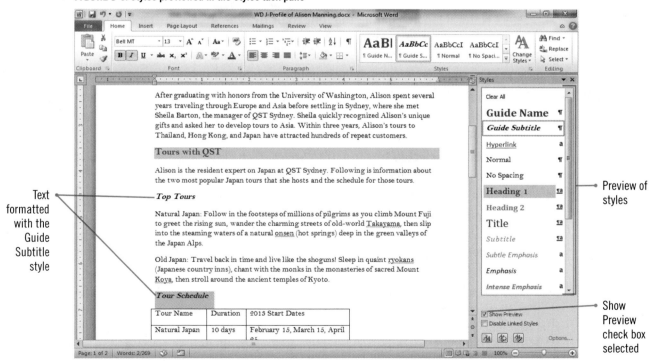

Creating Character and Linked Styles

A character style includes character format settings—such as font, font size, bold, and italic—that you name and save as a style. You apply a character style to selected text within a paragraph. Any text in the paragraph that is not formatted with the character style is formatted with the currently applied paragraph style. A linked style includes both character formats and paragraph formats, just like a paragraph style. The difference is that you can apply a linked style to an entire paragraph or to selected text within a paragraph. Linked styles are therefore very versatile. ▓▓▓▓▓ You create a character style called Tours to apply to each tour name and a linked style called QST to apply to each instance of QST Sydney.

STEPS

1. **Select the text** Natural Japan **in the section below Top Tours, press and hold [Ctrl], then select the text** Old Japan **at the beginning of the next paragraph**

   You use [Ctrl] to select all the text you wish to format with a new style.

2. **Click the** New Style button ▓, **type** Tours **in the Name text box, click the** Style type list arrow, **then select** Character

3. **Select these character formatting settings: the** Bell MT font, 12 pt, Bold, Italic, **and the** Olive Green, Accent 3, Darker 50% **font color, click** OK, **then click away from the text to deselect it**

   The text you selected is formatted with the Tours character style. You can modify an existing character style in the same way you modify a paragraph style. You decide that you'd prefer the text to be formatted with a different color.

4. **Select** Natural Japan, **change the font color to** Blue, Accent 1, Darker 50%, **right-click** Tours **in the Styles task pane to open the menu shown in Figure J-7, then click** Update Tours to Match Selection

   Both of the phrases formatted with the Tours character style are updated. You can also create a linked style.

QUICK TIP
Mouse over the options in the Text Effects gallery and then use the ScreenTips to help you make the correct selection.

5. **Scroll up and select** QST Sydney **in the paragraph below Tour Guide Career, click the** Text Effects list arrow ▓ **in the Font group, then select the** Gradient Fill – Orange, Accent 6, Inner Shadow **(last row, second column)**

6. **Right-click the selected text, point to** Styles, **then click** Save Selection as a New Quick Style

   The Create New Style from Formatting dialog box opens.

7. **Type** QST **as the style name, click** Modify, **click** Format, **click** Border, **click the** bottom border **in the Preview to add a thick green border line, then click** OK

   In the Create New Style from Formatting dialog box, you see that the Linked (paragraph and character) style type is automatically assigned when you save a selection as a new Quick Style. The style you created includes character formatting (the text effect format) and paragraph formatting (the border line).

8. **Click** OK, **click anywhere in the paragraph under Early Life, then click** QST **in the Styles task pane (you may need to scroll up the Styles task pane to view QST)**

   The entire paragraph is formatted with the new QST style, as shown in Figure J-8. Notice that both the character formatting and the paragraph formatting associated with the QST linked style are applied to the paragraph, but that only the character formatting associated with the QST linked style is applied to selected text. You prefer to apply the style just to selected text within a paragraph.

9. **Click the** Undo button ▓ **on the Quick Access toolbar, scroll to the paragraph below the Tours with QST heading, select** QST Sydney **in the paragraph, click** QST **in the Styles task pane, then save the document**

Working with Styles and Templates

FIGURE J-7: Updating the Tours character style

New font color
applied to
selected text

Update Tours to
Match Selection
option selected

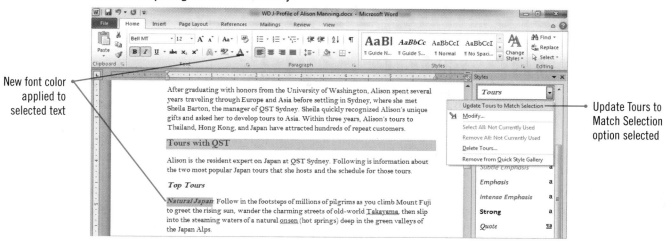

FIGURE J-8: QST linked style applied to a paragraph and to selected text

The QST linked
style formats
text with
character and
paragraph
formats when
applied to
an entire
paragraph

The QST linked
style formats
text with
character
formats only
when applied
to selected
text within a
paragraph

Paragraph
style

Linked style
can be applied
to either
selected text or
a paragraph

Character
style

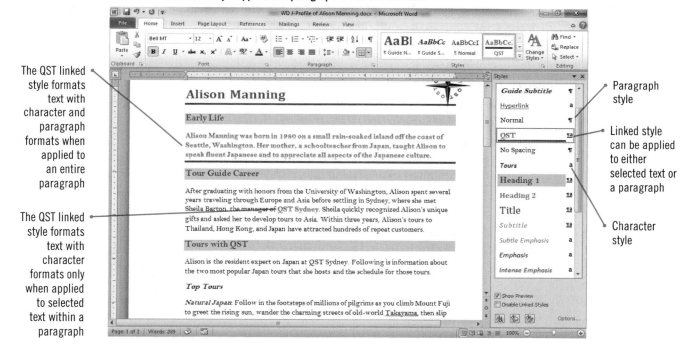

Identifying paragraph, character, and linked styles

Style types are identified in the Styles task pane by different symbols. Each paragraph style is marked with a paragraph symbol: ¶. You can apply a paragraph style just by clicking in any paragraph or line of text and selecting the style. The most commonly used predefined paragraph style is the Normal style. Each character style is marked with a character symbol: a. You apply a character style by clicking anywhere in a word or by selecting a phrase within a paragraph.

Predefined character styles include Emphasis, Strong, and Book Title. Each linked style is marked with both a paragraph symbol and a character symbol: ¶a. You can click anywhere in a paragraph to apply the linked style to the entire paragraph, or you can select text and then apply only the character formats associated with the linked style to the selected text. Predefined linked styles include Heading 1, Title, and Quote.

Creating Custom List and Table Styles

A list style includes settings that format a series of paragraphs so they appear related in some way. For example, you can create a list style that adds bullet characters to a series of paragraphs or sequential numbers to a list of items. A table style includes formatting settings for both the table grid and the table text. ▰▰▰▰▰ You create a list style called Tour List with a special bullet character, and then you create a table style called Tour Schedule.

STEPS

1. **Click to the left of Natural Japan in the Top Tours section, click the New Style button** ▦ **at the bottom of the Styles task pane, type** Tour List **as the style name, click the** Style type **list arrow, then click** List

   You can also click the Multilevel List button in the Paragraph group on the Home tab, and then click Define New List Style to open the Define New List Style dialog box and create a new style.

2. **Click the** Bullets button ▤, **click the** Insert symbol button ▨, **click the** Font list arrow, **click** Wingdings, **select the contents of the** Character code text box, **type** 81, **click** OK, **click the** Font color list arrow, **click** Blue, Accent 1, Darker 50%, **compare the Create New Style from Formatting dialog box to Figure J-9, then click** OK

   The Tour List style is applied to the text, and a blue plane symbol appears to the left of "Natural Japan".

3. **Click** Old **in the phrase "Old Japan", click the** Multilevel List button ▦, **move the mouse pointer over the style in the List Styles area and notice the ScreenTip reads Tour List, then click the** Tour List style

   The bullet character is added, the text is indented, and the spacing above the paragraph is removed so that the two list items appear closer together. By default, Word removes spacing between paragraphs formatted with a list style, which is part of the List Paragraph style. When you create a list style, the List style type is based on the List Paragraph style.

4. **Scroll down to view the table, click the** table move handle ⊕ **near the upper-left corner of the table to select the table, click the** New Style button ▦ **on the Styles task pane, type** Tour Schedule **in the Name text box, click the** Style type **list arrow, then click** Table

   The Create New Style from Formatting dialog box changes to show formatting options for a table.

5. **Refer to Figure J-10, select the** Bell MT font, **the** 12 pt font size, **a border width of** ½ pt, **a border color of** black (Automatic), **and a fill color of** Olive Green, Accent 3, Lighter 60%, **then click the** All Borders button ▦

6. **Click the** Apply formatting to list arrow, **click** Header row, **change the font color to** white **and the fill color to** Olive Green, Accent 3, Darker 50%, **click the** Align button list arrow, **click the** Align Center button ▤, **then click** OK

   The table is formatted with the new Tour Schedule table style, which includes a modified header row.

7. **Double-click the right edge of the table so all the text in each row fits on one line**

   You want the table centered between the left and right margins of the page, and you want the centering format to be part of the Tour Schedule style.

8. **Click the** Table Tools Design tab, **right-click the currently selected table style (far-left selection), click** Modify Table Style, **click** Format **in the lower-left corner of the dialog box, click** Table Properties, **click the** Center button **in the Alignment area, click** OK, **then click** OK

   The center format is part of the table style. The table appears as shown in Figure J-11.

9. **Click below the table to deselect it, then save the document**

FIGURE J-9: Create New Style from Formatting dialog box

Bullets button

List formatting applied to 1st level only

Explanation of formats applied to Tour List style

Font color list arrow

Insert symbol button

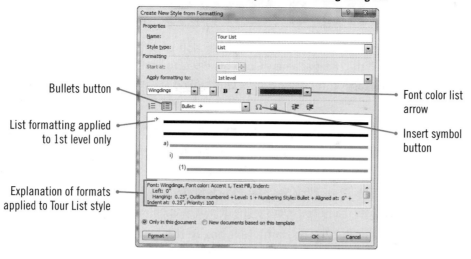

FIGURE J-10: Table formatting selections

Bell MT font and 12 pt font size

Border width list arrow

½ pt line weight and Automatic color

Apply Formatting to list arrow

Alignment list arrow

All Borders and Olive Green, Accent 3, Lighter 60% fill color

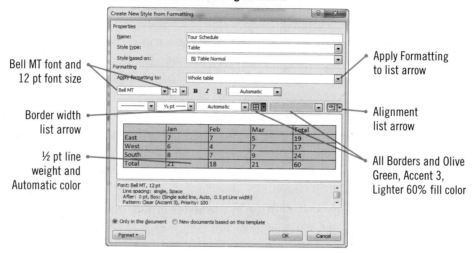

FIGURE J-11: Tour List and Tour Schedule styles applied

Tour Schedule table style in the Table Tools Design tab

Tour List style

Tour Schedule style

Styles pane includes only character, paragraph, and linked styles

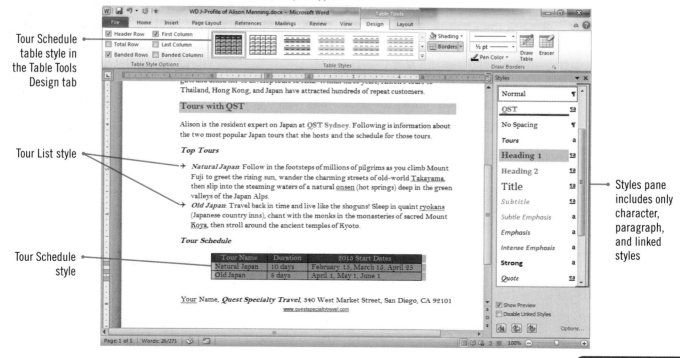

Creating a Quick Style Set

Once you have formatted a document with a selection of styles that includes both new and existing styles, you can save all the styles as a new Quick Style set. You can then apply the Quick Style set to format other documents.  You create a new Quick Style set called QST Profiles, and then apply it to another profile.

1. **Press [Ctrl][Home] to move to the top of the document, then click the Change Styles button in the Styles group**

2. **Point to Style Set, then click Save as Quick Style Set**
   The Save Quick Styles dialog box opens to the default location where Quick Style sets are saved.

3. **Type QST Profiles in the File name text box in the Save Quick Style Set dialog box, then click Save**

4. **Click the Change Styles button, then point to Style Set**
   The new QST Profiles Quick Style set appears in the list of Style Sets as shown in Figure J-12.

5. **Point to Colors, move the mouse over the various color schemes to see how the document changes, click Black Tie, then save the document**
   The color scheme has changed. You apply a new color scheme so the colors in that color scheme are available to you as you work on the document. You can apply the new QST Profiles Quick Style set to a new document.

6. **Open the file WD J-2.docx from the drive and folder where you store your Data Files, save it as WD J-Profile of Pierre Lamont, then open the Styles task pane if it is not already open**
   Pierre Lamont's profile is currently formatted with the Formal Quick Style set, one of the 13 predefined style sets. The Title style is applied to "Pierre Lamont", and the Heading 1 style is applied to the "Early Life", "Tour Guide Career", and "Tours with QST" headings.

7. **Click the Change Styles button in the Styles group, point to Style Set, then click QST Profiles**
   The QST Profiles Quick Style set is applied to the text in Pierre Lamont's profile, and all the new styles you created in previous lessons, except the Tour List and Tour Schedule styles, are available in the Styles gallery and the Styles task pane. Notice that the Black Tie color scheme you applied to Alison Manning's profile is not applied. Color schemes are not saved with a Quick Style set. You must reapply the color scheme.

8. **Click the Change Styles button in the Styles group, point to Colors, then click Black Tie**
   You need to apply the other styles associated with the QST Profile Quick Style set, including the Guide Name, Guide Subtitle, Tours, and QST styles. You will learn more about managing styles and apply the QST style, the Tour List style, and the Tour Schedule style in the next lesson.

9. **Apply the Guide Name, Guide Subtitle, and Tours styles to the text as shown in Figure J-13**

10. **Save the document**

FIGURE J-12: QST Profiles Quick Style set

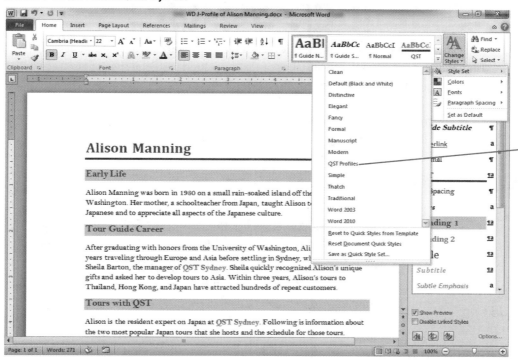

QST Profiles listed in the selection of Quick Style sets; your list may include other Quick Style sets

FIGURE J-13: Applying styles from the QST Profiles Quick Style set

Guide Name style applied to "Pierre Lamont"

Tours style applied to "Amazon Rainforest" and "Argentina Adventure"

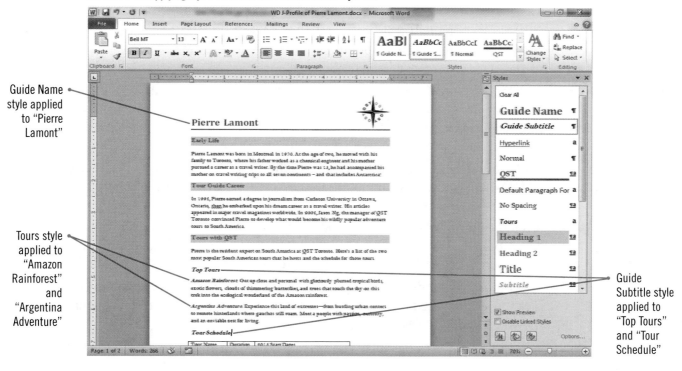

Guide Subtitle style applied to "Top Tours" and "Tour Schedule"

Managing Styles

You can manage styles in a variety of ways. For example, you can rename and delete styles, and you can use Find and Replace to find every instance of text formatted with one style and replace it with text formatted with another style. You can also copy styles from one document to another document. When you apply a Quick Style set to a document, all the list and table styles that you created are not automatically available. You need to copy list and table styles from one document to another document.  You use Find and Replace to find each instance of QST Toronto and replace it with the same text formatted with the QST style. You then work in the **Manage Styles dialog box** to copy the Tour List and the Tour Schedule styles from Alison Manning's profile to Pierre Lamont's profile.

STEPS

1. **Move to the top of the document, click Replace in the Editing group, type QST Toronto in the Find what text box, press [Tab], then type QST Toronto in the Replace with dialog box**

2. **Click More, click Format, click Style, scroll to view both QST Char and QST in the Replace Style dialog box, click QST Char as shown in Figure J-14, click OK, click Replace All, click OK, then click Close**

   Two versions of the QST style are listed in the Replace Style dialog box because the QST style is a linked style. The QST Char version of the QST linked style applies only the character formats associated with the QST style to the selected text.

3. **Click the Manage Styles button 🔘 at the bottom of the Styles task pane, then click Import/Export to open the Organizer dialog box**

   You copy styles from the document shown in the left side of the Organizer dialog box to a new document that you open in the right side of the Organizer dialog box. The document in the left side is the source file because it contains the styles you want to copy. The document in the right side is the target file because it receives the styles you copy. By default, the target file is the Normal template.

4. **Click Close File under the list box on the left, click Open File, then navigate to the drive and folder where you store your files**

   You do not see any Word documents listed because, by default, Word lists only templates.

5. **Click the All Word Templates list arrow, select All Word Documents, click WD J-Profile of Alison Manning.docx, then click Open**

   The styles assigned to Alison Manning's profile appear in the list box on the left side. This document contains the Tour List and Tour Schedule styles and is the source document. You need to select the target document.

6. **Click Close File under the list box on the right, click Open File, navigate to the drive and folder where you store your files, show all Word documents, click WD J-Profile of Pierre Lamont.docx, then click Open**

QUICK TIP
You can scroll the list of styles in the target file's list box to verify that the Tour List and the Tour Schedule styles are listed.

7. **Scroll the list of styles in the Alison Manning Profile document (left side of the Organizer dialog box), click Tour List, press and hold [Ctrl], click Tour Schedule to select both styles (see Figure J-15), click Copy, then click Close to exit the Organizer dialog box**

8. **Select the two tour descriptions (from Amazon Rainforest to Argentina Adventure), click the Multilevel List button ⊞ in the Paragraph group, then click the Tour List style shown under List Styles**

TROUBLE
If your name forces the text to a second line, make adjustments as needed so the contact information appears on two lines.

9. **Select the table, click the Table Tools Design tab, click the Tour Schedule table style, double-click the right edge of the table, enter your name where indicated below the table, click File, click Close, click Save, then close the Styles task pane**

   The file WD J-Profile of Alison Manning is again the active document.

Working with Styles and Templates

FIGURE J-14: Selecting a style in the Replace Style dialog box

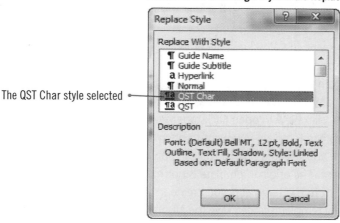

The QST Char style selected

FIGURE J-15: Managing styles using the Organizer dialog box

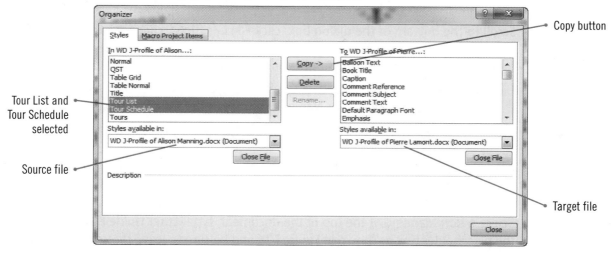

Copy button

Tour List and
Tour Schedule
selected

Source file

Target file

Renaming and deleting styles

To rename a style, right-click it in the Styles gallery, click Rename, type a new name, then press [Enter]. To delete a style from the Styles gallery, right-click the style, then click Remove from Quick Style Gallery. The style is deleted from the Styles gallery, but it is not deleted from your computer. You need to work in the Manage Styles

dialog box to delete a style from your system. Click the Manage Styles button at the bottom of the Styles task pane, select the style to delete, click Delete, then click OK to close the Manage Styles dialog box.

Creating a Template

A quick way to use all the styles contained in a document, including list and table styles, is to create a template. A template contains the basic structure of a document, including all the paragraph, character, linked, list, and table styles. You can create a template from an existing document, or you can create a template from scratch. Templates that you create are stored as **user templates**. To base a document on a user template, you click the File tab, click New to open Backstage view, click My templates in the Available Templates area, and then double-click the template you want to open. A new document that contains all the formats stored in the user template you selected opens. You can enter text into the document and then save it, just as you would any document. The original template is not modified. ▰▰▰ You create a new folder called Your Name Templates to store the templates you create in this unit, change the default location for user templates to the Your Name templates folder, save the Alison Manning profile as a user template, modify the template, and then open the template as a new document.

STEPS

1. **Click the** Start button 🪟 **on the taskbar, click** Computer, **navigate to the drive and folder where you store your files, click** New folder, **type** Your Name Templates **as the folder name, then press** [Enter]

   You want the Your Name Templates folder to be the default location for user templates. Then, when you save a document as a template, it is saved to the Your Name Templates folder by default.

2. **Close** Explorer, **click the** File tab, **click** Options, **then click** Advanced

   The Advanced option provides you with numerous ways to customize how you work with Word.

3. **Scroll to the bottom of the dialog box, click** File Locations, **click** User templates, **click** Modify, **navigate to the Your Name Templates folder, click the** Your Name Templates folder **to select it, then click** OK **until you are returned to the document**

4. **Click the** File tab, **click** Save As, **click the** Save as type list arrow, **click** Word Template (*.dotx), **then double-click** Your Name Templates **in the list of folders to open the folder**

5. **Select the** filename **in the File name text box, type** WD J-Profile Template, **then click** Save

   The file is saved as WD J-Profile Template.dotx to your default template location, which is the folder you called Your Name Templates. The .dotx filename extension identifies this file as a template file. Word automatically includes two additional folders in the Your Name Templates folder—the Document Themes and Live Content folders. You do not need to access the files in these folders.

6. **Select** Alison Manning **at the top of the document, type** [Enter Guide Name Here], **enter the placeholder text as shown in Figure J-16 and be sure to leave the contact information at the bottom of the document as part of the template, click** File, **click** Close, **then click** Save

   Now that you have created a template, you can use it to create a new document that contains all the styles and formatting you want.

7. **Click the** File tab, **click** New, **then click** My templates

   The Templates folder opens, and the template you saved is available.

8. **Verify that** WD J-Profile Template.dotx **is selected, verify that the Document option button in the Create New section is selected, then click** OK

   The template opens as a new document. You can enter text into this document and then save the document just as you would any document.

9. **Select the text** [Enter Guide Name Here], **type** Marion Keyes, **type text in the table and resize the column widths as shown in Figure J-17, type your name where indicated, save the document as** WD J-Profile of Marion Keyes **to the drive and folder where you store your files, click** File, **then click** Close

[Enter Guide Name Here]

Early Life

[Describe early life]

Tour Guide Career

[Describe tour guide's career]

Tours with QST

[Introduce two top tours and schedule]

Top Tours

[Describe top tours; format each tour name with the Tours style and format the list with the Tour List style]

Tour Schedule

Tour Name	Duration	2015 Start Dates

FIGURE J-17: **Table text for the new guide profile**

Tour Name	Duration	2015 Start Dates
France for Painters	10 days	July 1, August 1
Barging through Wales	8 days	July 12, August 15

Default location for user templates

By default, user templates are stored in the My templates folder. The path for this folder is: C:\Users\Administrator\AppData\Roaming\Microsoft\Templates. Note that a different folder might appear for Administrator, depending on how your computer system is set up. If the default location where user templates are saved has been changed, you can change back to the default location by selecting the User Templates folder in the File Locations section of the Advanced Options in the Word Options dialog box and then changing the location. The AppData folder is a hidden folder by default, so if you do not see the AppData folder, then use the Control Panel to change your folder settings to show hidden folders.

You can also create templates to distribute to others. These templates are called **workgroup templates**. You navigate to and select the location of a workgroup template in the File Locations section of the Advanced Options in the Word Options dialog box in the same way you navigate to and select the location of a user template.

Revising and Attaching a Template

You can modify a template just as you would any Word document. All new documents you create from the modified template will use the new settings. All documents that you created before you modified the template are not changed unless you open the Templates and Add-ins dialog box and direct Word to update styles automatically. ▰▰▰ You modify the Guide Title style in the Profile Template and then attach the revised template to a profile for Marsha Renfrew. You then update the profiles for the other tour guides with the revised template and delete the QST Profiles style set.

1. Click the File tab, click Open, navigate to and open the Your Name Templates folder, click WD J-Profile Template.dotx, click Open, right-click Guide Name in the Styles gallery, click Modify, change the font to Arial Rounded MT Bold, change the font size to 18 pt, then click OK

2. Select Early Life, change the font to Arial Rounded MT Bold, open the Styles gallery, right-click Heading 1, then click Update Heading 1 to Match Selection

   You need to resave the QST Profiles Quick Style set so that the new settings are available to new documents.

3. Click the Change Styles button, point to Style Set, click Save As Quick Style Set, click QST Profiles.dotx, click Save, click Yes, click the File tab, click Close, then click Save

4. Open the file WD J-3.docx from the drive and folder where you store your Data Files, save the file as WD J-Profile of Marsha Renfrew, then apply the Black Tie color scheme and the QST Profiles style set

   Colors schemes and Quick Style sets are not saved with templates. You need to attach the Profile Template to Marsha's profile so that you can apply all the new styles you created to the document. To do so you need to show the Developer tab.

5. Click the File tab, click Options, click Customize Ribbon, click the Developer check box in the list of Main Tabs as shown in Figure J-18, then click OK

   You use the Developer tab to work with advanced features such as form controls and templates.

6. Click the Developer tab on the Ribbon, click Document Template in the Templates group, click Attach, select WD J-Profile Template.dotx, click Open, click the Automatically update document styles check box, then click OK

   The Profile Template file is attached to Marsha Renfrew's profile. Now you can apply the styles associated with the Profile Template to Marsha's profile.

7. Click the Home tab, open the Styles task pane, apply styles as shown in Figure J-19, be sure your name is on the document, then save and close the document

8. Open the file WD J-Profile of Alison Manning.docx, click the Developer tab, click the Document Template button, click Attach, double-click WD J-Profile Template.dotx, click the Automatically update document styles check box to select it, click OK, enter your name where indicated, then save and close the document

9. Open the file WD J-Profile of Pierre Lamont.docx, attach WD J-Profile Template.dotx so Pierre Lamont's profile updates automatically, save and close the document, open and update WD J-Profile of Marion Keyes.docx, then save and close it

10. Open a new blank document, click the Change Styles button in the Styles group, point to Style Set, click Save as Quick Style Set, click QST Profiles.dotx, press [Delete], click Yes, click Cancel, click the File tab, click Options, click Customize Ribbon, click the Developer check box to deselect it, click OK, exit Word, then submit all your files to your instructor

Working with Styles and Templates

FIGURE J-18: Adding the Developer tab to the Ribbon

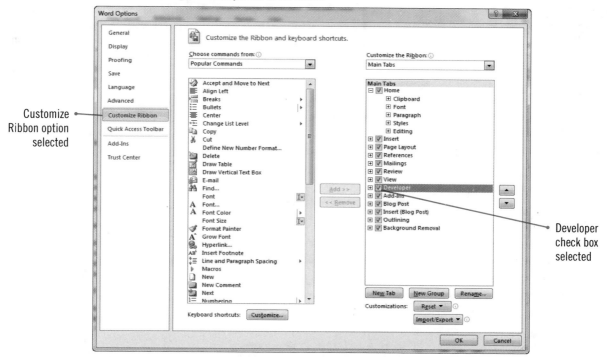

Customize Ribbon option selected

Developer check box selected

FIGURE J-19: Marsha Renfrew profile formatted with styles

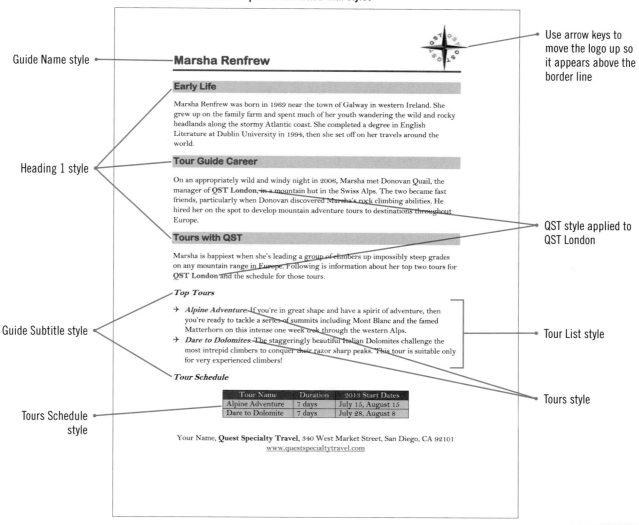

Guide Name style

Heading 1 style

Guide Subtitle style

Tours Schedule style

Use arrow keys to move the logo up so it appears above the border line

QST style applied to QST London

Tour List style

Tours style

Marsha Renfrew

Early Life

Marsha Renfrew was born in 1969 near the town of Galway in western Ireland. She grew up on the family farm and spent much of her youth wandering the wild and rocky headlands along the stormy Atlantic coast. She completed a degree in English Literature at Dublin University in 1994, then she set off on her travels around the world.

Tour Guide Career

On an appropriately wild and windy night in 2006, Marsha met Donovan Quail, the manager of QST London, in a mountain hut in the Swiss Alps. The two became fast friends, particularly when Donovan discovered Marsha's rock climbing abilities. He hired her on the spot to develop mountain adventure tours to destinations throughout Europe.

Tours with QST

Marsha is happiest when she's leading a group of climbers up impossibly steep grades on any mountain range in Europe. Following is information about her top two tours for QST London and the schedule for those tours.

Top Tours

→ *Alpine Adventure*: If you're in great shape and have a spirit of adventure, then you're ready to tackle a series of summits including Mont Blanc and the famed Matterhorn on this intense one week trek through the western Alps.

→ *Dare to Dolomites*: The staggeringly beautiful Italian Dolomites challenge the most intrepid climbers to conquer their razor sharp peaks. This tour is suitable only for very experienced climbers!

Tour Schedule

Tour Name	Duration	2013 Start Dates
Alpine Adventure	7 days	July 15, August 15
Dare to Dolomite	7 days	July 28, August 8

Your Name, **Quest Specialty Travel**, 340 West Market Street, San Diego, CA 92101
www.questspecialtytravel.com

Practice

Concepts Review

For current SAM information, including versions and content details, visit SAM Central (http://www.cengage.com/samcentral). If you have a SAM user profile, you may have access to hands-on instruction, practice, and assessment of the skills covered in this unit. Since various versions of SAM are supported throughout the life of this text, check with your instructor for the correct instructions and URL/Web site for accessing assignments.

Identify each of the items in Figure J-20.

FIGURE J-20

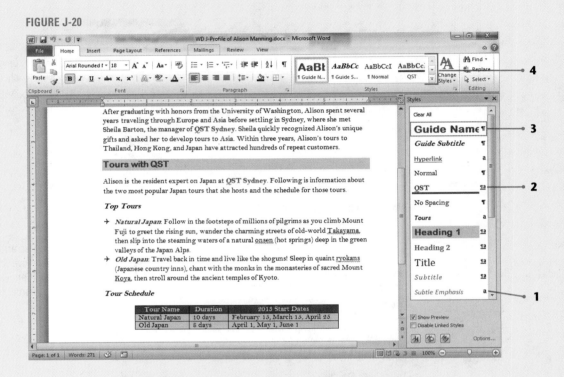

Match each term with the statement that best describes it.

5. **Quick Style set**
6. **Organizer dialog box**
7. **Template**
8. **Normal template**
9. **Character style**

a. A collection of character, paragraph, and linked styles that is named and available to all documents
b. Character formats that you name and store as a set
c. A file that contains the basic structure of a document in addition to selected styles; can be custom made
d. A file that contains the styles available to a new document in Word
e. Used to copy styles from a source document to a target document

Select the best answer from the list of choices.

10. What is available in the Quick Style gallery?
   a. Themes associated with a Quick Style set   **c.** Colors associated with a Quick Style set
   b. Styles associated with a Quick Style set   **d.** The Developer tab

11. Which of the following definitions best describes a paragraph style?
   a. Format settings applied only to selected text within a paragraph
   b. Format settings applied to a table grid
   c. Format settings applied to the structure of a document
   d. Format settings applied to all the text in a paragraph

12. How do you modify a style?
   a. Double-click the style in the Styles task pane.
   b. Right-click the style in the Styles gallery, then click Revise.
   c. Right-click the style in the Styles gallery, then click Modify.
   d. Click the style in the Styles task pane, then click New Style.

13. Which dialog box do you use to copy styles from one document to another?
   a. Organizer dialog box   **c.** Styles dialog box
   b. New Document dialog box   **d.** Modify Styles dialog box

14. Which tab do you use to attach a template to an existing document?
   a. Insert   **c.** Developer
   b. References   **d.** Page

Skills Review

1. Modify predefined styles.
   a. Start Word, open the file WD J-4.docx from the drive and folder where you store your Data Files, save it as **WD J-Puzzles_Shaped**, then open the Styles task pane.
   b. Modify the Normal style by changing the font to Times New Roman and the font size to 12 pt.
   c. Select the Animal Puzzles heading, then change the font to Arial Black, the font size to 16 pt, and the font color to Purple, Accent 4, Darker 50%.
   d. Remove the Before paragraph spacing, add After paragraph spacing, then add a 3 pt border line below the text in Purple, Accent 4, Darker 50%.
   e. Update the Heading 1 style so that it uses the new formats.

2. Create paragraph styles.
   a. Select the text "Shaped Jigsaw Puzzles" at the top of the document.
   b. Create a new style called **Puzzle Title** with the Arial Black font, 20 pt, and a bottom border of 3 pt, Purple, Accent 4, Darker 50%.
   c. Select "Summary of New Products," then create a new paragraph style called **Summary** that uses the Times New Roman font, 18 pt, and bold, and changes the font color to Purple, Accent 4, Darker 25%.
   d. Save the document.

3. Create character and linked styles.
   a. Create a new character style named **Puzzle Theme** that uses the Arial Black font, 12 pt, Italic, and the Purple, Accent 4, Darker 50% font color.
   b. Apply the Puzzle Theme style to "Elephant puzzle," Whale puzzle," "Italy puzzle," and "Great Britain puzzle" in the body text.
   c. Select "Puzzlemania" in the first paragraph, apply the Gradient Fill - Purple, Accent 4, Reflection text effect, open the Create New Style from Formatting dialog box, name the style **Company**, and select the Linked style type, then apply a 3-pt dark purple bottom border line.
   d. Apply the Company style to paragraph 2 (Elephant puzzle), undo the application, then apply the Company style just to the text "Puzzlemania" in the last paragraph.
   e. Save the document.

Skills Review (continued)

4. **Create custom list and table styles.**

   a. Click to the left of "Elephant puzzle", then define a new list style called **Puzzle List**. (*Hint*: Click the Multilevel List button in the Paragraph group on the Home tab, then click Define New List Style.)

   b. Change the list style to Bullet, open the Symbol dialog box, verify the Wingdings character set is active, type **182** in the Character code text box, then change the symbol color to Purple, Accent 4, Darker 50%.

   c. Apply the Puzzle List style to each paragraph that describes a puzzle: Whale puzzle, Italy puzzle, and Great Britain puzzle. (*Hint*: You access the Puzzle List style by clicking the Multilevel List button.)

   d. Select the table at the bottom of the document, then create a new table style called **Puzzle Table**.

   e. Select Purple, Accent 4, Lighter 80% for the fill color, change the border style to ½ pt and the border color to Automatic, then apply All Borders to the table.

   f. Format the header row with bold, the White font color, the Purple, Accent 4, Darker 50% fill color, and Center alignment.

   g. From the Table Tools Layout tab, modify the table properties of the current table so the table is centered between the left and right margins of the page, then save the document.

5. **Create a Quick Style set.**

   a. Save the current style set as **Puzzles**, then view the Puzzles style set in the list of Quick Style sets.

   b. Change the color scheme to Angles, then save the document.

   c. Open the file WD J-5.docx from the drive and folder where you store your Data Files, then save it as **WD J-Puzzles_3D**.

   d. Apply the Puzzles Quick Style set to the document, then apply the Angles color scheme.

   e. Apply the Puzzle Title style to the title, then apply the Summary style to "Summary of New Products".

   f. Apply the Puzzle Theme style to "Willow Tree puzzle", "Tulips puzzle", "Palazzo puzzle", and "Chalet puzzle", then save the document.

6. **Manage styles.**

   a. Position the insertion point at the beginning of the document, open the Replace dialog box, enter **Puzzlemania** in the Find what text box, then enter **Puzzlemania** in the Replace with dialog box.

   b. Open the More options area, select the Style option on the Format menu, select the Company Char style, then replace both instances of Puzzlemania with Puzzlemania formatted with the Company Char style.

   c. Open the Manage Styles dialog box from the Styles task pane, then click Import/Export to open the Organizer dialog box.

   d. Close the file in the left of the Organizer dialog box, then open the file WD J-Puzzles_Shaped.docx. Remember to navigate to the location where you save files and to change the Files of type to Word documents.

   e. Close the file in the right of the Organizer dialog box, then open the file WD J-Puzzles_3D.docx.

   f. Copy the Puzzle List and Puzzle Table styles from the WD J-Puzzles_Shaped document to the WD J-Puzzles_3D document, then close the Organizer dialog box and return to the document.

   g. In the file WD J-Puzzles_3D.docx, apply the Puzzle List style to each of the four puzzle descriptions.

   h. Select the table, use the Table Tools Design tab to apply the Puzzle Table style to the table, type your name where indicated at the end of the document, save the document, then close it.

   i. Close the Styles task pane.

Skills Review (continued)

7. Create a template.

a. In Windows Explorer, create a new folder called **Your Name Skills Review** in the drive and folder where you store your files.

b. Change the file location for user templates to the new folder you named Your Name Skills Review.

c. Save the current document (which should be WD J-Puzzles_Shaped) as a template called **WD J-Puzzle Descriptions.dotx** in the Your Name Skills Review folder.

d. Select "Shaped Jigsaw Puzzles" at the top of the page, type **[Enter Puzzle Category Here]**, then delete text and enter directions so the document appears as shown in Figure J-21. (*Hint:* If new text is formatted with the Puzzle Theme or Company style, select the formatted text and click the Clear Formatting button in the Font group on the Home tab.)

e. Save and close the template.

f. Create a new document based on the WD J-Puzzle Descriptions template.

g. Replace the title of the document with the text **Brain Teaser Puzzles**, save the document as **WD J-Puzzles_Brain Teaser** to the drive and folder where your store your files, then close it.

FIGURE J-21

8. Revise and attach a template.

a. Open the file WD J-Puzzle Descriptions.dotx template from the Your Name Skills Review folder, then modify the Heading 1 style so that the font is Comic Sans MS and bold. (*Note*: Be sure to open the template using the File and Open commands.)

b. Modify the Puzzle Title style by changing the font to Comic Sans MS and applying bold.

c. Resave the Puzzles Quick Style set.

d. Save and close the template.

e. Open the file WD J-6.docx from the drive and folder where your Data Files are located, save the file as **WD J-Puzzles_Landscape**, then select the Angles color scheme and apply the Puzzles Quick Style set.

f. Show the Developer tab on the Ribbon, open the Templates and Add-ins dialog box, attach the WD J-Puzzle Descriptions.dotx template, click the Automatically update document styles check box, then click OK.

g. Apply styles from the Puzzles Quick Style set that are associated with the WD J-Puzzle Descriptions template so that the WD J-Puzzles_Landscape document resembles the other documents you have formatted for this Skills Review (*Hint*: Remember to apply the Puzzle Title, Puzzle Theme, Summary, Puzzle List, and Puzzle Table styles, and to apply the Company style to all three instances of "Puzzlemania."

h. Enter your name where indicated, then save and close the document.

i. Open the file WD J-Puzzles_3D.docx, attach the updated template, automatically update document styles, enter your name where indicated, then save and close the document.

j. Update WD J-Puzzles_Shaped.docx and WD J-Puzzles_Brain Teaser with the modified template, enter your name where indicated, then save and close the documents.

k. In a new blank document in Word, open the Save Quick Style Set dialog box, delete the Puzzles style set, then remove the Developer tab from the Ribbon and exit Word.

l. Submit your files to your instructor.

Independent Challenge 1

You are the office manager of Digital Learning, a company that creates learning materials for delivery over the Internet. The annual company fun run is coming soon, and you need to inform the employees about the date and time of the run. To save time, you have already typed the text of the memo with some formatting. Now you need to change some of the styles, create a new Quick Style set, then use it to format another memo.

a. Start Word, open the file WD J-7.docx from the drive and folder where you store your Data Files, then save it as **WD J-Memo_Fun Run**.

b. Modify styles as shown in Table J-1.

TABLE J-1

style name	changes
Title	Berlin Sans FB font, 22-pt font size, Red, Accent 2, Darker 50%
Heading 1	Berlin Sans FB font, 14-pt font size, Red, Accent 2, Darker 25%

c. Change the color scheme to Module.

d. Save the style set as **Events**.

e. Select Your Name in the message header, type your name, save the document, then close it.

f. Open the file WD J-8.docx, save the document as **WD J-Memo_Holiday**, apply the Events Quick Style set, change the color scheme to Module, type your name where indicated, then save the document.

g. Remove the Events Quick Style set from the list of Quick Style sets, close the file and exit Word, then submit the files to your instructor.

Independent Challenge 2

As the owner of Le Bistro, an upscale café in San Francisco, you need to create two menus—one for winter and one for summer. You have already created an unformatted version of the winter menu. Now you need to format text in the winter menu with styles, save the styles in a new Quick Style set called Menus, then use the Menus Quick Style set to format text in the summer version of the menu. You also need to work in the Organizer dialog box to copy the list and table styles you created for the Winter Menu to the summer version of the menu.

a. Start Word, open the file WD J-9.docx from the drive and folder where you store your Data Files, then save it as **WD J-Le Bistro Winter Menu**. Apply the Waveform color scheme.

b. Select the title (Le Bistro Winter Menu), apply these formats: Arial, 18 pt, bold, a font color of Blue, Accent 1, Darker 50%, and Center alignment, then create a new style called **Menu Title** based on these formats. (*Hint*: Right-click the formatted text, point to Styles, click Save Selection as a New Quick Style, type Menu Title, then click OK.)

c. Select Appetizers, apply the formats Arial, 14 pt, bold, italic, a font color of Blue, Accent 1, Darker 25%, and a top and bottom border that has a 1 pt width with the same color as the text, then create a new paragraph style from the selection called **Menu Category**.

d. Click to the left of Brie (the first appetizer), then create a new list style called **Menu Item** that includes a bullet character from Wingdings symbol 84 (a stylized snowflake) that is colored Blue, Accent 1, Darker 50%.

e. Click the Multilevel List button, right-click the new Menu Item style in the List Styles area, click Modify, then in the Modify Style dialog box, click Format (bottom left), click Numbering, click More (bottom left), click the Add tab stop at: check box, select the contents of the text box, type **5.5**, click OK, then click OK.

f. Save the styles in a Quick Style set called **Menus**.

g. Apply the Menu Category style to each of the remaining main headings: Soups and Salads, Entrees, Desserts, and Opening Times.

h. Select the menu items in the Appetizers category, apply the Menu Item list style (remember to click the Multilevel List button), then apply the Menu Item list style to all the menu items in each category.

Independent Challenge 2 (continued)

i. Click anywhere in the table, then create a new table style called **Bistro Times** that fills the table cells with a light fill color of your choice and the header row with the corresponding dark fill color of your choice and the white font color, bold, and centering.

j. Modify the Bistro Times table style so that the table is centered between the left and right margins of the page.

k. Type your name where indicated at the bottom of the document, then save the document and keep it open.

l. Open the file WD J-10.docx, save it as **WD J-Le Bistro Summer Menu**, then apply the Menus Quick Style set.

m. Format the appropriate headings with the Menu Title and Menu Category styles. Note that the Menu Items list style and the Bistro Times table styles are not saved with the Menus Quick Style set. You need to copy them separately.

n. Change the color scheme to the color scheme of your choice. You do not need to select the same color scheme you applied to the winter menu.

o. Save the file, then open the Organizer dialog box from the Manage Styles dialog box. (*Hint*: Click Import/Export.)

p. In the Organizer dialog box, make WD J-Le Bistro Winter Menu.docx the source file and WD J-Le Bistro Summer Menu.docx the target file. Remember to select All Word Documents as the file type when opening the files.

q. Copy the Bistro Times table style and the Menu Item list style from the file WD J-Le Bistro Winter Menu.docx file to the WD J-Le Bistro Summer Menu.docx file, then close the Organizer dialog box.

r. In the Summer menu document, apply the Menu Item list style to the first appetizer (Goat cheeses).

s. Click the Multilevel List button, right-click the Menu Item style, click Modify, then change the bullet symbol for the Menu Item style to Wingdings 123 (a flower symbol).

t. Apply the updated Menu Item list style to all the menu items, apply the Bistro Times table style to the table, type your name where indicated at the bottom of the document, then remove the Menus style from the list of style sets.

Advanced Challenge Exercise

- In the Winter menu document, modify the Menu Title style so that it includes the Britannic Bold font and 20-point font size.
- Modify the Menu Category style so it includes the Gold, Accent 5, Darker 50% font color and a 1½ point top and bottom border in the same color.
- Modify the list style so that the bullet is diamond shape (character code 116) and Green, Accent 3, Darker 50%.
- Modify the table style so that the colors use variations on the Gold, Accent 5 color.
- Click text formatted with the Menu Category style, then change the name of the Menu Category style to **Category**. (*Hint:* Right-click the style name in the Styles gallery, click Rename, type the new name, then press [Enter].)

u. Save the documents, submit all files to your instructor, then close all files.

Independent Challenge 3

As a student in the business program at your local community college, you have volunteered to create a design for a bi-monthly class newsletter and another classmate has volunteered to write text for the first newsletter, which is to be distributed in October. First, you create a template for the newsletter, then you apply the template to the document containing the newsletter text.

a. In Word, modify the default location for user templates so that they are saved in the folder you created previously named Your Name Templates. This folder should be in the drive and folder where you store your files.

b. Open the file WD J-11.docx, save it as **WD J-Newsletter Template.dotx** to the Your Name Templates folder, then enter text and create styles as shown in Figure J-22.

FIGURE J-22

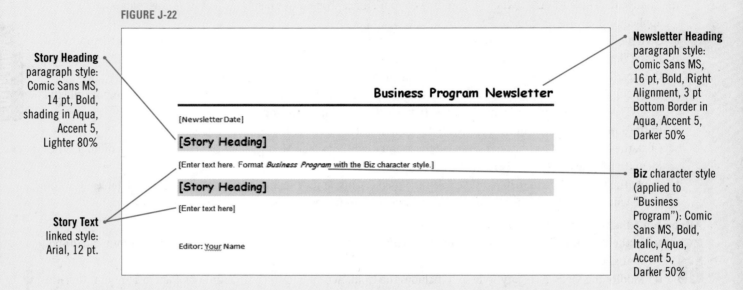

c. Save the style set as **Biz Program**.

d. Click to the left of the first [Story Heading], then create two columns from this point forward. (*Hint*: Click the Page Layout tab, click the Columns list arrow in the Page Setup group, click More Columns, then in the Columns dialog box, click two in the Presets section, click the Apply to list arrow, select This point forward, then click OK.)

e. Type your name where indicated, then save and close the template.

f. Start a new document based on the WD J-Newsletter Template, type **October 2013** in place of [Newsletter Date], **Class Projects** in place of the first [Story Heading] and **Upcoming Events** in place of the next [Story Heading].

g. Save the document as **WD J-Newsletter_October** to the drive and folder where you store your files, then close the document.

h. Open the file WD J-12.docx, save it as **WD J-Newsletter_December**, show the Developer tab on the Ribbon, attach the WD J-Newsletter Template.dotx to the document, apply the Biz Program Quick Style set, then apply styles and formatting where needed. Make sure you apply the Story Text style to all paragraphs of text that are not headings or the date.

i. Use the Replace feature to find every instance of Business Program (except Business Program in the Newsletter Heading) and replace it with Business Program formatted with the Biz Char style. (*Hint*: Use the Find Next command not the Replace All command.)

j. Apply the two-column format starting at the Class Projects heading. (*Note*: You need to apply the two-column format because options related to the structure of a document saved with a template are lost when you attach the template to an existing document.)

Independent Challenge 3 (continued)

k. Click at the end of the document (following your name), click the Page Layout tab, click Breaks, then click Continuous to balance the columns in the newsletter.

l. Modify the Story Text style so that the font size is 10 pt, then resave the Biz Program Quick Style set.

m. Save and close the document.

n. Open the file WD J-Newsletter Template.dotx, reapply the Biz Program Quick Style set so that the Story Text style changes, then modify the Newsletter Heading style so the font size is 22 pt.

o. Resave the Biz Program Quick Style set, then save and close the template.

p. Open the file WD J-Newsletter_October.docx, attach the updated template, then save and close the document.

q. Open the file WD J-Newsletter_ December.docx, then verify that the document is updated with the new style.

Advanced Challenge Exercise

- In the Class Projects section, select the list of dates and topics from November 15 to Security Issues, then convert the text to a table. (*Hint*: Click the Insert tab, click the Table list arrow, click Convert Text to Table, then click OK.)
- With the table selected, create a table style called **Projects**.
- Change the fill color for the entire table to Olive Green, Accent 3, Lighter 80.
- Select Editor, open the Style Inspector, open the Reveal Formatting task pane, note the addition of Bold and 12 pt to the selected text as seen in the Reveal Formatting task pane Font area, click Clear All in the Style Inspector to remove this additional formatting, then close all open task panes.

r. Save the document, delete the Biz Program Quick Style set, close the Developer tab, close the document and exit Word, then submit the files to your instructor.

Real Life Independent Challenge

This Independent Challenge requires an Internet connection.

From the Microsoft Office Templates Web site, you can access a variety of templates. You can import any template from the Web site directly into Word and then modify it for your own purposes. You decide to find and then modify a template for a business trip itinerary.

a. Start Word, click the File tab, click New, scroll down as needed and click More categories in the Office.com Templates area, or click More templates if all the categories are already showing, explore some of the documents available, then click Itineraries.

b. Select the template Business trip itinerary with meeting details, click Download, then save the document as **WD J-Itinerary from Microsoft Office Templates.docx**.

c. View the three pages of the itinerary template, delete the text and the tables on the last two pages, and then delete any blank pages so your document consists of one page.

d. Enter Your Company Name in place of Organization Name, then enter your name where indicated at the top of the second column in the itinerary table.

e. Fill in the second column so it contains information related to a business trip of your choice. You can make up the details. Note that you will need to apply the Body character style (check the Styles task pane) to some of the entries so that every entry uses the Body style.

f. Select a new color scheme for the document. (*Note*: You apply a new color scheme so that the colors in that color scheme are available to you as you work on the document.)

g. Modify the Heading 1 style by changing the font, font size, and color. Add a border line. You determine the settings.

h. Select Trip Description, check the name of the style that formats the text, then modify the style formatting so the text complements the formatting you created for Heading 1.

i. Save and close the document, exit Word, then submit the file to your instructor.

Visual Workshop

Create a new document, then type the text and create the tables shown in Figure J-23. Do not include any formatting. Select the Metro color scheme, apply the Title style to the title, then modify it so that it appears as shown in Figure J-23. Note that all the colors are variations of the Metro color theme, Turquoise, Accent 4, and the font style for the headings is Lucida Handwriting. Apply the Heading 1 style to the names of the price lists, then modify them so that they appear as shown in Figure J-23. Modify the Normal style so the font size is 14 pt. Create a table style called **Price List** that formats each table as shown in Figure J-23, then modify the column widths. Save the file as **WD J-Stress Free**, type **Prepared by Your Name** centered under the tables, submit a copy to your instructor, then close the document.

FIGURE J-23

Stress Free Aromatherapy

Essential Oils Price List

Produce #	Essential Oil	Price
6670	Cedar	$6.50
6672	Lavender	$8.00
6673	Ginger	$7.50
6674	Ylang Ylang	$6.00

Perfume Oils Price List

Produce #	Perfume Oil	Price
7760	Jasmine	$7.00
7780	Peppermint	$7.50
7790	Rose	$7.00
7792	Vanilla	$8.00
7795	Gardenia	$7.50

Prepared by Your Name

Working with Styles and Templates

Working with References

Word includes a variety of features that you can use to create and edit academic papers and articles. For example, you can use the AutoCorrect feature to simplify the typing of technical terms, you can use the Footnotes and Endnotes features to insert footnotes and endnotes that provide additional information, and you can use the Translate feature to translate text written in another language. In addition, you can add and manage citations, generate a bibliography or a works cited list, and generate tables of figures and authorities. You can even build and edit mathematical equations for inclusion in scientific and technical papers.  One of your duties as a special projects assistant at Quest Specialty Travel (QST) in San Diego is to compile reference materials that provide participants with background information about tour destinations. You use the AutoCorrect feature to insert text in an article for QST's Renaissance Art Tour to Italy, and then you add references and a table of figures to the article. You also create equations for an article on the pricing of QST tours.

OBJECTIVES

Work with AutoCorrect

Customize footnotes

Use the Translate feature

Work with citations

Modify citations and manage sources

Generate a bibliography

Create a table of figures

Work with equations

Working with AutoCorrect

The AutoCorrect feature is set up to automatically correct most typos and misspelled words. For example, if you type "teh" and press the Spacebar, the AutoCorrect feature inserts "the." The AutoCorrect feature also inserts symbols when you type certain character combinations. For example, if you type (r), the ® symbol appears. You can modify the list of AutoCorrect options, and you can create your own AutoCorrect entries. These entries can be a word, a phrase, or even a paragraph. You set up AutoCorrect to automatically enter the text you specify when you type a certain sequence of characters. For example, you could specify that "San Francisco, California" be entered each time you time "sfc." ▰▰▰ You are editing an article on the Renaissance artist Cellini, and you need to enter the term "Renaissance" in various places in the article. Since you know you will be working on several articles related to the Renaissance, you decide to create an AutoCorrect entry that will insert "Renaissance" each time you type "ren." You also use AutoCorrect to insert symbols, view the AutoFormat settings, and delete an entry from the AutoCorrect list.

STEPS

1. **Start Word, open the file WD K-1.docx from the drive and folder where you store your Data Files, save the file as WD K-Artist Article, click the File tab, click Options (below Help), then click Proofing**

   All the options related to how Word corrects and formats text appear in the Word Options dialog box.

2. **Click AutoCorrect Options**

   The AutoCorrect: English (U.S.) dialog box opens. By default the AutoCorrect tab is active.

3. **Scroll through the AutoCorrect list to view the predefined pairs of symbols and words**

   Notice how many symbols you can create with simple keystrokes. The AutoCorrect list is used in all the programs in the Microsoft Office suite, which means that any word you add or delete from the AutoCorrect list in one program is also added or deleted from all other Office programs. On the AutoCorrect tab, you can create a new AutoCorrect entry.

TROUBLE
If the insertion point is not blinking in the Replace text box, click the Replace text box to make it active.

4. **Type ren in the Replace text box, press [TAB], type Renaissance as shown in Figure K-1, click Add, click OK, then click OK**

   When you create an AutoCorrect entry, you need to enter an abbreviation that is not a real word. For example, you would not create an AutoCorrect entry for "Antarctic" from "ant" because every time you typed "ant," the word "Antarctic" would appear whether you wanted it to or not.

QUICK TIP
If you do not want an AutoCorrect entry to appear when you type its code, press [Backspace] after typing the code

5. **Press [Ctrl][F] to open the Navigation pane, type rest of the world, click to the left of world in the document, type ren, then press [Spacebar]**

   The word "Renaissance" is inserted.

6. **Press [Ctrl][End] to move to the end of the document, scroll up to view the table above the picture, then click in the blank table cell below Cost in the second row**

TROUBLE
If the Euro symbol does not appear, type 20AC, press and hold the [ALT] key, then press X.

7. **Type (e) to insert the symbol for the Euro currency, type 75.00, then use the AutoCorrect entry (e) to enter €85.00 in the blank cell of the third row as shown in Figure K-2**

8. **Click the File tab, click Options, click Proofing, then click AutoCorrect Options**

   As a courtesy to others who might use the computer you are currently working on, you delete the "ren" Autocorrect entry. If you are the only user of your computer, you can leave the entry so it is available for future use.

9. **Type ren in the Replace text box, click Delete, click Close, click OK, then save the document**

   The "ren" AutoCorrect entry is deleted from Word and all other Office applications.

FIGURE K-1: **Creating a new AutoCorrect entry**

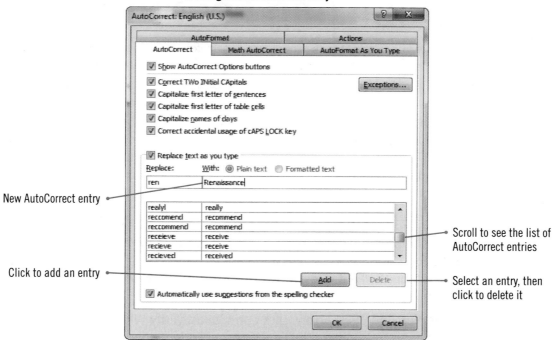

New AutoCorrect entry

Click to add an entry

Scroll to see the list of AutoCorrect entries

Select an entry, then click to delete it

FIGURE K-2: **Completed tour costs**

Tour	Description	Cost
The Gardens of Florence	Explore the great gardens of Florence, including the famous Boboli Gardens.	€75.00
Golden Artisans of Florence	Visit the workshops of three Florentine goldsmiths and marvel at their incredible skill.	€85.00

Symbol added automatically by AutoCorrect when (e) typed

Accessing AutoFormat options in the AutoCorrect dialog box

Two tabs in the AutoCorrect dialog box relate to how Word formats text that you type. From the AutoFormat tab, you can view the list of formats that Word applies automatically to text. For example, if you type straight quotes ("), Word inserts smart quotes ("). The AutoFormat As You Type tab shows some of the same options included in the AutoFormat tab along with some additional options, as shown in Figure K-3. Usually, you do not need to change the default options. However, if you do not want an option, you can click the check box next to the option to deselect it. For example, if you decide that you do not want Word to make an ordinal such as 1st into 1st, you can click the Ordinals (1st) with superscript check box to deselect it.

FIGURE K-3: **Options available in the AutoFormat As You Type dialog box**

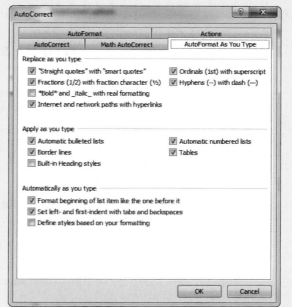

Customizing Footnotes

You use **footnotes** or **endnotes** to provide additional information or to acknowledge sources for text in a document. Footnotes appear at the bottom of the page on which the footnote reference appears and endnotes appear at the end of the document. Every footnote and endnote consists of a **note reference mark** and the corresponding note text. When you add, delete, or move a note, any additional notes in the document are renumbered automatically. You can customize footnotes by changing the number format, by adding a custom mark, or by modifying the numbering sequence. The footnotes in the current document are numbered using the A, B, C style and set to restart on every page. You change the numbering style of the footnotes to the 1, 2, 3 style and set the footnotes to number consecutively starting from "1." You then add a new footnote, and edit footnotes you inserted earlier.

STEPS

1. **Increase the zoom to 130%, scroll to the top of the document and notice as you scroll that the footnotes on each page start with "A," click the** References tab**, click the launcher** ⌐ **in the Footnotes group, click the** Number format list arrow**, then select the 1, 2, 3 number format**

2. **Click the** Numbering list arrow**, click** Continuous**, verify Whole document appears next to Apply changes to, compare the Footnote and Endnote dialog box to Figure K-4, then click** Apply

   The footnotes are numbered continuously through the document starting at "1".

3. **Type** rigorous training **in the Search Document text box in the Navigation pane, click after** training **in the document, then close the Navigation pane**

   The insertion point is positioned where you need to insert a new footnote.

4. **Click the** Insert Footnote button **in the Footnotes group, type** Artists began training at an early age. They first apprenticed with a master, as Cellini did at the age of fifteen.**, then scroll so you can see all three footnotes on the page**

   Figure K-5 shows the footnote area with the newly inserted footnote (footnote 2).

QUICK TIP
You can also click the footnote text to move directly to the footnote.

5. **Click in the line of text immediately above the footnote separator line, click the** Next Footnote button **in the Footnotes group to move to footnote 5, double-click 5 to move the insertion point to the footnote at the bottom of the page, click after the word** Clement**, press [Spacebar], type** VII**, then scroll up and click above the footnote separator**

6. **Press [Ctrl][G], click** Footnote **in the Go to what list, click in the** Enter footnote number text box**, type** 1**, click** Go To**, then click** Close

   The insertion point moves to the footnote 1 reference mark in the document.

7. **Press [Delete] two times to remove the footnote reference mark and its associated footnote text, then scroll down to see the newly labeled footnote 1**

   The original footnote reference mark 1 and its corresponding footnote are deleted, and the remaining footnote reference marks and their corresponding footnotes are renumbered starting with 1. By default, the Footnote Text style is applied to text in footnotes. You can also modify the appearance of the footnote text by changing the Footnote Text style.

8. **Click anywhere in the footnote at the bottom of a page,** right-click**, then click** Style

   The Style dialog box opens with Footnote Text already selected.

9. **Click** Modify**, click the** Format button **at the lower left of the dialog box, click** Paragraph**, reduce the After spacing to 6 pt, click the** Line spacing list arrow**, click** Single**, click** OK**, click** OK**, click** Apply**, then save the document**

   Text in all of the footnotes is now single spaced with 6 point After spacing.

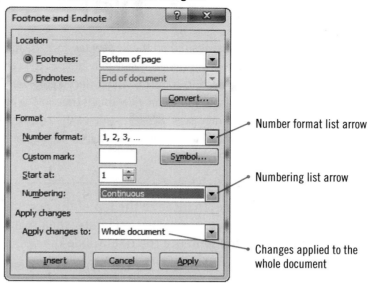

Number format list arrow

Numbering list arrow

Changes applied to the whole document

FIGURE K-5: Text for footnote 2

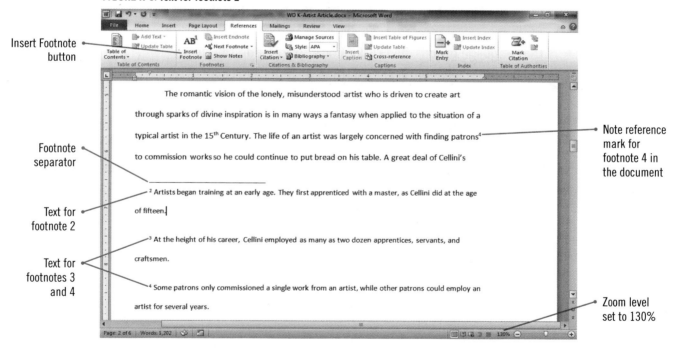

Insert Footnote button

Note reference mark for footnote 4 in the document

Footnote separator

Text for footnote 2

Text for footnotes 3 and 4

Zoom level set to 130%

Inserting endnotes

Click the Insert Endnote button in the Footnotes group on the References tab to insert a note reference mark for an endnote. When you click the Insert Endnote button, the insertion point moves to the end of your document so that you can enter text for the endnote in the same way you enter text for a footnote. You click above the endnote separator to return to the text of your document. You work in the Footnote and Endnote dialog box to modify options for endnotes.

Using the Translate Feature

You can use the Translate feature on the Review tab to translate single words or short passages of text into another language or from another language into English. You can also access Web-based translation services from Word when you need to translate longer documents that require a high degree of accuracy. Finally, you can use the Mini Translator to provide instant translations into 22 languages of single words or phrases that you move the pointer over. Some of the text in the article is written in Italian. You use the Translate feature to translate the text from Italian to English, and then you experiment with the Mini Translator feature.

STEPS

1. **Press [Ctrl][Home] to move to the top of the document, press [Ctrl][F] to open the Navigation pane, type produce sculpture, then select the text from Cellini to adornamenti at the end of the sentence (do not include the opening parenthesis)**

2. **Click the Review tab, then click the Translate button in the Language group**
   Three translation options are listed.

TROUBLE
You need to be connected to the Internet to work with the Translate feature.

3. **Click Translate Selected Text to open the Research task pane, verify that Italian (Italy) appears in the From text box, then if necessary, click the To list arrow and click English (U.S.)**
   A machine translation of the selected text appears in the Research task pane, as shown in Figure K-6. The translation is an approximation of the meaning and is not meant to be definitive.

4. **Close the Navigation pane, then close the Research task pane**

5. **Click the word goldsmith in the line above the Italian quote, click the Translate button in the Language group, then click Choose Translation Language**
   The Translation Language Options dialog box opens. You use this dialog box to set the options for translating the document or the options for the Mini Translator. You can also update the translation services available via a link in this dialog box.

6. **Click the Translate To: list arrow in the Choose Mini Translator language area, select Italian (Italy), then click OK**

7. **Click the Translate button, then click Mini Translator [Italian (Italy)] to turn on this feature**

8. **Move the pointer over and then slightly above goldsmith to view the Online Bilingual Dictionary, then note that the Italian translation is "orefice" as shown in Figure K-7**

9. **Click the Translate button in the Language group, click Mini Translator to turn the feature off, then save the document**

FIGURE K-6: Translating text

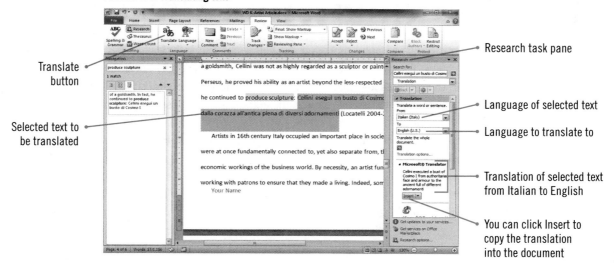

Translate button

Selected text to be translated

Research task pane

Language of selected text

Language to translate to

Translation of selected text from Italian to English

You can click Insert to copy the translation into the document

FIGURE K-7: Using the Mini Translator

Translation of "goldsmith" into Italian

Online Bilingual Dictionary tools; use ScreenTips to identify tools

Exploring the Research task pane

The Research task pane provides you with a variety of options for finding information. You can open the Research task pane from the Translate button, or you can open the Research task pane by clicking the Research button in the Proofing group on the Review tab. To find information about a specific topic, you enter keywords into the Search for text box, then click the list arrow to show the list of services. These services include dictionaries, thesauruses, and various Internet research Web sites. Figure K-8 shows the research sites that are available when "Italy" is entered in the Search text box and All Research Sites is selected. You can scroll through the list to find research sites that meet your needs.

FIGURE K-8: Options in the Research task pane

Working with Citations

The Citations & Bibliography group on the References tab includes features to help you keep track of the resources you use to write research papers and articles, as well as any document that includes information you obtained from other sources, such as books and Web sites. During the course of your research, you can create a source by entering information, such as the author, title, and year of publication, into a preset form. Word provides preset forms for 17 source types. As you work on a research paper, you can then insert a citation for an existing source or for a new source that you create. A **citation** is a short reference, usually including the author and page number, that gives credit to the source of a quote or other information included in a document. Citations are based on information you entered in the source form and are used to generate the bibliography or works cited page. Over time, you can accumulate hundreds of reference sources. You can use the Manage Sources feature to help you organize your sources. You have already inserted some citations into the artist article. Now you need to add two new sources—one to a book and one to a conference proceeding. You also need to format a long quote and include a placeholder citation.

STEPS

1. **Press [Ctrl][F] to open the Navigation pane, type** domestic security, **click after the ending quotation mark in the document, click the** References tab, **then click the** Insert Citation **button in the Citations & Bibliography group**

   A menu opens with a list of sources that have already been entered in the document. You can insert a citation to an existing source, or you can enter information to create a new source.

2. **Click** Add New Source, **click the** Type of Source list arrow **in the Create Source dialog box, scroll the list to view the types of sources available, then select** Book

   You enter information about the source in the Create Source dialog box. The fields provided in the preset form vary, depending on the type of source you selected.

3. **Complete the form with the information shown in Figure K-9**

4. **Click the** Show All Bibliography Fields check box **to expand the Create Source dialog box**

   You could enter more information about a source. The fields marked with a red asterisk are the recommended fields.

5. **Click** OK

   The citation (Wallace, 2011) appears following the text. The format of the citation, in this case (Author date), depends on which style, such as Chicago, MLA, or APA, you selected. The information in the citation is collected from its associated source form.

6. **Search for the text** sculptor's art, **click after the closing quotation mark, click the** Insert Citation button, **then click** Add New Source

7. **Click the** Type of Source list arrow, **select** Conference Proceedings, **complete the Create Source form with the information shown in Figure K-10, then click** OK

8. **Search for the text** you should know, **select the paragraph of text from "You should know..." to "...brief space of time."(include the quotation marks), click the** Home tab, **click the** More button ⬇ **in the Styles group to expand the Styles gallery, then select the** Intense Quote style **as shown in Figure K-11**

9. **Press [→] once to deselect the quotation, click [←] until the insertion point appears to the right of the quotation, click the** References tab, **click the** Insert Citation button, **click** Add New Placeholder, **click** OK, **then save the document**

   The citation (Placeholder1) appears. When you are writing a research paper, you sometimes insert a placeholder to indicate where you will insert a citation later.

FIGURE K-9: Entering a book source

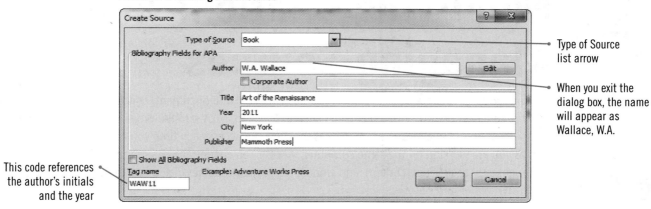

Type of Source
list arrow

When you exit the
dialog box, the name
will appear as
Wallace, W.A.

This code references
the author's initials
and the year

FIGURE K-10: Entering a Conference Proceedings source

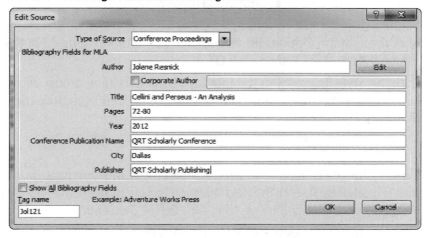

FIGURE K-11: Formatting a quote with the Intense Quote style

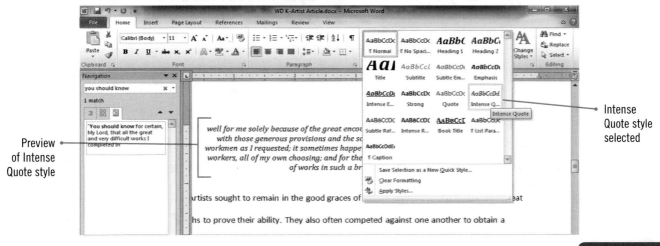

Intense
Quote style
selected

Preview
of Intense
Quote style

Working with References

Modifying Citations and Managing Sources

You can modify the contents of a citation you have inserted in a document, edit the source of the citation, and format a citation for specific guidelines such as Chicago, MLA, or APA. When you create a new source, the source is added to a master list of sources that you can access each time you create a new document as long as you are working on the same computer. ▓▓▓▓ You change the citation style of the citations in the document, edit the citation content, and work in the Manage Sources dialog box to edit and delete sources.

STEPS

1. **Search for Stevens using the Navigation pane, click Stevens in the document, then close the Navigation pane**

2. **Scroll up slightly so you can see a portion of the picture, click the field selection handle to select the entire citation (the citation is shaded in blue when it is selected), click the Style list arrow in the Citations & Bibliography group to show the list of citation styles, then click MLA Sixth Edition as shown in Figure K-12**

   The year is removed and the citation includes only the name of the author.

3. **Click the Citation Options list arrow, click Edit Citation, type 82 in the Pages text box as shown in Figure K-13, then click OK**

4. **Click the Style list arrow in the Citations & Bibliography group, click Chicago Fifteenth Edition, click the Citations Options list arrow, click Edit Citation, click the Year check box, then click OK**

   The year is suppressed, and the citation includes only the author's name and the page number of the reference, separated by a comma.

5. **Click outside the citation to deselect it, open the Navigation pane, find the text space of time, click (Placeholder1), click the field selection handle to select the entire citation, press [Delete], click the Insert Citation button, then click Cellini, Benvenuto as shown in Figure K-14**

6. **Click the citation, click the Citation Options list arrow, click Edit Citation, type 324-325 for the pages, click the Year check box to select it, click OK, then click outside the citation to deselect it**

   The citation changes to show the author name, a comma, and page numbers. The year is now suppressed in the citation.

7. **Search for domestic security, edit the Wallace citation to add 123 as the page number and suppress the year, then search for sculptor's art, and edit the Resnick citation to add 75 as the page number and suppress the year**

8. **Click Manage Sources in the Citations & Bibliography group**

   In the Source Manager dialog box, you can view a master list of sources, browse to select a different master list, and copy sources either from the master list to your current document or vice versa. You can also choose how to view sources, edit a source, add a new source, delete a source, and find a source. You notice that the entry for John Stevens should be John Stephens.

9. **Click the entry for Stevens in the Current list, click Edit, select Stevens, type Stephens, then click OK**

10. **Click Placeholder1 in the Current List, click Delete, click Close, then close the Navigation pane and save the document**

    The placeholder entry is removed from the document and will not be included when you generate a bibliography in the next lesson.

FIGURE K-12: Changing the citation style

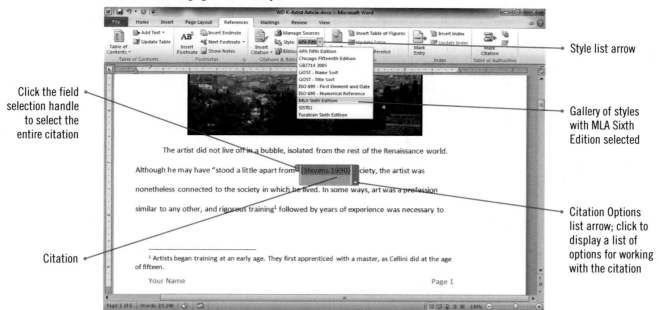

Style list arrow

Click the field selection handle to select the entire citation

Gallery of styles with MLA Sixth Edition selected

Citation

Citation Options list arrow; click to display a list of options for working with the citation

FIGURE K-13: Edit Citation dialog box

FIGURE K-14: Selecting an existing source

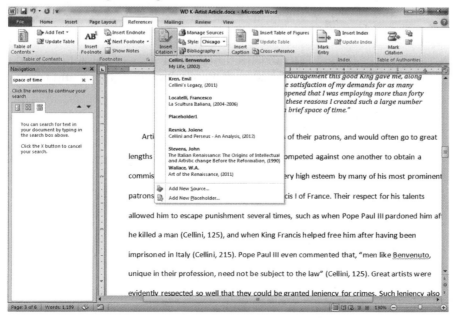

Generating a Bibliography

Once you have finished your research paper, you can assemble all your sources on a separate page or pages at the end of your document. You can choose to create a works cited list or a standard bibliography. A **works cited** page lists only the works that are included in citations in your document. A **bibliography** lists all the sources you used to gather information for the document. You can also choose the format that meets your needs, such as APA, MLA, or Chicago. By default, the references are listed in alphabetical order by author. You create a bibliography for the paper, then experiment with different formats. Finally, you remove a source and update the bibliography.

STEPS

1. **Press [Ctrl][End] to move to the bottom of the document, then press [Ctrl][Enter] to insert a page break following the picture**

2. **Click the Bibliography button in the Citations & Bibliography group, click Bibliography, then scroll up to see the bibliography**

   A field containing the bibliography is inserted. When you choose one of the built-in options, Word automatically inserts a title (Bibliography or Works Cited).

3. **Change the view to 100%, click below the bibliography, then compare the bibliography to Figure K-15**

   The references are listed in alphabetical order by author, and the title of each work in the bibliography is italicized according to the Chicago style.

4. **Click any entry to select the bibliography, click the Style list arrow in the Citations & Bibliography group on the References tab, then click MLA Sixth Edition**

   In a few moments, the bibliography is formatted according to MLA guidelines. The titles are underlined instead of italicized. The citations are also formatted in the MLA style. When you change the style for the bibliography, the style for the citations is also changed. Figure K-16 shows how the same entry is formatted according to three of the most common styles: MLA, Chicago, and APA.

5. **Click Manage Sources, then click the entry for Kren, Emil in the Current List**

   A check mark does not appear next to Emil Kren's name, indicating that his work was not cited in the article. However, you did use this source to gather information even though you did not cite it in the document. You leave the resource because you are generating a bibliography, which includes all documents you used to gather information.

6. **Click the entry for Jolene Resnick, click Edit, select Resnick, type Reznick, click OK, click Yes, then click Close**

7. **Click the Bibliography field, click Update Citations and Bibliography on the tab at the top of the Bibliography field, then click below the bibliography and compare it to Figure K-17**

   The bibliography is formatted in the MLA style, and the Resnick entry is updated to reflect the corrected spelling of Reznick.

8. **Save the document**

FIGURE K-15: Bibliography formatted in the Chicago style

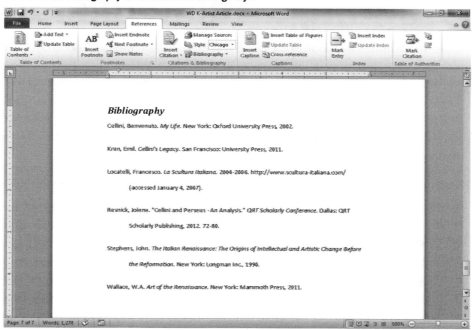

FIGURE K-16: Comparison of three common sourcing styles

Style	Example
MLA	Wallace, W.A. Art of the Renaissance. New York: Mammoth Press, 2011.
Chicago	Wallace, W.A. Art of the Renaissance. New York: Mammoth Press, 2011.
APA	Wallace, W. (2011). Art of the Renaissance. New York: Mammoth Press.

FIGURE K-17: Updated bibliography using the MLA format

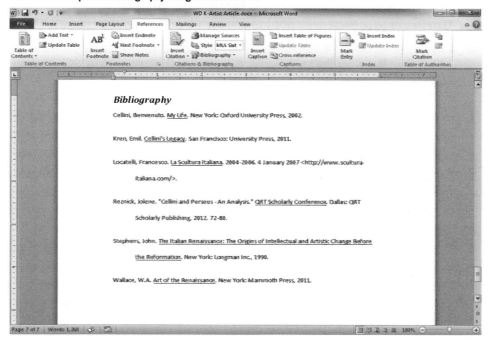

Creating a Table of Figures

A **table of figures** lists all the figures with captions that are used in a document. A **figure** is any object such as a chart, a picture, an equation, a table, or an embedded object to which you can add a caption. When you insert a table of figures, a list of all the figures with captions is generated along with the page number on which each figure is found. Only figures accompanied by captions formatted with the Caption style are included in a table of figures. By default, captions are formatted with the Caption style. ▰▰▰▰▰ You edit the caption attached to one of the pictures in the current document, generate a table of figures on a new page, and customize the appearance of the table of figures.

STEPS

1. **Press [Ctrl][Home], click the picture of Florence on page 1, click Insert Caption in the Captions group, type a colon (:), press [Spacebar], type Classic View of Florence, click the Position list arrow, click Above selected item, then click OK**

    You can modify the appearance of a figure caption by modifying its style.

2. **Select the text Figure 1: Classic View of Florence, click the Home tab, click the Line and Paragraph Spacing button in the Paragraph group, click Remove Space After Paragraph, right-click the selected text, point to Styles, click Update Caption to Match Selection, then scroll through the document to verify that spacing after each of the figure captions is reduced**

QUICK TIP

If your document includes a table of contents, the table of figures should be formatted using the same style as the table of contents, and it should appear after the table of contents.

3. **Press [Ctrl][Home], press [Ctrl][Enter] to insert a new page break, press [Ctrl][Home] and click the Clear Formatting button in the Font group, type Table of Figures, apply bold, centering, and 24-point, press [Enter] following the text, then clear the formatting**

4. **Click the References tab, click the Insert Table of Figures button in the Captions group, click the Formats list arrow, click Formal, then click OK**

    The table of figures is inserted. In addition to the Formal format, the Table of Figures style is applied to the table of figures by default. You can modify the Table of Figure style in the same way you modify other styles.

QUICK TIP

Drag the Hanging Indent marker to .5" on the ruler, then drag the First Line Indent marker to .5" on the ruler.

5. **Display the ruler bar if it is not displayed, click to the left of the first entry in the table of figures (Figure 1), then drag each of the left indent markers on the ruler bar to the .5" mark and the right tab marker on the ruler bar to the 5.5" mark as shown in Figure K-18**

6. **Click the Home tab, click the launcher in the Styles group, scroll and point to TABLE OF FIGURES (the last selection) in the Styles task pane, click the list arrow, click Update Table of Figures to Match Selection, then close the Styles task pane**

    The formatting of each entry in the table of figures is updated automatically to match the formatting applied to the first entry. When you make changes to the formatting of text in the table of figures, you need to update the style. If you do not update the style, your changes are lost when you update the table of figures.

TROUBLE

If too much space appears between the paragraphs, click the Show/Hide ¶ button in the Paragraph group on the Home tab, and delete the extra paragraph mark.

7. **Scroll to the Figure 2 caption in the document, select the caption, press [Delete], click the picture, press [Delete], then press [Delete] again to remove the extra blank line**

    After deleting a figure, you need to update the figure numbers and then update the table of figures.

8. **Scroll to the Figure 3 caption, select 3 in the figure caption (it will become highlighted in gray), click the References tab, click the Insert Caption button in the Captions group, click Numbering, click OK, then click Close**

    The figure caption numbers are updated to reflect the deletion of Figure 2.

9. **Press [Ctrl][Home], click in the table of figures, click Update Table in the Captions group, type your name in the footer, submit the file to your instructor, then save and close the document**

    The table of figures now includes four figures as shown in Figure K-19. Note that the new formatting you applied is maintained because you updated the Table of Figures style.

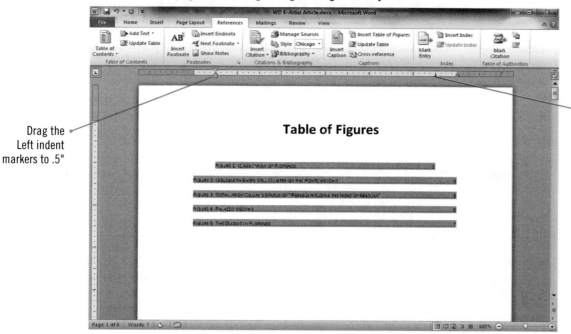

Drag the
Left indent
markers to .5"

Drag the
Right tab
marker
to 5.5"

FIGURE K-19: **Modified Table of Figures**

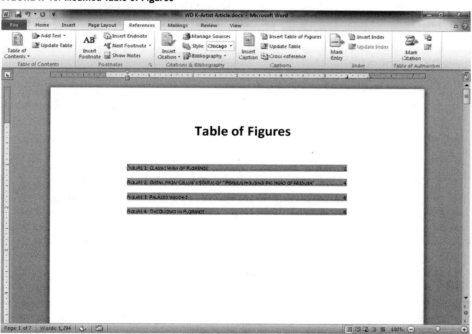

Table of authorities

A table of authorities lists all the cases, statutes, rules, and other legal references included in a legal document, along with the page on which each reference appears. To create a table of authorities, click the References tab, go to the first reference (called a citation) that you wish to include in the table of authorities, then click the Mark Citation button in the Table of Authorities group. After you have marked all the citations in the legal document, click the Insert Table of Authorities button in the Table of Authorities group to build the table of authorities. Word organizes and then displays each citation you marked by category.

Working with Equations

You use the Equations feature to insert mathematical and scientific equations using commands on the Equation Tools Design tab. You can also create your own equations that use a wide range of math structures including fractions, radicals, and integrals. When you select a structure, Word inserts a placeholder that you can then populate with symbols, values, or even text. If you write an equation that you want to use again, you can save the equation and then access it from a custom equation gallery. You can also use the Math AutoCorrect feature to type math symbols instead of selecting them from a gallery. For example, if you type \inc, Word inserts Δ, which is the increment symbol. You have prepared a short paper that uses the microeconomics concept of elasticity to describe the result of raising the price of the Renaissance Art Tour from $2,400 to $3,000. The paper includes several equations to express the economics concepts. You need to create one equation from scratch and then edit another equation.

STEPS

1. Open the file WD K-2.docx from the drive and folder where you store your Data Files, save the file as WD K-Tour Price Increase, select the text [Equation 1 to be created] below the third paragraph, then press [Delete]

2. Click the Insert tab, then click Equation in the Symbols group

   The Equation Tools Design tab opens. This tab is divided into three groups: Tools, Symbols, and Structures. Table K-1 describes the content of each group.

3. Click the Fraction button in the Structures group to show a selection of fraction structures, click the first fraction structure in the top row, then increase the zoom to 140%

   Increasing the zoom helps you see the components of the equation.

4. Press [←], then press [↑] to position the insertion point in the upper half of the fraction (the numerator)

5. Click the More button ⊽ in the Symbols group to expand the Symbols gallery, click the Basic Math list arrow on the title bar, click Greek Letters, then click the Delta symbol (Δ) as shown in Figure K-20

   You can select commonly used math symbols from eight galleries as follows: Basic Math, Greek Letters, Letter-Like Symbols, Operators, Arrows, Negated Relations, Scripts, and Geometry.

TROUBLE
Follow Step 3 to insert the fraction structure each time; use the keyboard arrow keys to move to different parts of the equation. If your insertion point moves outside the equation, click in the equation again.

6. Type Q, press [↓] to move to the bottom half of the fraction (the denominator), type Q, press [→], type an equal sign (=), then complete the equation as shown in Figure K-21, making sure to insert fraction structures as needed

7. Click anywhere in the next equation, be sure the Equation Tools Design tab is active, then click to the left of the top P in the first fraction

   The letter P looks like it is selected, and the insertion point flashes to the left of the letter P.

8. Click the dialog box launcher ⊡ in the Tools group, click Math AutoCorrect, scroll the list to see all the choices available, click OK, click OK, type \inc, then press [Spacebar]

   The Δ symbol is inserted when you type \inc. You use the Math AutoCorrect list to identify the shortcut keys you can use to enter symbols you use frequently.

9. Enter your name where indicated in the footer, submit your file to your instructor, then save and close the document

Working with References

FIGURE K-20: Selecting a symbol

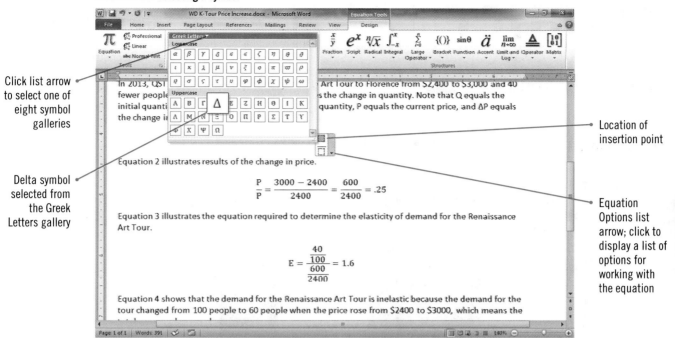

Click list arrow to select one of eight symbol galleries

Delta symbol selected from the Greek Letters gallery

Location of insertion point

Equation Options list arrow; click to display a list of options for working with the equation

Equation 2 illustrates results of the change in price.

$$\frac{P}{P} = \frac{3000 - 2400}{2400} = \frac{600}{2400} = .25$$

Equation 3 illustrates the equation required to determine the elasticity of demand for the Renaissance Art Tour.

$$E = \frac{\frac{40}{100}}{\frac{600}{2400}} = 1.6$$

Equation 4 shows that the demand for the Renaissance Art Tour is inelastic because the demand for the tour changed from 100 people to 60 people when the price rose from $2400 to $3000, which means the

FIGURE K-21: Completed Equation 1

$$\frac{\Delta Q}{Q} = \frac{100 - 40}{100} = \frac{60}{100}$$

TABLE K-1: Contents of the Equation Tools Design tab

group	description
Tools	• Use the Equation button to select a built-in equation
	• Select the equation style: Professional, Linear, or Normal Text
	• Click the launcher ▣ to access the Equation Options dialog box where you can specify equation settings and access the AutoCorrect list of symbols
Symbols	• Select commonly used mathematical symbols such as (±) and (∞)
	• Click the More button ▼ to show a gallery of symbols
	• Click the list arrow in the gallery to select the group for which you would like to see symbols
Structures	• Select common math structures, such as fractions and radicals
	• Click a structure button (such as the Fractions button) to select a specific format to insert in the equation for that structure

Practice

For current SAM information, including versions and content details, visit SAM Central (http://www.cengage.com/samcentral). If you have a SAM user profile, you may have access to hands-on instruction, practice, and assessment of the skills covered in this unit. Since various versions of SAM are supported throughout the life of this text, check with your instructor for the correct instructions and URL/Web site for accessing assignments.

Concepts Review

Label the numbered items shown in Figure K-22.

FIGURE K-22

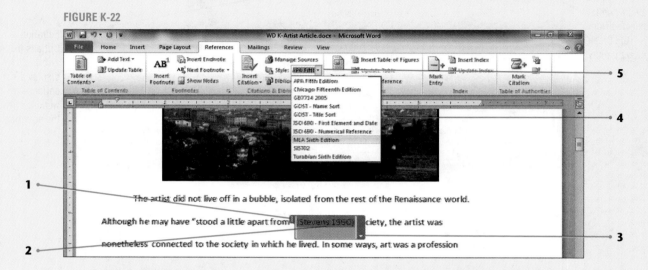

Match each term with the statement that best describes it.

6. **Table of Figures**
7. **Review**
8. **Table of Authorities**
9. **Footnote**
10. **Bibliography**
11. **Structures group**
12. **Citation**

a. List of references included in a document, such as an essay or report
b. Provides additional comments on information provided in the text
c. Tab that includes the Translate feature
d. Short reference, usually including the author and page number, that credits the source of a quote
e. List of objects, such as charts and pictures, included in a document
f. Location of fractions and radicals on the Equation Tools Design tab
g. List of references included in a legal document

Select the best answer from the list of choices.

13. **Which of the following selections in the Create Source dialog box do you select if you wish to enter information in a field not currently displayed?**
    a. Show Fields
    b. Show All Bibliography Fields
    c. Tag name
    d. No selection; only the currently showing fields are available for data entry

14. **Which of the following activities is *not* available in the Manage Sources dialog box?**
    a. Copy a source to your document
    b. Add a source
    c. Change the source style
    d. Delete a source

15. **From the Word Options dialog box, which option do you choose to work with the AutoCorrect feature?**
    a. General
    b. Display
    c. Advanced
    d. Proofing

Skills Review

1. Work with AutoCorrect.

a. Start Word, open the file WD K-3.docx from the drive and folder where you store your Data Files, then save the file as **WD K-History Term Paper**.

b Open the Word Options dialog box, open Proofing, then open the AutoCorrect dialog box.

c. Verify that the AutoCorrect tab is the active tab, type sc in the Replace text box, type **Saint Cyr** in the With text box, click Add, then exit all dialog boxes.

d. Search for **xx**, use the AutoCorrect keystroke to replace xx with **Saint Cyr**, then adjust the spacing and punctuation as needed. (*Hint*: Select xx, type **sc**, and press [Spacebar] to enter the AutoCorrect text.)

e. Repeat the process in Step d to replace xx in the next sentence, then check both inserts.

f. Double-click to the left of your name in the document footer, type **(c)** to insert the copyright symbol, then replace the your name placeholder with your name.

g. Delete the sc entry from the AutoCorrect Options dialog box.

2. Customize footnotes.

a. Change the Number format of the footnotes to the 1, 2, 3 number format and select the Continuous option for footnote numbering. Apply the formatting to the whole document.

b. Find the text "practical skills", then position the insertion point following the period after the word "skills."

c. Insert a footnote with the following text: **For example, training in textiles enabled girls to obtain employment in the factories**.

d. Edit footnote 1 so that **In the eighteenth century,** appears before "English girls" at the beginning of the footnote, then click above the separator line.

e. Go to footnote reference mark 4 in the document text, then delete the footnote reference mark.

f. Modify the style of the footnote text in the footnote area by changing the font size to 9 pt, the After spacing to 6 pt, and the line spacing to 1.5.

g. Click above the separator line, then save the document.

3. Use the Translate feature.

a. Find the text **This French quote**, then select the text from L'enseignement charitable... to ... à la vie extérieure at the end of the sentence (do not include the period).

b. Use the Translate feature to view a translation of the selected text from French to English.

c. Read the English translation, which is an approximate translation of the text.

d. Close the Navigation pane and Research task pane, click the word "schools" in the second line of the next paragraph, then turn on and use the Mini Translator to view the French translation of school (école).

e. Change the Mini Translator language to Spanish (International Sort), turn on the Mini Translator, then move the pointer over the word "schools" and note the Spanish translation to escuela.

f. Turn off the Mini Translator, then save the document.

4. Work with citations.

a. Find the text **roles in society**, insert a citation following the end quotation mark but before the period, select Add New Source, then enter information for a book in the Create Source dialog box as shown in Figure K-23.

b. Find the text **L'enseignement**, select the paragraph of French text (but not the citation), then apply the Quote style.

c. Find the text **popular education in England**, then after the quotation mark and before the period, insert a new citation placeholder.

d. Save the document.

FIGURE K-23

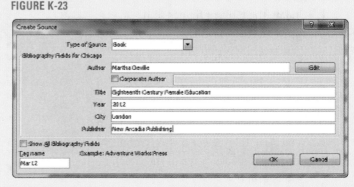

5. Modify citations and manage sources.

a. Find the text **roles in society**, then edit the citation so that it suppresses the year and includes 28 as the page number. Remember to click the citation to show the Citation Options list arrow.

b. Find the text **household activities**, then edit the citation so that it includes 93 as the page number.

c. Change the style to Chicago Fifteenth Edition, then edit the citation to suppress the display of the year.

d. Find the text **Placeholder**, select the Placeholder1 citation, then replace the placeholder with a citation using the Phyllis Stock source.

e. Edit the citation so that it suppresses the year and displays page 70.

f. Open the Source Manager dialog box, edit the entry for Wats so the name is **Watts**.

g. Delete the Placeholder 1 entry, then close the dialog box.

6. Generate a bibliography.

a. Move to the bottom of the document, and insert a page break.

b. Insert a bibliography, then scroll up to view it.

c. Change the style of the citations and bibliography to MLA Sixth Edition.

d. Open the Source Manager dialog box, then change the entry for Marsha Renfrew to Marion Renfrew.

e. Change the style of the bibliography back to Chicago Fifteenth Edition, then update the bibliography.

f. Enter your name where indicated in the document footer, save the document, submit a copy to your instructor, then close the document. The completed bibliography appears as shown in Figure K-24.

FIGURE K-24

7. Create a table of figures.

a. Open the file WD K-4.docx from the drive and folder where you store your Data Files, then save the file as **WD K-Common Equations**.

b. Click the selection handle of the second equation, then insert a caption that uses Equation as the label option and is positioned above the equation. Center the caption if necessary.

c. Select the caption for Equation 1, use the Mini toolbar to modify the caption so that the font color is Red, Accent 2, Darker 50%, then update the style to match the selected text.

d. Go to the top of the document, insert a page break, type **Table of Figures** at the top of the document, and format it with bold, 18 point, and center alignment.

e. Click below the title, clear the formatting, then insert a table of figures using the Distinctive format.

f. Click to the left of the first entry in the table of figures (Equation 1) to select it, then use the ruler bar to set the left margin at 1" and the right tab at 6".

g. Open the Styles task pane, update the Table of Figures style to match the selection, then close the Styles task pane.

h. Go to Equation 3, then delete the Equation 3 caption and the equation, and the blank line.

i. Select the 4 in Equation 4, then update the numbering of the captions. (*Hint*: You can right-click the caption number, then click Update Field.)

j. Update the table of figures so it appears as shown in Figure K-25, then save the document.

FIGURE K-25

8. Work with equations.

a. Go to the [Equation 1] placeholder, then replace it with an equation content control.

b. Type **A =**, then select the pi symbol ∏ from the uppercase area of the Greek Letters gallery.

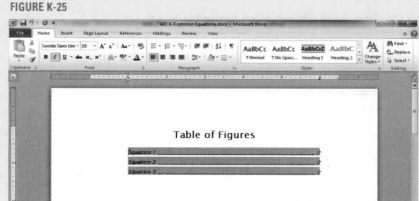

Skills Review (continued)

c. Open the Scripts gallery in the Structures group.

d. Select the first script structure, then type **r** in the large box, and **2** in the small box as shown in Figure K-26.

e. Enter your name where indicated in the document footer, save the document, submit the file to your instructor, then close it.

FIGURE K-26

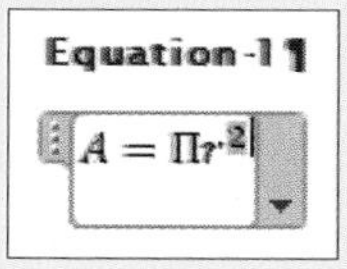

Independent Challenge 1

You have finished writing a paper about Prince Hal in Shakespeare's play *Henry IV: Part 1*. Now you use the References features to add source information. You create a new AutoCorrect entry, insert and modify footnotes, add new citations, and then modify existing citations. You also work in the Source Manager dialog box to organize sources, and then you generate and modify a bibliography.

a. Start Word, open the file WD K-5.docx from the drive and folder where you store your Data Files, then save it as **WD K-English Term Paper**.

b. Create an AutoCorrect entry that replaces **ssh** with **Shakespeare**, then search for each instance of **xx** and replace it with the **ssh** AutoCorrect entry. (*Note*: The document contains three instances of "xx.")

c. Go to the top of the document, find the text first instance of **chivalric code**, then add the footnote: **Chivalry is associated with the ideals of honor and courtly love held by medieval knights.**

d. Find footnote A, change the date 200 A.D. to **400 A.D.**, then change the number format for all the footnotes to 1, 2, 3.

e. Find the text **by his involvements**, then insert a citation for a journal article to the right of the ending quotation mark and before the ending period in the MLA Sixth Edition style from a new source with the information shown in Figure K-27. (*Note*: You need to click the Show All Bibliography Fields check box to view text boxes for all the information required.)

f. Edit the citation to add the page number **74**.

g. Find the text **Placeholder1**, then replace it with the Quinones citation that references page **84**.

h. Find the text **Placeholder2**, then replace it with a second Quinones citation that also references page **84**.

i. Find the text **with real virtue**, create the citation shown in Figure K-28, and insert it to the right of the quotation mark and before the ending period, then edit the citation to include pages 126–127.

j. In the Source Manager dialog box, make the following changes:
   - Delete the two placeholders.
   - Edit the source for *Shakespeare's Tudor History* by Tom Allenham so that the last name is McAlindon.
   - Create a new source for a book from the following information: Martha Danforth, *Prince Hal*, Mark One Publishing, Vancouver, 2012.

k. At the end of the document after the last paragraph, insert a new page, and then generate a new bibliography using the MLA Sixth Edition style.

FIGURE K-27

FIGURE K-28

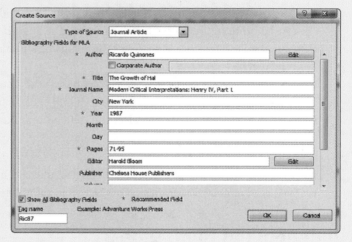

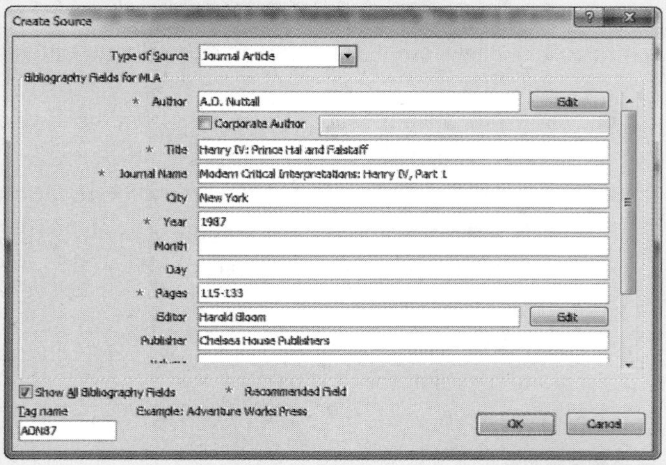

Independent Challenge 1 (continued)

Advanced Challenge Exercise

- In the Source Manager dialog box, search for all entries that include the text **Prince Hal**. (*Hint*: Type the search phrase in the Search text box to see the entries.)
- Edit the source for Martha Danforth so that the new title is **An Analysis of Prince Hal**, show all the Bibliography fields, then enter **BC** as the State/Province, **Canada** as the Country/Region, and **320** as the number of pages. (*Note*: You will need to scroll to see the Pages text box.)
- Answer Yes to update both your master list and the current document with the revised source, then update the bibliography.

l. Remove the **ssh** AutoCorrect entry from the AutoCorrect dialog box.

m. Type your name where indicated in the footer, submit the file to your instructor, then save and close the document.

Independent Challenge 2

You decide to further explore using the Translate feature. You open a document containing a short message in English. You translate the passage from English into Spanish and then from Spanish into French, and then compare the result with the original English text to check the accuracy of the translation.

a. Start Word, open the file WD K-6.docx from the drive and folder where you store your Data Files, then save it as **WD K-Translation Practice**.

b. Select the English message (begins "We are delighted…"), then use the Translate Selected Text feature to translate the selected text to Spanish.

c. Click in the table cell under English to Spanish, then click Insert in the Research task pane to insert the Spanish translation from the Research task pane into the English to Spanish cell in the table.

d. Close the Research task pane, select the Spanish translation, then use the Translate feature to translate the selected text into French.

e. Copy the translation in the Research task pane, and paste it into the table cell under Spanish to French. (*Hint*: Use the keyboard shortcuts [Ctrl][C] to copy and [Ctrl][V] to paste.)

f. Close the Research task pane, select the French translation in the table cell, use the Translate feature to translate the selected text back into English, then insert the English translation from the Research task pane into the table cell under Spanish to French to English.

g. Note how the meaning of the original English message has changed after two translations.

h. Type your name where indicated in the footer, submit a copy to your instructor, save it, then close it.

Independent Challenge 3

You are helping a teacher to prepare a worksheet showing some of the equations related to circles and spheres for a high school geometry class. The teacher has already entered some of the formulas into Word. She asks you to use the Equation feature to add a new formula and then to create a table of figures to list the formulas used in the document.

a. Start Word, open the file WD K-7.docx from the drive and folder where you store your Data Files, then save it as **WD K-Geometry Equations**.

b. Increase the zoom to 150% so you can easily see the formula as you work, then click below the Volume of a Sphere heading and create the Volume of a Sphere equation as follows:

- Click Equation on the Insert tab, then type **V**.
- Type an equal sign (=).
- Click the Fraction button in the Structures group in the Structures group, then select the first fraction style and highlight the top box.
- Type **4**, show the Basic Math symbols, then click the Pi (π) symbol.

Independent Challenge 3 (continued)

- Click the Script button in the Structures group, select the Superscript style (first selection), then type an **r** in the large box and a **3** in the small box.

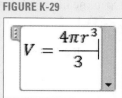

- Highlight the bottom box in the fraction, type **3**, then compare the completed formula to Figure K-29.

c. Add captions centered above each of the three equations so that each caption includes the caption number followed by a colon and the name of the equation. For example, caption 1 should be EQUATION 1: PERIMETER OF A CIRCLE. (*Hint*: Select Equation as the label type, and then type a colon and the caption title in the Caption text box in the Caption dialog box. To center the caption, press [Ctrl][e] immediately after you insert the caption.)

d. Modify the Caption style so that the font is 10 point and the font color is Rose, Accent 6, Darker 50%.

e. Below the heading SAMPLE EQUATIONS... at the top of the document, insert a table of figures using the style of your choice, insert a page break, then update the table of figures.

f. Modify the table of figures so that both the left and right sides are indented 1", then update the table of figures style. (*Note*: Update the Table of Figure style to match the selection in the Styles task pane.)

Advanced Challenge Exercise

- Click the first equation on page 2 (Perimeter of a Circle), then click its selection handle.
- From the Home tab, select the 16 point font size and the Rose, Accent 6, darker 50% font color.
- Use the Format Painter to apply the same formatting to the other two equations in the document.
- Click the third equation, click the selection handle, then change the equation to a Linear equation. (*Hint*: Click the Equation Options list arrow, then click Linear.)

g. Type your name where indicated in the document footer, submit the file to your instructor, then save and close the document.

Real Life Independent Challenge

The Internet is a vast storehouse of information. With just a few clicks and some keywords, you can find answers to just about any question. You have just started a job as a research assistant with Information Overload, a company in Tulsa, Oklahoma, that conducts research projects for local businesses. On your first day on the job, your supervisor asks you to demonstrate how you use the Internet to find answers to three questions he gives you. He then wants you to use the citation feature in Word to document each of the three Web sites you accessed to find the answers.

a. Start Word, open the file WD K-8.docx from the drive and folder where you store your Data Files, then save it as **WD K-Web Citations**.

b. Read the first question, then use your favorite search engine to find the information.

c. Copy a portion of the information (a paragraph at most) from the Web site you chose, then paste it below question 1 in the Web Citations document.

d. Select the copied text, clear the formatting and remove any hyperlinks (right-click the hyperlink, click Remove Hyperlink), then format the copied text with the Quote style.

e. Set the citations and bibliography style to APA Fifth Edition, then immediately following the quotation, insert a citation based on a new source you create by entering information about the Web site you used as a source. (*Hint*: To enter the Web site address, switch to the Web site, select the Web site address, press [Ctrl][C], switch back to the Create Source dialog box, click in the URL text box, then press [Ctrl][V].)

f. Repeat Steps b through e to find answers to the next two questions and to provide appropriate citations. Make sure you consult different Web sites to find the answers.

g. At the end of the document, generate a bibliography.

h. Enter your name where indicated in the footer, submit the file to your instructor, then save and close the document.

Visual Workshop

Open the file WD K-9.docx from the drive and folder where you store your Data Files, then save it as **WD K-Popular Culture Bibliography**. Open the Source Manager dialog box, then create a new entry using the information shown in Figure K-30. Generate the bibliography as shown in Figure K-31, then select the bibliography style (e.g., MLA Sixth Edition, APA Fifth Edition, Chicago Fifteenth Edition) so the format of the entries in the Figure K-31 matches the format of the entries in the bibliography you generated. Type your name where shown, submit the file to your instructor, then save and close the document.

FIGURE K-30

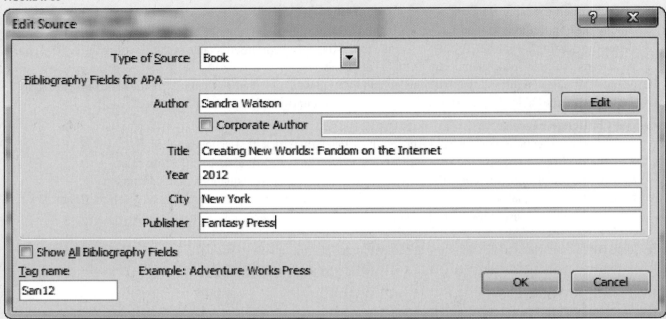

FIGURE K-31

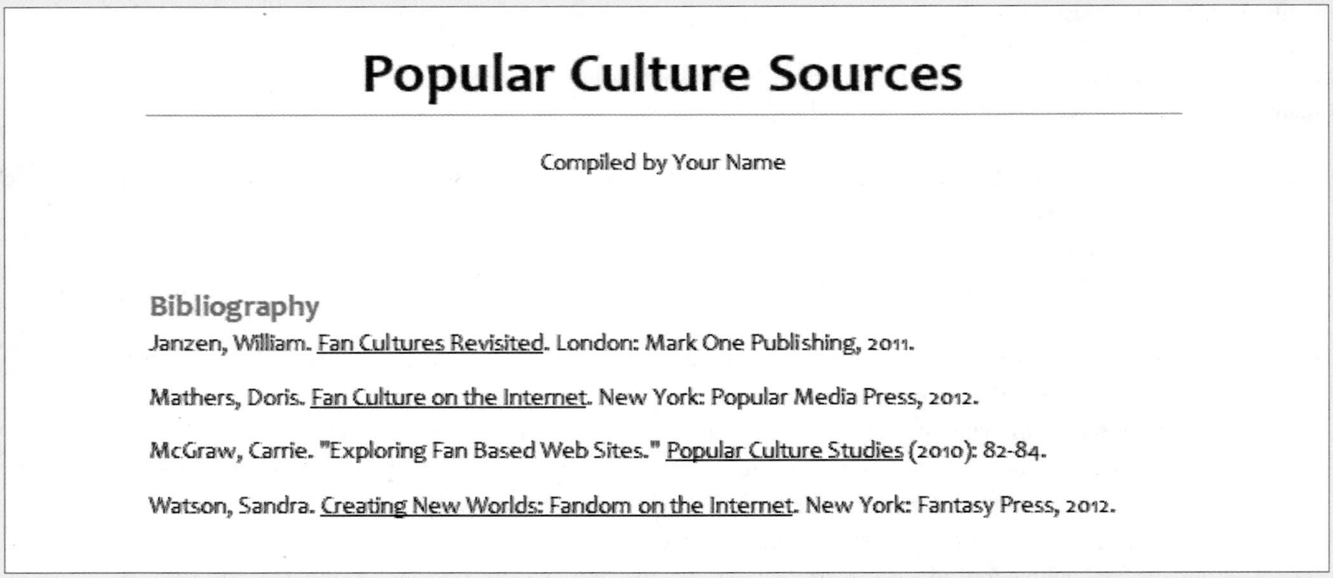

Popular Culture Sources

Compiled by Your Name

Bibliography

Janzen, William. Fan Cultures Revisited. London: Mark One Publishing, 2011.

Mathers, Doris. Fan Culture on the Internet. New York: Popular Media Press, 2012.

McGraw, Carrie. "Exploring Fan Based Web Sites." Popular Culture Studies (2010): 82-84.

Watson, Sandra. Creating New Worlds: Fandom on the Internet. New York: Fantasy Press, 2012.

Integrating Word with Other Programs

The Office suite includes several programs, each with its own unique purpose and characteristics. Sometimes information you want to include in a Word document is stored in files created with other Office programs, such as PowerPoint or Excel. For example, the report you are writing in Word might need to include a pie chart from a worksheet you created in Excel. You can embed information from other programs in a Word document, and you can create links between programs. Ron Dawson in the Marketing Department at the Quest Specialty Travel office in San Diego has started a report on how to market questspecialtytravel.com, QST's home on the World Wide Web. He asks you to supplement the report with embedded objects from PowerPoint and Excel, with information contained in another Word file, and with data included in files he created in Excel and Access. He then needs you to merge an Access data source with the cover letter that he will send along with the report to all the QST branch managers.

OBJECTIVES

Explore integration methods

Embed an Excel worksheet

Link an Excel chart

Embed a PowerPoint slide

Insert a Word file and hyperlinks

Import a table from Access

Manage document links

Merge with an Access data source

Exploring Integration Methods

You can integrate information created with other Office programs into a Word document in a variety of ways. Figure L-1 shows a five-page Word document containing shared information from PowerPoint, Excel, Access, and another Word document. The methods available for sharing information between programs include copy and paste, inserting files, object linking and embedding, and exporting Rich Text Format (.rtf) files from Access. Table L-1 describes each Office program and includes its associated file extension and icon. You review the various ways you can share information between programs.

DETAILS

You can share information in the following ways:

- **Copy and paste**

  You use the Copy and Paste commands to copy information from one program (the **source file**) and paste it into another program (the **destination file**). You usually use the Copy and Paste commands when you need to copy a small amount of text.

- **Insert a Word file**

  You can use the Object/Text from File command on the Insert tab to insert the text from an entire file into a Word document. The file types you can insert into Word include Word documents (.docx) or templates (.dotx), documents from previous versions of Word (.doc or .dot), documents saved in Rich Text Format (.rtf), and documents saved in a Web page format, such as .mht or .htm.

- **Object Linking and Embedding**

  The ability to share information with other programs is called **object linking and embedding (OLE)**. Two programs are involved in the OLE process. The **source program** is the program in which information is originally created, and the **destination program** is the program the information is copied to.

- **Objects**

  An **object** is self-contained information that can be in the form of text, spreadsheet data, graphics, charts, tables, or even sound and video clips. Objects are used to share information between programs. To insert an object, you use the Object command on the Insert tab. This command opens the Object dialog box where you can create an object from new or from an existing file. You can insert an object either as an embedded object or as a linked object.

- **Embedded objects**

  An **embedded object** is created either within a source program or within a destination program and then modified in the destination program using the tools of the source program. For example, you can create a PowerPoint slide in a Word document as an embedded object. Word is the destination program, and PowerPoint is the source program. To make changes to the PowerPoint slide, you double-click it, and the Ribbon associated with PowerPoint is activated. When you insert a file created in another program into a destination program, the file becomes an embedded object that you modify using the tools of the source program within the destination program.

- **Linked objects**

  A **linked object** is created in a source file, inserted in a destination file, and then linked to the source file. When you link an object, any changes you make to the data contained in the object in the source file are reflected in the destination file.

- **Exporting tables and reports from Access**

  You can export a table or a report from Access into Word using the Export command. This command produces a Rich Text Format (.rtf) file that you can open in Word and then modify using Word formatting tools. An Access table exported to an .rtf file and then opened in Word is the same as a Word table and can be formatted using Word table styles and other Word features.

FIGURE L-1: **Word document with shared information**

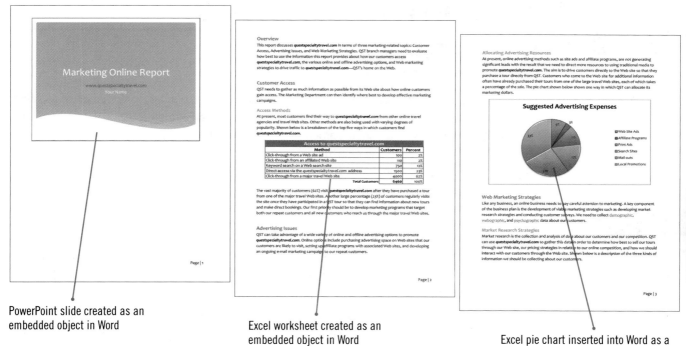

PowerPoint slide created as an embedded object in Word

Excel worksheet created as an embedded object in Word

Excel pie chart inserted into Word as a linked object that uses the Destination theme; the linked chart in Word can be updated to reflect changes made to the chart in Excel

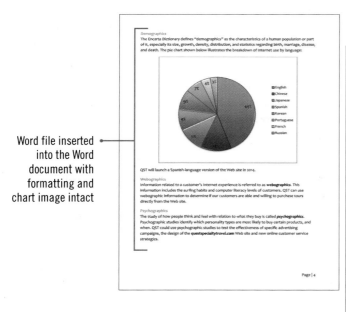

Word file inserted into the Word document with formatting and chart image intact

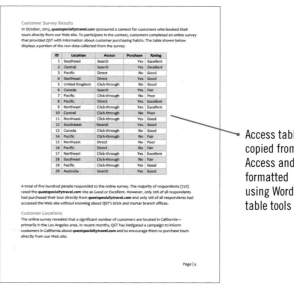

Access table copied from Access and then formatted using Word's table tools

TABLE L-1: **Common Office programs**

icon	program	extension	purpose
W	**Word**	.docx	To create documents and share information in print, e-mail, and on the Web
X	**Excel**	.xlsx	To create, analyze, and share spreadsheets and to analyze data with charts, PivotTable dynamic views, and graphs
P	**PowerPoint**	.pptx	To organize, illustrate, and provide materials in an easy-to-understand graphics format for delivery in a presentation or over the Internet
A	**Access**	.accdb	To store, organize, and share database information

Embedding an Excel Worksheet

An embedded object uses the features of another program such as Excel, but it is stored as part of the Word document. You embed an object, such as an Excel worksheet or a PowerPoint slide, in Word when you want to be able to edit the object using the source program commands but when you do *not* need changes made in the source file to be updated in the embedded Word object. You edit an embedded object directly in Word using commands on the Ribbon associated with the source program. ⬛⬛ The Online Marketing Report contains placeholder text and bookmarks to designate where you need to insert information created in other programs. Your first task is to embed an Excel worksheet.

STEPS

1. **Start Word, open the file WD L-1.docx from the drive and folder where you store your Data Files, save it as WD L-Online Marketing Report, then scroll through the report to note where you will insert content from other programs**

2. **Press [Ctrl][G] to open the Find and Replace dialog box with the Go To tab active, click Bookmark in the Go to what list, verify that "Customers" appears in the Enter bookmark name text box, click Go To, click Close, then press [Delete] to remove the placeholder text Excel Worksheet Here and position the insertion point on a blank line**

3. **Click the Insert tab, then click the Object button in the Text group**
    The Object dialog box opens. You use the Object dialog box to create a new object using the commands of a program other than Word or to insert an object created in another program.

4. **Click the Create from File tab, click the Browse button, navigate to the drive and folder where you store your Data Files, click WD L-2.xlsx, then click Insert**
    The path to the file WD L-2.xlsx is shown in the File name text box. Because you want to create an embedded object, you leave the Link to file check box blank, as shown in Figure L-2.

5. **Click OK, then double-click the embedded worksheet object**
    The embedded object opens in an Excel object window, and the Excel Ribbon opens in place of the Word Ribbon. The title bar at the top of the window contains the Word filename, indicating that you are still working within a Word file.

6. **Click cell B3, type 100, press [Enter], click cell B8, then click the Bold button 𝐁 in the Font group**
    The total number of customers shown in cell B8 increases by 62, from 6398 to 6460. Because you did not select the link option when you embedded the Excel file into the Word document, changes you make to the embedded file are not reflected in the original Excel file.

7. **Click the Page Layout tab, click the View check box under Gridlines in the Sheet Options group to deselect the check box, click Themes in the Themes group, then select Waveform**
    You turned off the display of gridlines so that only borders show in the worksheet. Then, you formatted the embedded Excel file to match the formatting of the Word document. The completed worksheet object appears in Word as shown in Figure L-3.

8. **Click to the right of the worksheet object to return to Word**
    The Excel Ribbon closes and the Word Ribbon opens. You double-click the Excel object when you want to make changes to the data. You click the Excel object once when you want to select the object to change the position of the object within the Word document.

    > **TROUBLE**
    > If text is on the same line as the Excel worksheet, click before "The" and press [Enter].

9. **Click the worksheet object to select it, click the Home tab, click the Center button ≡ in the Paragraph group, click below the worksheet object, then save the document**

FIGURE L-2: Create from File tab in the Object dialog box

Click to create an object from new, then select the type of object to create

The path to the Excel worksheet to be inserted in the Word document (your path will differ)

Click to browse to file location

Leave the Link to file check box blank for embedded objects

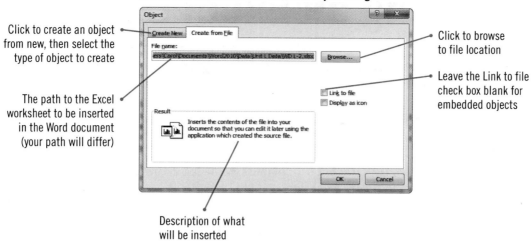

Description of what will be inserted

FIGURE L-3: Excel Worksheet embedded in Word document

Title bar verifies this is a Word window

Excel Ribbon

Excel worksheet selected so Excel Ribbon is active

Excel object window

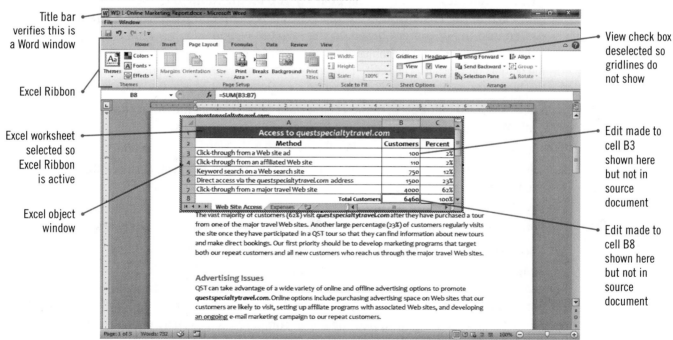

View check box deselected so gridlines do not show

Edit made to cell B3 shown here but not in source document

Edit made to cell B8 shown here but not in source document

Integrating Word with Other Programs

Linking an Excel Chart

The Paste command on the Home tab provides several options for integrating data from a source file into a destination file. When you select one of the paste link options, you create a linked object. The data copied from the source file in one program is pasted as a link into the destination file in another program. If you make a change to the data in the source file, the data in the linked object that you copied to the destination file is updated. You copy a pie chart from Excel and paste it into the Word report as a linked object.

STEPS

1. Press [Ctrl][G], click the Enter bookmark name list arrow, select Resources, click Go To, click Close, then delete the text Excel Pie Chart Here

2. Click the Start button 🌠 on the taskbar, point to All Programs, click Microsoft Office, click Microsoft Excel 2010, open the file WD L-2.xlsx from the drive and folder where you store your Data Files, then save it as WD L-Online Marketing Data

   Notice that the values in cells B3 and B8, which you changed in the embedded Excel worksheet object in the previous lesson, have not changed. Two programs (Word and Excel) are currently open, as indicated by their program buttons on your taskbar.

TROUBLE
Be sure a border with sizing handles surrounds the pie chart and all its related components. If only one component is selected, click outside the chart area, then repeat Step 3.

3. Click the Expenses tab at the bottom of the Excel worksheet, click any white area of the chart to select the pie chart and all its components, then click the Copy button 🖺 in the Clipboard group

4. Click the Microsoft Word program button on the taskbar to return to Word, click the Paste button list arrow in the Clipboard group on the Home tab, then move your mouse over each of the Paste Options to read each ScreenTip and preview how the chart will be pasted into the document based on the selected option

   Some of the options retain the formatting of the source program, and some options adopt the formatting of the destination program. The source program is Excel, which is currently formatted with the Office 2010 theme. The destination program is Word, which is currently formatted with the Waveform theme.

TROUBLE
If text is on the same line as the Excel chart, click before "Web" and press [Enter].

5. Click the Use Destination Theme & Link Data button 🖳 as shown in Figure L-4, then note that Web Site Ads account for 2% of the advertising expenses

   The chart is inserted using the destination theme, which is Waveform.

6. Click the Excel program button on the taskbar to return to Excel, click cell B2, type 9000, then press [Enter]

   The Web Site Ads slice increases to 9%.

TROUBLE
If the pie chart did not update, click the chart, click the Chart Tools Design tab, then click Refresh Data in the Data group

7. Return to Word, then verify that the Web Site Ads slice has increased to 9%

8. Click the Chart Tools Format tab, click Size if necessary to show the Shape Height and Shape Width text boxes, select the contents of the Shape Width text box in the Size group, type 6, press [Enter], click the Home tab, click the Center button 🖹 in the Paragraph group, click away from the pie chart object to deselect it, scroll up to view the Allocating Advertising Resources heading, compare the pie chart object to Figure L-5, then save the document

9. Switch to Excel, save and close the workbook, then exit Excel

   The WD L-Online Marketing Report in Word is again the active document.

FIGURE L-4: Selecting a link paste option

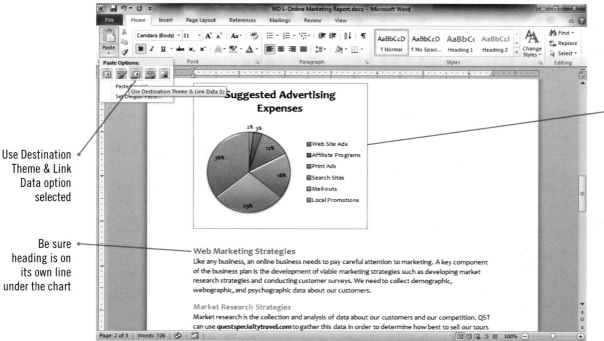

Use Destination Theme & Link Data option selected

Pasted chart uses the Waveform theme currently applied to the Word document

Be sure heading is on its own line under the chart

FIGURE L-5: Linked pie chart updated in Word

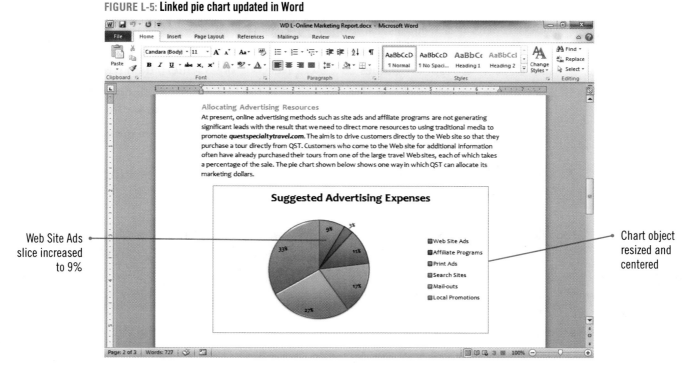

Web Site Ads slice increased to 9%

Chart object resized and centered

Using the Object dialog box to create a linked file

In addition to using the Paste options, you can create a linked object using the Object dialog box. Open the Object dialog box by clicking Object in the Text group on the Insert tab, and then click the Create from File tab. Click the Browse button, navigate to and then select the file you want to link, click the Link to file check box, then click OK. The active worksheet of the file you select is inserted in the destination file as a linked object.

You create a linked object using one of the options available on the Paste menu when you want to copy only a portion of a worksheet such as selected cells or a chart. You create a linked object using the Link to file check box in the Object dialog box when you want to insert the entire worksheet.

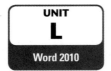

Embedding a PowerPoint Slide

You can share information between Word and PowerPoint in a variety of ways. You can use the Paste Special command to insert a slide as a linked or an embedded object into a Word document. You can also use the Create New tab in the Object dialog box to create a PowerPoint slide as an embedded object in Word, and then use the tools on the PowerPoint Ribbon to modify the slide in Word. ▰▰▰▰ You plan to distribute the Online Marketing Report at a conference where you will also deliver a PowerPoint presentation. You create a new PowerPoint slide and embed it in the title page, then you use the tools on the PowerPoint Ribbon to format the embedded object.

STEPS

1. **Press [Ctrl]Home], then press [Ctrl][Enter]**
    A new blank page appears. You want to embed a PowerPoint slide on the new blank page.

2. **Press [Ctrl][Home], click the Insert tab, then click Object in the Text group**
    The Object dialog box opens. The types of objects that you can create new in Word are listed in the Object type: list box.

3. **Scroll down, select Microsoft PowerPoint Slide in the Object type: list box as shown in Figure L-6, then click OK**
    A blank PowerPoint slide appears along with the PowerPoint Ribbon.

4. **Click the Click to add title text box, type Marketing Online Report, click the Click to add subtitle text box, type www.questspecialtytravel.com, press [Enter], then type your name**

5. **Click the Design tab, click the More button ⊡ in the Themes group to open the gallery of presentation designs, then scroll to and click Waveform as shown in Figure L-7**

6. **Click outside the slide, click the View tab, click One Page in the Zoom group, right-click the slide object, then click Format Object**

7. **Click the Size tab in the Format Object dialog box, select 100% in the Height text box in the Scale section, type 125, press [Tab], then click OK**
    The slide object is increased to 125% of its default size.

8. **Click the Home tab, click the Borders list arrow ⊞ ▾ in the Paragraph group, click Borders and Shading, click Box, click the width list arrow, click 1 pt, click OK, then click the Center button ☰ in the Paragraph group**

QUICK TIP
Scroll to page 2, click the body text to deselect the slide, then scroll to page 1 to view the slide with its border.

9. **Click away from the slide object to deselect it, return the Zoom to 100%, then save the document**
    The embedded PowerPoint slide appears in a Word document, as shown in Figure L-8.

Creating a PowerPoint presentation from a Word outline

When you create a PowerPoint presentation from a Word outline, the Word document is the source file and the PowerPoint document is the destination file. Text formatted with heading styles in the Word source file are converted to PowerPoint headings in the PowerPoint destination file. For example, each line of text formatted with the Heading 1 style becomes its own slide. To create a PowerPoint presentation from a Word outline, create and then save the outline in Word, close the document, then launch PowerPoint. In PowerPoint, click the New Slide list arrow, click Slides from Outline, navigate to the location where you stored the Word document, then double-click the filename. The Word outline is converted to a PowerPoint presentation, which you can modify in the same way you modify any PowerPoint presentation. Any changes you make to the presentation in PowerPoint are *not* reflected in the original Word document.

FIGURE L-6: **Create New tab in Object dialog box**

Microsoft
PowerPoint
Slide selected

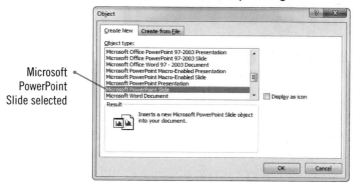

FIGURE L-7: **Waveform presentation design selected**

Word title bar

PowerPoint
Ribbon

Waveform theme; its
position in your
gallery might differ;
use ScreenTips to
locate theme

PowerPoint slide
object embedded
in Word

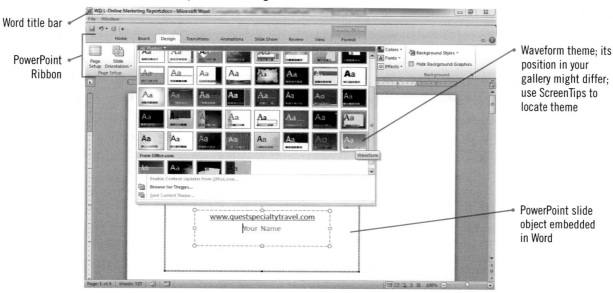

FIGURE L-8: **Completed embedded PowerPoint slide object in Word**

Word Ribbon

PowerPoint
Waveform design
applied to
embedded
PowerPoint slide

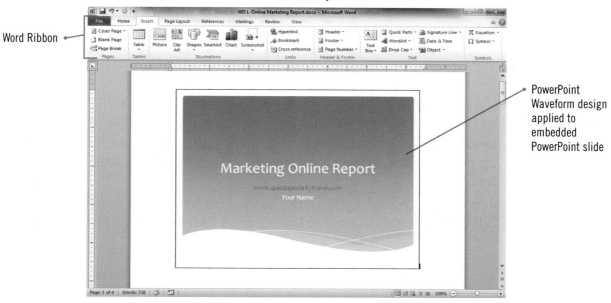

Integrating Word with Other Programs

Inserting a Word File and Hyperlinks

When you want to include the content of an entire Word document in another Word document, you use the Text from File Insert command to insert the entire Word file. When you insert an entire file into a document, the formatting applied to the destination file is also applied to the content you insert. The inserted file becomes part of the Word document, similar to an embedded object, and you cannot return to the original document from the inserted file. After inserting a file into a Word document and as a result expanding the document length, you can help readers navigate the content of a document quickly by creating hyperlinks from text in one part of the document to text in another location in the document. You insert a Word file, then you create hyperlinks and add ScreenTips to the hyperlinks.

STEPS

1. **Press [Ctrl][G], select the Research bookmark, click Go To, click Close, delete the text Word File Here, then be sure the insertion point is on a blank line**

2. **Click the Insert tab, click the Object list arrow in the Text group, then click Text from File**

3. **Navigate to the drive and folder where you store your Data Files, click WD L-3.docx, then click Insert**

   The content of the file WD L-3.docx file appears in your current document and is formatted with the Waveform theme. If you make changes to the text you inserted in this destination file, the changes will *not* be reflected in the file WD L-3.docx source file.

4. **Scroll up, select the title Market Research Methods (including the bottom border), press [Delete], select the Demographics heading, click the Home tab, click the More button** ⊡ **in the Styles group to show the Style gallery, click the Heading 3 style, then apply the Heading 3 style to the Webographics and Psychographics headings**

5. **Scroll up to the Web Marketing Strategies heading on page 3, select demographic in the third line of the paragraph, click the Insert tab, then click the Hyperlink button in the Links section**

   In the Insert Hyperlink dialog box, you can create a link to another file, to a Web page, or to a place in the current document. You can also create a link that creates a new document and a link that opens an e-mail client.

6. **Click Place in This Document**

   A list of all the places within a document you can create a hyperlink to appears in the Insert Hyperlink dialog box. The list includes all the headings and subheadings that are formatted with styles and the bookmarks already included in the document.

7. **Click Demographics as shown in Figure L-9, click ScreenTip, type Click here to move to information about demographics. as shown in Figure L-10, click OK, then click OK**

   The text demographic appears blue and underlined to indicate it is a hyperlink.

8. **Repeat Steps 5 through 7 to select and then create hyperlinks for the text webographic and psychographic, changing the ScreenTip as required so it matches its corresponding heading**

9. **Move the pointer over psychographic to show the ScreenTip as shown in Figure L-11, press Ctrl+Click as directed to move to the section on Psychographics, then save the document**

FIGURE L-9: Insert Hyperlink dialog box

Demographics selected

Place in This Document

List of places in this document that you can create a hyperlink to

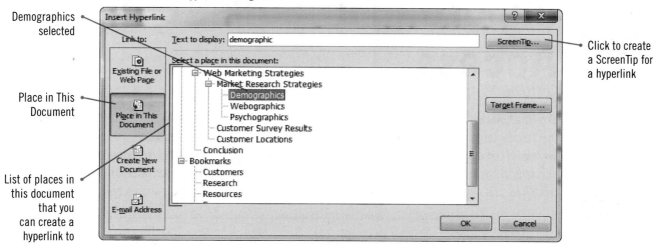

Click to create a ScreenTip for a hyperlink

FIGURE L-10: Entering text for a ScreenTip

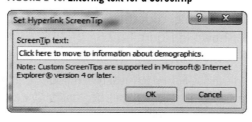

FIGURE L-11: Viewing a ScreenTip

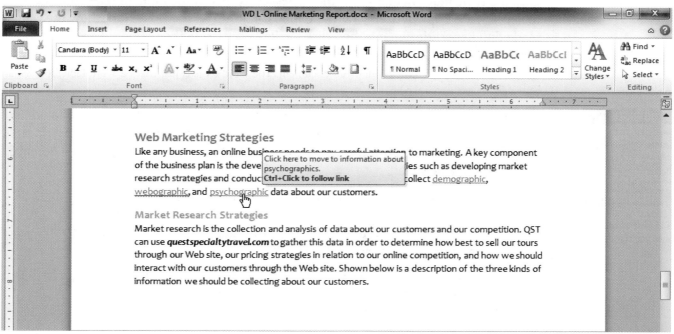

Importing a Table from Access

You can share information between Access and Word in a variety of ways. The most common method is to export an Access table or report to a Rich Text Format (.rtf) file. You can then open the .rtf file in Word and use Word's table features to format it just as you would format any table.  You have already created an Access database that contains information related to online survey results. You open the Access database and export the table containing the survey results to an .rtf file that you then open in Word. Next you copy the Word table into the Marketing Online Report and then format the table with a built-in table style.

1. **Press [Ctrl][G], select and go to the Survey bookmark, delete Access Table Here, be sure the insertion point is on a blank line, click the Start button ⊕ on the taskbar, point to All Programs, scroll to and click Microsoft Office, then click Microsoft Access 2010**

2. **In Access, click Open, navigate to the drive and folder where you store your Data Files, double-click WD L-4.accdb, then click Enable Content if prompted**

   The database file opens in Microsoft Access.

3. **Click Online Survey : Table, click the External Data tab, then click the More button in the Export group as shown in Figure L-12**

4. **Click Word**

   The Export – RTF File dialog box opens, as shown in Figure L-13. You use this dialog box to designate where you will save the exported file. You can also select options for exporting the file. When you are exporting to Word, only the second option is available.

5. **Click Browse, navigate to the drive and folder where you save your files, change the filename to WD L-Online Survey.rtf, click Save, click the Open the destination file after the export operation is complete check box to select it, then click OK**

   The .rtf file opens in a Word window.

6. **Click the table move handle ⊕ in the upper-left corner of the table to select the entire table, click the Copy button 📄 in the Clipboard group on the Home tab, show the Online Marketing Report document, then click the Paste button in the Clipboard group on the Home tab**

   The Word table is copied into your Word document. The Word table is just that—a Word table; it is *not* an embedded object or a linked object.

7. **Select the entire table again, click the Table Tools Design tab, click the Banded Columns check box in the Table Style Options group to deselect it, click the More button ▼ in the Table Styles group to view the table styles available, then select the Light Grid – Accent 3 (light green) table style**

8. **Double-click the column divider between Location and Access, click the Home tab, click the Center button ≡ in the Paragraph group, click away from the table to deselect it, save your document, submit the file to your instructor, then close it**

   The formatted table appears as shown in Figure L-14.

9. **Show the WD L-Online Survey.rtf document, close the document without saving it, switch to Access, click Close if the Export – RTF File dialog box is open, then exit Access**

   You don't need to save the WD L-Online Survey.rtf file because you've already copied the table.

FIGURE L-12: Options from the More button in the Export group

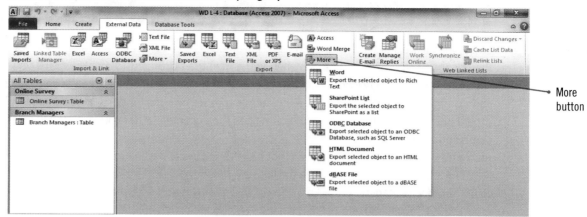

More button

FIGURE L-13: Export – RTF file dialog box

Location the file will be exported to; your path will differ

Export options; only the bold option is available for the file to be exported

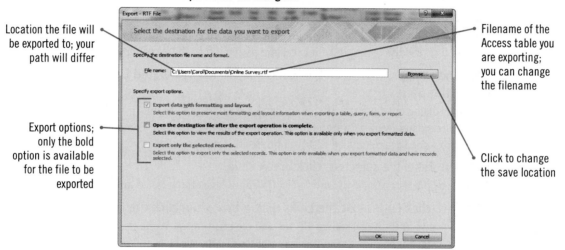

Filename of the Access table you are exporting; you can change the filename

Click to change the save location

FIGURE L-14: Table originally created in Access, then copied to and formatted in Word

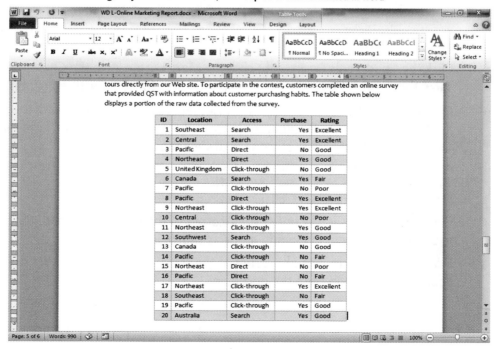

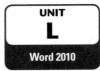

Managing Document Links

When you create a document that contains linked objects, you must include all source files when you copy the document to a new location or when you e-mail the document to a colleague. If you do not include source files, you (or your colleague) will receive error messages when trying to open the destination file. If you do not want to include source files when you move or e-mail a document containing links, then you should break the links before moving or e-mailing the document. After you break the links, the Update Links command cannot be used to update information in your destination file. Any changes you make to the source files after you break the links will not be reflected in the destination file. The objects in the destination file will appear as they do at the time the links are broken. ▰▰▰▰ You need to distribute the Word report to all QST branch managers. You keep a copy of the original report with the links intact, and then you save the report with a new name and break the links. You also view the entire report in Reading Layout view.

STEPS

1. **Open the document** WD L-Online Marketing Report, **then save it as** WD L-Online Marketing Report_Managers

    You do not want to send along the source file for the Excel pie chart, so you break the link that was created when you copied the pie chart from Excel and pasted it into the Word report.

2. **Click the** File tab, **then click** Edit Links to Files **in the Related Documents section of the Properties pane**

    The Links dialog box opens, as shown in Figure L-15. You can use the Links dialog box to update links, open source files, change source files, and break existing links. Notice that only one source file is listed in the Links dialog box—the Excel file called WD L-Online Marketing Data.xlsx.

3. **With the Excel file selected, click** Break Link

    A message appears asking if you are sure you want to break the selected link.

4. **Click** Yes, **click** OK **to exit the Links dialog box, then click the** Home tab

    The link between the Excel source file and the pie chart in the Word destination file is broken. Now if you make a change to the pie chart in the Excel source file, the pie chart in Word will not change.

5. **Scroll to the** Suggested Advertising Expenses pie chart **on page 3, then click the** pie chart

    The Word Ribbon is still active, and the Chart Tools contextual tabs are available. When you broke the link to the source file, Word converted the pie chart from a linked object to a chart object. You can use commands on the Design, Layout, and Format tabs to modify the chart object, but you cannot change the content of the pie chart.

6. **Click the** Chart Tools Design tab, **click the** More button ▾ **in the Chart Styles group to show the Chart Styles gallery, then click** Style 29 **(fourth row, fifth column)**

TROUBLE
What you see on your screen may differ. Remember, Full Screen Reading view shows the document so it is easy to read on the screen. Do not be concerned about page breaks or large areas of white space in this view.

7. **Click away from the chart, press** [Ctrl][Home], **click the** View tab, **click the** Full Screen Reading button **in the Document Views group to open the document in reading mode, then click the** Next Screen button ▶ **to view the report**

    In reading mode, you can comfortably read the document text and scroll from screen to screen using the Next Screen and Previous Screen buttons. As you scroll through the report in reading mode, you notice that page breaks appear in different places and that some parts of the graphics are cut off.

8. **Click** View Options **in the upper-right corner of the screen, then note the options available for working in reading mode as shown in Figure L-16**

9. **Click** Close **in the upper-right corner of the screen, save the document, submit a copy to your instructor, then close the document**

FIGURE L-15: Links dialog box

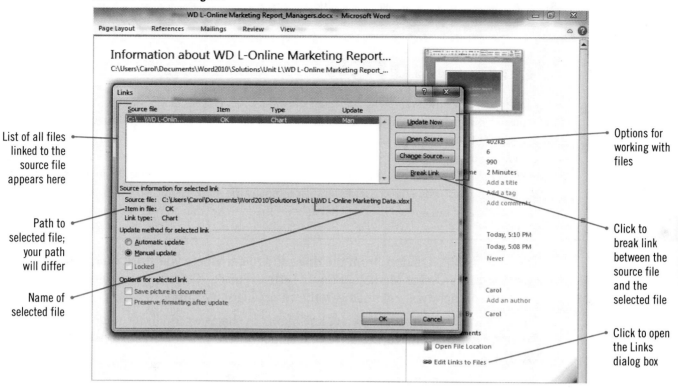

List of all files linked to the source file appears here

Options for working with files

Path to selected file; your path will differ

Name of selected file

Click to break link between the source file and the selected file

Click to open the Links dialog box

FIGURE L-16: Reading mode options

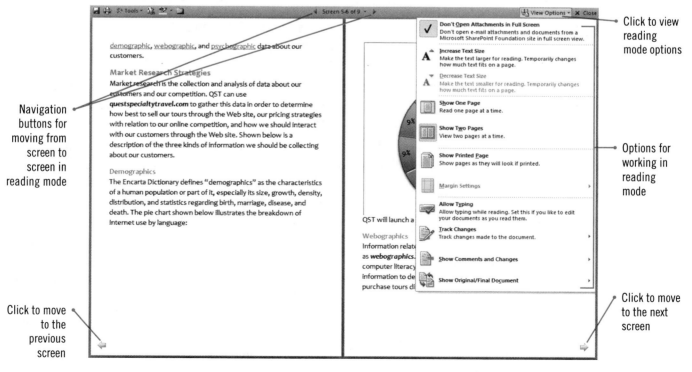

Navigation buttons for moving from screen to screen in reading mode

Click to view reading mode options

Options for working in reading mode

Click to move to the previous screen

Click to move to the next screen

Merging with an Access Data Source

Many businesses store the names and addresses of contacts, employees, and customers in an Access database. You can merge information contained in an Access database with a letter, a sheet of labels, or any merge document that you've created in Word. The data you merge with the destination file is the **data source**. When you use an existing database as your data source, you save time because you do not need to create a new data source. ▰▰▰▰ You need to mail a printed copy of the Online Marketing Report to all QST branch managers. First, you edit a cover letter to accompany the report, and then you merge the letter with the names and addresses of the QST branch managers that are stored in an Access database.

STEPS

1. **Open the file** WD L-5.docx **from the drive and folder where you store your Data Files, save it as** WD L-Online Marketing Cover Letter, **replace "Current Date" with today's date, scroll down, then type your name in the complimentary closing**

2. **Click the** Mailings tab, **click** Select Recipients **in the Start Mail Merge group, click** Use Existing List, **navigate to the drive and folder where you store your Data Files, click** WD L-4.accdb, **then click** Open

3. **Verify that** Branch Managers **is selected, then click** OK
   Most of the buttons on the Mailings tab are now active.

   > **TROUBLE**
   > Press [Enter] after <<AddressBlock>> if the text immediately follows the closing chevron.

4. **Delete the word** Address **near the top of the letter, be sure the insertion point is on a blank line, click the** Address Block **button in the Write & Insert Fields group, click the** Always include the country/region in the address **option button as shown in Figure L-17, then click** OK
   The <<AddressBlock>> field is inserted in the letter.

   > **TROUBLE**
   > Press [Enter] after <<GreetingLine>> if the text immediately follows the closing chevron.

5. **Delete the word** Greeting, **be sure the insertion point is on a blank line, click the** Greeting Line **button in the Write & Insert Fields group, click the** list arrow **next to Mr. Randall, scroll down and click** Joshua, **then click** OK

6. **Scroll to the last paragraph, click to the left of Please, click the** Insert Merge Field **button in the Write & Insert Fields group, click** FirstName, **click** Insert, **click** Close, **type a comma (,), press [Spacebar], then change Please to** please

7. **Click the** Preview Results **button in the Preview Results group, select the text in the address block from "Ms. Marilyn Clancy" to "United States," click the** Home **tab, click the Line and Paragraph Spacing button** [≡↕] **in the Paragraph group, click** Remove Space After Paragraph, **press the right arrow, then press [Enter] to move the greeting line down**
   Sometimes you need to adjust spacing when you view the results of a merge.

8. **Click the** Mailings **tab, then click the** Next Record **button** ▶ **in the Preview Results group until you have previewed all seven records**
   You've successfully merged the cover letter with the names and addresses of the branch managers. Now you can save just a selection of the letters.

9. **Click the** Finish & Merge **button in the Finish group, click** Edit Individual Documents, **click the** From **option button, enter 5 and 6, click** OK, **click the** View **tab, click** Two Pages, **compare the letters to Figure L-18, save the document as** WD L-Online Marketing Cover Letter_Merged, **then close it**

10. **Save the main document, submit all files to your instructor, close the file, then exit Word**

FIGURE L-17: Insert Address Block dialog box

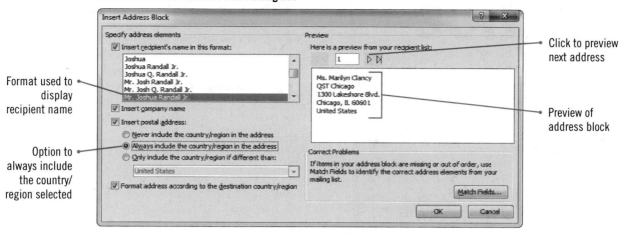

Format used to display recipient name

Option to always include the country/region selected

Click to preview next address

Preview of address block

FIGURE L-18: Merged cover letters in Two Pages view

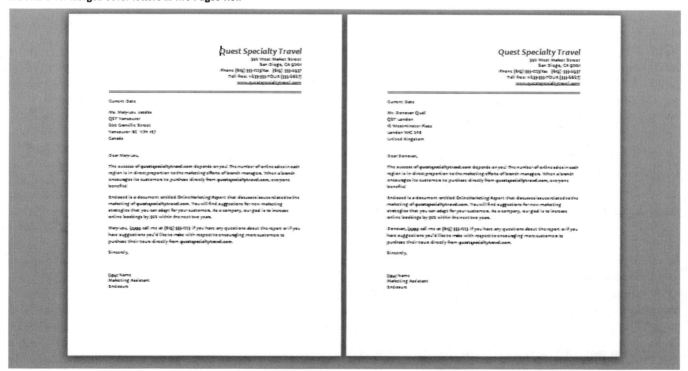

Opening a merge document

When you open the WD L-Online Marketing Cover Letter document, you will see a warning telling you that opening the document will run the SQL command: SELECT*FROM 'Branch Managers'. This warning means that Word will look for the list of recipients in the Branch Managers table in a database file. Click Yes. If the database is stored on your computer, the correct recipient list will be matched to the document. If the database is not stored in the location expected by Word, then you will need to navigate to the location where the database is stored and select it. If the database is not available, you will receive an error message and will not be able to complete the merge.

Practice

Concepts Review

For current SAM information, including versions and content details, visit SAM Central (http://www.cengage.com/samcentral). If you have a SAM user profile, you may have access to hands-on instruction, practice, and assessment of the skills covered in this unit. Since various versions of SAM are supported throughout the life of this text, check with your instructor for the correct instructions and URL/Web site for accessing assignments.

Refer to Figure L-19 to answer the questions that follow.

FIGURE L-19

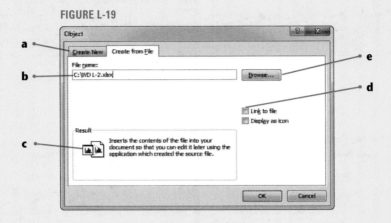

1. Which element do you click to create an Excel worksheet or PowerPoint slide directly in Word?
2. Which element describes the action being taken?
3. Which element points to the name of the file that will be inserted?
4. Which element do you click to link the inserted file to its source program?
5. Which element do you click to find the file you want to insert?

Match each term with the statement that best describes it.

6. OLE
7. Object
8. Destination theme
9. Embedded object
10. Source program

a. Describes the connection between linked objects
b. Doesn't change if the source document is edited
c. Self-contained information that can be in the form of text, graphics, and so on
d. Program that information is copied from
e. The Office theme applied to the contents of the destination program

Select the best answer from the list of choices.

11. What is the destination program?
    a. The program the information is copied from
    b. The program the information is copied to
    c. The program the information is created in
    d. The program containing new information

12. Which of the following statements is *not* true about an embedded object?
    a. An embedded object is created in a source file and inserted into a destination file.
    b. An embedded object becomes part of the destination file.
    c. Changes you make to an embedded object are reflected in the destination file.
    d. Changes you make to an embedded object are reflected in the source file.

13. Which command can be used to insert a linked object?
    a. Keep Source Formatting and Embed Workbook
    b. Keep Text Only
    c. Use Destination Theme & Link Data
    d. Picture

Skills Review

1. **Embed an Excel worksheet.**
   a. Start Word, open the file WD L-6.docx from the drive and folder where you store your Data Files, then save it as **WD L-Venture Tours Report**.
   b. Use the Go To command to find the Categories bookmark, then delete the placeholder text **Excel Worksheet** and be sure the insertion point is on a blank line. (*Note*: As you delete placeholder text throughout this Skills Review, always be sure the insertion point is on a blank line.)
   c. Click Object in the Text group on the Insert tab, click the Create from File tab, then use the Browse feature to insert the file WD L-7.xlsx from the drive and folder where you store your Data Files into the Word document.
   d. Edit the worksheet object. Change the value in cell B3 from 1400 to **1600**, then enhance the value in cell B8 with bold.
   e. Apply the Trek theme to the Excel workbook.
   f. In Word, center the worksheet object, then save the document.

2. **Link an Excel chart.**
   a. Use the Go To command to find the Popularity bookmark, then delete the placeholder text **Excel Chart**.
   b. Start Microsoft Excel, open the file WD L-7.xlsx from the drive and folder where you store your Data Files, then save it as **WD L-Venture Tours Data**.
   c. Show the Popularity worksheet, change the number of Backpacking Tours sold to **1600**, copy the column chart, switch to Word, preview the paste options, then paste the column chart using the Use Destination Theme & Link Data paste option.
   d. Switch to Excel, change the value in cell C5 from 2400 to **2500**, then save the workbook in Excel.
   e. In Word, verify that the Wilderness Canoeing column for Available Tours is now 2500, refreshing the data if the data does not update automatically.
   f. Switch to Excel, exit the program, then switch to the WD L-Venture Tours Report document if it is not the active document.

3. **Embed a PowerPoint slide.**
   a. Insert a blank page at the top of the document, then insert a PowerPoint slide as an embedded object on the new blank page.
   b. Enter the text **Venture Tours** as the slide title, then enter your name as the subtitle.
   c. Apply the Trek design to the embedded slide object.
   d. Click below the embedded slide object, then view the page in One Page view.
   e. Add a blank line below the slide object, increase the slide size by 110%, center the object, then save the document.

4. **Insert a Word file and hyperlinks.**
   a. Return to 100% view, then use the Go To command to find the Tours bookmark in WD L-Venture Tours Report.
   b. Remove the placeholder text **Word File**, then insert the file WD L-8.docx as a Text from File from the drive and folder where you store your Data Files.
   c. Scroll up to and delete the heading **Venture Tours**, including its bottom border, select the Sea Kayaking heading (currently formatted with the Heading 2 style), then apply the Heading 3 style to the heading.
   d. Apply the Heading 3 style to these other headings: Backpacking, Wildlife Photography, Wilderness Canoeing, and Mountain Biking.
   e. Scroll up to Category Descriptions, select Sea Kayaking in the first line, create a hyperlink to the Sea Kayaking heading, then create this ScreenTip: **Click here to move to the description of Sea Kayaking tours.**
   f. Create hyperlinks and ScreenTips for each of the remaining four tour categories: Backpacking, Wildlife Photography, Wilderness Canoeing, and Mountain Biking; test the hyperlinks, then save the document. (*Hint*: Copy the text for the Sea Kayaking ScreenTip, paste it into the ScreenTip text box for each entry, then change the name of the tour.)

5. **Import a table from Access.**
   a. Use the Go To command to find the Profile bookmark, then remove the placeholder text Access Table.
   b. Start Microsoft Access, then open the file WD L-9.accdb from the drive and folder where you store your Data Files, enabling content if prompted.

Skills Review (continued)

c. Export the Customer Profile table as an .rtf file called **WD L-Customer Profile.rtf** to the drive and folder where you store your files for this book, making sure to select the Open the destination file after the export operation is complete check box.

d. Copy the table from the .rtf file that opened in Word, and paste it into the Venture Tours Report document. (*Note*: The table breaks across two pages. You will adjust pagination shortly.)

e. Apply the Light Grid-Accent 4 table style to the table, deselect the Banded Rows check box, then reduce the column widths to fit the column content. (*Hint*: Mouse over the options in the Table Styles gallery, and use the ScreenTips to find the Light Grid-Accent 4 style.)

f. Press [Ctrl][Home], scroll through the document and adjust line spacing as needed. For example, add a page break before the Tour Popularity heading, remove the space before the Customer Profiles heading as needed being careful not to remove the style formatting, and then insert a page break at the Customer Survey Results heading.

g. Save the WD L-Venture Tours Report document, switch to and close the WD L-Customer Profile.rtf file without saving it, then switch to Access, click Close, then exit Access.

6. Manage document links.

a. Using the Word File tab, open the Links dialog box, then break the link to the WD L-Venture Tours Data.xlsx file.

b. Scroll to view the Tours Popularity column chart, then click the column chart.

c. Apply chart style 32, then select Chart Layout 1.

d. Click away from the chart, switch to Full Screen Reading view, use the Next Screen and Previous Screen buttons to view the document in reading mode, then exit Full Screen Reading view.

e. Enter your name where indicated in the document footer, save the document, submit a copy to your instructor, then close the document.

f. The completed report appears as shown in Figure L-20.

7. Merge with an Access data source.

a. Open the file WD L-10.docx from the drive and folder where you store your Data Files, save it as **WD L-Venture Tours Cover Letter**, then replace the place-holder text Current Date and Your Name with the appropriate information.

b. Click the Mailings tab, select the file WD L-9.accdb as the recipients list, then select the Tour Guides table.

c. Insert the Address Block to replace the word Address and accept the default settings.

d. Insert the Greeting Line with Joshua as the greeting line format to replace the word Greeting.

e. Click to the left of Please in the last paragraph, insert the FirstName field, type a comma (,), insert a space, then change Please to **please**.

FIGURE L-20

f. Preview the merge results, select the text of the first address in the address block, change the line spacing to 1.15 if that is not the current setting, then remove the After paragraph spacing so that no extra space appears between the lines in the inside address.

g. Press [Enter] following the address so a blank line appears between the address and the greeting line.

h. Preview all the records, finish the merge so that you edit letters **5** and **6**.

i. Save the two merged letters as **WD L-Venture Tours Cover Letter_Merged.docx**, then close the document.

j. Save and close the main document, submit all files to your instructor, then exit Word.

Independent Challenge 1

As a member of the Recreation Commission in Santa Fe, New Mexico, you are responsible for compiling the minutes of the monthly meetings. You have already written most of the text required for the minutes. Now you need to insert information from two sources. First, you insert a worksheet from an Excel file that shows the monies raised from various fundraising activities, and then you insert a Word file that the director of the commission has sent you for inclusion in the minutes.

a. Start Word, open the file WD L-11.docx from the drive and folder where you store your Data Files, then save it as **WD L-Recreation Commission Minutes**.

b. Go to the Fundraising bookmark, then insert the file WD L-12.xlsx from the drive and folder where you store your Data Files as an embedded object to replace EXCEL WORKSHEET. (*Hint*: Click the Create from File tab in the Object dialog box.)

c. Edit the worksheet object by changing the value in cell D5 from 800 to **700**, notice that the value in cell G5 is now 6000, then enhance the contents of cells A5 and A6 with bold.

d. Apply the Executive theme to the Excel workbook, then center the worksheet in Word.

e. Move the Recreation Council Report heading to page 2, press [Ctrl][End], press [Enter] and clear the formatting, then insert the file WD L-13.docx as a Text from File from the drive and folder where you store your Data Files.

f. Apply the Heading 1 style to the text **Director's Report**.

g. Type **Prepared by** followed by your name in the document footer.

Advanced Challenge Exercise

■ In the worksheet object, click cell A6, then press [↓] once to view another row in the worksheet.

■ In cell A7, type **Per Person**, click cell B7, enter the formula **=B6/B5**, then press [Enter].

■ Drag the lower-right corner of cell B7 across to cell F7 to fill cells C7 to F7 with the formula.

■ Bold the label in cell A7, select the range A1:G7, click the Borders list arrow, then click All Borders.

■ Drag the bottom middle of the worksheet object down slightly so that the new row 7 is visible as shown in Figure L-21.

■ Click outside the worksheet object.

h. Save the document, submit all files to your instructor, close the document, then exit Word.

FIGURE L-21

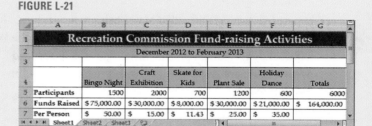

	A	B	C	D	E	F	G
1		Recreation Commission Fund-raising Activities					
2		December 2012 to February 2013					
3							
4		Bingo Night	Craft Exhibition	Skate for Kids	Plant Sale	Holiday Dance	Totals
5	Participants	1500	2000	700	1200	600	6000
6	Funds Raised	$75,000.00	$30,000.00	$8,000.00	$30,000.00	$21,000.00	$164,000.00
7	Per Person	$ 50.00	$ 15.00	$ 11.43	$ 25.00	$ 35.00	

Sheet1 / Sheet2 / Sheet3

Independent Challenge 2

You run a summer camp in Yosemite National Park for teenagers interested in taking on leadership roles at their schools and in their communities. You have started an outline for a report about this program in Word. You will continue to enhance the Word document so you can eventually use it to create a PowerPoint presentation.

a. Start Word, open the file WD L-14.docx from the drive and folder where you store your Data Files, then save it as **WD L-Yosemite Camp Report**.

b. Insert a new page above the first page in the document, then insert an embedded PowerPoint slide.

c. Add **Yosemite Camp Report** as the title and your name as the subtitle, then format the slide with the Hardcover design.

d. Center the slide object, and increase the slide size to 115%.

e. Deselect the slide, press [Ctrl][End], then press [Enter] once.

f. Start Excel, open the file WD L-15.xlsx from the drive and folder where you store your Data Files, then save it as **WD L-Yosemite Camp Data**.

g. Copy the chart, then paste it below the Student Enrollment heading using the Use Destination Theme & Link Data paste option.

h. In Excel, change the value in cell B3 from 1500 to **1900**, save and close the workbook, then exit Excel.

i. In Word, refresh the data if it did not update automatically, center the chart, add your name to the footer, then save the document.

Independent Challenge 2 (continued)

Advanced Challenge Exercise

- Go to the beginning of the document, then double-click the slide object to show the PowerPoint Ribbon.
- Format the slide background so it is filled with the Cork texture. (*Hint:* Click the Design tab, click the launcher in the Background group, click the Picture or texture fill option button, click the Texture list arrow, then select the required texture.)
- In Word, change the chart height to 2.7, center the chart, if it is not already centered, then move the chart and accompanying text up to page 2.

j. Open the Links dialog box, and break the link to the chart.

k. Save all open documents and workbooks, submit your files to your instructor, close all open documents, then exit Word.

Independent Challenge 3

You own a small Web-based business that sells art materials online. The business is growing—thanks in large part to the help you're receiving from several art stores in your area. You've decided to send a memo to the store managers every few months to describe the growth of the Web site. The memo will include a linked Excel worksheet and a table created in Access. Once you have completed the memo, you will merge it with a database containing the names of all the store managers who are helping to promote the Web site.

a. Start Word, open the file WD L-16.docx from the drive and folder where you store your Data Files and save it as **WD L-Arts Online Memo**.

b. Start Access, then open the file WD L-17.accdb from the drive and folder where you store your Data Files and enable content if requested.

c. Export the Access table called May 1 Sales to an .rtf file called WD L-May 1 Sales so the .rft file opens in Word.

d. In Word, copy the table in the .rtf file, then switch to the WD L-Arts Online Memo Word document, and paste the table below the paragraph that starts The table illustrated below....

e. Apply a table design of your choice with Banded Columns deselected, automatically adjust the column widths, then center the table.

f. Start Excel and open the file WD L-18.xlsx from the drive and folder where you store your Data Files, then save the Excel file as **WD L-Arts Online Data**.

g. Click the pie chart to select it, copy the pie chart, switch to the Arts Online Memo file in Word, then paste the worksheet below the paragraph that starts The pie chart shown below... using the Use Destination Theme & Link Data paste option.

h. In Excel, click cell F3, change the sale generated by the Georgia customer from 113.56 to **350.50**, press [Enter], then save the worksheet.

i. In the WD L-Arts Online Memo document, refresh the chart data if it did not update automatically, change the height of the chart to **2.5"**, then center it.

j. Break the link to the Excel chart.

k. Scroll to the top of the document, then replace the placeholder text with your name and today's date in the Memo heading.

l. Click after the To: in the Memo heading, open the Mailings tab, click the Select Recipients button, click Use Existing List, browse to the drive and folder where you store your Data Files, double-click WD L-17.accdb, then select the Retail Outlets table.

m. Insert an Address Block following To: that contains only the recipient's name. (*Hint:* Deselect the Insert company name check box and the Insert postal address check box in the Insert Address Block dialog box.)

n. Preview the recipients, then complete the merge so that records **3** and **4** can be edited.

o. Save the merged memos as **WD L-Arts Online Memo_Merged**, then close the file.

p. Save and close the main document in Word, close the .rtf file without saving it, submit your files to your instructor, then exit all open applications.

Real Life Independent Challenge

You can use the various applications in the Office suite in combination with Word to help you plan a special event in your life such as a party or a wedding. For example, you can enter the names and addresses of the people you plan to invite in an Access database and create a budget for the event in Excel. You could even create an invitation to the event in PowerPoint. To keep track of all the information related to the event, you can create a party planning document in Word. You open a Word document that contains tables and placeholders that you complete with information and objects related to an event of your choice.

Word 2010

a. Open the file WD L-19.docx from the drive and folder where you store your Data Files, save it as **WD L-Event Planning**, then apply the theme of your choice.

b. Complete the top table with the required information such as the type of party or event you are planning (for example, a wedding or a graduation party); the date, time, and location of the event; and the number of guests invited. You determine the required information.

c. Open WD L-20.accdb in Access, then save the database as **WD L-Event Guest List**. (*Hint*: Click the File tab, click Save Database As, then enter the name of the database and click Save.)

d. View the Guests table, enter information in the required fields for up to 10 guests you plan to invite to your event. (*Hint*: Press [Tab] to move from field to field in each record.) Close the table, then export it to an .rtf document called **WD L-Event Guests**.

e. Open WD L-Event Guests.rtf in Word, copy the table to the appropriate location in the Word Event Planning document, then format it attractively. Note that you can remove the ID column and adjust the spacing of the column headings so the information is easy to read.

f. Open WD L-21.xlsx, save it as **WD L-Event Data**, then close the file.

g. In the Word Event Planning document, delete Budget Items, then insert the Excel file WD L-Event Data.xlsx as a linked object. (*Hint*: To create the linked object, click Object in the Text group on the Insert tab, click the Create from File tab, browse to the WD L-Event Data.xlsx file, then be sure to click the Link to file check box to create the linked worksheet.)

h. Edit the data in the Costs worksheet to enter cost items appropriate to your event. For example, you can identify different categories or remove categories you don't want, and you can change the values assigned in the Cost column to the categories.

i. When you are finished working in the Cost worksheet, save and close the Excel file, then right-click the linked worksheet in Word and click Update Link if the data did not update automatically.

j. In Excel, open WD L-Event Data, click the Breakdown tab, copy the pie chart, switch to the WD L-Event Planning Word document, then paste the chart in the appropriate area of the document using the Use Destination Theme & Link Data paste option.

k. Return to Excel, change one of the values in the Costs worksheet related to the cost category of your choice, then save the worksheet.

l. Return to Word and refresh the chart data, then center the chart.

m. Scroll to and double-click the linked worksheet object to open its corresponding Excel worksheet, verify the change you made in Step k and then exit Excel, return to Word, right-click the linked worksheet, and then click Update Link to update the worksheet data.

n. Break the links to the Excel chart and the Excel worksheet.

o. Add your name to the footer in the Word document, view the document in Two Pages view, then adjust page breaks where needed.

p. Save all open files, submit your files to your instructor, close all documents, then exit all open applications.

Visual Workshop

Start a new document in Word, select the Slipstream theme, then enter and format the headings and text for the document shown in Figure L-22. Start Excel, open the file WD L-22.xlsx from the drive and folder where you store your Data Files, then save it as **WD L-Alabama Arts Cell Phone Data**. Copy the pie chart, paste it into the Word document using the Use Destination Theme & Link Data paste option, apply the chart style shown, then change the height and width to 3"× 6". Save the document as **WD L-Alabama Arts Cell Phone Report**. In Excel, change the value in cell B2 to **180**, then save the workbook. In Word, verify that the pie chart appears as shown in Figure L-22, then break the link to the Excel file. Type your name under the chart, submit your files to your instructor, close the document, close the workbook in Excel, then exit all programs.

FIGURE L-22

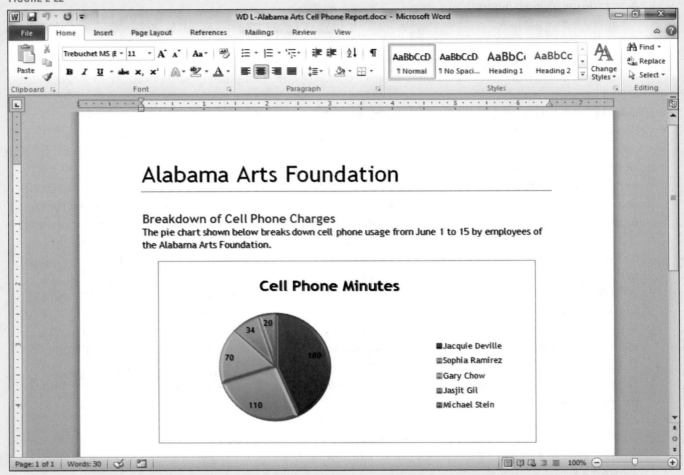

Exploring Advanced Graphics

Word includes features you can use to create and modify a variety of illustrations including charts, SmartArt diagrams, pictures, clip art, shapes, and screenshots. You can also apply a range of special effects to selected text and then enhance photographs by removing background objects and applying artistic effects. Finally, you can modify clip art pictures and work in the drawing canvas to combine them with other pictures and drawn objects. The Sydney branch of Quest Specialty Travel is excited about holding a series of tour presentations to promote tours to people in the Sydney area. Sheila Barton, the manager of QST Sydney, asks you to prepare a summary of the activities that QST Sydney completed in 2013. The summary will include text modified with text effects and other advanced font effects, a screen shot of the Quest Specialty Travel Web site, modified pictures, SmartArt graphics, and a drawing consisting of a modified clip art picture and four rotated shapes.

OBJECTIVES

Work with text effects

Create and modify screenshots

Modify a picture

Remove the background from a picture

Use artistic effects and layering options

Create SmartArt graphics

Edit clip art

Align, distribute, and rotate graphics

Working with Text Effects

You use the **Text Effects** feature to modify the appearance of any block of text in your document. Text effects are font enhancements that you can use in addition to the formats you are familiar with such as font style, font size, and font formats. You use text effects to apply fill and outline styles to selected text along with enhancements such as shadows, reflections, glows, and 3-D effects. You can also modify text with Character Spacing and OpenType settings from the Advanced tab of the Font dialog box. You open the document describing QST Sydney's year in review, apply a text effect to the document title, and then modify the text effect and save it as part of the Title style. You also experiment with some of the features in the Advanced tab of the Font dialog box to view their effect on selected text.

STEPS

TROUBLE
Read the ScreenTip that appears as you move the mouse pointer over each selection to find Gradient Fill - Blue, Accent 1.

1. **Start Word, open the file WD M-1.docx from the drive and folder where you store your Data Files, save it as WD M-QST Sydney Year in Review, select the title QST Sydney at the top of the document, click the Text Effects button A· in the Font group, then apply the Gradient Fill – Blue, Accent 1 text effect (third row, fourth column)**

2. **With the text still selected, click the launcher ⬚ in the Font group, then click Text Effects**
   In the Format Text Effects dialog box, you can modify a wide range of formats, such as text fill and outline, and apply additional formats, such as shadow, reflection, and 3-D effects.

3. **Click 3-D Format in the left pane, click the Top button, select the Art Deco bevel style (lower-right selection), select 4.5 pt in the Width text box, type 10 as shown in Figure M-1, click Close, click OK, then click away from the selected text**
   The changes you made are not that obvious because of the current font size of the text and the current font.

4. **Select QST Sydney again, click the Grow Font button A˙ in the Font group until 36 appears in the Font Size text box, click the Font list arrow, select Berlin Sans FB Demi, click the Font Color list arrow, then select Blue, Accent 1, Darker 50%**
   You can include the text effects as part of the Title style.

5. **Click the More button ⬚ in the Styles group to view the Styles Gallery, right-click Title, click Update Title to Match Selection, select 2013 Year in Review, open the Styles Gallery, apply the Title style, then click below the text to deselect it**

QUICK TIP
In the Advanced tab of the Font dialog box, you can adjust the character spacing and apply OpenType settings.

6. **Select the WEB SITE heading, click the launcher ⬚ in the Font group, then click the Advanced tab**

7. **Click the Spacing list arrow in the Character Spacing area, click Expanded, click OK, open the Styles Gallery, right click Heading 2, then click Update Heading 2 to Match Selection**
   All headings formatted with the Heading 2 style are updated to include the Expanded character spacing.

QUICK TIP
Information about which OpenType Features you can apply to a font can be obtained from the font designer, or you can experiment by applying OpenType settings to selected text.

8. **Select 2013 at the beginning of the first paragraph, click the launcher ⬚ in the Font group, click the Number spacing list arrow in the OpenType Features section, click Proportional, click the Number forms list arrow, then click Old-style**
   The numbers in 2013 appear slightly closer together and the bottom of the "3" drops below the other numbers. The **OpenType Features** include options that can be applied to any fonts that include designs for special features, such as ligatures, number spacing options, number form options, and stylistic sets. Table M-1 describes the four OpenType Features available and displays how text is changed according to which special feature is applied. Notice that some of the changes are very subtle.

9. **Click OK, click the Format Painter button ⬚ in the Clipboard group, click 2013 in the paragraph under the WEB SITE heading, save the document, then compare it to Figure M-2**

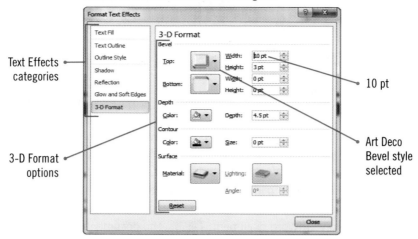

Text Effects categories

3-D Format options

10 pt

Art Deco Bevel style selected

FIGURE M-2: Text formatted with special effects

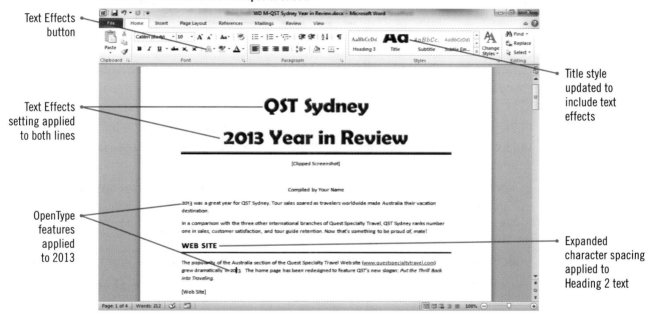

Text Effects button

Text Effects setting applied to both lines

OpenType features applied to 2013

Title style updated to include text effects

Expanded character spacing applied to Heading 2 text

TABLE M-1: OpenType Features

OpenType feature and options	description	sample changes	explanation of sample changes
Ligatures: None, Standard Only, Standard and Contextual, Historical and Discretionary, All	A combination of characters such as "ff" that is written as if it is a single character; each ligature option affects the character combination differently	No ligature: **ff** Standard Only ligature: **ff**	The ff cross-bars are joined in the Standard Only ligature
Number spacing: Default, Proportional, Tabular	The spacing between numbers; for example, an "8" is wider than a "1" and the spacing can be adjusted	Default: **18** Proportional: **18**	The bottom rule of the 1 has been dropped in proportional spacing
Number forms: Default, Lining, Old-style	The height of numbers; for example, Lining numbers all have the same height, while Old-style numbers flow above or below the line of the text, depending on the number	Default: **368** Old-style: **368**	The 3 dips below the 6 and 8 in Old-style
Stylistic sets: Default, Sets from 1 to 20 depending on the font	A set of formats that is applied to text in OpenType fonts to change the look of certain letters; some fonts can include up to 20 stylistic sets	Gabriola font default stylistic set: *The quick blue fox* Gabriola font stylistic set 7: *The quick blue fox*	The text becomes increasingly more ornate, depending on the stylistic set applied

Exploring Advanced Graphics

Creating and Modifying Screenshots

The Illustrations group on the Insert tab contains the buttons you use to create illustrations in one of six categories: pictures, clip art, shapes, SmartArt, charts, and screenshots. The **Screenshot** command can provide a gallery of screenshots of all open program windows, such as a Web site window, an Excel work-sheet window, and another Word window. You select the screenshot from the gallery and insert it into your document as a graphic object. A screenshot is a static image. If you take a screenshot of a Web page and then the contents of the Web page changes, the screenshot does not change. In addition to inserting a screenshot, you can also use the Screen Clipping option to select just a portion of a window and insert it as a graphic object into your Word document.  The document describing QST Sydney's year in review contains placeholders for two graphic objects that you will insert using the Screenshot and Screen Clipping commands. You want to include a screenshot of the Quest Specialty Travel Web site, so your first step is to open the Web site in your Web browser.

STEPS

1. **Start Internet Explorer or the Web browser you prefer, click in the Address text box, type www.questspecialtytravel.com, then press [Enter]**

   The Quest Specialty Travel Web site opens in the browser window.

2. **Return to the document in Word, press [Ctrl][F], type [Web Site], select the [Web Site] placeholder in the document (highlighted in yellow), then close the Navigation pane**

   The placeholder identifies the position where you will insert the screenshot.

3. **Click the Insert tab, then click the Screenshot button in the Illustrations group**

   A thumbnail of the window containing the Web page appears in the Available Windows gallery, as shown in Figure M-3. If you have additional windows active, then pictures of those windows will also appear in the Available Windows gallery.

4. **Click the thumbnail of the QST Web site window in the Available Windows gallery**

   The screenshot of the QST Web site window is inserted in the Word document as a graphic object. You can resize, position, and format the object just like you would any graphic object, such as a picture or a chart.

5. **Select the contents of the Width text box in the Size group, type 3.8, press [Enter], click the Home tab, click the Center button ≡, then click away from the screenshot to deselect it**

   In addition to the Screenshot feature, Word also has a Screen Clipping feature that you can use to insert just a portion of a screen into a Word document.

6. **Scroll to the top of the document, select the [Clipped Screenshot] placeholder, click the Insert tab, then click Screenshot**

7. **Click Screen Clipping**

   In a few seconds, the window containing the Web site fills the screen and is dimmed.

8. **Drag the pointer to select just the company slogan as shown in Figure M-4, then release the mouse button**

   When you release the mouse button, the screen clipping appears in the Word document at the selected loca-tion. If you do not like the appearance of the clipped screen, click the Undo button, then repeat Steps 6 to 8.

9. **Change the width of the screen clipping to 3", compare your screen to Figure M-5, make any spacing adjustments required, save the document, click the Web browser button on the taskbar, then close the Web browser**

> **TROUBLE**
> Press [Esc] if a win-dow other than the QST window opens, minimize all open windows except the QST window and your Word docu-ment, and then repeat Steps 6 and 7.

> **TROUBLE**
> If the Word screen does not open when you release the mouse button, click the Word button on the taskbar.

FIGURE M-3: Window available for a screenshot

The Web site open in the Web browser appears as an available window for a screenshot

Selected screenshot will be inserted at location of selected text

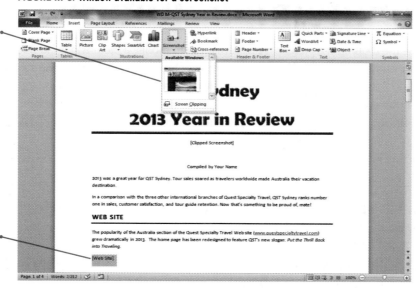

FIGURE M-4: Making a screen clipping

Web browser window appears dimmed when Screen Clipping option active

Drag the crosshair to select the portion of the screen to clip

FIGURE M-5: Completed screen clipping

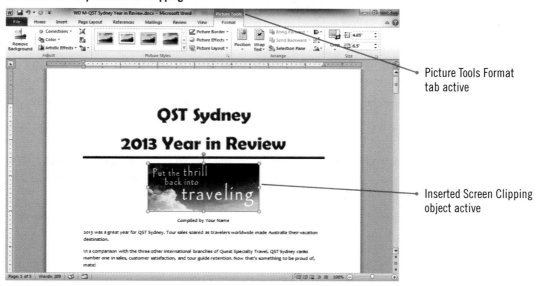

Picture Tools Format tab active

Inserted Screen Clipping object active

Exploring Advanced Graphics

Modifying a Picture

You use the tools on the Picture Tools Format tab to modify a picture in hundreds of different ways. You can crop a picture, change the picture shape, modify the picture border, and apply picture effects such as the Glow and Bevel effects. You can even add **alternative text** (also known as alt text) to a picture to provide a description of the picture for people who are visually impaired and using a screen reader to read the document. Finally, you can specify an exact position for the picture on the page. ▰▰▰ The document describing QST Sydney's year in review contains a picture of a pink flower. You use the picture tools to transform the picture into an interesting graphic object, add Alt Text, and then position the picture precisely.

STEPS

1. **Scroll to the Top Tours heading on page 2, then double-click the pink flower picture**
   By default, a picture inserted in a document is formatted with the Wrap Text setting called In Line with Text. This setting makes the picture part of the line of text it appears next to.

QUICK TIP
Click a picture to make the Picture Tools Format tab available. Double-click a picture to make the Picture Tools Format tab active.

2. **Click the Crop button in the Size group, then drag the lower-left crop mark up and to the right so the image appears as shown in Figure M-6**
   When you **crop** a picture, you drag the crop handle associated with the part of the picture you want to crop. If you don't like the crop effect, you can click the Undo button to undo your last crop action. A cropped picture is smaller than the original picture because you take away parts of the top, bottom, and/or sides of the picture. When you resize a picture, you make the entire picture smaller or larger.

3. **Click away from the picture to set the crop, click the pink flower picture again, click the Crop button list arrow in the Size group, point to Crop to Shape, then click the Oval shape in the top row of the Basic Shapes section (far-left selection)**
   The picture is cropped further in the shape of an oval.

4. **Click the launcher ▣ in the Picture Styles group**
   The Format Picture dialog box opens. In this dialog box, you can select options to modify the Fill, Line Color, Line Style, Shadow, Reflection, Glow and Soft Edges, 3-D Format, 3-D Rotation, Picture Corrections, Picture Color, Artistic Effects, Crop, and Text Box effects. You can also add Alt Text.

5. **Click Alt Text, click in the Title text box, type Pink Flower, press [Tab], type the description: Beautiful waterlily on the Mary River in Australia's Northern Territory., then click Close**
   The Alt Text will be visible to users who view the document with a screen reader.

6. **Click Picture Effects in the Picture Styles group, point to Bevel, then click the Convex bevel style (second row, third column)**
   A bevel effect is added to the picture.

7. **Click Picture Effects again, point to Bevel, click 3-D Options, change the Bevel Top Width setting to 15, click the Material button and select Dark Edge in the Special Effect section, click the Lighting button and select Two Point in the Special section, compare your Format Pictures dialog box to Figure M-7, then click Close**

8. **Click the Wrap Text button in the Arrange group, click Square, select the contents of the Shape Width text box in the Size group, type 1.6, then press [Enter]**
   The picture is resized, and the Square text wrapping makes the picture into a floating graphic. You apply Square text wrapping so you can position the picture any place in the document.

9. **Click the Position button in the Arrange group, click More Layout Options to open the Layout dialog box, modify the settings in your Layout dialog box to match those shown in Figure M-8, click OK, then save the document**
   You can position a graphic object horizontally and vertically on the page relative to a margin, column, line, or edge of the page.

FIGURE M-6: **Cropping a picture**

Gray shows area to be removed

The pointer changes to a crosshair as you drag

FIGURE M-7: **3-D effects applied to a picture**

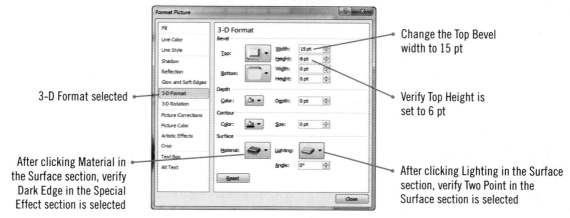

3-D Format selected

After clicking Material in the Surface section, verify Dark Edge in the Special Effect section is selected

Change the Top Bevel width to 15 pt

Verify Top Height is set to 6 pt

After clicking Lighting in the Surface section, verify Two Point in the Surface section is selected

FIGURE M-8: **Setting advanced positioning options for a graphic object**

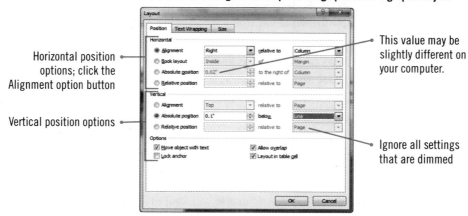

Horizontal position options; click the Alignment option button

Vertical position options

This value may be slightly different on your computer.

Ignore all settings that are dimmed

Using advanced positioning options

Word offers a variety of ways to position objects. You can use the Position tab in the Arrange group on the Picture Tools Format tab or the Drawing Tools Format tab to position the object in one of several predefined locations, such as Position in Middle Center with Square Text Wrapping. You can use the pointer to position an object anywhere on the page in a Word document unless the object has been formatted with the In Line with Text wrapping style. You can use the arrow keys on the keyboard to move an object by small increments. You can press [Ctrl] and use the arrow keys on the keyboard to move an object in very small increments. You can also use the Layout tab in the Format Object dialog box to position an object precisely in relation to the page, margin, column, paragraph, or line in a Word document.

Removing the Background from a Picture

You use the Remove Background feature to remove background objects from a photograph. For example, you can modify a photograph of a person standing in front of a landscape so that only the person is visible. ▓▓▓▓ The Year in Review document includes a photograph of a sleeping koala. You use the Remove Background feature to isolate just the koala from the surrounding leaves, and then in the next lesson you use artistic effects to superimpose the isolated koala over a new picture.

STEPS

QUICK TIP
This document contains two pictures of the koala. You will use the second picture in the next lesson.

1. **Scroll to the first picture of the koala under the Prize Winner heading on page 3, increase the zoom to 150%, then scroll so the picture fills the document window**

   You increase the zoom percentage when working with graphics so you can clearly see your changes.

2. **Click the koala picture to select it**

3. **Click Remove Background in the Adjust group**

   Most of the picture turns purple and only the koala and a section of the tree appear in full color, and the Background Removal tab becomes active. You use the buttons in the Refine group on the Background Removal tab to mark which areas of the photograph to keep and which areas to discard.

4. **Click the Mark Areas to Keep button in the Refine group, then move the mouse pointer over the picture**

   The mouse pointer changes to a pencil shape that you use to indicate which areas of the photograph to include.

QUICK TIP
When you mark an area to include or to remove, you can simply click and drag to draw a line across the area. You do not need to be precise.

5. **Click the area of the tree near the koala's left paw and drag the pencil down as shown in Figure M-9, then release the mouse button**

   A portion of the tree reappears. A dotted line showing where you dragged the pointer appears on the tree trunk. The dotted line includes an Include marker, which is a circle with a plus symbol. The Include marker indicates that the line identifies the area of the picture to keep. A Remove marker appears as a circle with a minus symbol. You use the Remove marker to indicate which areas of the picture you want to remove. The markers give a hint about whether something is part of the foreground that you want to keep or part of the background that you want to remove.

TROUBLE
The process of removing a background takes some time. You do not need to match Figure M-10 exactly.

6. **Mark additional areas of the tree to keep as indicated by the Include markers shown in Figure M-10, then click the Mark Areas to Remove button to remove areas that you don't want to include as indicated by the lines with Remove markers shown in Figure M-10**

   The best way to learn more about the Remove Background tools is to spend time experimenting with them. Remember that you can use the Undo button on the Quick Access toolbar to undo any action that produces a result you don't want. Notice that in the koala picture some areas of the picture appear connected. For example, when you try to remove the top of the tree trunk, a portion of the leaves might appear. When this happens, click the Undo button, then reverse the order you mark things. Use the Mark Areas to Remove pointer to mark the portion of leaves as an area you want to remove and use the Mark Areas to Keep pointer to mark the top of the tree trunk as an area to include.

QUICK TIP
If you want to start over, click the Reset Picture button in the Adjust group to return the picture to its original settings.

7. **When you are satisfied that the picture appears similar to Figure M-10, click the Keep Changes button in the Close group**

   The picture appears similar to Figure M-11. If you do not like the picture you have created, click the Remove Background button again and then use the Mark Areas to Keep, Mark Areas to Remove, and Undo buttons to further refine the picture.

8. **Save the document**

FIGURE M-9: Selecting an area of a photograph to keep

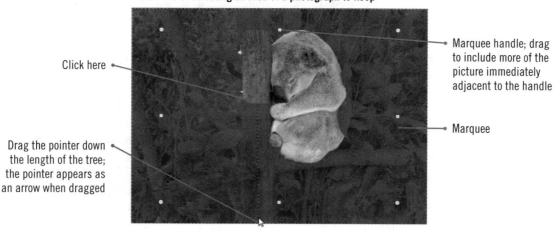

Click here

Marquee handle; drag to include more of the picture immediately adjacent to the handle

Marquee

Drag the pointer down the length of the tree; the pointer appears as an arrow when dragged

FIGURE M-10: Marking multiple areas to keep and remove

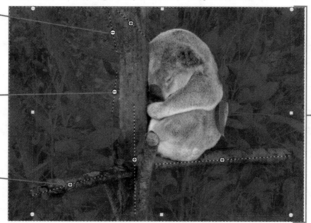

Mark this area to remove before marking the top of the tree trunk to keep

Remove marker is a minus sign that indicates areas marked for removal

Include marker is a plus sign that indicates areas marked for inclusion

The location of the Include and Remove markers will be different on your screen, depending on how you marked areas to keep and remove

FIGURE M-11: Portion of a picture isolated from the background

Compressing pictures

When you add a picture to a document, you increase the file size of your document—sometimes quite dramatically. You can use the Compress Pictures command to reduce the file size of the picture. When you apply this command, you can choose to reduce the image resolution and you can specify to delete all cropped areas of a picture. To compress a picture, select it, click the Picture Tools Format tab, click the Compress Pictures button in the Adjust group, then specify the resolution you want to use. For example, you may choose 220 dpi (dots per inch) for pictures that you want to print and 96 dpi for a picture that you want to send in an e-mail. If you have more than one picture in a document, you can specify that you wish to apply compression options to every picture in the document.

Using Artistic Effects and Layering Options

In the Adjust group on the Picture Tools Format tab, you can choose to apply one of 23 artistic effects to a picture, correct the brightness and contrast, modify the color saturation, and sharpen or soften the appearance of a photograph. When you include two or more photographs or graphic objects in your document, you can use the options in the Arrange group on the Picture Tools Format tab to specify how the objects should appear in relation to each other. For example, you can choose to layer objects in order to show one object partially on top of another object. You can also use the **Selection and Visibility pane** to help you layer objects. ▰▰▰ You want to combine two versions of the koala bear picture. First, you apply an artistic effect to the untouched picture of the koala, and then you use layering options to superimpose the picture of the koala with the background removed over the picture of the koala with the artistic effect applied.

STEPS

QUICK TIP
You can move the mouse pointer over each of the artistic effects to view how the photograph changes.

1. Scroll to and click the untouched photograph of the koala, then click Artistic Effects in the Adjust group

2. Click the Mosaic Bubbles effect as shown in Figure M-12

3. Click Corrections in the Adjust group, then click the Brightness: +20% Contrast: –20% option (second row, fourth column) in the Brightness and Contrast area

4. Reduce the zoom to 60%, click the Wrap Text button in the Arrange group, click Through, click the top picture of the koala, click the Wrap Text button, then click Through

   You changed the wrapping of both pictures so you can superimpose one picture on top of the other picture.

5. Press the down arrow [↓] to move the selected picture down so that it exactly covers the koala with the Mosaic Bubbles artistic effect as shown in Figure M-13

   The picture of the koala with the background removed is superimposed over the picture formatted with the Mosaic Bubbles artistic effect. You show the Selection and Visibility pane and experiment with the layering options.

QUICK TIP
You can rename objects in the Selection and Visibility pane so they have meaningful names, such as "koala background removed". You can also widen the Selection and Visibility pane.

6. Increase the zoom to 100%, click Selection Pane in the Arrange group, click the eye icon 👁 to the right of the currently selected picture in the Selection Pane

   The photograph of the koala with the background removed is hidden from view. The eye icon is a toggle button that toggles the status of an object between show and hide. The Selection and Visibility pane shows the objects on the current page along with the stacking order of those objects. The picture listed at the top of the pane is the picture on top, which in this example is the photograph of the koala with the background removed.

QUICK TIP
You can also use the re-order buttons at the bottom of the Selection and Visibility pane to change the layering of pictures.

7. Click the eye icon 👁 again to show the koala with the background removed, click the koala picture, click the Picture Tools Format tab, click the Send Backward list arrow in the Arrange group, click Send to Back, notice how the photograph of the koala with the background removed seems to disappear and the pictures in the Selection Pane are re-ordered, click the Bring Forward list arrow, then click Bring to Front

   The koala picture with the background removed is back on top, and it is listed first in the Selection and Visibility pane.

8. Click the second picture listed in the Selection and Visibility pane, click Color in the Adjust group, click Saturation 200% in the Color Saturation area (top row), then close the Selection and Visibility pane

9. Click above the picture, press [Delete] once to remove the extra blank line, compare the completed pictures to Figure M-14, then save the document

FIGURE M-12: Applying the Mosaic Bubbles artistic effect

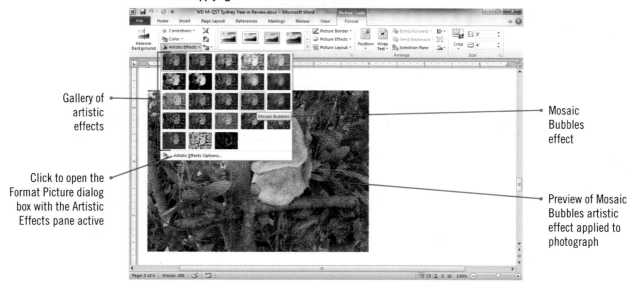

Gallery of artistic effects

Click to open the Format Picture dialog box with the Artistic Effects pane active

Mosaic Bubbles effect

Preview of Mosaic Bubbles artistic effect applied to photograph

FIGURE M-13: Moving one picture on top of another picture

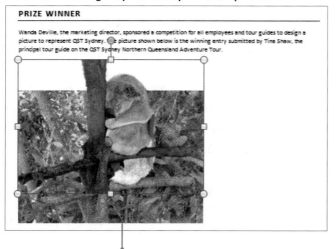

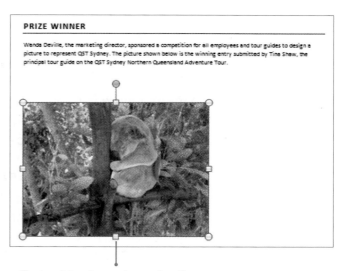

After applying text wrapping to both pictures, the bottom picture moves up and under the other picture

The top picture is superimposed on the bottom picture

FIGURE M-14: Completed pictures appear as one picture

Pictures moved up together when blank line deleted

Creating SmartArt Graphics

You create a **SmartArt graphic** when you want to provide a visual representation of information that you can communicate using bullet points. A SmartArt graphic combines shapes with text. Figure M-15 describes when to use each of the eight categories of SmartArt graphics and shows an example of each. Once you have selected a SmartArt category, you select a layout and then type text in each of the SmartArt shapes or in the text pane. You can further modify a SmartArt graphic by changing fill colors, shape styles, and layouts. ▰▰▰▰ You include two SmartArt graphics in the QST Sydney Year in Review document: a picture graphic and an organizational chart.

STEPS

1. **Scroll up to page 2, then click the picture immediately below the Top Tours paragraph**

   You can create a SmartArt picture graphic from any picture inserted in a document, and then you can add additional pictures to the graphic.

2. **Click the Picture Tools Format tab, click Picture Layout in the Picture Styles group, move your mouse pointer over each of the picture layouts to see how the selected picture changes, click the Bending Picture Blocks layout (second row, fourth column), then click Text Pane in the Create Graphic group if the Text Pane is not open**

   Two SmartArt Tools tabs appear with the Design tab active. You use commands on these tabs to add more pictures to the graphic and to apply formatting.

3. **Click Add Shape in the Create Graphic group, click Add Shape again, click the picture icon ▦ for the second shape in the Text Pane to open the Insert Picture dialog box, navigate to the location where you store your Data Files, double-click WD M-2.jpg, click the picture icon ▦ in the last shape in the Text Pane, then double-click WD M-3.jpg**

4. **Click next to the top bullet, type Red Centre Tour, press the [↓], enter text in the Text Pane for the other two pictures as shown in Figure M-16, close the Text Pane, click away from the SmartArt graphic, then click a white area of the graphic to select it**

TROUBLE
Click Wrap Text in the Arrange group if you do not see Arrange.

5. **Click the SmartArt Tools Format tab, click Arrange, click Wrap text, click Square, click the Size button if you do not see the Shape Height and Shape Width text boxes, change the Height of the graphic to 5" and the Width to 6.5", click the SmartArt Tools Design tab, click the Bending Picture Caption layout in the Layouts group, then use your arrow keys and the mouse pointer to move the graphic down so that it appears below the flower picture**

6. **Click away from the graphic to deselect it, press [Ctrl][F], type Personnel, press [Enter], select the [Organization Chart] placeholder, close the Navigation pane, click the Insert tab, click the SmartArt button in the Illustrations group, click Hierarchy, select the Hierarchy style, click OK, click in the top box, type Sheila Barton, press [Shift][Enter], then type Manager**

   You press [Shift][Enter] to move to a new line in the same box.

QUICK TIP
Click the Undo button 🔄 on the Quick Access toolbar if you do not like where a shape is added.

7. **Click the box below and to the right, click the Add Shape list arrow in the Create Graphic group, then click Add Shape Below**

   The Add Shape menu provides options (such as below, after, and above) for adding more shapes to your SmartArt graphic. The new shape is added based on the currently selected box and the menu selection.

8. **Click the Change Colors button in the SmartArt Styles group, select Colorful Range – Accent Colors 2 to 3, click the More button ▾ in the SmartArt Styles group, then click Inset**

9. **Enter text so the organization chart appears as shown in Figure M-17, making sure to press [Shift][Enter] after you type each name, then save the document**

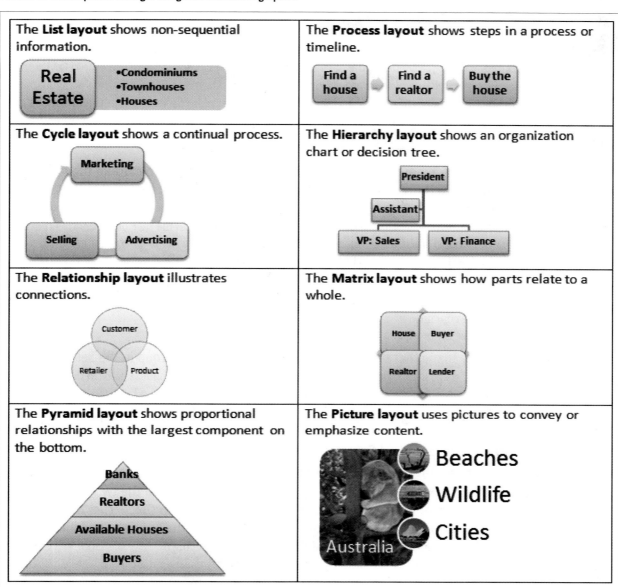

The **List layout** shows non-sequential information.	The **Process layout** shows steps in a process or timeline.
The **Cycle layout** shows a continual process.	The **Hierarchy layout** shows an organization chart or decision tree.
The **Relationship layout** illustrates connections.	The **Matrix layout** shows how parts relate to a whole.
The **Pyramid layout** shows proportional relationships with the largest component on the bottom.	The **Picture layout** uses pictures to convey or emphasize content.

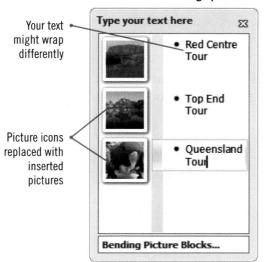

Your text might wrap differently

Picture icons replaced with inserted pictures

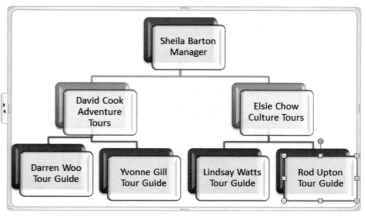

Word 2010

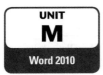

Editing Clip Art

A clip art picture is made up of many objects that are grouped together into one picture. When you edit a clip-art picture, you are really editing the objects that make up the picture. ▆▆▟▆▆ The Year in Review document contains a clip art picture of an award ribbon that was inserted from the Clip Organizer. First, you ungroup the picture into its component objects, and then you change the color of selected objects and remove an object. Finally, you use the Edit Shape feature to change the shape of one of the objects in the picture.

STEPS

1. **Increase the zoom to 200%, scroll down to view the clip art picture of the ribbon, use the scroll bars to center the ribbon picture in the document window, right-click the picture, click Edit Picture, then click Yes in response to the warning**

   The picture is contained in a drawing canvas. A gray border encloses the edge of the drawing canvas, and the Drawing Tools Format tab becomes available. The **drawing canvas** is an area for creating or modifying graphics, such as the shapes that make up a clip art picture.

2. **Click the Drawing Tools Format tab, then click Selection Pane in the Arrange group**

   The Selection and Visibility pane opens and shows all the objects that make up the ribbon picture. The objects are contained in one group named Canvas. You can click the icon to the left of the word "Canvas" to collapse the list or expand the list.

3. **Click any shape that begins with Freeform in the Canvas group in the Selection Pane**

   Selecting a shape in the Selection and Visibility pane selects the corresponding shape in the image. In a clip art picture that contains so many objects, you will find it easier to select shapes by clicking them in the picture.

4. **Click the tip of any black star point to select the entire black star shape as shown in Figure M-18, close the Selection Pane, click the Shape Fill button list arrow, then click Green in the Standard Colors section**

   The black star shape is filled with green. You continue to modify shapes that make up the clip art image.

5. **Click the black object that makes up the background of one of the two ribbon shapes, change its color to Green, repeat for the other black ribbon shape, click the 1 in the center of the black circle, change its color to White, then click the red circle and press [Delete]**

   The ribbon appears as shown in Figure M-19. In addition to changing the color of shapes, you can use the Edit Points feature to change the shape of any of the objects that make up the clip art picture. When you work with the Edit Points feature, you often expand the Drawing canvas so you have more room to work.

6. **Drag the left, right, and top dotted edges of the Drawing canvas to provide more white space as shown in Figure M-20, click the large green star shape, click the Edit Shape button ⌞ॱ in the Insert Shapes group, then click Edit Points**

   Black squares appear around the edges of the shape. These squares identify the shape's **wrap points**. You can click and drag any of these wrap points to redraw any shape included in a clip art picture. Some pictures contain hundreds of wrap points, and editing each one can be a long process.

7. **Drag a star point up until it extends to the top of the drawing canvas, then use Figure M-21 as a guide to redraw the remaining star points so you have adjusted a total of five star points**

   After you modify specific objects that make up a clip art picture, you can group all the objects back into one object that you can easily size and position.

8. **Click a blank area of the drawing canvas, click the Home tab, click Select in the Editing group, then click Select All**

9. **Click the Drawing Tools Format tab, click the Group button ⊞ in the Arrange group, click Group, then save the document**

   The modified clip art picture is complete.

FIGURE M-18: Selecting one object in an ungrouped clip art picture

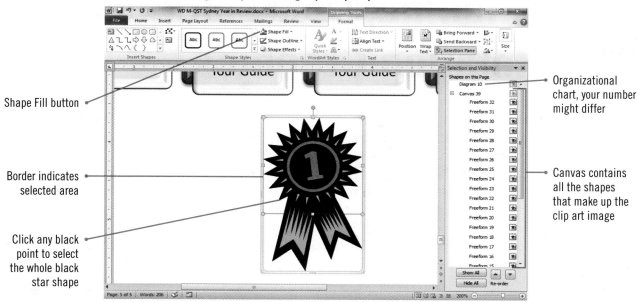

Shape Fill button

Border indicates
selected area

Click any black
point to select
the whole black
star shape

Organizational
chart, your number
might differ

Canvas contains
all the shapes
that make up the
clip art image

FIGURE M-19: Clip art picture enhanced with new fill colors

Drag dotted area on
the left edge

FIGURE M-20: Resizing the drawing canvas

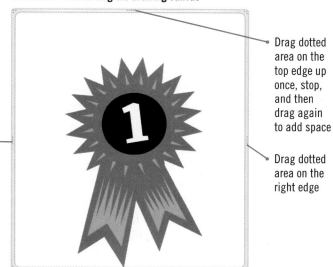

Drag dotted
area on the
top edge up
once, stop,
and then
drag again
to add space

Drag dotted
area on the
right edge

FIGURE M-21: Modifying five star points

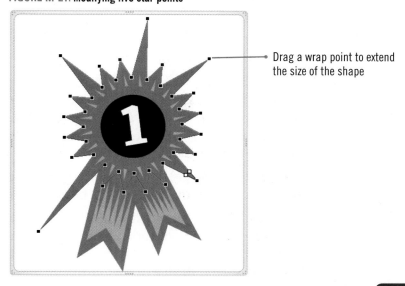

Drag a wrap point to extend
the size of the shape

Exploring Advanced Graphics

Word 319

Aligning, Distributing, and Rotating Graphics

The Align button in the Arrange group on the Drawing Tools Format tab includes commands you can use to change the relative positioning of two or more objects. For example, you can use the Align Left command to align several drawn objects along their left sides. You can use the Distribute Vertically or the Distribute Horizontally command to display three or more objects so that the same amount of space appears between each object. The Rotate button in the Arrange group includes commands you can use to rotate or flip an object. For example, suppose you insert a clip art picture of a cat stalking to the right. You can use the Flip Horizontal command to flip the cat so that it stalks to the left, or you can use the Rotate option to make the cat stalk uphill or downhill. 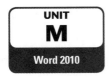 You decide to include a series of small stars that are aligned and distributed vertically along the left edge of the drawing canvas containing the clip art picture that you modified in the previous lesson. You also want to rotate the stars.

STEPS

1. **Click outside the Drawing canvas, click the Insert tab, click Shapes in the Illustrations group, then select the 5-Point Star shape in the Stars and Banners section (first row, fourth column)**

2. **Point to a white area above and to the left of the ribbon picture, then draw a star similar to the star shown in Figure M-22**

3. **Click the More button ⊽ in the Shape Styles group to show the selection of shape styles, then click the Moderate Effect – Orange, Accent 6 style (second to last row, last column)**
   The star is filled with an attractive gradient fill that includes a shadow.

4. **Click the Size button on the Drawing Tools tab if you do not see the launcher ⬚, click the Size dialog box launcher ⬚, click the Lock aspect ratio check box to select it, set the Absolute Height at .3", press [Tab] to set the Width automatically, compare the Layout dialog box to Figure M-23, then click OK**
   By selecting the Lock aspect ratio check box, you make sure that the Width is calculated in proportion to the Height you enter (or vice versa).

5. **Press [Ctrl][C] to copy the star, press [Ctrl][V] to paste a copy of the star, repeat two times so you have four stars, then position the bottom star as shown in Figure M-24**
   You don't need to worry about positioning the star exactly because you will use the Align and Distribute commands to set the positions of all four stars at once.

6. **Press and hold [Ctrl], click each star until all four stars are selected, click the Align button ⬚ ▾ in the Arrange group, then click Align Left**
   The left edge of each star is on the same plane as the other stars.

7. **Verify all four stars are still selected, click the Align button ⬚ ▾, click Distribute Vertically, click the Group button ⬚ in the Arrange group, then click Group**
   The Distribute Vertically command places the stars so that the distance between each star is equal. You group the stars into one shape so that you can rotate all four stars at once and then position them.

8. **Click the Rotate button ⬚ ▾ in the Arrange group, click Rotate Left 90°, reduce the zoom to 100%, then position the rotated stars below the clip art picture**

TROUBLE
The Many Pages button looks like a computer with several pages displayed on the monitor.

9. **Click the View tab, click Zoom, click the Many Pages button, drag to show 1 × 4 pages, click OK, turn on formatting marks and make adjustments to the spacing so your pages resemble Figure M-25, enter your name where indicated at the top of the document, save the document, submit the file to your instructor, then close the document**

FIGURE M-22: **Star shape drawn**

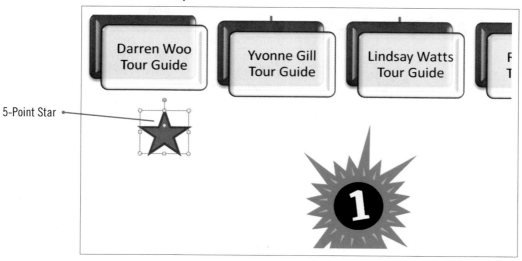

5-Point Star

FIGURE M-23: **Setting a specific size for an object**

Absolute height is .3"

Absolute width adjusted to .3"; your value may differ slightly

Lock aspect ratio option selected

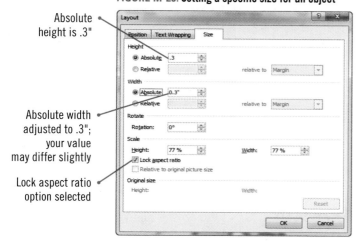

FIGURE M-24: **Positioning a graphic object**

Star positioned

FIGURE M-25: **Completed document**

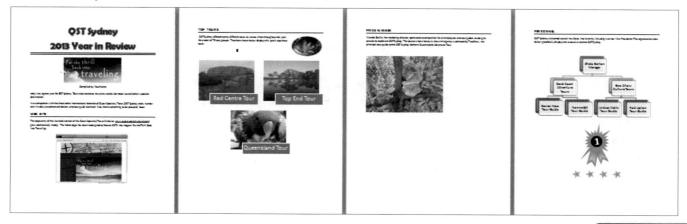

Exploring Advanced Graphics

Practice

Concepts Review

For current SAM information, including versions and content details, visit SAM Central (http://www.cengage.com/samcentral). If you have a SAM user profile, you may have access to hands-on instruction, practice, and assessment of the skills covered in this unit. Since various versions of SAM are supported throughout the life of this text, check with your instructor for the correct instructions and URL/Web site for accessing assignments.

Label the numbered items shown in Figure M-26.

FIGURE M-26

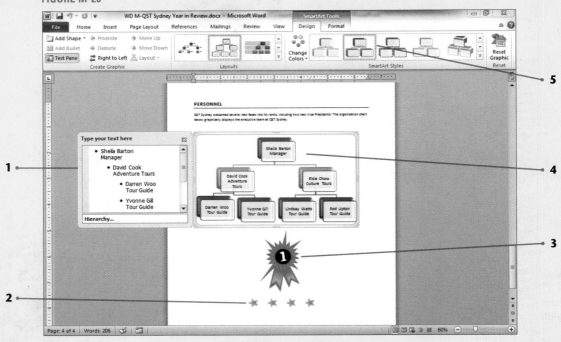

Match each term with the statement that best describes it.

6. **Drawing canvas**
7. **Edit Picture**
8. **Edit Points**
9. **Distribute Vertically**
10. **Align Left**
11. **Target**

a. Select to edit the drawing points on an object
b. Type of SmartArt graphic
c. Evenly spaces three or more objects
d. Select to modify the individual objects that make up a clip art picture
e. Arranges two or more objects along the same plane
f. Enclosed box that can contain a variety of graphics objects

Select the best answer from the list of choices.

12. **In the Advanced tab of the Font dialog box, what selection increases the spacing between characters?**
    a. Proportional
    b. Expanded
    c. Condensed
    d. Ligatures
13. **Which type of SmartArt diagram do you use to show relationships that progress from a single entity at the top to multiple entities at the bottom?**
    a. Process
    b. Cycle
    c. Hierarchy
    d. Relationship
14. **How do you select two or more non-adjacent objects?**
    a. Press and hold [Ctrl], then click each object in turn.
    b. Click each object in turn.
    c. Press and hold [Alt], then click each object in turn.
    d. Click Edit in the Arrange group, then click Select.

Exploring Advanced Graphics

Skills Review

1. Work with text effects.

a. Start Word, open the file WD M-4.docx from the drive and folder where you store your Data Files, then save it as **WD M-Island Trading Report**.

b. Apply the Gradient Fill – Lime, Accent 6, Inner Shadow text effect to the Island Trading Report title.

c. Open the Format Text Effects dialog box, then modify the text effect by applying the Circle bevel style to the top with a width of 10 pt.

d. Increase the font size of the title to 28 pt, then apply the Arial Black font.

e. Update the Title style to match the selection, then apply the Title style to "Year End Analysis".

f. Scroll to and select the Web Design heading, open the Advanced tab in the Font dialog box, then apply the Expanded character spacing.

g. Update the Heading 1 style to match the selection.

h. Select Way to Go Team! (the line above the Web Design heading), apply the Gabriola font, open the Advanced tab in the Font dialog box, apply Stylistic Set 6, increase the font size to 18 pt, then center the text.

i. Save the document.

2. Create and modify screenshots.

a. Open WD M-5.docx from the drive and folder where you store your Data Files.

b. Return to the Island Trading Report in Word, then select the [Home Page Design] placeholder.

c. View the available windows for a screenshot, verify that the Word document you just opened appears as the first available thumbnail, then click Screen Clipping.

d. Clip the picture so only the representation of the Web page is included.

e. Change the width of the inserted clip picture to 3.8", center the picture, then apply a black border. (*Note*: The picture will appear on page 1 of the report after you complete the next section.)

f. Save the document, then close WD M-5.docx without saving it.

3. Modify a picture.

a. Click the picture of the flower on page 1, then crop it so that it appears as shown in Figure M-27.

b. Crop the picture to the Diamond shape.

c. In the Format Picture dialog box, open the Alt Text pane, then enter **Flower** in the Title text box and replace Flower.jpg with **A pink hibiscus in Hawaii.** as the description.

d. Modify the picture effects to use the Slope Bevel with the following settings in the Bevel 3-D options: Top Width of 15 pt and Metal Material.

e. Change the text wrapping to Square, open the Size tab in the Layout dialog box, click the Lock aspect ratio check box to deselect it, then set the height of the picture to 1.5" and the width of the picture to 1.6".

f. Using the Position tab in the Layout dialog box, specify the horizontal alignment as Right relative to the column, then save the document. Note that the screen clipping should now fit on page 1.

FIGURE M-27

located throughout the Hawaiian Islands 9

4. Remove the background from a picture.

a. Scroll to the first picture of the sailboat on page 3.

b. Remove the background and make adjustments until only the sailboat appears as shown in Figure M-28.

c. Save the document.

FIGURE M-28

5. Use artistic effects and layering options.

a. Scroll down until the two sailboats pictures are in the document window, adjust the zoom as needed to see both pictures, then apply the Watercolor Sponge artistic effect to the second picture.

b. Apply the Brightness: 0% (Normal) Contrast: +20% correction.

c. Change the wrapping option to Through for both pictures, then move the picture of the single sailboat over the picture of the two sailboats.

Skills Review (continued)

d. Use the Selection and Visibility pane to select the photograph of the two sailboats, then use the Bring Forward command to change the order of the two pictures.

e. Apply the 400% Saturation color effect to the picture of the two sailboats, then place the single sailboat in front, close the Selection and Visibility pane, and save the document.

6. Create SmartArt graphics.

a. Scroll up to page 2, click the photograph (not the clip art image) below the New Supplier Countries paragraph, then apply the Picture Accent Blocks picture layout.

b. Add two new shapes using Add Shape After, then insert WD M-6.jpg in the new top shape and WD M-7.jpg in the new bottom shape from the drive and folder where you store you Data Files.

c. In the Text Pane, enter three captions as follows: **Japan, Australia, Thailand**.

d. Apply the Square wrapping option, and change the height of the graphic to 4" and the width to 6".

e. Apply the Ascending Picture Accent Process layout (third row, fourth column).

f. Find the [Organization Chart] placeholder, insert an organization chart using the Hierarchy layout in the Hierarchy category, type **Anita Chau** in the top box, press [Shift][Enter], then type **President**.

g. Click the box below and to the left, add a shape after, then add a shape below the new box.

h. Enter text so the organization chart appears as shown in Figure M-29, making sure to press [Shift][Enter] after typing each name.

i. Apply the Polished SmartArt style, change the colors of the organization chart to Colorful – Accent Colors, then save the document.

FIGURE M-29

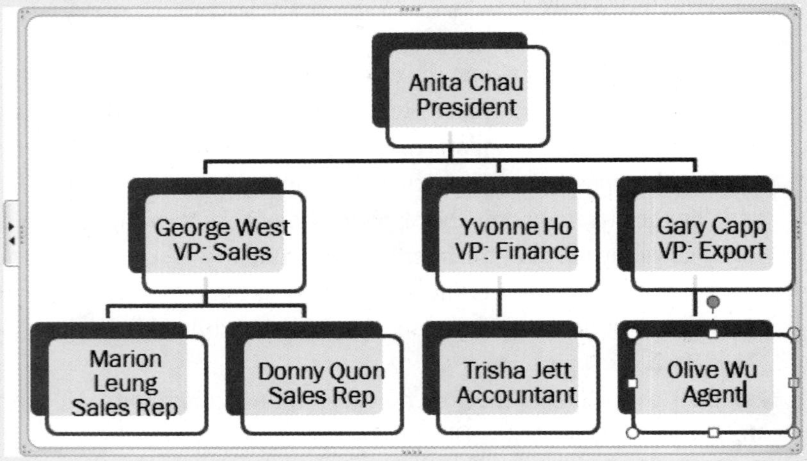

FIGURE M-30

7. Edit clip art.

a. Scroll up to the New Supplier Countries heading, click the green globe figure, then edit it to convert it into a graphic (answer Yes to the warning).

b. Using Figure M-30 as your guide, increase the zoom, remove the green square, remove all the objects that make up the rocket ship shape, then use the wrap points function to modify the appearance of the two feet.

c. Select and then group the objects into one object.

d. Save the document.

8. Align, distribute, and rotate graphics.

a. Draw a sun shape in a blank area to the right of the clip art picture and outside the drawing canvas, then apply the Subtle Effect – Lime, Accent 6 shape style.

b. Open the Size tab in the Layout dialog box, select the Lock aspect ratio check box to select it, then set the absolute height of the shape at .3".

c. Copy the sun shape twice so that there is a total of three sun shapes.

d. Use the Align and Distribute functions to show all three suns evenly spaced above the drawing canvas containing the clip art picture. (*Note*: Move one star to the right side of the clip art picture, then select all three suns and apply align left and distribute horizontally options. If the suns do not align as expected, click the Align Selected Objects option on the Align menu in the Arrange Group on the Drawing Tools Format tab.)

e. Group the three suns into one picture.

f. Click the clip art picture, view the rotate options, then click Flip Horizontal.

Skills Review (continued)

g. Change the wrapping of the drawing canvas to Square, then position the objects on page 2 as shown in the completed document in Figure M-31.

h. Preview the document and view each of the four pages, enter your name where indicated at the top of the document, save the document, submit the file to your instructor, then close the document.

FIGURE M-31

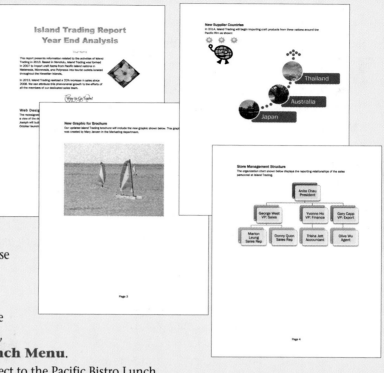

Independent Challenge 1

You have just been hired to design a menu for Pacific Bistro, a new restaurant situated on an island off the coast of Washington state. You use text effects to enhance text in the document, and then you use the Remove Background and Artistic Effects features to modify a photograph.

a. Start Word, open the file WD M-8.docx from the drive and folder where you store your Data Files, then save it as **WD M-Pacific Bistro Lunch Menu**.

b. Apply the Gradient Fill – Gold Accent 1 text effect to the Pacific Bistro Lunch Menu title, increase the font size to 28 pt, then apply the Offset Diagonal Bottom Left shadow style. (*Hint*: Click the Text Effects button, point to Shadow, then click the first row, third column, in the Outer section.)

c. Update the Menu Title style to match the selection.

d. Select "Appetizers", then change the character spacing on the Advanced tab of the Font dialog box to Expanded by 2 pt. (*Hint:* Select 1 pt in the By text box, then type **2 pt**.) Update the Category style to match the selection so that all the menu items use the expanded character spacing.

e. Select $6.95 (the first price in the Appetizers section), then change the OpenType setting for Number forms to Old-style. Update the Price style to match the selection. (*Note:* With the Old-style number form applied, the placement of numbers varies depending on the number combinations; for example, the "95" in "6.95" dips below the "6" but are even with the "4" in "4.95.")

f. Scroll to the bottom of the document, select the picture of the kayak on page 1, then remove the background so only the orange kayak remains.

g. Scroll to the second page, apply the Cutout artistic effect to the second photograph of the kayak, then change the color to Aqua, Accent color 2 Light in the Recolor section that appears when you click Color in the Adjust group.

h. Use the Corrections feature to select the Brightness: + 20% Contrast: +40% Correction.

i. Change the picture style to Bevel Rectangle, then apply the Circle Bevel picture effect.

FIGURE M-32

j. Change the wrapping to Through, then scroll up and change the wrapping of the kayak picture with the background removed to Through.

k. Use arrow keys and the mouse pointer to position the orange kayak over the aqua picture. Use the Selection and Visibility pane and the Bring Forward and Send Backward features to help you position the two pictures in relation to each other so the completed picture appears as shown in Figure M-32.

l. Type your name where indicated at the top of the document, save and close the document, submit the file to your instructor, then close the document.

Exploring Advanced Graphics

Independent Challenge 2

You have just started working for Growing Green, a tour company based in Connecticut that takes visitors on guided tours of local gardens and provides gardening advice. One of your jobs is to prepare the company's annual report. Before you format the entire report, you gather some of the information required. First, you insert and modify a screenshot of the graphic created by a coworker that will be featured on the report's title page, and then you create an organization chart to show the company personnel.

a. Start Word, open the file WD M-9.docx from the drive and folder where you store your Data Files, then save it as **WD M-Growing Green Report** to the drive and folder where you store your Data Files.

b. Open WD M-10.docx, then view the WD M-Growing Green Report document again.

c. Select the [Screenshot] placeholder, then use the Screenshot command to take a screen clipping of the picture in WD M-10.docx. Include only the picture from WD M-10.docx, not any of the text, in the screenshot.

d. In the WD M-Growing Green Report document, add a 3 pt Dark Green, Accent 5 border to the screen clipping, change the picture's width to 6", then center it.

e. Insert a page break to move the Organization Chart heading to the next page, left align the heading if it is not already left aligned, select the [Organization chart] placeholder, then insert a SmartArt graphic that uses the Horizontal Hierarchy style in the Hierarchy category.

FIGURE M-33

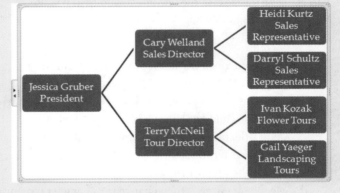

f. Refer to Figure M-33 to enter the text and add or remove the boxes required for your organization chart. Remember to press [Shift][Enter] after you type a name so that you can enter the position.

g. Apply the Cartoon SmartArt style from the SmartArt Tools Design tab.

Advanced Challenge Exercise

- Click the box for Jessica Gruber, right-click, click Format Shape, then change the fill color to Dark Green, Accent 5, Darker 50%.

- Change the fill color of the two second-level boxes to the Lighter 40% shade of the same Green color, and change the text color to black. (*Hint*: You need to enhance each box separately.)

- Click a white area of the chart, change the width of the entire chart to 7", then change the text wrapping to Through.

- Double-click below the organization chart, click the Clip Art button on the Insert tab, search for **flower** (you must be connected to the Internet to find suitable clip art), then insert the clip art picture (not a photograph) of the flower you prefer. (Hint: Choose a simple clip art picture that will be easy to modify.)

- Use the Edit Picture command to ungroup the picture, enlarge the drawing canvas to provide more workspace, and then modify the clip art picture in some way. For example, you can remove some of the objects that make up the picture and change the fill color of other objects. (*Hint*: If the picture "jumps" to the top of the page when you edit it, drag it back to a blank area of the screen.)

- Select all the components of the picture and group them into one object, change the wrapping for the drawing canvas to Through, then position the drawing canvas with the picture in a blank area of the organization chart. Note that you can slightly overlap any of the boxes, if you wish. (*Hint*: Be sure to drag the border of the drawing canvas to move both the drawing canvas and the picture.)

h. Type your name where indicated in the document footer, save the document, close the WD M-10.docx document without saving it, submit the WD M-Growing Green Report to your instructor, then close the document.

Independent Challenge 3

You work as a teacher's aide at an elementary school. Your supervisor has asked you to create a worksheet that children can color, according to the labels. You've downloaded the clip art picture to use in the worksheet. Now you need to modify the picture, draw and rotate an AutoShape, and then add some text objects.

a. Start Word, open the file WD M-11.docx from the drive and folder where you store your Data Files, then save it as **WD M-Learning Colors Picture**.

b. Drag a corner handle of the balloon picture to increase its size to approximately 5" × 5" using the settings on the horizontal and vertical ruler bars to help you. (*Note*: Change the zoom setting as needed to meet your needs as you work.)

c. Right-click the picture of the balloons, select Edit Picture (answer Yes), then remove the colored shape from each balloon.

d. Refer to Figure M-34 to complete the picture, according to the following instructions.

e. Outside and to the right of the drawing canvas containing the balloons, draw and format the three sun AutoShapes: First draw one sun AutoShape, and set the height at 1.3" with the lock aspect ratio option selected. (*Hint*: Select the Lock aspect ratio button before you enter 1.3 in the Height text box.)

f. Remove the fill color and change the line color to black, copy and paste the two other sun AutoShapes, use the vertical distribute option to set an equal space between each of the suns, and then use the pointer to drag the middle sun just behind the far-right balloon. (*Hint*: To place the sun behind the balloon, select the Send Behind Text layering option.)

g. As shown in Figure M-34, add text boxes and draw black, 3 pt lines, copying and pasting where needed to reduce drawing time. Type text in the text boxes and format it in Calibri, 18 pt. (*Note*: Remove the border around each text box and move text boxes as needed to ensure they do not block other parts of the picture.)

FIGURE M-34

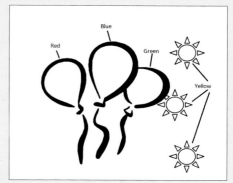

Advanced Challenge Exercise

- Use the Edit Points function to modify each of the three balloons so that each balloon shape is closed.
- Be sure there is no gap in the oval shape.
- Increase the zoom so that you can see the points you are dragging. Click away from the picture to see the progress, then use Edit Points again to refine your efforts.

h. Double-click below the Drawing canvas, type **Prepared by** followed by your name, and then center the text.

i. Save the document, submit the file to your instructor, then close the document.

Real Life Independent Challenge

You can use the many options available in the Picture Tools Format tab to modify the appearance of your photographs. You can then use the modified photographs to enhance invitations, posters, and photo albums. You decide to explore the options on the Picture Tools Format tab and then to use at least four different options to format two photographs. As you format the photographs, you keep track of the options you have selected.

a. Open the file WD M-12.docx from the drive and folder where you store your Data Files, then save it as **WD M-Picture Effects**. This document contains two photographs and space for you to specify the options you use to modify the photographs.

b. Use the Rotate function to show the second of the two pictures vertically.

c. Use four features to modify each of the two pictures. For example, you can choose to change the shape of the picture; modify picture effects such as glows, bevels, and reflections; apply a picture correction; change the picture color; or apply an artistic effect. As you work, note the modifications you make in the table provided under the photograph. For example, if you add a Cool Slant Bevel picture effect, enter **Picture Effects: Bevel** in the Feature column, then enter **Cool Slant** in the Setting column.

d. Type your name where indicated in the footer, save the document, submit the file to your instructor, then close the document.

Visual Workshop

You are working with the Web Development Group at SnugglePets.com to plan and launch a new Web site that sells exotic stuffed animals. You've created a Target SmartArt graphic that illustrates the steps toward the goal of launching the Web site. Open the file WD M-13.docx from the drive and folder where you store your Data Files, then save it as **WD M-Web Launch Target Graphic**. Apply the Gradient Fill – Green, Accent 4, Reflection text effect to the document title. Edit the crocodile picture so that it appears as shown in Figure M-35. With the crocodile in the drawing canvas, remove the reflection shape, then change the color of the crocodile's body to Indigo, Accent 6, Darker 50%. After you have modified the picture, regroup it and change the wrapping to Square. Use the Basic Target SmartArt graphic in the Relationship category to create the Target graphic. (*Hint*: Be sure to use the text pane to enter the text and add shapes before you apply a color or style to the graphic.) Select the color scheme and SmartArt style shown. Enclose the SmartArt graphic in a 6 pt green border. Change the wrapping to Square, and use the mouse to position the graphic and the picture. Add your name, save the document, submit the file to your instructor, then close the document.

FIGURE M-35

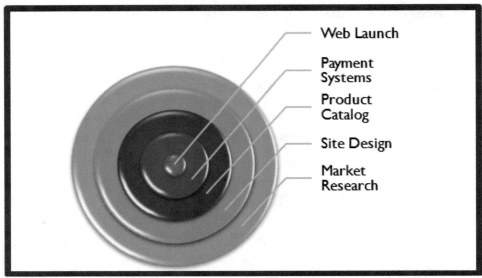

Exploring Advanced Graphics

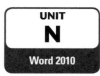

Building Forms

Word provides the tools you need to build forms that users can complete within a Word document. A **form** is a structured document with spaces reserved for entering information. You create a form as a template that includes labeled spaces—called **content controls**—into which users type information. The form template can include a variety of content controls including Rich Text content controls, Building Block Gallery content controls, and even a Date Picker content control. Once you have created a form, you can protect it so that users can enter information into the form, but they cannot change the structure of the form itself. Ron Dawson in the Marketing Department wants to create a form to survey the managers of the various Quest Specialty Travel (QST) branches worldwide. You start by creating the form template.

OBJECTIVES

Construct a form template

Add Text content controls

Add Date Picker and Check Box content controls

Add Drop-Down and Picture content controls

Add a Building Block Gallery content control

Insert Legacy Tools controls

Format and protect a form

Fill in a form as a user

Constructing a Form Template

A Word form is created as a **form template**, which contains all the components of the form. As you learned in an earlier unit, a **template** is a file that contains the basic structure of a document, such as the page layout, headers and footers, and graphic elements. The structure of a form template usually consists of a table that contains labels and two types of controls: content controls and Legacy Tools controls. A **label** is a word or phrase such as "Date" or "Location" that tells people who fill in the form the kind of information required for a given field. A **control** is the placeholder that you, as the form developer, insert into the form. You insert a control to contain the data associated with the label. Figure N-1 shows a completed form template containing several different types of controls. ▰▰▰ You need to create the basic structure of the form in Word, and then you save the document as a template to a new folder that you create.

STEPS

1. **Start Word, click the** File tab, **click** New, **then click** My templates **in the Available Templates section to open the New dialog box**

2. **Be sure** Blank Document **is selected, click the** Template option button **in the Create New section, then click** OK

   A new document appears in the document window, and Template1 appears on the title bar.

   > **QUICK TIP**
   > To apply the Title style, click the More button ⊡ in the Styles group on the Home tab, then click Title.

3. **Click the** Page Layout tab, **click** Themes, **click** Concourse, **type** Marketing Survey, **press** [Enter], **select the text, then apply the Title style and center the text**

4. **Click below the title, click the** Insert tab, **click** Table, **click** Insert Table, **enter 4 for the number of columns and 8 for the number of rows, click** OK, **type** Name, **press** [Tab] **twice, type** Position, **select the** first three rows **of the table, then reduce the width of columns 1 and 3 as shown in Figure N-2**

   > **QUICK TIP**
   > To merge cells, select the cells to merge, click the Table Tools Layout tab, then click Merge Cells in the Merge group.

5. **Enter the remaining labels and merge cells to create the form shown in Figure N-3**

   Once you have created the structure for your form, you can save it as a template. First, you create a new folder to contain the template and then you specify this folder as the location of user templates so that Word can find it.

6. **Minimize Word, click the** Start button **on the taskbar, click** Computer, **navigate to the drive and folder where you store your Data Files, click** New folder **on the menu bar, type** Your Name Form Templates **as the folder name, then press** [Enter]

   You set this new folder as the default location for user templates so all templates are stored automatically in the same location and so you do not need to navigate to the folder each time you save a template. A **user template** is any template that you create.

7. **Close Windows Explorer, return to Template1 in Word, click the** File tab, **click** Options, **click** Advanced, **then scroll to the bottom of the Word Options dialog box**

   > **QUICK TIP**
   > Write down the default location so you have the information available when you reset the File Location for User Templates to the default location.

8. **Click** File Locations, **click** User templates, **click** Modify, **navigate to the Your Name Form Templates folder, click to select the folder, then click** OK **until you are returned to the document**

9. **Click the** Save button 🔲 **on the Quick Access toolbar, verify that "Marketing Survey.dotx" appears in the File name text box, change the filename to** WD N-Marketing Survey.dotx, **then click** Save

   Word saves the template to the new folder you created.

Building Forms

FIGURE N-1: **Form construction**

Rich Text content control

Legacy Tools Text Form Field into which users can enter only a three-digit number

Combo Box content control; a list arrow appears when users move to the field

Building Block Gallery content control contains text and a SmartArt graphic

Legacy Tools Text Form Field formatted for upper case and includes a Help message that appears on the status bar when a user moves to the field

Plain Text content control formatted with the Strong style

Date Picker content control; a calendar appears when users move to the field

Drop-Down List content control; a list arrow appears when users move to the field

Picture content control; a user can insert a picture file

Check Box content control; a check mark appears when a user clicks the box

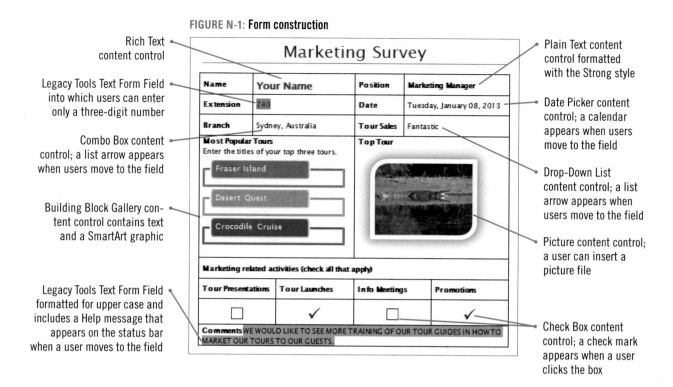

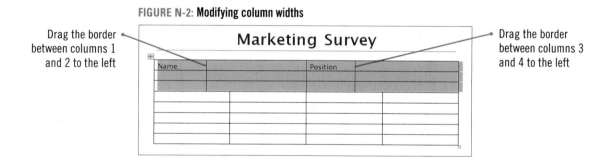

FIGURE N-2: **Modifying column widths**

Drag the border between columns 1 and 2 to the left

Drag the border between columns 3 and 4 to the left

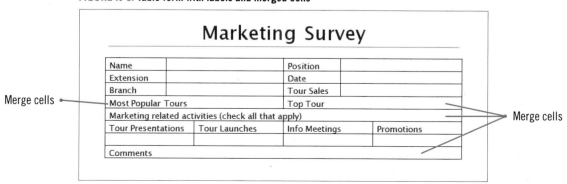

FIGURE N-3: **Table form with labels and merged cells**

Merge cells

Merge cells

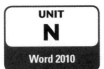
Adding Text Content Controls

Once you have created a structure for your form, you need to designate the locations where you want users to enter information. You insert text content controls in the table cells where users enter text information, such as their names or positions. Two types of text content controls are available. You use the **Rich Text content control** when you want formatting, such as bold or a different font size, automatically applied to text as users enter it in the content control. You can also apply a style, such as the Title style, to a Rich Text content control. You generally use the **Plain Text content control** when you do not need formatting applied to the text that users enter. However, if you want to format a Plain Text content control, you can specify that a style be automatically applied to text as users enter it. You use the Developer tab to access all the commands you use to create and work with forms in Word. ▨▨▨ You display the Developer tab on the Ribbon, then you insert text content controls in the table cells where you need users to enter text.

STEPS

1. **Click the File tab, click Options, click Customize Ribbon, click the Developer check box in the list of main tabs on the right side of the Word Options dialog box to select it, then click OK**

   The Developer tab becomes available on the Ribbon. The Controls group on the Developer tab contains the buttons you use to create and modify the various elements of a form. Table N-1 describes each content control button in the Controls group.

2. **Click the Developer tab, click Design Mode in the Controls group to make Design Mode active, click in the blank table cell to the right of Name, then click the Rich Text Content Control button Aa in the Controls group**

   A Rich Text content control is inserted. When completing the form, the user will be able to enter text into this content control.

3. **Click Properties in the Controls group**

   The Content Control Properties dialog box opens.

4. **Type Full Name as the title of the content control, press [Tab], type Name as the tag, then click OK**

   You can use the same title for more than one content control, but you must assign a unique tag to each content control. The tag is used to help Word distinguish between different content controls that may have the same title. You can view tags only in Design Mode.

5. **Click Full Name to select the entire content control, click the Home tab, change the font size to 16 point, click the Bold button B, click the Font Color list arrow A⋅, then select Red, Accent 2, Darker 25%**

6. **Click the Developer tab, select the text Click here to enter text. between the two tags, then type Enter your full name here. as shown in Figure N-4**

7. **Press [Tab] two times to move to the blank cell to the right of Position, then click the Plain Text Content Control button Aa in the Controls group**

8. **Click Properties in the Controls group, type Job, press [Tab], type Job, click the Use a style to format contents check box, click the Style list arrow, select Strong as shown in Figure N-5, then click OK**

   If you want text entered in a Plain Text content control to appear formatted when the user fills in the form, you must apply a paragraph style. If you apply formats, such as bold and font size, to the Plain Text content control, the formatting will be lost when the form is opened and filled in by a user. You can format both Rich Text and Plain Text content controls with a paragraph style. The Strong paragraph style that you applied to the Plain Text content control will show when you fill in the form as a user.

9. **Select Click here to enter text. between the two Job tags, type Enter your job title here., then save the template**

FIGURE N-4: Rich Text content control

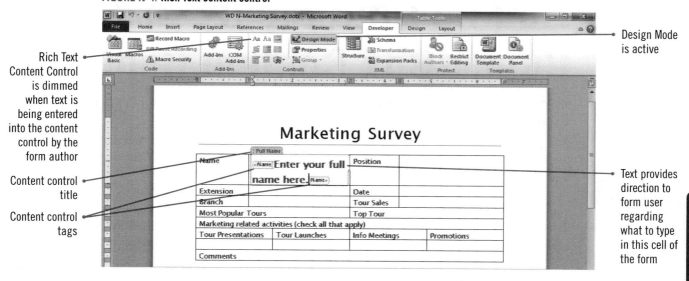

Rich Text Content Control is dimmed when text is being entered into the content control by the form author

Content control title

Content control tags

Design Mode is active

Text provides direction to form user regarding what to type in this cell of the form

FIGURE N-5: Content Control Properties dialog box

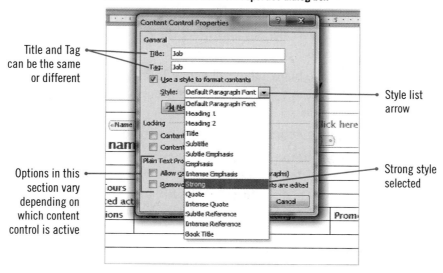

Title and Tag can be the same or different

Options in this section vary depending on which content control is active

Style list arrow

Strong style selected

TABLE N-1: Buttons in the Controls group

button	use to
Aa	Insert a Rich Text content control when you want to apply formatting, such as bold, to text users type
Aa	Insert a Plain Text content control to apply a style to text users type or to display text as plain, unformatted text
🖼	Insert a Picture content control when you want users to be able to insert a picture file
🗂	Insert a Building Block Gallery content control when you want to insert a custom building block, such as a cover page or a SmartArt graphic
📑	Insert a Combo Box content control when you want users to select from a list or be able to add a new item
📑	Insert a Drop-Down List content control to provide users with a list of restricted choices
📅	Insert a Date Picker content control when you want to include a calendar control that users can use to select a specific date
☑	Insert a Check Box content control when you want to insert a check box that users can click to indicate a selection
🔧	Insert controls from the Legacy Tools options when you want additional control over the content that can be entered into a control; if you have programming experience, you can insert ActiveX Controls into forms using the Legacy Tools button

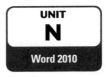
Adding Date Picker and Check Box Content Controls

The **Date Picker content control** provides users with a calendar from which they can select a date. The **Check Box content control** inserts a check box that users can click to insert an "X" or another symbol of your choice such as a check mark. You want the form to include a Date Picker content control that users click to enter the current date and Check Box content controls that users can click to indicate their preferences among a selection of options.

STEPS

1. **Click in the blank table cell to the right of Date, then click the Date Picker Content Control button** in the Controls group

2. **Click Properties in the Controls group, type Current Date as the title and Date as the tag, click the date format shown in Figure N-6, then click OK**

   You will see the calendar in a later lesson when you complete the form as a user.

3. **Select the contents of the Current Date content control, then type the message Click the down arrow to show a calendar and select the current date.**

   Users see this message when they fill in the form.

4. **Scroll to and click the blank table cell below Tour Presentations, then click the Check Box Content Control button** in the Controls group

   A check box appears in the cell.

5. **Click Properties, type Activity, press [Tab], then type Check Box**

6. **Click the Use a style to format contents check box, click the Style list arrow, then select Title**

   If you want the check box to appear larger than the default size in the form, you need to modify it with a style that includes a large font size. You can also choose what character is inserted in the check box when a user clicks it.

7. **Click Change next to the Checked symbol label, click the Font list arrow in the Symbol dialog box, click Wingdings if that is not the active font, select the contents of the Character code text box, type 252, click OK, then click OK**

   A check mark symbol will appear in the check box when a user filling in the form clicks it.

8. **Click Activity to select the check box content control, press [Ctrl][C], press [→] to deselect the check box, press [→] to move to the next cell, press [Ctrl][V], press [→], press [Ctrl][V], press [→], then press [Ctrl][V]**

   A check box appears under each of the four marketing activities.

9. **Click to the left of the row to select the entire row, press [Ctrl][E] to center each of the check boxes, click away from the selected row, then save the document**

   The Check Box and Date Picker content controls appear as shown in Figure N-7.

Building Forms

FIGURE N-6: **Selecting a date format**

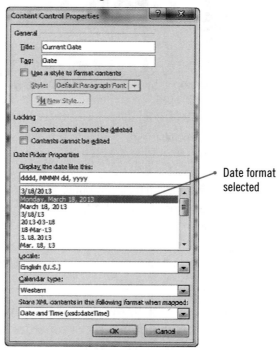

Date format
selected

FIGURE N-7: **Table form with the Date Picker and Check Box content controls added**

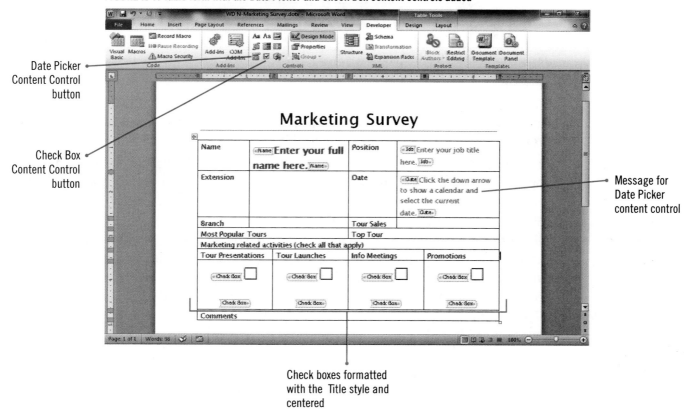

Date Picker
Content Control
button

Check Box
Content Control
button

Message for
Date Picker
content control

Check boxes formatted
with the Title style and
centered

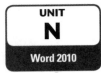
Adding Drop-Down and Picture Content Controls

You can choose from two drop-down content controls: the **Combo Box content control** and the **Drop-Down List content control**. Both drop-down content controls provide users with a list of choices. Users can only select from the list of choices in the Drop-Down List content control. In the Combo Box content control, users can select an item from the list of choices or they can type a new item. You can also insert a Picture content control into a form. In the completed form, users click the Picture content control and then insert a picture they have stored on their computer. ▰▰▰▰ As QST continues to grow, new branch locations are opening on a regular basis. You insert a Combo Box content control next to the Branch table cell so users can select the location of their QST branch if it is listed or type in the location of their branch if it is not listed. You then insert a Drop-Down List content control so users can select an adjective to describe overall tour sales. Finally, you insert a Picture content control in the Top Tour table cell.

1. **Click in the blank table cell to the right of Branch, click the Combo Box Content Control button 🖾 in the Controls group, click Properties in the Controls group, type Branch Location, press [Tab], then type Branch**

2. **Click Add, type London, England, then click OK**
   London, England, will be the first choice users see when they click the Combo Box content control.

3. **Click Add, type San Diego, California, then click OK**

4. **Refer to Figure N-8 to add three more branch locations to the Content Control Properties dialog box: Sydney, Australia; Vancouver, Canada; and New York, USA**

5. **Click San Diego, California, click Modify, change California to USA, click OK, click New York, USA, click Move Up until the entry appears immediately below London, England**
   The list is now in alphabetical order.

6. **Click OK**

7. **Click in the blank table cell to the right of Tour Sales, click the Drop-Down List Content Control button 🖾 in the Controls group, click Properties, complete the Content Control Properties dialog box as shown in Figure N-9, then click OK**

8. **Click Design Mode in the Controls group to turn off Design Mode, click to the right of Top Tour, press [Enter], then click the Picture Content Control 🖾 in the Controls group**
   You need to turn off Design Mode before you insert a Picture content control or a Building Block Gallery content control so that the controls work when you fill in the form.

9. **Click the blue background square representing the picture, click the Picture Tools Format tab, click the More button 🔽 in the Picture Styles group, click Rounded Diagonal Corner, White in the Picture Styles group, then click the Developer tab**
   You applied a picture style to the Picture content control, as shown in Figure N-10. When a user inserts a picture in the form, this picture style will be applied to the inserted picture.

10. **Save the template**

FIGURE N-8: Entries for the Combo Box content control

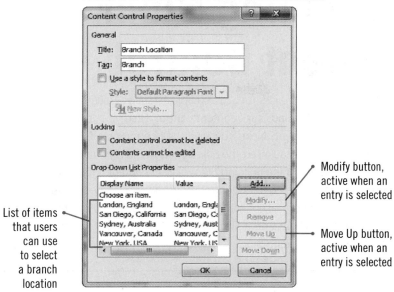

FIGURE N-9: Entries for the Drop-Down List content control

List of items that users can use to select a branch location

Modify button, active when an entry is selected

Move Up button, active when an entry is selected

FIGURE N-10: Picture style selected

Design Mode must be turned off when inserting a Picture content control

Content control tags are not visible when Design Mode is turned off

Combo Box content control

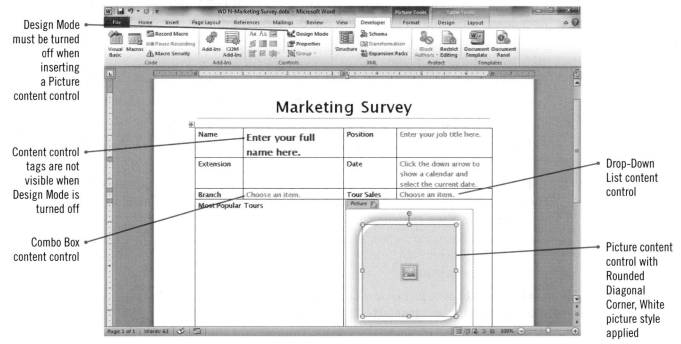

Drop-Down List content control

Picture content control with Rounded Diagonal Corner, White picture style applied

Adding a Building Block Gallery Content Control

A **Building Block Gallery content control** can contain both text and objects, such as pictures and SmartArt graphics. You must follow several steps to use a Building Block content control. First, you create the content you want to be the building block in a new document. Next, you save the content as a Quick Part to the General gallery (or any gallery of your choice). Then, you insert the Building Block Gallery content control into the form. Finally, you use the Quick Parts list arrow on the Building Block Gallery content control to insert the Quick Part you created into the form. Just like Picture content controls, you always work with Design Mode turned off when you are working with Building Block Gallery content controls.  You create a Building Block Gallery content control that contains instructions and a SmartArt graphic that users can modify when they fill out the form. You start by creating a new building block.

STEPS

1. **Click the File tab, click New, then click Create**

   You create a new blank document that will contain the new building block you want to appear in the form.

2. **Type the text Enter the titles of your top three tours., press [Enter], click the Insert tab, click SmartArt in the Illustrations group, click List in the list of SmartArt types, then click Vertical Box List as shown in Figure N-11**

3. **Click OK, click the Change Colors button, then select Colorful - Accent Colors (first selection in the Colorful section)**

4. **Click in the text above the SmartArt graphic, press [Ctrl][A] to select the contents of the document, click the Insert tab, click the Quick Parts list arrow in the Text group, then click Save Selection to Quick Part Gallery**

5. **Type Tour List as the building block name, click OK, save the document as WD N-Marketing Survey Building Block to the location where you save the files for this book (but *not* to the Your Name Form Templates folder), then close the document**

   TROUBLE
   If a warning message opens, click Yes.

6. **Verify that WD N-Marketing Survey.dotx is the active document, click to the right of Most Popular Tours, press [Enter], click the Developer tab, then verify that the Design Mode button is not active**

7. **Click the Building Block Gallery Content Control button in the Controls group, click the Quick Parts list arrow on the Building Block Gallery content control title tab as shown in Figure N-12, then click Tour List**

   Notice that a different color scheme is applied to the SmartArt graphic because you applied the Concourse theme to the form when you created it. The default Office theme was applied when you created the SmartArt graphic in a new document.

8. **Click the white area just below Enter to select the graphic (a gray box appears around the graphic to indicate it is selected), scroll down if necessary, then drag the lower-right corner handle up and to the left to change the width of the graphic to about 3" as shown in Figure N-13**

9. **Click outside the SmartArt graphic, then save the template**

FIGURE N-11: Selecting the Vertical Box List SmartArt graphic

Vertical Box List

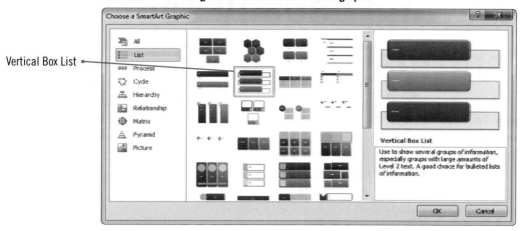

FIGURE N-12: Selecting the Tour List building block

Design Mode
must be turned
off when
inserting a
Building Block
content control

Quick Parts
list arrow

Tour List
building block
(you may see
other building
blocks in the
General section)

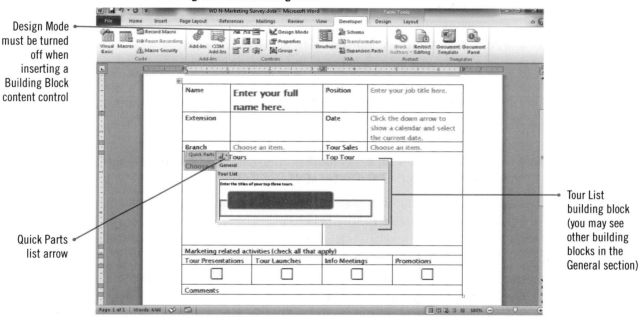

FIGURE N-13: Resizing the Tour List building block

Drag the
lower-right sizing
handle up to
reduce the size of
the SmartArt
graphic to
about 3"

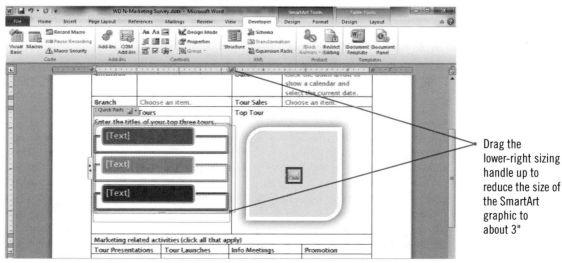

Inserting Legacy Tools Controls

The Legacy Tools button in the Controls group on the Developer tab provides access to a selection of **Legacy Tools controls**. Some of the Legacy Tools controls, such as the **Text control** and the **Drop-Down Form Field control**, are similar to the content controls you have already worked with. You use Legacy Tools when you need more control over how the content control is configured. 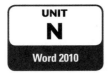 First, you insert a **Text Form Field control** that you limit to three numerical characters, and then you insert another Text Form Field control to contain comments and a Help message.

STEPS

1. **Click the Design Mode button in the Controls group to turn Design Mode back on, click in the blank table cell to the right of Extension, then click the Legacy Tools button 🖳 in the Controls group**

    The selection of Legacy Forms controls and ActiveX controls opens, as shown in Figure N-14.

QUICK TIP

Legacy Tools controls are inserted as a field, which appears as a gray shaded box, and do not include a title bar or tags.

2. **Click the Text Form Field button abl to insert a form field**

    You use the Text Form Field control when you need to control exactly what data a user can enter into the placeholder.

3. **Double-click the text form field to open the Text Form Field Options dialog box**

    In the Text Form Field Options dialog box, you define the type and characteristics of the data that users can enter into the Text Form Field control.

4. **Click the Type list arrow, click Number, then click the Maximum length up arrow to set the maximum length of the entry at 3**

5. **Click the Default number text box, type 100, compare your Text Form Field Options dialog box to Figure N-15, then click OK**

    Users will only be able to enter a 3-digit number in the form field. If users do not enter a number, the default setting of 100 will appear.

6. **Scroll to the last row of the table (contains "Comments"), click to the right of Comments, then press [Spacebar]**

7. **Click the Legacy Tools button 🖳, click the Text Form Field button abl, double-click the text form field, click the Text format list arrow, then click Uppercase**

8. **Click the Add Help Text button to open the Form Field Help Text dialog box, click the Type your own: option button, then type Provide suggestions to help us improve our marketing efforts. as shown in Figure N-16**

    The Help message will appear in the status bar when users click in the Text Form Field control.

9. **Click OK, click OK, then save the template**

ActiveX controls

The Legacy Tools button also provides you with access to ActiveX controls that you can use to offer options to users or to run macros or scripts that automate specific tasks. You need to have some experience with programming to use most of the ActiveX controls.

FIGURE N-14: Inserting a Text Form Field control

Text Form Field button

Legacy Tools button

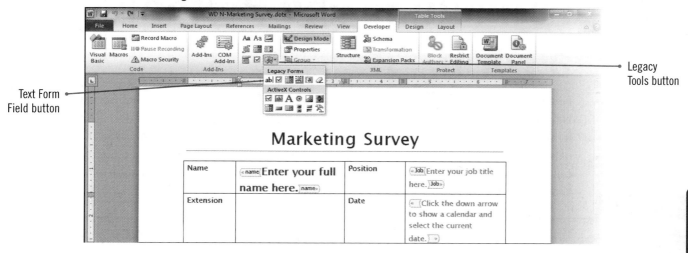

FIGURE N-15: Text Form Field Options dialog box

Type list arrow

Up arrow

100 entered as the Default number

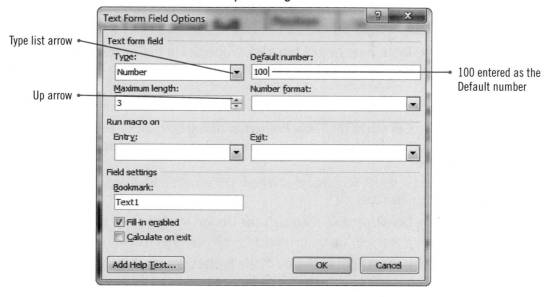

FIGURE N-16: Adding Help text

Type your own: option button

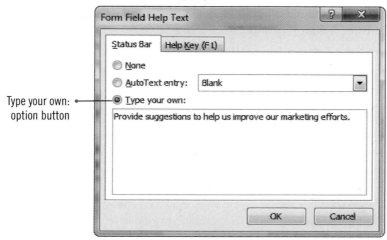

Formatting and Protecting a Form

Forms should be easy to read on-screen so that users can fill them in quickly and accurately. You can enhance a table containing form fields, and you can modify the magnification of a document containing a form so that users can easily see the form fields. You can then protect a form so that users can enter only the data required but are *not* able to change the structure of the form. When a form is protected, information can be entered only in form fields. ▰▰▰ You enhance the field labels, modify the table form, then protect and save the template.

STEPS

QUICK TIP
Instead of using the Format Painter, you can use the [Ctrl] key to select each label, then click the Bold button.

1. **Scroll up and select** Name **in the first cell of the table, click the** Home tab, **click the** Bold **button** **B** **in the Font group, double-click the** Format Painter button **, then use the Format Painter to enhance all the field labels with bold**

2. **Click the** Format Painter button **to turn off formatting, reduce the zoom to 60%, select the first three rows in the table, press and hold [Ctrl], then select the last four rows in the table**

3. **Click the** Table Tools Layout tab, **click** Properties **in the Table group, click the** Row tab, **click the** Specify height check box, **select the contents of the** Specify height text box, **then type .45**

   You work in the Table Properties dialog box to quickly format nonadjacent rows in a table.

TROUBLE
Don't worry that the table has extended to two pages. It will fit on one page when Design Mode is turned off.

4. **Click the** Cell tab **in the Table Properties dialog box, click** Center **in the Vertical alignment section, click** OK, **then click any cell containing a label (for example,** Name**) to deselect the rows**

   The height of the rows is increased to at least .45", and all the labels and content controls are centered vertically within each table cell.

5. **Click the** Developer tab, **then click the** Design Mode button **to turn off Design Mode**

   Before you protect a document, you must be sure Design Mode is turned off.

6. **Click the** Restrict Editing button **in the Protect group, click the** check box **in the Editing restrictions section, click the** No changes (Read only) list arrow, **then click** Filling in forms **as shown in Figure N-17**

7. **Click** Yes, Start Enforcing Protection

8. **Type** cengage, **press [Tab], then type** cengage

   You enter a password so that a user cannot unprotect the form and change its structure. You can only edit the form if you enter the "cengage" password when prompted.

9. **Click** OK, **close the Restrict Formatting and Editing task pane, compare the completed form template to Figure N-18, save the template, then close it**

Protecting documents with formatting and editing restrictions

You protect a form so that users can enter data only in designated areas. You can also protect a document. To protect a document, click the Developer tab, click the Restrict Editing button, then choose the restriction settings you wish to apply. To restrict formatting, you click the Limit formatting to a selection of styles check box, then click Settings. You then choose the styles that you do not want users to use when formatting a document. For example, you can choose to prevent users from using the Heading 1 style or some of the table styles. For editing restrictions, you can specify that users may only make tracked changes or insert comments, or you can select No changes (read only) when you want to prevent users from making any changes to a document.

Design Mode must be turned off before protecting a form

Restrict Editing must be selected to protect a form

Filling in forms selected

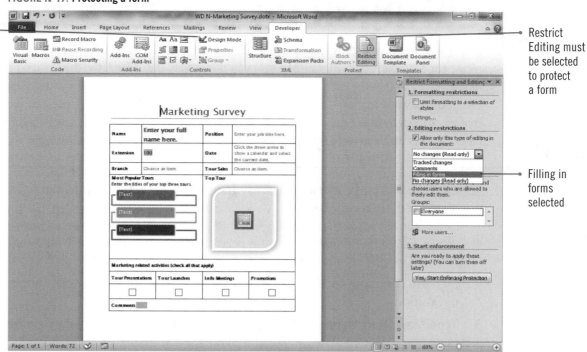

Word 2010

FIGURE N-18: Completed form template

Filling in a Form as a User

Before you distribute a form template to users, you need to test it to ensure that all the elements work correctly. For example, you want to make sure you can modify the SmartArt in the Building Block Gallery content control and that the Help text you entered appears in the status bar when you move to the Comments cell. You also want to make sure that selections appear in the list boxes, that you can insert a picture, and that you can easily select the check boxes.  You open a new document based on the template, then fill in the form as if you were the Sydney branch manager.

STEPS

1. **Click the File tab, click New, click My templates, verify that WD N-Marketing Survey.dotx is selected, then click OK**

   Notice that the WD N-Marketing Survey.dotx file opens as a Word document, as indicated by the filename that appears on the title bar. The insertion point highlights the content control following Name. The form is protected, so you can enter information only in spaces that contain content controls or check boxes.

2. **Increase the zoom to 100%, type your name, then click the content control to the right of Position**

3. **Type Marketing Manager, double-click 100 next to Extension, then type 240**

   Notice how Marketing Manager appears bold because you applied the Strong style when you inserted the Plain Text content control.

4. **Click the content control to the right of Date, click the down arrow, click the left arrow or right arrow to move to January 2013 as shown in Figure N-19, then click 8**

   The date of Tuesday, January 08, 2013, is entered.

   > **QUICK TIP**
   > Users could also click the content control and type a new branch name because the content control is a Combo Box content control.

5. **Click the content control to the right of Branch, click the list arrow, click Sydney, Australia, click the content control to the right of Tour Sales, click the list arrow, then click Fantastic**

6. **Click the red box in the SmartArt graphic, type Fraser Island, click the orange box, type Desert Quest, click the blue box, then type Crocodile Cruise**

7. **Click the picture icon in the Picture content control in the Top Tour cell, navigate to the drive and folder where you store your Data Files, then double-click WD N-1.jpg**

8. **Click the check box below Tour Launches, click the check box below Promotions, verify that the insertion point appears next to Comments, note the message that appears on the status bar, then type the comment text shown in Figure N-20, noting that it will appear in lower case as you type**

9. **Press [Tab] to view the text in uppercase, switch to 60% view, compare the completed form to Figure N-21, save the document with the name WD N-Sydney Survey to the drive and folder where you save your files for this book, submit the file to your instructor, then close the document**

Editing a form template

Before you can edit a form template, you need to unprotect it. Open the form template, click the Developer tab, click the Restrict Editing button in the Protect group, click Stop Protection, then enter the correct password, if prompted. You can make changes to the structure of the form by inserting new controls and labels, and modifying the formatting. You protect the form again, and then save the template.

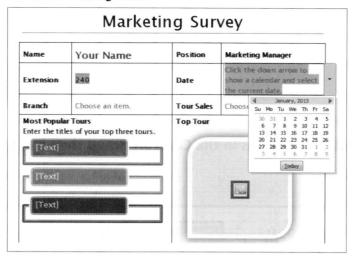

Help text
appears on the
status bar

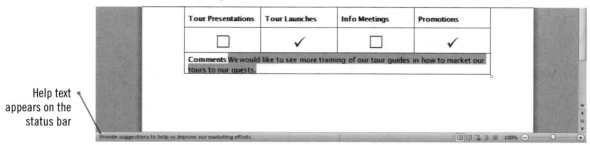

Skills Review (continued)

c. On the next line, insert a SmartArt graphic using the Target List type from the List category (in the last line of the selection of graphics in the List category).

d. Apply the Cartoon SmartArt style, then apply the Colorful Range - Accent Colors 4 to 5 color scheme.

e. Click the text above the SmartArt graphic, then press [Ctrl][A] to select all the text and the SmartArt graphic.

f. Save the selection to the Quick Parts gallery as a building block called **Program Profile**.

g. Save the document as **WD N-Business Program Building Block** to the drive and folder where you save your files for this book (but *not* to the Your Name Forms Template folder), then close the document.

h. Verify that Design Mode is not active, then insert a Building Block Gallery content control in the blank cell below Program Profile in the form template.

i. Use the Quick Parts list arrow to select Program Profile, then use your mouse to reduce the size of the SmartArt graphic. It should fit the space in column 3 so that the widths of column 1 and column 2 are similar. Be sure the form fits on one page. The SmartArt graphic will be approximately 3" wide and 1" high. You may need to reduce the zoom so that you can see and then resize the graphic.

j. Save the template.

6. Insert Legacy Tools controls.

a. Turn on Design Mode, then insert a Text Form Field control from the Legacy Tools in the blank cell to the right of Student Number.

b. Double-click the control to open the Text Form Field Options dialog box, change the type to Number, change the Maximum length to **7**, then enter **1234567** as the default.

c. Insert a Text Form Field control from the Legacy Tools in the blank cell to the right of Comments.

d. Specify that the format should be uppercase, then add the help text: **Provide additional details if necessary**.

e. Save the template.

7. Format and protect a form.

a. Turn off Design Mode, then apply bold to all the labels in the form template.

b. Change the view to 60%, select the table, then change the row height to at least .4".

c. Vertically center text in all the cells. (*Hint*: Use the Cell tab in the Table Properties dialog box.)

d. Protect the document for users filling in forms using the password **skills**, then save and close the template.

8. Fill in a form as a user.

a. Start a new blank document based on the WD N-Change of Grade Notification.dotx template, then complete the form as shown in Figure N-24. Insert WD N-2.jpg (or your own picture if you wish) in the Picture content control.

b. Save the document as **WD N- Grade Change Completed** to the drive and folder where you store your files for this book, submit the file to your instructor, then close the document.

FIGURE N-24

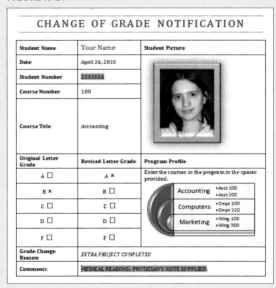

Independent Challenge 1

You work for the owner of Watson Consultants, a communications consulting company that assists businesses in the creation and development of business reports and proposals. The owner and some of the managers of the company often travel to meet with clients. Your boss asks you to create an itinerary form that managers can complete in Word to help them keep track of their travel details.

a. Start Word and open the file WD N-3.docx from the drive and folder where you store your Data Files. Save it as a template called **WD N-Itinerary Form** to the Your Name Form Templates folder that you created to complete the lessons in this unit. (Refer to the first lesson in this unit, if necessary.)

Independent Challenge 1 (continued)

b. Make Design Mode active, then insert a Rich Text content control in the blank table cell to the right of the Name label. Enter **Full Name** as the title and **Name** as the tag, then format the control with 14 pt, bold, and italic.

c. Insert a Date Picker control in the blank table cell to the right of Report Date. Enter **Date** as the title and tag, then select the date format that corresponds with June 30, 2013.

d. Click the Date content control title bar, then copy the content control to each of the seven cells in column 1 below the Date label.

e. Insert a Drop-Down List content control in the blank table cell to the right of Department. Enter **Department** as the title and tag, then add three selections: **Sales**, **Accounting**, and **Human Resources**. Put the three entries in alphabetical order.

f. Insert a text form field from the Legacy Tools in the blank table cell to the right of Extension. Specify the type as Number, a Maximum length of **3**, and **200** as the Default number.

g. Insert a Plain Text content control in the blank table cell to the right of Purpose of Travel. Enter **Travel Purpose** for the title and **Travel** for the tag, then apply the Intense Emphasis style.

h. Insert a Drop-Down List content control in the blank table cell to the right of Location. Enter **Location** as the title and tag, add three selections: **North America**, **Europe**, and **Asia**, then arrange them in alphabetical order.

i. Insert a Combo Box content control in the first cell below Category. Enter **Category** as the title and tag, then add three selections: **Transportation**, **Hotel**, **Meeting**. Enter the text **Choose an item or type your own** between the two tags.

j. Copy the content control, then paste it into each of the next six cells in the Category column.

k. Insert a Plain Text content control in the first cell below Details. Enter **Details** as the title and tag, change the style to Subtle Emphasis, then copy the control and paste it into each of the next six cells in the Details column.

FIGURE N-25

l. Exit Design Mode, then insert a Picture content control in the blank cell to the right of Picture of Location. Apply the Drop Shadow Rectangle picture style.

m. Apply bold to all the form labels, then center the three labels: Date, Category, and Details.

n. Protect the form using the Filling in forms selection, enter **challenge1** as the password, then save and close the template.

o. Open a new document based on the template, then complete the form with appropriate information, inserting WD N-4.jpg for the picture. Figure N-25 shows an example of a completed form.

p. Save the form as **WD N-Paris Itinerary**, submit a copy to your instructor, then close the document.

Independent Challenge 2

You are the Office Manager at Lakeside Regional Securities, a company that has just instituted parking regulations for staff wanting to park in the new staff parking lot. Any staff member who wants to park in the lot must purchase a parking permit. You decide to create a Word form that staff members complete to purchase a parking permit. You create the form as a Word template saved on the company's network. Staffers can open a new Word document based on the template, then complete the form in Word, or they can print the form and fill it in by hand.

a. Start Word and open the file WD N-5.docx from the drive and folder where you store your Data Files. Save it as a template called **WD N-Parking Permit Requisition** to the Your Name Form Templates folder that you created to complete the lessons in this unit. (Refer to the first lesson in this unit, if necessary.)

b. Be sure Design Mode is active, then insert content controls with appropriate titles and tags (you choose) as follows:

Location	Content Control
Date	Date Picker content control using the 5-May-13 format
Name	Plain Text content control formatted with the style of your choice
Department	Drop-Down List content control with four entries (for example, Accounting, Sales) in alphabetical order

Independent Challenge 2 (continued)

Extension   Plain Text content control formatted with the style of your choice

Full-time, Part-time, etc.   Check Box content control in each of the four Status cells formatted with the Heading 1 style and using the check mark symbol of your choice

  c. Exit Design Mode, right-align the contents of all four of the Status cells, then apply bold to all the labels.

Advanced Challenge Exercise

- Add a new row at the bottom of the form, enter **Payment** in the first cell, then apply bold if necessary.
- Select the next three blank cells, click the Clear Formatting button on the Home tab, merge the three cells into one cell, then split the newly merged cell into three cells. (*Note*: This creates three cells of equal width, independent of the cells above them.)
- Click in the second cell in the last row, click the Design Mode button to turn it on, show the selection of Legacy Tools, then click the Option Button (ActiveX Control) button in the ActiveX Controls section. (*Note*: In a form containing a selection of option buttons, users can select just one button.)
- Click the Properties button, widen the Properties panel as needed to see all the text in column 2, select the OptionButton1 text next to Caption in the list of properties, then type **Payroll**.
- Repeat the procedure to insert two more option button ActiveX controls in cells 3 and 4 with the captions **Debit** and **Cash**.
- Close the Properties panel.
- Select just the cell containing Status, then use your mouse to reduce its width to .5".
- Click the Design Mode button to exit design mode, save the template, then answer yes if a message regarding macros appears.
- Select the row containing the option buttons, then increase its height to .5" with center vertical alignment.

  d. Protect the form for filling in forms, click OK to bypass password protection when prompted, then save and close the template.

  e. Open a new document based on the template, then complete the form as a user with appropriate information you provide.

  f. Save the document as **WD N-Completed Parking Requisition** to the drive and folder where you store your files for this book, submit a copy to your instructor, close the document, then exit Word.

Independent Challenge 3

You work for a company called Write Right! that conducts business writing and communications seminars for corporate and government clients in the Houston area. One way you can measure the success of the seminars is to ask clients to complete a feedback form after they participate in a seminar. You decide to create a Word form that you can e-mail to clients.

  a. Start Word and open the file WD N-6.docx from the drive and folder where your Data Files are located. Save it as a template called **WD N-Seminar Evaluation Form** to the Your Name Form Templates folder that you created to complete the lessons in this unit. (Refer to the first lesson in this unit, if necessary.)

  b. Switch to Design Mode, then insert and format controls as described below using titles and tags of your choice:

Location	Content Control
Name	Rich Text content control formatted with Heading 1
Seminar Date	Date Picker content control using the date format of your choice
Instructor	Drop-Down List content control with the names of four instructors (for example, Mary Prentiss, Doreen Jefferson); put the names in alphabetical order by last name
Subject	Combo Box content control with entries for three subjects in alphabetical order: Viral Marketing, Business Writing, and Leadership Skills; include the text **Select an item or enter a new subject.** between the form tags as a direction to users
Rankings	Check Box content control in each of the 16 blank cells for the ranking of course elements. Format the content controls with the Heading 1 style, and select the check mark character of your choice. *Hint*: Insert and modify the first check box content control, then copy and paste it to the remaining table cells.

Independent Challenge 3 (continued)

c. Save the template, then create a new blank document.

d. Type the text: **Enter three words that summarize your experience at your Write Right! seminar.**

e. Press [Enter], then insert the Converging Radial SmartArt graphic from the Relationship category.

f. Type **Write Right!** in the circle shape, then apply the SmartArt style and color of your choice.

g. Select all the text and the SmartArt graphic, then save it as a building block called **Seminar Evaluation** in the Quick Parts gallery in the General category. (*Hint*: Be sure to click in the text above the SmartArt and use [Ctrl][A] to select all content for the building block.)

h. Save the Word document as **WD N-Seminar Building Block** to the location where you save files for this book (but not to the Your Name Form Templates folder).

i. In the form template, turn off Design Mode, then insert the Seminar Evaluation building block in the last row of the table.

j. Reduce the size of the SmartArt graphic so it fills the row without overlapping the edges of the table and the entire form remains on one page.

k. Select the entire table, then change the cell alignment so all the text is centered vertically.

l. Center all the check boxes and the numbers above them.

Advanced Challenge Exercise

- Turn Design Mode on, then delete one of the instructors from the Drop-Down List content control.
- Apply the table style of your choice to the entire table; experiment with the table style options (Header Row, Banded Columns, etc.) until you are satisfied with the appearance of your form.
- Turn off Design Mode, verify that the form remains on one page, then increase the width of the SmartArt graphic so it appears centered within the table cell.

m. Protect the form for filling in forms, click OK to bypass password protection when prompted, then save and close the template.

n. Open a new document based on the template, then complete the form as a user with appropriate information you provide.

o. Save the document as **WD N-Completed Seminar Evaluation Form** to the drive and folder where you store the files for this book, submit it to your instructor, then close the document.

Real Life Independent Challenge

Microsoft Word includes a large number of form templates that you can adapt to meet the needs of your company or organization. You can learn a great deal about form design by studying how the form templates are constructed. To complete this independent challenge, you decide to find and complete one of the form templates included with Microsoft Office Word.

a. Open Word, click the File tab, click New, click Forms in the list of document types in the Office.com Templates section, then explore the various categories and forms available.

b. Click Business, scroll to and click the Interpersonal/organizational skills assessment, then click Download. The form was created with controls from the Legacy Tools selection.

c. Delete the text box containing Your Logo Here, type the name of your company, organization, or school in place of Company Name, center the text you just typed, then increase the font size to 20 point.

d. Select the first row containing black shading, press and hold the [Ctrl] key, select all the rows that contain black shading on both pages, then change the shading color to a color of your choice (for example, Purple, Accent 4, Darker 25%).

e. Protect the form using the filling in forms setting, password protect the form or click OK to bypass password protection, then save the document as a template called **WD N-Assessment Form** to the Your Name Form Templates folder. Answer OK at the prompt.

f. Close the template, then start a new document based on the template.

g. Type your name where indicated, complete the form with an assessment of your own interpersonal and organizational skills, save the form as **WD N-Completed Assessment Form** and submit it to your instructor, then close the form. (*Note*: You can use the [Tab] key to move from field to field in a form created with Legacy Tools controls.)

h. Open the Your Name Form Templates folder, then delete the Interpersonal-organizational skills assessment.dot template and any other templates you may have downloaded (but not the LiveContent, Document Themes, and SmartArt Graphics folders that were created when you created the various templates in this unit).

Visual Workshop

You work for Culture Crawl Tours, Inc., a tour company that specializes in taking small groups of travelers on study tours that focus on the history and culture of a region. You need to create a form that clients can complete after they have returned from a tour. Work in Design Mode to create and enhance a form template similar to the one shown in Figure N-26. Note that the Slipstream theme and the Modern style set are applied to the document. You can determine an appropriate title and tag for each control. Make Tour Guide a drop-down list with three names entered and make Tour Name a drop-down list with four tour names entered: **New York Culture**, **Renaissance Art Tour**, **Asian History Tour**, and **Chicago Architecture Tour** entered. Use the check box symbol of your choice. Save the SmartArt graphic as a building block called **Tour Preferences** in the General category in the Quick Parts gallery. You don't need to save the document containing the building block. Make sure you exit Design Mode before you insert the Building Block Gallery content control and the Picture content controls. Use styles, apply formatting, and make adjustments to controls as needed so that the form fits on one page. Save the template as **WD N-Tour Feedback Form** to the Your Name Form Templates folder containing all the form templates you've created for this unit. Protect the form, do not password protect it, close the template, then open a new document based on the template. Complete the form as a user who took the Chicago tour, inserting WD N-7.jpg as the picture, then save the completed form as **WD N-Completed Tour Feedback Form** to the drive and folder where you store your files for this book, submit a copy to your instructor, then close the document.

FIGURE N-26

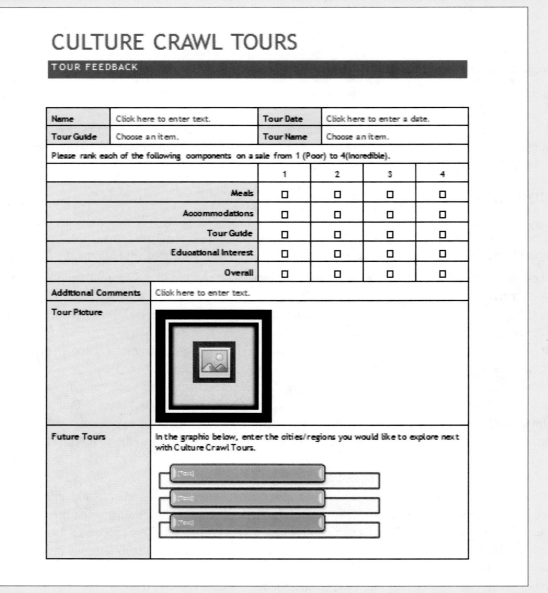

Building Forms

Collaborating with Coworkers

Files You Will Need:

WD O-1.docx
WD O-2.docx
WD O-3.docx
WD O-4.docx
WD O-5.docx
WD O-6.docx
WD O-7.docx
WD O-8.docx
WD O-9.docx
WD O-10.docx
WD O-11.docx
WD O-12.docx

Word includes a variety of commands designed to let you work on a document as part of a team. You can include comments and tracked changes in a document, compare documents to see differences between them as tracked changes, and combine the compared documents into a new document that colleagues can review and approve. You can also use Find and Replace options to edit special characters and formatting. Finally, you can add a digital signature to a document that confirms to the recipient the file is from you. ▰▰▰ Paula Watson in the Marketing Department at Quest Specialty Travel in New York has written several questions for an online survey that visitors to the Quest Specialty Travel Web site can complete. You collaborate with Paula to refine the survey so you can submit it to other colleagues for additional input.

OBJECTIVES

Explore collaboration options

Include comments in a document

Track changes

Work with tracked changes

Manage reviewers

Compare documents

Use advanced find and replace options

Sign a document digitally

Exploring Collaboration Options

You can collaborate with colleagues in different ways. For example, you can distribute printed documents that show all the changes made by one or more colleagues, along with the comments they have made, or you can share the electronic file of the document, which also shows the changes and comments. In addition, you can collaborate with coworkers over the Internet by working with the Word Office Web Apps on Windows Live. ▰▰▰▰▰ Before you start working with Paula to develop questions for an online survey, you investigate collaborative features available in Word.

DETAILS

The collaborative features in Word include the following:

• **Review tab**

The Review tab provides access to commands that allow you to share a document with two or more people. The collaboration commands are included in four groups on the Review tab: Comments, Tracking, Changes, and Compare.

• **Insert comments**

You insert comments into a document when you want to ask questions or provide additional information. When several people work on the same document, their comments appear in colored balloons. Each reviewer is assigned a unique color automatically. The colored comment balloons appear along the right side of the document in Print Layout view. Figure O-1 shows a document containing comments made by two people.

• **Track changes**

When you share documents with colleagues, you need to be able to show them where you have inserted and deleted text. In Word, inserted text appears in the document as underlined text in the color assigned to the person who made the insertion. This same color identifies that person's deletions and comment balloons. For example, if Paula's comment balloons are blue, then the text she inserts in a document will also be blue, and the text she deletes will be marked with a blue strikethrough. The default setting for text that is deleted is to show the deleted text as strikethrough and the default setting for text that is inserted is to show the inserted text as underlined. Figure O-1 includes both new text and deleted text.

• **Compare and combine documents**

You use the Compare command to compare documents based on the same original document to show the differences between them. The Compare command is often used to show the differences between an original document and an edited copy of the original. The differences between the two documents are shown as tracked changes. The Combine command is also used to combine the changes and comments of multiple reviewers into a single document when each reviewer edits the document using a separate copy of the original.

• **Collaborate online**

If you are a business user of Word 2010, you can use SharePoint Workspace 2010 to access a coauthoring feature that allows you to work collaboratively on a document with one or more people at the same time. You can edit files in real time, discuss revisions among team members, and review the work done by each person on a team. If you are a home user of Word 2010, you can sign into a Windows Live account and use the Word Office Web App to work collaboratively with another user. You can save a document directly from Word to Windows Live by clicking Save & Send on the File tab, clicking Save to Web, signing into your Windows Live account, and then saving the document. Figure O-2 shows a document open in the Word Web App in a Web browser. In the Word Web App, you can perform simple functions such as typing and formatting text, and inserting pictures, tables, clip art, and hyperlinks.

Collaborating with Coworkers

FIGURE O-1: Document showing tracked changes and comments

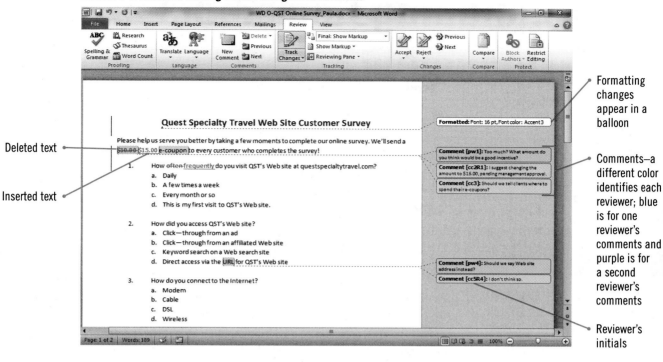

Deleted text

Inserted text

Formatting changes appear in a balloon

Comments—a different color identifies each reviewer; blue is for one reviewer's comments and purple is for a second reviewer's comments

Reviewer's initials

FIGURE O-2: Document in Word Web App

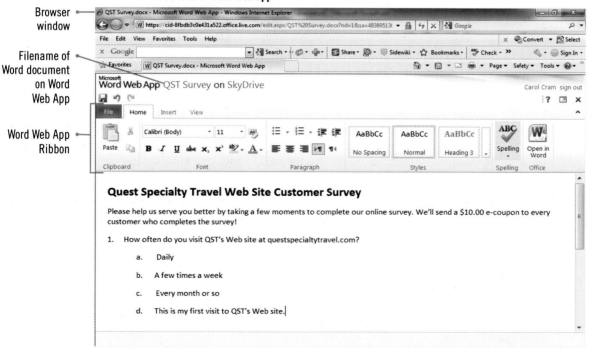

Browser window

Filename of Word document on Word Web App

Word Web App Ribbon

Including Comments in a Document

Sometimes when you review a document that someone else has written, you want to insert a comment about the document text, the document formatting, or any number of other related issues. A **comment** is contained in a comment balloon that appears along the right side of your document by default. Comment marks and shading appear in the document at the point where you inserted the comment. A line connects the end comment mark and the comment balloon. The **Reviewing pane** is used to view comments. The Reviewing pane can be set to display tracked changes at the left of the document window or below the document window. ▰▰▰▰ Your colleague, Paula Watson, has prepared a document containing a list of survey questions, and she has inserted some comments for your review. You open the document, add a new comment, edit one of the comments that Paula inserted, then delete a comment.

STEPS

1. **Start Word, open the file WD O-1.docx from the drive and folder where you store your Data Files, then save it as WD O-QST Online Survey_Paula**

   The comments that Paula inserted appear in colored balloons in the right margin of the document. Comment marks (parentheses that surround the text associated with the comment) and shading indicate the location of a comment.

2. **Click the Review tab, select the word e-coupon in the first paragraph, then click the New Comment button in the Comments group**

   The word "e-coupon" is shaded, and a comment balloon appears in the right margin in a color that is different from Paula's comment. Your initials or the initials assigned to your computer appear in the balloon.

3. **Type Should we tell users where to spend their e-coupons?**

   Your comment appears in a new balloon, as shown in Figure O-3.

4. **Click in the first comment balloon (starts with "Too much?"), click the New Comment button in the Comments group, type I suggest changing the amount to $15.00, pending management approval. in the new balloon, then click anywhere outside the comment balloon**

   A comment balloon with your response appears between the two existing comments. You click in a comment balloon, and then click the New Comment button in the Comments group to keep the original comment and the response together. Note that the balloon has the code R1 after your initials to indicate that the comment is a response to comment 1.

5. **Scroll down as needed, click in Paula's second comment balloon ("Should we say..."), click the New Comment button in the Comments group, then in the new balloon type I don't think so.**

QUICK TIP
When you click in a comment balloon, the balloon becomes a darker shade of its original color.

6. **Click in the comment you inserted in Step 3 that contains the text "Should we tell users..." next to paragraph 1, select users, then type clients**

7. **Scroll down as needed, click the comment balloon containing the text "I'm using the new name..." attached to Best Picks in question 4, then click the Delete button in the Comments group**

   The comment is removed from the document.

8. **Click Reviewing Pane in the Tracking group, reduce the zoom to 80% so you can see the comments, then compare your screen to Figure O-4**

9. **Close the Reviewing pane, return to 100% view, then save the document**

FIGURE O-3: Comment balloons

New Comment
button

Text shaded at
point where
comment
added

Paula's
comment;
you may
see a
different
color

New comment
inserted by
you; different
initials will
appear

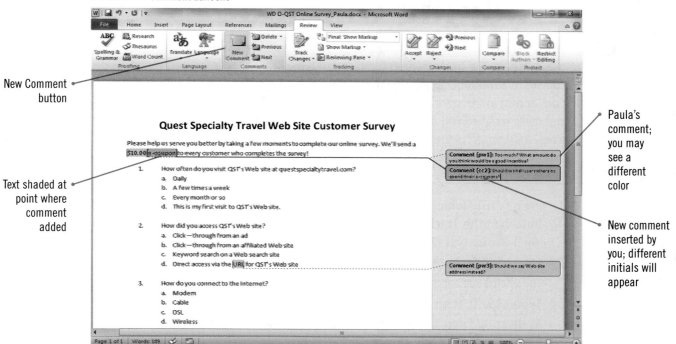

FIGURE O-4: Comments in the Reviewing pane

The name that
appears here
depends on the
settings in the
Word Options
dialog box for
the computer
you are using

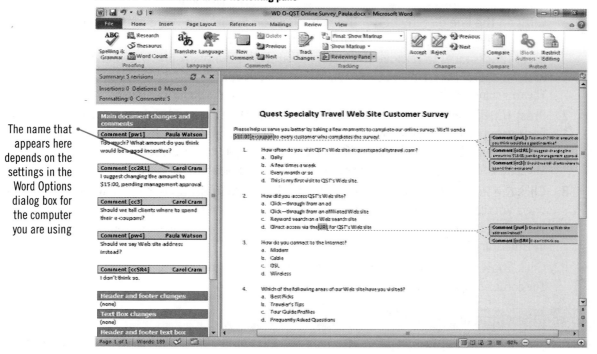

Tracking Changes

When you work on a document with two or more people, you want to be able to see any changes they have made. You use the Track Changes command to show deleted text and inserted text. By default, deleted text appears as strikethrough and inserted text appears underlined in the document. Both insertions and deletions appear in the color assigned to the reviewer. You go through the survey that Paula prepared and make some editing changes to the text and to some of the formatting. You also move selected text to a new location. All of these changes are tracked so that each person who opens the document next can see exactly what changes you made.

1. **Press [Ctrl][Home] to move to the top of the document, then click the Track Changes button in the Tracking group**

   Now, when the Track Changes button is active, every change you make to the document will appear in colored text.

2. **Select $10.00 in the first paragraph, then press [Delete]**

   The deleted text appears as strikethrough. The strikethrough line is the same color as your comment balloon.

3. **Type $15.00, then press [Spacebar]**

   As shown in Figure O-5, the inserted text appears underlined and in the same color as the color of the comment balloons you inserted in the previous lesson.

4. **Select often in question 1, then type frequently**

   The deleted text appears as strikethrough, and the text "frequently" appears in colored underlined text.

5. **Scroll down the document to question 5, select the text from "Have you" to the blank line above question 6 as shown in Figure O-6, click the Home tab, then click the Cut button ✂ in the Clipboard group**

   The text you selected appears as deleted text, and the questions have been renumbered.

6. **Click on the line directly below the new question 5, click the Paste button in the Clipboard group, click after "Improvement" (option d. in question 5.), press [Enter], then press [Backspace] to remove the letter "e" and create a blank line between the questions**

   As shown in Figure O-7, both the cut text and the pasted text appear in a new color and are double-underlined. The new color and the double underlining indicate that the text has been moved.

7. **Press [Ctrl][Home], select the title of the document, click the Shrink Font button A⁻ in the Font group once to shrink the font to 16 pt, click the Font Color list arrow A⁻, select Olive Green, Accent 3, Darker 50%, then press the [◄] to deselect the text**

   The formatting changes appear in a new balloon next to the selected text.

8. **Click the Review tab, click Show Markup in the Tracking group to show a menu with the ways you can view tracked changes in a document, then click Comments**

   The comments are no longer visible in the document. You can also choose not to view formatting changes, insertions, and/or deletions.

9. **Click Show Markup, click Comments, then save the document**

   The document appears as shown in Figure O-8.

Track Changes and the Clipboard

If Track Changes is on when you are pasting items from the Clipboard, each item you paste is inserted in the document as a tracked change. If you cut an individual item and then paste it from the Clipboard in a new location, the item is inserted in a new color and with double underlining, which indicates that the item has been moved. If, however, you use the Paste All button on the Clipboard to paste all the items on the Clipboard at once, the items are pasted in the document as inserted text at the location of the insertion point. When you use the Paste All button, the items are pasted in the order in which you collected them, from the first item you collected (the item at the bottom of the Clipboard) to the most recent item you collected (the item at the top of the Clipboard).

FIGURE O-5: Text inserted with Track Changes feature active

Track Changes button active

Deleted text

The line in the margin indicates there is a change made to this line of text

New text inserted

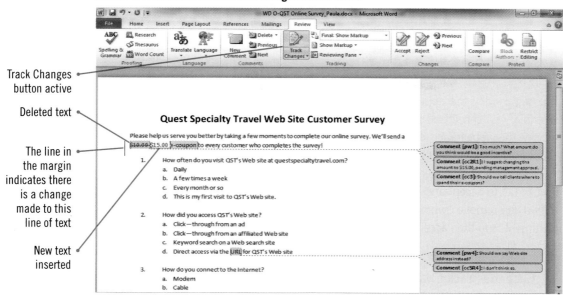

FIGURE O-6: Selected text

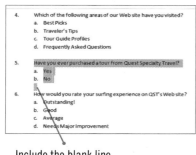

Include the blank line in the selection

FIGURE O-7: Tracked changes formatting for moved text

Cut text

Question renumbered

Pasted text

FIGURE O-8: Document with formatting and text tracked changes

Formatting changes appear in a balloon

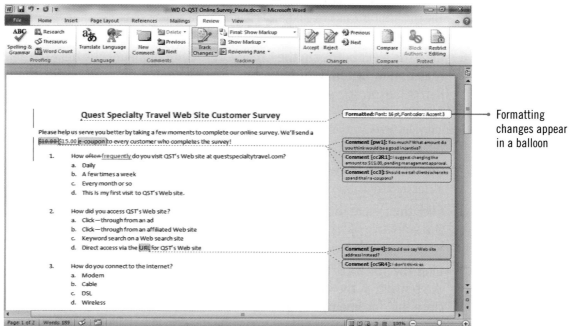

Working with Tracked Changes

You can modify the appearance of tracked changes using the Track Changes Options dialog box. For example, you can change the formatting of insertions and select a specific color for them, and you can modify the appearance of the comment balloons. When you receive a document containing tracked changes, you can accept or reject the changes. When you accept a change, inserted text becomes part of the document and deleted text is permanently removed. You use the buttons in the Changes group on the Review tab to accept and reject changes in a document, and you use the buttons in the Comments group to find and remove comments. ⬛⬛⬛ You decide to modify the appearance of the tracked changes in the document. You then accept or reject the tracked changes and remove all the comments.

STEPS

1. **Click the Track Changes list arrow in the Tracking group, then click Change Tracking Options**

   The Track Changes Options dialog box opens.

2. **Click the Insertions list arrow, click Double underline, then in the Balloons section at the bottom of the Track Changes Options dialog box, change the Preferred width of the balloon to 2"**

   The Track Changes Options dialog box appears, as shown in Figure O-9.

3. **Click OK, press [Ctrl][Home], then click the Next button in the Changes group to move to the first tracked change in the document**

   The insertion point highlights the title because you modified the formatting.

4. **Click the Accept list arrow in the Changes group, then click Accept and Move to Next**

   The formatting changes to the title are accepted, and the insertion point moves to the deleted text ($10.00) in the first paragraph.

5. **Click the Accept button to accept the deletion, click the Accept button again to accept the new amount ($15.00), then click the Delete button in the Comments group to delete the comment**

   The comment is removed, and the amount $15.00 appears in black text in the document, which indicates that it has been accepted as the new amount.

6. **Click the Next button in the Changes group to highlight the next tracked change (deletion of "often"), click the Reject button in the Changes group, then click the Reject button again**

   Question 1 is restored to its original wording. You can continue to review and accept or reject changes individually, or you can choose to accept the remaining changes in the document.

7. **Click the Accept list arrow in the Changes group, click Accept All Changes in Document, then scroll to the end of the document**

   All the tracked changes in the document are accepted, including the question that was moved and renumbered.

8. **Click the Delete list arrow in the Comments group, then click Delete All Comments in Document**

   Scroll through the document. Notice that all tracked changes and comments are removed from the document.

9. **Click the Track Changes button in the Tracking group to turn off Track Changes, scroll to the bottom of the document, type your name at the end of the document, then save and close the document, but do not exit Word**

   The completed document appears as shown in Figure O-10.

FIGURE O-9: Track Changes Options dialog box

Insertions markup changed to Double underline

Balloon width changed to 2"

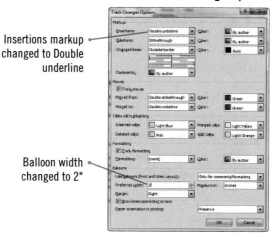

FIGURE O-10: Completed document with tracked changes accepted and comments deleted

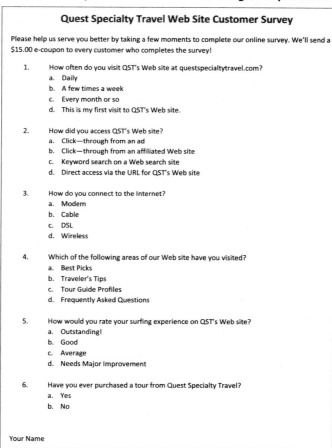

Quest Specialty Travel Web Site Customer Survey

Please help us serve you better by taking a few moments to complete our online survey. We'll send a $15.00 e-coupon to every customer who completes the survey!

1. How often do you visit QST's Web site at questspecialtytravel.com?
   a. Daily
   b. A few times a week
   c. Every month or so
   d. This is my first visit to QST's Web site.

2. How did you access QST's Web site?
   a. Click—through from an ad
   b. Click—through from an affiliated Web site
   c. Keyword search on a Web search site
   d. Direct access via the URL for QST's Web site

3. How do you connect to the Internet?
   a. Modem
   b. Cable
   c. DSL
   d. Wireless

4. Which of the following areas of our Web site have you visited?
   a. Best Picks
   b. Traveler's Tips
   c. Tour Guide Profiles
   d. Frequently Asked Questions

5. How would you rate your surfing experience on QST's Web site?
   a. Outstanding!
   b. Good
   c. Average
   d. Needs Major Improvement

6. Have you ever purchased a tour from Quest Specialty Travel?
   a. Yes
   b. No

Your Name

Distributing documents for revision

When you work with several people on a document, you can e-mail each person a copy of the document and ask for his or her input. To send the active document, click the File tab, click Save & Send, be sure Send Using E-mail is selected, then click Send as Attachment in the Send Using E-mail pane. If you are using Outlook as your e-mail client, the Outlook client window opens. The current document filename appears in the subject line, and the current document is attached to the e-mail message. If you are already connected to the Internet, you just enter the e-mail address(es) of the recipient(s) in the To: and Cc: text boxes, type a message in the message window, and then click Send.

Managing Reviewers

You use commands on the Review tab to help you collaborate with one or more people and to manage how you work with multiple reviewers. For example, you can choose to display tracked changes and comments associated with one reviewer, with several reviewers, or with all reviewers. You can also choose how you would like your own username and initials to appear in a document that you have reviewed. Finally, you can choose how you want to review the changes made to a document. You sent a copy of the QST Online Survey document you completed in the previous lesson to Darren Grant, who edited the document and then sent it to Susan Won for her input. Susan then sent the edited document back to you. You view the changes they made and add a few more changes of your own.

STEPS

1. **Open the file WD O-2.docx from the drive and folder where you store your Data Files, save the document as WD O-QST Online Survey_Darren and Susan, click the Review tab, then click the Track Changes button to turn on tracked changes if the feature is not active**

2. **Click the Final: Show Markup list arrow in the Tracking group as shown in Figure O-11, click Final, note that all the changes are accepted, click the Final list arrow, then click Final: Show Markup**

   All the comments and tracked changes are again visible.

3. **Click the Show Markup button in the Tracking group, point to Balloons, click Show All Revisions Inline, then move your pointer over sw2 in paragraph 1 to view the comment made by Susan as shown in Figure O-12**

   Instead of being contained in balloons, the comments are contained within the document.

4. **Click the Show Markup button in the Tracking group, point to Balloons, click Show Revisions in Balloons, note that both the comments and the deletions appear in balloons, click the Show Markup button again, point to Balloons, then click Show Only Comments and Formatting in Balloons to return to the default view**

5. **Click the Show Markup button, then point to Reviewers**

   As shown in Figure O-13, a list of the reviewers who worked on the document appears, along with the color assigned to each reviewer.

6. **Click the check box next to Susan Won to deselect it, then scroll through the document**

   Only the changes made by Darren Grant are visible. You can choose to view comments for all reviewers, for several reviewers, or for an individual reviewer.

QUICK TIP
You can also change the username and initials by clicking the File tab, and then clicking Options to open the Word Options dialog box.

7. **Click the Track Changes list arrow, click Change User Name to open the Word Options dialog box, select the contents of the User name text box, type your name, press [Tab], type your initials, then click OK**

8. **Click the Accept button once to accept the deletion in the title, click the Accept button again to accept the insertion of QST, select e-coupon, then type gift certificate**

   The text "e-coupon" is marked as deleted, and the text "gift certificate" is marked as inserted.

TROUBLE
To delete all comments, click any comment, click the Delete list arrow in the Comments group, then click Delete All Comments in Document

9. **Click the Show Markup button, point to Reviewers, note that your name appears as one of the reviewers, click the check box next to Susan Won to select it, then accept all changes and delete all comments in the document**

10. **Turn off track changes, type your name where indicated at the end of the document, save the document, then close the document, but do not exit Word**

FIGURE O-11: Changing the Markup view

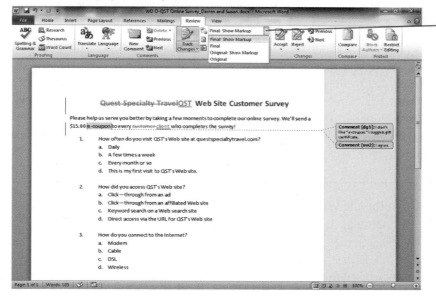

Final: Show Markup list arrow

FIGURE O-12: Showing a comment

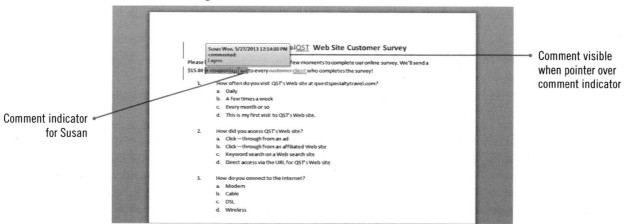

Comment visible when pointer over comment indicator

Comment indicator for Susan

FIGURE O-13: Showing reviewers

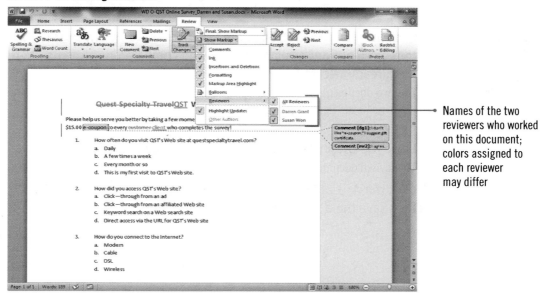

Names of the two reviewers who worked on this document; colors assigned to each reviewer may differ

Comparing Documents

The Compare feature in Word allows you to compare two documents at one time so you can determine where changes have been made. Word shows the differences between the two documents as tracked changes. After identifying the documents you want to compare, you can choose to show the changes in the original document, in the revised document, or combined into one new document. ▰▰▰▰▰ Ron Dawson, your boss at QST, has reviewed the latest version of the QST Online Survey. You use the Compare feature to check the changes that Ron made against the WD O-QST Online Survey_Darren and Susan document.

STEPS

1. **Open the file WD O-3.docx from the drive and folder where you store your Data Files, type your name at the end of the document, then save it as WD O-QST Online Survey_Ron**

   Ron changed the value of the gift certificate from $15.00 to $25.00 before he turned on track changes. As a result, the change does not appear as a tracked change. After he turned on track changes, he added "within 30 days of receipt" to paragraph one and changed "Good" to "Very Good" in question 5 b.

2. **Click the File tab, click Close, click the Review tab, click the Compare button in the Compare group, then click Compare**

   The Compare Documents dialog box opens. In this dialog box, you specify which two documents you want to compare.

3. **Click the Browse button 🖼 in the Original document section, navigate to the location where you save the files for this unit, then double click WD O-QST Online Survey_Darren and Susan**

4. **Click the Browse button 🖼 in the Revised document section, then double-click WD O-QST Online Survey_Ron**

5. **Select the name in the Label changes with text box in the Revised document section, type Ron Dawson, then click More to show the options available for comparing documents**

   The edited Compare Documents dialog box is shown in Figure O-14. Check marks identify all the document settings that will be compared. If you do not want one of the settings to be included in the comparison, you can uncheck the check box next to that setting. By default, the changes are shown in a new document.

   <blockquote>TROUBLE
If your document opens in a split screen as shown in Figure O-15, read but do not complete Step 7.</blockquote>

6. **Click OK, then click Yes to accept the warning**

   The new document that opens shows the difference between the two documents being compared as tracked changes, including the change Ron made to the price of the gift certificate price before he turned on tracked changes.

   <blockquote>TROUBLE
Close the Reviewing pane if it opens to the left of the compared document.</blockquote>

7. **Click the Compare button in the Compare group, point to Show Source Documents to see the options available for viewing compared documents, then click Show Both if it is not already selected**

   The two documents appear in a split screen, as shown in Figure O-15. The original document appears in the top pane to the right of the compared document and the revised document that incorporates Ron's changes appears in the lower pane.

8. **Close the Original document, then close the Revised document**

   The revised document with tracked changes now fills the screen.

9. **Click the Accept list arrow in the Changes group, click Accept All Changes in Document, then save the document as WD O-QST Online Survey_Final**

Collaborating with Coworkers

FIGURE O-14: Compare Documents dialog box

WD O-QST Online Survey_Darren and Susan.docx

WD O-QST Online Survey_Ron.docx

Click to toggle between showing less options and more options

Changes in the document reviewed by Ron will be labeled with Ron Dawson's name

Insertions and deletions are compared by default and cannot be deselected

Document settings that can be compared or deselected and not compared

Where changes will appear

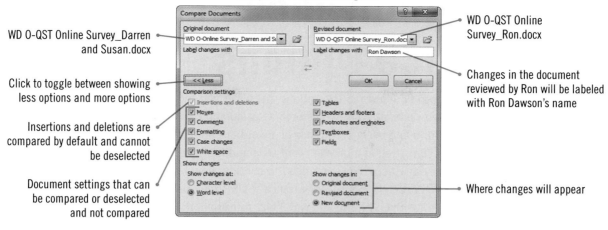

FIGURE O-15: Comparing documents

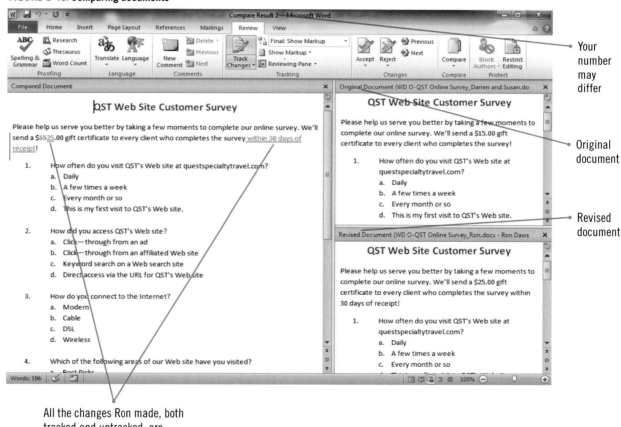

Your number may differ

Original document

Revised document

All the changes Ron made, both tracked and untracked, are shown as tracked changes in the Compared Document

Word 2010

Using Advanced Find and Replace Options

Word offers advanced find and replace options that allow you to search for and replace formats, special characters, and even nonprinting elements such as paragraph marks (¶) and section breaks. For example, you can direct Word to find every occurrence of a word or phrase of unformatted text, and then replace it with the same text formatted in a different font style and font size. You are pleased with the final version of the survey questions. Now you need to consider how best to format the questions for delivery over the Internet. You decide to bold every instance of QST. You use Find and Replace to find every instance of QST, then replace it with QST formatted with bold. You also notice that an em dash (—) appears between the words "Click" and "through" in two entries in question 2. You use Find and Replace to replace the em dash with the smaller en dash (–).

STEPS

1. **Click the Track Changes button to deselect it, click the Home tab, then click the Replace button in the Editing group**
   The Find and Replace dialog box opens.

2. **Type QST in the Find what text box, press [Tab], type QST, then click More**
   The Find and Replace dialog box expands, and a selection of additional commands appears.

3. **Click the Format button at the bottom of the Find and Replace dialog box, click Font to open the Replace Font dialog box, click Bold in the Font style list, then click OK**
   The format settings for the replacement text QST appear in the Find and Replace dialog box, as shown in Figure O-16.

4. **Click Find Next, move the dialog box as needed to see the selected text, click Replace All, click OK, click Close, then scroll up and click in the first paragraph to deselect the text**
   Every instance of QST is replaced with **QST**.

5. **Press [Ctrl][H] to open the Find and Replace dialog box with the Replace tab active, press [Delete], click the Special button at the bottom of the dialog box, then click Em Dash**

6. **Press [Tab] to move to the Replace with text box, click Special, then click En Dash**
   Codes representing the em dash and en dash are entered in the Find what and Replace with text boxes on the Replace tab in the Find and Replace dialog box.

7. **Click the No Formatting button at the bottom of the Find and Replace dialog box**
   As shown in Figure O-17, the codes for special characters appear in the Find what and Replace with text boxes, and the formatting assigned to the text in the Replace with text box is removed.

8. **Click Find Next, click Replace All, click Yes if prompted, click OK, then click Close**
   Two em dashes (—) are replaced with en dashes (–).

9. **Save the document**

FIGURE O-16: **Find and Replace dialog box**

Formatting to
apply to the
replaced text

Format button

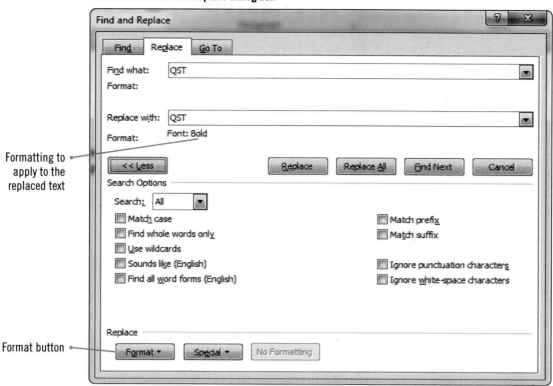

FIGURE O-17: **Special characters entered**

Em dash code

En dash code

Special button

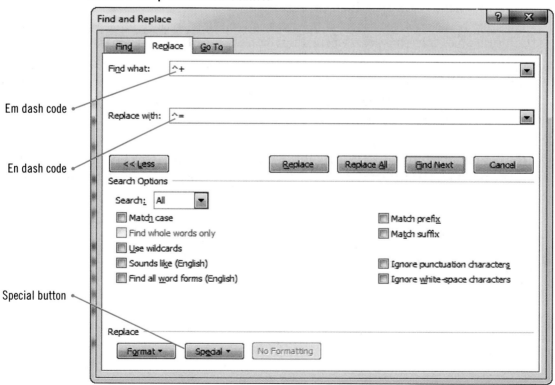

Signing a Document Digitally

You can authenticate yourself as the author of a document by inserting a digital signature. A **digital signature** is an electronic stamp that you attach to a document to verify that the document is authentic and that the content of the document has not been changed or tampered with since it was digitally signed. When you insert a digital signature line into a Word document, you specify who can sign the document and include instructions for the signer. When the designated signer receives an electronic copy of the document, he or she sees the signature line and a notification that a signature is requested. The signer clicks the signature line to sign the document digitally, and then either types a signature, selects a digital image of his or her signature, or uses a Tablet PC to write a signature. A document that has been digitally signed becomes read-only so that no one else can make changes to the content. ▰▰▰ You add a digital signature to the online survey.

STEPS

1. Press **[Ctrl][End]** to move to the bottom of the document, select **your name**, press **[Delete]**, press **[Backspace]** two times to move the insertion point up so it appears just below question 6, click the **Insert tab**, then click **Signature Line** in the Text group

2. Read the information about digital signatures that appears, then click **OK**

   The Signature Setup dialog box opens. You enter information about the person who can sign the document in this dialog box.

3. Type your name in the Suggested signer text box in the Signature Setup dialog box as shown in Figure O-18, then click **OK**

   A space for your signature appears at the position of the insertion point.

4. Double-click the **signature line**, read the message that appears, then click **OK**

5. Type **your name**, click **Sign**, then click **OK**

   The signature appears at the bottom of the document, and an information bar appears at the top of the document window, which includes a message that the file is marked as final and an Edit Anyway button.

6. Click the **File tab**, click **Close**, click the **File tab**, open **WD O-QST Online Survey_Final.docx** again, then try to type text

   You are not able to type text because the document has been digitally signed, and the document is marked as final, as shown in Figure O-19.

7. Click **Edit Anyway** in the information bar at the top of the document, click **Yes** to remove the digital signature, click **OK**, click the **Review tab**, click the **Track Changes list arrow**, click **Change Tracking Options**, return the options to the default settings: **Underline** for insertions and **3"** for the balloon width, then click **OK**

8. Scroll to the bottom of the document, double-click the **signature line**, click **OK**, type your name, click **Sign**, then click **OK**

9. Click **File**, click **Close**, submit a copy of the file and the other three files you created in this unit to your instructor, then exit Word

FIGURE 0-18: Signature Setup dialog box

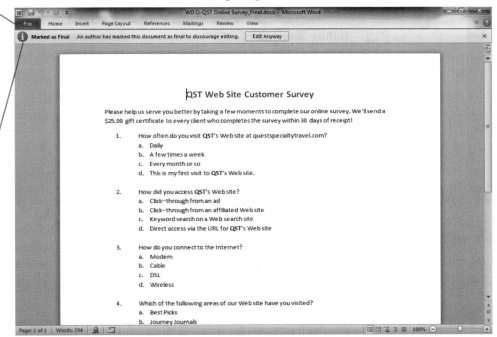

FIGURE 0-19: Document marked as final after digital signature added

The Ribbon is minimized; most commands on the Ribbon are not available because the document is marked as final

The information bar shows that the document is marked as final

Acquiring a digital ID

You can acquire a digital ID from two sources. First, you can purchase a digital ID from a Microsoft partner. Other people can use this type of digital ID to verify that your digital signature is authentic. The Microsoft partner that issues the digital ID ensures the authenticity of the person or organization that acquires the digital ID. Second, you can create your own digital ID, as you did in this lesson. Other people cannot verify the authenticity of a digital ID that you create yourself. If you open a document that you digitally signed, you will see the digital signature. However, if someone else opens a document that you digitally signed using a digital ID that you created, the person will see an error message. This message tells the user that the digital ID cannot be verified as authentic.

   e. Accept the deletion of "objects d'art" and the insertion of "décor items".

   f. Reject the change to "home-based".

   g. Accept all the remaining changes in the document, then delete all the comments in the document.

   h. Turn off Track Changes, make any additional adjustments, such as deleting blank lines between paragraphs as needed, type your name at the bottom of the document where indicated, then save and close the document.

4. Manage reviewers.

   a. Open the file WD O-5.docx from the drive and folder where you store your Data Files, then save the document as **WD O-Company Description_Wendy and David**.

   b. Show the document in Final view, scroll to view the document, return to Final: Show Markup view, change to Show All Revisions Inline, then mouse over an inline comment to view the comment in the document.

   c. Return to the Show Only Comments and Formatting in Balloons view.

   d. Show the list of reviewers, then deselect David Vance.

   e. Change the user name to your name and your initials if necessary.

   f. Show the changes made by David Vance.

   g. Move to the beginning of the document, use commands on the Review tab to accept the addition of "and professional," delete the two comments in paragraph 1, then reject the change to "lifestyle".

   h. Accept all remaining changes in the document, then delete all comments in the document.

   i. Turn off track changes if it is active, save the document, then close the document.

5. Compare documents.

   a. Open the file WD O-6.docx from the drive and folder where you store your Data Files, then save it as **WD O-Company Description_Merilee.** Note that Merilee has made several changes, including changing the amount of the loan request in the Expansion Plans section from $50,000 to $80,000.

   b. Close the document, but do not exit Word, open the Compare Documents dialog box, select WD O-Company Description_Wendy and David as the original document, then select WD O-Company Description_Merilee as the revised document.

   c. Enter **Merilee Owens** in the Label changes with text box in the Revised document area.

   d. Click OK to create the Compared Document, click Yes to accept tracked changes, then show both documents (Original and Revised) if they are not already open. (*Note*: Your compared document window may open with the Reviewing pane active, and the original and revised documents open in the right pane.)

   e. Close the original and revised documents, then close the Reviewing pane if it is open.

   f. Accept all changes to the document, then save the document as **WD O-Company Description_Final**.

6. Use advanced find and replace options.

   a. Verify that Track Changes is turned off, move to the top of the document, open the Replace dialog box, then enter **The Design Place** in the Find what text box.

   b. Expand the dialog box if necessary, type **The Design Place** in the Replace with dialog box, then set the formatting as Bold Italic.

   c. Find and replace all instances of The Design Place with *The Design Place*.

   d. Move to the top of the document, replace the contents of the Find what text box with the symbol for a Manual Line Break. (*Hint:* Click Special, then click Manual Line Break.)

   e. Remove the contents of the Replace with text box so nothing appears in the text box, then remove the formatting assigned to the text.

   f. Find and replace every Manual Line Break with nothing, close the Find and Replace dialog box, then save the document. (*Note*: You will make one replacement.)

7. Sign a document digitally.

   a. Move to the bottom of the document, then insert a signature line.

   b. Type your name in the Signature Setup dialog box.

   c. Open the Sign dialog box, and type your name in the Sign dialog box.

   d. Close the document, open the document again, then try to type text.

Skills Review (continued)

e. Compare your document to the one shown in Figure O-21.

f. Click Edit Anyway, click Yes, click OK, open the Track Changes Options dialog box, return the options to the default settings: Green for Moved text (two places), and 3" balloon width appearing in the right margin.

g. Double-click the signature line and digitally sign the document again, close the document, submit the files you created in this Skills Review to your instructor, then exit Word.

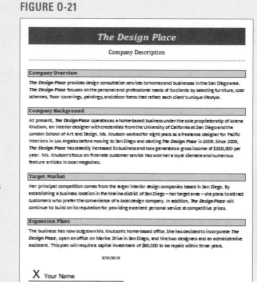

Independent Challenge 1

You work for Tech Savvy Solutions, a large application service provider based in Birmingham, England. The company is sponsoring a conference called E-Business Solutions for local businesses interested in enhancing their online presence. Two of your coworkers have been working on a preliminary schedule for the conference. They ask for your input.

a. Start Word, open the file WD O-7.docx from the drive and folder where you store your Data Files, then save it as **WD O-Conference Schedule**.

b. Scroll through the document to read the comments and view the changes made by William Jones and Joan McDonald.

c. Change the user name to your name and initials if necessary.

d. In the 9:00 to 10:00 entry, select "E-Payment Systems", then insert a comment with the text **I suggest we change the name of this session to E-Cash in the Second Decade.**

e. Be sure the Track Changes feature is active.

f. Starting with the first comment, make all the suggested changes, including the change you suggested in your comment. Be sure to capitalize "continental" in Continental Breakfast.

g. Type your name where indicated at the bottom of the document, go to the top of the document, then accept all the changes.

Advanced Challenge Exercise

- Show only formatting changes.
- Open the Reviewing pane and review the information in the Detail Summary near the top of the Reviewing pane.
- Center the two lines of text that refer to the location of the event, then increase the size of the text to 14 pt.
- Notice how the information in the Reviewing pane changes as you track changes.
- Center and bold "Conference Schedule."
- Change the Theme to Technic, then note if the change of theme is recorded as a formatting change.
- Change Show Markup so all the boxes are checked, then accept all the changes.
- Close the Reviewing pane.

h. Delete all the comments in the document.

i. Save the document, submit a copy to your instructor, then close the document.

Independent Challenge 2

You work as an editor for Gillian Markham, a freelance author currently writing a series of articles related to e-commerce. Gillian sent you a draft of her Web Security Issues article that contains changes she has made and changes made by her colleague Jasjit Singh. You need to review the changes made by Gillian and Jasjit and then prepare the final document. Gillian has also asked you to use the Find and Replace feature to apply formatting to selected text included throughout the article.

a. Start Word, open the file WD O-8.docx from the drive and folder where you store your Data Files, then save it as **WD O-Web Security Issues Article**.

Independent Challenge 2 (continued)

b. Turn on Track Changes, then scroll through the document to get a feeling for its contents.

c. Open the Reviewing pane. Notice there were two reviewers—Gillian Markham and Jasjit Singh. Close the Reviewing pane.

d. Find and accept the first change that is not a comment—the addition of "Access Control."

e. Find, read, and then accept all the remaining changes.

f. Move back to the top of the document, move to the first comment, read it, then as requested in the comment, move the last sentence in paragraph 1 to the end of the article (following the Validity head and its paragraph), as its own paragraph.

g. Move to the comment about switching the Protection and Access Control sections, then perform the action requested.

h. Make the change requested in the Identification paragraph.

i. Delete all the comments from the document, then accept all the changes.

j. Turn off the Track Changes feature.

k. Show the paragraph marks, scroll through the document, then remove extra paragraph marks between paragraphs, if necessary.

l. Scroll to the top of the document, then use the Find and Replace feature to find all instances of "Web" and replace it with "Web" formatted in Italic.

m. Clear formatting assigned to the text in the Replace with text box, then close the Find and Replace dialog box.

n. At the bottom of the document, add a digital signature containing your name.

o. Close the document, then submit a copy to your instructor.

Independent Challenge 3

The Alpine Challenge School in Banff, Alberta offers teens and young adults courses in various winter and summer mountain sports. As the course programmer, you are responsible for approving all the course descriptions included on the school's Web site. Two of your colleagues, Gordon Liu and Cecil Gomez, have each revised descriptions of the three summer courses offered at the school. You use the Compare feature so that you can see the changes made by the reviewers. You review the changes and make some additional changes.

a. Start Word, open these files from the drive and folder where you store your Data Files, then save them as indicated: WD O-9.docx as **WD O-Summer Courses_Gordon.docx**, and WD O-10.docx as **WD O-Summer Courses_Cecil.docx**. Close both files.

b. Use the Compare feature to compare the WD O-Summer Courses_Gordon (select as the Original document) and WD O-Summer Courses_Cecil (select as the Revised document).

c. Show both documents used in the comparison to the right of the Compared Document.

d. Show just the compared document.

e. Change the user name to your name if necessary, turn on Track Changes, then make the following changes:

   i. Replace "thrill" in the paragraph on Rock Climbing with an appropriate synonym. (*Hint:* Right-click "thrill," point to Synonyms, then select a synonym such as "excitement," or "delight.")

   ii. Replace "expedition" in the Mountaineering paragraph with an appropriate synonym.

   iii. Replace "proficient" in the Kayaking paragraph with an appropriate synonym.

f. Accept all the changes, then save the document as **WD O-Summer Courses_Final.docx**.

Advanced Challenge Exercise

■ Be sure the Track Changes feature is active, then change the name of the Mountaineering Course to **Wilderness Survival**.

■ Password protect the document for Track Changes with the password **banff**. (*Hint:* Click the Restrict Editing button in the Protect group on the Review tab, click the Allow only this type of editing in the document check box in the Editing restrictions section, select Tracked changes, click Yes, Start Enforcing Protection, enter the password two times as requested, then click OK.)

■ Try to accept the tracked change to verify that the file is protected.

■ Unprotect the document, then accept the tracked change.

Independent Challenge 3 (continued)

g. Turn off Track Changes if necessary, save the document, then add a digital signature at the bottom of the document using your name.

h. Close the document, then submit a copy to your instructor.

Real Life Independent Challenge

This Independent Challenge requires an Internet connection.

From Word 2010 you can go directly to SkyDrive on Windows Live on the Internet and work with a Word file using the Word Web App. The Word Web App does not include all of the features and functions included with the full Office version of its associated application. However, you can use the Word Web App from any computer that is connected to the Internet, even if Microsoft Word 2010 is not installed on that computer. You obtain a Windows Live account (if you do not already have one), upload a file from Word to SkyDrive on Windows Live, and then explore how you can work with Word Web App to modify the file.

a. Open your Web browser, type **home.live.com** in the Address bar, then press [Enter].

b. If you do not have a Windows Live account, follow the instructors to sign up for a Windows Live account using your e-mail address, then close your Web browser. If you do have a Windows Live account, use that account to complete the remaining steps.

c. Start Word, open the file WD O-11.docx from the drive and folder where you store your Data Files, then save it as **WD O-Work Plan**.

d. Click the File tab, click Save & Send, then click Save to Web. In a moment, the Save to Windows Live SkyDrive pane opens on the right side of the window (*Note*: If you are not already signed in to Windows Live, you will need to sign in.) To sign in, click Sign In, type the e-mail address you use to access your Windows Live account, press [Tab], type your password, then click OK.

e. Click the link to Windows Live SkyDrive, click your e-mail address and enter your password as directed, click Sign In, switch to Word, then close WD O-Work Plan.

f. Switch to your Web browser, then in Windows Live SkyDrive, click My Documents, click Add files, click Select documents from your computer, navigate to the location where you saved WD O-Work Plan, then double-click WD O-Work Plan.

g. Click Continue, click WD O-Work Plan, then click Edit in Browser. (*Note*: The document is ready for editing in the Word Web App. You can perform limited functions in the Word Web App to make edits to the document.)

h. In the Word Web App, select "Marketing" in the heading and change it to **Work**, add your name in the subtitle, then change the deadline for the first task to **March 20**.

i. Click Open in Word in the Office group, click Save, then click OK in response to the message.

j. Click Enable Editing on the Protected View bar near the top of the document window if prompted then save the document as **WD O_Work Plan Revised** to the location where you save files for this book. (*Hint*: Click the File tab, click Save As, then navigate to the location where you save the files for this book. If you click Save on the Quick Access toolbar, the file will be saved to your Windows Live SkyDrive account.)

k. Select the table and apply the table design of your choice, save the document, submit your file to your instructor, then close the document.

l. Exit the Web browser.

Visual Workshop

You work for a company called Tropical Art that sells gardening supplies and plants. Your coworker has prepared a mission statement for the company, and she asks you to edit it. Open the file WD O-12.docx from the drive and folder where you store your Data Files, then save it as **WD O-Tropical Art Mission Statement**. Turn on the Track Changes feature, then change the Track Changes Options and add changes so that the edited mission statement appears as shown in Figure O-22. (*Hint:* Change the color of insertions to Red and select the Double-underline style.) Save the document and turn off Track Changes, add a digital signature containing your name, close the document, then submit a copy to your instructor. (Be sure to change the Track Changes Options back to the default: Underline insertions with the color set to By author.)

FIGURE O-22

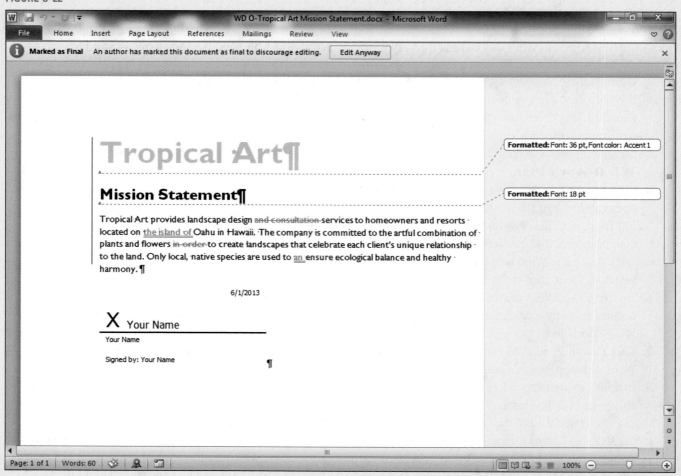

Customizing Word

Files You Will Need:

WD P-1.docx
WD P-2.docx
WD P-3.docx
WD P-4.docx
WD P-5.docx
WD P-6.docx
WD P-7.docx
WD P-8.docx
WD P-9.docx
WD P-10.docx
WD P-11.docx
WD P-12.docx

You can customize Word in a variety of ways to suit your working style and to help you use Word efficiently. You can create a new tab for the Ribbon that contains buttons for commands you use frequently, you can change the default spelling options, and you can create keyboard shortcuts for specific tasks. You can also create a watermark to designate a document with a category such as "Draft," add customized page borders, include line numbers in a document, modify how words are hyphenated, and use options on the View tab to view and work in two or more documents at the same time. Finally, you can save files in different formats for sharing with others and explore Help to find answers to Word-related questions.  Ron Dawson in the Marketing Department at Quest Specialty Travel in San Diego has asked you to produce a booklet of excerpts from travel journals created by clients who have taken a QST tour. You have received travel journals from several clients, but each journal is formatted differently. You create a new tab for the Ribbon that contains the commands you will use to format the journals and then you customize the appearance of buttons on the new tab, modify default settings to help you work efficiently, create keyboard shortcuts to automate document formatting tasks, and add a watermark and page border. Finally, you work in two windows, explore the file save options, and use Help to provide the steps required to create entries for an AutoText gallery.

OBJECTIVES

Create a new tab

Customize buttons

Modify Word options

Create keyboard shortcuts

Add a watermark and a page border

Work with document windows

Save in alternate file formats

Apply Word Help

Creating a New Tab

You can create a new Ribbon tab that consists of groups containing only the commands you specify. You can also customize the Quick Access toolbar to include additional buttons that you use frequently. ▰▰▰ Over time, you will be formatting dozens of journals submitted by QST clients. You want every journal to use a common format, so to save time, you create a new Ribbon tab that includes only the commands you need to format a journal.

STEPS

1. **Open the file WD P-1.docx from the drive and folder where you store your Data Files, then save it as WD P-Journal_Pacific Odyssey Tour.docx**

2. **Click the File tab, click Options, then click Customize Ribbon**

   The Word Options dialog box opens with the Customize the Ribbon and keyboard shortcuts pane the active pane. You use this pane to create a new tab and then to choose commands to place into groups on the new tab.

3. **Click the New Tab button, click New Tab (Custom) in the list of tabs, click the Rename button, type Journals, then click OK**

   The new tab is called Journals. You need to add groups to the tab to contain commands.

4. **Click New Group (Custom) under Journals (Custom), click the Rename button, type Document, then click OK**

   Now that you have created a group for the Journals tab, you can add commands to it. You move commands from the list box on the left side to the list box on the right side of the Word Options dialog box. By default, the list of popular commands appears in the Choose commands from list.

5. **Click the Popular Commands list arrow, then click All Commands**

   The hundreds of commands you can use to develop and format documents in Word are listed in alphabetical order. You plan to add two commands to the Document group: Footer and Page Border.

6. **Scroll to and click Footer, click the Add button, scroll to and click Page Borders, then click the Add button**

   The two commands associated with the Document group on the new Journals tab appear as shown in Figure P-1.

7. **Click Journals (Custom), click the New Group button, click the Rename button, type Text, click OK, then add the following commands to the Text group: Hyphenation Options, Line Numbers, Spelling & Grammar, and Text Effects (the second of the two Text Effects selections with the Home Tab | Font | Text Effects (TextEffectsGallery) ScreenTip)**

   The ScreenTip describes the exact function of the command. The Text Effects command you selected will show the Text Effects Gallery when clicked.

8. **Click Journals (Custom), create a new group called Graphics, then add the Change Shape button for WordArt Tools (first selection) and Watermark**

   The list of main tabs appears as shown in Figure P-2.

9. **Click OK, click the Journals tab, compare the Journals tab to Figure P-3, then save the document**

   The Change Shape button in the Graphics group is grayed out. This button will be active when a WordArt object is selected.

Customizing the Quick Access toolbar

To customize the Quick Access toolbar, click the File tab, click Options, then click Quick Access Toolbar. The three buttons included by default on the Quick Access toolbar appear in the far-right pane. These buttons are Save, Undo, and Redo. To add a new command to the Quick Access toolbar, select the command from the list to the left, then click Add. To remove a button from the Quick Access toolbar, select it and click Remove.

FIGURE P-1: **Adding buttons to a new group**

All Commands selected

Add button

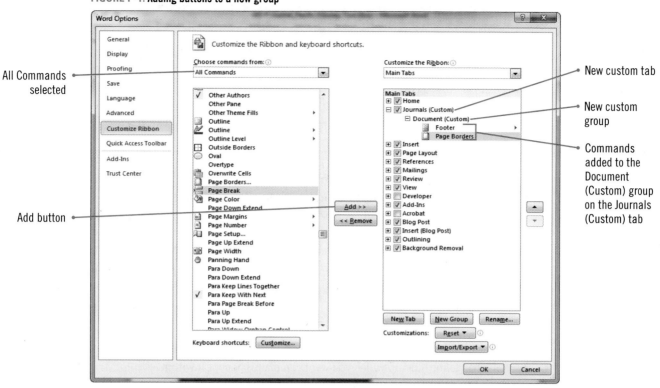

New custom tab

New custom group

Commands added to the Document (Custom) group on the Journals (Custom) tab

FIGURE P-2: **Groups and commands on the Journals custom tab**

Your Home group may be expanded

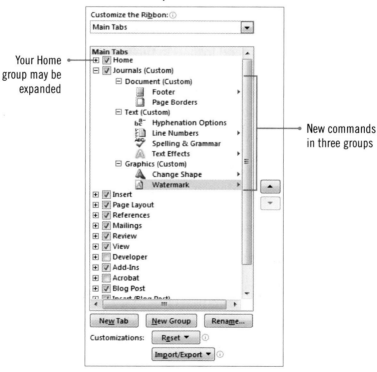

New commands in three groups

FIGURE P-3: **Table form with labels and merged cells**

Customizing Word

Customizing Buttons

You can change the name of any button that you add to a custom group. You can also change the icon associated with a button you add to a custom group. However, you cannot change the names of buttons or the icons associated with the buttons on the default Ribbon. Now that you have created the new Journals tab and added commands to three new groups on this custom tab, you customize the commands on the Journals tab by changing button names and the icons associated with them.

1. **Click the File tab, click Options, then click Customize Ribbon**

2. **Click the Popular Commands list arrow, then click Tool Tabs**

   The list of all the Tool tabs, such as the Drawing Tools tab and the SmartArt Tools tab, along with all the commands associated with each tab appears. When you are not sure exactly what command you want to include on a custom Ribbon tab, you can browse the commands on the specific set of tabs that interests you.

3. **Click the Format expand icon ⊞ under Picture Tools, click the Picture Styles expand icon ⊞, then click the Picture Effects expand icon ⊞**

   All the commands associated with the Picture Styles command on the Picture Tools tab are listed, as shown in Figure P-4.

4. **Click Bevel, click Graphics (Custom) in the list of tabs to the right, then click Add**

   You can change the order in which you want commands to appear within a group.

5. **Click Bevel, then drag the mouse pointer up to move Bevel above Change Shape**

   You can further customize a button by renaming it and identifying a unique icon to associate with it.

6. **Click the Document (Custom) expand icon ⊞, click Page Borders, click the Rename button, type Border, click the icon shown in Figure P-5, then click OK**

7. **Click the Watermark expand icon ⊞ in the Graphics (Custom) group to view the commands associated with the Watermark button, click Watermark, click the Rename button, type Draft, click the icon shown in Figure P-6, then click OK**

8. **Click OK to exit the Word Options dialog box and return to the document**

   The revised Journals toolbar appears as shown in Figure P-7.

9. **Click the picture at the end of the document, click the Bevel button in the Graphics group on the Journals tab, click the Divot style (bottom left option) in the Bevel section, click away from the picture to deselect it, then save the document**

FIGURE P-4: Commands associated with the Picture Effects command

Click the Expand icon to show the list of associated commands

Expand icon changes to a Collapse icon when clicked

Bevel command

Groups on the Journals tab are collapsed

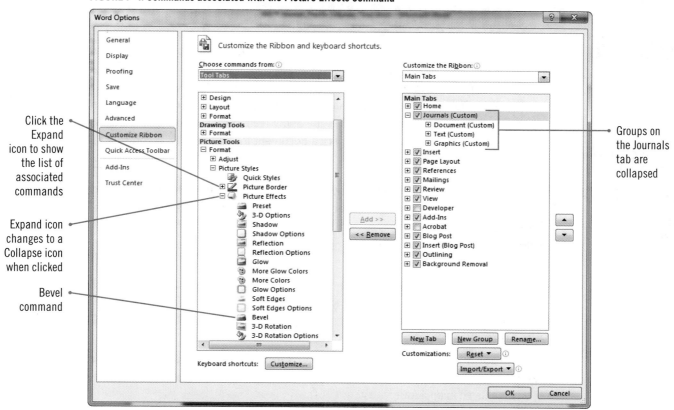

FIGURE P-5: Selecting an icon for the Border button

Icon selected for the Border button

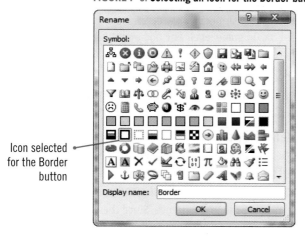

FIGURE P-6: Selecting an icon for the Draft button

Icon selected for the Draft button

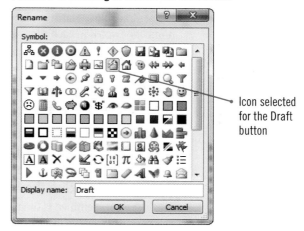

FIGURE P-7: Updated Journals tab

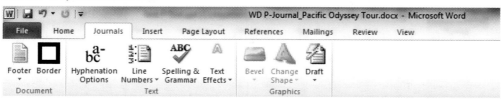

Modifying Word Options

Word includes many default settings designed to meet the needs of most users. You can modify default settings by selecting or deselecting options in the Word Options dialog box. ▰▰▰ After working with Word for several months, you have identified some default options that do not suit your working style. You work in the Word Options dialog box to change the number of recent documents you can view on the File menu, modify a Spelling option, specify that the Show readability statistics dialog box appears each time you check the spelling, then set Word to check a document for both grammar and style errors.

QUICK TIP

By default, recent documents are not displayed on the File menu.

1. **Click the File tab, click Recent, click the Quickly access this number of Recent Documents check box at the bottom of the Recent Documents pane to select it, click in the text box, type 3, then press [Enter]**

   A list of three recent documents appears on the File menu.

2. **Click Options**

   In addition to customizing the Ribbon and the Quick Access toolbar, you can access eight other categories in the Word Options dialog box. In Unit J, you used the Advanced option to change the location where templates are stored, and in Unit O, you used the General option to change the user name and initials associated with a computer.

3. **Click Proofing, then click the Ignore words in UPPERCASE check box to deselect it**

   Now when you use the Spelling command to check the spelling of a document, Word will check the spelling of words entered in uppercase.

4. **Click the Show readability statistics check box to select it, click OK, click the Spelling & Grammar button in the Text group on the Journals tab, then correct the spelling errors**

   Notice that "COPYWRIGHT" is identified as a spelling error because you changed the option so that Word checks the spelling of words entered in uppercase.

5. **Click OK, then compare the Readability Statistics dialog box to Figure P-8**

   In the Readability Statistics dialog box, Word displays the number of words in the document, the average number of words in each sentence, and the Flesch-Kincaid grade level. The document contained some grammatical errors that were not identified. You can also set Word to check grammar and style.

QUICK TIP

Table P-1 lists some of the other categories available via Options on the File tab.

6. **Click OK, click the File tab, click Options, click Proofing, click the Writing Style list arrow in the When correcting spelling and grammar in Word section of the dialog box, then click Grammar & Style if it is not already set to Grammar & Style**

7. **Click Settings, scroll down and view the default options that Word checks when Grammar & Style are selected, click the Use of first person check box to select it, click OK, click Recheck Document, click Yes, click OK, press [Ctrl][Home] to move to the top of the document, then click the Spelling & Grammar button in the Text group**

   The first error identified is the use of the first person "I" in the first sentence. Since these are journal entries, you decide that you'd like to keep the first person after all.

8. **Click Options, click Settings, click the Use of first person check box to deselect it, click OK, then click OK**

   The next error is the use of "they're" instead of "their." The suggested correction does not work.

9. **Select they're in the Contraction Use box, type their, then click Next Sentence**

   The next error is the use of passive voice.

10. **Select The day was spent in the Passive Voice box, type I spent the day, click Next Sentence, click OK, click OK, then save the document**

FIGURE P-8: Readability Statistics dialog box

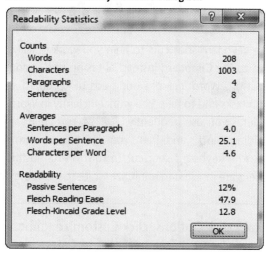

TABLE P-1: Some categories available via Options on the File tab

category	options to change	category	options to change
General	• User interface • User name • Start-up	Language	• Editing languages • Display and Help languages
Display	• Page display • Formatting marks • Printing options	Advanced	• Editing options • Cut, copy, and paste • Image size and quality • Document content • Display • Print • Save • Fidelity • General • Compatibility
Proofing	• AutoCorrect • Spelling • Spelling and Grammar • Exceptions	Add-Ins	• List of programs included with or added to Word
Save	• Save documents • Offline editing options • Fidelity for sharing	Trust Center	• Privacy • Security • Microsoft Word Trust Center

Creating and using custom dictionaries

You can use a custom dictionary to prevent Microsoft Word from flagging words that are spelled correctly but that do not appear in Word's main dictionary. For example, you can create a custom dictionary to contain terms you use frequently, such as medical terms, technical terms, or surnames. To create a new custom dictionary, click the File tab, click Options, click Proofing, click the Custom Dictionaries button, click New, type a name for the custom dictionary, save it, then click Edit Word List to add words to the new custom dictionary. If you do not want a custom dictionary to be activated for a particular document, you can remove the check mark that appears next to it in the Custom Dictionaries dialog box.

Creating Keyboard Shortcuts

You may already use keyboard shortcuts to help you work quickly in Word. For example, you might press [Ctrl][C] to copy text to the Clipboard instead of taking one hand from the keyboard and using the mouse to click the Copy button. Word includes hundreds of keyboard shortcuts that you can use to streamline document formatting tasks and to help you work efficiently in Word. You can also create your own keyboard shortcuts for procedures you use frequently. You create a keyboard shortcut that you can use to create a footer building block, and then you use several common keyboard shortcuts to format the document, including the keyboard shortcut to turn on full justification. Finally, you modify hyphenation options so that hyphens are inserted to minimize white space in the document that now uses full justification.

STEPS

1. **Click the File tab, click Options, click Customize Ribbon, click Customize next to Keyboard shortcuts, then click Insert Tab in the list of Categories**

   All the commands associated with the Insert tab are listed in alphabetical order in the Commands box.

2. **Click CreateFooterBlockFromSel in the list of Commands**

   This command will create a footer building block from currently selected text and then make the footer block available in the list of Quick Parts.

3. **Click in the Press new shortcut key: text box, then press [ALT][F]**

   Notice that the [Alt][F] keyboard shortcut is unassigned, as shown in Figure P-9, which means it is available for you to use. You always want to check if a keyboard shortcut is assigned and then decide if you want to reassign the shortcut to a different command. For example, you would likely keep [Ctrl][B] as the keyboard shortcut for the Bold command rather than use it for another procedure such as adding a border.

4. **Click Assign, click Close, click OK, select COPYRIGHT Quest Specialty Travel above the picture, press [Alt][F], then click OK**

   You've created a new building block that you can use to enter the selected text in a footer.

5. **Press [Delete] to remove the selected text, click the Footer button in the Document group on the Journals tab, click Blank, then click the Quick Parts button in the Insert group of the Header & Footer Tools tab**

6. **Click Building Blocks Organizer, click Name to put all the building blocks in alphabetical order, scroll to and click COPYRIGHT, click Insert, click the Close Header and Footer button in the Close group, then scroll to view the footer**

   The footer text is inserted.

TROUBLE
The > symbol appears above the period on your keyboard.

7. **Double-click in the footer area, click after Travel in the Copyright line, press [Tab] once, type your name, close the footer and move to the top of the document, select Pacific Odyssey Tour, click the Journals tab, click the Text Effects button in the Text group, select Gradient Fill – Blue, Accent 1 (third row, fourth column), then press [Ctrl][Shift][>] five times to increase the font size**

8. **Press [Ctrl][A] to select all the text in the document, press [Ctrl][5] to turn on 1.5 line spacing, then press [Ctrl][J] to turn on full justification**

   When full justification is turned on, extra space is inserted in lines so that every line is the exact same width. You can turn on hyphenation to minimize these extra spaces.

9. **Click the Hyphenation Options button in the Text group, complete the dialog box as shown in Figure P-10, click OK, click anywhere in the text to deselect it, then save the document**

   Hyphens are added where appropriate, and most extra spacing is removed.

FIGURE P-9: **Customize Keyboard dialog box**

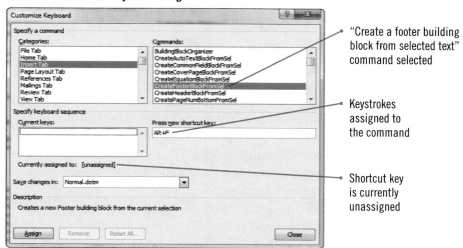

"Create a footer building block from selected text" command selected

Keystrokes assigned to the command

Shortcut key is currently unassigned

FIGURE P-10: **Hyphenation dialog box**

Automatically hyphenate document selected

Hyphenation zone changed to .1"

Finding keyboard shortcuts

You access the list of Word's keyboard shortcuts from the Help menu. Click the Help button in the upper-right corner of the document window, type keyboard shortcuts, then press [Enter]. Click the link to Keyboard shortcuts for Microsoft Word. In the article that appears, all the keyboard shortcuts you can access in Word are described. Figure P-11 shows some common keyboard shortcuts.

FIGURE P-11: **Some common keyboard shortcuts**

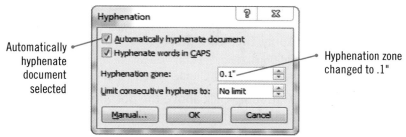

function	keyboard shortcut		function	keyboard shortcut
Bold text	[Ctrl][B]		Print a document	[Ctrl][P]
Center text	[Ctrl][e]		Redo or repeat an action	[Ctrl][Y]
Copy text	[Ctrl][C]		Save a document	[Ctrl][S]
Cut text	[Ctrl][X]		Select all text	[Ctrl][A]
Open a document	[Ctrl][O]		Turn on double spacing	[Ctrl][2]
Paste text	[Ctrl][V]		Undo an action	[Ctrl][Z]

Adding a Watermark and a Page Border

You can customize the appearance of a document by including a watermark and a page border. A **watermark** is a picture or other type of graphic object that appears lightly shaded behind text in a document. For example, you could include a company logo as a watermark on every page of a company report, or you could create "Confidential" as a WordArt object that appears in a very light gray behind the text of an important letter or memo. A **page border** encloses one or more pages of a document. You can create a box border using a variety of line styles and colors, or you can insert one of Word's preset art borders. 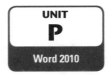 You add a watermark consisting of the text "DRAFT" that will appear lightly shaded behind the document text, you modify the text using the Change Shape button in the Graphics group on the Journals tab, and then you add a page border.

STEPS

1. **Click the** Draft button **in the Graphics group on the Journals tab, then click** Custom Watermark

2. **Click the** Text watermark option button, **click the** ASAP list arrow **in the Text text box, then select** DRAFT

3. **Click the** Horizontal option button, **compare the Printed Watermark dialog box to Figure P-12, click** Apply, **then click** Close

   If you want to make additional changes to the watermark, you can access it by opening the document header. Both the watermark and the document header are on a drawing layer.

4. **Switch to 70% view, double-click above the document title to open the header area, then click any part of Draft that appears below the text**

5. **Click the** Journals tab, **click the** Change Shape button **in the Graphics group, then click the** Cascade Down shape **(row four, column six in the Warp section)**

   You can also modify the watermark using any of the tools on the Drawing Tools tab. For example, you can modify the transparency settings and fill color, and add special effects such as a reflection or shadow.

6. **Double-click anywhere in the document to close the header area**

7. **Click the** Border button **in the Document group, click** Box, **scroll to and click the** Thick-Thin border **in the Style list box (ninth selection from the top), click the** Color list arrow, **click** Blue, Accent 1, Darker 25%, **then compare the Borders and Shading dialog box to Figure P-13**

8. **Click** OK, **then save the document**

   The document appears in 70% view as shown in Figure P-14. This document is the formatted journal you will refer to when you want to format other journal entries.

FIGURE P-12: **Printed Watermark dialog box**

To add a picture watermark, click the Picture watermark option button and select a picture file

Text watermark selected

DRAFT selected

Horizontal selected

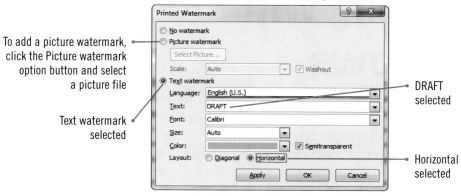

FIGURE P-13: **Selecting a page border**

Thick-Thin border style selected

New color selected

Preview of border

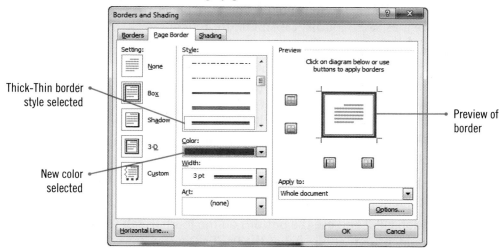

FIGURE P-14: **Document modified with a watermark and page border**

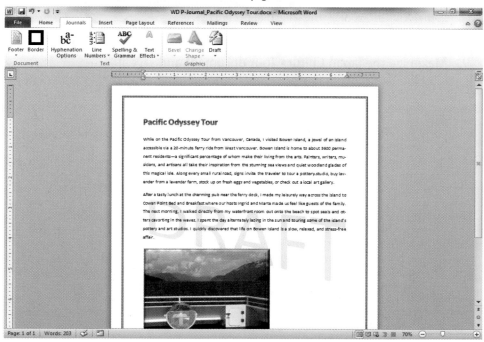

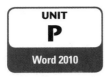

UNIT P
Word 2010

Working with Document Windows

You use options in the Window group on the View tab to help you work easily with two or more documents at once. You can view two documents side by side, split a current document into two windows, and place a copy of the current document in a new window. ▰▰▰ You have created the new Journals tab and modified other settings so that you can quickly format every journal document you receive. To help you format a new journal document, you display it side by side with the formatted journal document so you can easily see what changes you need to make. You also turn on line numbers so that you can quickly determine the length of the two documents.

STEPS

1. **Open the file WD P-2.docx from the drive and folder where you store your Data Files, then save it as WD P-Journal_Japan Culture Tour.docx**

2. **Click the View tab, click View Side by Side in the Window group, then scroll up if necessary so you can see the title of both documents**

   Notice that synchronous scrolling is turned on, which means that the windows scroll together. When you work with two windows side by side, you generally need to turn off synchronous scrolling so that you can view different parts of each document at the same time.

3. **Click Window on the Ribbon in the Japan Culture Tour document if the Window group is not displayed, then click Synchronous Scrolling to deselect it**

4. **Change the view to 70%, then click the Journals tab on the Ribbon in the Japan Culture Tour document**

5. **Refer to Table P-2 and use the buttons on the Journals tab to modify the Japan Culture Tour document so that it matches the Pacific Odyssey Tour document**

6. **Click the Line Numbers button in the Text group, then click Continuous**

7. **Click in the Pacific Odyssey Tour document, then add continuous line numbers**

   The two documents appear as shown in Figure P-15. By turning on line numbers you can see at a glance that both documents contain the same number of lines.

8. **Press [Ctrl][S] to save the Pacific Odyssey Tour document, then minimize it**

9. **Maximize the Japan Culture Tour document and save it**

FIGURE P-15: Documents viewed side by side

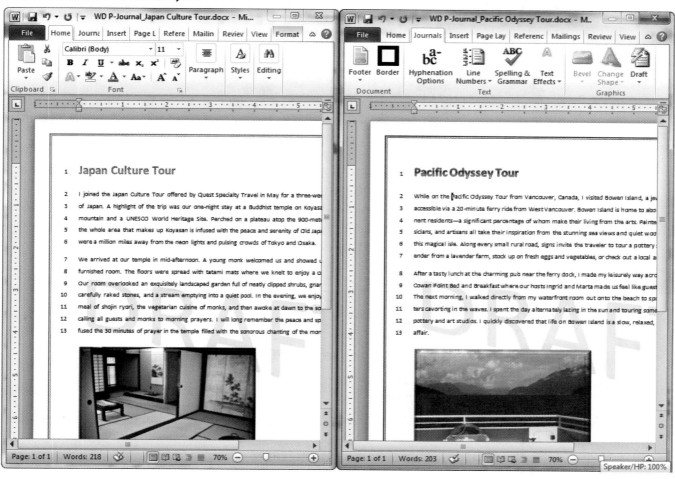

TABLE P-2: Changes to make to the Japan Culture Tour document

location	change
Whole Document	Use the Border button to add a Thick-Thin double border that is formatted with the Orange, Accent 6, Darker 25% color
Spelling & Grammar	Use the Spelling & Grammar button to check the spelling and grammar in the document: • Correct spelling errors and accept the two hyphen suggestions (three-week and 900-meter), ignore Japanese words (koya, koyasan, etc.), and change UNASCO to UNESCO • Ignore the two passive voice errors
Footer	Insert the COPYRIGHT building block in the footer followed by [Tab] and your name; delete any extra blank lines
Watermark	Use the Draft button to insert the DRAFT watermark with the Horizontal option selected
Watermark Shape	Use the Change Shape button to change the shape of the Draft button to Cascade Down
Document Title	Use the Text Effects button to apply the Gradient Fill – Orange, Accent 6, Inner Shadow text effect to "Japan Culture Tour," then use [Ctrl][Shift][>] to increase the font size so the titles of the two documents match
Line Spacing	Select all the text, then use the [Ctrl][5] keyboard shortcut to change the spacing for the entire document to 1.5 spacing
Hyphenation	Turn on full justification using [Ctrl][J], then turn on hyphenation with a hyphenation zone of .1
Picture Format	Use the Bevel button to apply the Divot bevel style

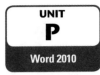
Saving in Alternate File Formats

By default, Word saves all documents with the .docx extension. You can also choose to save a Word document in other formats such as PDF and RTF. You save a document as a **PDF (Portable Document Format)** file when you want to send it to people who may not have Word installed on their computers. You also use the PDF file format for documents that you want to post on a Web site. People can download a document saved as a PDF file and view it using Acrobat Reader, a free program available for download from Adobe. You use the **RTF (Rich Text Format)** file type when you want to limit the file size of a document and you want to share it with people who may not have access to Word. An RTF file can be opened, viewed, and edited in virtually any word processing program. ▓▓▓▓ You save the current document as a PDF file and view it in Acrobat Reader, and then you save another copy of the document as an RTF file. Finally, you take a screenshot of the Journals tab you created in this unit.

STEPS

1. **Click the** File tab, **then click** Save As
   The Save As dialog box opens.

2. **Click the** Save as type list arrow, **then click** PDF **as shown in Figure P-16**

3. **Click the** text **to the right of Authors, press** [Backspace] **to delete any text that may appear, then type your name**

> **TROUBLE**
> If Acrobat Reader is not installed on your system, follow prompts to install it or go to Step 6.

4. **Click the** Open file after publishing check box **to select it if it is not already checked, then click** Save
   In a few moments, the document opens in Acrobat Reader. You can choose to print the PDF version of the file from Acrobat or you can close it.

5. **Click** File **on the menu bar in Acrobat Reader, then click** Close
   You can also access file-saving options using the Save & Send option on the File tab.

6. **Click** File, **click** Save & Send, **click** Change File Type **in the File Types section, click** Rich Text Format (*.rtf) **in the Other File Types section, click** Save As, **click** Save, **read the warning that appears, then click** Continue
   The text effect you applied to the document title is removed in the .rtf file. However, the larger font size is retained.

7. **Click** File, **click** Close, **then verify that WD P-Pacific Odyssey Journals.docx is again the active document and that the Journals tab is the active tab**

8. **Press** [Ctrl][N] **to start a new blank document, click the** Insert tab, **click the** Screenshot button **in the Illustrations group, click** Screen Clipping, **then drag to clip only the Journals tab as shown in Figure P-17**

9. **Save the document as** WD P-Journals Tab
   The document contains the screen clipping of the Journals tab.

FIGURE P-16: Selecting PDF in the Save As dialog box

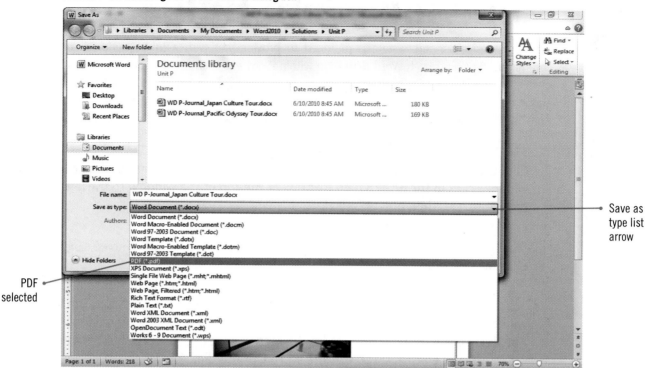

PDF selected

Save as type list arrow

FIGURE P-17: Creating a screen clipping of the Journals tab

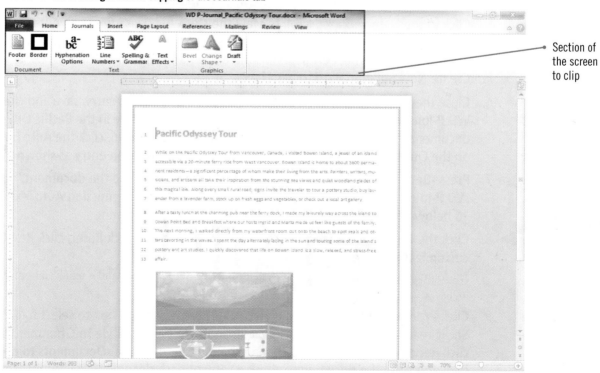

Section of the screen to clip

Applying Word Help

Word's extensive support system is designed to provide you with help on hundreds of features and commands. You can search Word Help from within Word and then modify your windows so that you can quickly try the steps suggested to perform a specific task. You search Word Help for information about the new AutoText feature, add the AutoText button to the Quick Access toolbar, then insert an AutoText entry into the two journal documents. Finally, you delete the Journals tab and restore all defaults.

STEPS

1. Click the **Microsoft Word Help button** in the upper-right corner of the document window, click in the **Search help text box** at the top of the window to the left of bing, type **AutoText**, then press **[Enter]**

2. Click **Add AutoText in Word**

   The page includes the steps required to add the AutoText command to the Quick Access toolbar and to create a new AutoText entry.

3. Click the **Restore Down button** if your Word Help window is maximized, scroll to the heading **Add AutoText from a gallery**, use the mouse to size and position the Word Help window as shown in Figure P-18, follow the steps included in the Help window to add AutoText to the Quick Access toolbar (in Step 3, click **Quick Access Toolbar** instead of Customize), then click **OK** to exit the Word Options dialog box

   The AutoText button appears on the Quick Access toolbar as shown in Figure P-19

   TROUBLE
   Move the window containing the Help steps to see the screen as you type.

4. Double-click below the screenshot of the Journals tab, then type the following text: **A customer of Quest Specialty Travel has written this journal entry about his or her experiences on a QST tour. The customer has provided QST with permission to reproduce the journal entry on its Web site and in print materials.**

5. Click in the **Help window**, scroll to view the steps for creating a new AutoText entry, then follow the first three steps to create the text you typed in Step 4 as an AutoText entry using the text **Journal Permission** as the entry name, and then clicking **OK** to close the Create New Building Block dialog box

   TROUBLE
   If the picture disappears, click the Undo button on the Quick Access toolbar, then repeat Step 6, making sure the insertion point is on line 16.

6. Close the Help window, add your name below the AutoText entry, save and close the WD P-Journals Tab document, double-click below the picture in the Pacific Odyssey Tour document, press **[Enter]** until the insertion point is on line 16, click the **AutoText button** on the Quick Access toolbar, then click the Journal Permission entry as shown in Figure P-20

7. Press **[Backspace]** to remove line number 19, save and close the document, open **WD P-Journal_ Japan Culture Tour.docx**, add the Journal Permission AutoText entry at line 16 below the picture, remove line 19, then save the document

   QUICK TIP
   If you wish to keep the Journals tab on your system, select it, then click Remove. The tab is removed from the Ribbon but it is stored with Custom Tabs and Groups. Repeat the process to remove the AutoText command from the Quick Access toolbar.

8. Click the **File tab**, click **Options**, click **Customize Ribbon**, click **Reset**, click **Reset all customizations**, then click **Yes**

   The Journals tab is removed from your system, and the AutoText command is removed from the Quick Access toolbar.

9. Click **Proofing**, click the **Ignore words in UPPERCASE check box** to select it, deselect the **Show readability statistics check box**, change the Writing Style to **Grammar Only**, click **OK**, click **Recent** on the File menu, change the number of Recent Documents to access to **0**, save and close the document, submit a copy of each document to your instructor, exit Word, then if prompted click **Don't Save**, click **Cancel**, then click **Don't Save** twice more

   The warnings refer to the keyboard shortcut you created in a previous lesson and to the building blocks you created. You don't need to save these changes.

FIGURE P-18: Resizing the Help window

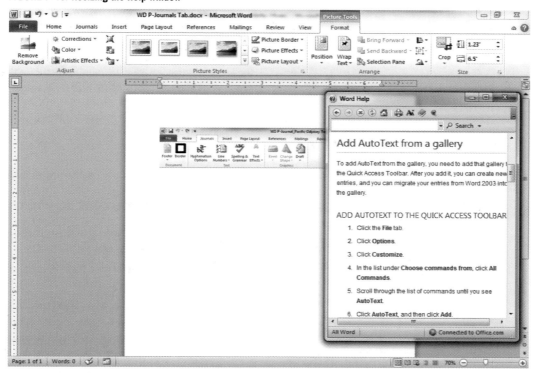

FIGURE P-19: AutoText button added to the Quick Access toolbar

AutoText button

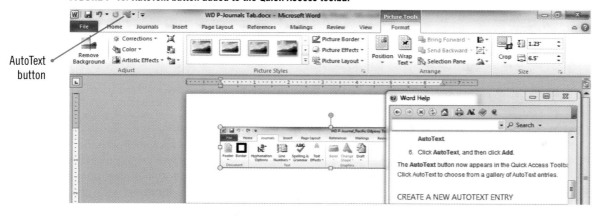

FIGURE P-20: Selecting an AutoText entry

AutoText entry

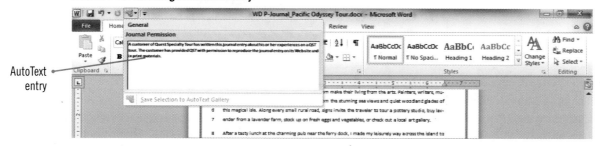

Getting Help from the Internet

When you cannot find a solution to a Word problem in Help, you can often find answers by searching the Internet. Thousands of tutorials, blogs, discussion groups, forums, and white papers contain information on virtually every aspect of Word from automatically checking for errors to working with Zoom options. The key to success is to enter as many relevant keywords as possible into your search engine. For example, if you want to find out how to use the hyphenation option, enter "How do I turn on hyphenation in Word?" Entering search terms in the form of a question often yields excellent results.

Practice

Concepts Review

Refer to Figure P-21 to answer the following questions.

FIGURE P-21

Which element do you click

a. to include a command on a Ribbon tab?

b. to show the list of command groups?

c. to customize the Quick Access toolbar?

d. to remove all customized tabs from your system?

e. when you want to create a shortcut, such as [Alt][F]?

Match each term with the statement that best describes it.

6. **New Group**
7. **Watermark**
8. **Quick Access toolbar**
9. **Customize**
10. **Options**
11. **RTF**

a. Can contain buttons of your choice
b. Use to set up a group for commands on a new Ribbon tab
c. Graphic or text that appears lightly shaded behind text
d. Button used to access the Customize Keyboard dialog box
e. File format that can be opened and edited in any word processing program
f. Contains categories such as General, Advanced, and Proofing

Select the best answer from the list of choices.

12. **How do you create a new Ribbon tab?**
    a. Right-click the Ribbon, then click New Tab.
    b. In the Customize the Ribbon and keyboard shortcuts pane of the Word Options dialog box, click New Ribbon.
    c. In the Customize the Ribbon and keyboard shortcuts pane of the Word Options dialog box, click New Tab.
    d. In the Add-Ins pane of the Word Options dialog box, click Add Tab.
13. **How do you restore the default Ribbons and Quick Access toolbar?**
    a. In the Customize the Ribbon and keyboard shortcuts pane of the Word Options dialog box, click Reset.
    b. Right-click the new Ribbon tab, then click Delete.
    c. Open the template containing the Ribbons tabs, then select the new tab and press Delete.
    d. In the Customize the Ribbon and keyboard shortcuts pane of the Word Options dialog box, click the new tab, then click Remove.

Skills Review

1. Create a new tab.

  a. Start Word, open the file WD P-3.docx from the drive and folder where you store your Data Files, then save it as **WD P-Press Release_Lake Towers Hotel**. (*Note*: Spelling and grammar errors in the document are intentional. You will correct these errors later in the Skills Review.)

  b. Using the File tab, open the Word Options dialog box, then open the Customize the Ribbon and keyboard shortcuts pane.

  c. Create a new tab called **Hotels**.

  d. Rename the new group on the Hotels tab **Format**, then add the following commands: Header, Hyphenation Options, Line Numbers, Page Borders, and Spelling & Grammar.

  e. Create a new group on the Hotels tab called **Visuals**, then add the Shading, Shadow (third selection for Text Effect), Shape Fill (first selection for WordArt), and Watermark commands.

  f. Exit the Word Options dialog box, then save the document.

2. Customize buttons.

  a. Using the File tab, open the Word Options dialog box, then open the Customize the Ribbon and keyboard shortcuts pane.

  b. Show the list of Tool Tabs, expand the Picture Tools Format tab, expand Picture Styles, add Quick Styles to the Visuals group on the Hotels tab, then move Quick Styles above Shading.

  c. Expand the Format group on the Hotels tab, then change the name of the Header command to **Hotel Name**.

  d. Change the name of the Quick Styles command in the Visuals group on the Hotels tab to **Clip Art**, then select the icon in the second row of the Symbols that resembles an artist's palette.

  e. Click OK to accept the changes and close the Word Options dialog box, then display the Hotels tab. Compare your updated Hotels tab to the one shown in Figure P-22.

  f. Click the picture, use the Clip Art button to apply the Drop Shadow Rectangle picture style to the clip art picture, then save the document.

FIGURE P-22

3. Modify Word options.

  a. Using the Recent options on the File tab, change the number of recent documents displayed on the File tab to 5.

  b. Using the Word Options dialog box, change the Proofing options as follows:

    • Check the spelling of words in UPPERCASE

    • Show the readability statistics

  c. Return to the document.

  d. Use the Spelling & Grammar command on the Hotels tab to correct the errors, then save the document.

4. Create keyboard shortcuts.

  a. Use the Customize Ribbon option in the Word Options dialog box to open the Customize Keyboard dialog box.

  b. Select the Insert Tab option in the Categories list box, then select the CreateHeaderBlockFromSel command in the Command list box.

  c. Enter [ALT][H] as the new shortcut key for creating a header building block from currently selected text, then assign the shortcut key.

  d. Return to the document, select Lake Towers Hotel Press Release at the bottom of the document, then use the [Alt][H] command to make it a building block called **Press Release**.

  e. Delete the selected text, then use the Hotel Name button on the Hotels tab to insert a Blank header.

  f. Insert the Press Release building block into the header.

  g. Select the document title, then use the Shadow button on the Hotels tab to apply the Offset Diagonal Bottom Right shadow style.

  h. Select the address line, then use the Shading button to shade the line of text with Blue, Accent 1, Lighter 80%.

  i. Use the [Ctrl][Shift][<] keystroke combination to reduce the font size of the address text by three increments.

  j. Use [Ctrl][A] to select all the text, press [Ctrl][2] to turn on double spacing, then press [Ctrl][J] to turn on full justification.

  k. Use the Hyphenation Options button to turn on hyphenation and set the hyphenation zone at .15.

  l. Save the document.

Skills Review (continued)

5. **Add a watermark and a page border.**

   a. Use the Watermark button to add a custom Text watermark to the document using the text SAMPLE with the default positioning (Diagonal).

   b. Open the header area in the document, click the SAMPLE watermark, then use the Shape Fill button on the Hotels tab to fill the watermark with Blue, Accent 1, Lighter 60%.

   c. Exit the header, then use the Page Borders button to add the art border shown in the completed document in Figure P-23. (*Hint*: You will need to scroll almost to the bottom of the Art border selections.)

   d. Set the width of the art border to 20 pt, then save the document.

   FIGURE P-23

6. **Work with document windows.**

   a. Open the file WD P-4.docx from the drive and folder where you store your Data Files, then save it as **WD P- Press Release_Saskatoon Classic Hotel.docx**.

   b. View the document windows side by side, turn off synchronous scrolling, then adjust the view to a percentage that allows you to see most of the document without scrolling.

   c. Use the buttons on the Hotels tab to modify the Saskatoon Classic Hotel document so that it matches the Lake Towers Hotel document as described in Table P-3.

TABLE P-3

location	change
Whole Document	Use the Page Borders button to add the same art border with the 20 pt width
Spelling & Grammar	Use the Spelling & Grammar button to check the spelling and grammar in the document; ignore people's names and passive voice suggestions, but accept all other corrections suggested
Header	Insert the Press Release building block in the header, then change "Lake Towers" to **Saskatoon Classic**
Watermark	Use the Watermark button to insert the SAMPLE watermark
Watermark Fill	Use the Fill Color button to change the fill color of custom text SAMPLE to match the Lake Towers Hotel document
Document Title	Use the Shadow button to apply the same shadow effect to "Saskatoon Classic Hotel" as you applied to "Lake Towers Hotel"
Address Line	Use the Shading button to apply the required shading to the address line, then use [CTRL][SHIFT][<] three times to reduce the font size of the address line so the two documents match
Line Spacing	Select all the text, then use the Ctrl][2] keyboard shortcut to change the line spacing to Double
Hyphenation	Turn on full justification, then turn on hyphenation with a hyphenation zone of .15
Clip Art Picture	Use the Clip Art button to apply the correct picture style to the clip art picture

   d. Use the Line Number button to turn on continuous line numbering in both documents, then verify that both documents contain 15 lines. Remove any blank lines, if necessary.

   e. Save and minimize the Lake Towers Hotel document, then maximize the Saskatoon Classic Hotel document and save it.

7. **Save in alternate file formats.**

   a. Save the document as a PDF file using your name as the author, then close the file after it opens in Acrobat Reader.

   b. Use the Save & Send option on the File tab to change the file type for the current document to Rich Text Format, note the formatting removed from the document title when the RTF file opens, then close the document.

   c. Verify that WD P-Press Release_Lake Towers Hotel.docx is again the active document with the Hotels tab active, press [Ctrl][N] to start a new blank document, then use the Screenshot button to take a screen clipping of the Hotels tab.

   d. Save the document as **WD P-Hotels Tab**.

Skills Review (continued)

8. **Apply Word Help.**

   a. Open the Microsoft Word Help dialog box, search for AutoText, then open the Help window containing the steps required to add AutoText to the Quick Access toolbar and create an AutoText entry.

   b. Resize the Window containing the Help steps, then follow the steps to add AutoText to the Quick Access toolbar. (*Hint*: In Step 3, remember to click Quick Access Toolbar instead of Customize.)

   c. Double-click below the screenshot of the Hotels tab, then type the following text: **This hotel provides a 100% money-back customer satisfaction guarantee to all its guests. Details about the guarantee appear on the hotel's Web site**.

   d. In the Help window, scroll to view the steps for creating a new AutoText entry, then follow the first three steps to create the text you typed in Step c as an AutoText entry using the text **Guarantee** as the entry name.

   e. Close the Help window, type your name below the AutoText entry, save and close the WD P-Hotels Tab document, then press [Enter] following the last line of text (line 15) in the Lake Towers Hotel document to create a new line (line 16).

   f. Use the AutoText button on the Quick Access toolbar to add the Guarantee entry.

   g. Press [Backspace] to remove line number 18, type your name in the footer area, then save and close the document.

   h. Open WD P-Press Release_Saskatoon Classic Hotel.docx, add the Guarantee AutoText entry at line 16 below the last line of text, remove line 18, then type your name in the footer area.

   i. Reset all customizations, then restore the default settings for Proofing: the Ignore words in UPPERCASE check box is selected, and the Show readability statistics check box is deselected.

   k. Reset the Recent option so that 0 recent documents are listed in the File menu.

   l. Save and close the document, submit a copy of the document (.docs) files you created in this unit to your instructor, exit Word, then if prompted click Don't Save in response to the message informing you of changes made that affect the global template, click Cancel, then click Don't Save twice more.

Independent Challenge 1

As the office manager of the Black Belt Academy, you prepare a gift certificate that you can e-mail to new members. You create a new Ribbon tab called Academy that contains the commands you'll use most often to personalize each certificate and then you format two gift certificates and save them as PDF documents.

   a. Start Word, use the File tab to open the Word Options dialog box, view the Customize the Ribbon and keyboard short-cuts pane, create a new tab called **Academy**, then change the name of the custom group to **Text**.

   b. Add the following buttons to the Text group: Bold, Font Size, and Font Color. Move Font Color so the three buttons are in alphabetical order.

   c. Create a new group on the Academy tab called **Shapes**, then add the Change Shape button (second selection), the Shape Fill button for Shape Styles (third selection), the Shapes button (first selection), and the Weight (first selection) to the Shapes group.

   d. Close the Word Options dialog box, open the file WD P-5.docx, then save it as **WD P-Gift Certificate_Sally Yang**.

   e. Click the hexagon shape, click the Change Shape button on the Academy tab, then select the Explosion 2 shape in the Stars and Banners category.

   f. Type **Sally** in the shape, press [Shift][Enter], type **Yang**, then select the text and use the buttons in the Text group on the Academy toolbar to enhance the text with Bold, 14 pt, and the font color of your choice.

   g. Use the Shape Fill button to select a light fill color of your choice.

   h. Use the Shapes button to draw a straight line that starts to the right of "To:" and extends just to the left of the explosion shape.

   i. Draw another line next to "Date:," then use the Weight button to change the width of the two lines to 2¼ pt.

   j. Click next to "To:," type **Sally Yang, 500 West 4th Street, Green Bay, WI**, increase the font size to 14 pt, click next to "Date:," type the current date, then use your arrow keys as needed to move the lines under the text.

   k. Type **Prepared by** followed by your name centered below the last line of text, then save the document.

   l. Open the file WD P-6.docx, then save it as **WD P-Gift Certificate_Shadi Khosani**.

   m. Show the two windows side by side, then use the Academy tab to format the gift certificate for Shadi so that it is similar to but not exactly the same as Sally's, entering **Shadi Khosani, 250 Lake Drive, Green Bay, WI** next to "To:,".

Independent Challenge 1 (continued)

n. Use [Ctrl][N] to start a new document, insert a screen clipping showing only the Academy toolbar, then add your name below the screen clipping. Save the document as **WD P-Academy Tab**, then close it.

o. Save both certificate documents as PDF files using your name as the author each time, remove the Academy tab from your system, save and close all documents, submit them to your instructor, then exit Word.

Independent Challenge 2

You work for Blossom Florists in Nashville, Tennessee, which has moved to a new location. As a result, several letters include an incorrect address in the letterhead. You create an AutoText entry that replaces the outdated information with the correct information and then create a keyboard shortcut to insert the AutoText entry in a new letter. You also create a keyboard shortcut for adding a border to the two letters. Finally, you change some settings so that the picture in each file is saved at a lower resolution, thereby using less storage space.

a. Start Word, open the file WD P-7.docx from the drive and folder where you store your Data Files, then save it as **WD P-Catalog Request_McDonald**.

b. Use Word Help as needed to add AutoText to the Quick Access toolbar.

c. Select the current address, type **140 Mainline Avenue, Nashville, TN 37205**, then use the address line to create an AutoText entry called **Blossom**.

d. Open the file WD P-8.docx from the drive and folder where you store your Data Files, save it as **WD P-Catalog Request_Fane**, then replace the current address with the Blossom AutoText entry.

e. Open the Customize Keyboard dialog box, then create and assign a keyboard shortcut using the keystrokes of your choice that will add a page border to a document. (*Hint*: The required command is called FormatPageBordersAndShading and is located on the Page Layout Tab.)

f. Use the keyboard shortcut to add an art border to the Fane letter, then modify the width of the page border.

g. Show the two windows containing the two letters side by side, and use the keyboard shortcut you created to add the same art border with the same settings to the McDonald letter.

h. From the McDonald letter, go to the Advanced area of the Word Options dialog box, scroll to Image Size and Quality, then verify that WD P-Catalog Request_McDonald.docx is in the text box to the right of Image Size and Quality.

i. Deselect the Do not compress images in the file check box, then set the default target output to 96 ppi. These changes reduce the file size of the picture in the document, which reduces the file size of the entire document.

j. Exit the Word Options dialog box, then apply the same settings for image size and quality to the Fane document.

Advanced Challenge Exercise

- In the Fane document, click above the date, then use the keyboard shortcut you created to open the Borders and Shading dialog box with the Page Border tab active.
- Click Horizontal Line, select the line style you prefer, then click OK.
- Click the line to select it, then drag the lower-middle sizing handle down slightly to increase the height of the line to approximately 1/8 of an inch.
- Copy the line, then paste it in the appropriate location in the McDonald document.

k. Enter your name in the closing where indicated in both letters, save the letters, submit a copy of both letters to your instructor, then close them.

Independent Challenge 3

You've just started working for Organics Forever, a company that delivers fresh, organic fruits and vegetables to its customers in Seattle. The price lists distributed to customers are all contained within tables; however, the tables are not formatted very attractively. You decide to create a custom tab called Organics that will contain all the commands you need to format the price list tables. The tab will also include commands for adding a watermark and a theme.

a. Open the file WD P-9.docx from the drive and folder where you store your Data Files, then save it as **WD P-Price Lists_Produce**.

b. Create a new custom tab called **Organics** that contains two groups: **Table** and **Document**.

c. Show the commands associated with the Table Tools Design tab and expand all groups, then add at least five commands to the Table group. Choose commands based on how you would like to format the price list tables.

Independent Challenge 3 (continued)

d. Show the commands associated with the Table Tools Layout tab, expand all groups, and add the Sort command and at least two other table layout commands to the Table group on the Organics tab.

e. Change the name of the Sort command to **Codes**, assign it an icon, then alphabetize the commands.

f. Change to show All Commands in the left pane, then add the Themes command and the Watermark command to the Document group.

g. Use the commands in the Table group on the Organics tab to format each of the two tables in the same way. If you need to change the commands on the Organics tab, access the Customize the Ribbon and keyboard shortcuts pane of the Word Options dialog box and add or delete commands.

h. Use the Codes command in the Table group on the Organics tab to sort all the entries in each table in numerical order by code. (*Hint*: In the Sort dialog box, select Column 1 to sort by and click the Header row option button to select it.)

i. Use the Watermark command in the Document group on the Organics tab to add the Confidential watermark using the horizontal orientation, open the header area, then drag the watermark so it appears below the two tables.

j. Use the Themes command in the Document group on the Organics tab to add the theme of your choice.

k. Open the file WD P-10.docx, then save it as **WD P-Price Lists_Dairy and Meat**.

l. Show the two windows containing the two documents side by side, then use the buttons on the Organics tab to format the Dairy and Meat document so it looks the same as the Produce Price Lists document.

m. Create a new document containing a screen clipping of the Organics tab, then save the document as **WD P-Organics Tab**.

Advanced Challenge Exercise:

- Open the Customize the Ribbon and keyboard shortcuts pane in the Word Options dialog box.
- Click the Organics (Custom) tab, then click Remove. The tab is removed from the list of main tabs, but it is not removed from your system.
- Click the Popular Commands list arrow, then click Custom Tabs and Groups.
- Press the Prt Scr button on your keyboard (the key could also be called PrtScrn, Prt Sc or another combination).
- Click OK, then press [Ctrl][V] to paste a picture showing the Custom Tabs and Groups pane in the Word Options dialog box to the WD P-OrganicsTab.docx file.

n. Add your name to all documents, save the documents, submit a copy of each document to your instructor, then exit Word, answering Don't Save if requested to save the normal template.

Real Life Independent Challenge

You can search the Internet to find information on just about any Word function or task. Even a search for information about very difficult or obscure options or tasks usually yields results—often in the form of postings to forums and blogs or in online tutorials. You will use the Internet to search for information about two Word-related topics of your choice and then select and describe search results. Make sure the results you choose provide information about topics related to Word 2010.

a. Open the file WD P-11.docx from the drive and folder where you store your Data Files, then save it as **WD P-Internet Search Results**.

b. In the appropriate areas of the table, enter a brief description of the two topics you wish to find information about. Make the topics as specific as possible. For example, you may wish to find out how to add text to a table of contents or how to use continuous section breaks. If you wish, select a topic related to a problem you may have had working with Word, such as creating a cross-reference or understanding citation styles. You are free to choose any topic you wish.

c. Open the Web browser you like to use, then conduct a search for information about the topic you identified.

d. Follow links to some of the search results returned or conduct a different search using slightly different keywords if the search results are not useful. You may need to conduct several searches to find useable results.

e. Select one search result for each topic that provides information about the topic. The search result can be information posted in a forum or on a blog posting or it can be in the form of an online tutorial.

f. Briefly describe (approximately 50 words) the information presented in each of the two search results you selected.

g. Use keyboard shortcuts to copy the Web site addresses of the two search results you selected from your browser window and paste then in the appropriate table cells.

h. Type your name in the subtitle, save the document, submit a copy to your instructor, then close the document.

Visual Workshop

Open the file WD P-12.docx from the drive and folder where you store your Data Files, then save the file as **WD P-Birthday Card**. Create a new tab called **BirthdayCard** that includes the buttons and groups shown in Figure P-24. Use the BirthdayCard tab to format the birthday card so that it appears as shown in Figure P-25. Note that you use the Apply Styles button to apply the Title style to "Happy Birthday" and the Heading 1 style to "Pacific Parasailing" and the Center button to center all the text. Apply the font color of your choice to "Happy Birthday." Create a screenshot of the BirthdayCard tab in a new document called **WD P-BirthdayCard Tab**. Add your name to both documents, save the documents, submit them to your instructor, then close the documents. Remove the BirthdayCard tab from your system, then exit Word.

FIGURE P-24

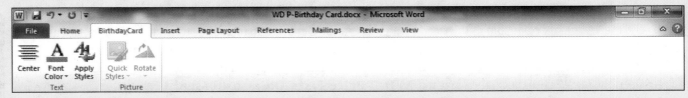

FIGURE P-25

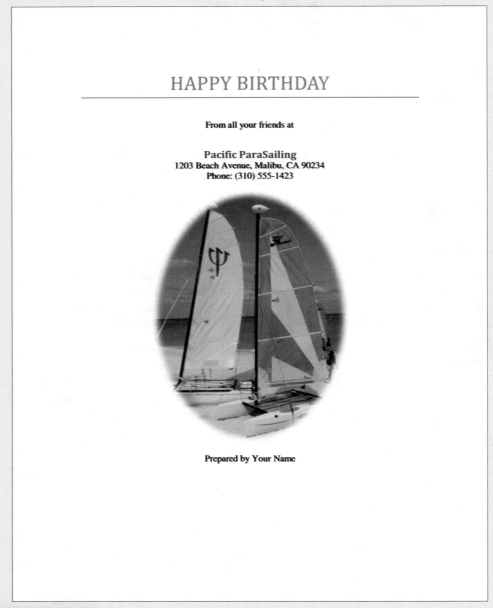

HAPPY BIRTHDAY

From all your friends at

Pacific ParaSailing
1203 Beach Avenue, Malibu, CA 90234
Phone: (310) 555-1423

Prepared by Your Name

Automating Worksheet Tasks

Files You Will Need:

EX I-1.xlsx

EX I-2.xlsx

A **macro** is a named set of instructions you can create that performs tasks automatically, in an order you specify. You create macros to automate Excel tasks that you perform frequently. Because they perform tasks rapidly, macros can save you a great deal of time. For example, if you usually enter your name and date in a worksheet footer, you can record the keystrokes in an Excel macro that enters the text and inserts the current date automatically when you run the macro. In this unit, you will plan and design a simple macro, then record and run it. You will then edit the macro and explore ways to make it more easily available as you work.  Kate Morgan, the North America regional vice president of sales at Quest, wants you to create a macro for the sales division. The macro needs to automatically insert text that identifies the worksheet as a sales division document.

OBJECTIVES

Plan a macro

Enable a macro

Record a macro

Run a macro

Edit a macro

Assign keyboard shortcuts to macros

Use the Personal Macro Workbook

Assign a macro to a button

Planning a Macro

You create macros for Excel tasks that you perform frequently. For example, you can create a macro to enter and format text or to save and print a worksheet. To create a macro, you record the series of actions using the macro recorder built into Excel, or you write the instructions in a special programming language. Because the sequence of actions in a macro is important, you need to plan the macro carefully before you record it. ▰▰▰▰ Kate wants you to create a macro for the sales division that inserts the text "Quest Sales" in the upper-left corner of any worksheet. You work with her to plan the macro.

DETAILS

To plan a macro, use the following guidelines:

- **Assign the macro a descriptive name**

  The first character of a macro name must be a letter; the remaining characters can be letters, numbers, or underscores. Letters can be uppercase or lowercase. Spaces are not allowed in macro names; use underscores in place of spaces. Press [Shift][-] to enter an underscore character. Kate wants you to name the macro "DivStamp". See Table I-1 for a list of macros that could be created to automate other tasks at Quest.

- **Write out the steps the macro will perform**

  This planning helps eliminate careless errors. Kate writes a description of the macro she wants, as shown in Figure I-1.

- **Decide how you will perform the actions you want to record**

  You can use the mouse, the keyboard, or a combination of the two. Kate wants you to use both the mouse and the keyboard.

- **Practice the steps you want Excel to record, and write them down**

  Kate has written down the sequence of actions she wants you to include in the macro.

- **Decide where to store the description of the macro and the macro itself**

  Macros can be stored in an active workbook, in a new workbook, or in the **Personal Macro Workbook**, a special workbook used only for macro storage. Kate asks you to store the macro in a new workbook.

FIGURE I-1: Paper description of planned macro

Macro to create stamp with the division name

Name:	DivStamp
Description:	Adds a stamp to the top left of the worksheet, identifying it as a Quest sales worksheet

Steps:
1. Position the cell pointer in cell A1.
2. Type Sales Division, then click the Enter button.
3. Click the Format button, then click Format Cells.
4. Click the Font tab, under Font style click Bold; under Underline click Single; under Color click Red; then click OK.

TABLE I-1: Possible macros and their descriptive names

description of macro	descriptive name for macro
Enter a frequently used proper name, such as "Kate Morgan"	KateMorgan
Enter a frequently used company name, such as Quest	Company_Name
Print the active worksheet on a single page, in landscape orientation	FitToLand
Add a footer to a worksheet	FooterStamp
Add totals to a worksheet	AddTotals

Enabling a Macro

Because a macro may contain a **virus**—destructive software that can damage your computer files—the default security setting in Excel disables macros from running. Although a workbook containing a macro will open, if macros are disabled, they will not function. You can manually change the Excel security setting to allow macros to run if you know a macro came from a trusted source. When saving a workbook with a macro, you need to save it as a macro-enabled workbook with the extension .xlsm. Kate asks you to change the security level to enable all macros. You will change the security level back to the default setting after you create and run your macros.

STEPS

1. **Start Excel, click the** Save button 🔲 **on the Quick Access toolbar, in the Save As dialog box click the** Save as type list arrow, **click** Excel Macro-Enabled Workbook (*.xlsm), **then in the File name text box type** EX I-Macro Workbook

2. **Navigate to the drive and folder where you store your Data Files, then click** Save
   The security settings that enable macros are available on the Developer tab. The Developer tab does not appear by default, but you can display it by customizing the Ribbon.

3. **Click the** File tab, click Options, **then click** Customize Ribbon **in the category list**
   The Customize the Ribbon options open in the Excel Options dialog box, as shown in Figure I-2.

4. **Click the** Developer check box **in the Main Tabs area on the right side of the screen to select it, then click** OK
   The Developer tab appears on the Ribbon. You are ready to change the security settings.

5. **Click the** Developer tab, **then click the** Macro Security button **in the Code group**
   The Trust Center dialog box opens, as shown in Figure I-3.

6. **Click** Macro Settings **if necessary, click the** Enable all macros (not recommended; potentially dangerous code can run) option button **to select it, then click** OK
   The dialog box closes. Macros remain enabled until you disable them by deselecting the Enable all macros option. As you work with Excel, you should disable macros when you are not working with them.

FIGURE I-2: Excel Options dialog box

Select to display the Developer tab

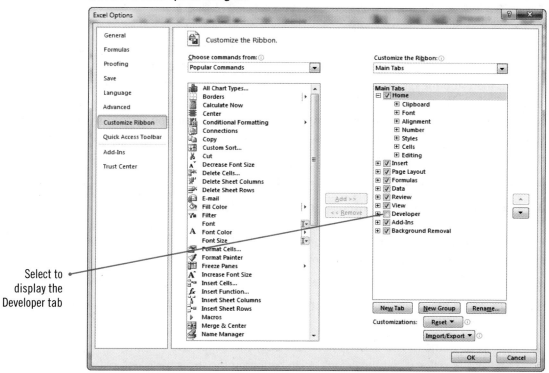

FIGURE I-3: Trust Center dialog box

Click to enable all macros

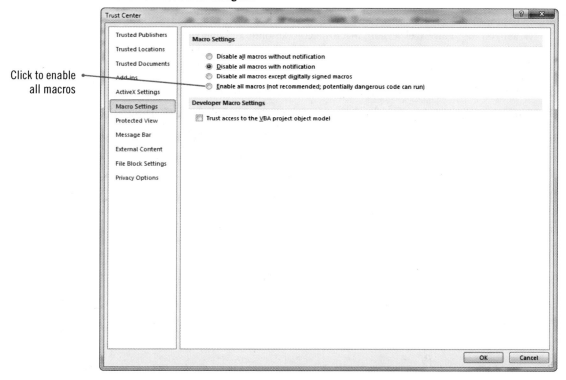

Disabling macros

To prevent viruses from running on your computer, you should disable all macros when you are not working with them. To disable macros, click the Developer tab, then click the Macro Security button in the Code group. Clicking any of the first three options disables macros. The first option disables all macros without notifying you. The second option notifies you when macros are disabled, and the third option allows only digitally signed macros to run.

Recording a Macro

The easiest way to create a macro is to record it using the Excel Macro Recorder. You turn the Macro Recorder on, name the macro, enter the keystrokes and select the commands you want the macro to perform, then stop the recorder. As you record the macro, Excel automatically translates each action into program code that you can later view and modify. You can take as long as you want to record the macro; a recorded macro contains only your actions, not the amount of time you took to record it. ▰▰▰ Kate wants you to create a macro that enters a division "stamp" in cell A1 of the active worksheet. You create this macro by recording your actions.

STEPS

1. **Click the Record Macro button 🖾 on the left side of the status bar**

   The Record Macro dialog box opens, as shown in Figure I-4. The default name Macro1 is selected. You can either assign this name or enter a new name. This dialog box also lets you assign a shortcut key for running the macro and assign a storage location for the macro.

2. **Type DivStamp in the Macro name text box**

3. **If the Store macro in list box does not display "This Workbook", click the list arrow and select This Workbook**

4. **Type your name in the Description text box, then click OK**

   The dialog box closes, and the Record Macro button on the status bar is replaced with a Stop Recording button. Take your time performing the steps below. Excel records every keystroke, menu selection, and mouse action that you make.

5. **Press [Ctrl][Home]**

   When you begin an Excel session, macros record absolute cell references. By beginning the recording with a command to move to cell A1, you ensure that the macro includes the instruction to select cell A1 as the first step, in cases where A1 is not already selected.

6. **Type Quest Sales in cell A1, then click the Enter button ✔ on the Formula Bar**

7. **Click the Home tab, click the Format button in the Cells group, then click Format Cells**

8. **Click the Font tab, in the Font style list box click Bold, click the Underline list arrow and click Single, click the Color list arrow and click the Red, Accent 2 Theme color (first row, sixth color from the left), then compare your dialog box to Figure I-5**

9. **Click OK, click the Stop Recording button ▣ on the left side of the status bar, click cell D1 to deselect cell A1, then save the workbook**

   Figure I-6 shows the result of recording the macro.

FIGURE I-4: **Record Macro dialog box**

Type macro name here

Type your name and description of macro here

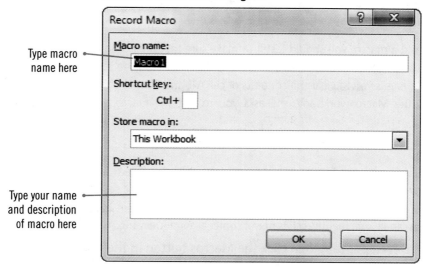

FIGURE I-5: **Font tab of the Format Cells dialog box**

Macro will apply these formatting attributes to the text

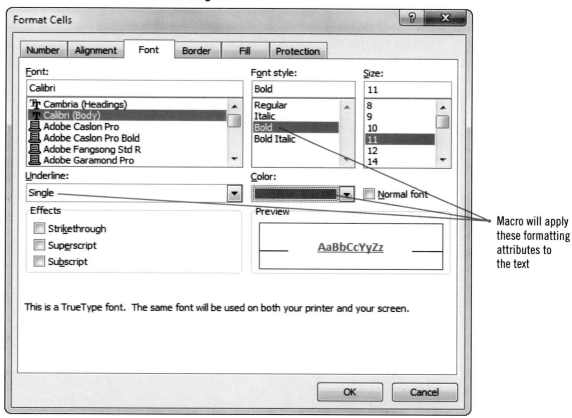

FIGURE I-6: **Sales Division stamp**

	A	B	C
1	Quest Sales		
2			
3			

Running a Macro

Once you record a macro, you should test it to make sure that the actions it performs are correct. To test a macro, you **run** (play) it. You can run a macro using the Macros button in the Code group of the Developer tab. ▰▰▰▰ Kate asks you to clear the contents of cell A1, and then test the DivStamp macro. After you run the macro in the Macro workbook, she asks you to test the macro once more from a newly opened workbook.

STEPS

1. **Click cell A1, click the Home tab if necessary, click the Clear button 🗑️ in the Editing group, click Clear All, then click any other cell to deselect cell A1**

    When you delete only the contents of a cell, any formatting still remains in the cell. By using the Clear All option you can be sure that the cell is free of contents and formatting.

2. **Click the Developer tab, then click the Macros button in the Code group**

    The Macro dialog box, shown in Figure I-7, lists all the macros contained in the open workbooks. If other people have used your computer, other macros may be listed.

3. **Make sure DivStamp is selected, as you watch cell A1 click Run, then deselect cell A1**

    The macro quickly plays back the steps you recorded in the previous lesson. When the macro is finished, your screen should look like Figure I-8. As long as the workbook containing the macro remains open, you can run the macro in any open workbook.

4. **Click the File tab, click New, then in the Blank Workbook area click Create**

    Because the EX I-Macro Workbook.xlsm is still open, you can use its macros.

5. **Deselect cell A1, click the Macros button in the Code group, make sure 'EX I-Macro Workbook.xlsm'!DivStamp is selected, click Run, then deselect cell A1**

    When multiple workbooks are open, the macro name in the Macro dialog box includes the workbook name between single quotation marks, followed by an exclamation point, indicating that the macro is outside the active workbook. Because you only used this workbook to test the macro, you don't need to save it.

6. **Close Book2.xlsx without saving changes**

    The EX I-Macro Workbook.xlsm workbook remains open.

Automating Worksheet Tasks

FIGURE I-7: Macro dialog box

Lists macros stored in open workbooks

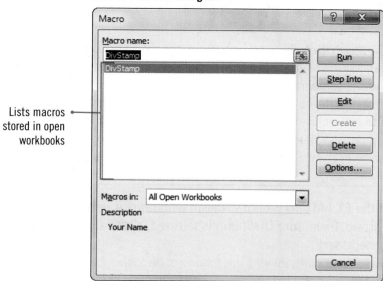

FIGURE I-8: Result of running DivStamp macro

Formatted text inserted into cell A1

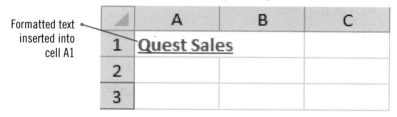

Running a macro automatically

You can create a macro that automatically performs certain tasks when the workbook in which it is saved is opened. This is useful for actions you want to do every time you open a workbook. For example, you may import data from an external data source into the workbook or format the worksheet data in a certain way. To create a macro that will automatically run when the workbook is opened, you need to name the macro Auto_Open and save it in the workbook.

Automating Worksheet Tasks

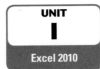
Editing a Macro

When you use the Macro Recorder to create a macro, the program instructions, called **program code**, are recorded automatically in the **Visual Basic for Applications (VBA)** programming language. Each macro is stored as a **module**, or program code container, attached to the workbook. After you record a macro, you might need to change it. If you have a lot of changes to make, it might be best to record the macro again. But if you need to make only minor adjustments, you can edit the macro code directly using the **Visual Basic Editor**, a program that lets you display and edit your macro code. Kate wants you to modify the DivStamp macro to change the point size of the department stamp to 14.

STEPS

1. **Make sure the EX I-Macro Workbook.xlsm workbook is open, click the Macros button in the Code group, make sure DivStamp is selected, click Edit, then maximize the Code window, if necessary**

   The Visual Basic Editor starts, showing three windows: the Project Explorer window, the Properties window, and the Code window, as shown in Figure I-9.

TROUBLE

If the Properties window does not appear in the lower-left portion of your screen, click the Properties Window button 🔲 in the Visual Basic Standard toolbar, then resize it as shown in the figure if necessary.

2. **Click Module 1 in the Project Explorer window if it's not already selected, then examine the steps in the macro, comparing your screen to Figure I-9**

   The name of the macro and your name appear at the top of the module window. Below this area, Excel has translated your keystrokes and commands into macro code. When you open and make selections in a dialog box during macro recording, Excel automatically stores all the dialog box settings in the macro code. For example, the line .FontStyle = "Bold" was generated when you clicked Bold in the Format Cells dialog box. You also see lines of code that you didn't generate directly while recording the DivStamp macro, for example, .Name = "Calibri".

3. **In the line .Size = 11, double-click 11 to select it, then type 14**

   Because Module1 is attached to the workbook and not stored as a separate file, any changes to the module are saved automatically when you save the workbook.

QUICK TIP

You can return to Excel without closing the module by clicking the View Microsoft Excel button 🔲 on the Visual Basic Editor toolbar.

4. **Review the code in the Code window**

5. **Click File on the menu bar, then click Close and Return to Microsoft Excel**

   You want to rerun the DivStamp macro to make sure the macro reflects the change you made using the Visual Basic Editor. You begin by clearing the division name from cell A1.

6. **Click cell A1, click the Home tab, click the Clear button ② in the Editing group, then click Clear All**

QUICK TIP

Another way to start the Visual Basic Editor is to click the Developer tab, then click the Visual Basic button in the Code group.

7. **Click any other cell to deselect cell A1, click the Developer tab, click the Macros button in the Code group, make sure DivStamp is selected, click Run, then deselect cell A1**

   The department stamp is now in 14-point type, as shown in Figure I-10.

8. **Save the workbook**

FIGURE I-9: Visual Basic Editor showing Module1

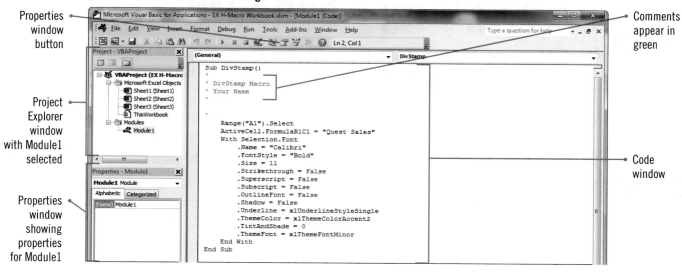

Properties window button

Project Explorer window with Module1 selected

Properties window showing properties for Module1

Comments appear in green

Code window

FIGURE I-10: Result of running edited DivStamp macro

Font size is enlarged to 14 point

	A	B	C
1	Quest Sales		
2			
3			
4			

Adding comments to Visual Basic code

With practice, you will be able to interpret the lines of macro code. Others who use your macro, however, might want to review the code to, for example, learn the function of a particular line. You can explain the code by adding comments to the macro. **Comments** are explanatory text added to the lines of code. When you enter a comment, you must type an apostrophe (') before the comment text. Otherwise, the program tries to interpret it as a command. On the screen, comments appear in green after you press [Enter], as shown in Figure I-9. You can also insert blank lines as comments in the macro code to make the code more readable. To do this, type an apostrophe, then press [Enter].

Assigning Keyboard Shortcuts to Macros

For macros that you run frequently, you can run them by using shortcut key combinations instead of the Macro dialog box. You can assign a shortcut key combination to any macro. Using shortcut keys saves you time by reducing the number of actions you need to take to run a macro. You assign shortcut key combinations in the Record Macro dialog box.  Kate also wants you to create a macro called Region to enter the company region into a worksheet. You assign a shortcut key combination to run the macro.

STEPS

1. **Click cell B2**

   You want to record the macro in cell B2, but you want the macro to enter the region of North America anywhere in a worksheet. Therefore, you do not begin the macro with an instruction to position the cell pointer, as you did in the DivStamp macro.

2. **Click the Record Macro button 🖳 on the status bar**

   The Record Macro dialog box opens. Notice the option Shortcut key: Ctrl+ followed by a blank box. You can type a letter (A–Z) in the Shortcut key text box to assign the key combination of [Ctrl] plus that letter to run the macro. Because some common Excel shortcuts use the [Ctrl][letter] combination, such as [Ctrl][C] for Copy, you decide to use the key combination [Ctrl][Shift] plus a letter to avoid overriding any of these shortcut key combinations.

3. **With the default macro name selected, type Region, click the Shortcut key text box, press and hold [Shift], type C, then in the Description box type your name**

   You have assigned the shortcut key combination [Ctrl][Shift][C] to the Region macro. After you create the macro, you will use this shortcut key combination to run it. Compare your screen with Figure I-11. You are ready to record the Region macro.

4. **Click OK to close the dialog box**

5. **Type North America in cell B2, click the Enter button ✓ on the formula bar, press [Ctrl][I] to italicize the text, click the Stop Recording button 🔳 on the status bar, then deselect cell B2**

   North America appears in italics in cell B2. You are ready to run the macro in cell A5 using the shortcut key combination.

6. **Click cell A5, press and hold [Ctrl][Shift], type C, then deselect the cell**

   The region appears in cell A5, as shown in Figure I-12. The macro played back in the selected cell (A5) instead of the cell where it was recorded (B2) because you did not begin recording the macro by clicking cell B2.

FIGURE I-11: Record Macro dialog box with shortcut key assigned

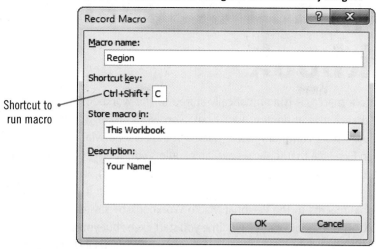

Shortcut to run macro

FIGURE I-12: Result of running the CompanyName macro

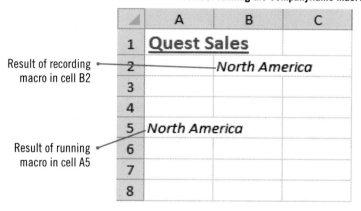

Result of recording macro in cell B2

Result of running macro in cell A5

Using relative referencing when creating a macro

By default, Excel records absolute cell references in macros. You can record a macro's actions based on the relative position of the active cell by clicking the Use Relative References button in the Code group prior to recording the action. For example, when you create a macro using the default setting of absolute referencing, bolding the range A1:D1 will always bold that range when the macro is run. However, if you click the Use Relative References button when recording the macro before bolding the range, then running the macro will not necessarily result in bolding the range A1:D1. The range that will be

bolded will depend on the location of the active cell when the macro is run. If the active cell is A4, then the range A4:D4 will be bolded. Selecting the Use Relative References button highlights the button name, indicating it is active, as shown in Figure I-13. The button remains active until you click it again to deselect it. This is called a **toggle**, meaning that it acts like an off/on switch: it retains the relative reference setting until you click it again to turn it off or you exit Excel.

FIGURE I-13: Relative Reference button selected

Use Relative References button selected

Using the Personal Macro Workbook

When you create a macro, it is automatically stored in the workbook in which you created it. But if you wanted to use that macro in another workbook, you would have to copy the macro to that workbook. Instead, it's easier to store commonly used macros in the Personal Macro Workbook. The **Personal Macro Workbook** is an Excel file that is always available, unless you specify otherwise, and gives you access to all the macros it contains, regardless of which workbooks are open. The Personal Macro Workbook file is automatically created the first time you choose to store a macro in it, and is named PERSONAL.XLSB. You can add additional macros to the Personal Macro Workbook by saving them in the workbook. By default, the PERSONAL.XLSB workbook opens each time you start Excel, but you don't see it because Excel designates it as a hidden file. Kate often likes to print her worksheets in landscape orientation with 1" left, right, top, and bottom margins. She wants you to create a macro that automatically formats a worksheet for printing this way. Because she wants to use this macro in future workbooks, she asks you to store the macro in the Personal Macro Workbook.

STEPS

1. **Click the Record Macro button 🖳 on the status bar**
   The Record Macro dialog box opens.

2. **Type FormatPrint in the Macro name text box, click the Shortcut key text box, press and hold [Shift], type F, then click the Store macro in list arrow**
   You have named the macro FormatPrint and assigned it the shortcut combination [Ctrl][Shift][F]. This Workbook storage option is selected by default, indicating that Excel automatically stores macros in the active workbook, as shown in Figure I-14. You can also choose to store the macro in a new workbook or in the Personal Macro Workbook.

TROUBLE
If a dialog box appears saying that a macro is already assigned to this shortcut combination, choose another letter for a keyboard shortcut. If a dialog box appears with the message that a macro named FormatPrint already exists, click Yes to replace it.

3. **Click Personal Macro Workbook, in the Description text box enter your name, then click OK**
   The recorder is on, and you are ready to record the macro keystrokes.

4. **Click the Page Layout tab, click the Orientation button in the Page Setup group, click Landscape, click the Margins button in the Page Setup group, click Custom Margins, then enter 1 in the Top, Left, Bottom, and Right text boxes**
   Compare your margin settings to Figure I-15.

5. **Click OK, then click the Stop Recording button 🖳 on the status bar**
   You want to test the macro.

TROUBLE
You may have to wait a few moments for the macro to finish. If you are using a different letter for the shortcut key combination, type that letter instead of the letter F.

6. **Activate Sheet2, in cell A1 type Macro Test, press [Enter], press and hold [Ctrl][Shift], then type F**
   The FormatPrint macro plays back the sequence of commands.

7. **Preview Sheet2 and verify that the orientation is landscape and the margins are 1" on the left, right, top, and bottom**

8. **Click the Home tab, then save the workbook**

FIGURE I-14: **Record Macro dialog box showing macro storage options**

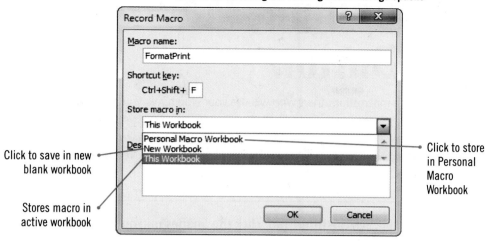

Click to save in new blank workbook

Stores macro in active workbook

Click to store in Personal Macro Workbook

FIGURE I-15: **Margin settings for the FormatPrint macro**

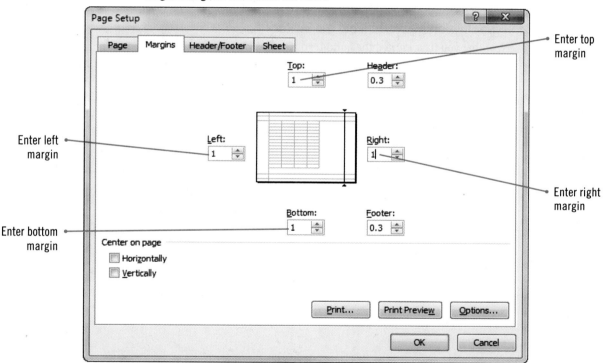

Enter top margin

Enter left margin

Enter right margin

Enter bottom margin

Excel 2010

Working with the Personal Macro Workbook

Once you use the Personal Macro Workbook, it opens automatically each time you start Excel so you can add macros to it. By default, the Personal Macro Workbook is hidden in Excel as a precautionary measure so you don't accidentally delete anything from it. If you need to delete a macro from the Personal Macro Workbook, click the View tab, click Unhide in the Window group, click PERSONAL.XLSB, then click OK. To hide the Personal Macro Workbook, make it the active workbook, click the View tab, then click Hide in the Window group. If you should see a message that Excel is unable to record to your Personal Macro Workbook, check to make sure it is enabled: Click the File tab, click Options, click Add-ins, click Disabled Items, then click Go. If your Personal Macro Workbook is listed in the Disabled items dialog box, click its name, then click Enable.

Assigning a Macro
to a Button

When you create macros for others who will use your workbook, you might want to make the macros more visible so they're easier to use. In addition to using shortcut keys, you can run a macro by assigning it to a button on your worksheet. Then when you click the button the macro will run. To make it easier for people in the sales division to run the DivStamp macro, Kate asks you to assign it to a button on the workbook. You begin by creating the button.

STEPS

1. **Click Sheet3, click the Insert tab, click the Shapes button in the Illustrations group, then click the first rectangle in the Rectangles group**
   The mouse pointer changes to a + symbol.

2. **Click at the top-left corner of cell A8, and drag the pointer to the lower-right corner of cell B9**
   Compare your screen to Figure I-16.

3. **Type Division Macro to label the button**
   Now that you have created the button, you are ready to assign the macro to it.

4. **Right-click the new button, then on the shortcut menu click Assign Macro**
   The Assign Macro dialog box opens.

5. **Click DivStamp under "Macro name", then click OK**
   You have assigned the DivStamp macro to the button.

6. **Click any cell to deselect the button, then click the button**
   The DivStamp macro plays, and the text Quest Sales appears in cell A1, as shown in Figure I-17.

7. **Save the workbook, preview Sheet3, close the workbook, then exit Excel, clicking No when asked to save changes to the Personal Macro Workbook**

8. **Submit the workbook to your instructor**

FIGURE I-16: **Button shape**

Rectangle shape will
become button

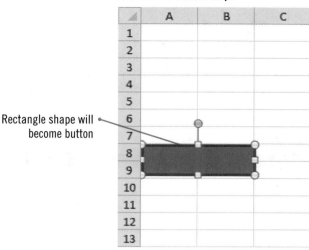

FIGURE I-17: **Sheet3 with the Sales Division text**

Result of running macro
using the button

Quest Sales

Division Macro

Formatting a macro button

You can format macro buttons using 3-D effects, clip art, photographs, fills, and shadows. To format a button, right-click it and select Format Shape from the shortcut menu. In the Format Shape dialog box you can select from many features such as Fill, Line Color, Line Style, Shadow, Reflection, Glow and Soft Edges, 3-D Format, 3-D Rotation, Picture Color, and Text Box. To add an image to the button, click Fill, then click the Picture or texture fill option button. To insert a picture from a file, click File, select a picture, then click Insert. To insert a clip art picture, click Clip Art, select a picture, then

click OK. You may need to resize your button to fully display a picture. You may also want to move the text on the button if it overlaps the image. Figure I-18 shows a button formatted with clip art.

FIGURE I-18: **Button formatted with clip art**

Format

Automating Worksheet Tasks

Practice

Concepts Review

For current SAM information, including versions and content details, visit SAM Central (http://www.cengage.com/samcentral). If you have a SAM user profile, you may have access to hands-on instruction, practice, and assessment of the skills covered in this unit. Since various versions of SAM are supported throughout the life of this text, check with your instructor for the correct instructions and URL/Web site for accessing assignments.

FIGURE I-19

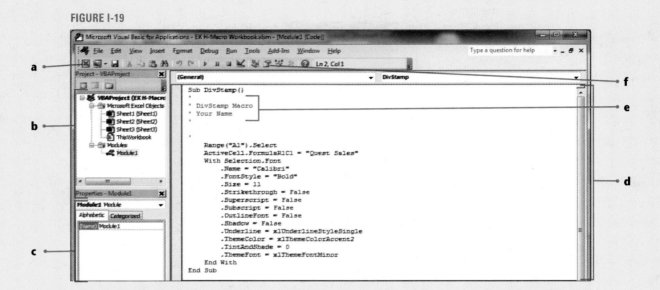

1. Which element do you click to return to Excel without closing the module?
2. Which element points to comments?
3. Which element points to the Properties Window button?
4. Which element points to the Code window?
5. Which element points to the Properties window?
6. Which element points to the Project Explorer window?

Match each term or button with the statement that best describes it.

7. **Virus**
8. **Macro**
9. **Personal Macro Workbook**
10. **Comments**
11. **Visual Basic Editor**

a. Set of instructions that performs a task in a specified order
b. Statements that appear in green explaining the macro
c. Destructive software that can damage computer files
d. Used to make changes to macro code
e. Used to store frequently used macros

Select the best answer from the list of choices.

12. **Which of the following is the best candidate for a macro?**
    a. Nonsequential tasks
    b. Often-used sequences of commands or actions
    c. Seldom-used commands or tasks
    d. One-button or one-keystroke commands
13. **You can open the Visual Basic Editor by clicking the _____ button in the Macro dialog box.**
    a. Programs
    b. Edit
    c. Modules
    d. Visual Basic Editor
14. **A Macro named _____ will automatically run when the workbook it is saved in opens.**
    a. Auto_Open
    b. Default
    c. Macro1
    d. Open_Macro

15. **Which of the following is *not* true about editing a macro?**
    a. You edit macros using the Visual Basic Editor.
    b. You can type changes directly in the existing program code.
    c. A macro cannot be edited and must be recorded again.
    d. You can make more than one editing change in a macro.

16. **Why is it important to plan a macro?**
    a. Planning helps prevent careless errors from being introduced into the macro.
    b. Macros can't be deleted.
    c. It is impossible to edit a macro.
    d. Macros won't be stored if they contain errors.

17. **Macros are recorded with relative references:**
    a. In all cases.
    b. Only if the Use Relative References button is selected.
    c. By default.
    d. Only if the Use Absolute References button is not selected.

18. **You can run macros:**
    a. From the Macro dialog box.
    b. From shortcut key combinations.
    c. From a button on the worksheet.
    d. Using all of the above.

19. **Macro security settings can be changed using the _____ tab.**
    a. Developer
    b. Home
    c. Security
    d. Review

Skills Review

1. **Plan and enable a macro.**
    a. You need to plan a macro that enters and formats your name and e-mail address in a worksheet.
    b. Write out the steps the macro will perform.
    c. Write out how the macro could be used in a workbook.
    d. Start Excel, open a new workbook, then save it as a Macro-Enabled workbook named **EX I-Macros** in the drive and folder where you store your Data Files. (*Hint*: The file will have the file extension .xlsm.)
    e. Use the Excel Options feature to display the Developer tab if it is not showing in the Ribbon.
    f. Using the Trust Center dialog box, enable all macros.

2. **Record a macro.**
    a. You want to record a macro that enters and formats your name and e-mail address in the range A1:A2 in a worksheet using the steps below.
    b. Name the macro **MyEmail**, store it in the current workbook, and make sure your name appears as the person who recorded the macro.
    c. Record the macro, entering your name in cell A1 and your e-mail address in cell A2. (*Hint*: You need to press [Ctrl][Home] first to ensure cell A1 will be selected when the macro runs.)
    d. Resize column A to fit the information entirely in that column.
    e. Add an outside border around the range A1:A2 and format the font using red from the Standard Colors.
    f. Add bold formatting to the text in the range A1:A2.
    g. Stop the recorder and save the workbook.

3. **Run a macro.**
    a. Clear cell entries and formats in the range affected by the macro, then resize the width of column A to 8.43.
    b. Run the MyEmail macro to place your name and e-mail information in the range A1:A2.
    c. On the worksheet, clear all the cell entries and formats generated by running the MyEmail macro. Resize the width of column A to 8.43.
    d. Save the workbook.

Skills Review (continued)

4. Edit a macro.

   a. Open the MyEmail macro in the Visual Basic Editor.

   b. Change the line of code above the last line from Selection.Font. Bold = True to Selection.Font.Bold = False.

   c. Use the Close and Return to Microsoft Excel option on the File menu to return to Excel.

   d. Test the macro on Sheet1, and compare your worksheet to Figure I-20 verifying that the text is not bold.

   e. Save the workbook.

FIGURE I-20

	A	B
1	Your Name	
2	yourname@yourschool.edu	
3		
4		
5		

5. Assign keyboard shortcuts to macros.

   a. You want to record a macro that enters your e-mail address in italics with a font color of green, without underlining, in the selected cell of a worksheet, using the steps below.

   b. Record the macro called **EmailStamp** in the current workbook, assigning your macro the shortcut key combination [Ctrl][Shift][E], storing it in the current workbook, with your name in the description.

   c. After you record the macro, clear the contents and formats from the cell containing your e-mail address that you used to record the macro.

   d. Use the shortcut key combination to run the EmailStamp macro in a cell other than the one in which it was recorded. Compare your macro result to Figure I-21. Your e-mail address may appear in a different cell.

   e. Save the workbook.

FIGURE I-21

	E	F	G
	yourname@yourschool.edu		

6. Use the Personal Macro Workbook.

   a. Using Sheet1, record a new macro called **FitToLand** and store it in the Personal Macro Workbook with your name in the Description text box. If you already have a macro named FitToLand replace that macro. The macro should set the print orientation to landscape.

   b. After you record the macro, display Sheet2, and enter **Test data for FitToLand macro** in cell A1.

   c. Preview Sheet2 to verify that the orientation is set to portrait.

   d. Run the FitToLand macro. (You may have to wait a few moments.)

   e. Add your name to the Sheet2 footer, then preview Sheet2 and verify that it is now in Landscape orientation.

   f. Save the workbook.

7. Assign a macro to a button.

   a. Enter **Button Test** in cell A1 of Sheet3.

   b. Using the rectangle shape, draw a rectangle in the range A7:B8. Compare your worksheet to Figure I-22.

   c. Label the button with the text **Landscape**.

   d. Assign the macro PERSONAL.XLSB!FitToLand to the button.

   e. Verify that the orientation of Sheet3 is set to portrait.

   f. Run the FitToLand macro using the button.

   g. Preview the worksheet, and verify that it is in landscape view.

   h. Add your name to the Sheet3 footer, then save the workbook.

   i. Close the workbook, exit Excel without saving the FitToLand macro in the Personal Macro Workbook, then submit your workbook to your instructor.

FIGURE I-22

	A	B	C
1	Button Test		
2			
3			
4			
5			
6			
7		Landscape	
8			
9			

Independent Challenge 1

As a computer-support employee of Smith and Jones Consulting Group, you need to develop ways to help your fellow employees work more efficiently. Employees have asked for Excel macros that can do the following:

- Adjust the column widths to display all column data in a worksheet.
- Place the company name of Smith and Jones Consulting Group in the header of a worksheet.

Independent Challenge 1 (continued)

a. Plan and write the steps necessary for each macro.

b. Start Excel, open the Data File EX I-1.xlsx from the drive and folder where you store your Data Files, then save it as a macro-enabled workbook called **EX I-Consulting**.

c. Check your macro security on the Developer tab to be sure that macros are enabled.

d. Create a macro named **ColumnFit**, save it in the EX I-Consulting.xlsm workbook, assign the ColumnFit macro a shortcut key combination of [Ctrl][Shift][C], and add your name in the description area for the macro. Record the macro using the following instructions:

- Record the ColumnFit macro to adjust a worksheet's column widths to display all data. (*Hint*: Select the entire sheet, click the Home tab, click the Format button in the Cells group, select AutoFit Column Width, then click cell A1 to deselect the worksheet.)
- End the macro recording.

e. Format the widths of columns A through G to 8.43, then test the ColumnFit macro with the shortcut key combination [Ctrl][Shift][C].

f. Create a macro named **CompanyName**, and save it in the EX I-Consulting.xlsm workbook. Assign the macro a shortcut key combination of [Ctrl][Shift][D], and add your name in the description area for the macro.

g. Record the CompanyName macro. The macro should place the company name of Smith and Jones Consulting Group in the center section of the worksheet header.

FIGURE I-23

h. Enter **CompanyName test data** in cell A1 of Sheet2, and test the CompanyName macro using the shortcut key combination [Ctrl][Shift][D]. Preview Sheet2 to view the header.

i. Edit the CompanyName macro in the Visual Basic Editor to change the company name from Smith and Jones Consulting Group to **Smith Consulting Group**. Close the Visual Basic Editor and return to Excel.

j. Add a rectangle button to the Sheet3 in the range A6:B7. Label the button with the text **Company Name**.

k. Assign the CompanyName macro to the button.

l. Enter **New CompanyName Test** in cell A1. Use the button to run the CompanyName macro. Preview the worksheet checking the header to be sure it is displaying the new company name. Compare your screen to Figure I-23.

Advanced Challenge Exercise

- Format the button using the fill color of your choice. (*Hint*: Right-click the button and select Format Shape from the shortcut menu.)
- Format the button to add the 3-D effect of your choice.
- Add a shadow in the color of your choice to the button.

m. Enter your name in the footers of all three worksheets. Save the workbook, close the workbook, then submit the workbook to your instructor and exit Excel.

Independent Challenge 2

You are an assistant to the VP of Sales at American Beverage Company, a distributor of juices, water, and soda to supermarkets. As part of your work, you create spreadsheets with sales projections for different regions of the company. You frequently have to change the print settings so that workbooks print in landscape orientation with custom margins of 1" on the top and bottom. You also add a header with the company name on every worksheet. You have decided that it's time to create a macro to streamline this process.

a. Plan and write the steps necessary to create the macro.

b. Check your macro security settings to confirm that macros are enabled.

Independent Challenge 2 (continued)

c. Start Excel, create a new workbook, then save it as a macro-enabled file named **EX I-Sales Macro** in the drive and folder where you store your Data Files.

d. Create a macro that changes the page orientation to landscape, adds custom margins of 1" on the top and bottom of the page, adds a header of **American Beverage Company** in the center section formatted as Bold with a font size of 14 points. Name the macro **Format**, add your name in the description, assign it the shortcut key combination [Ctrl][Shift][W], and store it in the current workbook.

e. Go to Sheet2 and enter the text **Format Test** in cell A1. Test the macro using the shortcut key combination of [Ctrl][Shift][W]. Preview Sheet2 to check the page orientation, margins, and the header.

f. Enter the text **Format Test** in cell A1 of Sheet3, add a rectangular button with the text Format Worksheet to run the Format macro, then test the macro using the button.

g. Preview the Visual Basic code for the macro.

h. Save the workbook, close the workbook, exit Excel, then submit the workbook to your instructor.

Independent Challenge 3

You are the eastern region sales manager of Bio Pharma, a biotech consulting firm. You manage the California operations and frequently create workbooks with data from the office locations. It's tedious to change the tab names and colors every time you open a new workbook, so you decide to create a macro that will add the office locations and colors to your three default worksheet tabs, as shown in Figure I-24.

FIGURE I-24

a. Plan and write the steps to create the macro described above.

b. Start Excel and open a new workbook.

c. Create the macro using the plan you created in Step a, name it **SheetFormat**, assign it the shortcut key combination [Ctrl][Shift][Z], store it in the Personal Macro Workbook, and add your name in the description area.

d. After recording the macro, close the workbook without saving it.

e. Open a new workbook, then save it as a macro-enabled workbook named **EX I-Office Test** in the drive and folder where you store your Data Files. Use the shortcut key combination of [Ctrl][Shift][Z] to test the macro in the new workbook.

f. Unhide the PERSONAL.XLSB workbook. (*Hint*: Click the View tab, click the Unhide button in the Window group, then click PERSONAL.XLSB.)

g. Edit the SheetFormat macro using Figure I-25 as a guide, changing the San Diego sheet name to Berkeley. (*Hint*: There are three instances of San Diego that need to be changed.)

FIGURE I-25

```
Sub SheetFormat()
'
' SheetFormat Macro
' Your Name
'
' Keyboard Shortcut: Ctrl+Shift+Z
'
    Sheets("Sheet1").Select
    Sheets("Sheet1").Name = "San Francisco"
    Sheets("San Francisco").Select
    With ActiveWorkbook.Sheets("San Francisco").Tab
        .Color = 12611584
        .TintAndShade = 0
    End With
    Sheets("Sheet2").Select
    Sheets("Sheet2").Name = "Los Angeles"
    Sheets("Los Angeles").Select
    With ActiveWorkbook.Sheets("Los Angeles").Tab
        .Color = 65535
        .TintAndShade = 0
    End With
    Sheets("Sheet3").Select
    Sheets("Sheet3").Name = "Berkeley"
    Sheets("Berkeley").Select
    With ActiveWorkbook.Sheets("Berkeley").Tab
        .Color = 10498160
        .TintAndShade = 0
    End With
End Sub
```

Independent Challenge 3 (continued)

h. Open a new workbook, then save it as a macro-enabled workbook named **EX I-Office Test New** in the drive and folder where you store your Data Files. Test the edited macro using the shortcut key combination of [Ctrl][Shift][Z].

i. Add a new sheet in the workbook, and name it **Code**. Copy the SheetFormat macro code from the Personal Macro Workbook, and paste it in the Code sheet beginning in cell A1. Save the workbook, close the workbook, then submit the EX I-Office Test New workbook to your instructor.

j. Hide the PERSONAL.XLSB workbook. (*Hint*: With the PERSONAL.XLSB workbook active, click the View tab, then click the Hide button in the Window group.)

k. Close the workbook, click No to save the PERSONAL.XLSB changes, then exit Excel.

Real Life Independent Challenge

Excel can be a helpful tool in keeping track of hours worked at a job or on a project. A macro can speed up the repetitive process of entering a formula to total your hours each week.

a. Start Excel, create a new workbook, then save it as **EX I-Hours** in the drive and folder where you store your Data Files. Be sure to save it as a macro-enabled file.

b. If necessary, change your security settings to enable macros.

c. Use Table I-2 as a guide in entering labels and hours into a worksheet tracking your work or project effort.

d. Create a macro named **TotalHours** in the cell adjacent to the Total label that can be activated by the [Ctrl][Shift][T] key combination. Save the macro in the EX I-Hours workbook, and add your name in the description area.

e. The TotalHours macro should do the following:
- Total the hours for the week.
- Boldface the Total amount and the Total label to its left.

f. Test the macro using the key combination [Ctrl][Shift][T].

g. Add a button to the range A11:B12 with the label **Total**.

h. Assign the TotalHours macro to the Total button.

i. Test the macro using the button.

j. Enter your name in the footer, then save your workbook.

k. Open the macro in the Visual Basic Editor, and preview the macro code.

TABLE I-2

Monday	5
Tuesday	8
Wednesday	5
Thursday	8
Friday	9
Saturday	5
Sunday	0
Total	

Advanced Challenge Exercise

- Edit the macro code to add a comment with a description of your work or project.
- Add another comment with your e-mail address.
- Above the keyboard comment enter the comment **Macro can be run using the Total button**.

l. Return to Excel, save and close the workbook, exit Excel, then submit the workbook to your instructor.

Visual Workshop

Start Excel, open the Data File EX I-2.xlsx from the drive and folder where you store your Data Files, then save it as a macro-enabled workbook called **EX I-Payroll**. Create a macro with the name **TotalHours** in the EX I-Payroll workbook that does the following:

- Totals the weekly hours for each employee by totaling the hours for the first employee and copying that formula for the other employees
- Adds a row at the top of the worksheet and inserts a label of **Hours** in a font size of 14 point, centered across all columns
- Adds your name in the worksheet footer

Compare your macro results to Figure I-26. Test the macro, edit the macro code as necessary, then save the workbook. Submit the workbook to your instructor.

FIGURE I-26

	A	B	C	D	E	F	G	H	I	J
1	Hours									
2		Monday	Tuesday	Wednesday	Thursday	Friday	Saturday	Sunday	Total	
3	Mary Jones	8	2	8	8	2	2	0	30	
4	Jack McKay	4	8	7	8	8	5	1	41	
5	Keith Drudge	5	4	6	5	4	4	0	28	
6	Sean Lavin	7	6	5	6	6	2	2	34	
7	Kerry Baker	9	6	8	7	6	6	0	42	
8	Justin Regan	6	3	6	3	3	7	0	28	
9	Carol Hodge	7	5	2	6	8	5	3	36	
10	Rick Thomas	2	7	8	6	7	2	0	32	
11	Kris Young	0	4	4	4	4	4	1	21	
12	Lisa Russell	7	8	2	8	8	1	0	34	
13										

Enhancing Charts

Although Excel offers a variety of eye-catching chart types, you can customize your charts for even greater impact. In this unit, you learn to enhance your charts by manipulating chart data, formatting axes, and rotating the chart. You clarify your data display by adding a data table, special text effects, and a picture. You also show trends in data using sparklines and trendlines. As you enhance your charts, keep in mind that too much customization can be distracting. Your goal in enhancing charts should be to communicate your data more clearly and accurately.  Quest's vice president of sales, Kate Morgan, has requested charts comparing sales in the Quest regions over the first two quarters. You will produce these charts and enhance them to improve their appearance and make the worksheet data more accessible.

OBJECTIVES

Customize a data series

Change a data source and add data labels

Format the axes of a chart

Add a data table to a chart

Rotate a chart

Enhance a chart with WordArt and pictures

Add sparklines to a worksheet

Identify data trends

Customizing a Data Series

A **data series** is the sequence of values that Excel uses to **plot**, or create, a chart. You can format the data series in a chart to make the chart more attractive and easier to read. As with other Excel elements, you can change the data series borders, patterns, or colors. ▨▨▨▨ Kate wants you to create a chart showing the sales for each region in January and February. You begin by creating a column chart, which you will customize to make it easier to compare the sales for each region.

STEPS

1. **Start Excel, open the file EX J-1.xlsx from the drive and folder where you store your Data Files, then save it as EX J-Region Sales**

   To begin, Kate wants to see how each region performed over January and February. The first step is to select the data you want to appear in the chart. In this case, you want the row labels in cells A3:A6 and the data for January and February in cells B2:C6, including the column labels.

2. **Select the range A2:C6**

TROUBLE

If your chart over-laps the worksheet data, you can drag its edge to move it below row 6.

3. **Click the Insert tab, click the Column button in the Charts group, then click the 3-D Clustered Column chart (the first chart in the 3-D Column group)**

   The column chart compares the January and February sales for each branch, as shown in Figure J-1. You decide to display the data so that it is easier to compare the monthly sales for each branch.

4. **Click the Switch Row/Column button in the Data group**

   The legend now contains the region data, and the horizontal axis groups the bars by month. Kate can now easily compare the branch sales for each month. The graph will be easier to read if the U.S. data series is plotted in a color that is easier to distinguish.

QUICK TIP

You can also format a data series by click-ing the data series on the chart, clicking the Chart Tools Layout tab, then clicking the Format Selection button in the Current Selec-tion group.

5. **Right-click the Jan U.S. data series bar (the far-left bar on the graph), click Format Data Series from the shortcut menu, click Fill in the left pane of the Format Data Series dialog box, click the Solid fill option button, click the Color list arrow, select Purple, Accent 6 in the Theme Colors group, then click Close**

6. **Point to the edge of the chart, then drag the chart to place its upper-left corner in cell A8**

   You can resize a chart by dragging its corner sizing handles. When a chart is resized this way, all of the elements are resized to maintain its appearance.

7. **Drag the chart's lower-right sizing handle to fit the chart in the range A8:H23, then compare your chart to Figure J-2**

8. **Save the workbook**

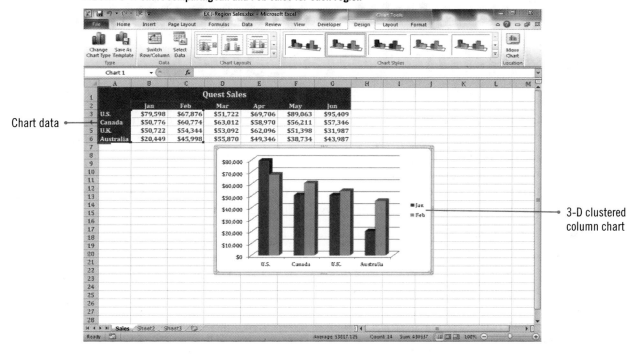

Chart data

3-D clustered column chart

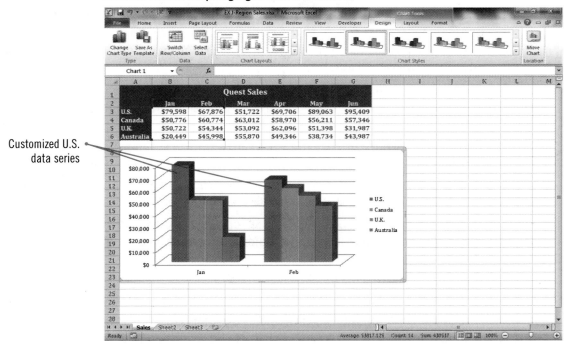

Customized U.S. data series

Adding width and depth to data series

You can change the gap depth and the gap width in 3-D bar or column charts by right-clicking one of the data series of the chart then clicking Format Data Series from the shortcut menu. With Series Options selected in the left pane of the Format Data Series dialog box, you can move the Gap Depth and Gap Width sliders from No

Gap (or 0%) to Large Gap (or 500%). Increasing the gap width adds space between each set of data on the chart by increasing the width of the chart's data series. Increasing the gap depth adds depth to all categories of data.

Changing a Data Source and Adding Data Labels

As you update your workbooks with new data, you may also need to add data series to (or delete them from) a chart. Excel makes it easy to revise a chart's data source and to rearrange chart data. To communicate chart data more clearly, you can add descriptive text, called a **data label**, which appears above a data marker in a chart.  Kate wants you to create a chart showing the branch sales for the first quarter. You need to add the March data to your chart so that it reflects the first-quarter sales. Kate asks you to add data labels to clarify the charted data and to make the chart more attractive. It will be easier to compare the branch sales in a 3-D column chart that is not clustered.

STEPS

1. **Click the Chart Tools Design tab if necessary, click the Change Chart Type button in the Type group, in the Change Chart Type dialog box click 3-D Column (the last chart in the first row), then click OK**

    The chart bars are no longer clustered. You want to change the data view to compare branch sales for each month in the new chart type.

2. **Click the Switch Row/Column button in the Data group**

    The labels that were in the legend are now on the horizontal axis. You want to add the March data to the chart.

> **QUICK TIP**
>
> You can also add data to a chart by clicking the Select Data button in the Data group of the Chart Tools Design tab, selecting the new range of cells in the Select Data Source dialog box, then click OK.

3. **Click the edge of the chart to select it if necessary, then drag the lower-right corner of the data border in worksheet cell C6 to the right to include the data in column D**

    The March data series appears on the chart, as shown in Figure J-3. You want to make the columns more attractive and decide to use one of the preformatted chart styles.

4. **Click the More button ⊡ in the Chart Styles group, then click Style 26**

    The January data bars are now a maroon color, and all of the data bars have shadows. You want to add data labels to your chart indicating the exact amount of sales each bar represents.

> **QUICK TIP**
>
> You can also add data labels by clicking the Chart Tools Design tab, clicking the More button in the Chart Layouts group, and selecting a chart layout with data labels.

5. **Click the Chart Tools Layout tab, click the Data Labels button in the Labels group, click More Data Label Options, then drag the dialog box to the right of the chart**

    Data labels on the chart show the exact value of each data point above each bar. The data labels are hard to read against the dark shadows of the columns. You decide to add a white background fill to the labels.

6. **With the Jan data labels selected, click Fill in the Format Data Labels dialog box, click the Solid fill option button to select it, click the Color list arrow, then click White, Background1 (the first theme color)**

    The January data labels now have a white background.

7. **Click one of the Feb data labels on the chart, click Fill in the Format Data labels dialog box, click the Solid fill option button, click one of the Mar data labels on the chart, click Fill in the Format Data labels dialog box, click the Solid fill option button, then click Close**

    The data labels are still difficult to read because they are crowded together. You decide to resize the chart to add space between the columns.

8. **Drag the chart's lower-right sizing handle to fit the chart in the range A8:L30, then compare your chart to Figure J-4**

FIGURE J-3: **Chart with March data series added**

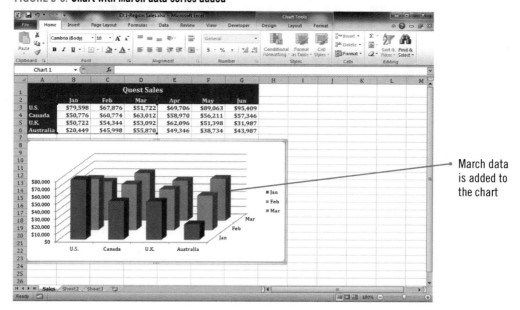

March data
is added to
the chart

FIGURE J-4: **Chart with data labels**

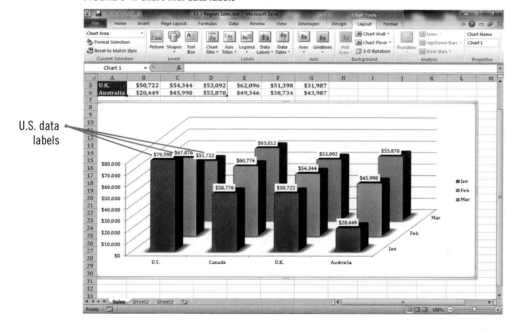

U.S. data
labels

Moving, removing, and formatting legends

To change the position of a legend or to remove it, click the Chart Tools Layout tab, click the Legend button in the Labels group, then select the desired legend position or select None to remove the legend. To format a legend's position, fill, border color and style, or shadows, click More Legend Options at the bottom of the Legend menu. You can add textured fills or pictures and customize the border and shadow characteristics. If you position the Format Legend dialog box next to the legend, you can use the Excel Live Preview feature to try out different effects, such as those shown in Figure J-5. To change a legend's font size, right-click the legend text, click Font on the shortcut menu, then adjust the font size in the Font dialog box. You can also drag a legend to any location.

FIGURE J-5: **Formatted legend**

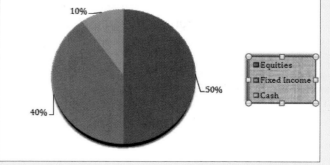

Formatting the Axes of a Chart

Excel plots and formats chart data and places the chart axes within the chart's **plot area**. Data values in two-dimensional charts are plotted on the vertical y-axis (often called the **value axis** because it usually shows value levels). Categories are plotted on the horizontal x-axis (often called the **category axis** because it usually shows data categories). Excel creates a scale for the value (*y*) axis based on the highest and lowest values in the series and places intervals along the scale. A three-dimensional (3-D) chart, like the one in Figure J-6, has a third axis displaying the chart's depth. You can override the Excel default formats for chart axes at any time by using the Format Axis dialog box.  Kate asks you to increase the maximum number on the value axis and change the axis number format. She would also like you to add axes titles to explain the plotted data.

STEPS

1. **Click the chart to select it if necessary, click the** Chart Tools Layout tab**, click the** Axes button **in the Axes group, point to** Primary Vertical Axis**, then click** More Primary Vertical Axis Options

   The Format Axis dialog box opens. The minimum, maximum, and unit Axis Options are set to Auto, and the default scale settings appear in the text boxes on the right. You can override any of these settings by clicking the Fixed option buttons and entering new values.

2. **With Axis Options selected in the list on the left, click the** Fixed option button **in the Maximum line, press [Tab], in the Fixed text box type** 90000**, then click** Close

   Now 90,000 appears as the maximum value on the value axis, and the chart bar heights adjust to reflect the new value. Next, you want the vertical axis values to appear without additional zeroes to make the chart data easier to read.

3. **Click the** Axes button **in the Axes group, point to** Primary Vertical Axis**, then click** Show Axis in Thousands

   The values are reduced to two digits and the word "Thousands" appears in a text box to the left of the values. You decide that vertical and horizontal axis titles would improve the clarity of the chart information.

4. **Click the** Axis Titles button **in the Labels group, point to** Primary Vertical Axis Title**, then click** Rotated Title

   A text box containing the text "Axis Title" appears on the vertical axis, next to "Thousands".

5. **Type** Sales**, then click outside the text box to deselect it**

   The word "Sales" appears in the Vertical axis label. You decide to label the horizontal axis.

6. **Click the** Axis Titles button **in the Labels group, point to** Primary Horizontal Axis Title**, click** Title Below Axis**, type** Regions**, then click outside the text box to deselect it**

7. **Drag the** Thousands text box **on the vertical axis lower in the Chart Area to match Figure J-7, then deselect it**

FIGURE J-6: **Chart elements in a 3-D chart**

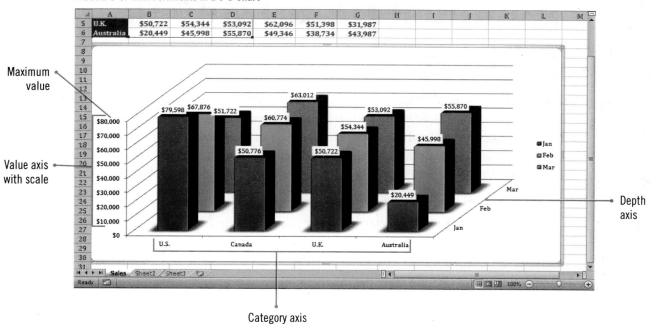

Maximum value

Value axis with scale

Category axis

Depth axis

FIGURE J-7: **Chart with formatted axes**

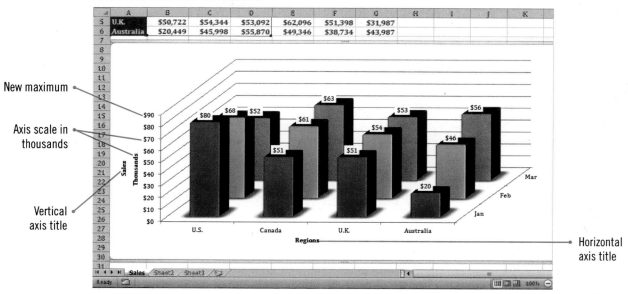

New maximum

Axis scale in thousands

Vertical axis title

Horizontal axis title

Adding a Data Table to a Chart

A **data table** is a grid containing the chart data, attached to the bottom of a chart. Data tables are useful because they display—directly on the chart itself—the data you used to generate a chart. It's good practice to add data tables to charts that are stored separately from worksheet data. You can display data tables in line, area, column, and bar charts, and print them automatically along with a chart.  Kate wants you to move the chart to its own worksheet and add a data table to emphasize the chart's first-quarter data.

STEPS

1. **Click the chart object to select it if necessary, click the Chart Tools Design tab, then click the Move Chart button in the Location group**

   The Move Chart dialog box opens. You want to place the chart on a new sheet named First Quarter.

2. **Click the New sheet option button, type First Quarter in the New sheet text box, then click OK**

QUICK TIP

You can also add a data table by clicking the Chart Tools Design tab, and selecting a chart with a data table from the Chart Layouts gallery.

3. **Click the Chart Tools Layout tab, click the Data Table button in the Labels group, then click Show Data Table with Legend Keys**

   A data table with the first-quarter data and a key to the legend appears at the bottom of the chart, as shown in Figure J-8. The data table would stand out more if it were formatted.

4. **Click the Data Table button in the Labels group, then click More Data Table Options**

   The Format Data Table dialog box opens.

QUICK TIP

To hide a data table, click the Data Table button in the Labels group, then click None.

5. **Click Border Color in the left pane, click the Solid line option button to select it, click the Color list arrow, click the Orange, Accent2 color in the Theme Colors section, click Close, then click the chart area to deselect the data table**

   The data table now has orange borders. The left side of the data table contains legend keys, showing which series each color represents, so you don't need the legend that appears on the right of the chart.

QUICK TIP

You can also remove a legend by clicking the Legend button in the Labels group of the Chart Tools Layout tab and clicking None.

6. **Click the legend to select it, then press [Delete]**

   Now the only legend for the chart is part of the data table, as shown in Figure J-9.

7. **Save the workbook**

FIGURE J-8: Chart with data table

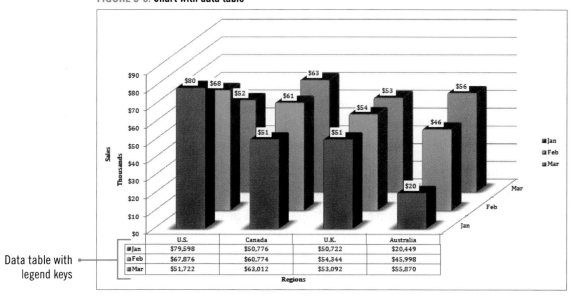

Data table with legend keys

FIGURE J-9: Chart with formatted data table

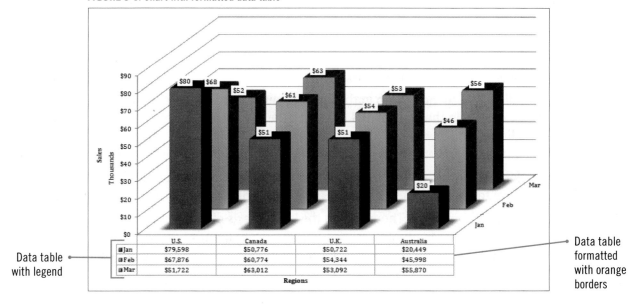

Data table with legend

Data table formatted with orange borders

Using the Modeless Format dialog box

Many of the buttons on the Chart Tools Layout tab have a More ...Options command at the bottom of the menu that appears when you click them. For example, clicking the Data Table button allows you to click More Data Table Options. The Format dialog box that opens when you click it allows you to format the selected data table. But while the dialog box is open, you can also click and format other elements. The Format dialog boxes are **modeless,** which means that when they are open, you can click on other chart elements and then change their formatting in the same dialog box, whose options adjust to reflect the selected element. You are not restricted to changing only one object—you are not in a single **mode** or limited set of possible choices. For example if the Format Data Table dialog box is open and you click a data label, the dialog box changes to Format Data Labels. If you click the legend, the dialog box becomes the Format Legend dialog box, allowing you to modify the legend characteristics.

Rotating a Chart

Three-dimensional (3-D) charts do not always display data in the most effective way. In many cases, one or more of a chart's data points can obscure the view of other data points, making the chart difficult to read. By rotating and/or changing the chart's depth, you can make the data easier to understand.  Kate wants you to rotate the chart and increase the depth. You will begin by hiding the data table so it doesn't overlap the view of the data.

STEPS

1. **Click the chart to select it if necessary, click the Chart Tools Layout tab, click the Data Table button in the Labels group, then click None**

2. **Click the 3-D Rotation button in the Background group, then if necessary click 3-D Rotation in the list on the left pane of the Format Chart Area dialog box**
   The 3-D rotation options are shown in Figure J-10.

3. **In the Chart Scale section, click the Right Angle Axes check box to deselect it, double-click the X: text box in the Rotation section, then enter 50**
   The X: Rotation setting rotates the chart to the left and right. You can also click the Left and Right buttons or the up and down arrows to rotate the chart.

QUICK TIP
You can also click the Up and Down buttons in the Rotation area of the dialog box to rotate the chart up and down.

4. **Double-click the Y: text box, then enter 30**
   The Y: Rotation setting rotates the chart up and down. You decide to change the depth of the columns.

5. **Double-click the Depth (% of base) text box in the Chart Scale section, then enter 200, then click Close**
   Deleting the data table removed the legend so you decide to add a legend to the chart. Also, the axes titles need to be adjusted for the new chart layout.

6. **Click the Legend button in the Labels group, click Show Legend at Bottom, right-click the text Sales in the vertical axis title, click the Font Size list arrow in the Mini toolbar, then click 18**
   The vertical axis label is now easier to read. You will format the horizontal axis similarly.

7. **Right-click the text Regions in the horizontal axis title, click the Font Size list arrow in the Mini toolbar, click 18, then drag the Regions title closer to the horizontal axis**

8. **Right-click the text Thousands in the vertical axis display units label, click the Font Size list arrow in the Mini toolbar, click 14, drag the Thousands title closer to the vertical axis, drag the Sales title to the left of the Thousands title, then compare your chart to Figure J-11.**
   The chart columns now appear deeper and less crowded, with labels positioned in the correct place, making the chart easier to read.

9. **Save the workbook**

Making 3-D charts easier to read

In addition to rotating a chart, there are other ways to view smaller data points that may be obscured by larger data markers in the front of a 3-D chart. To reverse the order in which the data series are charted, you can click the Axes button in the Axes group of the Chart Tools Layout tab, point to Depth Axis, click More Depth Axis Options, click the Series in reverse order check box in the Format Axis dialog box to select it, then click Close. Another way to see smaller data series in the back of a 3-D chart is to add transparency to the large data markers in the front of the chart. To do this, right-click the data series that you want to make transparent, click Format Data Series on the shortcut menu, click Fill in the Format Data Series dialog box, click either the Solid fill or Gradient fill option buttons, move the slider on the Transparency bar to a percentage that allows you to see the other data series on the chart, then click Close. If you have a picture on the chart's back wall, adding transparency to the series in front of it makes more of the picture visible.

FIGURE J-10: 3-D Rotation options

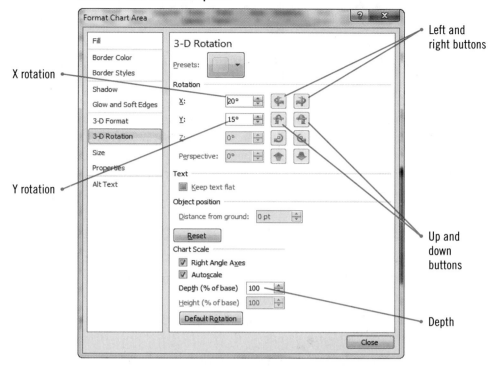

X rotation

Y rotation

Left and right buttons

Up and down buttons

Depth

FIGURE J-11: Chart with increased depth and rotation

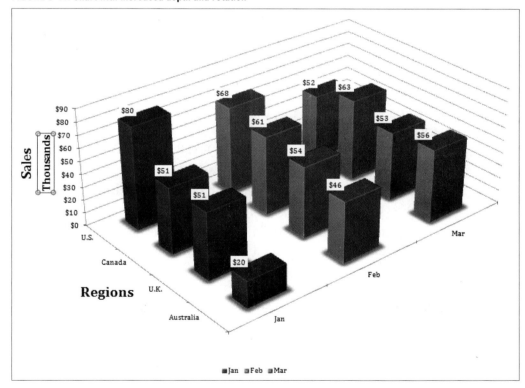

Charting data accurately

The purpose of a chart is to help viewers to interpret the worksheet data. When creating charts, you need to make sure that your chart accurately portrays your data. Charts can sometimes misrepresent data and thus mislead people. For example, you can change the y-axis units or its starting value to make charted sales values appear larger than they are. Even though you may have correctly labeled the sales values on the chart, the height of the data points will lead people viewing the chart to think the sales are higher than the labeled values. So use caution when you modify charts to make sure you accurately represent your data.

Enhancing a Chart with WordArt and Pictures

You can enhance your chart or worksheet titles using **WordArt**, which is preformatted text. Once you've added WordArt text, you can edit or format it by adding 3-D effects and shadows. WordArt text is a shape rather than text. This means that you cannot treat WordArt objects as if they were labels entered in a cell; that is, you cannot sort, use the spell checker, or use their cell references in formulas. You can further enhance your chart by adding a picture to one of the chart elements. Kate wants you to add a WordArt title to the first-quarter chart. She also wants you to add the Quest logo to the chart. You will begin by adding a title to the chart.

STEPS

QUICK TIP

To delete a chart title, right-click it, then select Delete from the shortcut menu. You can also select the chart title and press [Delete].

1. **Click the chart to select it if necessary, click the Chart Tools Layout tab, click the Chart Title button in the Labels group, then click Above Chart**

   A chart title text box appears above the chart.

2. **With the Chart Title text box selected, type First Quarter Sales, then click the Enter button ✓ on the Formula Bar**

3. **Click the Chart Tools Format tab, then click the More button ⊡ in the WordArt Styles group**

   The WordArt Gallery opens, as shown in Figure J-12. This is where you select the style for your text.

4. **Click Fill – White, Outline – Accent 1 (the fourth style in the first row), then click outside the chart title to deselect it**

   The title text becomes formatted with outlined letters. You decide the chart would look better if the gridlines were not visible.

5. **Click the Chart Tools Layout tab, click the Gridlines button in the Axes group, click Primary Horizontal Gridlines, then click None**

   Kate wants you to add the Quest logo to the back wall of the chart to identify the company data.

QUICK TIP

You can also enhance a chart by adding a picture to the data markers, chart area, plot area, legend, or chart floor.

6. **Click the chart to select it if necessary, click the Chart Tools Format tab, click the Chart Elements list arrow in the Current Selection group, then click Back Wall**

   The back wall of the chart is selected, as shown by the four small circles on its corners.

7. **Click the Format Selection button in the Current Selection group, click the Picture or texture fill option button to select it in the Format Wall dialog box, click File, navigate to the location where you store your Data Files, click the chartlogo.gif file, click Insert, then click Close**

8. **Click the Insert tab, click the Header & Footer button in the Text group, click the Custom Footer button, enter your name in the Center section, click OK, then click OK again**

   The Quest logo appears on the back wall of the chart. Compare your chart to Figure J-13.

Adding WordArt to a worksheet

You can use WordArt to add interest to the text on a worksheet. To insert WordArt, click the Insert tab, click the WordArt button in the Text group, choose a WordArt Style from the gallery, then replace the WordArt text "Your Text Here" with your text. You can use the Text Fill list arrow in the WordArt Styles group to add a solid, picture, gradient, or texture fill to your text. The Text Outline list arrow in the WordArt Styles group allows you to add color, weight, and dashes to the text outline. You can use the Text Effects button in the WordArt Styles group to add shadows, reflections, glows, bevels, 3-D rotations, and transformations to the WordArt text.

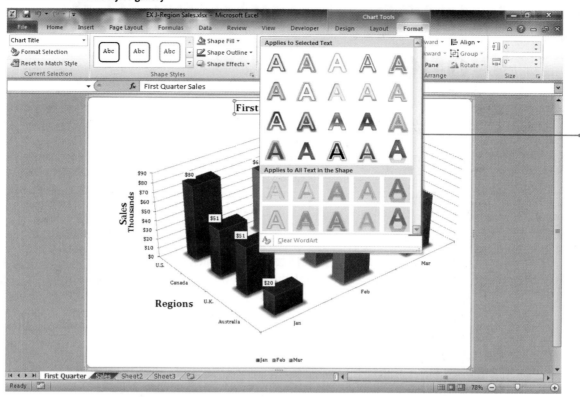

Select style from the gallery

Title formatted with WordArt

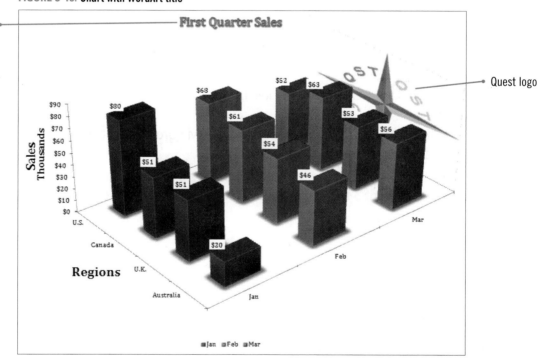

Quest logo

Rotating chart labels

You can rotate the category labels on a chart so that longer labels won't appear crowded. Select the Category Axis on the chart, click the Chart Tools Format tab, click the Format Selection button in the Current Selection group, click Alignment in the left pane of the dialog box, click the Text direction list arrow, then select the rotation option for the labels. Rotating labels works best in two-dimensional charts because labels on three-dimensional charts often overlap as they are moved. You can also select a custom angle for horizontally aligned axis labels on two-dimensional charts.

Excel 2010

Adding Sparklines to a Worksheet

You can enhance your worksheets by adding sparklines to the worksheet cells. **Sparklines** are miniature charts that show data trends in a worksheet range such as sales increases or decreases. Sparklines are also used to highlight maximum and minimum values in a range of data. Sparklines usually appear close to the data they represent. Any changes that you make to a worksheet are reflected in the sparklines that represent the data. After you add sparklines to a worksheet, you can change the sparkline and color. You can also format high and low data points in special colors. ▦▦▦ Kate wants you to add sparklines to the Sales worksheet to illustrate the sales trends for the first half of the year.

STEPS

1. **Click the Sales sheet, click cell H3 to select it, click the Insert tab if necessary, click Line in the Sparklines group, verify that the insertion point is in the Data Range text box, select the range B3:G3 on the worksheet, then click OK**

    A sparkline showing the sales trend for the U.S. appears in cell H3. You can copy the sparkline to cells representing other regions.

2. **With cell H3 selected, drag the fill handle to fill the range H4:H6**

    The sparklines for all four regions are shown in Figure J-14. You decide to change the sparklines to columns.

3. **Click cell H3, then click the Column button in the Type group of the Sparkline Tools Design tab**

    All of the sparklines in column H appear as columns. The column heights represent the values of the data in the adjacent rows. You want the sparklines to appear in a theme color.

QUICK TIP
You can also change the color scheme of your sparklines by choosing a format from the Style gallery on the Sparkline Tools Design tab.

4. **Click the Sparkline Color list arrow in the Style group, then click Indigo Accent 5 from the Theme colors**

    The sparklines match the worksheet format. You want to highlight the high and low months using theme colors.

5. **Click the Marker Color list arrow in the Style group, point to High Point, then select Orange Accent 2 from the Theme Colors**

6. **Click the Marker Color list arrow in the Style group, point to Low Point, select Olive Green Accent 3 from the Theme Colors, then compare your worksheet to Figure J-15**

Creating a chart template

After you create a custom chart with specific formatting, you can save it as a chart template. You can create future charts based on your saved chart templates, and they will reflect your custom formatting. Chart templates have .crtx as their file extension. If you use a custom chart frequently, you can save the template as the default chart type. To save a chart as a chart template, click the Chart Tools Design tab, click Save As Template in the Type group, enter a file-name in the Save Chart Template dialog box, then click Save. Your chart template will be saved in the Microsoft\Templates\Charts folder. When you want to format a chart like your chart template, you need to apply the template. Select your chart, click the Insert tab, click a chart type in the Charts group, click All Chart Types, click the Templates folder in the Change Chart Type dialog box, select a template in the My Templates area, then click OK.

FIGURE J-14: **Sales trend sparklines**

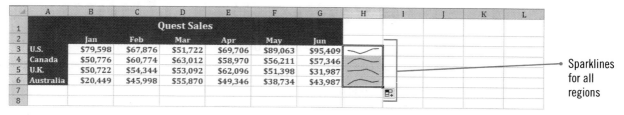

Sparklines for all regions

FIGURE J-15: **Formatted sparklines**

	A	B	C	D	E	F	G	H	I	J	K	L
1				Quest Sales								
2		Jan	Feb	Mar	Apr	May	Jun					
3	U.S.	$79,598	$67,876	$51,722	$69,706	$89,063	$95,409					
4	Canada	$50,776	$60,774	$63,012	$58,970	$56,211	$57,346					
5	U.K.	$50,722	$54,344	$53,092	$62,096	$51,398	$31,987					
6	Australia	$20,449	$45,998	$55,870	$49,346	$38,734	$43,987					
7												
8												

Formatted Sparklines

Identifying Data Trends

You often use charts to visually represent data over a period of time. To emphasize patterns in data, you can add trendlines to your charts. A **trendline** is a series of data points on a line that shows data values representing the general direction in a data series. In some business situations, you can use trendlines to predict future data based on past trends.  Kate wants you to compare the U.S. and U.K. sales performance over the first two quarters and to project sales for each region in the following 3 months, assuming past trends. You begin by charting the 6-months sales data in a 2-D Column chart.

STEPS

1. **On the Sales sheet select the range A2:G6, click the Insert tab, click the Column button in the Charts group, then click the Clustered Column button (the first chart in the 2-D Column group)**

2. **Drag the chart left until its upper-left corner is at the upper-left corner of cell A8, then drag the middle-right sizing handle right to the border between column G and column H**
   You are ready to add a trendline for the U.S. data series.

3. **Click the U.S. January data point (the far-left column in the chart) to select the U.S. data series, click the Chart Tools Layout tab, click the Trendline button in the Analysis group, then click Linear Trendline**

   A linear trendline identifying U.S. sales trends in the first 6 months is added to the chart, along with an entry in the legend identifying the line. You need to compare the U.S. sales trend with the U.K. sales trend.

4. **Click the U.K. January data point (the third column in the chart) to select the U.K. data series, click the Trendline button, then click Linear Trendline**

   The chart now has two trendlines, making it easy to compare the sales trends of the U.S. and the U.K. branches. Now you want to project the next 3-months sales for the U.S. and U.K. sales branches based on the past 6-month trends.

5. **Click the U.S. data series trendline, click the Trendline button, then click More Trendline Options**

   The Format Trendline dialog box opens, as shown in Figure J-16.

6. **In the Forecast section, enter 3 in the Forward text box, click Close, click the U.K. data series trendline, click the Trendline button, click More Trendline Options, enter 3 in the Forward text box, then click Close**

   The trendlines project an additional 3 months, predicting the future sales trends for the U.S. and U.K. regions, assuming that past trends continue. The two trendlines look identical, so you decide to format them.

7. **Click the U.S. data series trendline, click the Trendline button, click More Trendline Options, click the Custom option button in the Trendline Name section, then type U.S. Trends in the Custom text box**

8. **Click Line Color in the left pane of the dialog box, click the Solid line option button, click the Color list arrow, select Red in the Standard colors section, click Line Style in the left pane, click the Dash type list arrow, select the Dash option, then click Close**

   The U.S. data series trendline is now a red dashed line and is clearly identified in the legend.

9. **Select the U.K. data series trendline, repeat Steps 7 and 8 but use the name U.K. Trends and a Purple dashed line, then click outside the chart and go to cell A1**

10. **Enter your name in the center section of the Sales sheet footer, save the workbook, preview the Sales sheet, close the workbook, submit the workbook to your instructor, then exit Excel**

    The completed worksheet is shown in Figure J-17

> **TROUBLE**
> If you have trouble selecting the trendline, you can click the Chart Tools Layout tab, click the Chart Elements list arrow in the Current Selection group, then select Series "U.S." Trendline 1.

FIGURE J-16: Format Trendline dialog box

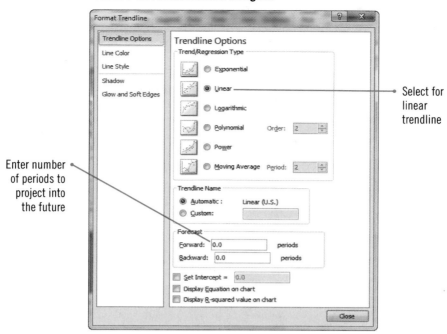

Enter number of periods to project into the future

Select for linear trendline

FIGURE J-17: Sales chart with trendlines for U.S. and U.K. data

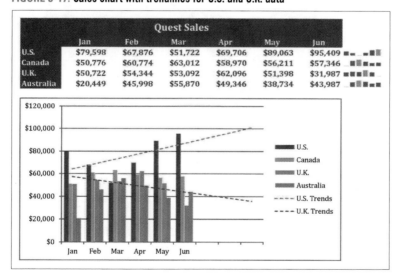

Choosing the right trendline for your chart

Trendlines can help you forecast where your data is headed and understand its past values. This type of data analysis is called **regression analysis** in mathematics. You can choose from four types of trendlines: Linear, Exponential, Linear Forecast, and Two-Period Moving Average. A **linear trendline** is used for data series with data points that have the pattern of a line. An exponential trendline is a curved line that is used when data values increase or decrease quickly. You cannot use an exponential trendline if your data contains negative values. A linear forecast trendline is a linear trendline with a two-period forecast. A two-period moving average smooths out fluctuations in data by averaging the data points.

Practice

For current SAM information, including versions and content details, visit SAM Central (http://www.cengage.com/samcentral). If you have a SAM user profile, you may have access to hands-on instruction, practice, and assessment of the skills covered in this unit. Since various versions of SAM are supported throughout the life of this text, check with your instructor for the correct instructions and URL/Web site for accessing assignments.

Concepts Review

1. Which element points to the vertical axis title?
2. Which element points to the vertical axis?
3. Which element points to the chart title?
4. Which element points to the chart legend?
5. Which element points to a data label?
6. Which element points to the horizontal category axis?

FIGURE J-18

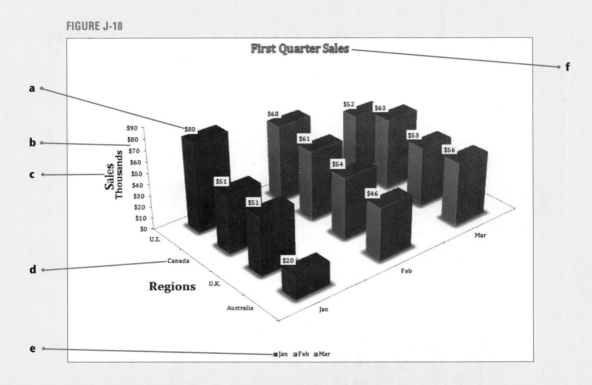

Match each term with the statement that best describes it.

7. Plot area	a. Category axis
8. Data series	b. Miniature charts that show data trends
9. X-axis	c. Line charts that can be used to predict future data
10. Sparklines	d. Sequence of values plotted on a chart
11. Trendlines	e. Location holding data charted on the axes

Select the best answer from the list of choices.

12. Which of the following is true regarding WordArt?

a. WordArt is a shape.

b. Cell references to WordArt can be used in formulas.

c. Spelling errors in WordArt can be detected by the spell checker.

d. Cells containing WordArt can be sorted.

13. Descriptive text that appears above a data marker is called a:

a. Data label.

b. Data series.

c. High point.

d. Period.

14. A chart's scale:

a. Always has a maximum of 80000.

b. Can be adjusted.

c. Always has a minimum of 0.

d. Always appears in units of 10.

15. Which Chart Tools tab is used to format the axes of a chart?

a. Layout

b. Design

c. Insert

d. Format

16. What is a data table?

a. The data used to create a chart, displayed in a grid

b. A customized data series

c. A grid with chart data displayed above a chart

d. A three-dimensional arrangement of data on the y-axis

Skills Review

1. Customize a data series.

a. Start Excel, open the file EX J-2.xlsx from the drive and folder where you save your Data Files, then save it as **EX J-Pastry Sales**.

b. With the Sales sheet active, select the range A2:D6.

c. Create a 3-D column chart using the selected data. (*Hint*: Do not choose the 3-D clustered column chart.)

d. Move and resize the chart to fit in the range A8:G20.

e. Change the color of the January data series to a light blue color in the Standard Colors group.

f. Save the workbook.

2. Change a data source and add data labels.

a. Add the April, May, and June data to the chart.

b. Change the chart view by exchanging the row and column data.

c. Resize the chart to fill the range A8:J28 to display the new data.

d. Change the chart view back to show the months in the legend by exchanging the row and column data. Add data labels to your chart. Delete the data labels for all but the June series. (*Hint*: Click one of the data labels in the series, then press [Delete].) Move any June data labels that are difficult to view.

e. Save the workbook.

3. Format the axes of a chart.

a. Change the vertical axis major unit to 1000. (*Hint*: Use the Format Axis dialog box to set the Major unit to a fixed value of 1000.)

b. Change the display of the vertical axis values to Thousands, then move the Thousands label lower along the axis so it appears centered between $2 and $4.

c. Set the value axis maximum to 5000.

d. Add a horizontal axis title below the chart. Label the axis **Products**.

e. Move the horizontal axis title so it appears between the Cookies and Brownies axis labels.

f. Save the workbook.

Skills Review (continued)

4. Add a data table to a chart.

  a. Move the chart to its own sheet named **Sales Chart**.

  b. Add a data table with legend keys.

  c. Move the horizontal axis title up to a location above the data table between the Cookies and Brownies axis labels.

  d. Format the data table to change the border color to the standard color purple.

  e. Save the workbook, then compare your screen to Figure J-19.

5. Rotate a chart.

  a. Remove the data table and adjust the axes titles as necessary.

  b. Set the X: rotation to 70 degrees.

  c. Set the Y: rotation to 20 degrees.

  d. Change the depth to 180% of the base.

  e. Adjust the axes titles. Add a white fill to the June data labels to make them visible. Save the workbook.

6. Enhance a chart with WordArt and pictures.

  a. Add a chart title of **Pastry Sales** to the top of the chart. Format the chart title with WordArt Fill – None, Outline - Accent 2 (the second style on the first line).

  b. Position the new title approximately half way across the top of the chart and closer to the chart.

  c. Select the legend. Format the legend with the picture cookie.gif from the drive and folder where you store your Data Files.

  d. Increase the size of the legend to show the picture of the cookie. Compare your chart to Figure J-20.

  e. Add your name to the chart footer, then save the workbook.

7. Add Sparklines to a worksheet.

  a. On the Sales worksheet, add a Line sparkline to cell H3 that represents the data in the range B3:G3.

  b. Copy the sparkline in cell H3 into the range H4:H6.

  c. Change the sparklines to columns.

  d. Change the Sparkline color to Blue-Gray, Accent 6 (the last color in the top row of Theme colors).

  e. Save the workbook.

8. Identify data trends.

  a. Create a 2-D line chart using the data in the range A2:G6, then move and resize the chart to fit in the range A8:G20.

  b. Add a linear trendline to the Muffins data series.

  c. Change the trendline color to red and the line style to Square Dot.

  d. Set the forward option to six periods to view the future trend, increase the width of the chart to the border between columns J and K, deselect the chart, then compare your screen to Figure J-21.

FIGURE J-19

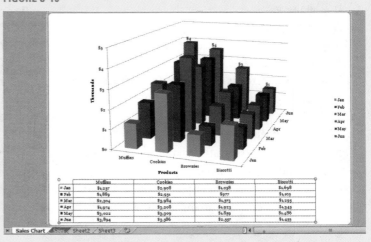

FIGURE J-20

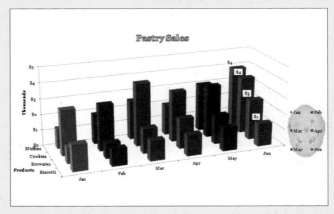

FIGURE J-21

Enhancing Charts

Skills Review (continued)

e. Add your name to the center footer section, save the workbook, preview the worksheet, close the workbook, then submit the workbook to your instructor.

f. Exit Excel.

Independent Challenge 1

You are the assistant to the vice president of marketing at the Metro-West Philharmonic located outside of Boston. The vice president has asked you to chart some information from a recent survey of the Philharmonic's customers. Your administrative assistant has entered the survey data in an Excel worksheet, which you will use to create two charts.

a. Start Excel, open the file titled EX J-3.xlsx from the drive and folder where you store your Data Files, then save it as **EX J-Customer Demographics**.

b. Using the data in A2:B7 of the Education Data worksheet, create a 3-D pie chart (the first chart in the 3-D Pie group) on the worksheet.

c. Move the chart to a separate sheet named **Education Chart**. Format the chart using chart Style 34.

d. Add a title of **Education Data** above the chart. Format the title using WordArt Gradient Fill – Dark Red, Accent 1 (fourth style in the third row). Change the chart title font to a size of 28, and center it over the chart.

e. Add data labels to the outside end of the data points. Format the legend text in a 14-point font. (*Hint*: Use the font options on the Home tab or the Mini toolbar.)

f. Select the Bachelor's degree pie slice by clicking the chart, then clicking the Bachelor's degree slice. Change the slice color to the standard color of Olive Green, Accent 3 from the Theme colors. (*Hint*: On the Chart Tools Format tab, click the Format Selection button in the Current Selection group and use the Format Data Point dialog box.) Compare your chart to Figure J-22.

g. On the Income Data worksheet, use the data in A2:B6 to create a standard clustered column (the first chart in the 2-D Column group) chart.

h. Delete the legend. (*Hint*: Select the legend and press [Delete].)

i. Place the chart on a new sheet named **Income Chart**. Format the chart using chart Style 7.

j. Add a chart title of **Income Data** above the chart, and format the title using WordArt Style Gradient Fill - Blue, Accent 4, Reflection.

k. Title the category axis **Income**. Format the category axis title in 18-point bold. (*Hint*: Use the font options on the Home tab or use the Mini toolbar.)

FIGURE J-22

Education Data

l. Enter your name in the center sections of the footers of the Income Chart and Education Chart sheets.

m. Save the workbook, preview the Income Chart and the Education Chart sheets.

n. Close the workbook, submit the workbook to your instructor, and exit Excel.

Independent Challenge 2

You manage the Chicago Athletic Club, which offers memberships for swimming, tennis, and fitness. You also offer a full membership that includes all of the activities at the club. The club owner has asked you to assemble a brief presentation on the membership data over the past 4 years while it has been under your management. You decide to include a chart showing the memberships in each category as well as an analysis of trends in memberships.

a. Start Excel, open the file titled EX J-4.xlsx from the drive and folder where you store your Data Files, then save it as **EX J-Memberships**.

Independent Challenge 2 (continued)

b. Create a clustered bar chart (the first chart in the 2-D Bar group) on the worksheet, comparing the membership enrollments in the four types of memberships. Format the chart using chart Style 7.

c. Change the row and column data so the years are shown in the legend.

d. Add a chart title of **Membership Data** above the chart, and format it using WordArt Style Gradient Fill – Green, Accent 4, Reflection.

e. Add Line sparklines to cells F4:F7 showing the membership trend from 2010 to 2013, moving the chart as necessary.

f. Format the sparklines using Sparkline Style Accent 5 (no dark or light).

g. Add a new membership type of **Family** in row 8 of the worksheet with the following data:

Year	Membership
2010	1445
2011	1877
2012	1925
2013	2557

h. Add the new data to the bar chart. Copy the sparklines into cell F8.

i. Move the chart to a sheet named **Membership Chart**.

j. Add a horizontal axis title of **Number of Memberships**, and format the title in 18-point bold font.

k. Add a data table with legend keys to the chart. Delete the legend on the right side of the chart. Format the data table lines to be displayed in Tan, Accent 6 (the last Theme color in the top row). Compare your chart to Figure J-23.

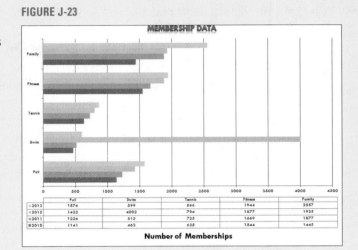

FIGURE J-23

Advanced Challenge Exercise

■ Use the Format Data Series dialog box to add a border color of Tan Accent 6, Darker 50% to the bars that represent the year 2010 in the chart.

■ Add a top circle bevel of width 10 pt. to the bars that represent the year 2013 in the chart.

■ Add a border to the plot area of the chart with the color of Gold, Accent 5.

l. Enter your name in the center section of the Membership Chart sheet footer, save the workbook, then preview the sheet.

m. Close the workbook, submit the workbook to your instructor, then exit Excel.

Independent Challenge 3

You manage the Pine Hills Pro Shop. You meet twice a year with the store owner to discuss store sales trends. You decide to use a chart to represent the sales trends for the department's product categories. You begin by charting the sales for the first 5 months of the year. Then you add data to the chart and analyze the sales trend using a trendline. Lastly, you enhance the chart by adding a data table, titles, and a picture.

a. Start Excel, open the file EX J-5.xlsx from the drive and folder where you store your Data Files, then save the workbook as **EX J-Golf Sales**.

b. Create a 3-D column chart on the worksheet showing the May through July sales information. Move the upper-left corner of the chart to cell A8 on the worksheet.

c. Format the May data series using the color yellow on the standard colors.

d. Add the Aug, Sep, and Oct data to the chart.

e. Move the chart to its own sheet named **May - Oct**.

Independent Challenge 3 (continued)

f. Rotate the chart with an X:Rotation of 40 degrees, a Y Rotation of 50 degrees, a perspective of 15 and the Depth (% of base) of 200.

g. Add a chart title of **May - October Sales** above the chart. Format the chart title using the WordArt Style Gradient Fill – Green, Accent1.

h. Add a rotated title of **Sales** in 20-point bold to the vertical axis.

i. Change the value axis scale to a maximum of **4000**.

j. Insert the golfball.gif picture from the drive and folder where your Data Files are stored into the legend area of the chart. Move the legend lower in the chart area and increase its width. Compare your chart to Figure J-24.

FIGURE J-24

Advanced Challenge Exercise

- Move the legend to the upper-left side of the chart.
- Change the value axis scale to increment by 500.
- Remove the primary horizontal gridlines. Add a gradient fill of your choice to the plot area.

k. Enter your name in the center footer section of the chart sheet, save the workbook, then preview the chart.

l. Close the workbook, submit the workbook to your instructor, then exit Excel.

Real Life Independent Challenge

This Independent Challenge requires an Internet connection.

Stock charts are used to graph a stock's high, low, and closing prices. You will create a stock chart using 4 weeks of high, low, and close prices for a stock that you are interested in tracking.

a. Start Excel, save a new workbook as **EX J-Stock Chart** in the drive and folder where you store your Data Files.

b. Use your Web browser to research the weekly high, low, and close prices for a stock over the past 4 weeks. (*Hint*: You may need to search for historical prices.)

c. Create a worksheet with the data from your chart. Enter the column labels **Date**, **High**, **Low**, and **Close** in columns A, B, C, and D. In the Date column, enter the Friday dates for the past 4 weeks starting with the oldest date. In columns B, C, and D, enter the high, low, and closing prices for your stock. Apply a document theme and formatting of your choice.

d. Create a High-Low-Close stock chart using your worksheet data. (*Hint*: To find the stock charts, click the Other Charts button.)

e. Format the horizontal axis to change the major unit to 7 days.

f. Change the color of the high-low lines to the standard color of red.

g. Add a rotated vertical axis title of **Stock Price**. Format the title in 14-point bold.

h. Format the Close data series in a color of purple from the standard colors and a size of 5. (*Hint*: You can change the size using the Marker Options in the Format Data Series dialog box.)

i. Add a chart title with your stock name above the chart. Format the title with a WordArt style of your choice from the WordArt Styles gallery. Change the vertical axis minimum and maximum values as necessary to view the chart lines.

j. Format the chart area using a gradient fill and transparency of your choice. Move the chart so it is below the worksheet data, leaving a couple of empty worksheet rows between the data and the chart.

k. Add Line sparklines to the cell below the Closing prices in the worksheet to show the trend of the stock over the past month. Format the sparklines in a color of your choice.

l. Enter your name in the center footer section of the worksheet, save the workbook, then preview the worksheet.

m. Close the workbook, submit the workbook to your instructor, then exit Excel.

Visual Workshop

Open the file EX J-6.xlsx from the drive and folder where you store your Data Files, and create the custom chart shown in Figure J-25. Save the workbook as **EX J-Organic Sales**. Study the chart and worksheet carefully to make sure you select the displayed chart type with all the enhancements shown. Enter your name in the center section of the worksheet footer, then preview the worksheet in landscape orientation on one page. Submit the workbook to your instructor.

FIGURE J-25

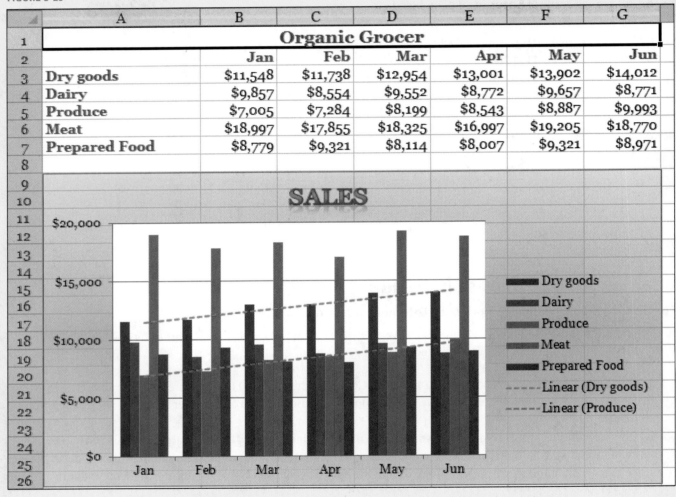

	A	B	C	D	E	F	G
1	Organic Grocer						
2		Jan	Feb	Mar	Apr	May	Jun
3	Dry goods	$11,548	$11,738	$12,954	$13,001	$13,902	$14,012
4	Dairy	$9,857	$8,554	$9,552	$8,772	$9,657	$8,771
5	Produce	$7,005	$7,284	$8,199	$8,543	$8,887	$9,993
6	Meat	$18,997	$17,855	$18,325	$16,997	$19,205	$18,770
7	Prepared Food	$8,779	$9,321	$8,114	$8,007	$9,321	$8,971

Using What-if Analysis

Each time you use a worksheet to explore different outcomes for Excel formulas, you are performing a **what-if analysis**. For example, what would happen to a firm's overall expense budget if company travel expenses decreased by 30 percent? Using Excel, you can perform a what-if analysis in many ways. In this unit, you learn to track what-if scenarios and generate summary reports using the Excel Scenario Manager. You design and manipulate data tables to project outcomes. Also, you use the Goal Seek feature to solve a what-if analysis. Finally, you use Solver to perform a complex what-if analysis involving multiple variables and use the Analysis ToolPak to generate descriptive statistics about your data. Kate Morgan, the vice president of sales at Quest, is meeting with the U.S. region manager to discuss sales projections for the first half of the year. Kate asks you to help analyze the U.S. sales data in preparation for her meeting.

OBJECTIVES

Define a what-if analysis

Track a what-if analysis with Scenario Manager

Generate a scenario summary

Project figures using a data table

Use Goal Seek

Set up a complex what-if analysis with Solver

Run Solver and summarize results

Analyze data using the Analysis ToolPak

Defining a What-if Analysis

By performing a what-if analysis in a worksheet, you can get immediate answers to questions such as "What happens to profits if we sell 25 percent more of a certain product?" or "What happens to monthly payments if interest rates rise or fall?". A worksheet you use to produce a what-if analysis is often called a **model** because it acts as the basis for multiple outcomes or sets of results. To perform a what-if analysis in a worksheet, you change the value in one or more **input cells** (cells that contain data rather than formulas), then observe the effects on dependent cells. A **dependent cell** usually contains a formula whose resulting value changes depending on the values in the input cells. A dependent cell can be located either in the same worksheet as the changing input value or in another worksheet.  Kate Morgan has received projected sales data from regional managers. She has created a worksheet model to perform an initial what-if analysis, as shown in Figure K-1. She thinks the U.S. sales projections for the months of February, March, and April should be higher. You first review the guidelines for performing a what-if analysis.

DETAILS

When performing a what-if analysis, use the following guidelines:

- **Understand and state the purpose of the worksheet model**

  Identify what you want to accomplish with the model. What problem are you trying to solve? What questions do you want the model to answer for you? Kate's Quest worksheet model is designed to total Quest sales projections for the first half of the year and to calculate the percentage of total sales for each Quest region. It also calculates the totals and percentages of total sales for each month.

- **Determine the data input value(s) that, if changed, affect the dependent cell results**

  In a what-if analysis, changes in the content of the data input cells produces varying results in the output cells. You will use the model to work with three data input values: the February, March, and April values for the U.S. region, in cells C3, D3, and E3, respectively.

- **Identify the dependent cell(s) that will contain results**

  The dependent cells usually contain formulas, and the formula results adjust as you enter different values in the input cells. The results of two dependent cell formulas (labeled Total and Percent of Total Sales) appear in cells H3 and I3, respectively. The totals for the months of February, March, and April in cells C7, D7, and E7 are also dependent cells, as are the percentages for these months in cells C8, D8, and E8.

- **Formulate questions you want the what-if analysis to answer**

  It is important that you know the questions you want your model to answer. In the Quest model, you want to answer the following questions: (1) What happens to the U.S. regional percentage if the sales for the months of February, March, and April are each increased by $5000? (2) What happens to the U.S. regional percentage if the sales for the months of February, March, and April are each increased by $10,000?

- **Perform the what-if analysis**

  When you perform the what-if analysis, you explore the relationships between the input values and the dependent cell formulas. In the Quest worksheet model, you want to see what effect a $5000 increase in sales for February, March, and April has on the dependent cell formulas containing totals and percentages. Because the sales amounts for these months are located in cells C3, D3, and E3, any formula that references the cells is directly affected by a change in these sales amounts—in this case, the total formulas in cells H3, C7, D7, and E7. Because the formula in cell I3 references cell H3, a change in the sales amounts affects this cell as well. The percentage formulas in cells C8, D8, and E8 will also change because they reference the total formulas in cells C7, D7, and E7. Figure K-2 shows the result of the what-if analysis described in this example.

Data input values →

	A	B	C	D	E	F	G	H	I
1	2014 Projected Sales								
2		Jan	Feb	Mar	Apr	May	Jun	Total	Percent of Total Sales
3	U.S.	$91,473	$65,189	$67,423	$62,564	$102,926	$91,244	$480,819	30.32%
4	Canada	$65,068	$72,326	$76,244	$71,353	$68,015	$69,388	$422,394	26.64%
5	U.K.	$61,373	$65,756	$64,241	$72,716	$62,191	$42,334	$368,611	23.25%
6	Australia	$36,843	$55,657	$61,552	$59,708	$46,868	$53,224	$313,852	19.79%
7	Total	$254,757	$258,928	$269,460	$266,341	$280,000	$256,190	$1,585,676	
8	Percent of Total Sales	16.07%	16.33%	16.99%	16.80%	17.66%	16.16%		
9									
10									

Dependent cell formulas

A1   fx   2014 Projected Sales

Changed input values →

	A	B	C	D	E	F	G	H	I
1	2014 Projected Sales								
2		Jan	Feb	Mar	Apr	May	Jun	Total	Percent of Total Sales
3	U.S.	$91,473	$70,189	$72,423	$67,564	$102,926	$91,244	$495,819	30.98%
4	Canada	$65,068	$72,326	$76,244	$71,353	$68,015	$69,388	$422,394	26.39%
5	U.K.	$61,373	$65,756	$64,241	$72,716	$62,191	$42,334	$368,611	23.03%
6	Australia	$36,843	$55,657	$61,552	$59,708	$46,868	$53,224	$313,852	19.61%
7	Total	$254,757	$263,928	$274,460	$271,341	$280,000	$256,190	$1,600,676	
8	Percent of Total Sales	15.92%	16.49%	17.15%	16.95%	17.49%	16.01%		
9									

Changed formula results

Excel 2010

Tracking a What-if Analysis with Scenario Manager

A **scenario** is a set of values you use to observe different worksheet results. For example, you might plan to sell 100 of a particular item, at a price of $5 per item, producing sales results of $500. But what if you reduced the price to $4 or increased it to $6? Each of these price scenarios would produce different sales results. A changing value, such as the price in this example, is called a **variable**. The Excel Scenario Manager simplifies the process of what-if analysis by allowing you to name and save multiple scenarios with variable values in a worksheet. Kate asks you to use Scenario Manager to create scenarios showing how a U.S. sales increase can affect total Quest sales over the 3-month period of February through April.

1. **Start Excel, open the file EX K-1.xlsx from the drive and folder where you store your Data Files, then save it as EX K-Sales**

   The first step in defining a scenario is choosing the changing cells. **Changing cells** are those that will vary in the different scenarios.

2. **With the Projected Sales sheet active, select range C3:E3, click the Data tab, click the What-If Analysis button in the Data Tools group, then click Scenario Manager**

   The Scenario Manager dialog box opens with the following message: No Scenarios defined. Choose Add to add scenarios. You decide to create three scenarios. You want to be able to easily return to your original worksheets values, so your first scenario contains those figures.

3. **Click Add, drag the Add Scenario dialog box to the right if necessary until columns A and B are visible, then type Original Sales Figures in the Scenario name text box**

   The range in the Changing cells box shows the range you selected, as shown in Figure K-3.

4. **Click OK to confirm the scenario range**

   The Scenario Values dialog box opens, as shown in Figure K-4. The existing values appear in the changing cell boxes. Because you want this scenario to reflect the current worksheet values, you leave these unchanged.

5. **Click OK**

   The Scenario Manager dialog box reappears with the new scenario, named Original Sales Figures, listed in the Scenarios box. You want to create a second scenario that will show the effects of increasing sales by $5,000.

6. **Click Add; in the Scenario name text box type Increase Feb, Mar, Apr by 5000; verify that the Changing cells text box reads C3:E3, then click OK; in the Scenario Values dialog box, change the value in the $C$3 text box to 70189, change the value in the $D$3 text box to 72423, change the value in the $E$3 text box to 67564, then click Add**

   You are ready to create a third scenario. It will show the effects of increasing sales by $10,000.

7. **In the Scenario name text box, type Increase Feb, Mar, Apr by 10000 and click OK; in the Scenario Values dialog box, change the value in the $C$3 text box to 75189, change the value in the $D$3 text box to 77423, change the value in the $E$3 text box to 72564, then click OK**

   The Scenario Manager dialog box reappears, as shown in Figure K-5. You are ready to display the results of your scenarios in the worksheet.

8. **Make sure the Increase Feb, Mar, Apr by 10000 scenario is still selected, click Show, notice that the percent of U.S. sales in cell I3 changes from 30.32% to 31.62%; click Increase Feb, Mar, Apr by 5000, click Show, notice that the U.S. sales percent is now 30.98%; click Original Sales Figures, click Show to return to the original values, then click Close**

9. **Save the workbook**

FIGURE K-3: Add Scenario dialog box

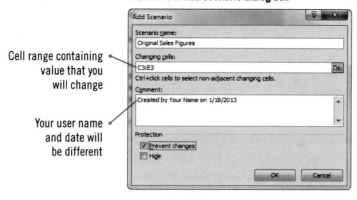

Cell range containing value that you will change

Your user name and date will be different

FIGURE K-4: Scenario Values dialog box

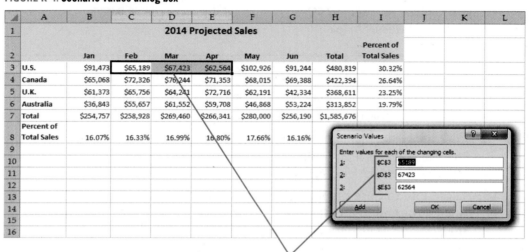

Changing cell boxes with original values

FIGURE K-5: Scenario Manager dialog box with three scenarios listed

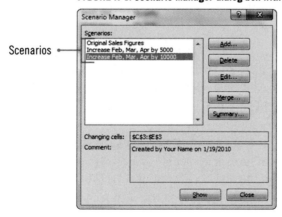

Scenarios

Merging scenarios

Excel stores scenarios in the workbook and on the worksheet in which you created them. To apply scenarios from another worksheet or workbook into the current worksheet, click the Merge button in the Scenario Manager dialog box. The Merge Scenarios dialog box opens, letting you select scenarios from other locations. When you click a sheet name in the sheet list, the text under the sheet list tells you how many scenarios exist on that sheet. To merge scenarios from another workbook, such as those sent to you in a workbook by a coworker, open the other workbook file, click the Book list arrow in the Merge Scenarios dialog box, then click the workbook name. When you merge workbook scenarios, it's best if the workbooks have the same structure, so that there is no confusion of cell values.

Generating a Scenario Summary

Although it may be useful to display the different scenario outcomes when analyzing data, it can be difficult to keep track of them. In most cases, you will want to refer to a single report that summarizes the results of all the scenarios in a worksheet. A **scenario summary** is an Excel table that compiles data from the changing cells and corresponding result cells for each scenario. For example, you might use a scenario summary to illustrate the best, worst, and most likely scenarios for a particular set of circumstances. Using cell naming makes the summary easier to read because the names, not the cell references, appear in the report. ▓▓▓▓ Now that you have defined Kate's scenarios, she needs you to generate and print a scenario summary report. You begin by creating names for the cells in row 2 based on the labels in row 1, so that the report will be easier to read.

STEPS

1. **Select the range B2:I3, click the** Formulas tab, **click the** Create from Selection button **in the** Defined Names group, **click the** Top row check box **to select it if necessary, then click** OK

   Excel creates the names for the data in row 3 based on the labels in row 2. You decide to review them.

   > **QUICK TIP**
   > You can also click the Name box list arrow on the formula bar to view cell names.

2. **Click the** Name Manager button **in the** Defined Names group

   The eight labels appear, along with other workbook names, in the Name Manager dialog box, confirming that they were created, as shown in Figure K-6. Now you are ready to generate the scenario summary report.

3. **Click** Close **to close the Name Manager dialog box, click the** Data tab, **click the** What-If Analysis button **in the** Data Tools group, **click** Scenario Manager, **then click** Summary **in the Scenario Manager dialog box**

   Excel needs to know the location of the cells that contain the formula results that you want to see in the report. You want to see the results for U.S. total and percentage of sales, and on overall Quest sales.

4. **With the** Result cells text box selected, **click cell** H3 **on the worksheet, type** , **(a comma), click cell** I3, **type** , **(a comma), then click cell** H7

   With the report type and result cells specified, as shown in Figure K-7, you are now ready to generate the report.

   > **QUICK TIP**
   > To see the Comments for each scenario, which by default contain the creator name and creation date, click the plus sign to the left of row 3.

5. **Click** OK

   A summary of the worksheet's scenarios appears on a new sheet titled Scenario Summary. The report shows outline buttons to the left of and above the worksheet so that you can hide or show report details. Because the Current Values column shows the same values as the Original Sales Figures column, you decide to delete column D.

6. **Right-click the** column D heading, **then click** Delete **in the shortcut menu**

   Next, you notice that the notes at the bottom of the report refer to the column that no longer exists. You also want to make the report title and labels for the result cells more descriptive.

7. **Select the range** B13:B15, **press [Delete], select cell** B2, **edit its contents to read** Scenario Summary for U.S. Sales, **click cell** C10, **then edit its contents to read** Total U.S. Sales

   > **QUICK TIP**
   > The scenario summary is not linked to the worksheet. If you change the values in the worksheet, you must generate a new scenario summary.

8. **Click cell** C11, **edit its contents to read** Percent U.S. Sales, **click cell** C12, **edit its contents to read** Total Quest Sales, **then click cell** A1

   The completed scenario summary is shown in Figure K-8.

9. **Add your name to the center section of the Scenario Summary sheet footer, change the page orientation to landscape, then save the workbook and preview the worksheet**

Using What-if Analysis

FIGURE K-6: Name Manager dialog box displaying new names

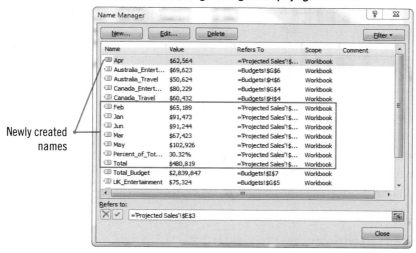

Newly created names

FIGURE K-7: Scenario Summary dialog box

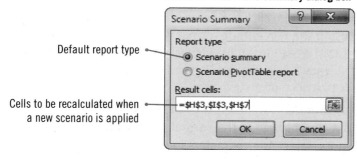

Default report type

Cells to be recalculated when a new scenario is applied

FIGURE K-8: Completed Scenario Summary report

Report is in outline format

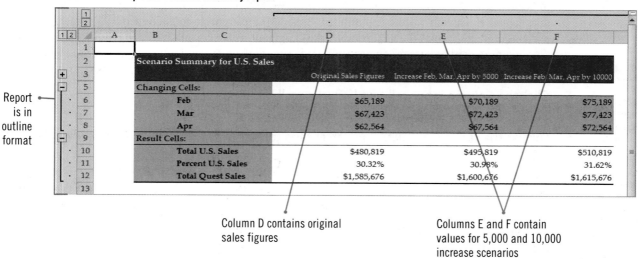

Column D contains original sales figures

Columns E and F contain values for 5,000 and 10,000 increase scenarios

Projecting Figures Using a Data Table

Another way to answer what-if questions in a worksheet is by using a data table. A **data table** is a range of cells that simultaneously shows the varying resulting values when one or more input values is changed in a formula. For example, you could use a data table to display your monthly mortgage payment based on several different interest rates. A **one-input data table** is a table that shows the result of varying one input value, such as the interest rate. ![] Now that you have completed Kate's analysis, she wants you to find out how the U.S. sales percentage would change as U.S. total sales increased.

1. **Click the Projected Sales sheet tab, enter Total U.S. Sales in cell K1, widen column K to fit the label, in cell K2 enter 480819, in cell K3 enter 530819, select the range K2:K3, drag the fill handle to select the range K4:K6, then format the values using the Accounting number format with zero decimal places**

   You begin setting up your data table by entering the total U.S. sales from cell H3 and then increasing the amount by increments of $50,000. These are the **input values** in the data table. With the varying input values listed in column K, you enter a formula reference to cell I3 that you want Excel to use in calculating the resulting percentages (the **output values**) in column L, based on the possible sales levels in column K.

2. **Click cell L1, type =, click cell I3, click the Enter button ✓ on the formula bar, then format the value in cell L1 using the Percentage format with two decimal places**

   The value in cell I3, 30.32%, appears in cell L1, and the cell name =Percent_of_Total_Sales appears in the formula bar, as shown in Figure K-9. Because it isn't necessary for users of the data table to see the value in cell L1, you want to hide the cell's contents from view.

3. **With cell L1 selected, click the Home tab, click the Format button in the Cells group, click Format Cells, click the Number tab in the Format Cells dialog box if necessary, click Custom under Category, select any characters in the Type box, type ;;; (three semicolons), then click OK**

   The three semicolons hide the values in a cell. With the table structure in place, you can now generate the data table showing percentages for the varying sales amounts.

4. **Select the range K1:L6, click the Data tab, click the What-If Analysis button in the Data Tools group, then click Data Table**

   You have highlighted the range that makes up the table structure. The Data Table dialog box opens, as shown in Figure K-10. This is where you indicate in which worksheet cell you want the varying input values (the sales figures in column K) to be substituted. Because the percentage formula in cell I3 (which you just referenced in cell L1) uses the total sales in cell H3 as input, you enter a reference to cell H3. You place this reference in the Column input cell text box, rather than in the Row input cell text box, because the varying input values are arranged in a column in your data table structure.

5. **Click the Column input cell text box, click cell H3, then click OK**

   Excel completes the data table by calculating percentages for each sales amount.

6. **Format the range L2:L6 with the Percentage format with two decimal places, then click cell A1**

   The formatted data table is shown in Figure K-11. It shows the sales percentages for each of the possible levels of U.S. sales. By looking at the data table, Kate determines that if she can increase total U.S. sales to over $700,000, the U.S. division will then comprise about 40% of total Quest sales for the first half of 2014.

7. **Add your name to the center section of the worksheet footer, change the worksheet orientation to landscape, then save the workbook and preview the worksheet**

FIGURE K-9: One-input data table structure

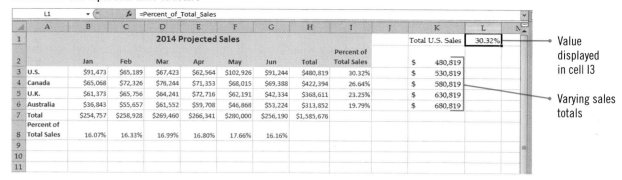

Value displayed in cell I3

Varying sales totals

FIGURE K-10: Data Table dialog box

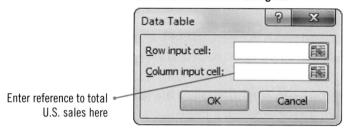

Enter reference to total U.S. sales here

FIGURE K-11: Completed data table with resulting values

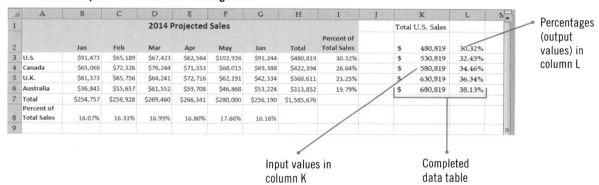

Percentages (output values) in column L

Input values in column K

Completed data table

Creating a two-input data table

A **two-input data table** shows the resulting values when two differ-ent input values are varied in a formula. You could, for example, use a two-input data table to calculate your monthly car payment based on varying interest rates and varying loan terms, as shown in Figure K-12. In a two-input data table, different values of one input cell appear across the top row of the table, while different values of the second input cell are listed down the left column. You create a two-input data table the same way that you created a one-input data table, except you enter both a row and a column input cell. In the example shown in Figure K-12, the two-input data table struc-ture was created by first entering the number of payments in the range B6:D6 and rates in the range A7:A19. Then the data table val-ues were created by first selecting the range A6:D19, clicking the Data tab, clicking the What-If Analysis button in the Data Tools group, then clicking Data Table. In the Data Table dialog box, the row input value is the term in cell C2. The column input value is the

interest rate in cell B2. You can check the accuracy of these values by cross-referencing the values in the data table with those in row 2 where you can see that an interest rate of 7% for 36 months has a monthly payment of $617.54.

FIGURE K-12: Two-input data table

	A	B	C	D
1	Loan Amount	Interest Rate	# Payments	Monthly Payment
2	$ 20,000.00	7.00%	36	$617.54
3				
4		Car Payment for $20,000 Loan		
5			Term	
6		36	48	60
7	6.48%	$612.80	$474.11	$391.14
8	6.61%	$613.98	$475.31	$392.35
9	6.74%	$615.17	$476.52	$393.58
10	6.87%	$616.35	$477.72	$394.80
11	7.00%	$617.54	$478.92	$396.02
12	7.13%	$618.73	$480.13	$397.25
13	7.26%	$619.92	$481.34	$398.48
14	7.39%	$621.11	$482.55	$399.71
15	7.52%	$622.31	$483.76	$400.95
16	7.65%	$623.50	$484.98	$402.19
17	7.78%	$624.70	$486.20	$403.43
18	7.91%	$625.90	$487.41	$404.67
19	8.04%	$627.10	$488.63	$405.91

Using Goal Seek

You can think of goal seeking as a what-if analysis in reverse. In a what-if analysis, you might try many sets of values to achieve a certain solution. To **goal seek**, you specify a solution, then ask Excel to find the input value that produces the answer you want. "Backing into" a solution in this way, sometimes referred to as **backsolving**, can save a significant amount of time. For example, you can use Goal Seek to determine how many units must be sold to reach a particular sales goal or to determine what expense levels are necessary to meet a budget target. After reviewing her data table, Kate has a follow-up question: What January U.S. sales target is required to bring the January Quest sales percentage to 17%, assuming the sales for the other regions don't change? You use Goal Seek to answer her question.

STEPS

1. **Click cell B8**

   The first step in using Goal Seek is to select a goal cell. A **goal cell** contains a formula in which you can substitute values to find a specific value, or goal. You use cell B8 as the goal cell because it contains the percent formula.

2. **Click the Data tab, click the What-If Analysis button in the Data Tools group, then click Goal Seek**

   The Goal Seek dialog box opens. The Set cell text box contains a reference to cell B8, the percent formula cell you selected in Step 1. You need to indicate that the figure in cell B8 should equal 17%.

3. **Click the To value text box, then type 17%**

   The value 17% represents the desired solution you want to reach by substituting different values in the By changing cell.

4. **Click the By changing cell text box, then click cell B3**

   You have specified that you want cell B3, the U.S. January amount, to change to reach the 17% solution, as shown in Figure K-13.

5. **Click OK**

   The Goal Seek Status dialog box opens with the following message: "Goal Seeking with Cell B8 found a solution." By changing the sales amount in cell B3 to $109,232, Goal Seek achieves a January percentage of 17.

6. **Click OK, then click cell A1**

   Changing the sales amount in cell B3 changes the other dependent values in the worksheet (B7, H3, I3, and H7) as shown in Figure K-14.

7. **Save the workbook, then preview the worksheet**

> **QUICK TIP**
> Before you select another command, you can return the worksheet to its status prior to the Goal Seek by pressing [Ctrl][Z].

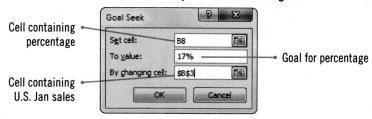

Cell containing
percentage → Set cell: B8

To value: 17% ← Goal for percentage

Cell containing
U.S. Jan sales → By changing cell: $B$3

FIGURE K-14: **Worksheet with new dependent values**

	A	B	C	D	E	F	G	H	I	J
1				**2014 Projected Sales**						
2		Jan	Feb	Mar	Apr	May	Jun	Total	Percent of Total Sales	
3	U.S.	$109,232	$65,189	$67,423	$62,564	$102,926	$91,244	$498,578	31.09%	
4	Canada	$65,068	$72,326	$76,244	$71,353	$68,015	$69,388	$422,394	26.34%	
5	U.K.	$61,373	$65,756	$64,241	$72,716	$62,191	$42,334	$368,611	22.99%	
6	Australia	$36,843	$55,657	$61,552	$59,708	$46,868	$53,224	$313,852	19.57%	
7	Total	$272,516	$258,928	$269,460	$266,341	$280,000	$256,190	$1,603,435		
8	Percent of Total Sales	17.00%	16.15%	16.81%	16.61%	17.46%	15.98%			
9										
10										
11										

New target values calculated
by Goal Seek

New dependent values

Excel 2010

Setting up a Complex What-if Analysis with Solver

The Excel Solver is an **add-in** program that provides optional features. It must be installed before you can use it. Solver finds the best solution to a problem that has several inputs. The cell containing the formula is called the **target cell**, or **objective**. As you learned earlier, cells containing the values that vary are called "changing cells." Solver is helpful when you need to perform a complex what-if analysis involving multiple input values or when the input values must conform to specific limitations or restrictions called **constraints**. ▰▰▰▰ Kate decides to fund each region with the same amount, $757,500, to cover expenses. She adjusts the travel and entertainment allocations to keep expenditures to the allocated amount of $757,500. You use Solver to help Kate find the best possible allocation.

STEPS

TROUBLE

If Solver is not on your Data tab, click the File tab, click Options, click Add-Ins, in the list of Add-ins click Solver Add-in, click Go, in the Add-Ins dialog box click the Solver Add-in check box to select it, then click OK.

1. **Click the Budgets sheet tab**

   This worksheet is designed to calculate the travel, entertainment, and other budgets for each region. It assumes fixed costs for communications, equipment, advertising, salaries, and rent. You use Solver to change the entertainment and travel amounts in cells G3:H6 (the changing cells) to achieve your target of a total budget of $3,030,000 in cell I7 (the target cell). You want your solution to include a constraint on cells G3:H6 specifying that each region is funded $757,500. Based on past budgets, you know there are two other constraints: the travel budgets must include at least $80,000, and the entertainment budgets must include at least $93,000. It is a good idea to enter constraints on the worksheet for documentation purposes, as shown in Figure K-15.

2. **Click the Data tab, then click the Solver button in the Analysis group**

   In the Solver Parameters dialog box opens, you indicate the target cell with its objective, the changing cells, and the constraints under which you want Solver to work. You begin by entering your total budget objective.

TROUBLE

If your Solver Parameters dialog box has entries in the By Changing Cells box or in the Subject to the Constraints box, click Reset All, click OK, then continue with Step 3.

3. **With the insertion point in the Set Objective text box, click cell I7 in the worksheet, click the Value Of option button, double-click the Value Of text box, then type 3,030,000**

   You have specified an objective of $3,030,000 for the total budget. In typing the total budget figure, be sure to type the commas.

4. **Click the By Changing Variable Cells text box, then select the range G3:H6 on the worksheet**

   You have told Excel which cells to vary to reach the goal of $3,030,000 total budget. You need to specify the constraints on the worksheet values to restrict the Solver's answer to realistic values.

5. **Click Add, with the insertion point in the Cell Reference text box in the Add Constraint dialog box, select the range I3:I6 in the worksheet, click the list arrow in the dialog box, click =, then with the insertion point in the Constraint text box click cell C9**

   As shown in Figure K-16, the Add Constraint dialog box specifies that cells in the range I3:I6, the total region budget amounts, should be equal to the value in cell C9. Next, you need to add the constraint that the budgeted entertainment amounts should be at least $93,000.

QUICK TIP

If your solution needs to be an integer, you can select it in the Add Constraint dialog box.

6. **Click Add, with the insertion point in the Cell Reference text box select the range G3:G6 in the worksheet, click the list arrow, select >=, with the insertion point in the Constraint text box click cell C11**

   Next, you need to specify that the budgeted travel amounts should be greater than or equal to $80,000.

7. **Click Add, with the insertion point in the Cell Reference text box select the range H3:H6, select >=, with the insertion point in the Constraint text box click cell C10, then click OK**

   The Solver Parameters dialog box opens with the constraints listed, as shown in Figure K-17. In the next lesson, you run Solver and generate solutions to the budget constraints.

FIGURE K-15: Worksheet set up for a complex what-if analysis

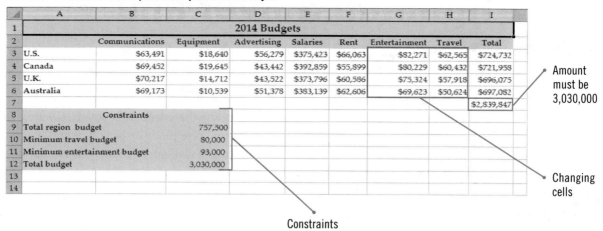

	A	B	C	D	E	F	G	H	I
1				2014 Budgets					
2		Communications	Equipment	Advertising	Salaries	Rent	Entertainment	Travel	Total
3	U.S.	$63,491	$18,640	$56,279	$375,423	$66,063	$82,271	$62,565	$724,732
4	Canada	$69,452	$19,645	$43,442	$392,859	$55,899	$80,229	$60,432	$721,958
5	U.K.	$70,217	$14,712	$43,522	$373,796	$60,586	$75,324	$57,918	$696,075
6	Australia	$69,173	$10,539	$51,378	$383,139	$62,606	$69,623	$50,624	$697,082
7									$2,839,847
8		Constraints							
9	Total region budget		757,500						
10	Minimum travel budget		80,000						
11	Minimum entertainment budget		93,000						
12	Total budget		3,030,000						
13									
14									

Amount must be 3,030,000

Changing cells

Constraints

FIGURE K-16: Adding constraints

Cells containing region budget amounts

Value in cell C9 should be 757,500

FIGURE K-17: Completed Solver Parameters dialog box

Target cell

Target value

Changing cells

Constraints on worksheet values

Running Solver and Summarizing Results

After entering all the parameters in the Solver Parameters dialog box, you can run Solver to find a solution. In some cases, Solver may not be able to find a solution that meets all of your constraints. Then you would need to enter new constraints and try again. Once Solver finds a solution, you can choose to create a summary of the solution or a special report displaying the solution. You have finished entering the parameters in the Solver Parameters dialog box. ▓▓▓▓ Kate wants you to run Solver and create a summary of the solution on a separate worksheet.

STEPS

1. **Make sure your Solver Parameters dialog box matches Figure K-17 in the previous lesson**

2. **Click Solve**

   The Solver Results dialog box opens, indicating that Solver has found a solution, as shown in Figure K-18. The solution values appear in the worksheet, but you decide to save the solution values in a summary worksheet and display the original values in the worksheet.

3. **Click Save Scenario, enter Adjusted Budgets in the Scenario Name text box, click OK, in the Solver Results dialog box click the Restore Original Values option button, then click OK to close the Solver Results dialog box**

   The Solver Results dialog box closes, and the original values appear in the worksheet. You will display the Solver solution values on a separate sheet.

4. **Click the What-If Analysis button in the Data Tools group, click Scenario Manager, with the Adjusted Budgets scenario selected in the Scenario Manager dialog box click Summary, then click OK**

   The Solver results appear on the Scenario Summary 2 worksheet, as shown in Figure K-19. To keep the budget at $3,030,000 and equally fund each region, the travel and entertainment budget allocations are calculated in column E labeled Adjusted Budgets. You want to format the solution values on the worksheet.

5. **Select Column A, click the Home tab if necessary, click the Delete button in the Cells group, right-click the Scenario Summary 2 sheet tab, click Rename on the shortcut menu, type Adjusted Budgets, then press [Enter]**

6. **Select the range A16:A18, press [Delete], select the range A2:D3, click the Fill Color list arrow, then click Blue, Accent 2**

7. **Select the range A5:D15, click the Fill Color list arrow, click Blue, Accent 2, Lighter 80%, right-click the row 1 header to select the row, click Delete, select cell A1, then enter Solver Solution**

   The formatted Solver solution is shown in Figure K-20.

8. **Enter your name in the center section of the worksheet footer, save the workbook, then preview the worksheet**

   You have successfully found the best budget allocations using Solver.

FIGURE K-18: Solver Results dialog box

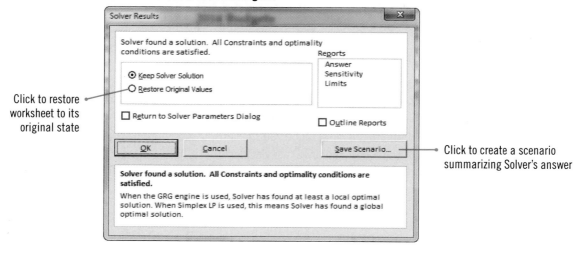

Click to restore worksheet to its original state

Click to create a scenario summarizing Solver's answer

FIGURE K-19: Solver Summary

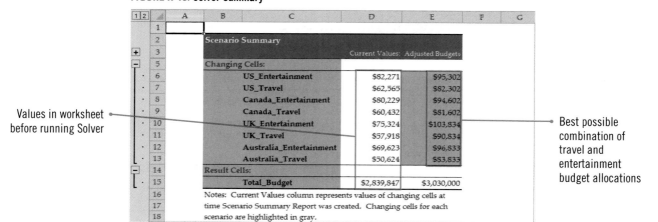

Values in worksheet before running Solver

Best possible combination of travel and entertainment budget allocations

FIGURE K-20: Formatted Solver Summary

Understanding Answer Reports

Instead of saving Solver results as a scenario, you can select from three types of answer reports in the Solver Results window. One of the most useful is the Answer Report, which compares the original values with the Solver's final values. The report has three sections. The top section has the target cell information; it compares the original value of the target cell with the final value. The middle section of the report contains information about the adjustable cells. It lists the original and final values for all cells that were changed to reach the target value. The last report section has information about the constraints. Each constraint that was added into Solver is listed in the Formula column along with the cell address and a description of the cell data. The Cell Value column contains the Solver solution values for the cells. These values will be different from your worksheet values if you restored the original values to your worksheet rather than keeping Solver's solution. The Status column contains information on whether the constraints were binding or not binding in reaching the solution. If a solution is not binding, the slack—or how far the result is from the constraint value—is provided. Frequently, the answer report shows equality constraints as nonbinding with a slack of zero.

Analyzing Data Using the Analysis ToolPak

The Analysis ToolPak is an Excel add-in that contains many statistical analysis tools. The Descriptive Analysis tool in the Data Analysis dialog box generates a statistical report including mean, median, mode, minimum, maximum, and sum for an input range you specify on your worksheet. ▓▓▓▓ After reviewing the projected sales figures for the Quest regions, Kate decides to statistically analyze the projected regional sales totals submitted by the managers. You use the Analysis ToolPak to help her generate the sales statistics.

STEPS

TROUBLE

If Data Analysis is not on your Data tab, click the File tab, click Options, click Add-Ins, in the list of Add-ins click Analysis ToolPak, click Go, in the Add-Ins dialog box click the Analysis ToolPak check box to select it, then click OK.

1. **Click the Projected Sales sheet tab, click the Data tab, then click the Data Analysis button in the Analysis group**
   The Data Analysis dialog box opens, listing the available analysis tools.

2. **Click Descriptive Statistics, then click OK**
   The Descriptive Statistics dialog box opens, as shown in Figure K-21.

3. **With the insertion point in the Input Range text box, select the range H3:H6 on the worksheet**
   You have told Excel to use the total projected sales cells in the statistical analysis. You need to specify that the data is grouped in a column and the results should be placed on a new worksheet named Region Statistics.

QUICK TIP

Selecting the New Worksheet Ply option places the statistical output on a new worksheet in the workbook.

4. **Click the Columns option button in the Grouped By: area if necessary, click the New Worksheet Ply option button in the Output options section if necessary, then type Region Statistics in the text box**
   You want to add the summary statistics to the new worksheet.

QUICK TIP

If there are fewer than four data values, the Kurtosis will display the DIV/0! error value.

5. **Click the Summary statistics check box to select it, then click OK**
   The statistics are generated and placed on the new worksheet named Region Statistics. Table K-1 describes some of the statistical values provided in the worksheet. Column A is not wide enough to view the labels, and the worksheet needs a descriptive title.

6. **Widen column A to display the row labels, then edit the contents of cell A1 to read Total Projected Sales Jan – Jun**

7. **Enter your name in the center section of the Region Statistics footer, preview the report, save the workbook, close the workbook, then exit Excel**

8. **Submit the workbook to your instructor**
   The completed report is shown in Figure K-22.

Choosing the right tool for your data analysis

The Analysis ToolPak offers 19 options for data analysis. ANOVA, or the analysis of variance, can be applied to one or more samples of data. The regression option creates a table of statistics from a least-squares regression. The correlation choice measures how strong of a linear relationship exists between two random variables. A moving average is often calculated for stock prices or any other data that is time sensitive. Moving averages display long-term trends by smoothing out short-term changes. The Random Number Generation creates a set of random numbers between values that you specify. The Rank and Percentile option creates a report of the ranking and percentile distribution.

FIGURE K-21: **Descriptive Statistics dialog box**

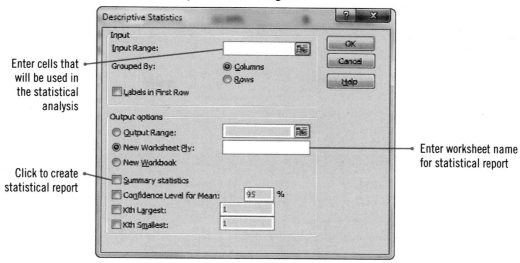

Enter cells that will be used in the statistical analysis

Enter worksheet name for statistical report

Click to create statistical report

FIGURE K-22: **Completed Report**

Total Projected Sales Jan - Jun	
Mean	400858.7
Standard Error	39394.23
Median	395502.5
Mode	#N/A
Standard Deviation	78788.46
Sample Variance	6.21E+09
Kurtosis	-0.54301
Skewness	0.342022
Range	184725.8
Minimum	313852
Maximum	498577.8
Sum	1603435
Count	4

TABLE K-1: **Descriptive statistics**

statistic	definition
Mean	The average of a set of numbers
Median	The middle value of a set of numbers
Mode	The most common value in a set of numbers
Standard Deviation	The measure of how widely spread the values in a set of numbers are; if the values are all close to the mean, the standard deviation is close to zero
Range	The difference between the largest and smallest values in a set of numbers
Minimum	The smallest value in a set of numbers
Maximum	The largest value in a set of numbers
Sum	The total of the values in a set of numbers
Count	The number of values in a set of numbers
Skewness	The measure of the asymmetry of the values in a set of numbers
Sample Variance	The measure of how scattered the values in a set of numbers are from an expected value
Kurtosis	The measure of the peakedness or flatness of a distribution of data

Practice

Concepts Review

For current SAM information, including versions and content details, visit SAM Central (http://www.cengage.com/samcentral). If you have a SAM user profile, you may have access to hands-on instruction, practice, and assessment of the skills covered in this unit. Since various versions of SAM are supported throughout the life of this text, check with your instructor for the correct instructions and URL/Web site for accessing assignments.

FIGURE K-23

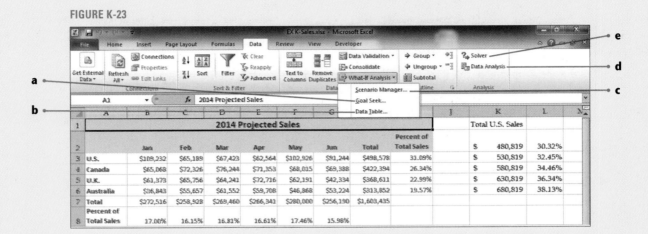

1. Which element do you click to perform a statistical analysis on worksheet data?
2. Which element do you click to create a range of cells showing the resulting values with varied formula input?
3. Which element do you click to perform a what-if analysis involving multiple input values with constraints?
4. Which element do you click to name and save different sets of values to forecast worksheet results?
5. Which element do you click to find the input values that produce a specified result?

Match each term with the statement that best describes it.

6. One-input data table
7. Solver
8. Goal Seek
9. Scenario summary
10. Two-input data table

a. Add-in that helps you solve complex what-if scenarios with multiple input values
b. Separate sheet with results from the worksheet's scenarios
c. Generates values resulting from varying two sets of changing values in a formula
d. Helps you backsolve what-if scenarios
e. Generates values resulting from varying one set of changing values in a formula

Select the best answer from the list of choices.

11. To hide the contents of a cell from view, you can use the custom number format:
   a. ;;;
   b. —
   c. Blank
   d. " "
12. The _____ button in the Scenario Manager dialog box allows you to bring scenarios from another workbook into the current workbook.
   a. Combine
   b. Add
   c. Import
   d. Merge

13. When you use Goal Seek, you specify a _____, then find the values that produce it.

   a. Row input cell   **c.** Solution

   b. Column input cell   **d.** Changing value

14. In Solver, the cell containing the formula is called the:

   a. Changing cell.   **c.** Input cell.

   b. Target cell.   **d.** Output cell.

15. Which of the following Excel add-ins can be used to generate a statistical summary of worksheet data?

   a. Solver   **c.** Analysis ToolPak

   b. Lookup Wizard   **d.** Conditional Sum

Skills Review

1. Define a what-if analysis.

   a. Start Excel, open the file EX K-2.xlsx from the drive and folder where you store your Data Files, then save it as **EX K-Repair**.

   b. Examine the Auto Repair worksheet to determine the purpose of the worksheet model.

   c. Locate the data input cells.

   d. Locate any dependent cells.

   e. Examine the worksheet to determine problems the worksheet model can solve.

2. Track a what-if analysis with Scenario Manager.

   a. On the Auto Repair worksheet, select the range B3:B5, then use the Scenario Manager to set up a scenario called **Most Likely** with the current data input values.

   b. Add a scenario called **Best Case** using the same changing cells, but change the Labor cost per hour in the $B$3 text box to **80**, change the Parts cost per job in the $B$4 text box to **65**, then change the Hours per job value in cell $B$5 to **1.5**.

   c. Add a scenario called **Worst Case**. For this scenario, change the Labor cost per hour in the $B$3 text box to **95**, change the Parts cost per job in the $B$4 text box to **80**, then change the Hours per job in the $B$5 text box to **3**.

   d. If necessary, drag the Scenario Manager dialog box to the right until columns A and B are visible.

   e. Show the Worst Case scenario results, and view the total job cost.

   f. Show the Best Case scenario results, and observe the job cost. Finally, display the Most Likely scenario results.

   g. Close the Scenario Manager dialog box.

   h. Save the workbook.

3. Generate a scenario summary.

   a. Create names for the input value cells and the dependent cell using the range A3:B7.

   b. Verify that the names were created.

   c. Create a scenario summary report, using the Cost to complete job value in cell B7 as the result cell.

   d. Edit the title of the Summary report in cell B2 to read **Scenario Summary for Auto Repair**.

   e. Delete the Current Values column.

   f. Delete the notes beginning in cell B11. Compare your worksheet to Figure K-24.

   g. Return to cell A1, enter your name in the center section of the Scenario Summary sheet footer, save the workbook, then preview the Scenario Summary sheet.

FIGURE K-24

	A	B	C	D	E	F
1						
2		Scenario Summary for Auto Repair				
3				Most Likely	Best Case	Worst Case
5		**Changing Cells:**				
6		Labor_cost_per_hour		$90.00	$80.00	$95.00
7		Parts_cost_per_job		$70.00	$65.00	$80.00
8		Hours_per_job		2.00	1.50	3.00
9		**Result Cells:**				
10		Cost_to_complete_job		$250.00	$185.00	$365.00

Independent Challenge 1 (continued)

■ Enter your name in the center section of the Scenario Summary 2 sheet footer, save the workbook, then preview the Advanced Scenario Summary.

h. Close the workbook, exit Excel, then submit the workbook to your instructor.

Independent Challenge 2

You are a CFO at Northern Interactive, an interactive media consulting company based in Minneapolis. The company president has asked you to prepare a loan summary report for a business expansion. You need to develop a model to show what the monthly payments would be for a $500,000 loan with a range of interest rates. You will create a one-input data table that shows the results of varying interest rates in 0.2% increments, then you will use Goal Seek to specify a total payment amount for this loan application.

a. Start Excel, open the file EX K-4.xlsx from the drive and folder where you store your Data Files, then save it as **EX K-Capital Loan Payment Model**.

b. Reference the monthly payment amount from cell B9 in cell E4, and format the contents of cell E4 as hidden.

c. Using cells D4:E13, create a one-input data table structure with varying interest rates for a 5-year loan. Use cells D5:D13 for the interest rates, with 9% as the lowest possible rate and 10.6% as the highest. Vary the rates in between by 0.2%. Use Figure K-28 as a guide.

d. Generate the data table that shows the effect of varying interest rates on the monthly payments. Use cell B5, the Annual Interest Rate, as the column input cell. Format the range E5:E13 as currency with two decimal places.

FIGURE K-28

	A	B	C	D
1	**Northern Interactive**			
2				
3				
4	Loan Amount	$500,000.00		Interest Rate
5	Annual Interest Rate	9.80%		9.00%
6	Term in Months	60		9.20%
7				9.40%
8				9.60%
9	Monthly Payment:	$10,574.39		9.80%
10	Total Payments:	$634,463.11		10.00%
11	Total Interest:	$134,463.11		10.20%
12				10.40%
13				10.60%
14				

e. Select cell B10 and use Goal Seek to find the interest rate necessary for a total payment amount of $600,000. Use cell B5, the Annual Interest Rate, as the By changing cell. Accept the solution found by Goal Seek.

Advanced Challenge Exercise

■ Reference the monthly payment amount from cell B9 in cell A13, and format the contents of cell A13 as hidden.
■ Using cells A13:C22, create a two-input data table structure with varying interest rates for 10- and 15-year terms. Use Figure K-29 as a guide.
■ Generate the data table that shows the effect of varying interest rates and loan terms on the monthly payments. (*Hint*: Use cell B6, Term in Months, as the row input cell, and cell B5, the Annual Interest Rate, as the column input cell.)
■ Format the range B14:C22 as currency with two decimal places.

FIGURE K-29

	A	B	C	D	E	F
1	**Northern Interactive**					
2						
3						
4	Loan Amount	$500,000.00		Interest Rate		
5	Annual Interest Rate	7.42%		9.00%	$10,379.18	
6	Term in Months	60		9.20%	$10,427.78	
7				9.40%	$10,476.51	
8				9.60%	$10,525.38	
9	Monthly Payment:	$10,000.00		9.80%	$10,574.39	
10	Total Payments:	$600,000.00		10.00%	$10,623.52	
11	Total Interest:	$100,000.00		10.20%	$10,672.79	
12				10.40%	$10,722.20	
13			120	180	10.60%	$10,771.74
14	7.00%					
15	7.25%					
16	7.50%					
17	7.75%					
18	8.00%					
19	8.25%					
20	8.50%					
21	8.75%					
22	9.00%					
23						

f. Enter your name in the center section of the worksheet footer, save the workbook, then preview the worksheet.

g. Close the workbook, exit Excel, then submit the workbook to your instructor.

Independent Challenge 3

You are the owner of Home Health, a home medical products company based in Boston. You are considering adding local delivery service to your business. You decide on a plan to purchase a combination of vans, sedans, and compact cars that can deliver a total of 1500 cubic feet of products. You want to first look at how the interest rate affects the monthly payments for each vehicle type you are considering purchasing. To do this, you use Goal Seek. You need to keep the total monthly payments for all of the vehicles at or below $6,000. You use Solver to help find the best possible combination of vehicles.

a. Start Excel, open the file EX K-5.xlsx from the drive and folder where you store your Data Files, then save it as **EX K-Vehicle Purchase**.

b. Use Goal Seek to find the interest rate that produces a monthly payment for the van purchase of $1,650, and write down the interest rate that Goal Seek finds. Record the interest rate in cell A19, enter **Interest rate for $1650 van payment** in cell B19, then reset the interest rate to its original value.

c. Use Goal Seek to find the interest rate that produces a monthly payment for the sedan purchase of $950. Record the interest rate in cell A20, enter **Interest rate for $950 sedan payment** in cell B20, then reset the interest rate to its original value of 6.75%.

d. Use Goal Seek to find the interest rate that produces a monthly payment for the compact purchase of $790. Record the interest rate in cell A21, enter **Interest rate for $790 compact payment** in cell B21, then reset the interest rate to its original value.

e. Assign cell B8 the name **Quantity_Van**, name cell C8 **Quantity_Sedan**, name cell D8 **Quantity_Compact**, and name cell B15 **Total_Monthly_Payments**. Use Solver to set the total delivery capacity of all vehicles to 1500. Use the quantity to purchase, cells B8:D8, as the changing cells. Specify that cells B8:D8 must be integers. Make sure that the total monthly payments amount in cell B15 is less than or equal to $6,000.

f. Generate a scenario named **Delivery Solution** with the Solver values, and restore the original values in the worksheet. Create a scenario summary using the Delivery Solution scenario, delete the notes at the bottom of the solution, and edit cell B2 to contain **Solver Solution**.

g. Enter your name in the center footer section of both worksheets. Preview both worksheets, then save the workbook.

h. Close the workbook, then submit the workbook to your instructor.

Real Life Independent Challenge

You decide to take out a loan for a new car. You haven't decided whether to finance the car for 3, 4, or 5 years. You will create scenarios for car loans with the different terms, using interest rates at your local lending institution. You will summarize the scenarios to make them easy to compare.

a. Start Excel, open the file EX K-6.xlsx from the drive and folder where you store your Data Files, then save it as **EX K-Car Payment**.

b. Research the interest rates for 3-year, 4-year, and 5-year auto loans at your local lending institution. Record your 48-month interest rate in cell B3 of the worksheet. Change the data in cell B2 to the price of a car you would like to purchase, then widen columns as necessary.

c. Create cell names for the cells B2:B9 based on the labels in cells A2:A9.

d. Create a scenario named **48 months** to calculate the monthly payment for your loan amount, using the 48-month term and the corresponding interest rate at your lending institution.

e. Create a scenario named **36 months** to calculate the monthly payment for your loan amount, using the 36-month term and the corresponding interest rate at your lending institution.

f. Create a scenario named **60 months** to calculate the monthly payment for your loan amount, using the 60-month term and the corresponding interest rate at your lending institution.

g. Generate a scenario summary titled **Scenario Summary for Car Purchase** that summarizes the payment information in cells B7:B9 for the varying interest rates and terms. Delete the Current Values column in the report and the notes at the bottom of the report.

h. Enter your name in the center section of the scenario summary footer, then preview the scenario summary.

i. Enter your name in the center section of the Loan sheet footer, then preview the Loan sheet.

j. Save the workbook, close the workbook, then exit Excel and submit the workbook to your instructor.

Visual Workshop

Open the file EX K-7.xlsx from the drive and folder where you save your Data Files, then save it as **EX K-Atlanta Manufacturing**. Create the worksheet shown in Figure K-30. (*Hint*: Use Goal Seek to find the Hourly labor cost to reach the total profit in cell H11 in the figure and accept the solution.) Then generate descriptive statistics for the products' total profits on a worksheet named **Manufacturing Profits**, as shown in Figure K-31. Add your name to the center footer section of each sheet, change the orientation of the Profit sheet to landscape, then preview and print both worksheets.

FIGURE K-30

	A	B	C	D	E	F	G	H
1	Atlanta Manufacturing							
2	January Production							
3	Hourly Labor Cost	$61.18						
4								
5								
6	Product Number	Hours	Parts Cost	Cost to Produce	Retail Price	Unit Profit	Units Produced	Total Profit
7	NA1547	8	$452	$ 941.43	$1,695.00	$ 753.57	327	$ 246,417.12
8	CB5877	10	$214	$ 825.79	$1,588.00	$ 762.21	407	$ 310,220.07
9	QW5287	15	$384	$1,301.68	$1,995.00	$ 693.32	321	$ 222,554.82
10	TY8894	17	$610	$1,650.04	$2,544.00	$ 893.96	247	$ 220,807.99
11	Total Profit							$ 1,000,000.00
12								

FIGURE K-31

	A	B
1	Profit Statistics	
2		
3	Mean	250000
4	Standard Error	20905.95
5	Median	234486
6	Mode	#N/A
7	Standard Deviation	41811.9
8	Sample Variance	1.75E+09
9	Kurtosis	2.254124
10	Skewness	1.575897
11	Range	89412.07
12	Minimum	220808
13	Maximum	310220.1
14	Sum	1000000
15	Count	4
16		

Analyzing Data with PivotTables

Files You Will Need:

EX L-1.xlsx
EX L-2.xlsx
EX L-3.xlsx
EX L-4.xlsx
EX L-5.xlsx
EX L-6.xlsx
EX L-7.xlsx

Excel PivotTables and PivotCharts let you summarize large quantities of data in a compact layout. You can interact with the PivotTable or PivotChart to explore the relationships within your data and display your findings in an easy-to-understand format. Excel includes two PivotTable features: PivotTable reports and PivotChart reports. In this unit, you plan, design, create, update, and change the layout and format of a PivotTable report and a PivotChart report. Kate Morgan, the vice president of sales at Quest, is preparing for the annual meeting for the United States region. She decides to analyze product sales in Quest's Chicago, New York, and Miami branches over the past year. Kate asks you to create a PivotTable to summarize the 2013 sales data by quarter, product, and branch. She then has you illustrate the information using a PivotChart.

OBJECTIVES

Plan and design a PivotTable report

Create a PivotTable report

Change a PivotTable's summary function and design

Filter and sort PivotTable data

Update a PivotTable report

Change a PivotTable's structure and format

Create a PivotChart report

Use the GETPIVOTDATA function

Planning and Designing a PivotTable Report

The Excel **PivotTable Report** feature lets you summarize large amounts of columnar worksheet data in an interactive table format. You can freely rearrange, or "pivot," parts of the table structure around the data to summarize any data values within the table by category. Creating a PivotTable report (often called a PivotTable) involves only a few steps. Before you begin, however, you need to review the data and consider how a PivotTable can best summarize it. ▓▓▓▓ Kate asks you to design a PivotTable to display Quest's sales information for its branches in the United States. You begin by reviewing guidelines for creating PivotTables.

DETAILS

Before you create a PivotTable, think about the following guidelines:

- **Review the source data**

  Before you can effectively summarize data in a PivotTable, you need to understand the source data's scope and structure. The source data does not have to be defined as a table, but should be in a table-like format. That is, it should have column headings, should not have any blank rows or columns, and should have the same type of data in each column. To create a meaningful PivotTable, make sure that one or more of the fields has repeated information so that the PivotTable can effectively group it. Also be sure to include numeric data that the PivotTable can total for each group. The data columns represent categories of data, which are called **fields**, just as in a table. You are working with sales information that Kate received from Quest's U.S. branch managers, shown in Figure L-1. Information is repeated in the Product ID, Category, Branch, and Quarter columns, and numeric information is displayed in the Sales column, so you will be able to summarize this data effectively in a PivotTable.

- **Determine the purpose of the PivotTable and write the names of the fields you want to include**

  The purpose of your PivotTable is to summarize sales information by quarter across various branches. You want your PivotTable to summarize the data in the Product ID, Category, Branch, Quarter, and Sales columns, so you include those fields in your PivotTable.

- **Determine which field contains the data you want to summarize and which summary function you want to use**

  You want to summarize sales information by summing the Sales field for each product in a branch by quarter. You'll do this by using the Excel SUM function.

- **Decide how you want to arrange the data**

  The PivotTable layout you choose is crucial to delivering the message you intend. Product ID will appear in the PivotTable columns, Branch and Quarter will appear in rows, and the PivotTable will summarize Sales figures, as shown in Figure L-2.

- **Determine the location of the PivotTable**

  You can place a PivotTable in any worksheet of any workbook. Placing a PivotTable on a separate worksheet makes it easier to locate and prevents you from accidentally overwriting parts of an existing sheet. You decide to create the PivotTable as a new worksheet in the current workbook.

FIGURE L-1: Sales worksheet

	A	B	C	D	E	F
1	United States Sales					
2	Product ID	Category	Branch	Quarter	Sales	
3	240	Travel Accessory	Chicago	1	$ 2,300.56	
4	240	Travel Accessory	Chicago	2	$ 5,767.76	
5	240	Travel Accessory	Chicago	3	$ 4,883.65	
6	240	Travel Accessory	Chicago	4	$ 5,697.45	
7	110	Travel Insurance	Chicago	1	$ 980.65	
8	110	Travel Insurance	Chicago	2	$ 2,634.69	
9	110	Travel Insurance	Chicago	3	$ 2,400.74	
10	110	Travel Insurance	Chicago	4	$ 3,612.93	
11	340	Tour	Chicago	1	$ 8,995.43	
12	340	Tour	Chicago	2	$ 7,976.43	
13	340	Tour	Chicago	3	$ 8,232.65	
14	340	Tour	Chicago	4	$ 8,631.98	
15	780	Travel Accessory	Chicago	1	$ 999.65	
16	780	Travel Accessory	Chicago	2	$ 2,334.56	
17	780	Travel Accessory	Chicago	3	$ 2,210.32	
18	780	Travel Accessory	Chicago	4	$ 1,245.67	
19	640	Travel Insurance	Chicago	1	$ 1,289.65	
20	640	Travel Insurance	Chicago	2	$ 6,434.56	
21	640	Travel Insurance	Chicago	3	$ 6,110.32	
22	640	Travel Insurance	Chicago	4	$ 6,345.67	
23	510	Tour	Chicago	1	$ 999.43	
24	510	Tour	Chicago	2	$ 1,954.43	
25	510	Tour	Chicago	3	$ 2,412.65	
26	510	Tour	Chicago	4	$ 2,661.98	
27	240	Travel Accessory	Miami	1	$ 1,394.32	
28	240	Travel Accessory	Miami	2	$ 3,231.80	
29	240	Travel Accessory	Miami	3	$ 3,511.65	

Data with repeated
information

Numeric data

FIGURE L-2: Example of a PivotTable report

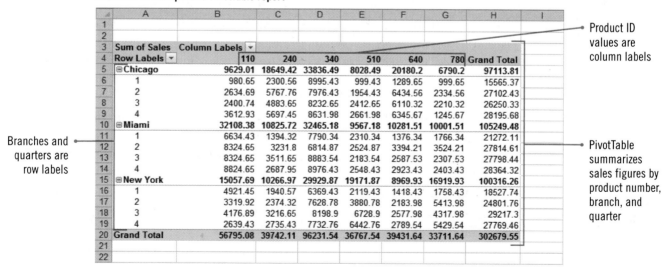

	A	B	C	D	E	F	G	H	I
1									
2									
3	Sum of Sales	Column Labels							
4	Row Labels	110	240	340	510	640	780	Grand Total	
5	⊟Chicago	9629.01	18649.42	33836.49	8028.49	20180.2	6790.2	97113.81	
6	1	980.65	2300.56	8995.43	999.43	1289.65	999.65	15565.37	
7	2	2634.69	5767.76	7976.43	1954.43	6434.56	2334.56	27102.43	
8	3	2400.74	4883.65	8232.65	2412.65	6110.32	2210.32	26250.33	
9	4	3612.93	5697.45	8631.98	2661.98	6345.67	1245.67	28195.68	
10	⊟Miami	32108.38	10825.72	32465.18	9567.18	10281.51	10001.51	105249.48	
11	1	6634.43	1394.32	7790.34	2310.34	1376.34	1766.34	21272.11	
12	2	8324.65	3231.8	6814.87	2524.87	3394.21	3524.21	27814.61	
13	3	8324.65	3511.65	8883.54	2183.54	2587.53	2307.53	27798.44	
14	4	8824.65	2687.95	8976.43	2548.43	2923.43	2403.43	28364.32	
15	⊟New York	15057.69	10266.97	29929.87	19171.87	8969.93	16919.93	100316.26	
16	1	4921.45	1940.57	6369.43	2119.43	1418.43	1758.43	18527.74	
17	2	3319.92	2374.32	7628.78	3880.78	2183.98	5413.98	24801.76	
18	3	4176.89	3216.65	8198.9	6728.9	2577.98	4317.98	29217.3	
19	4	2639.43	2735.43	7732.76	6442.76	2789.54	5429.54	27769.46	
20	Grand Total	56795.08	39742.11	96231.54	36767.54	39431.64	33711.64	302679.55	
21									
22									

Product ID
values are
column labels

Branches and
quarters are
row labels

PivotTable
summarizes
sales figures by
product number,
branch, and
quarter

Excel 2010

Creating a PivotTable Report

Once you've planned and designed your PivotTable report, you can create it. After you create the PivotTable, you **populate** it by adding fields to areas in the PivotTable. A PivotTable has four areas: the Report Filter, which is the field by which you want to filter, or show selected data in, the PivotTable; the Row Labels, which contain the fields whose labels will describe the values in the rows; the Column Labels, which appear above the PivotTable values and describe the columns; and the Values, which summarize the numeric data. ▰▰▰▰ With the planning and design stage complete, you are ready to create a PivotTable that summarizes sales information. Kate will use the information in her presentation to the branch managers in the Chicago, New York, and Miami offices.

STEPS

1. **Start Excel if necessary, open the file EX L-1.xlsx from the drive and folder where you store your Data Files, then save it as EX L-US Sales**

   This worksheet contains the year's sales information for Quest's U.S. branches, including Product ID, Category, Branch, Quarter, and Sales. The records are sorted by branch.

2. **Click the Insert tab, then click the PivotTable button in the Tables group**

   The Create PivotTable dialog box opens, as shown in Figure L-3. This is where you specify the type of data source you want to use for your PivotTable: an Excel Table/Range or an external data source such as a database file. You also specify where you want to place the PivotTable.

3. **Make sure the Select a table or range option button is selected and the range Sales!$A$2:$E$74 appears in the Table/Range text box, make sure the New Worksheet option button is selected, then click OK**

   The PivotTable appears on the left side of the worksheet and the PivotTable Field List pane appears on the right, as shown in Figure L-4. You populate the PivotTable by clicking field check boxes in the Field List pane. The diagram area at the bottom of the PivotTable Field List task pane represents the main PivotTable areas and helps you track field locations as you populate the PivotTable. You can also drag fields among the diagram areas to change the PivotTable layout.

   > **QUICK TIP**
   > To remove a field from a PivotTable, click the field's check box to uncheck it.

4. **Click the Branch field check box in the PivotTable Field List**

   Because the Branch field is nonnumeric, Excel adds it to the Row Labels area.

5. **Click the Product ID check box in the PivotTable Field List pane**

   The Product ID field name appears in the Values area in the diagram area, and the Product ID information is automatically added to the PivotTable. But because the data type of the Product ID field is numeric, the field is added to the Values area of the PivotTable and the Product ID values are summed. Instead, you want the Product IDs as column headers in the PivotTable.

6. **Click the Sum of Product ID list arrow in the Values area at the bottom of the PivotTable Field List, then choose Move to Column Labels**

   The Product ID field becomes a column label, causing the Product ID values to appear in the PivotTable as column headers. You can also drag fields to place them directly in the area you choose.

   > **QUICK TIP**
   > You can click the Collapse Outline button [−] next to the branch names to collapse the outline and hide the quarter details. You can display hidden quarter values by clicking the Expand Outline button [+] next to any field name on a PivotTable to expand an outline.

7. **Drag the Quarter field from the top of the PivotTable Field List and drop it below the Branch field in the Row Labels area at the bottom, then select the Sales field check box in the PivotTable Field List**

   You have created a PivotTable that totals U.S. sales, with the Product IDs as column headers and Branches and Quarters as row labels. Adding the Quarter field as a row label below the Branches field displays the quarters below each branch in the Row Labels area of the PivotTable. Because the data in the Sales field is numeric, the Sales field is added to the Values area. SUM is the Excel default function for data fields containing numbers, so Excel automatically calculates the sum of the sales in the PivotTable. The PivotTable tells you that Miami sales of Product #110 were twice the New York sales level and more than three times the Chicago sales level. Product #340 was the best selling product overall, as shown in the Grand Total row. See Figure L-5.

8. **Save the workbook**

Analyzing Data with PivotTables

FIGURE L-3: Create PivotTable dialog box

Data source you want to use for the PivotTable •

Location where you want to place PivotTable •

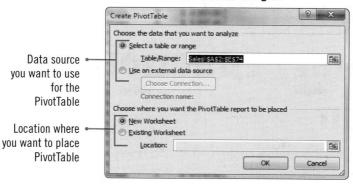

FIGURE L-4: New PivotTable ready to receive field data

PivotTable •

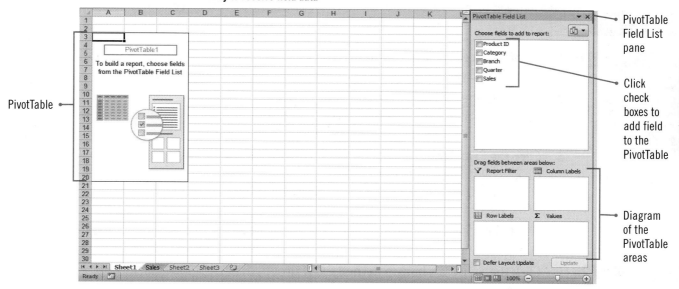

• PivotTable Field List pane

• Click check boxes to add field to the PivotTable

• Diagram of the PivotTable areas

FIGURE L-5: New PivotTable with fields in place

Miami sales for this product are twice as high as New York and three times Chicago's sales

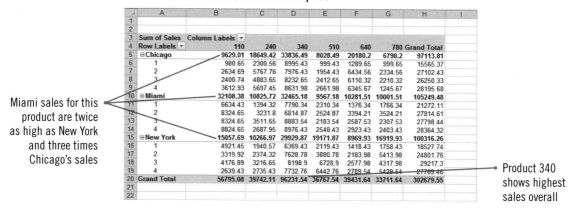

Product 340 shows highest sales overall

Changing the PivotTable layout

The default layout for PivotTables is the compact form; the row labels are displayed in a single column, and the second-level field items (such as the quarters in the U.S. Sales example) are indented for readability. You can change the layout of your PivotTable by clicking the PivotTable Tools Design tab, clicking the Report Layout button in the Layout group, then clicking either Show in Outline Form or Show in Tabular Form. The tabular form and the outline form show each row label in its own column. The outline form places subtotals at the top of every column. The tabular and outline layouts take up more space on a worksheet than the compact layout.

Changing a PivotTable's Summary Function and Design

A PivotTable's **summary function** controls what calculation Excel uses to summarize the table data. Unless you specify otherwise, Excel applies the SUM function to numeric data and the COUNT function to data fields containing text. However, you can easily change the SUM function to a different summary function. ▰▰▰ Kate wants you to calculate the average sales for the U.S. branches using the AVERAGE function, and to improve the appearance of the PivotTable for her presentation.

STEPS

1. **Right-click cell A3, then point to Summarize Values By in the shortcut menu**

   The menu shows that the Sum function is selected by default, as shown in Figure L-6.

2. **Click Average**

   The data area of the PivotTable shows the average sales for each product by branch and quarter, and cell A3 now contains "Average of Sales". You want to view the PivotTable data without the subtotals.

3. **Click the PivotTable Tools Design tab, click the Subtotals button in the Layout group, then click Do Not Show Subtotals**

   After reviewing the data, you decide that it would be more useful to sum the sales information than to average it. You also want to redisplay the subtotals.

4. **Right-click cell A3, point to Summarize Values By in the shortcut menu, then click Sum**

   Excel recalculates the PivotTable—in this case, summing the sales data instead of averaging it.

5. **Click the Subtotals button in the Layout group, then click Show all Subtotals at Top of Group**

   In the same way that tables have styles available to quickly format them, PivotTables have a gallery of styles to choose from. You decide to add a PivotTable style to the PivotTable to improve its appearance.

6. **Click the More button ⊽ in the PivotTable Styles gallery, then click Pivot Style Light 13**

   To further improve the appearance of the PivotTable, you will remove the unnecessary headers of "Column Labels" and "Row Labels".

7. **Click the PivotTable Tools Options tab, then click the Field Headers button in the Show group**

   The data would be more readable if it were in currency format.

8. **Click any sales value in the PivotTable, click the Field Settings button in the Active Field group, click Number Format in the Value Field Settings dialog box, select Currency in the Category list, make sure Decimal places is 2 and Symbol is $, click OK, then click OK again**

   You decide to give the PivotTable sheet a more descriptive name. When you name a PivotTable sheet, it is best to avoid using spaces in the name. If a PivotTable name contains a space, you must put single quotes around the name if you refer to it in a function.

9. **Rename Sheet1 PivotTable, add your name to the worksheet footer, save the workbook, then preview the worksheet**

   The PivotTable is easier to read now that it is formatted as shown in Figure L-7.

FIGURE L-6: Shortcut menu showing Sum function selected

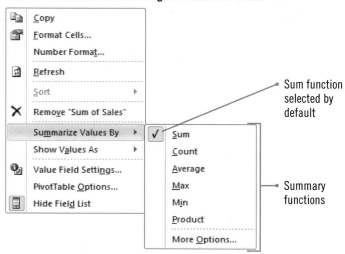

FIGURE L-7: Formatted PivotTable

	A	B	C	D	E	F	G	H	I
1									
2									
3	Sum of Sales								
4		110	240	340	510	640	780	Grand Total	
5	⊟Chicago	$9,629.01	$18,649.42	$33,836.49	$8,028.49	$20,180.20	$6,790.20	$97,113.81	
6	1	$980.65	$2,300.56	$8,995.43	$999.43	$1,289.65	$999.65	$15,565.37	
7	2	$2,634.69	$5,767.76	$7,976.43	$1,954.43	$6,434.56	$2,334.56	$27,102.43	
8	3	$2,400.74	$4,883.65	$8,232.65	$2,412.65	$6,110.32	$2,210.32	$26,250.33	
9	4	$3,612.93	$5,697.45	$8,631.98	$2,661.98	$6,345.67	$1,245.67	$28,195.68	
10	⊟Miami	$32,108.38	$10,825.72	$32,465.18	$9,567.18	$10,281.51	$10,001.51	$105,249.48	
11	1	$6,634.43	$1,394.32	$7,790.34	$2,310.34	$1,376.34	$1,766.34	$21,272.11	
12	2	$8,324.65	$3,231.80	$6,814.87	$2,524.87	$3,394.21	$3,524.21	$27,814.61	
13	3	$8,324.65	$3,511.65	$8,883.54	$2,183.54	$2,587.53	$2,307.53	$27,798.44	
14	4	$8,824.65	$2,687.95	$8,976.43	$2,548.43	$2,923.43	$2,403.43	$28,364.32	
15	⊟New York	$15,057.69	$10,266.97	$29,929.87	$19,171.87	$8,969.93	$16,919.93	$100,316.26	
16	1	$4,921.45	$1,940.57	$6,369.43	$2,119.43	$1,418.43	$1,758.43	$18,527.74	
17	2	$3,319.92	$2,374.32	$7,628.78	$3,880.78	$2,183.98	$5,413.98	$24,801.76	
18	3	$4,176.89	$3,216.65	$8,198.90	$6,728.90	$2,577.98	$4,317.98	$29,217.30	
19	4	$2,639.43	$2,735.43	$7,732.76	$6,442.76	$2,789.54	$5,429.54	$27,769.46	
20	Grand Total	$56,795.08	$39,742.11	$96,231.54	$36,767.54	$39,431.64	$33,711.64	$302,679.55	
21									
22									

Using the Show buttons

To display and hide PivotTable elements, you can use the buttons in the Show group on the PivotTable Tools Options tab. For example, the Field List button will hide or display the PivotTable Field List pane. The +/– Buttons button will hide or display the Expand and Collapse Outline buttons, and the Field Headers button will hide or display the Row and Column Label headers on the PivotTable.

Filtering and Sorting PivotTable Data

When you worked with Excel tables, you used filters to hide and display table data. You can restrict the display of PivotTable data using a **Slicer**, graphic object with a set of buttons that allow you to easily filter your PivotTable data to show only the data you need. For example, you can use the buttons in a slicer to show only data about a specific product in your PivotTable. You can also filter a PivotTable using a **report filter**, which lets you filter PivotTable data using a list arrow to show data based on one or more field values. For example, if you add a field with monthly data to the Report Filter area, you can filter a PivotTable so that only data representing the January sales appears in the PivotTable. In addition to filtering PivotTable data, you can also sort PivotTable data to organize it in ascending or descending order. ▰▰▰ Kate wants you to sort the PivotTable so she can see sales data about specific products for specific quarters.

1. **Click cell H5, click the PivotTable Tools Options tab if necessary, then click the Sort button in the Sort & Filter group**

   The Sort By Value dialog box opens. As you select options in the dialog box, the Summary information at the bottom of the dialog box changes to describe the sort results using your field names.

2. **Click the Largest to Smallest option button to select it in the Sort options section, make sure the Top to Bottom option button is selected in the Sort direction section, review the sort description in the Summary section of the dialog box, then click OK**

   The branches are arranged in the PivotTable in decreasing order of total sales from top to bottom. You want to easily display the sales for specific product IDs.

> **QUICK TIP**
> You can select multiple values on a slicer by pressing [Ctrl] while clicking buttons on a Slicer.

3. **Click any cell in the PivotTable, click the Insert Slicer button in the Sort & Filter group, click the Product ID check box in the Insert Slicers dialog box to select it, then click OK**

   A slicer appears containing a column of buttons representing the Product ID numbers as shown in Figure L-8. Slicers can be formatted using different styles and formatting options. See Table L-1 for a summary of slicer formatting options. You decide to filter the data so it displays the data for only the Product ID 510.

4. **Click the 510 button in the Slicer shape**

   The PivotTable filters the sales data to display the Product ID 510 data only, as shown in Figure L-9. In the Slicer shape, the Clear Filter symbol changes, indicating the PivotTable is filtered to display the selected field. You decide to clear the filter and remove the Slicer shape from the PivotTable worksheet.

> **QUICK TIP**
> You can also click the Hide All button in the Selection and Visibility pane to remove Slicer shapes.

5. **Click the Clear Filter button 🏹 in the Slicer shape, click the Selection Pane button in the Arrange group of the Slicer Tools Options tab, click the Visibility button 🔲 in the Selection and Visibility pane, then close the Selection and Visibility pane**

   You want to display the PivotTable data by quarter using a Report Filter.

> **TROUBLE**
> If the PivotTable Field List is not visible, click the PivotTable Tools Options tab, and click the Field List button in the Show group.

6. **In the PivotTable Field List, click the Quarter field list arrow in the Row Labels area, then select Move to Report Filter**

   The Quarter field moves up to cell A1, and a list arrow and the word "(All)" appear in cell B1. The list arrow allows you to filter the data in the PivotTable by Quarter. "(All)" indicates that the PivotTable currently shows data for all quarters. You decide to filter the data so it displays the data for only the fourth quarter.

7. **In the PivotTable cell B1, click the Quarter list arrow, click 4, then click OK**

   The PivotTable filters the sales data to display the fourth quarter only, as shown in Figure L-10. The Quarter field list arrow changes to a filter symbol. A filter symbol also appears to the right of the Quarter field in the PivotTable Field List pane, indicating that the PivotTable is filtered and summarizes only a portion of the PivotTable data.

8. **Save the workbook**

FIGURE L-8: Slicer for Product ID field

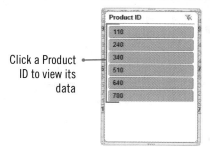

Click a Product
ID to view its
data

FIGURE L-9: PivotTable filtered by Product ID

Only data for
Product ID 510
appears in
PivotTable

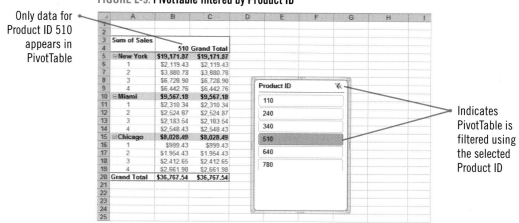

Indicates
PivotTable is
filtered using
the selected
Product ID

FIGURE L-10: PivotTable filtered by fourth quarter

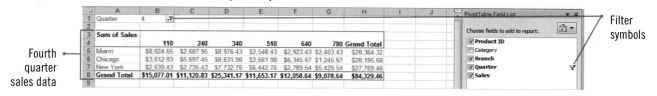

Fourth
quarter
sales data

Filter
symbols

TABLE L-1: Options for formatting slicers

to	action	group/command/key
Apply a slicer style	Click Slicer Tools Options tab	Slicer Styles group
Change button order	Click Slicer Tools Options tab	Slicer group/Slicer Settings button
Change caption name	Click Slicer Tools Options tab	Slicer group/Slicer Caption text box
Change slicer size, or columns	Click Slicer Tools Options tab	Buttons group
Change slicer position	Right-click slicer	Size and Properties command
Delete slicer	Click slicer's edge	[Delete] key

Filtering PivotTables using multiple values

You can select multiple values when filtering a PivotTable report using a report filter. After clicking a field's report filter list arrow in the top section of the PivotTable Field List or in cell B1 on the PivotTable itself, click the Select Multiple Items check box at the bottom of the filter selections. This allows you to select multiple values for the filter. For example, selecting 1 and 2 as the report filter in a PivotTable with quarters would display all of the data for the first two quarters. You can also select multiple values for the row and column labels by clicking the Row Label list arrow or the Column Label list arrow in cells A4 and B3 on the PivotTable and selecting the data items that you want to display.

Updating a PivotTable Report

The data in a PivotTable report looks like typical worksheet data. Because the PivotTable data is linked to a **data source** (the data you used to create the PivotTable), however, the values and results in the PivotTable are read-only values. That means you cannot move or modify a part of a PivotTable by inserting or deleting rows, editing results, or moving cells. To change PivotTable data, you must edit the items directly in the data source, then update, or **refresh**, the PivotTable to reflect the changes. ▰▰▰▰ Kate just learned that sales information for a custom group tour sold in New York during the fourth quarter was never entered into the Sales worksheet. Kate asks you to add information about this tour to the data source and PivotTable. You start by inserting a row for the new information in the Sales worksheet.

STEPS

1. **Click the Sales sheet tab**
   By inserting the new row in the correct position by branch, you will not need to sort the data again.

2. **Right-click the row 51 heading, then click Insert on the shortcut menu**
   A blank row appears as the new row 51, and the data in the old row 51, moves down to row 52. You now have room for the tour data.

3. **Enter the data for the new tour in row 51 using the following information**

Product ID	450
Category	Tour
Branch	New York
Quarter	4
Sales	3010.04

   The PivotTable does not yet reflect the additional data.

4. **Click the PivotTable sheet tab, then verify that the Quarter 4 data appears**
   The fourth quarter list does not currently include the new tour information, and the grand total is $84,329.46. Before you refresh the PivotTable data, you need to make sure that the cell pointer is located within the PivotTable range.

5. **Click anywhere within the PivotTable if necessary, click the PivotTable Tools Options tab, then click the Refresh button in the Data group**
   The PivotTable now contains a column for the new product ID, which includes the new tour information, in column H, and the grand total has increased by the amount of the tour's sales ($3,010.04) to $87,339.50, as shown in Figure L-11.

6. **Save the workbook**

Grouping PivotTable data

You can group PivotTable data to analyze specific values in a field as a unit. For example, you may want to group sales data for quarters one and two to analyze sales for the first half of the year. To group PivotTable data, you need to first select the rows and columns that you want to group, click the PivotTable Tools Options tab, then click the Group Selection button in the Group group. After you group data you can summarize it by clicking the Field Settings button in the Active Field group, clicking the Custom button in the Field Settings dialog box, selecting the function that you want to use to summarize the data, then clicking OK. You can click the Collapse Outline button ⊟ next to the group name to collapse the group and show the function results. You can click the Expand Outline button ⊞ next to the group name to display the rows or columns in the group. To ungroup data, select the Group name in the PivotTable, then click the Ungroup button in the Group group.

FIGURE L-11: Updated PivotTable report

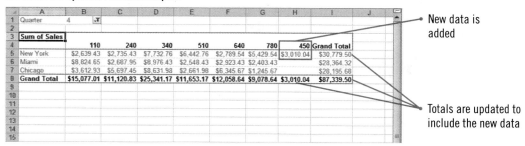

New data is added

Totals are updated to include the new data

FIGURE L-12: Insert Calculated Field dialog box

New field name

Formula to increase sales by 10%

Fields you can use in the formula

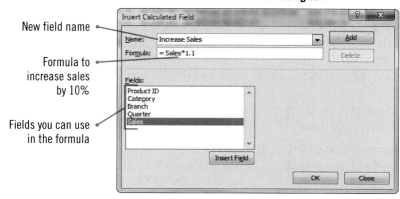

FIGURE L-13: PivotTable with Calculated Field

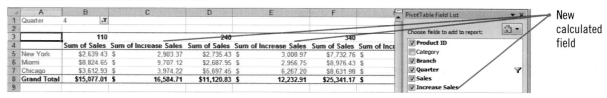

New calculated field

Adding a calculated field to a PivotTable

You can use formulas to analyze PivotTable data in a field by adding a calculated field. A calculated field appears in the PivotTable Field List pane and can be manipulated like other PivotTable fields. To add a calculated field, click any cell in the PivotTable, click the PivotTable Tools Options tab, click the Fields, Items, & Sets button in the Calculations group, then click Calculated Field. The Insert Calculated Field dialog box opens. Enter the field name in the Name text box, click in the Formula text box, click a field name in the Fields list that you want to use in the formula, and click Insert Field. Use standard arithmetic operators to enter the formula you want to use. For example Figure L-12 shows a formula to increase Sales data by 10 percent. After entering the formula in the Insert Calculated Field dialog box, click Add, then click OK. The new field with the formula results appears in the PivotTable, and the field is added to the PivotTable Field List as shown in Figure L-13.

Changing a PivotTable's Structure and Format

What makes a PivotTable such a powerful analysis tool is the ability to change the way data is organized in the report. You can easily change the structure of a PivotTable by adding fields or by moving fields to new positions in the PivotTable. ▰▰▰ Kate asks you to include category information in the sales report. She is also interested in viewing the PivotTable in different arrangements to find the best organization of data for her presentation.

STEPS

1. **Make sure that the PivotTable sheet is active, that the active cell is located anywhere inside the PivotTable, and that the PivotTable Field List is visible**

QUICK TIP
You can change the amount an inner row is indented by clicking the Options button in the PivotTable group on the PivotTable Tools Options tab, clicking the Layout & Format tab, then changing the number for the character(s) in the Layout section.

2. **Click the Category check box in the PivotTable Field List**

   Because the category data is nonnumeric, it is added to the Row Labels area. The PivotTable displays the category sales information for each branch. When you have two row labels, the data is organized by the values in the outer field and then by the data in the inner field. The inner field values are indented to make them easy to distinguish from the outer field. You can move fields within an area of a PivotTable by dragging and dropping them to the desired location. When you drag a field, the pointer appears with a PivotTable outline attached to its lower-right corner.

3. **In the diagram section of the PivotTable Field List, locate the Row Labels area, then drag the Category field up and drop it above the Branch field**

   The category field is now the outer or upper field, and the branch field is the inner or lower field. The PivotTable is restructured to display the sales data by the category values and then the branch values within the category field. The subtotals now reflect the sum of the categories, as shown in Figure L-14. You can also move fields to new areas in the PivotTable.

4. **In the diagram area of the PivotTable Field List, drag the Category field from the Row Labels area to the Column Labels area, then drag the Product ID field from the Column Labels area to the Row Labels area below the Branch field**

   The PivotTable now displays the sales data with the category values in the columns and then the product IDs grouped by branches. The product ID values are indented below the branches because the Product ID field is the inner row label.

QUICK TIP
As you move fields around in a PivotTable, you can control when the PivotTable structure is updated to reflect your changes. Click the Defer Layout Update check box at the bottom of the PivotTable Field List window. When you are ready to update the PivotTable, click the Update button.

5. **In the diagram area of the PivotTable Field List, drag the Category field from the Column Labels area to the Report Filter area above the Quarter field, then drag the Product ID field from the Row Labels area to the Column Labels area**

   The PivotTable now has two filters. The upper filter, Category, summarizes data using all of the categories. Kate asks you to display the tour sales information for all quarters.

6. **Click the Category list arrow in cell B1 of the PivotTable, click Tour, click OK, click the Quarter filter list arrow, click All, then click OK**

   The PivotTable displays sales totals for the Tour category for all quarters. Kate asks you to provide the sales information for all categories.

7. **Click the Category filter arrow, click All, then click OK**

   The completed PivotTable appears as shown in Figure L-15.

8. **Save the workbook, change the page orientation of the PivotTable sheet to landscape, then preview the PivotTable**

FIGURE L-14: PivotTable structured by branches within categories

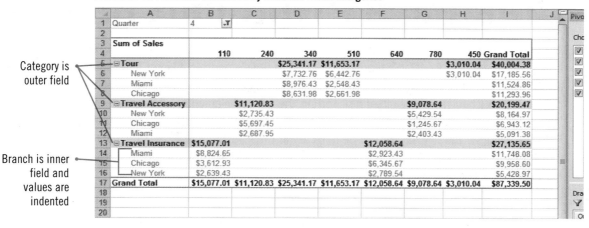

Category is outer field → (pointing to Tour, Travel Accessory, Travel Insurance rows)

Branch is inner field and values are indented → (pointing to Miami, Chicago, New York rows)

	A	B	C	D	E	F	G	H	I	J
1	Quarter	4 ⊤								
2										
3	Sum of Sales									
4		110	240	340	510	640	780	450	Grand Total	
5	⊟Tour			$25,341.17	$11,653.17			$3,010.04	$40,004.38	
6	New York			$7,732.76	$6,442.76			$3,010.04	$17,185.56	
7	Miami			$8,976.43	$2,548.43				$11,524.86	
8	Chicago			$8,631.98	$2,661.98				$11,293.96	
9	⊟Travel Accessory		$11,120.83				$9,078.64		$20,199.47	
10	New York		$2,735.43				$5,429.54		$8,164.97	
11	Chicago		$5,697.45				$1,245.67		$6,943.12	
12	Miami		$2,687.95				$2,403.43		$5,091.38	
13	⊟Travel Insurance	$15,077.01				$12,058.64			$27,135.65	
14	Miami	$8,824.65				$2,923.43			$11,748.08	
15	Chicago	$3,612.93				$6,345.67			$9,958.60	
16	New York	$2,639.43				$2,789.54			$5,428.97	
17	Grand Total	$15,077.01	$11,120.83	$25,341.17	$11,653.17	$12,058.64	$9,078.64	$3,010.04	$87,339.50	
18										
19										
20										

FIGURE L-15: Completed PivotTable report

	A	B	C	D	E	F	G	H	I
1	Category	(All) ▾							
2	Quarter	(All) ▾							
3									
4	Sum of Sales								
5		110	240	340	510	640	780	450	Grand Total
6	Miami	$32,108.38	$10,825.72	$32,465.18	$9,567.18	$10,281.51	$10,001.51		$105,249.48
7	New York	$15,057.69	$10,266.97	$29,929.87	$19,171.87	$8,969.93	$16,919.93	$3,010.04	$103,326.30
8	Chicago	$9,629.01	$18,649.42	$33,836.49	$8,028.49	$20,180.20	$6,790.20		$97,113.81
9	Grand Total	$56,795.08	$39,742.11	$96,231.54	$36,767.54	$39,431.64	$33,711.64	$3,010.04	$305,689.59
10									

Adding conditional formatting to a PivotTable

You can add conditional formatting to a PivotTable to make it easier to compare the data values. The conditional formatting is applied to cells in a PivotTable the same way as it is to non-PivotTable data. The conditional formatting rules follow the PivotTable cells when you move fields to different areas of the PivotTable. Figure L-16 shows a PivotTable that uses data bars to visually display the sales data.

FIGURE L-16: PivotTable with Conditional Formatting

5		110	240	340	510	640	780	450
6	Miami	$32,108.38	$10,825.72	$32,465.18	$9,567.18	$10,281.51	$10,001.51	
7	New York	$15,057.69	$10,266.97	$29,929.87	$19,171.87	$8,969.93	$16,919.93	$3,010.04
8	Chicago	$9,629.01	$18,649.42	$33,836.49	$8,028.49	$20,180.20	$6,790.20	
9	Grand Total	$56,795.08	$39,742.11	$96,231.54	$36,767.54	$39,431.64	$33,711.64	$3,010.04
10								

Creating a PivotChart Report

A **PivotChart report** is a chart that you create from data or from a PivotTable report. Table L-2 describes how the elements in a PivotTable report correspond to the elements in a PivotChart report. When you create a PivotChart directly from data, Excel automatically creates a corresponding PivotTable report. If you change a PivotChart report by filtering or sorting the charted elements, Excel updates the corresponding PivotTable report to show the new data values. You can move the fields of a PivotChart using the PivotTable Field List window; the new layout will be reflected in the PivotTable. Kate wants you to chart the fourth quarter tour sales and the yearly tour sales average for her presentation. You create the PivotChart report from the PivotTable data.

STEPS

1. **Click the Category list arrow in cell B1, click Tour, click OK, click the Quarter list arrow, click 4, then click OK**

   The fourth quarter tour sales information appears in the PivotTable. You want to create the PivotChart from the PivotTable information you have displayed.

2. **Click any cell in the PivotTable, click the PivotTable Tools Options tab, then click the PivotChart button in the Tools group**

   The Insert Chart dialog box opens and shows a gallery of chart types.

3. **Click the Clustered Column chart if necessary, then click OK**

   The PivotChart appears on the worksheet as shown in Figure L-17. The chart has Field buttons that enable you to filter and sort a PivotChart in the same way that you do a PivotTable. It will be easier to view the PivotChart if it is on its own sheet.

   > **QUICK TIP**
   > You can sort and filter the axis and legend fields by clicking their field button list arrows on the PivotChart and selecting a sort or filter option.

4. **Click the Move Chart button in the Location group, click the New sheet option button, type PivotChart in the text box, click OK**

   The chart represents the fourth quarter tour sales. Kate asks you to change the chart to show the average sales for all quarters.

5. **Click the Quarter field button at the top of the PivotChart, click All, then click OK**

   The chart now represents the sum of tour sales for the year as shown in Figure L-18. You can change a PivotChart's summary function to display averages instead of totals.

   > **TROUBLE**
   > If the PivotTable Field List is not visible, click the PivotChart Tools Analyze tab, then click the Field List button to display it.

6. **Click the Sum of Sales list arrow in the Values area of the PivotTable Field List, click Value Field Settings, click Average on the Summarize Values by tab, then click OK**

   The PivotChart report recalculates to display averages. The chart would be easier to understand if it had a title.

7. **Click the PivotChart Tools Layout tab, click the Chart Title button in the Labels group, click Above Chart, type Average Tour Sales, press [Enter], then drag the chart title border to center the title over the columns if necessary**

   You are finished filtering the chart data and decide to remove the field buttons.

   > **TROUBLE**
   > If you click the Field Buttons list arrow then you need to click Hide All to remove the filter buttons.

8. **Click the PivotChart Tools Analyze tab, then click the Field Buttons button in the Show/Hide group**

9. **Enter your name in the PivotChart sheet footer, save the workbook, then preview the PivotChart report**

   The final PivotChart report displaying the average tour sales for the year is shown in Figure L-19.

FIGURE L-17: PivotChart with fourth quarter tour sales

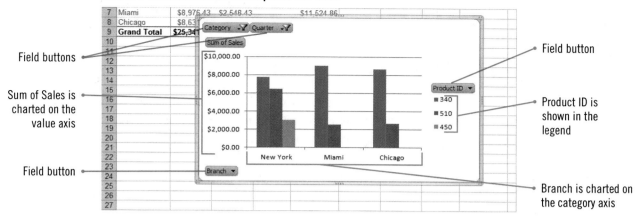

Field buttons

Sum of Sales is charted on the value axis

Field button

Field button

Product ID is shown in the legend

Branch is charted on the category axis

FIGURE L-18: PivotChart displaying tour sales for the year

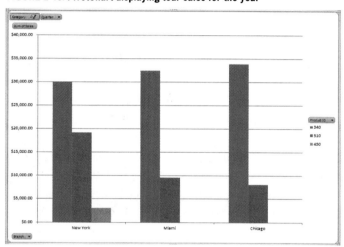

FIGURE L-19: Completed PivotChart report

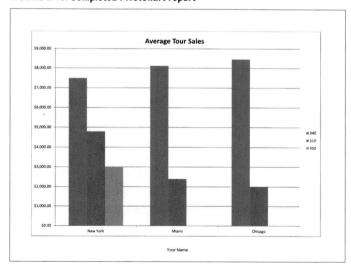

TABLE L-2: PivotTable and PivotChart elements

PivotTable items	PivotChart items
Row labels	Axis fields (categories)
Column labels	Legend fields (series)
Report filters	Report filters

Using the GETPIVOTDATA Function

Because you can rearrange a PivotTable so easily, you can't use an ordinary cell reference when you want to reference a PivotTable cell in another worksheet. The reason is that if you change the way data is displayed in a PivotTable, the data moves, rendering an ordinary cell reference incorrect. Instead, to retrieve summary data from a PivotTable, you need to use the Excel GETPIVOTDATA function. See Figure L-20 for the GETPIVOTDATA function format. ▨▨▨▨ Kate wants to include the yearly sales total for the Chicago branch in the Sales sheet. She asks you to retrieve this information from the PivotTable and place it in the Sales sheet. You use the GETPIVOTDATA function to retrieve this information.

STEPS

1. **Click the PivotTable sheet tab**
   The sales figures in the PivotTable are average values for tours. You decide to show sales information for all categories and change the summary information back to Sum.

2. **Click the Category filter arrow in cell B1, click All, then click OK**
   The PivotChart report displays sales information for all categories.

3. **Right-click cell A4 on the PivotTable, point to Summarize Values By on the shortcut menu, then click Sum**
   The PivotChart report recalculates to display sales totals. Next, you want to include the total for sales for the Chicago branch in the Sales sheet by retrieving it from the PivotTable.

4. **Click the Sales sheet tab, click cell G1, type Total Chicago Sales:, click the Enter button ✔ on the formula bar, click the Home tab, click the Align Text Right button ▤ in the Alignment group, click the Bold button B in the Font group, then adjust the width of column G to display the label in cell G1**
   You want the GETPIVOTDATA function to retrieve the total Chicago sales from the PivotTable. Cell I8 on the PivotTable contains the data you want to return to the Sales sheet.

5. **Click cell G2, type =, click the PivotTable sheet tab, click cell I8 on the PivotTable, then click ✔**
   The GETPIVOTDATA function, along with its arguments, is inserted into cell G2 of the Sales sheet, as shown in Figure L-21. You want to format the sales total.

6. **Click the Accounting Number Format button $ in the Number group**
   The current sales total for the Chicago branch is $97,113.81. This is the same value displayed in cell I8 of the PivotTable.

7. **Enter your name in the Sales sheet footer, save the workbook, then preview the first page of the Sales worksheet**

8. **Close the file, exit Excel, then submit the workbook to your instructor**
   The Sales worksheet is shown in Figure L-22.

FIGURE L-20: Format of GETPIVOTDATA function

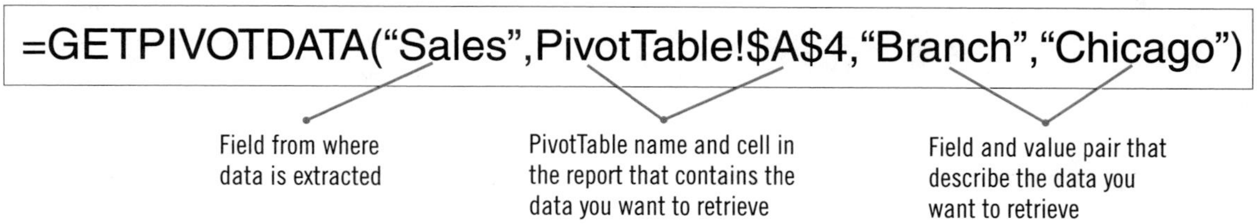
=GETPIVOTDATA("Sales",PivotTable!$A$4,"Branch","Chicago")
Field from where data is extracted
PivotTable name and cell in the report that contains the data you want to retrieve
Field and value pair that describe the data you want to retrieve

FIGURE L-21: GETPIVOTDATA function in the Sales sheet

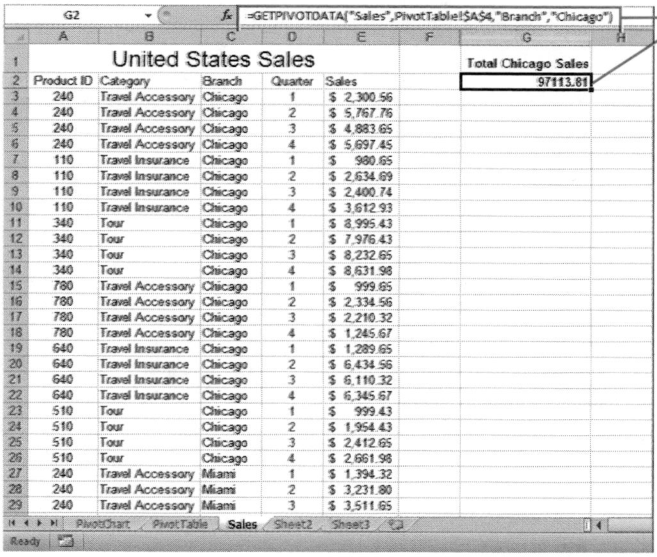
G2
=GETPIVOTDATA("Sales",PivotTable!$A$4,"Branch","Chicago")
Total Chicago Sales
97113.81
PivotChart
PivotTable
Sales
Sheet2
Sheet3
Ready

	A	B	C	D	E
1		United States Sales			
2	Product ID	Category	Branch	Quarter	Sales
3	240	Travel Accessory	Chicago	1	$ 2,300.56
4	240	Travel Accessory	Chicago	2	$ 5,767.76
5	240	Travel Accessory	Chicago	3	$ 4,883.65
6	240	Travel Accessory	Chicago	4	$ 5,697.45
7	110	Travel Insurance	Chicago	1	$ 980.65
8	110	Travel Insurance	Chicago	2	$ 2,634.69
9	110	Travel Insurance	Chicago	3	$ 2,400.74
10	110	Travel Insurance	Chicago	4	$ 3,612.93
11	340	Tour	Chicago	1	$ 8,995.43
12	340	Tour	Chicago	2	$ 7,976.43
13	340	Tour	Chicago	3	$ 8,232.65
14	340	Tour	Chicago	4	$ 8,631.98
15	780	Travel Accessory	Chicago	1	$ 999.65
16	780	Travel Accessory	Chicago	2	$ 2,334.56
17	780	Travel Accessory	Chicago	3	$ 2,210.32
18	780	Travel Accessory	Chicago	4	$ 1,245.67
19	640	Travel Insurance	Chicago	1	$ 1,289.65
20	640	Travel Insurance	Chicago	2	$ 6,434.56
21	640	Travel Insurance	Chicago	3	$ 6,110.32
22	640	Travel Insurance	Chicago	4	$ 6,345.67
23	510	Tour	Chicago	1	$ 999.43
24	510	Tour	Chicago	2	$ 1,954.43
25	510	Tour	Chicago	3	$ 2,412.65
26	510	Tour	Chicago	4	$ 2,661.98
27	240	Travel Accessory	Miami	1	$ 1,394.32
28	240	Travel Accessory	Miami	2	$ 3,231.80
29	240	Travel Accessory	Miami	3	$ 3,511.65

Function is entered into the formula bar, and the result is placed in the cell

FIGURE L-22: Completed Sales worksheet showing total Chicago sales

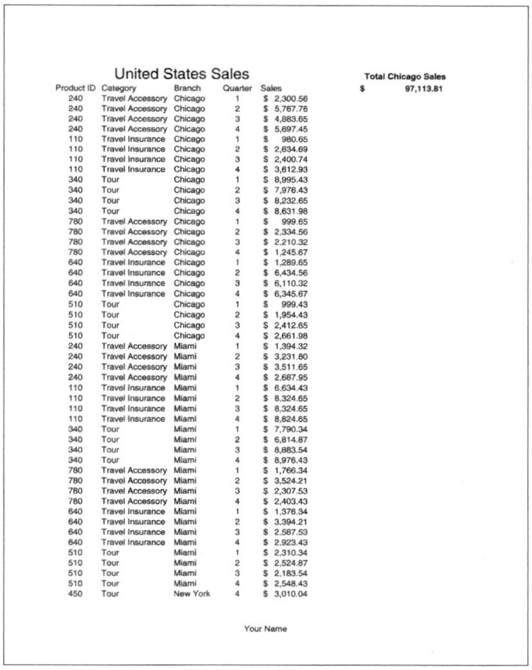

United States Sales

Total Chicago Sales $ 97,113.81

Product ID	Category	Branch	Quarter	Sales
240	Travel Accessory	Chicago	1	$ 2,300.56
240	Travel Accessory	Chicago	2	$ 5,767.76
240	Travel Accessory	Chicago	3	$ 4,883.65
240	Travel Accessory	Chicago	4	$ 5,697.45
110	Travel Insurance	Chicago	1	$ 980.65
110	Travel Insurance	Chicago	2	$ 2,634.69
110	Travel Insurance	Chicago	3	$ 2,400.74
110	Travel Insurance	Chicago	4	$ 3,612.93
340	Tour	Chicago	1	$ 8,995.43
340	Tour	Chicago	2	$ 7,976.43
340	Tour	Chicago	3	$ 8,232.65
340	Tour	Chicago	4	$ 8,631.98
780	Travel Accessory	Chicago	1	$ 999.65
780	Travel Accessory	Chicago	2	$ 2,334.56
780	Travel Accessory	Chicago	3	$ 2,210.32
780	Travel Accessory	Chicago	4	$ 1,245.67
640	Travel Insurance	Chicago	1	$ 1,289.65
640	Travel Insurance	Chicago	2	$ 6,434.56
640	Travel Insurance	Chicago	3	$ 6,110.32
640	Travel Insurance	Chicago	4	$ 6,345.67
510	Tour	Chicago	1	$ 999.43
510	Tour	Chicago	2	$ 1,954.43
510	Tour	Chicago	3	$ 2,412.65
510	Tour	Chicago	4	$ 2,661.98
240	Travel Accessory	Miami	1	$ 1,394.32
240	Travel Accessory	Miami	2	$ 3,231.80
240	Travel Accessory	Miami	3	$ 3,511.65
240	Travel Accessory	Miami	4	$ 2,687.95
110	Travel Insurance	Miami	1	$ 6,634.43
110	Travel Insurance	Miami	2	$ 8,324.65
110	Travel Insurance	Miami	3	$ 8,324.65
110	Travel Insurance	Miami	4	$ 8,824.65
340	Tour	Miami	1	$ 7,790.34
340	Tour	Miami	2	$ 6,814.87
340	Tour	Miami	3	$ 8,883.54
340	Tour	Miami	4	$ 8,976.43
780	Travel Accessory	Miami	1	$ 1,766.34
780	Travel Accessory	Miami	2	$ 3,524.21
780	Travel Accessory	Miami	3	$ 2,307.53
780	Travel Accessory	Miami	4	$ 2,403.43
640	Travel Insurance	Miami	1	$ 1,376.34
640	Travel Insurance	Miami	2	$ 3,394.21
640	Travel Insurance	Miami	3	$ 2,587.53
640	Travel Insurance	Miami	4	$ 2,923.43
510	Tour	Miami	1	$ 2,310.34
510	Tour	Miami	2	$ 2,524.87
510	Tour	Miami	3	$ 2,183.54
510	Tour	Miami	4	$ 2,548.43
450	Tour	New York	4	$ 3,010.04

Your Name

Working with PivotTable versions

PivotTables created using Excel 2010 have a version of 12, which is the same version used in Excel 2007 PivotTables. PivotTables created using Excel 2002 and Excel 2003 have a version of 10 which has fewer PivotTable features. If you are working in Compatibility Mode in Excel 2010 by saving a workbook in an earlier Excel format, any PivotTable that you create will have a version of 10, but if you save the PivotTable file as an .xlsx file and reopen it, the PivotTable will be upgraded to version 12 when it is refreshed.

Practice

Concepts Review

For current SAM information, including versions and content details, visit SAM Central (http://www.cengage.com/samcentral). If you have a SAM user profile, you may have access to hands-on instruction, practice, and assessment of the skills covered in this unit. Since various versions of SAM are supported throughout the life of this text, check with your instructor for the correct instructions and URL/Web site for accessing assignments.

FIGURE L-23

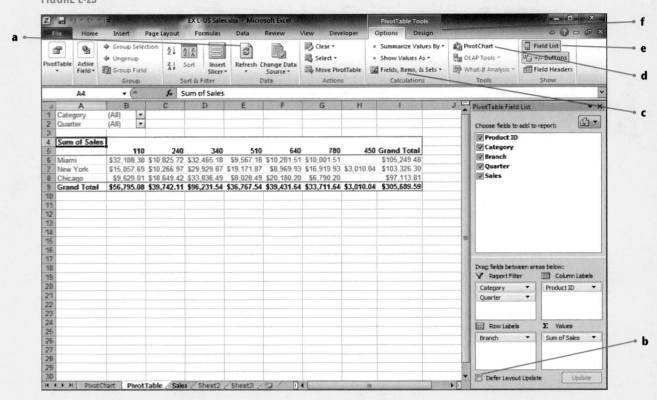

1. **Which element do you click to create a chart based on the data in a PivotTable?**
2. **Which element do you click to create a calculated field in a PivotTable?**
3. **Which element do you click to control when PivotTable changes will occur?**
4. **Which element do you click to display a gallery of PivotTable Styles?**
5. **Which element do you click to update a PivotTable?**
6. **Which element do you click to display or hide the PivotTable Field List pane?**

Match each term with the statement that best describes it.

7. **Slicer**	**a.** Retrieves information from a PivotTable
8. **PivotTable Row Label**	**b.** Default layout for a PivotTable
9. **Summary function**	**c.** PivotTable filtering tool
10. **Compact form**	**d.** PivotChart axis field
11. **GETPIVOTDATA function**	**e.** Determines if data is summed or averaged

Select the best answer from the list of choices.

12. When a numeric field is added to a PivotTable, it is placed in the _____ area.

  a. Row Labels   **c.** Column Labels

  b. Values   **d.** Report Filter

13. Which PivotTable report area allows you to display only certain data using a list arrow?

  a. Values   **c.** Row Labels

  b. Column Labels   **d.** Report Filter

14. To make changes to PivotTable data, you must:

  a. Drag a column header to the column area.   **c.** Edit cells in the source list, and then refresh the PivotTable.

  b. Create a page field.   **d.** Edit cells in the PivotTable, then refresh the source list.

15. When a nonnumeric field is added to a PivotTable, it is placed in the _____ area.

  a. Values   **c.** Column Labels

  b. Report Filter   **d.** Row Labels

16. The default summary function for data fields containing numbers in an Excel PivotTable is:

  a. Count.   **c.** Sum.

  b. Max.   **d.** Average.

Skills Review

1. Plan and design a PivotTable report.

  a. Start Excel, open the file titled EX L-2.xlsx from the drive and folder where you store your Data Files, then save it as **EX L-Product Sales**.

  b. Review the fields and data values in the worksheet.

  c. Verify that the worksheet data contains repeated values in one or more fields.

  d. Verify that there are not any blank rows or columns in the range A1:E25.

  e. Verify that the worksheet data contains a field that can be summed in a PivotTable.

2. Create a PivotTable report.

  a. Create a PivotTable report on a new worksheet using the Sales worksheet data in the range A1:E25.

  b. Add the Product ID field in the PivotTable Field List pane to the Column Labels area.

  c. Add the Sales field in the PivotTable Field List pane to the Values Area.

  d. Add the Store field in the PivotTable Field List pane to the Row Labels area.

  e. Add the Sales Rep field in the PivotTable Field List pane to the Row Labels area below the Store field.

3. Change a PivotTable's summary function and design.

  a. Change the PivotTable summary function to Average.

  b. Rename the new sheet **Sales PivotTable**.

  c. Change the PivotTable Style to Pivot Style Medium 13. Format the sales values in the PivotTable as Currency with a $ symbol and two decimal places.

  d. Enter your name in the center section of the PivotTable report footer, then save the workbook.

  e. Change the Summary function back to Sum. Remove the headers "Row Labels" and "Column Labels."

4. Filter and sort PivotTable data.

  a. Sort the stores in ascending order by total sales.

  b. Use a Slicer to filter the PivotTable to display sales for only the Portland store.

  c. Clear the filter and then display sales for only the DC store.

  d. Clear the filter and then display the Selection and Visibility pane. Turn off the visibility of the Store Slicer shape, and close the Selection and Visibility pane.

  e. Add the Region field to the Report Filter area in the PivotTable Field List pane. Use the Report Filter to display sales for only the East region. Display sales for all regions.

  f. Save the workbook.

Skills Review (continued)

5. Update a PivotTable report.

  a. With the Sales PivotTable sheet active, note the NY total for Product ID 300.

  b. Activate the Sales sheet, and change K. Lyons's sales of Product ID 300 in cell D7 to **$9,000**.

  c. Refresh the PivotTable so it reflects the new sales figure.

  d. Verify the NY total for Product ID 300 increased by $157.

  e. Save the workbook.

6. Change a PivotTable's structure and format.

  a. In the PivotTable Field List, drag the Product ID field from the Column Labels area to the Row Labels area.

  b. Drag the Sales Rep field from the Row Labels area to the Column Labels area.

  c. Drag the Store field from the Row Labels area to the Report Filter area.

  d. Drag the Product ID field back to the Column Labels area.

  e. Drag the Store field back to the Row Labels area.

  f. Remove the Sales Rep field from the PivotTable.

  g. Compare your completed PivotTable to Figure L-24, save the workbook.

7. Create a PivotChart report.

  a. Use the existing PivotTable data to create a Clustered Column PivotChart report.

  b. Move the PivotChart to a new worksheet, and name the sheet **PivotChart**.

  c. Add the title **Total Sales** above the chart.

  d. Filter the chart to display only sales data for Product ID 300. Display the sales data for all Product IDs. Hide all of the Field Buttons.

  e. Add your name to the center section of the PivotChart sheet footer. Compare your PivotChart to Figure L-25, save the workbook.

8. Use the GETPIVOTDATA function.

  a. In cell D27 of the Sales sheet type = , click the Sales PivotTable sheet, click the cell that contains the grand total for LA, then press [Enter].

  b. Review the GETPIVOTDATA function that you entered in cell D27.

  c. Enter your name in the Sales sheet footer, compare your Sales sheet to Figure L-26, save the workbook, then preview the sales worksheet.

  d. Close the workbook and exit Excel.

  e. Submit the workbook to your instructor.

FIGURE L-24

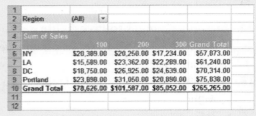

FIGURE L-25

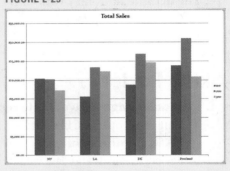

FIGURE L-26

	A	B	C	D	E
1	Product ID	Region	Store	Sales	Sales Rep
2	100	West	LA	$10,934	H. Jeung
3	200	West	LA	$16,512	H. Jeung
4	300	West	LA	$18,511	H. Jeung
5	100	East	NY	$11,989	K. Lyons
6	200	East	NY	$9,750	K. Lyons
7	300	East	NY	$9,000	K. Lyons
8	100	West	Portland	$13,998	M. Holak
9	200	West	Portland	$20,550	M. Holak
10	300	West	Portland	$15,690	M. Holak
11	100	East	DC	$10,850	J. Forum
12	200	East	DC	$16,225	J. Forum
13	300	East	DC	$19,331	J. Forum
14	100	West	LA	$4,655	D. Janes
15	200	West	LA	$6,850	D. Janes
16	300	West	LA	$3,778	D. Janes
17	100	East	NY	$8,400	L. Sorrento
18	200	East	NY	$10,500	L. Sorrento
19	300	East	NY	$8,234	L. Sorrento
20	100	West	Portland	$9,900	T. Leni
21	200	West	Portland	$10,500	T. Leni
22	300	West	Portland	$5,200	T. Leni
23	100	East	DC	$7,900	M. Gregoire
24	200	East	DC	$10,700	M. Gregoire
25	300	East	DC	$5,308	M. Gregoire
26					
27			LA Sales for July:	$61,240	
28					

Independent Challenge 1

You are the accountant for the Service Department of an automobile dealer. The Service Department employs three technicians that service cars purchased at the dealership. Until recently, the owner had been tracking the technicians' hours manually in a log. You have created an Excel worksheet to track the following basic information: service date, technician name, job #, job category, hours, and warranty information. The owner has asked you to analyze the billing data to provide information about the number of hours being spent on the various job categories. He also wants to find out how much of the technicians' work is covered by warranties. You will create a PivotTable that sums the hours by category and technician. Once the table is completed, you will create a column chart representing the billing information.

  a. Start Excel, open the file titled EX L-3.xlsx from the drive and folder where you store your Data Files, then save it as **EX L-Service**.

Independent Challenge 1 (continued)

FIGURE L-27

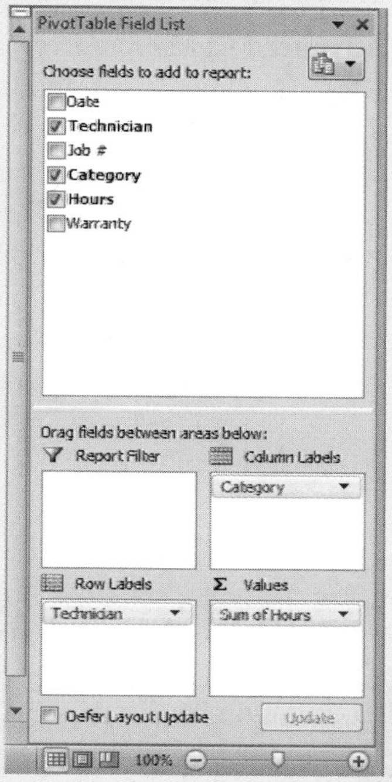

b. Create a PivotTable on a separate worksheet that sums hours by technician and category. Use Figure L-27 as a guide.

c. Name the new sheet **PivotTable**, and apply the Pivot Style Medium 14.

d. Add a Slicer to filter the PivotTable using the category data. Display only service data for the category Level 1. Remove the filter, and remove the Category Slicer visibility.

e. Add the Warranty field to the Report Filter area of the PivotTable. Display only the PivotTable data for jobs covered by warranties.

f. Remove the headers of "Column Labels" and "Row Labels" from the PivotTable.

g. Create a clustered column PivotChart that shows the warranty hours. Move the PivotChart to a new sheet named **PivotChart**.

h. Add the title **Warranty Hours** above the chart.

i. Change the PivotChart filter to display hours where the work was not covered by a warranty. Edit the chart title to read **Nonwarranty Hours**.

j. Hide the field buttons on the chart.

k. Add your name to the center section of the PivotTable and PivotChart footers, then save the workbook. Preview the PivotTable and the PivotChart.

l. Close the workbook and exit Excel. Submit the workbook to your instructor.

Independent Challenge 2

You are the owner of an office supply store called Office Solutions based in Miami. You sell products at the store as well as online. You also take orders by phone from your catalog customers. You have been using Excel to maintain a sales summary for the second quarter sales of the different types of products sold by the company. You want to create a PivotTable to analyze and graph the sales in each product category by month and type of order.

a. Start Excel, open the file titled EX L-4.xlsx from the drive and folder where you store your Data Files, then save it as **EX L-Office Solutions**.

b. Create a PivotTable on a new worksheet named **PivotTable** that sums the sales amount for each category across the rows and each type of sale down the columns. Add the month field as an inner row label. Use Figure L-28 as a guide.

FIGURE L-28

c. Move the month field to the Report Filter location. Display the sum of sales data for the month of April.

d. Turn off the grand totals for the columns. (*Hint*: Use the Grand Totals button on the Design tab and choose On for Rows Only.)

e. Change the summary function in the PivotTable to Average.

f. Format the sales values using the Currency format with two decimal places and the $ symbol.

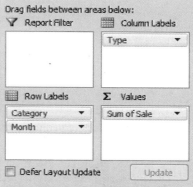

g. On the Sales worksheet, change the April online paper sales in cell D3 to $28,221. Update the PivotTable to reflect this increase in sales.

h. Sort the average sales of categories from smallest to largest using the grand total of sales.

i. Create a stacked column PivotChart report for the average April sales data for all three types of sales.

j. Change the PivotChart to display the June sales data.

k. Move the PivotChart to a new sheet, and name the chart sheet **PivotChart**.

l. Add the title **Average June Sales** above your chart.

Independent Challenge 2 (continued)

Advanced Challenge Exercise

- On the PivotTable, move the Month field from the Report Filter to the Row Label area of the PivotTable below the Category field. Add a Slicer to filter the PivotTable by month.
- Use the Slicer to display the April and May sales data. (*Hint*: You can select multiple fields in the Slicer shape by holding [Ctrl] and clicking the field names.)
- Format the Slicer shape using the Slicer Style Dark 1 in the Slicer Styles gallery on the Slicer Tools Options tab.
- Remove the Row Labels and Column Labels headers in cells A4 and B3.
- Check the PivotChart to be sure that the new data is displayed.
- Change the chart title to describe the charted sales.

m. Add your name to the center section of the PivotTable and PivotChart worksheet footers, save the workbook, then preview the PivotTable and the PivotChart.

n. Close the workbook and exit Excel. Submit the workbook to your instructor.

Independent Challenge 3

You are the North American sales manager for a drug store supply company with sales offices in the United States and Canada. You use Excel to keep track of the staff in the San Francisco, Los Angeles, Chicago, St. Louis, Toronto, Montreal, Vancouver, Boston, and New York offices. Management asks you to provide a summary table showing information on your sales staff, including their locations, status, and titles. You will create a PivotTable and PivotChart summarizing this information.

a. Start Excel, open the file titled EX L-5.xlsx from the drive and folder where you store your Data Files, then save it as **EX L-Sales Employees**.

b. On a new worksheet, create a PivotTable that shows the number of employees in each city, with the names of the cities listed across the columns, the titles listed down the rows, and the status indented below the titles. (*Hint*: Remember that the default summary function for cells containing text is Count.) Use Figure L-29 as a guide. Rename the new sheet **PivotTable**.

FIGURE L-29

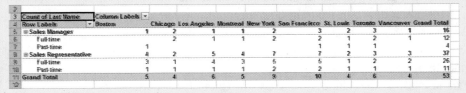

c. Change the structure of the PivotTable to display the data as shown in Figure L-30.

d. Add a report filter using the region field. Display only the U.S. employees.

e. Create a clustered column PivotChart from the PivotTable and move the chart to its own sheet named PivotChart. Rearrange the fields to create the PivotChart shown in Figure L-31.

f. Add the title **U.S. Sales Staff** above the chart.

g. Add the Pivot Style Light 18 style to the PivotTable.

h. Insert a new row in the Employees worksheet above row 7. In the new row, add information reflecting the recent hiring of Kathy Crosby, a full-time sales manager at the Boston office. Update the PivotTable to display the new employee information.

i. Add the label **Total Chicago Staff** in cell G1 of the Employees sheet. Widen column G to fit the label.

FIGURE L-30

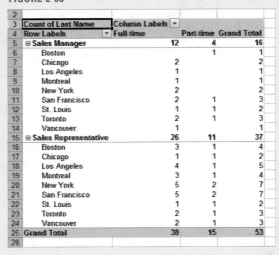

Independent Challenge 3 (continued)

j. Enter a function in cell H1 that retrieves the total number of employees located in Chicago from the PivotTable. Change the page orientation of the Employees sheet to landscape.

FIGURE L-31

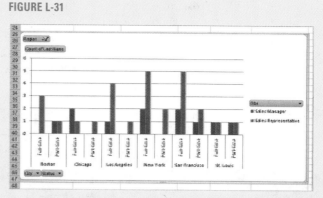

Advanced Challenge Exercise

- Use a Slicer to filter the PivotTable to display only the data for the cities of Boston, Chicago, Los Angeles, and San Francisco.
- Change the Slicer caption from City to **Sales Office**. (*Hint*: Use the Slicer Settings button in the Slicer group of the Slicer Tools Option tab.)
- Add another Slicer for the Title field to display only the sales representatives.
- Display the Visibility pane, and use the Re-order buttons at the bottom of the pane to move the Sales Office Slicer to the top of the list of Shapes.
- Verify that the number of Chicago employees in cell H1 of the Employees sheet is now 2.

k. Add your name to the center section of all three worksheet footers, save the workbook, then preview the PivotTable, the first page of the Employee worksheet, and the PivotChart.

l. Close the workbook and exit Excel. Submit the workbook to your instructor.

Real Life Independent Challenge

PivotTables can be effective tools for analyzing your personal investments. You will use a PivotTable and a PivotChart to represent the short-term trend for four stocks by summarizing the performance of the stocks over five business days. You will use a PivotTable function to display each stock's weekly high, and you will use a PivotChart to represent each stock's five-day performance.

a. Start Excel, open the file EX L-6.xlsx, then save it as **EX L-Stocks** in the drive and folder where you save your Data Files.

b. If you have stock information available you can replace the data in the file with your own data.

c. Create a PivotTable on a new worksheet that sums the stock prices for each stock across the rows and for each day down the columns. Rename the PivotTable sheet **PivotTable**.

d. Format the sales figures as Currency with two decimal places, and apply the Pivot Style Light 20 format.

e. Turn off the grand totals for both the rows and columns.

f. Add the Exchange field to the Report Filter area of the PivotTable. Display only the NASDAQ data, then redisplay the data from both exchanges.

g. Create a clustered column PivotChart report from your data. Move the PivotChart to its own sheet named **PivotChart**. Change the column chart to a clustered bar chart. (*Hint*: Use the Change Chart Type button.)

h. Add grand totals for the rows of the PivotTable. Change the summary function to MAX, then change the label in cell G4 from Grand Total to **Highest Price**. Widen column G to fit the label.

i. Enter the label **Highest Price** in cell F1 of the Stocks sheet. Widen column F to fit the label. Enter the MSFT stock symbol in cell F2. If you are using your own data, enter one of your stock symbols in cell F2.

j. Enter a function in cell G2 that retrieves the highest price for the stock in cell F2 over the past five days from the PivotTable.

k. Change the structure of the PivotTable, moving the Day field to the Row Labels area below the Stock field and Exchange to the Column Labels area. Verify that the highest price for the MSFT stock (or your own stock if you are using personal data) is still correct on the Stocks worksheet.

l. Change the PivotChart type to a line.

m. Add your name to the center section of the footer for the PivotChart, the PivotTable, and the Stocks worksheet, save the workbook, then preview the three worksheets.

n. Close the workbook and exit Excel. Submit the workbook to your instructor.

Visual Workshop

Open the file EX L-7.xlsx from the drive and folder where you store your Data Files, then save it as **EX L-Real Estate**. Using the data in the workbook, create the PivotTable shown in Figure L-32 on a worksheet named PivotTable, then generate a PivotChart on a new sheet named PivotChart as shown in Figure L-33. (*Hint*: The PivotTable has been formatted using the Pivot Style Medium 12.) Add your name to the PivotTable and the PivotChart footers, then preview the PivotTable and the PivotChart. Save the workbook, close the workbook, exit Excel, then submit the workbook to your instructor.

FIGURE L-32

	Sum of Sales	Jan	Feb	Mar	Grand Total
5	⊟DC	$37,522,921.00	$104,517,200.00	$109,525,142.00	$251,565,263.00
6	Commercial	$4,511,899.00	$6,505,556.00	$8,504,845.00	$19,522,300.00
7	Land	$17,505,645.00	$30,503,133.00	$38,515,452.00	$86,524,230.00
8	Residential	$15,505,377.00	$67,508,511.00	$62,504,845.00	$145,518,733.00
9	⊟Miami	$48,830,890.00	$108,522,460.00	$68,143,450.00	$225,496,800.00
10	Commercial	$2,742,221.00	$9,030,458.00	$9,049,554.00	$20,822,233.00
11	Land	$25,043,225.00	$80,489,557.00	$19,045,454.00	$124,578,236.00
12	Residential	$21,045,444.00	$19,002,445.00	$40,048,442.00	$80,096,331.00
13	⊟NY	$117,564,007.00	$81,054,224.00	$128,071,884.00	$326,690,115.00
14	Commercial	$8,018,009.00	$3,015,222.00	$11,025,664.00	$22,058,895.00
15	Land	$70,518,444.00	$50,027,452.00	$40,025,444.00	$160,571,340.00
16	Residential	$39,027,554.00	$28,011,550.00	$77,020,776.00	$144,059,880.00
17	Grand Total	$203,917,818.00	$294,093,884.00	$305,740,476.00	$803,752,178.00

FIGURE L-33

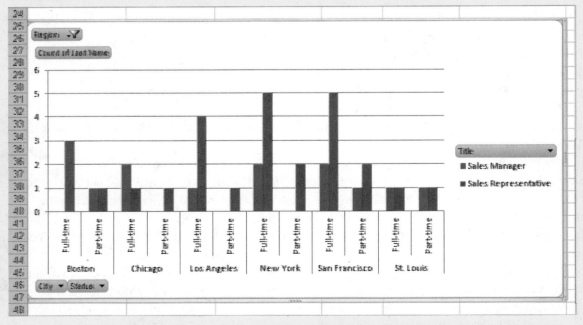

Exchanging Data with Other Programs

In a Windows environment, you can freely exchange data among Excel and most other Windows programs, a process known as integration. In this unit, you plan a data exchange between Excel and other Microsoft Office programs. Quest's upper management has asked Kate Morgan, the vice president of sales, to research the possible purchase of Service Adventures, a small company specializing in combining travel with volunteer work for corporate employees. Kate is reviewing the organization's files and developing a presentation on the feasibility of acquiring the company. To complete this project, Kate asks you to help set up the exchange of data between Excel and other programs.

OBJECTIVES

Plan a data exchange

Import a text file

Import a database table

Insert a graphic file in a worksheet

Embed a workbook in a Word document

Link a workbook to a Word document

Link an Excel chart to a PowerPoint slide

Import a table into Access

Planning a Data Exchange

Because the tools available in Microsoft Office programs are designed to be compatible, exchanging data between Excel and other programs is easy. The first step involves planning what you want to accomplish with each data exchange. ▰▰▰▰ Kate asks you to use the following guidelines to plan data exchanges between Excel and other programs in order to complete the business analysis project.

DETAILS

To plan an exchange of data:

- **Identify the data you want to exchange, its file type, and, if possible, the program used to create it**

  Whether the data you want to exchange is a graphics file, a database file, a worksheet, or consists only of text, it is important to identify the data's **source program** (the program used to create it) and the file type. Once you identify the source program, you can determine options for exchanging the data with Excel. Kate needs to analyze a text file containing the Service Adventures tour sales. Although she does not know the source program, Kate knows that the file contains unformatted text. A file that consists of text but no formatting is sometimes called an **ASCII** or **text** file. Because ASCII is a universally accepted file format, Kate can easily import an ASCII file into Excel. See Table M-1 for a partial list of other file formats that Excel can import. Excel can also import older file formats as well as templates, backup files, and workspace files that are easily accessible in Excel.

- **Determine the program with which you want to exchange data**

  Besides knowing which program created the data you want to exchange, you must also identify which program will receive the data, called the **destination program**. This determines the procedure you use to perform the exchange. You might want to insert a graphic object into an Excel worksheet or add a spreadsheet to a Word document. Kate received a database table of Service Adventures' corporate customers created with the Access database program. After determining that Excel can import Access tables and reviewing the import procedure, she imports the database file into Excel so she can analyze it using Excel tools.

- **Determine the goal of your data exchange**

  Windows offers two ways to transfer data within and between programs that allow you to retain some connection with the source program. These data transfer methods use a Windows feature known as **object linking and embedding**, or **OLE**. The data to be exchanged, called an **object**, may consist of text, a worksheet, or any other type of data. You use **embedding** to insert a copy of the original object in the destination document and, if necessary, to subsequently edit this data separately from the source document. This process is illustrated in Figure M-1. You use **linking** when you want the information you inserted to be updated automatically if the data in the source document changes. This process is illustrated in Figure M-2. You learn more about embedding and linking later in this unit. Kate has determined that she needs to use both object embedding and object linking for her analysis and presentation project.

- **Set up the data exchange**

  When you exchange data between two programs, it is often best to start both programs before starting the exchange. You might also want to tile the program windows on the screen either horizontally or vertically so that you can see both during the exchange. You will work with Excel, Word, Access, and PowerPoint when exchanging data for this project.

- **Execute the data exchange**

  The steps you use will vary, depending on the type of data you want to exchange. Kate is ready to have you start the data exchanges for the business analysis of Service Adventures.

FIGURE M-1: Embedded object

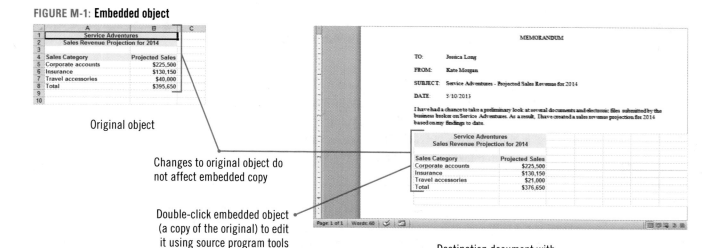

Original object

Changes to original object do
not affect embedded copy

Double-click embedded object
(a copy of the original) to edit
it using source program tools

Destination document with
embedded copy of worksheet

FIGURE M-2: Linked object

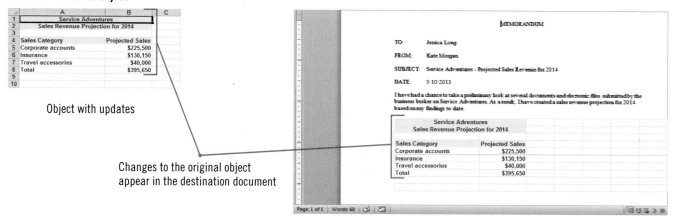

Object with updates

Changes to the original object
appear in the destination document

Destination document

TABLE M-1: Importable file formats and extensions

file format	file extension(s)	file format	file extension(s)
Access	.mdb, .accdb	All Data Sources	.odc, .udl, .dsn
Text	.txt, .prn, .csv, .dif, .sylk	OpenDocument Spreadsheet	.ods
Query	.iqy, .dqy, .oqy, .rqy	XML	.xml
Web page	.htm, .html, .mht, .mhtml	dBASE	.dbf

Importing a Text File

You can import data created in other programs into Excel by opening the file, as long as Excel can read the file type. After importing the file, you use the Save As command on the Office menu to save the data in Excel format. Text files use a tab or space as the **delimiter**, or column separator, to separate columns of data. When you import a text file into Excel, the Text Import Wizard automatically opens and describes how text is separated in the imported file. ▓▓▓▓ Now that Kate has planned the data exchange, she wants you to import a tab-delimited text file containing ranch and profit data from Service Adventures.

STEPS

1. **Start Excel if necessary, click the File tab, click Open, then navigate to the folder containing your Data Files**

   The Open dialog box shows only those files that match the file types listed in the Files of type box—usually Microsoft Excel files. In this case, however, you're importing a text file.

2. **Click All Excel Files, click Text Files (*.prn; *.txt; *.csv), click EX M-1.txt, then click Open**

   The first Text Import Wizard dialog box opens, as shown in Figure M-3. Under Original data type, the Delimited option button is selected. In the Preview of file box, line 1 indicates that the file contains two columns of data: Branch and Profit. No changes are necessary in this dialog box.

3. **Click Next**

   The second Text Import Wizard dialog box opens. Under Delimiters, Tab is selected as the delimiter, indicating that tabs separate the columns of incoming data. The Data preview box contains a line showing where the tab delimiters divide the data into columns.

4. **Click Next**

   The third Text Import Wizard dialog box opens with options for formatting the two columns of data. Under Column data format, the General option button is selected. The Data preview area shows that both columns will be formatted with the General format. This is the best formatting option for text mixed with numbers.

5. **Click Finish**

   Excel imports the text file into the blank worksheet as two columns of data: Branch and Profit.

6. **Maximize the Excel window if necessary, click the File tab, click Save As, in the Save As dialog box navigate to the folder containing your Data Files, click the Save as type list arrow, click Excel workbook (*.xlsx), change the filename to EX M-Branch Profit, then click Save**

   The file is saved as an Excel workbook, and the new name appears in the title bar. The sheet tab automatically changes to the name of the imported file, EX M-1. The worksheet information would be easier to read if it were formatted and if it showed the total profit for all regions.

7. **Double-click the border between the headers in columns A and B, click cell A8, type Total Profit, click cell B8, on the Home tab click the Sum button Σ in the Editing group, then click the Enter button ✓ on the formula bar**

8. **Rename the sheet tab Profit, center the column labels, apply bold formatting to them, format the data in column B using the Currency style with the $ symbol and no decimal places, then click cell A1**

   Figure M-4 shows the completed worksheet, which analyzes the text file data you imported into Excel.

9. **Add your name to the center section of the worksheet footer, save the workbook, preview the worksheet, close the workbook, then submit the workbook to your instructor**

FIGURE M-3: First Text Import Wizard dialog box

Original data is delimited

Two column headings

Preview of data

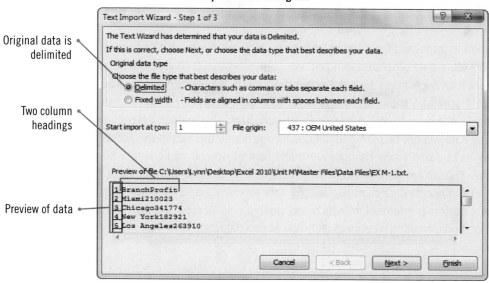

FIGURE M-4: Completed worksheet with imported text file

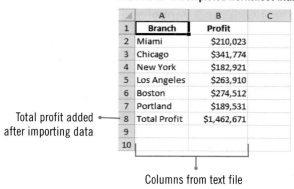

	A	B	C
1	**Branch**	**Profit**	
2	Miami	$210,023	
3	Chicago	$341,774	
4	New York	$182,921	
5	Los Angeles	$263,910	
6	Boston	$274,512	
7	Portland	$189,531	
8	Total Profit	$1,462,671	
9			
10			

Total profit added after importing data

Columns from text file

Importing files using other methods

Another way to open the Text Import Wizard to import a text file into Excel is to click the Data tab, click the From Text button in the Get External Data group, select a data source in the Import Text File dialog box, then click Import. You can also drag the icon representing a text file on the Windows desktop into a blank worksheet window. Excel will create a worksheet from the data without using the Wizard.

Importing a Database Table

In addition to importing text files, you can also use Excel to import data from database tables. A **database table** is a set of data organized using columns and rows that is created in a database program. A **database program** is an application, such as Microsoft Access, that lets you manage large amounts of data organized in tables. Figure M-5 shows an Access table. To import data from an Access table into Excel, you can copy the table in Access and paste it into an Excel worksheet. This method places a copy of the Access data into Excel; the data will not be refreshed in Excel if you change the data in the Access file. If you need the data in Excel to be updated when changes are made to it in Access, you create a connection, or a **link**, to the database. This allows you to work with current data in Excel without recopying the data from Access whenever the Access data changes. ▟▟▙▟ Kate received a database table containing Service Adventures' corporate customer information, which was created with Access. She asks you to import this table into an Excel workbook, creating a connection to the Access data. She would also like you to format, sort, and total the data.

STEPS

1. **Click the File Tab, click New, then click Create**
   A new workbook opens, displaying a blank worksheet for you to use to import the Access data.

TROUBLE
If your screen does not show the From Access button in the Get External Data group, click the Get External Data button, click From Access, then navigate to the folder containing your Data Files. The Add-Ins you have installed and your screen resolution will affect the configuration of your Data tab.

2. **Click the Data tab, click the From Access button in the Get External Data group, then navigate to the folder containing your Data Files if necessary**

3. **Click EX M-2.accdb, click Open, verify that the Table option button and the Existing worksheet button are selected, then click OK in the Import Data dialog box**
   Excel inserts the Access data into the worksheet as a table with the table style Medium 2 format applied, as shown in Figure M-6.

4. **Rename the sheet tab Customer Information, then format the data in columns F and G with the Currency format with the $ symbol and no decimal places**
   You are ready to sort the data using the values in column G.

5. **Click the cell G1 list arrow, then click Sort Smallest to Largest**
   The records are reorganized in ascending order according to the amount of the 2013 orders.

6. **Click the Table Tools Design tab if necessary, click the Total Row check box in the Table Style Options group to select it, click cell F19, click the cell F19 list arrow next to cell F19, select Sum from the drop-down function list, then click cell A1**
   Your completed worksheet should match Figure M-7.

7. **Add your name to the center section of the worksheet footer, change the worksheet orientation to landscape, save the workbook as EX M-Customer Information, then preview the worksheet**

FIGURE M-5: Access Table

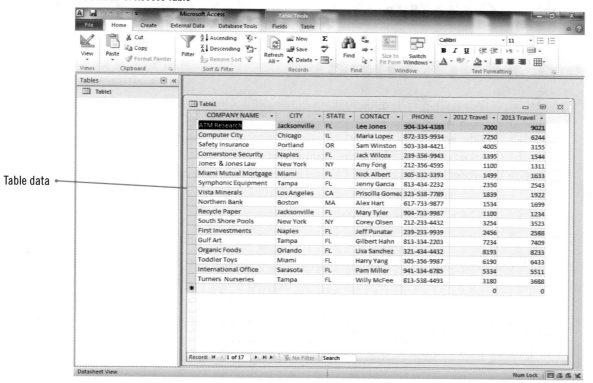

Table data

FIGURE M-6: Imported Access table

	A	B	C	D	E	F	G	H
1	COMPANY NAME	CITY	STATE	CONTACT	PHONE	2012 Travel	2013 Travel	
2	ATM Research	Jacksonville	FL	Lee Jones	904-334-4388	7000	9021	
3	Computer City	Chicago	IL	Maria Lopez	872-335-9934	7250	6244	
4	Safety Insurance	Portland	OR	Sam Winston	503-334-4421	4005	3155	
5	Cornerstone Security	Naples	FL	Jack Wilcox	239-356-9943	1395	1544	
6	Jones & Jones Law	New York	NY	Amy Fong	212-356-4595	1100	1311	
7	Miami Mutual Mortgage	Miami	FL	Nick Albert	305-332-3393	1499	1633	
8	Symphonic Equipment	Tampa	FL	Jenny Garcia	813-434-2232	2350	2543	
9	Vista Minerals	Los Angeles	CA	Priscilla Gomez	323-538-7789	1839	1922	
10	Northern Bank	Boston	MA	Alex Hart	617-733-9877	1534	1699	
11	Recycle Paper	Jacksonville	FL	Mary Tyler	904-733-9987	1100	1234	
12	South Shore Pools	New York	NY	Corey Olsen	212-233-4432	3254	3523	
13	First Investments	Naples	FL	Jeff Punatar	239-233-9939	2456	2588	
14	Gulf Art	Tampa	FL	Gilbert Hahn	813-334-2203	7234	7409	
15	Organic Foods	Orlando	FL	Lisa Sanchez	321-434-4432	8193	8233	
16	Toddler Toys	Miami	FL	Harry Yang	305-356-9987	6190	6433	
17	International Office	Sarasota	FL	Pam Miller	941-334-6785	5334	5511	
18	Turners Nurseries	Tampa	FL	Willy McFee	813-538-4493	3180	3688	
19								

FIGURE M-7: Completed worksheet containing imported data

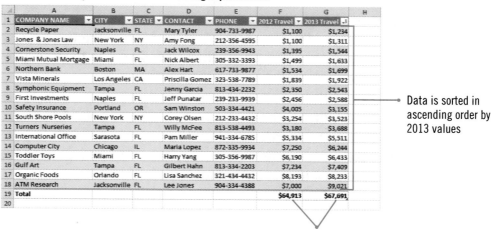

	A	B	C	D	E	F	G	H
1	COMPANY NAME	CITY	STATE	CONTACT	PHONE	2012 Travel	2013 Travel	
2	Recycle Paper	Jacksonville	FL	Mary Tyler	904-733-9987	$1,100	$1,234	
3	Jones & Jones Law	New York	NY	Amy Fong	212-356-4595	$1,100	$1,311	
4	Cornerstone Security	Naples	FL	Jack Wilcox	239-356-9943	$1,395	$1,544	
5	Miami Mutual Mortgage	Miami	FL	Nick Albert	305-332-3393	$1,499	$1,633	
6	Northern Bank	Boston	MA	Alex Hart	617-733-9877	$1,534	$1,699	
7	Vista Minerals	Los Angeles	CA	Priscilla Gomez	323-538-7789	$1,839	$1,922	
8	Symphonic Equipment	Tampa	FL	Jenny Garcia	813-434-2232	$2,350	$2,543	
9	First Investments	Naples	FL	Jeff Punatar	239-233-9939	$2,456	$2,588	
10	Safety Insurance	Portland	OR	Sam Winston	503-334-4421	$4,005	$3,155	
11	South Shore Pools	New York	NY	Corey Olsen	212-233-4432	$3,254	$3,523	
12	Turners Nurseries	Tampa	FL	Willy McFee	813-538-4493	$3,180	$3,688	
13	International Office	Sarasota	FL	Pam Miller	941-334-6785	$5,334	$5,511	
14	Computer City	Chicago	IL	Maria Lopez	872-335-9934	$7,250	$6,244	
15	Toddler Toys	Miami	FL	Harry Yang	305-356-9987	$6,190	$6,433	
16	Gulf Art	Tampa	FL	Gilbert Hahn	813-334-2203	$7,234	$7,409	
17	Organic Foods	Orlando	FL	Lisa Sanchez	321-434-4432	$8,193	$8,233	
18	ATM Research	Jacksonville	FL	Lee Jones	904-334-4388	$7,000	$9,021	
19	Total					$64,913	$67,691	
20								

Data is sorted in ascending order by 2013 values

Totals for 2012 and 2013 orders

Excel 2010

Inserting a Graphic File in a Worksheet

A graphic object, such as a drawing, logo, or photograph, can greatly enhance your worksheet's visual impact. You can insert a picture into a worksheet and then format it using the options on the Format tab.  Kate wants you to insert the Quest logo at the top of the customer worksheet. The company's graphic designer created the graphic and saved it in JPG format. You insert and format the image on the worksheet. You start by creating a space for the logo on the worksheet.

STEPS

1. **Select rows 1 through 5, click the Home tab, then click the Insert button in the Cells group**
   Five blank rows appear above the header row, leaving space to insert the picture.

2. **Click cell A1, click the Insert tab, then click the Picture button in the Illustrations group**
   The Insert Picture dialog box opens. You want to insert a picture that already exists in a file. The file you will insert has a .jpg file extension, so it is called a "jay-peg" file. JPEG files can be viewed in a Web browser.

3. **Navigate to the folder containing your Data Files, click EX M-3.jpg, then click Insert**
   Excel inserts the image and displays the Picture Tools Format tab. The small circles around the picture's border are sizing handles. Sizing handles appear when a picture is selected; you use them to change the size of a picture.

4. **Position the pointer over the sizing handle in the logo's lower-right corner until the pointer becomes ⤡, then click and drag the corner up and to the left so that the logo's outline fits within rows 1 through 5**
   Compare your screen to Figure M-8. You decide to remove the logo's white background.

   QUICK TIP
   The Remove Background button removes the entire background of an image and doesn't allow you to select a color to make transparent.

5. **With the image selected, click the Color button in the Adjust group of the Picture Tools Format tab, click Set Transparent Color, then use ✎ to click the white background on the logo**
   The logo is now transparent, and shows the worksheet gridlines behind it. You decide that the logo will be more visually interesting with a frame and a border color.

6. **With the image selected, click the More button ⊽ in the Picture Styles group, point to several styles and observe the effect on the graphic, click the Reflected Beveled, White style (the third from the right in the last row), click the Picture Border button in the Picture Styles group, then click Blue, Accent 1, Lighter 40% in the Theme Colors group**
   You decide to add a glow to the image.

7. **Click the Picture Effects button in the Picture Styles group, point to Glow, point to More Glow Colors, click Blue, Accent 1, Lighter 80% in the Theme Colors group, resize the logo as necessary to fit it in rows 1 through 5, then drag the logo above the column D data**
   You decide to add an artistic effect to the image.

8. **Click the Artistic Effects button in the Adjust group, click Light Screen (First effect in the third row), then click cell A1**
   Compare your worksheet to Figure M-9.

9. **Save the workbook, preview the worksheet, close the workbook, exit Excel, then submit the workbook to your instructor**

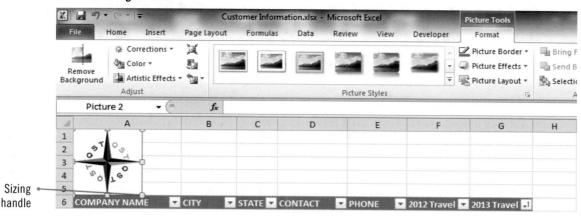

Sizing handle

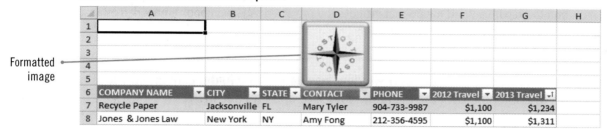

Formatted image

Formatting SmartArt graphics

SmartArt graphics provide another way to visually communicate information on a worksheet. A **SmartArt graphic** is a professionally designed illustration with text and graphics. Each SmartArt type communicates a kind of information or relationship, such as a list, process, or hierarchy. Each type has various layouts you can choose. For example, you can choose from 4 pyramid layouts, 16 process layouts, or 31 picture layouts, allowing you to illustrate your information in many different ways. To insert a SmartArt graphic into a worksheet, click the Insert tab, then click the SmartArt button in the Illustrations group. In the Choose a SmartArt Graphic dialog box,

choose from eight SmartArt types: List, Process, Cycle, Hierarchy, Relationship, Matrix, Pyramid, and Picture. The dialog box also describes the type of information that is appropriate for each selected layout. After you choose a layout and click OK, a SmartArt object appears on your worksheet. As you enter text in the text entry areas, the graphics automatically resize to fit the text. The SmartArt Tools Design tab lets you choose color schemes and styles for your SmartArt. You can add effects to SmartArt graphics using choices on the SmartArt Tools Format tab. Figure M-10 shows examples of SmartArt graphics.

FIGURE M-10: Examples of SmartArt graphics

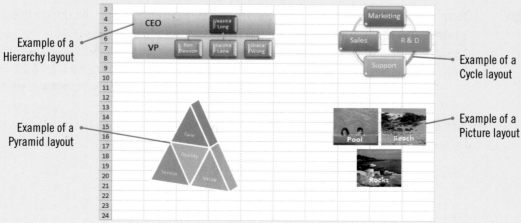

Example of a Hierarchy layout

Example of a Cycle layout

Example of a Pyramid layout

Example of a Picture layout

Excel 2010

Embedding a Workbook in a Word Document

Microsoft Office programs work together to make it easy to copy an object (such as text, data, or a graphic) in a source program and then insert it into a document in a different program (the destination program). If you insert the object using a simple Paste command, however, you retain no connection to the source program. That's why it is often more useful to embed objects rather than simply paste them. Embedding allows you to edit an Excel workbook from within the source program using that program's commands and tools. If you send a Word document with an embedded workbook to another person, you do not need to send a separate Excel file with it. All the necessary information is embedded in the Word document. When you embed information, you can either display the data itself or an icon representing the data; users double-click the icon to view the embedded data. An icon is often used rather than the data when the file is sent electronically.  Kate decides to update Jessica Long, the CEO of Quest, on the project status. She asks you to prepare a Word memo that includes the projected sales workbook embedded as an icon. You begin by starting Word and opening the memo.

STEPS

1. **Open a Windows Explorer window, navigate to the folder containing your Data Files, then double-click the file EX M-4.docx to open the file in Word**

    The memo opens in Word.

2. **Click the File tab, click Save As, navigate to the folder containing your Data Files, change the file name to EX M-Service Adventures Memo, then click Save**

    You want to embed the workbook below the last line of the document.

3. **Press [Ctrl][End], click the Insert tab, click the Object button in the Text group, then click the Create from File tab**

    Figure M-11 shows the Create from File tab in the Object dialog box. You need to indicate the file you want to embed.

4. **Click Browse, navigate to the drive and folder where you store your Data Files, click EX M-5.xlsx, click Insert, then select the Display as icon check box**

    You will change the icon label to a more descriptive name.

> **QUICK TIP**
> To display a different icon to represent the file, click the Change Icon button in the Object dialog box, scroll down the icon list in the Change Icon dialog box, and select any icon.

5. **Click Change Icon, select the text in the Caption text box, type Projected Sales, then click OK twice**

    The memo contains an embedded copy of the sales projection data, displayed as an icon, as shown in Figure M-12.

> **TROUBLE**
> If the Excel program window does not come to the front automatically, click the Excel icon in the taskbar.

6. **Double-click the Projected Sales icon on the Word memo, then maximize the Excel window and the worksheet window if necessary**

    The Excel program starts and displays the embedded worksheet, with its location displayed in the title bar, as shown in Figure M-13. Any changes you make to the embedded object using Excel tools are not reflected in the source document. Similarly, if you open the source document in the source program, changes you make are not reflected in the embedded copy.

7. **Click the File tab, click Close, exit Excel, click the Word File tab, then click Save to save the memo**

FIGURE M-11: Object dialog box

Click this tab to embed an existing file

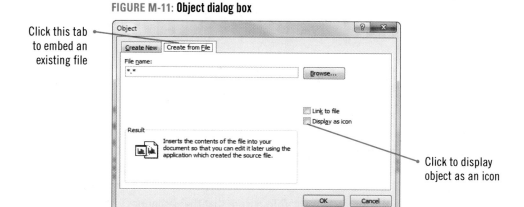

Click to display object as an icon

FIGURE M-12: Memo with embedded worksheet

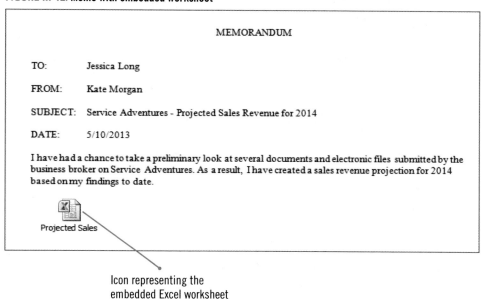

Icon representing the embedded Excel worksheet

FIGURE M-13: Embedded worksheet opened in Excel

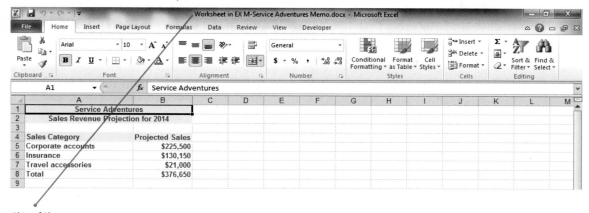

Location of the embedded worksheet

Excel 2010

Linking a Workbook to a Word Document

Linking a workbook to another file retains a connection with the original document as well as the original program. When you link a workbook to another program, the link contains a connection to the source document so that, when you double-click it, the source document opens for editing. Once you link a workbook to another program, any changes you make to the original workbook (the source document) are reflected in the linked object. Kate realizes she may need to make some changes to the workbook she embedded in the memo to Jessica. To ensure that these changes will be reflected in the memo, she feels you should use linking instead of embedding. She asks you to delete the embedded worksheet icon and replace it with a linked version of the same workbook.

STEPS

1. **With the Word memo still open, click the Projected Sales Worksheet icon to select it if necessary, then press [Delete]**

   The workbook is no longer embedded in the memo. The linking process is similar to embedding.

2. **Make sure the insertion point is below the last line of the memo, click the Insert tab, click the Object button in the Text group, then click the Create from File tab in the Object dialog box**

QUICK TIP

If you want to link part of an existing worksheet to another file, in the destination document paste the information as a link using one of the link options from the Paste Options list. You can also use the Paste button list arrow in the Clipboard group.

3. **Click Browse, navigate to the drive and folder where you store your Data Files, click EX M-5.xlsx, click Insert, select the Link to file check box, then click OK**

   The memo now displays a linked copy of the sales projection data, as shown in Figure M-14. In the future, any changes made to the source file, EX M-5, will also be made to the linked copy in the Word memo. You verify this by making a change to the source file and viewing its effect on the Word memo.

4. **Click the File tab, click Save, then close the Word memo, exit Word, then close any open Excel windows if necessary**

TROUBLE

If you get an error message, exit Excel and repeat the step.

5. **Start Excel, open the file EX M-5.xlsx from the drive and folder where you store your Data Files, click cell B7, type 40,000, then press [Enter]**

   You want to verify that the same change was made automatically to the linked copy of the workbook.

TROUBLE

If your link didn't update, right click the Excel data and select Update Links on the shortcut menu.

6. **Start Word, open the EX M-Service Adventures Memo.docx file from the drive and folder where you store your Data Files, then click Yes if asked if you want to update the document's links**

   The memo displays the new value for Travel accessories, and the total has been updated as shown in Figure M-15

7. **Click the Insert tab, click the Header button in the Header & Footer group, click Edit Header, type your name in the Header area, then click the Close Header and Footer button in the Close group**

8. **Save the Word memo, preview it, close the file, exit Word, then submit the file to your instructor**

9. **Close the Excel worksheet without saving it, then exit Excel**

FIGURE M-14: Memo with linked worksheet

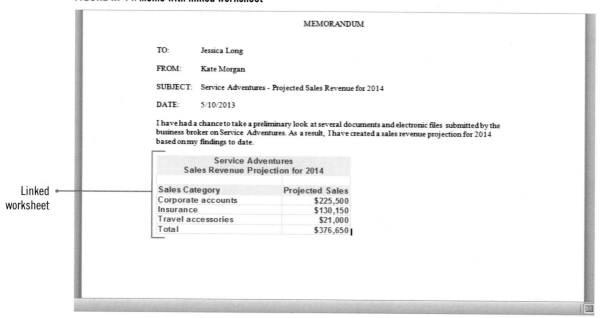

Linked
worksheet

MEMORANDUM

TO: Jessica Long

FROM: Kate Morgan

SUBJECT: Service Adventures - Projected Sales Revenue for 2014

DATE: 5/10/2013

I have had a chance to take a preliminary look at several documents and electronic files submitted by the
business broker on Service Adventures. As a result, I have created a sales revenue projection for 2014
based on my findings to date.

Service Adventures
Sales Revenue Projection for 2014

Sales Category	Projected Sales
Corporate accounts	$225,500
Insurance	$130,150
Travel accessories	$21,000
Total	$376,650

FIGURE M-15: Memo with link updated

MEMORANDUM

TO: Jessica Long

FROM: Kate Morgan

SUBJECT: Service Adventures - Projected Sales Revenue for 2014

DATE: 5/10/2013

I have had a chance to take a preliminary look at several documents and electronic files submitted by the
business broker on Service Adventures. As a result, I have created a sales revenue projection for 2014
based on my findings to date.

Service Adventures
Sales Revenue Projection for 2014

Sales Category	Projected Sales
Corporate accounts	$225,500
Insurance	$130,150
Travel accessories	$40,000
Total	$395,650

Values update to match
those in the source
document

Managing links

When you open a document containing linked data, you are asked if you want to update the linked data. You can manage the updating of links by clicking the File tab, and clicking Edit Links to Files in the right pane. The Links dialog box opens, allowing you to change a link's update from the default setting of automatic to manual. The Links dialog box also allows you to change the link source, permanently break a link, open the source file, and manually update a link. If you send your linked files to another user, the links will be broken because the linked file path references the local machine where you inserted the links. Because the file path will not be valid on the recipient user's machine, the links will no longer be updated when the user opens the destination document. To correct this, recipients who have both the destination and source documents can use the Links dialog box to change the link's source in the destination document to their own machines. Then the links will be automatically updated when they open the destination document in the future.

Linking an Excel Chart to a PowerPoint Slide

Microsoft PowerPoint is a **presentation graphics** program that you can use to create slide show presentations. PowerPoint slides can include a mix of text, data, and graphics. Adding an Excel chart to a slide can help to illustrate data and give your presentation more visual appeal. ▚▚▚ Kate asks you to add an Excel chart to one of the PowerPoint slides, illustrating the 2014 sales projection data. She wants you to link the chart in the PowerPoint file.

STEPS

1. **Start PowerPoint, then open the file EX M-6.pptx from the drive and folder where you store your Data Files, then save it as EX M-Management Presentation**

   The presentation appears in Normal view and contains three panes, as shown in Figure M-16. You need to open the Excel file and copy the chart that you will paste in the PowerPoint presentation.

2. **Start Excel, open the file EX M-7.xlsx from the drive and folder where you store your Data Files, right-click the Chart Area on the Sales Categories sheet, click Copy on the shortcut menu, then click the PowerPoint program button on the taskbar to display the presentation**

   You need to add an Excel chart to Slide 2, "2014 Sales Projections." To add the chart, you first need to select the slide on which it will appear.

TROUBLE
If you don't see Copy on the shortcut menu, you may have clicked the Plot area rather than the Chart area. Clicking the white area surrounding the pie will display the Copy command on the menu.

3. **Click Slide 2 in the left pane, right-click Slide 2 in the slide pane, then click the Use Destination Theme & Link Data button (third from the right) in the Paste Options group**

   A pie chart illustrating the 2014 sales projections appears in the slide. The chart matches the colors and fonts in the presentation, which is the destination document. You decide to edit the link so it will update automatically if the data source changes.

4. **Click the File tab, click Edit Links to Files at the bottom of the right pane, in the Links dialog box click the Automatic option button, then click Close**

   You want to apply a style to the chart before saving the PowerPoint file.

QUICK TIP
The default setting for updating links in PowerPoint file is Manual.

5. **Click the Chart Tools Design tab, click the More button in the Chart Styles group, click Style 26 in the Chart Styles gallery, click the Save button 🖫 on the Quick Access toolbar, then close the file**

   Kate has learned that the sales projections for the Travel accessories category has increased based on late sales for the current year.

6. **Switch to Excel, click the Sales sheet tab, change the Travel accessories value in cell B7 to 45,000, then press [Enter]**

   You decide to reopen the PowerPoint presentation to check the chart data.

QUICK TIP
To update links in an open PowerPoint file, click the File tab, click Edit Links to Files in the right pane, click the link in the Links list, click Update Now, then click Close.

7. **Switch to PowerPoint, open the file EX M-Management Presentation.pptx, click Update Links, click Slide 2 in the left pane, then point to the Travel accessories pie slice**

   The ScreenTip shows that the chart has updated to display the revised Travel accessories value, $45,000, you entered in the Excel workbook. Slide Show view displays the slide on the full screen the way the audience will see it.

8. **Click the Slide Show button 🖵 on the status bar**

   The finished sales projection slide is complete, as shown in Figure M-17.

9. **Press [Esc] to return to Normal view; with Slide 2 selected click the Insert tab, click the Header & Footer button in the Text group, select the Footer check box, type your name in the Footer text box, click Apply, save and close the presentation, close the Excel file without saving it, exit PowerPoint and Excel, then submit the file to your instructor**

FIGURE M-16: Presentation in Normal view

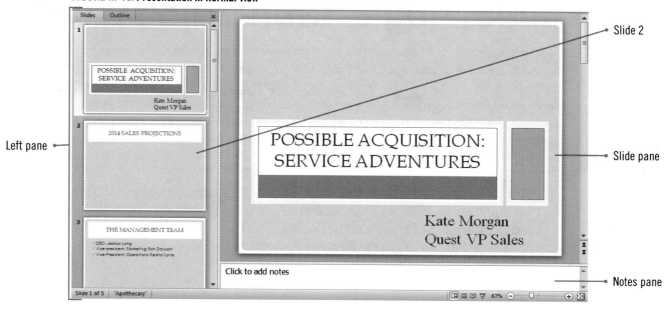

Left pane

Slide 2

Slide pane

Notes pane

FIGURE M-17: Completed Sales Projections slide in Slide Show view

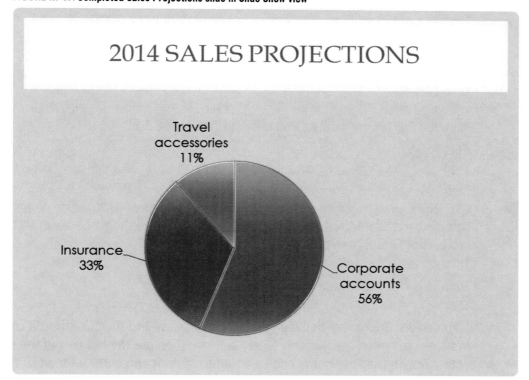

Importing a Table into Access

If you need to analyze Excel data using the more extensive tools of a database, you can import the table into Microsoft Access. When you import Excel table data into Access, the data becomes an Access table using the same field names as the Excel table. In the process of importing an Excel table, Access specifies a primary key for the new table. A **primary key** is the field that contains unique information for each record (row) of information. Kate has just received a workbook containing salary information for the managers at Service Adventures, organized in a table. She asks you to convert the Excel table to a Microsoft Access table.

STEPS

1. **Click the** Start button **on the taskbar, point to** All Programs, **click** Microsoft Office, **click** Microsoft Access 2010; **with the** Blank database button **selected in the Available Templates section, change the filename in the File Name text box to** EX M-SA Management, **click the** Browse button 📂 **next to the filename, navigate to the drive and folder where you store your Data Files, click** OK, **then click** Create

   The database window for the EX M-SA Management database opens. You are ready to import the Excel table data.

2. **Click the** External Data tab, **then click the** Excel button **in the Import & Link group**

   The Get External Data - Excel Spreadsheet dialog box opens, as shown in Figure M-18. This dialog box allows you to specify how you want the data to be stored in Access.

3. **Click the** Browse button, **navigate to the drive and folder where you store your Data Files, click** EX M-8.xlsx, **click** Open, **if necessary click the** Import the source data into a new table in the current database option button, **then click** OK

   The first Import Spreadsheet Wizard dialog box opens, with the Compensation worksheet selected, and a sample of the sheet data in the lower section. In the next dialog box, you indicate that you want to use the column headings in the Excel table as the field names in the Access database.

4. **Click** Next, **make sure the** First Row Contains Column Headings check box **is selected, then click** Next

   The Wizard allows you to review and change the field properties by clicking each column in the lower section of the window. You will not make any changes to the field properties.

5. **Click** Next

   The Wizard allows you to choose a primary key for the table. The table's primary key field contains unique information for each record; the ID Number field is unique for each person in the table.

QUICK TIP
Specifying a primary key allows you to retrieve data more quickly in the future.

6. **Click the** Choose my own primary key option, **make sure "ID Number" appears in the text box next to the selected option button, click** Next, **note the name assigned to the new table, click** Finish, **then click** Close

   The name of the new Access table ("Compensation") appears in the Navigation pane.

7. **Double-click** Compensation: **in the Navigation Pane**

   The data from the Excel worksheet appears in a new Access table, as shown in Figure M-19.

8. **Double-click the** border **between the Monthly Salary and the Click to Add column headings to widen the Monthly Salary column, then use the last row of the table to enter your name in the First Name and Last Name columns and enter 0 for an ID Number**

9. **Click the** Save button 🔲 **on the Quick Access toolbar, close the file, then exit Access**

FIGURE M-18: **Get External Data – Excel Spreadsheet dialog box**

Data source

Specify how you want data to be stored in Access

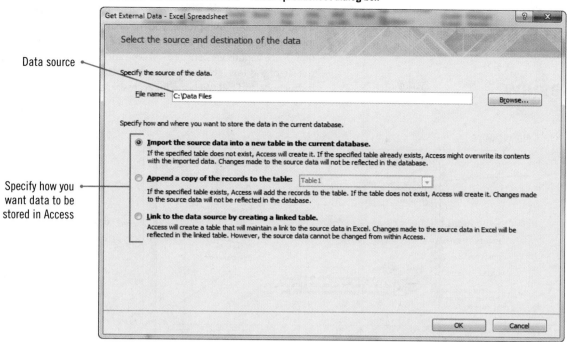

FIGURE M-19: **Completed Access table**

Access table

Primary key

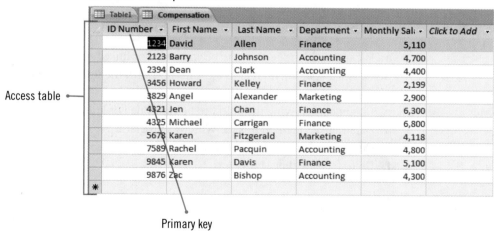

Practice

Concepts Review

For current SAM information, including versions and content details, visit SAM Central (http://www.cengage.com/samcentral). If you have a SAM user profile, you may have access to hands-on instruction, practice, and assessment of the skills covered in this unit. Since various versions of SAM are supported throughout the life of this text, check with your instructor for the correct instructions and URL/Web site for accessing assignments.

FIGURE M-20

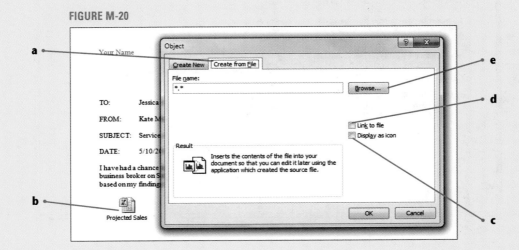

1. Which element do you click to insert an existing object into a Word document rather than creating a new file?
2. Which element do you click to embed information that can be viewed by double-clicking an icon?
3. Which element do you double-click to display an embedded Excel workbook?
4. Which element do you click to find a file to be embedded or linked?
5. Which element do you click to insert an object that maintains a connection to the source document?

Match each term with the statement that best describes it.

6. **Embedding**
7. **Source document**
8. **Destination document**
9. **Presentation graphics program**
10. **Linking**
11. **OLE**

a. File from which the object to be embedded or linked originates
b. Copies an object and retains a connection with the source program and source document
c. Document receiving the object to be embedded or linked
d. Data transfer method used in Windows programs
e. Copies an object and retains a connection with the source program only
f. Used to create slide shows

Select the best answer from the list of choices.

12. **An ASCII file:**
    a. Contains text but no formatting.
    b. Contains formatting but no text.
    c. Contains a PowerPoint presentation.
    d. Contains an unformatted worksheet.
13. **An object consists of:**
    a. A worksheet only.
    b. Text, a worksheet, or any other type of data.
    c. Text only.
    d. Database data only.
14. **A column separator in a text file is called a(n):**
    a. Object.
    b. Link.
    c. Delimiter.
    d. Primary key.

15. To view a workbook that has been embedded as an icon in a Word document, you need to:

a. Drag the icon.

b. Double-click the icon.

c. Click View, then click Worksheet.

d. Click File, then click Open.

16. A field that contains unique information for each record in a database table is called a(n):

a. ID Key.

b. Primary key.

c. First key.

d. Header key.

Skills Review

1. Import a text file.

a. Start Excel, open the tab-delimited text file titled EX M-9.txt from the drive and folder where you store your Data Files, then save it as a Microsoft Office Excel workbook with the name **EX M-West Street Tea**.

b. Widen the columns as necessary so that all the data is visible.

c. Format the data in columns B and C using the Currency style with two decimal places.

d. Center the column labels and apply bold formatting, as shown in Figure M-21.

e. Add your name to the center section of the worksheet footer, save the workbook, preview the worksheet, close the workbook, then submit the workbook to your instructor.

FIGURE M-21

	A	B	C	D
1	**Item**	**Cost**	**Price**	
2	Pot, small	$8.55	$17.50	
3	Pot, large	$10.15	$27.00	
4	Pot, decorated	$15.55	$27.70	
5	Pot, china	$20.15	$31.90	
6	Basket, small	$14.95	$27.80	
7	Basket, large	$20.80	$33.90	
8	Kettle, small	$18.75	$28.45	
9	Kettle, large	$24.30	$33.75	
10	Mug, large	$1.95	$5.70	
11				

2. Import a database table.

a. In Excel, use the From Access button in the Get External Data group on the Data tab to import the Access Data File EX M-10.accdb from the drive and folder where you store your Data Files, then save it as a Microsoft Excel workbook named **EX M-February Budget**.

b. Rename the sheet with the imported data **Budget**.

c. Change the column labels so they read as follows: **Budget Category**, **Budget Item**, **Month**, and **Amount Budgeted**.

d. Adjust the column widths as necessary.

e. Add a total row to the table to display the sum of the budgeted amounts in cell D26.

f. Apply the Medium 5 Table Style. Format range D2:D26 using the Accounting style, the $ symbol, and no decimal places.

g. Save the workbook, and compare your screen to Figure M-22.

FIGURE M-22

	A	B	C	D
1	**Budget Category**	**Budget Item**	**Month**	**Amount Budgeted**
2	Compensation	Benefits	Feb	$ 62,000
3	Compensation	Bonuses	Feb	$ 29,110
4	Compensation	Commissions	Feb	$ 21,610
5	Compensation	Conferences	Feb	$ 77,654
6	Compensation	Promotions	Feb	$ 65,570
7	Compensation	Payroll Taxes	Feb	$ 14,980
8	Compensation	Salaries	Feb	$ 43,240
9	Compensation	Training	Feb	$ 59,600
10	Facility	Lease	Feb	$ 48,200
11	Facility	Maintenance	Feb	$ 61,310
12	Facility	Other	Feb	$ 58,230
13	Facility	Rent	Feb	$ 75,600
14	Facility	Telephone	Feb	$ 61,030
15	Facility	Utilities	Feb	$ 58,510
16	Supplies	Food	Feb	$ 61,430
17	Supplies	Computer	Feb	$ 45,290
18	Supplies	General Office	Feb	$ 42,520
19	Supplies	Other	Feb	$ 55,200
20	Supplies	Outside Services	Feb	$ 47,010
21	Equipment	Computer	Feb	$ 47,210
22	Equipment	Other	Feb	$ 41,450
23	Equipment	Cash Registers	Feb	$ 53,630
24	Equipment	Software	Feb	$ 63,590
25	Equipment	Telecommunications	Feb	$ 57,170
26	**Total**			$ 1,251,144
27				

3. Insert a graphic file in a worksheet.

a. Add four rows above row 1 to create space for an image.

b. In rows 1 through 4, insert the picture file EX M-11.gif from the drive and folder where you store your Data Files.

c. Resize and reposition the picture as necessary to make it fit in rows 1 through 4.

d. Apply the Moderate frame, White style, and change the border color to Purple, Accent 4, Lighter 60%. Resize the picture to fit the image and the border in the first four rows. Center the picture in the range A1:D4.

e. Compare your worksheet to Figure M-23, add your name to the center section of the worksheet footer, preview the workbook, save and close the workbook, then submit the workbook to your instructor.

FIGURE M-23

	A	B	C	D
1				
2				
3				
4				
5	**Budget Category**	**Budget Item**	**Month**	**Amount Budgeted**
6	Compensation	Benefits	Feb	$ 62,000
7	Compensation	Bonuses	Feb	$ 29,110

Skills Review (continued)

4. Embed a workbook in a Word document.

  a. Start Word, create a memo header addressed to your instructor, enter your name in the From line, enter **February Salaries** as the subject, and enter the current date in the Date line.

  b. In the memo body, use the Object dialog box to embed the workbook EX M-12.xlsx from the drive and folder where you store your Data Files, displaying it as an icon with the caption **Salary Details**.

  c. Save the document as **EX M-February Salaries** in the drive and folder where you store your Data Files, then double-click the icon to verify that the workbook opens. (*Hint*: If the workbook does not appear after you double-click it, click the Excel icon on the taskbar.)

  d. Close the workbook and return to Word.

  e. Compare your memo to Figure M-24.

5. Link a workbook to a Word document.

  a. Delete the icon in the memo body.

  b. In the memo body, link the workbook EX M-12.xlsx, displaying the data, not an icon.

  c. Save the document, then note that Mindy Guan's salary is $6,800. Close the document.

  d. Open the EX M-12.xlsx workbook in Excel, and change Mindy Guan's salary to **$8,800**.

  e. Open the **EX M-February Salaries** document in Word, update the links, and verify that Mindy Guan's salary has changed to $8,800 and that the new total salaries amount is $50,940, as shown in Figure M-25. (*Hint*: If the dialog box does not open, giving you the opportunity to update the link, then right-click the worksheet object and click Update Links.)

  f. Save the **EX M-February Salaries** document, preview the memo, close the document, exit Word, then submit the document to your instructor.

  g. Close the EX M-12 workbook without saving changes, then exit Excel.

6. Link an Excel chart to a PowerPoint slide.

  a. Start PowerPoint.

  b. Open the PowerPoint file EX M-13.pptx from the drive and folder where you store your Data Files, then save it as **EX M-Budget Meeting**.

  c. Display Slide 2, February Expenditures.

  d. Link the chart, using the formatting for the destination file, from the Excel file EX M-14.xlsx from the drive and folder where you store your Data Files to Slide 2. Edit the link to be updated automatically. Save and close the Ex M-Budget Meeting file.

  e. Change the Equipment amount on Sheet1 of the file EX M-14 to $200,000, open the EX M-Budget Meeting file, updating the links, and verify the Equipment percentage changed from 12% to 15% on Slide 2.

  f. Add a footer to Slide 2 with your name, then view the slide in Slide Show view. Resize the chart to fit on the slide if necessary. Compare your slide to Figure M-26.

  g. Press [Esc] to return to Normal view.

  h. Save the presentation, exit PowerPoint, close EX M-14 without saving it, then submit the presentation to your instructor.

FIGURE M-24

> Memo
>
> To: Your Instructor
>
> From: Your Name
>
> Subject: February Salaries
>
> Date: 1/29/2013
>
> The February salaries are provided in the worksheet below:
>
> Salary Details

FIGURE M-25

> Memo
>
> To: Your Instructor
>
> From: Your Name
>
> Subject: February Salaries
>
> Date: 1/29/2013
>
> The February salaries are provided in the worksheet below:

West Street Tea Salary Summary			
First Name	**Last Name**	**Position**	**Salary**
Mindy	Guan	Manager	$ 8,800
John	Kelley	Manager	$ 6,500
Mary	O'Riley	Manager	$ 6,600
Sally	Walkman	Sales Associate	$ 7,600
Sarah	Jaffee	Custodian	$ 7,040
Kathy	Alexander	Sales Associate	$ 6,900
Greg	Holak	Sales Associate	$ 7,500
		Total	$ 50,940

FIGURE M-26

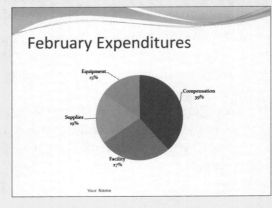

February Expenditures

Skills Review (continued)

7. Import a table into Access.

a. Start Access.

b. Create a blank database named **EX M-Budget** on the drive and folder where you store your Data Files.

c. Use the External Data tab to import the Excel table in the file EX M-15.xlsx from the drive and folder where you store your Data Files. Use the first row as column headings, store the data in a new table, let Access add the primary key, and use the default table name February Budget.

d. Open the February Budget table in Access, and widen the columns as necessary to fully display the field names and field information.

e. Enter your name in the Budget Category column of row 25 in the table, save the database file, compare your screen to Figure M-27, exit Access, then submit the database file to your instructor.

FIGURE M-27

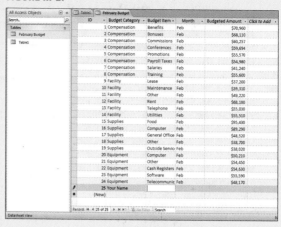

Independent Challenge 1

You are a real estate agent for the Sarasota branch of West Coast Realty. You have been asked to give a presentation to the regional manager about your sales in the past month. To illustrate your sales data, you will add an Excel chart to one of your slides, showing the different types of property sales and the sales amounts for each type.

a. Start Excel, create a new workbook, then save it as **EX M-June Sales** in the drive and folder where you store your Data Files.

b. Enter the property types and the corresponding sales amounts shown in Table M-2 into the EX M-June Sales workbook. Name the sheet with the sales data **Sales**.

c. Create a 3-D pie chart from the sales data on a new sheet named **Chart**. Format it using Chart Layout 1 and Style 2. Increase the font size of the data labels to 14 and apply bold formatting. (*Hint*: Click a data label on the chart and then use the Mini toolbar.) Delete the chart title. Your chart should look like Figure M-28.

d. Copy the chart to the Clipboard.

e. Start PowerPoint, open the PowerPoint Data File EX M-16.pptx from the drive and folder where you store your Data Files, then save it as **EX M-Sales Presentation**.

f. Link the Excel chart to Slide 2 using the destination theme. Use the sizing handles to change the size if necessary, and drag the chart to position it in the center of the slide if necessary.

g. View the slide in Slide Show view, then press [Esc] to end the show.

h. Add a footer to Slide 2 with your name, then save the presentation.

i. Close the presentation, exit PowerPoint, then submit the PowerPoint file to your instructor.

j. Save the workbook, then close the workbook, and exit Excel.

TABLE M-2

property type	sales
Condominium	$3,300,400
Single-family	$6,700,200
Land	$2,500,200

FIGURE M-28

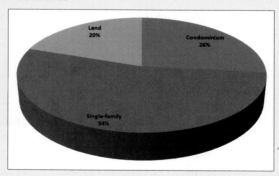

Independent Challenge 2

You are opening a new fitness center, Total Fitness, in San Francisco, California. The owner of a fitness center in the area is retiring and has agreed to sell you a text file containing his list of supplier information. You need to import this text file into Excel so that you can manipulate the data. Later, you will convert the Excel file to an Access table so that you can give it to your business partner who is building a supplier database.

Independent Challenge 2 (continued)

a. Start Excel, open the file EX M-17.txt from the drive and folder where you store your Data Files, then save it as an Excel file named **EX M-Fitness Suppliers**. (*Hint*: This is a tab-delimited text file.)

b. Adjust the column widths as necessary. Rename the worksheet **Suppliers**.

c. Create a table using data on the Suppliers sheet, and apply the Table Style Light 18 format.

d. Sort the worksheet data in ascending order by Supplier. Your worksheet should look like Figure M-29.

e. Add your name to the center section of the worksheet footer, save and close the workbook, then exit Excel.

FIGURE M-29

	A	B	C	D	E	F	G
1	Supplier	Address	City	State	Zip	Phone	Contact
2	Ace Equipment	2 Jean St	Oakland	CA	94611	510-422-9923	R. Jurez
3	All Equipment	PO Box 9870	Milpitas	CA	94698	408-345-9343	F. Gerry
4	Best Start	102 Lake Dr	San Diego	CA	93112	212-223-9934	S. Werthen
5	Cool Equipment	232 Corn Ave	Daly City	CA	94623	415-465-7855	O. Rolins
6	East Coast Equipment	343 Upham St	Los Angeles	CA	93111	213-887-4456	P. Newhall
7	Fitness Pro	223 Main St	Ventura	CA	93143	213-332-5568	A. Blume
8	Handley Exercise	44 West St	Brisbane	CA	94453	415-223-9912	H. Jones
9	Jones Equipment	394 19th Ave	San Francisco	CA	94554	415-444-9932	L. Smith
10	Sports Plus	33 Jackson St	Fresno	CA	96899	608-332-8790	J. Jerry
11	Sports Pro	998 Little St	San Francisco	CA	94622	415-665-7342	W. Kitter
12	Sports Unlimited	77 Sunrise St	Malibu	CA	93102	213-223-5432	J. Walsh
13	West Coast Sports	8 High St	San Jose	CA	94671	408-332-9981	K. McGuire

f. Start Access, create a new blank database on the drive and folder where you store your Data Files. Name the new database **EX M-Suppliers**.

g. Use the External Data tab to import the Excel file EX M-Fitness Suppliers from the drive and folder where you store your Data Files. Use the column labels as the field names, store the data in a new table, let Access add the primary key, and accept the default table name.

h. Open the Suppliers table and AutoFit the columns. (Table1 will be removed when the file is closed.)

i. Enter your name in the Supplier column in row 13, save and then close the table, and exit Access.

Advanced Challenge Exercise

- Create a copy of the EX M-Fitness Suppliers.xlsx file with the name **EX M-Fitness Suppliers_ACE** on the drive and folder where you store your Data Files.
- Using Access, create a new blank database named **EX M-Suppliers_ACE** on the drive and folder where your store your Data Files. Link the Excel data in the EX M-Fitness Suppliers _ACE file to the EX M-Suppliers_ACE database file.
- Close the database file, open the EX M-Fitness Suppliers _ACE.xlsx file, and change the contact for the Ace Equipment supplier to J. Smith. Save and close the Excel file.
- Open the EX M-Suppliers_ACE database, and verify that the contact name was updated in the Suppliers table, then close the table and exit Access.

j. Submit the database file to your instructor.

Independent Challenge 3

You are the newly hired manager at People Alliance, a mutual funds firm specializing in consumer products. An employee, Karen Holden, has completed a two-year training period as an assistant and you would like to promote her to an associate position with a higher salary. You have examined the salaries of the other associates in the company and will present this information to the vice president of Human Resources, requesting permission to grant Karen a promotion and an increase in salary.

a. Start Word, open the Word file EX M-18.docx from the drive and folder where you store your Data Files, then save it as **EX M-Promotion**.

b. Add your name to the From line of the memo, and change the date to the current date.

c. At the end of the memo, embed the workbook EX M-19.xlsx as an icon from the drive and folder where you store your Data Files. Change the caption for the icon to **Salaries**. Double-click the icon to verify that the workbook opens.

d. Close the workbook, return to Word, delete the Salaries icon, and link the workbook EX M-19 to the memo, displaying the data, not an icon.

e. Save the EX M-Promotion memo, and close the file.

f. Open the EX M-19 workbook, and change Karen Holden's salary to $55,000.

g. Open the EX M-Promotion memo, update the links, and make sure Karen Holden's salary is updated.

Independent Challenge 3 (continued)

Advanced Challenge Exercise

- Delete the worksheet at the bottom of the Promotion memo. Copy the range A1:C10 from Sheet1 of the EX M-19 workbook to the Clipboard. (*Tip*: You are not copying the gross salary information because you do not want it to appear in the memo.)
- Return to the EX M-Promotion memo, and use the Paste Special dialog box to paste a link to the range A1:C10 from EX M-19 that is on the Clipboard. Use Figure M-30 as a guide. Save and close the memo.
- Change Karen Holden's position to Associate in the EX M-19 workbook. Verify the new position information is displayed in the EX M-Promotion memo when the memo is opened with the links updated.

FIGURE M-30

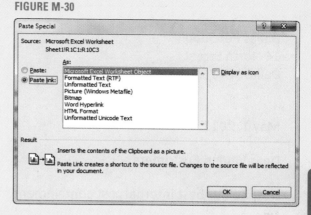

h. Save and close the memo. Exit Word and submit the memo to your instructor.

i. Close EX M-19 without saving the changes to Karen Holden's information, then exit Excel.

Real Life Independent Challenge

You decide to create a daily schedule of your pet's activities to give to the person who will care for your pet when you go on vacation. As part of this schedule, you record the times and corresponding activities that your pet engages in daily. You also record when medicine should be taken. You will include the schedule in a Word document that provides your contact information. You decide to link the workbook so that schedule changes will be reflected in the information you provide to the pet sitter.

a. Start Excel, open the file EX M-20.xlsx from the drive and folder where you store your Data Files, then save it as **EX M-Schedule**.

b. Use the structure of the worksheet to record your pet's schedule. Change the data in columns A and B to reflect your pet's times and activities. If you do not have any data to enter, create your own or use the data provided on the worksheet.

c. Save and close the EX M-Schedule workbook, then exit Excel.

d. Open the Data File EX M-21.docx from the drive and folder where you store your Data Files, then save it as **EX M-Contact Information**.

e. Enter your name at the bottom of the document. Change the document data to reflect your destination and contact information. If you do not have any data to enter, use the provided document data.

f. Below the line "Here is a schedule of Junior's daily activities:", create a linked version of the worksheet to the EX M-Schedule workbook.

g. Save the file, then preview the EX M-Contact Information document.

h. Close the Word document, exit Word, then submit the Word document to your instructor.

Advanced Challenge Exercise

- Open the EX M-Schedule.xlsx workbook from the drive and folder where you store your Data Files. Add rows at the top of the worksheet to display a picture of your pet. Add as many rows as necessary. Insert a picture of your pet in the new rows. You can use the picture EX M-22.gif if you don't have a picture.
- Resize the picture, and move it to the top center of the new worksheet rows. Use the rotation options of your choice to rotate the picture. (*Hint*: You can rotate a picture by clicking the Rotate button in the Arrange group on the Picture Tools Format tab.)
- Use the picture effects options of your choice to change the picture.
- Save the workbook and preview the sheet.
- Close the workbook, exit Excel, then submit the workbook to your instructor.

Visual Workshop

Create the document shown in Figure M-31 by opening the Word file EX M-23.docx and linking the data from the Excel file EX M-24.xlsx. Replace Management in the last line of the document with your name. Save the document as **EX M-Price Increase**, close the document, exit Word and Excel. Submit the file to your instructor.

FIGURE M-31

Dallas Pet Supply
14 North Street
Dallas, TX 75201

May 1, 2013

Dear Valued Customers,

Despite our best internal cost containment measures we have experienced cost increases in transportation and materials. To address these costs we will increase the prices for the products listed below on orders received and shipped after June 1, 2013.

Product	Item Code	Price
Dog Bed Large	A324	$152.99
Dog Bed Small	A325	$131.57
Dog Brush Set	A251	$35.94
Dog Crate Large	A409	$139.99
Dog Crate Medium	A407	$121.22
Dog Crate Small	A408	$108.57
Cat Bed	B101	$105.99
Cat Play Set	B211	$42.99
Dog Collar	A135	$25.19
Cat Collar	B132	$20.36
Cat Post	B755	$19.99
Dog Toy Set	A884	$39.54

Thank you for your understanding and continued business.

Regards,

Your Name

Sharing Excel Files and Incorporating Web Information

Increasingly, Excel users share workbooks with others, over the Web as well as on private networks. Sharing workbooks allows others to review, revise, and provide feedback on worksheet data. In addition, users frequently incorporate up-to-date information from the Web into their workbooks and prepare their own data for posting on the Web. Kate Morgan, the vice president of sales for Quest, wants to share information with corporate office employees and branch managers using the company's intranet and the Web.

OBJECTIVES

Share Excel files

Set up a shared workbook for multiple users

Track revisions in a shared workbook

Apply and modify passwords

Work with XML schemas

Import and export XML data

Run Web queries to retrieve external data

Import and export HTML data

Sharing Excel Files

Microsoft Excel provides many different ways to share spreadsheets with people in your office, in your organization, or anywhere on the Web. When you share workbooks, you have to consider how you will protect information that you don't want everyone to see and how you can control revisions others will make to your files. Also, some information you want to use might not be in Excel format. For example, there is a great deal of information published on the Web in HTML format, so Excel allows you to import HTML to your worksheets. You can also export your worksheet data in HTML format. However, many companies find the XML format to be more flexible than HTML for storing and exchanging data, so they are increasingly using XML to store and exchange data both internally and externally. Excel allows you to easily import and export XML data as well. You can also retrieve data from the Web using queries. Figure N-1 shows methods of importing to and exporting from workbooks. Kate considers the best way to share her Excel workbooks with corporate employees and branch managers.

DETAILS

To share worksheet information, consider the following issues:

- **Allowing others to use a workbook**

    While many of your workbooks are for your own use, you will want to share some of them with other users. When users **share** your workbooks, they can simultaneously open them from a network server, modify them electronically, and return their revisions to you for incorporation with others' changes. You can view each user's name and the date each change was made. To share a workbook, you need to turn on the sharing feature for that workbook. Kate wants to obtain feedback on Quest sales data from the branch managers, so she sets up her workbook so others can use it.

- **Controlling access to workbooks on a server**

    When you place a workbook on a network server, you will probably want to control who can open and change it. You can do this using Excel passwords. Kate assigns a password to her workbook, then posts the workbook on the Quest server. She gives the corporate staff and branch managers the password, so only they can open the workbook and revise it.

- **HTML data**

    You can paste data from a Web page into a worksheet and then manipulate and format it using Excel. You can also save Excel workbook information in HTML format so you can publish it on an intranet or on the Web. Kate decides to publish the worksheet with the North American sales information in HTML format on the company intranet, as shown in Figure N-2

- **Working with XML data**

    Importing and storing data in XML format allows you to use it in different situations. For example, a company might store all of its sales data in an XML file and make different parts of the file available to various departments such as marketing and accounting. These departments can extract information that is relevant to their purposes from the file. A subset of the same XML file might be sent to vendors or other business associates who only require certain types of sales data stored in the XML file. Kate decides to import XML files that contain sales information from the Miami and New York branches to get a sales summary for Quest's eastern region.

- **Using an Excel query to retrieve data from the Web**

    You can use built-in Excel queries to import up-to-date stock quotes and currency rates from the MSN Money Web site. These queries import data from the Web into an Excel workbook, where you can organize and manipulate the information using Excel spreadsheet and graphics tools. Kate decides to use a query to get currency rate information for her analysis of the sales data from the Quest Canada branches, as shown in Figure N-3.

FIGURE N-1: Importing and exporting data

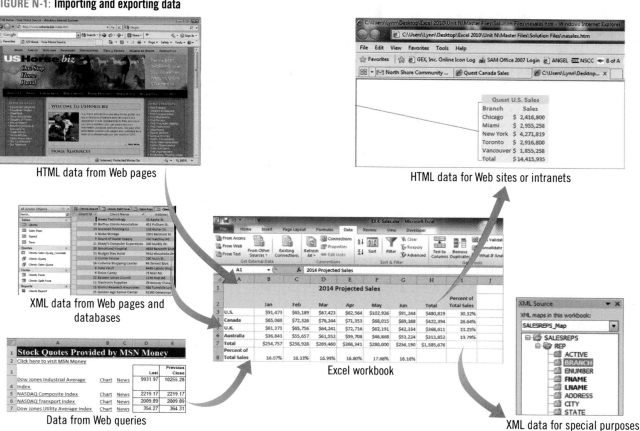

HTML data from Web pages

HTML data for Web sites or intranets

XML data from Web pages and databases

Excel workbook

Data from Web queries

XML data for special purposes

FIGURE N-2: North America sales information displayed in a Web browser

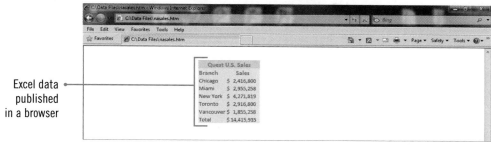

Excel data published in a browser

FIGURE N-3: Data retrieved from the Web using a Web query

Excel worksheet with imported currency information

Sharing Excel Files and Incorporating Web Information

Setting Up a Shared Workbook for Multiple Users

You can make an Excel file a **shared workbook** so that several users can open and modify it at the same time. This is useful for workbooks that you want others to review on a network server, where the workbook is equally accessible to all network users. When you share a workbook, you can have Excel keep a list of all changes to the workbook, which you can view and print at any time. ▓▓▓ Kate wants to get feedback from selected corporate staff and branch managers before presenting the information at the next corporate staff meeting. She asks you to help her put a shared workbook containing customer and sales data on the company's network. You begin by making her Excel file a shared workbook.

STEPS

1. **Start Excel, open the file EX N-1.xlsx from the drive and folder where you store your Data Files, then save it as EX N-Sales Information**

   The workbook with the sales information opens, displaying two worksheets. The first contains tour sales data for the Quest U.S. branches; the second is a breakdown of the branch sales by sales associate.

2. **Click the Review tab, then click the Share Workbook button in the Changes group**

   The Share Workbook dialog box opens, as shown in Figure N-4.

> 3. **Click the Editing tab, if necessary**

   The dialog box lists the names of people who are currently using the workbook. You are the only user, so your name, or the name of the person entered as the computer user, appears, along with the current date and time.

> 4. **Click to select the check box next to Allow changes by more than one user at the same time. This also allows workbook merging., then click OK**

   A dialog box appears, asking if you want to save the workbook. This will resave it as a shared workbook.

5. **Click OK**

   Excel saves the file as a shared workbook. The title bar now reads EX N-Sales Information.xlsx [Shared], as shown in Figure N-5. This version replaces the unshared version.

QUICK TIP

The Advanced tab of the Share Workbook dialog box allows you to specify the length of time the change history is saved and when the file will be updated with the changes.

QUICK TIP

To return a shared workbook to unshared status, click the Review tab, click the Share Workbook button in the Changes group, then deselect the Allow changes by more than one user at the same time option on the Editing tab of the Share Workbook dialog box.

Sharing workbooks using Excel Web App

The Excel Web App is an online program that lets you collaborate on Excel workbooks with others using a Web browser, without needing the Excel program installed on any users' computers. You need a Windows Live ID to access Windows Live SkyDrive where you store and access your Excel workbooks. To post your workbook to Windows Live SkyDrive from Excel, click the File tab, click Save & Send, click Save to Web, if necessary sign in using your Windows Live ID username and password, click the folder where you want to save the document, then click Save As. Assign a filename and online folder destination, then click Save.

FIGURE N-4: **Share Workbook dialog box**

Select to allow multiple users of the workbook at the same time

Current users of the workbook

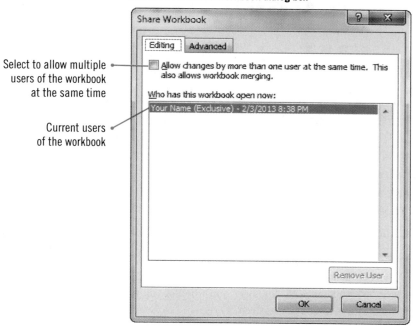

FIGURE N-5: **Shared workbook**

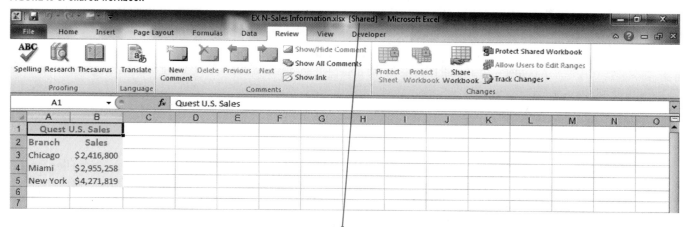

Title bar indicates the workbook is shared

Merging workbooks

Instead of putting the shared workbook on a server to be shared simultaneously, you might want to distribute copies to your reviewers via e-mail. Once everyone has entered their changes and returned their workbook copies to you, you can merge the changed copies into one master workbook that contains everyone's changes. Each copy you distribute must be designated as shared, and the Change History feature on the Advanced tab of the Share Workbook dialog box must be activated. Occasionally a conflict occurs when two users are trying to edit the same cells in a shared workbook. In this case, the second person to save the file will see a Resolve Conflicts dialog box and need to choose Accept Mine or Accept Other. To merge workbooks, you need to add the Compare and Merge Workbooks command to the Quick Access toolbar by clicking the File tab, clicking Options, and clicking Quick Access toolbar. Click All Commands in the Choose commands from list, click Compare and Merge Workbooks, click Add, then click OK. Once you get the changed copies back, open the master copy of the workbook, then click the Compare and Merge Workbooks button on the Quick Access toolbar. The Select Files to Merge Into Current Workbook dialog box opens. Select the workbooks you want to merge (you can use the [Ctrl] key to select more than one workbook), then click OK.

Tracking Revisions in a Shared Workbook

When you share workbooks, it is often helpful to **track** modifications, or identify who made which changes. You can accept the changes you agree with, and if you disagree with any changes you can reject them. When you activate the Excel change tracking feature, changes appear in a different color for each user. Each change is identified with the username and date. In addition to highlighting changes, Excel keeps track of changes in a **change history**, a list of all changes that you can place on a separate worksheet so you can review them all at once. Kate asks you to set up the shared Sales Information workbook so that Excel tracks all future changes. You then open a workbook that is on the server and review its changes and the change history.

STEPS

1. **Click the Track Changes button in the Changes group, then click Highlight Changes**

   The Highlight Changes dialog box opens, as shown in Figure N-6, allowing you to turn on change tracking. You can also specify which changes to highlight and whether you want to display changes on the screen or save the change history in a separate worksheet.

2. **Click to select the Track changes while editing check box if necessary, remove check marks from all other boxes except for Highlight changes on screen, click OK, then click OK in the dialog box that informs you that you have yet to make changes**

   Leaving the When, Who, and Where check boxes blank allows you to track all changes.

3. **Click the Sales by Rep sheet tab, change the sales figure for Sanchez in cell C3 to 290,000, press [Enter], then move the mouse pointer over the cell you just changed**

   A border with a small triangle in the upper-left corner appears around the cell you changed, and a ScreenTip appears with the date, the time, and details about the change, as shown in Figure N-7.

4. **Save and close the workbook**

   Jose Silva has made changes to a version of this workbook. You want to open this workbook and view the details of these changes and accept the ones that appear to be correct.

5. **Open the file EX N-2.xlsx from the drive and folder where you store your Data Files, save it as EX N-Sales Information Edits, click the Review tab if necessary, click the Track Changes button in the Changes group, click Accept/Reject Changes, click the When check box in the Select Changes to Accept or Reject dialog box to deselect it, then click OK**

   You will accept the first four changes that Jose made to the workbook and reject his last change. You also want to see a list of all changes.

6. **Click Accept four times to approve the first four changes, click Reject to undo Jose's fifth change, click the Track Changes button in the Changes group, click Highlight Changes, click the When check box in the Highlight Changes dialog box to deselect it, click to select the List changes on a new sheet check box, then click OK**

   A new sheet named History opens, as shown in Figure N-8, with Jose's changes in a filtered list. Because saving the file closes the History sheet, you need to copy the information to a new worksheet.

7. **Copy the range A1:I6 on the History sheet, click the Insert Worksheet button next to the History sheet tab, on the new sheet click cell A1, click the Home tab, click the Paste button in the Clipboard group, widen columns E, F, H, and I to display the information in the columns, then rename the new sheet tab Saved History**

8. **Add a footer with your name to the Saved History sheet, save and close the workbook, then submit the workbook to your instructor**

   The Saved History sheet shows all of Jose's changes to the workbook.

FIGURE N-6: **Highlight Changes dialog box**

Select to show
changes to the
worksheet

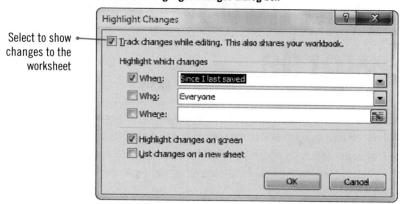

FIGURE N-7: **Tracked change**

Triangle in corner
indicates cell has
been changed

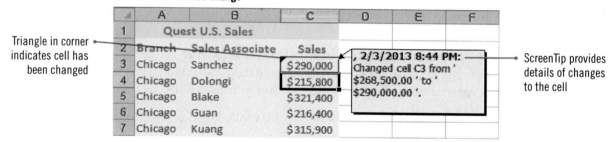

ScreenTip provides
details of changes
to the cell

FIGURE N-8: **History sheet tab with change history**

Details of
changes
to the
worksheet

History
tab

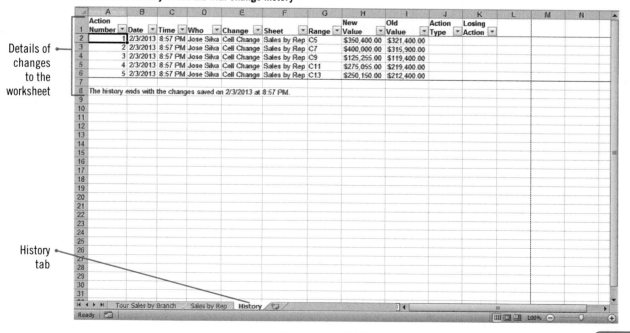

Applying and Modifying Passwords

When you place a shared workbook on a server, you may want to use a password so that only authorized people will be able to open it or make changes to it. However, it's important to remember that *if you lose your password, you will not be able to open or change the workbook.* Passwords are case sensitive, so you must type them exactly as you want users to type them, with the same spacing and using the same case. For security, it is a good idea to include uppercase and lowercase letters and numbers in a password. ▓▓▓▓▓ Kate wants you to put the workbook with sales information on one of the company's servers. You decide to save a copy of the workbook with two passwords: one that users will need to open it, and another that they will use to make changes to it.

STEPS

QUICK TIP
You can also use a password to encrypt the contents of a workbook by clicking the File tab, clicking Protect Workbook in the middle pane, clicking Encrypt with Password, and entering a password.

1. **Open the file EX N-1.xlsx from the drive and folder where you store your Data Files, click the File Tab, click Save As, click the Tools list arrow in the bottom of the Save As dialog box, then click General Options**

   The General Options dialog box opens, with two password boxes: one to open the workbook, and one to allow changes to the workbook, as shown in Figure N-9.

2. **In the Password to open text box, type QSTmanager01**

   Be sure to type the letters in the correct cases. This is the password that users must type to open the workbook. When you enter passwords, the characters you type are masked with bullets (• • •) for security purposes.

QUICK TIP
You can press [Enter] rather than clicking OK after entering a password. This allows you to keep your hands on the keyboard.

3. **Press [Tab], in the Password to modify text box, type QSTsales02, then click OK**

   This is the password that users must type to make changes to the workbook. A dialog box asks you to verify the first password by reentering it.

4. **Enter QSTmanager01 in the first Confirm Password dialog box, click OK, enter QSTsales02 in the second Confirm Password dialog box, then click OK**

5. **Change the filename to EX N-Sales Information PW, if necessary navigate to the location where you store your Data Files, click Save, then close the workbook**

QUICK TIP
To delete a password, reopen the General Options dialog box, highlight the symbols for the existing password, press [Delete], click OK, change the filename, then click Save.

6. **Reopen the workbook EX N-Sales Information PW, enter the password QSTmanager01 when prompted for a password, click OK, then enter QSTsales02 to obtain write access**

   The Password dialog box is shown in Figure N-10. Obtaining write access for a workbook allows you to modify it.

7. **Click OK, change the sales figure for the Chicago branch in cell B3 to 2,500,000, then press [Enter]**

   You were able to make this change because you obtained write access privileges using the password "QSTsales02".

8. **Save and close the workbook**

FIGURE N-9: General Options dialog box

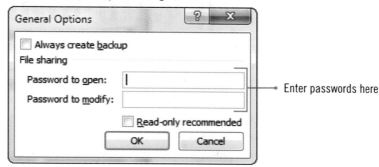

Enter passwords here

FIGURE N-10: Password entry prompt

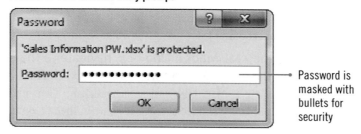

Password is masked with bullets for security

Creating strong passwords for Excel workbooks

Strong passwords will help to protect your workbooks from security threats. A **strong password** has at least 14 characters that are not commonly used. Although your password needs to be easy to remember, it should be difficult for other people to guess. Avoid using your birthday, your pet's name, or other personal information in your password. Also avoid dictionary words and repeated characters. Instead, mix the types of characters using uppercase and lowercase letters, numbers, and special characters such as @ and %. Microsoft offers an online password checker to test your passwords for security. See Table N-1 for rules and examples for creating strong passwords.

TABLE N-1: Rules for creating strong passwords

rule	example
Include numbers	5qRyz8O6w
Add symbols	lQx!u%z7q9
Increase complexity	4!%5Zq^c6#
Use long passwords	Z7#l%2!q9!6@i9&Wb

Working with XML Schemas

Using Excel you can import and export XML data and analyze it using Excel tools. To import XML data, Excel requires a file called a schema that describes the structure of the XML file. A **schema** contains the rules for the XML file by listing all of the fields in the XML document and their characteristics, such as the type of data they contain. A schema is used to **validate** XML data, making sure the data follows the rules given in the file. Once a schema is attached to a workbook, a schema is called a **map**. When you map an element to a worksheet, you place the element name on the worksheet in a specific location. Mapping XML elements allows you to choose the XML data from a file with which you want to work in the worksheet. ▓▓▓▓▓ Kate has been given XML files containing sales information from the U.S. branches. She asks you to prepare a workbook to import the sales representatives' XML data. You begin by adding a schema to a worksheet that describes the XML data.

STEPS

1. **Create a new workbook, save it as EX N-Sales Reps in the drive and folder where you store your Data Files, click the Developer tab, then click the Source button in the XML group**

   The XML Source pane opens. This is where you specify a schema, or map, to import. A schema has the extension .xsd. Kate has provided you with a schema she received from the IT Department describing the XML file structure.

2. **Click XML Maps at the bottom of the task pane**

   The XML Maps dialog box opens, listing the XML maps or schemas in the workbook. There are no schemas in the Sales Reps workbook at this time, as shown in Figure N-11.

3. **Click Add in the XML Maps dialog box, navigate to the drive and folder containing your Data Files in the Select XML Source dialog box, click EX N-3.xsd, click Open, then click OK**

   The schema elements appear in the XML Source task pane. Elements in a schema describe data similarly to the way field names in an Excel table describe the data in their columns. You choose the schema elements from the XML Source pane with which you want to work on your worksheet and map them to the worksheet. Once on the worksheet, the elements are called fields.

4. **Click the BRANCH element in the XML Source task pane and drag it to cell A1 on the worksheet, then use Figure N-12 as a guide to drag the FNAME, LNAME, SALES, and ENUMBER fields to the worksheet**

   The mapped elements appear in bolded format in the XML Source pane. The fields on the worksheet have filter arrows because Excel automatically creates a table on the worksheet as you map the schema elements. You decide to remove the ENUMBER field from the table.

5. **Right-click the ENUMBER element in the XML Source task pane, then click Remove element**

   ENUMBER is no longer formatted in bold because it is no longer mapped to the worksheet. This means that when XML data is imported, the ENUMBER field will not be populated with data. However, the field name remains in the table on the worksheet.

6. **Drag the table resizing arrow to the left to remove cell E1 from the table**

   Because you plan to import XML data from different files, you want to be sure that data from one file will not overwrite data from another file when it is imported into the worksheet. You also want to be sure that Excel validates the imported data against the rules specified in the schema.

7. **Click any cell in the table, click the Developer tab, then click the Map Properties button in the XML group**

   The XML Map Properties dialog box opens, as shown in Figure N-13.

8. **Click the Validate data against schema for import and export check box to select it, if necessary click the Append new data to existing XML tables option button to select it, then click OK**

   You are ready to import XML data into your worksheet.

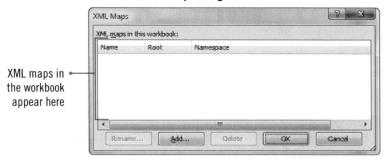

XML maps in the workbook appear here

FIGURE N-12: **XML elements mapped to the worksheet**

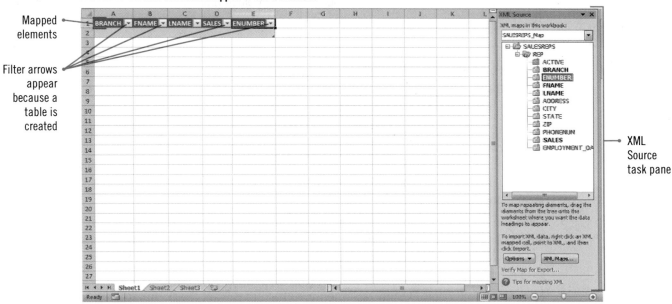

Mapped elements

Filter arrows appear because a table is created

XML Source task pane

Excel 2010

FIGURE N-13: **XML Map Properties dialog box**

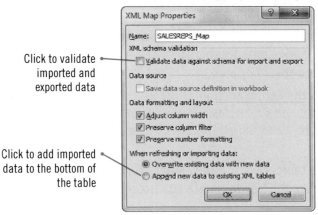

Click to validate imported and exported data

Click to add imported data to the bottom of the table

Learning more about XML

XML is a universal data format for business and industry information sharing. Using XML, you can store structured information related to services, products, or business transactions and easily share and exchange the information with others. XML provides a way to express structure in data. Structured data is tagged, or marked up, to indicate its content. For example, an XML data marker (tag) that contains an item's cost might be named COST. Excel's ability to work with XML data allows you to access the large amount of information stored in the XML format. For example, organizations have developed many XML applications with a specific focus, such as MathML (Mathematical Markup Language) and RETML (Real Estate Transaction Markup Language).

Importing and Exporting XML Data

After the mapping is complete, you can import any XML file with a structure that conforms to the workbook schema. The mapped elements on the worksheet will fill with (or be **populated** with) data from the XML file. If an element is not mapped on the worksheet, then its data will not be imported. Once you import the XML data, you can analyze it using Excel tools. You can also export data from an Excel workbook to an XML file.  Kate asks you to combine the sales data for the Miami and New York branches that are contained in XML files. She would like you to add a total for the combined branches and export the data from Excel to an XML file.

STEPS

1. **Click cell A1, click the Developer tab if necessary, then click the Import button in the XML group**

   The Import XML dialog box opens.

2. **Navigate to the folder containing your Data Files if necessary, click EX N-4.xml, then click Import**

   The worksheet is populated with data from the XML file that contains the Miami sales rep information. Excel only imports data for the mapped elements. You decide to add the sales rep data for the New York branch to the worksheet.

3. **Click the Import button in the XML group, navigate to the folder containing your Data Files in the Import XML dialog box if necessary, click EX N-5.xml, then click Import**

   The New York branch sales rep data is added to the Miami branch data. You decide to total the sales figures for all sales reps.

4. **Click the Table Tools Design tab, then click the Total Row check box to select it**

   The total sales amount of 4999777 appears in cell D25. You decide to format the table.

5. **Select the range of cells D2:D25, click the Home tab, click the Accounting Number Format button $ in the Number group, click the Decrease Decimal button in the Number group twice, click the Table Tools Design tab, click the More button in the Table Styles group, select Table Style Light 18, then click cell A1**

   Compare your completed table to Figure N-14.

6. **Enter your name in the center section of the worksheet footer, then preview the table**

   You will export the combined sales rep data as an XML file. Because not all of the elements in the schema were mapped to fields in your Excel table, you do not want the data exported from the table to be validated against the schema.

7. **Click any cell in the table, click the Developer tab, click the Map Properties button in the XML group, then click the Validate data against schema for import and export check box to deselect it**

   The Map Properties dialog box with the validation turned off is shown in Figure N-15. You are ready to export the XML data.

8. **Click OK, click the Export button in the XML group, navigate to the folder containing your Data Files in the Export XML dialog box, enter the name EX N-East Reps in the File name text box, click Export, then save and close the workbook**

   The sales data is saved in your Data File location in XML format, in the file called EX N-East Reps.xml.

FIGURE N-14: Completed table with combined sales rep data

Imported data is formatted

Total sales

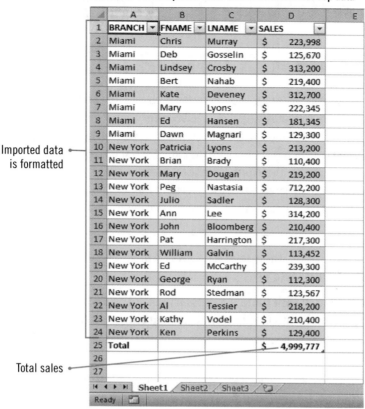

	A	B	C	D	E
1	BRANCH	FNAME	LNAME	SALES	
2	Miami	Chris	Murray	$ 223,998	
3	Miami	Deb	Gosselin	$ 125,670	
4	Miami	Lindsey	Crosby	$ 313,200	
5	Miami	Bert	Nahab	$ 219,400	
6	Miami	Kate	Deveney	$ 312,700	
7	Miami	Mary	Lyons	$ 222,345	
8	Miami	Ed	Hansen	$ 181,345	
9	Miami	Dawn	Magnari	$ 129,300	
10	New York	Patricia	Lyons	$ 213,200	
11	New York	Brian	Brady	$ 110,400	
12	New York	Mary	Dougan	$ 219,200	
13	New York	Peg	Nastasia	$ 712,200	
14	New York	Julio	Sadler	$ 128,300	
15	New York	Ann	Lee	$ 314,200	
16	New York	John	Bloomberg	$ 210,400	
17	New York	Pat	Harrington	$ 217,300	
18	New York	William	Galvin	$ 113,452	
19	New York	Ed	McCarthy	$ 239,300	
20	New York	George	Ryan	$ 112,300	
21	New York	Rod	Stedman	$ 123,567	
22	New York	Al	Tessier	$ 218,200	
23	New York	Kathy	Vodel	$ 210,400	
24	New York	Ken	Perkins	$ 129,400	
25	Total			$ 4,999,777	
26					
27					

Sheet1 / Sheet2 / Sheet3

Ready

FIGURE N-15: XML Map Properties dialog box

Click to deselect the validation of exported data

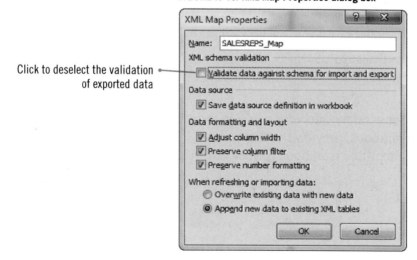

XML Map Properties

Name: SALESREPS_Map

XML schema validation

☐ Validate data against schema for import and export

Data source

☑ Save data source definition in workbook

Data formatting and layout

☑ Adjust column width
☑ Preserve column filter
☑ Preserve number formatting

When refreshing or importing data:

○ Overwrite existing data with new data
◉ Append new data to existing XML tables

OK   Cancel

Importing XML data without a schema

You can import XML data without a schema, and Excel will create one for you. In this situation all of the XML elements are mapped to the Excel worksheet, and the data in all of the fields is populated using the XML file. When a schema is not used, you are unable to validate the data that is imported. You also need to delete all of the fields in the table that you will not use in the worksheet, which can be time consuming.

Running Web Queries to Retrieve External Data

Often you'll want to incorporate information from the Web into an Excel worksheet for analysis. Using Excel, you can obtain data from a Web site by running a **Web query** and save that information in an existing or new Excel workbook. You must be connected to the Internet to run a Web query. You can save Web queries to use them again later; a saved query has an .iqy file extension. Several Web query files come with Excel. ▨▨▨▨ As part of an effort to summarize the North American sales for Quest, Kate needs to obtain currency rate information for the Canadian dollar to adjust the data from the Toronto and Vancouver branches. She asks you to run a Web query to obtain the most current currency rate information from the Web.

STEPS

TROUBLE

Depending on your screen's settings and the Add-Ins you have installed, you might not see an Existing Connections button; you may instead see a Get External Data button. If so, click the Get External Data button, then click Existing Connections.

1. **Create a new workbook, then save it as EX N-Currency Rates in the drive and folder where you store your Data Files**

2. **Close the XML Source task pane if necessary, click the Data tab, then click the Existing Connections button in the Get External Data group**

   The Existing Connections dialog box opens, with all of the connections displayed, including the queries that come with Excel.

3. **Scroll down if necessary, click MSN MoneyCentral Investor Currency Rates in the Connection files on this computer area if necessary, then click Open**

   The Import Data dialog box opens, as shown in Figure N-16. Here you specify the worksheet location where you want the imported data to appear.

QUICK TIP

You can also incorporate information from a Web page by inserting a screenshot into an Excel worksheet. Click the Screenshot button on the Insert tab, click Screen Clipping, then select the area on the Web page that you want to insert. The screenshot is inserted as a picture in the worksheet.

4. **Make sure the Existing worksheet option button is selected, click cell A1 if necessary to place =$A$1 in the Existing worksheet text box, then click OK**

   Currency rate information from the Web is placed in the workbook, as shown in Figure N-17. Kate wants you to obtain the previous closing exchange rate of the Canadian dollar.

5. **Click the Canadian Dollar to US Dollar link**

   A Web page opens in your browser displaying currency rate details for the Canadian dollar, as shown in Figure N-18.

6. **Close your browser window, add your name to the center footer section of the worksheet, save the workbook, preview the first page of the worksheet, close the workbook, exit Excel, then submit the workbook to your instructor**

FIGURE N-16: Import Data dialog box

Location on worksheet where
imported data will appear

FIGURE N-17: Currency rates quote

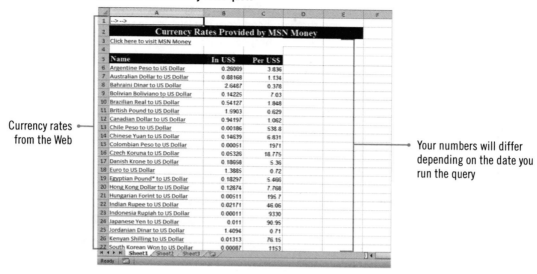

Currency rates
from the Web

Your numbers will differ
depending on the date you
run the query

FIGURE N-18: Rate details for the Canadian dollar

Your values
will differ
depending
on the date
you run
the query

Creating your own Web queries

The easiest way to retrieve data from a particular Web page on a regular basis is to create a customized Web query. Click the Data tab, click the From Web button in the Get External Data group (or click the Get External Data button and click the From Web button). In the Address text box in the New Web Query dialog box, type the address of the Web page from which you want to retrieve data, then click Go. Click the yellow arrows next to the information you want to bring into a worksheet or click the upper-left arrow to import the entire page, verify that the information that you want to import has a green checkmark next to it, then click Import. The Import Data dialog box opens and allows you to specify where you want the imported data placed in the worksheet. You can save a query for future use by clicking the Save Query button 🖫 in the New Web Query dialog box before you click Import. The query is saved as a file with an .iqy file extension.

Importing and Exporting HTML Data

Although you can open HTML files directly in Excel, most often the information that you want to include in a worksheet is published on the Web and you don't have the HTML file. In this situation you can import the HTML data by copying the data on the Web page and pasting it into an Excel worksheet. This allows you to bring in only the information that you need from the Web page to your worksheet. Once the HTML data is in your worksheet, you can analyze the imported information using Excel features. You can also export worksheet data as an HTML file that you can then share on a Web site. ▓▓▓▓ The Toronto and Vancouver branch managers have published the Canada branch sales information on the company intranet. Kate asks you to import the published sales data into an Excel worksheet so she can summarize it using Excel tools. She also wants you to export the summarized data to an HTML file she can post on the company intranet.

STEPS

1. **In Windows Explorer, navigate to the drive and folder containing your Data Files, double-click the EX N-6.htm file to open it in your browser, then copy the two table rows on the Web page containing the Toronto and Vancouver sales information**
   You are ready to paste the information from the Web page into an Excel worksheet.

2. **Start Excel, open the file EX N-1.xlsx from the drive and folder where you store your Data Files, then save it as EX N-North America Sales**

3. **Right-click cell A6 on the Tour Sales by Branch sheet, click the Match Destination Formatting button 📋 in the Paste Options list**
   The Canada sales information is added to the U.S. sales data. You decide to total the sales and format the new data.

4. **Click cell A8, type Total, press [Tab], click the Sum button Σ in the Editing group, then press [Enter]**

5. **Select the range A5:B5, click the Format Painter button 🖌 in the Clipboard group, select the range A6:B8, then click cell A1**
   Compare your worksheet to Figure N-19. Kate is finished with the analysis and formatting of the North America branches. She wants the combined information published in a Web page.

6. **Click the File tab, then click Save As**
   The Save As dialog box opens. This dialog box allows you to specify what workbook components you want to publish.

7. **Navigate to the folder containing your Data Files if necessary, click the Save as type list arrow, click Web Page (*.htm; *.html), edit the filename to read nasales.htm, click the Selection: Sheet option button, click Publish, then click Publish again**
   The HTML file is saved in your Data Files folder. To avoid problems when publishing your pages to a Web server, it is best to use lowercase characters, omit special characters and spaces, and limit your filename to eight characters with an additional three-character extension.

8. **In Windows Explorer, navigate to the drive and folder containing your Data Files, then double-click the file nasales.htm**
   The HTML version of your worksheet opens in your default browser, similar to Figure N-20.

9. **Close your browser window, click the Excel window to activate it if necessary, enter your name in the center footer section of the Tour Sales by Branch worksheet, save the workbook, preview the worksheet, close the workbook, exit Excel, then submit the workbook and the Web page file to your instructor**

FIGURE N-19: **Worksheet with North America sales data**

Formatted table with two rows added from HTML file →

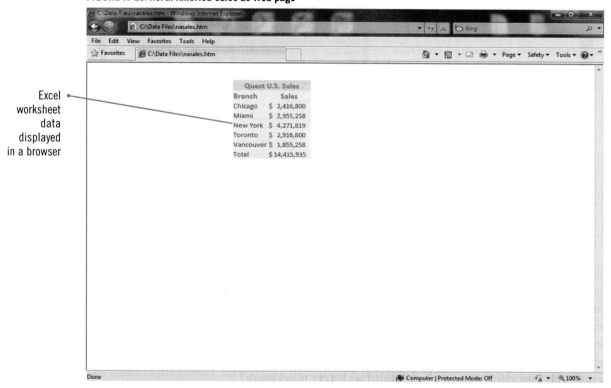

	A	B
1	Quest U.S. Sales	
2	Branch	Sales
3	Chicago	$ 2,416,800
4	Miami	$ 2,955,258
5	New York	$ 4,271,819
6	Toronto	$ 2,916,800
7	Vancouver	$ 1,855,258
8	Total	$14,415,935
9		
10		

FIGURE N-20: **North America Sales as Web page**

Excel worksheet data displayed in a browser →

Adding Web hyperlinks to a worksheet

In Excel worksheets, you can create hyperlinks to information on the Web. Every Web page is identified by a unique Web address called a Uniform Resource Locator (URL). To create a hyperlink to a Web page, click the cell for which you want to create a hyperlink, click the Insert tab, click the Hyperlink button in the Links group, under Link to: make sure Existing File or Web Page is selected, specify the target for the hyperlink (the URL) in the Address text box, then click OK. If there is text in the cell, the text format changes to become a blue underlined hyperlink or the color the current workbook theme uses for hyperlinks. If there is no text in the cell, the Web site's URL appears in the cell.

Skills Review (continued)

4. Work with XML schemas.

  a. Create a new workbook, then save it as **EX N-Contact Information** in the drive and folder where you store your Data Files.

  b. Open the XML Source pane, and add the XML schema EX N-8.xsd to the workbook.

  c. Map the FNAME element to cell A1 on the worksheet, LNAME to cell B1, PHONENUM to cell C1, and EMPLOYMENT_DATE to cell D1.

  d. Remove the EMPLOYMENT_DATE element from the map, and delete the field from the table.

  e. Use the XML Map Properties dialog box to make sure imported XML data is validated using the schema.

5. Import and export XML data.

  a. Import the XML file EX N-9.xml into the workbook.

  b. Sort the worksheet list in ascending order by LNAME.

  c. Add the Table Style Medium 10 to the table, and compare your screen to Figure N-23.

  d. Enter your name in the center section of the worksheet footer, save the workbook, then preview the worksheet.

  e. Use the XML Map Properties dialog box to turn off the validation for imported and exported worksheet data, export the worksheet data to an XML file named **EX N-Contact**, save and close the workbook.

FIGURE N-23

	A	B	C
1	FNAME	LNAME	PHONENUM
2	Kim	Crosby	503-302-1163
3	Jim	Gormley	503-367-4156
4	Ellen	Jones	503-392-8163
5	Linanne	MacMillan	503-932-9966
6	Kathy	Malloney	503-272-9456
7	Kris	Manney	503-722-9163
8	Bob	Nelson	503-322-3163
9	Mary	Shilling	503-322-3163
10			

6. Run Web queries to retrieve external data.

  a. Create a new workbook, then save it as **EX N-Quotes** in the location where you store your Data Files.

  b. Use the Existing Connections dialog box to select the MSN MoneyCentral Investor Major Indices Web query.

  c. Specify that you want to place the data in cell A1 of the current worksheet. Compare your screen to Figure N-24. (You may see Invalid symbols and question mark symbols in the worksheet, but don't be concerned with these.)

  d. Enter your name in the center section of the worksheet header, set the worksheet orientation to landscape, preview the worksheet, then save the workbook.

  e. Close the workbook, and submit the workbook to your instructor.

FIGURE N-24

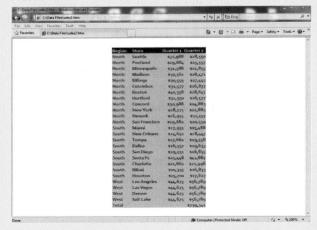

7. Import and export HTML data.

  a. Open the file EX N-7.xlsx from the drive and folder where you store your Data Files, then save it as **EX N-Sales2**.

  b. Open the file EX N-10.htm in your browser from the drive and folder where you store your Data Files. Copy the data in the four rows of the Web page (not the column headings), and paste it below the data in the Sales sheet of the EX N-Sales2 workbook.

  c. On the Sales sheet, enter **Total** in cell A27, and use **AutoSum** in cell D27 to total the values in column D.

  d. Adjust the formatting for the new rows to match the other rows on the Sales sheet, add your name to the center section of the worksheet footer, save the workbook, then preview the Sales sheet.

  e. Save the data on the Sales sheet as an HTML file with the name **sales2.htm**.

  f. Exit Excel, open the sales2.htm file in your browser, compare your screen to Figure N-25, close your browser, then submit the sales2.htm file to your instructor.

FIGURE N-25

Sharing Excel Files and Incorporating Web Information

Independent Challenge 1

New England State College has two campuses, North and South. The deans of the campuses work together on the scheduling of classes using shared Excel workbooks. As the registrar for the college, you are preparing the fall schedule as a shared workbook for the two campus deans. They will each make changes to the location data, and you will review both workbooks and accept their changes.

a. Start Excel, open the file EX N-11.xlsx from the drive and folder where you store your Data Files, then save it as **EX N-NESC**. The workbook has been shared so the other dean can modify it. Close the workbook.

b. Open the file EX N-12.xlsx from the drive and folder where you store your Data Files, then save it as **EX N-North**. This workbook is a copy of the original that has been reviewed and changed.

c. Use the Accept or Reject dialog box to accept the change made to the workbook. Save and close the workbook.

d. Open the file EX N-13.xlsx from the drive and folder where you store your Data Files, then save it as **EX N-South**. This workbook has also been reviewed and changed.

e. Use the Accept or Reject dialog box to accept the workbook change.

f. Use the Highlight Changes dialog box to highlight the change on the screen. Review the ScreenTip details.

g. Use the Highlight Changes dialog box to create a History worksheet detailing the change to the workbook. Copy the information about the change in the range A1:I2, and paste it in Sheet2. Widen the column widths as necessary, and rename Sheet2 to **History Sheet**.

h. Add your name to the center section of the History sheet footer, then preview the History worksheet. Save and close the workbook. Submit the EX N-South.xlsx workbook to your instructor.

Independent Challenge 2

The Charleston Athletic Club is a fitness center with five fitness facilities. As the general manager you are responsible for setting and publishing the membership rate information. You decide to run a special promotion offering a 10 percent discount off the current membership prices. You will also add two new membership categories to help attract younger members. The membership rate information is published on the company Web site. You will copy the rate information from the Web page and work with it in Excel to calculate the special discounted rates. You will save the new rate information as an HTML file so it can be published on the Web.

a. Open the file EX N-14.htm from the drive and folder where you store your Data Files to display it in your browser.

b. Start Excel, create a new workbook, then save it as **EX N-Rates** in the drive and folder where you store your Data Files.

c. Copy the five rows of data, including the column headings from the table in the EX N-14 file, and paste them in the EX N-Rates workbook. Adjust the column widths and formatting as necessary. Close the EX N-14.htm file.

d. Add the new membership data from Table N-2 in rows 6 and 7 of the worksheet.

e. Enter **Special** in cell C1, and calculate each special rate in column C by discounting the prices in column B by 10%. (*Hint*: Multiply each price by .90.)

f. Format the price information in columns B and C with the Accounting format using the $ symbol with two decimal places.

g. Add the passwords **Members11** to open the EX N-Rates workbook and **Fitness01** to modify it. Save and close the workbook, then reopen it by entering the passwords.

h. Verify that you can modify the workbook by formatting the worksheet using the Office Theme and a fill with the Theme color Olive Green, Accent 3, Lighter 80%. Compare your worksheet data to Figure N-26.

i. Add your name to the center footer section of the worksheet, save the workbook, then preview the worksheet.

j. Save the worksheet data in HTML format using the name **prices.htm**. Close the workbook and exit Excel.

k. Open the prices.htm page in your browser and print the page.

l. Close your browser. Submit the prices.htm file to your instructor.

TABLE N-2

Teen	350
Youth	200

FIGURE N-26

	A	B	C	D	E	F	G
1	**Membership**	**Price**	**Special**				
2	Family	$ 1,000.00	$ 900.00				
3	Adult	$ 750.00	$ 675.00				
4	Senior	$ 300.00	$ 270.00				
5	College	$ 470.00	$ 423.00				
6	Teen	$ 350.00	$ 315.00				
7	Youth	$ 200.00	$ 180.00				
8							
9							

Independent Challenge 3

You are the director of development at a local performing arts nonprofit institution. You are preparing the phone lists for your annual fundraising phone-a-thon. The donor information for the organization is in an XML file, which you will bring into Excel to organize. You will use an XML schema to map only the donors' names and phone numbers to the worksheet. This will allow you to import the donor data and limit the information that is distributed to the phone-a-thon volunteers. You will also import information about the donors from another XML file. You will export your worksheet data as XML for future use.

a. Start Excel, create a new workbook, then save it as **EX N-Donors** in the drive and folder where you store your Data Files.

b. Add the map EX N-15.xsd from the drive and folder where you store your Data Files to the workbook.

c. Map the FNAME element to cell A1, LNAME to cell B1, and PHONENUM to cell C1.

d. Import the XML data in file EX N-16.xml from the drive and folder where you store your Data Files. Make sure the data is validated using the schema as it is imported.

e. Add the Table Style Light 19 to the table. Change the field name in cell A1 to **FIRST NAME**, change the field name in cell B1 to **LAST NAME**, and change the field name in cell C1 to **PHONE NUMBER**. Widen the columns as necessary to accommodate the full field names.

f. Sort the table in ascending order by LAST NAME. Compare your sorted table to Figure N-27.

FIGURE N-27

	A	B	C
1	FIRST NAME	LAST NAME	PHONE NUMBER
2	Peg	Alexander	312-765-8756
3	Ernie	Atkins	773-167-4156
4	Kerry	Bradley	773-220-9456
5	Steve	Connolly	312-322-3163
6	Brenda	Duran	312-322-3163
7	Kevin	Gonzales	773-379-0092
8	Amy	Land	312-299-4298
9	Julio	Mendez	312-765-8756
10	Lisa	Ng	312-932-9966
11	Martin	Zoll	312-765-8756
12			

g. Open the XML Map Properties dialog box to verify the Overwrite existing data with new data option button is selected. Map the ACTIVE element to cell D1. Import the XML data in file EX N-16.xml again.

h. Map the CONTRIB_DATE element to cell E1. Import the XML data in file EX N-16.xml a third time. Change the field name in cell E1 to **LAST DONATION**, and widen the column to accommodate the full field name.

i. Filter the table to show only active donors. Compare your filtered table to Figure N-28.

j. Export the worksheet data to an XML file named **EX N-Phone List**.

FIGURE N-28

	A	B	C	D	E	F
1	FIRST NAME	LAST NAME	PHONE NUMBER	ACTIVE	LAST DONATION	
2	Kerry	Bradley	773-220-9456	TRUE	Jan-10	
4	Lisa	Ng	312-932-9966	TRUE	Jan-10	
7	Kevin	Gonzales	773-379-0092	TRUE	Nov-11	
9	Martin	Zoll	312-765-8756	TRUE	Dec-10	
10	Peg	Alexander	312-765-8756	TRUE	Nov-09	
11	Julio	Mendez	312-765-8756	TRUE	Dec-10	
12						

Advanced Challenge Exercise

- Remove the filter for the Active field.
- Add the map EX N-17.xsd from the drive and folder where you store your Data Files to the worksheet.
- Using the INFO_Map, map the DNUMBER element to cell F1 and LEVEL to cell G1.
- Import the XML data in file EX N-18.xml from the drive and folder where you store your Data Files.
- Change the field name in cell F1 to **DONOR NUMBER**.
- Add the Table Style Light 19 to the new table data.
- Filter the table to display only information for Excellent and Above Average Levels. Compare your worksheet to Figure N-29.

FIGURE N-29

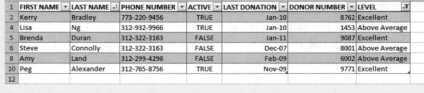

	A	B	C	D	E	F	G	H
1	FIRST NAME	LAST NAME	PHONE NUMBER	ACTIVE	LAST DONATION	DONOR NUMBER	LEVEL	
2	Kerry	Bradley	773-220-9456	TRUE	Jan-10	8762	Excellent	
4	Lisa	Ng	312-932-9966	TRUE	Jan-10	1453	Above Average	
5	Brenda	Duran	312-322-3163	FALSE	Jan-11	9087	Excellent	
6	Steve	Connolly	312-322-3163	FALSE	Dec-07	8001	Above Average	
8	Amy	Land	312-299-4298	FALSE	Feb-09	6002	Above Average	
10	Peg	Alexander	312-765-8756	TRUE	Nov-09	9771	Excellent	
12								

k. Enter your name in the center section of the worksheet footer, preview the worksheet in landscape orientation, then save the workbook.

l. Close the workbook, exit Excel, then submit the workbook to your instructor.

Real Life Independent Challenge

You can track the history of a stock using published Web quotes that can be entered into Excel worksheets for analysis. To eliminate the data entry step, you will use the MSN MoneyCentral Investor Stock Quotes Web query in Excel. You will run the query from an Excel workbook using the symbol of a stock that you are interested in following. The stock information will be automatically inserted into your worksheet.

a. Start Excel, create a new workbook, then save it as **EX N-Stock Analysis** in the drive and folder where you store your Data Files.

b. Run the Web Query MSN MoneyCentral Investor Stock Quotes to obtain a quote for Microsoft's stock by entering the symbol for Microsoft, **MSFT**, in the Enter Parameter Value dialog box, as shown in Figure N-30.

FIGURE N-30

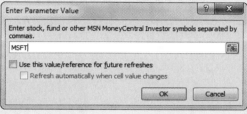

c. Use the Symbol Lookup hyperlink in the query results to find the symbol of a company that you are interested in researching.

d. Use Sheet2 of the workbook to run the Web Query MSN MoneyCentral Investor Stock Quotes to obtain a quote for the company symbol you found in the preceding step.

e. Place the name of the company that you are researching in cell A20. Use the name in cell A20 to add a hyperlink to the company's Web site. (*Hint*: Click the Insert tab, then click the Hyperlink button in the Links group.)

f. Test the link, then close the browser and return to the workbook.

g. Enter your name in the center section of the Sheet2 footer.

h. Display the chart of your stock by clicking the Chart link on Sheet2.

Advanced Challenge Exercise

- Without closing the Browser display of your chart, return to the workbook.
- Beginning in cell A1 of Sheet3, insert a screenshot of your stock's 6m chart from the opening Web page. (*Hint*: Click the Screenshot button on the Insert tab, click Screen Clipping, then select the chart on the Web page.)
- Enter your name in the center section of the Sheet3 footer.

i. Preview each worksheet in the workbook in landscape orientation.

j. Close the workbook, close your browser, exit Excel, then submit the workbook to your instructor.

Visual Workshop

Start Excel, create a new workbook, then save it as **EX N-Bay.xlsx** in the drive and folder where you store your Data Files. Open the file EX N-19.htm in your browser from the drive and folder where you store your Data Files. Create the Web page shown in Figure N-31 by pasting the information from the Web page into your EX N-Bay.xlsx file, formatting it, adding the fourth quarter information, adding the totals, replacing Your Name with your name, then saving it as an HTML file named **bay.htm**. Add your name to the footer of Sheet1 of the EX N-Bay.xlsx workbook, and preview the worksheet. Submit the bay.htm file and the EX N-Bay.xlsx workbook to your instructor. (*Hint*: The colors are in the Office theme.)

FIGURE N-31

Customizing Excel and Advanced Worksheet Management

Excel includes numerous tools and options that can help you work as efficiently as possible. In this unit, you will learn how to use some of these elements to find errors and hide the details of worksheet summaries. You'll also find out how to eliminate repetitive typing chores, save calculation time when using a large worksheet, and customize basic Excel features. Finally, you'll learn how to document your workbook and save it in a format that makes it easy to reuse. Quest's vice president of sales, Kate Morgan, asks you to help with a variety of spreadsheet-related tasks. You will use Excel tools and options to help Kate perform her work quickly and efficiently.

OBJECTIVES

Audit a worksheet

Control worksheet calculations

Group worksheet data

Use cell comments

Create custom AutoFill lists

Customize Excel workbooks

Customize the Excel Screen

Create and apply a template

Auditing a Worksheet

Because errors can occur at any stage of worksheet development, it is important to include auditing as part of your workbook-building process. The Excel **auditing** feature helps you track errors and check worksheet logic. The Formula Auditing group on the Formulas tab contains several error-checking tools to help you audit a worksheet. ▓▓▓▓ Kate asks you to help identify errors in the worksheet that tracks sales for the two Canadian branches to verify the accuracy of year-end totals and percentages.

STEPS

TROUBLE
You will fix the for-mula errors that appear in cells O5 and O6.

1. **Start Excel, open the file EX O-1.xlsx from the drive and folder where you store your Data Files, then save it as EX O-Canada Sales**

2. **Click the Formulas tab, then click the Error Checking button in the Formula Auditing group**

   The Error Checking dialog box opens and alerts you to a Divide by Zero Error in cell O5, as shown in Figure O-1. The formula reads =N5/N8, indicating that the value in cell N5 will be divided by the value in cell N8. In Excel formulas, blank cells have a value of zero. This error means the value in cell N5 cannot be divided by the value in cell N8 (zero) because division by zero is not mathematically possible. To correct the error, you must edit the formula so that it references cell N7, the total of sales, not cell N8.

3. **Click Edit in Formula Bar in the Error Checking dialog box, edit the formula to read =N5/N7, click the Enter button ✔ on the formula bar, then click Resume in the Error Checking dialog box**

   The edited formula produces the correct result, .55371, in cell O5. The Error Checking dialog box indicates another error in cell N6, the total Vancouver sales. The formula reads =SUM(B6:L6) and should be =SUM(B6:M6). The top button in the Error Checking dialog box changes to "Copy Formula from Above". Since this formula in the cell N5 is correct, you will copy it.

4. **Click Copy Formula from Above**

   The Vancouver total changes to $328,430 in cell N6. The Error Checking dialog box finds another division-by-zero error in cell O6. You decide to use another tool in the Formula Auditing group to get more information about this error.

5. **Close the Error Checking dialog box, then click the Trace Precedents button in the Formula Auditing group**

   Blue arrows called **tracer arrows** point from the cells referenced by the formula to the active cell as shown in Figure O-2. The arrows help you determine if these cell references might have caused the error. The tracer arrows extend from the error to cells N6 and N8. To correct the error, you must edit the formula so that it references cell N7 in the denominator, the sales total, not cell N8.

6. **Edit the formula in the formula bar to read =N6/N7, then click ✔ on the formula bar**

   The result of the formula, .44629, appears in cell O6. The November sales for the Vancouver branch in cell L6 is unusually high compared with sales posted for the other months. You can investigate the other cells in the sheet that are affected by the value of cell L6 by tracing the cell's **dependents**—the cells that contain formulas referring to cell L6.

7. **Click cell L6, then click the Trace Dependents button in the Formula Auditing group**

   The tracer arrows run from cell L6 to cells L7 and N6, indicating that the value in cell L6 affects the total November sales and the total Vancouver sales. You decide to remove the tracer arrows and format the percentages in cells O5 and O6.

8. **Click the Remove Arrows button in the Formula Auditing group, select the range O5:O6, click the Home tab, click the Percent Style button % in the Number group, click the Increase Decimal button ⟐ twice, return to cell A1, then save the workbook**

   Now that all the errors have been identified and corrected, you are finished auditing the worksheet.

FIGURE O-1: Error Checking dialog box

Cell containing error and formula →

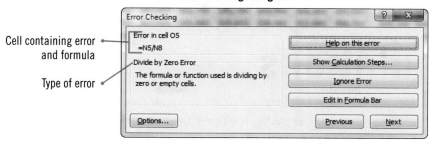

Type of error →

FIGURE O-2: Worksheet with traced error

Quest Canada
2013 Sales Summary

Branch	Jan	Feb	Mar	Apr	May	Jun	Jul	Aug	Sep	Oct	Nov	Dec	Total	Percent
Toronto	$38,248	$35,982	$38,942	$41,980	$15,232	$32,557	$31,790	$40,786	$33,992	$31,102	$35,022	$31,852	$407,485	0.55371
Vancouver	$26,798	$22,841	$27,349	$30,943	$32,791	$22,921	$21,941	$20,812	$28,341	$22,841	$50,711	$20,141	$528,430	#DIV/0!
Total	$65,046	$58,823	$66,291	$72,923	$48,023	$55,478	$53,731	$61,598	$62,333	$53,943	$85,733	$51,993	$735,915	

Tracer arrows from cells that are referenced by the formula

Watching and evaluating formulas

As you edit your worksheet, you can watch the effect that cell changes have on selected worksheet formulas. Select the cell or cells that you want to watch, click the Formulas tab, click the Watch Window button in the Formula Auditing group, click Add Watch in the Watch Window, then click Add. The Watch Window displays the workbook name, worksheet name, the cell address you want to watch, the current cell value, and its formula. As cell values that "feed into" the formula change, the resulting formula value in the

Watch Window changes. To delete a watch, you can select the cell information in the Watch Window and click Delete Watch. You can also step through the evaluation of a formula, selecting the cell that contains a formula and clicking the Evaluate Formula button in the Formula Auditing group. The formula appears in the Evaluation Window of the Evaluate Formula dialog box. As you click the Evaluate button, the cell references are replaced with their values and the formula result is calculated.

Controlling Worksheet Calculations

Whenever you change a value in a cell, Excel automatically recalculates all the formulas in the worksheet based on that cell. This automatic calculation is efficient until you create a worksheet so large that the recalculation process slows down data entry and screen updating. Worksheets with many formulas, data tables, or functions may also recalculate slowly. In these cases, you might want to selectively determine if and when you want Excel to perform calculations. You do this by applying the **manual calculation** option. Once you change the calculation mode to manual, Excel applies manual calculation to all open worksheets. Because Kate knows that using specific Excel calculation options can help make worksheet building more efficient, she asks you to review the formula settings in the workbook and change the formula calculations from automatic to manual calculation.

STEPS

QUICK TIP
You can also change the formula calculation to manual by clicking the Calculations Options button in the Calculation group on the Formulas tab and clicking Manual.

1. **Click the File tab, click Options, then click Formulas in the list of options**

   The options related to formula calculation and error checking appear, as shown in Figure O-3.

2. **Under Calculation options, click to select the Manual option button**

   When you select the Manual option, the Recalculate workbook before saving check box automatically becomes active and contains a check mark. Because the workbook will not recalculate until you save or close and reopen the workbook, you must make sure to recalculate your worksheet before you print it and after you finish making changes.

3. **Click OK**

   Kate informs you that the December total for the Toronto branch is incorrect. You adjust the entry in cell M5 to reflect the actual sales figure.

4. **Click cell M5**

   Before making the change to cell M5, notice that in cell N5 the total for the Toronto branch is $407,485, and the Toronto percent in cell O5 is 55.37%.

5. **Type 40,598, then click the Enter button ☑ on the formula bar**

   The total and percent formulas are *not* updated. The total in cell N5 is still $407,485 and the percentage in cell O5 is still 55.37%. The word "Calculate" appears in the status bar to indicate that a specific value in the worksheet did indeed change and that the worksheet must be recalculated.

QUICK TIP
The Calculate Now command recalculates the entire workbook. You can also manually recalculate by pressing [F9] to recalculate the workbook or [Shift][F9] to recalculate only the active sheet.

6. **Click the Formulas tab, click the Calculate Sheet button 🖩 in the Calculation group, click cell A1, then save the workbook**

   The total in cell N5 is now $416,231 instead of $407,485, and the percentage in cell O5 is now 55.90% instead of 55.37%. The other formulas in the worksheet affected by the value in cell M5 changed as well, as shown in Figure O-4. Because this is a relatively small worksheet that recalculates quickly, you will return to automatic calculation.

7. **Click the Calculations Options button in the Calculation group, then click Automatic**

   Now any additional changes you make will automatically recalculate the worksheet formulas.

QUICK TIP
To automatically recalculate all worksheet formulas except one- and two-input data tables, click Automatic Except for Data Tables.

8. **Place your name in the center section of the worksheet footer, then save the workbook**

FIGURE O-3: Excel formula options

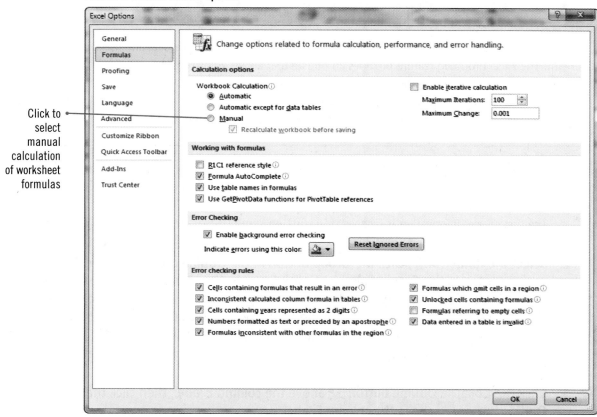

Click to select manual calculation of worksheet formulas

FIGURE O-4: Worksheet with updated values

	A	B	C	D	E	F	G	H	I	J	K	L	M	N	O
1					**Quest Canada**										
2					2013 Sales Summary										
3															
4	Branch	Jan	Feb	Mar	Apr	May	Jun	Jul	Aug	Sep	Oct	Nov	Dec	Total	Percent
5	Toronto	$38,248	$35,982	$38,942	$41,980	$15,232	$32,557	$31,790	$40,786	$33,992	$31,102	$35,022	$40,598	$416,231	55.90%
6	Vancouver	$26,798	$22,841	$27,349	$30,943	$32,791	$22,921	$21,941	$20,812	$28,341	$22,841	$50,711	$20,141	$328,430	44.10%
7	Total	$65,046	$58,823	$66,291	$72,923	$48,023	$55,478	$53,731	$61,598	$62,333	$53,943	$85,733	$60,739	$744,661	
8															

Updated values

Excel 2010

Grouping Worksheet Data

You can create groups of rows and columns on a worksheet to manage your data and make it easier to work with. The Excel grouping feature provides an outline that allows you to easily expand and collapse groups to show or hide selected worksheet data. You can turn off the outline symbols if you are using the condensed data in a report. ██████ Kate needs to give Jessica Long, the Quest CEO, the quarterly sales totals for the Canadian branches. She asks you to group the worksheet data by quarters.

STEPS

1. **Click the Quarterly Summary sheet, select the range B4:D7, click the Data tab, click the Group button in the Outline group, click the Columns option button in the Group dialog box, then click OK**

   The first quarter information is grouped, and **outline symbols** that are used to hide and display details appear over the columns, as shown in Figure O-5. You continue to group the remaining quarters.

2. **Select the range F4:H7, click the Group button in the Outline group, click the Columns option button in the Group dialog box, click OK, select the range J4:L7, click the Group button in the Outline group, click the Columns option button in the Group dialog box, click OK, select the range N4:P7, click the Group button in the Outline group, click the Columns option button in the Group dialog box, click OK, then click cell A1**

   All four quarters are grouped. You decide to use the outline symbols to expand and collapse the first quarter information.

3. **Click the Collapse Outline button ⊟ above the column E label, then click the Expand Outline button ⊞ above the column E label**

   Clicking the (-) symbol temporarily hides the Q1 detail columns, and the (-) symbol changes to a (+) symbol. Clicking the (+) symbol expands the Q1 details and redisplays the hidden columns. The Column Level symbols in the upper-left corner of the worksheet are used to display and hide levels of detail across the entire worksheet.

4. **Click the Column Level 1 button ①**

   All of the group details collapse, and only the quarter totals are displayed.

5. **Click the Column Level 2 button ②**

   You see the quarter details again. Kate asks you to hide the quarter details and the outline symbols for her summary report.

6. **Click ①, click the File tab, click Options, click Advanced in the list of options, scroll to the Display options for this worksheet section, verify that Quarterly Summary is displayed as the worksheet name, click the Show outline symbols if an outline is applied check box to deselect it, then click OK**

   The quarter totals without outline symbols are shown in Figure O-6.

7. **Enter your name in the center footer section, save the workbook, then preview the worksheet**

FIGURE O-5: First quarter data grouped

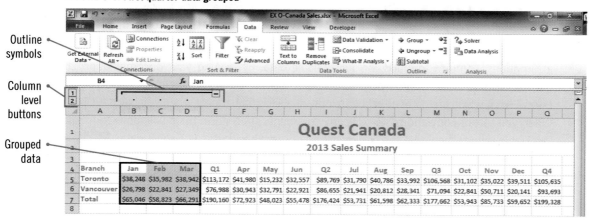

Outline symbols

Column level buttons

Grouped data

FIGURE O-6: Quarter summary

	A	E	I	M	Q	R	S
1		Quest Canada					
2		2013 Sales Summary					
3							
4	Branch	Q1	Q2	Q3	Q4		
5	Toronto	$113,172	$89,769	$106,568	$105,635		
6	Vancouver	$76,988	$86,655	$71,094	$93,693		
7	Total	$190,160	$176,424	$177,662	$199,328		
8							

Applying and creating custom number and date formats

When you use numbers and dates in worksheets or calculations, you can apply the Excel custom number formats, or create your own custom formats. To apply a custom cell format, click the Home tab, click the Format button in the Cells group, then click Format Cells. If necessary, click the Number tab in the Format Cells dialog box, click Custom in the Category list, then click the format you want. A number format can have four parts, each one separated by semicolons: [positive numbers];[negative numbers];[zeroes];[text]. You don't need to specify all four parts. Many of the custom formats contain codes: # represents any digit and 0 represents a digit that will always be displayed, even if the digit is 0. An underscore adds space for alignment. For example, the value –3789 appears as (3,789) if the cell is formatted as #,##0 _); (#,##0). To create your own custom format, click a format that resembles the one you want and customize it in the Type text box. For example, you could edit the #,##0_);[Red](#,##0) format to show negative numbers in blue by changing it to read #,##0_);[Blue](#,##0).

Using Cell Comments

If you plan to share a workbook with others, it's a good idea to **document**, or make notes about, basic assumptions, complex formulas, or questionable data. By reading your documentation, a coworker can quickly become familiar with your workbook. The easiest way to document a workbook is to use **cell comments**, which are notes attached to individual cells that appear when you place the pointer over a cell. When you sort or copy and paste cells, any comments attached to them will move to the new location. In PivotTable reports, however, the comments do not move with the worksheet data. ██████ Kate thinks one of the figures in the worksheet may be incorrect. She asks you to add a comment for Mark Ng, the Toronto branch manager, pointing out the possible error. You will start by checking the default settings for comments in a workbook.

STEPS

1. **Click the File tab if necessary, click Options, click Advanced in the list of options, scroll to the Display section, click the Indicators only, and comments on hover option button to select it in the "For cells with comments, show:" section if necessary, then click OK**

   The other options in the "For cells with comments, show:" area allow you to display the comment and its indicator or no comments.

2. **Click the Sales sheet tab, click cell F5, click the Review tab, then click the New Comment button in the Comments group**

   The Comment box opens, as shown in Figure O-7. Excel automatically includes the computer's username at the beginning of the comment. The username is the name that appears in the User name text box of the Excel Options dialog box. The white sizing handles on the border of the Comment box allow you to change the size of the box.

3. **Type Is this figure correct? It looks low to me., then click outside the Comment box**

   A red triangle appears in the upper-right corner of cell F5, indicating that a comment is attached to the cell. People who use your worksheet can easily display comments.

4. **Place the pointer over cell F5**

   The comment appears next to the cell. When you move the pointer outside of cell F5, the comment disappears. Kate asks you to add a comment to cell L6.

5. **Right-click cell L6, click Insert Comment on the shortcut menu, type Is this increase due to the new marketing campaign?, then click outside the Comment box**

   Kate asks you to delete a comment and edit a comment. You start by displaying all worksheet comments.

6. **Click cell A1, then click the Show All Comments button in the Comments group**

   The two worksheet comments are displayed on the screen, as shown in Figure O-8.

7. **Click the Next button in the Comments group, with the comment in cell F5 selected click the Delete button in the Comments group, click the Next button in the Comments group, click the Edit Comment button in the Comments group, type Mark – at the beginning of the comment in the Comment box, click cell A1, then click the Show All Comments button in the Comments group**

   The Show All Comments button is a toggle button: You click it once to display comments, then click it again to hide comments. You decide to preview the worksheet and the cell comment along with its associated cell reference on separate pages.

8. **Click the File tab, click Print, click Page Setup at the bottom of the Print pane, click the Sheet tab, under Print click the Comments list arrow, click At end of sheet, click OK, then click the Next Page arrow at the bottom of the preview pane to view the comments**

   Your comment appears on a separate page after the worksheet.

9. **Save the workbook**

FIGURE O-7: **Comment box**

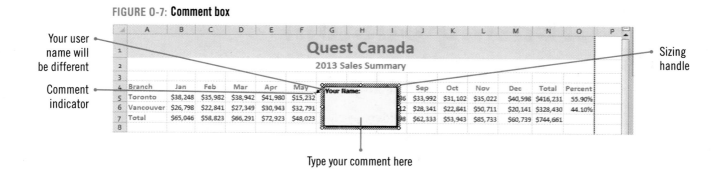

FIGURE O-7: **Comment box**

Your user name will be different

Comment indicator

Sizing handle

Type your comment here

FIGURE O-8: **Worksheet with comments displayed**

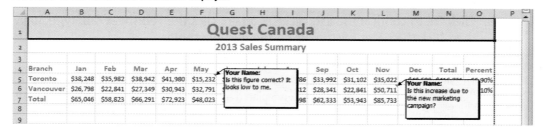

Changing the way you work with Excel

As you work with Excel you may want to change some of the settings to suit your personal preferences. For example, you may want to change the Excel color scheme from blue to black or silver. Or you may want to turn off the Mini toolbar, which provides quick access to formatting options when you select text. Other options you may want to change are the Live Preview feature or the way the ScreenTips are displayed. You can change these settings by clicking the File tab, clicking Options, and selecting your settings in the General area of the Excel Options dialog box. Some settings have a small "i" next to them, which displays more information on the feature as you hover your mouse pointer over it.

Creating Custom AutoFill Lists

Whenever you need to type a list of words regularly, you can save time by creating a custom list. Then you can simply enter the first value in a blank cell and drag the fill handle. Excel enters the rest of the information for you. Figure O-9 shows examples of custom lists that are built into Excel as well as a user-created custom list. ⬛⬛⬛ Kate often has to enter a list of Quest's sales representatives' names in her worksheets. She asks you to create a custom list to save time in performing this task. You begin by selecting the names in the worksheet.

1. Click the **Jan sheet tab**, then select the range **A5:A24**

2. Click the **File tab**, click **Options**, click **Advanced**, scroll down to the General section, then click **Edit Custom Lists**

   The Custom Lists dialog box displays the custom lists that are already built into Excel, as shown in Figure O-10. You want to define a custom list containing the sales representatives' names you selected in column A. The Import list from cells text box contains the range you selected in Step 1.

3. Click **Import**

   The list of names is highlighted in the Custom lists box and appears in the List entries box. You decide to test the custom list by placing it in a blank worksheet.

4. Click **OK** to confirm the list, click **OK** again, click the **Feb sheet tab**, type **Sullivan** in cell A1, then click the **Enter button** ✔ on the formula toolbar

5. Drag the **fill handle** to fill the range **A2:A20**

   The highlighted range now contains the custom list of sales representatives you created. Kate informs you that sales representative Bentz has been replaced by a new representative, Linden. You update the custom list to reflect this change.

6. Click the **File tab**, click **Options**, click **Advanced**, scroll down to the General section, click **Edit Custom Lists**, click the list of sales representatives names in the Custom lists box, change **Bentz** to **Linden** in the List entries box, click **OK** to confirm the change, then click **OK** again

   You decide to check the new list to be sure it is accurate.

7. Click cell **C1**, type **Sullivan**, click ✔ on the formula toolbar, drag the **fill handle** to fill the range **C2:C20**

   The highlighted range contains the updated custom list of sales representatives, as shown in Figure O-11. You've finished creating and editing your custom list, and you need to delete it from the Custom Lists dialog box in case others will be using your computer.

8. Click the **File tab**, click **Options**, click **Advanced**, scroll down to the General section, click **Edit Custom Lists**, click the list of sales representatives' names in the Custom lists box, click **Delete**, click **OK** to confirm the deletion, then click **OK** two more times

9. Save and close the workbook

FIGURE O-9: **Sample custom lists**

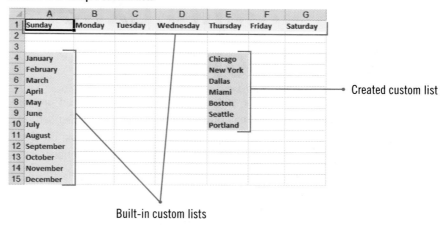

Created custom list

Built-in custom lists

FIGURE O-10: **Custom Lists dialog box**

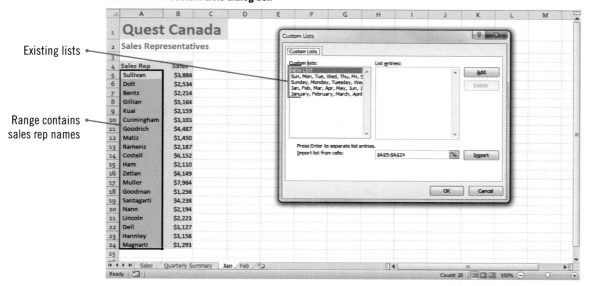

Existing lists

Range contains
sales rep names

FIGURE O-11: **Custom lists with names of sales representatives**

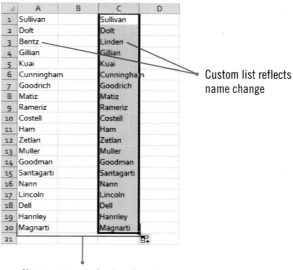

Custom list reflects
name change

Names generated using the
custom list

Customizing Excel Workbooks

The Excel default settings for editing and viewing a worksheet are designed to meet the needs of the majority of Excel users. You may find, however, that a particular setting doesn't always fit your particular needs, such as the default number of worksheets in a workbook, the default worksheet view, or the default font. You have already used the Advanced category of Excel Options to create custom lists and the Formulas category to switch to manual calculation. The General category of the Excel Options dialog box contains features that are commonly used by a large number of Excel users, and you can use it to further customize Excel to suit your work habits and needs. The most commonly used categories of the Excel Options are explained in more detail in Table O-1. [illegible] Kate is interested in customizing workbooks to allow her to work more efficiently. She asks you to use a blank workbook to explore features that will help her better manage her data.

TROUBLE

If you are working on a school computer, check with your instructor or the lab administrator before changing the workbook settings in this lesson.

QUICK TIP

Excel's default text style is the body font, which is Calibri unless it is changed by the user.

1. **Click the File tab, click New, then click Create**

   In the last workbook you prepared for Kate you had to add a fourth worksheet. You would like to have four worksheets displayed rather than three when a new workbook is opened.

2. **Click the File tab, click Options, in the "When creating new workbooks" area of the General options, select 3 in the Include this many sheets text box, then type 4**

   You can change the default font Excel uses in new workbooks, as shown in Figure O-12.

3. **Click the Use this font list arrow, then select Arial**

   You can also change the standard workbook font size.

4. **Click the Font size list arrow, then select 12**

   Kate would rather have new workbooks open in Page Layout view.

5. **Click the Default view for new sheets list arrow, select Page Layout View, click OK to close the Excel Options dialog box, then click OK to the message about quitting and restarting Excel**

   These default settings take effect after you exit and restart Excel.

6. **Close the workbook, exit Excel, then start Excel again**

   A new workbook opens with four sheet tabs in Page Layout view and a 12-point Arial font, as shown in Figure O-13. Now that you have finished exploring the Excel workbook Options, you need to reestablish the original Excel settings.

7. **Click the File tab, click Options, in the "When creating new workbooks" area of the General options, select 4 in the Include this many sheets text box, enter 3, click the Use this font list arrow, select Body Font, select 12 in the Font size text box, type 11, click the Default view for new sheets list arrow, select Normal View, click OK twice, then close the workbook and exit Excel**

FIGURE O-12: General category of Excel options

Standard font defaults

Number of worksheets in a new workbook

The user name for the computer

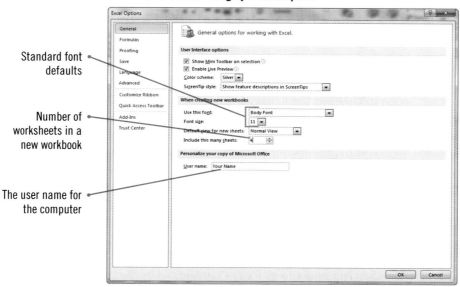

FIGURE O-13: Workbook with new default settings

New default font is 12-point Arial

Worksheet is in Page Layout view

New workbook has four worksheets

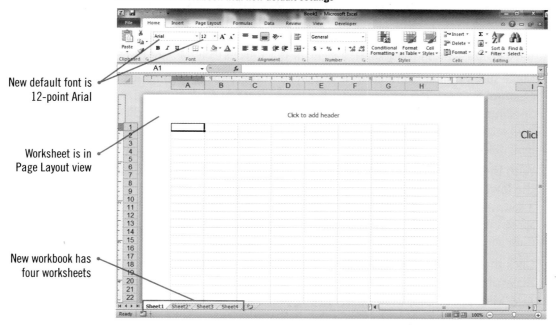

TABLE O-1: Categories of Excel options

category	allows you to
General	Change the user name and the workbook screen display
Formulas	Control how the worksheet is calculated, how formulas appear, and error checking settings and rules
Proofing	Control AutoCorrect and spell-checking options
Save	Select a default format and location for saving files, and customize AutoRecover settings
Language	Control the languages displayed and allows you to add languages
Advanced	Create custom lists as well as customize editing and display options
Customize Ribbon	Add tabs and groups to the Ribbon
Quick Access Toolbar	Add commands to the Quick Access toolbar
Add-Ins	Install Excel Add-in programs such as Solver and Analysis ToolPak
Trust Center	Change Trust Center settings to protect your Excel files

Customizing the Excel Screen

While the Quick Access toolbar and the Ribbon give you easy access to many useful Excel features, you might have other commands that you want to have readily available to speed your work. The Excel Options dialog box allows you to add commands to the Quick Access toolbar. It also lets you create your own tabs and groups on the Ribbon and customize the built-in Ribbon tabs and groups. You can use these options to quickly access commands you use frequently. For example, you might want to add the Spelling, Open, or Print Preview commands to the Quick Access toolbar, or create a tab on the Ribbon with commands you use on a particular monthly report. ░░░░░ Kate is interested in customizing the Quick Access toolbar to include spell checking. She would also like you to add a new tab to the Ribbon with accessibility tools.

STEPS

QUICK TIP

Your Quick Access toolbar might show more commands if a previous user has already customized it. You can continue with the lesson.

QUICK TIP

You can change the order of the buttons on the toolbar using the Move Up button ▲. You can remove buttons from the toolbar by selecting the icon and clicking the Remove button.

1. **Start Excel, then save the new file as** EX O-Customized **in the drive and folder where you store your Data Files**

2. **Click the** Customize Quick Access Toolbar button ▼ **on the Quick Access toolbar, then click** More Commands

   The Excel Options dialog box opens with the Quick Access Toolbar option selected as shown in Figure O-14. You want to add the spell checking feature to the Quick Access toolbar for the EX O-Customized workbook.

3. **Make sure Popular Commands is displayed in the Choose commands from list, click the Customize Quick Access Toolbar list arrow, select For EX O-Customized.xlsx, click the Spelling command in the Popular Commands list, click Add, then click OK**

   The Spelling button now appears on the Quick Access toolbar to the right of the Save, Undo, and Redo buttons, which appear by default. Kate wants you to add a tab to the Ribbon with a group of accessibility tools.

4. **With the Home tab selected, click the** File tab, **click** Options, **click** Customize Ribbon, **on the lower-right side of the Excel Options dialog box click** New Tab

   A new tab named New Tab (Custom) is displayed in the listing of Main Tabs below the Home tab. A new tab appears in the list after the currently selected tab. Under the new tab is a new group named New Group (Custom). You want to add accessibility tools to the new group.

5. **Click the** Choose commands from list arrow, **click** Commands Not in the Ribbon, **click** Accessibility Checker, **click** Add, **click** Alt Text, **click** Add, **scroll down, click** Zoom In, **click** Add, **click** Zoom Out, **then click** Add

   Four accessibility tools are in the custom group on the new custom tab. You decide to rename the tab and the group to identify the buttons.

6. **Click** New Tab (Custom) **in the Main Tabs area, click** Rename, **in the Rename dialog box type** Accessibility, **click** OK, **click** New Group (Custom) **below the Accessibility tab, click** Rename, **in the Rename dialog box type** Accessibility Tools **in the Display name text box, click** OK, **then click** OK again

   The new custom tab appears in the Ribbon, just to the right of the Home tab. You decide to check it to verify it contains the buttons you want.

7. **Click the** Accessibility tab, **compare your tab to Figure O-15, click the** Zoom In button, **then click the** Zoom Out button

   You will reset the Ribbon to the default settings.

8. **Click the** File tab, **click** Options, **click** Customize Ribbon, **on the lower-right side of the Excel Options dialog box click** Reset, **click** Reset all customizations, **click** Yes, **click** OK, **save the workbook, then close it and exit Excel**

FIGURE O-14: Quick Access Toolbar category of Excel options

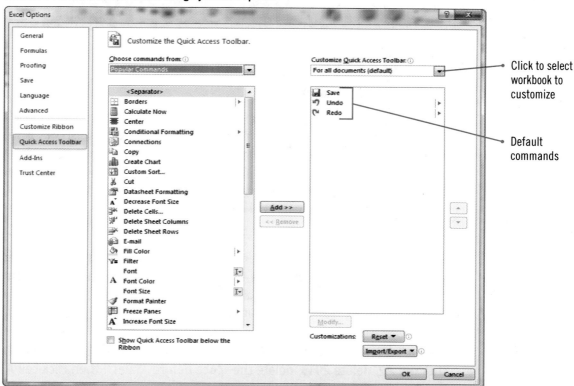

FIGURE O-15: Workbook with new Accessibility Tab

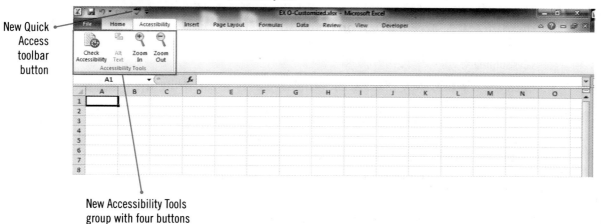

New Quick Access toolbar button

New Accessibility Tools group with four buttons

Customizing the Quick Access toolbar

You can quickly add a button from the Ribbon to the Quick Access toolbar by right-clicking it and selecting Add to Quick Access Toolbar. Right-clicking a Ribbon button also allows you to quickly customize the Ribbon and the Quick Access toolbar. You can also move the Quick Access toolbar from its default position and minimize the Ribbon.

Excel 2010

Creating and Applying a Template

A template is a workbook with an .xltx file extension that contains text, formulas, macros, and formatting that you use repeatedly. Once you save a workbook as a template, it provides a model for creating a new workbook without your having to reenter standard data. You create workbooks *based on* a template. A workbook based on a template has the same content, formulas, and formatting you defined in the template, and is saved in the .xlsx format. The template file itself remains unchanged. 🖬🖳🖳 Kate plans to use the same formulas, titles, and row and column labels from the Sales worksheet for subsequent yearly worksheets. She asks you to create a template that will allow her to quickly prepare these worksheets.

STEPS

1. **Start Excel, open the file EX O-Canada Sales.xlsx from the drive and folder where you store your Data Files, then delete the Quarterly Summary, Jan, and Feb sheets.**

   The workbook now contains only the Sales sheet. You decide to use the Sales sheet structure and formulas as the basis for your new template. You want to leave the formulas in row 7 and in columns N and O so future users will not have to re-create them. But you want to delete the comment, the sales data, and the year 2013.

2. **Right-click cell L6, click Delete Comment, select the range B5:M6, press [Delete], double-click cell A2, delete 2013, delete the space before "Sales", then click cell A1**

   The divide-by-zero error messages in column O are only temporary and will disappear as soon as Kate opens a document based on the template, saves it as a workbook, and begins to enter next year's data.

3. **Click the Page Layout tab, click the Themes button in the Themes group, click Executive**

   You want the worksheet colors to match the new Quest colors.

4. **Click the Home tab, click the Fill Color list arrow 🖌▾ in the Fonts group, click Ice Blue, Background 2 (third from left in the Theme Colors), click the Select All button 🔲 in the upper-left corner of the worksheet, click the Font Color list arrow A▾ in the Font group, click Gray-50%, Accent 6 (last on right), then click on the worksheet to deselect the range**

   The completed template is shown in Figure O-16. You will save the template so Kate can use it for next year's sales summary.

5. **Click the File tab, click Save As, click the Save as type list arrow, then click Excel Template (*.xltx)**

   Excel adds the .xltx extension to the filename and automatically switches to the Templates folder. If you are using a computer on a network, you may not have permission to save to the Templates folder, so you save it to your Data File location.

6. **Navigate to your Data Files folder, click Save, then close the workbook and exit Excel**

   Kate asks you to test the new template. To do this, you open a workbook based on the Canada Sales template, also known as **applying** the template, and test it by entering data in the Sales worksheet.

7. **In Windows Explorer, navigate to your Data Files folder, then double click the EX O-Canada Sales.xltx to open a workbook based on the template**

   The workbook name is EX O-Canada Sales1 as shown in Figure O-17. You want to make sure the formulas are working correctly.

8. **Click cell B5, enter 100, click cell B6, enter 200, select the range B5:B6 and use the fill handle to copy the data into the range C5:M6**

9. **Save the workbook as EX O-Template Test, close the workbook, exit Excel, then submit the workbook to your instructor**

   The completed EX O-Template Test workbook is shown in Figure O-18.

FIGURE O-16: Completed template

Temporary divide-by-zero messages

FIGURE O-17: Workbook based on template

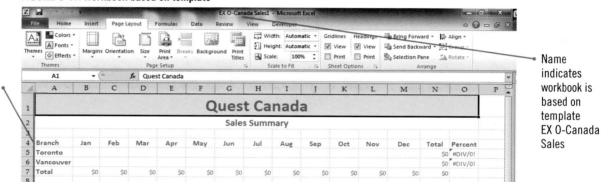

Workbook based on template contains the template's content, formatting, and formulas

Name indicates workbook is based on template EX O-Canada Sales

FIGURE O-18: Completed template test

Quest Canada
Sales Summary

Branch	Jan	Feb	Mar	Apr	May	Jun	Jul	Aug	Sep	Oct	Nov	Dec	Total	Percen
Toronto	$100	$100	$100	$100	$100	$100	$100	$100	$100	$100	$100	$100	$1,200	33.33%
Vancouver	$200	$200	$200	$200	$200	$200	$200	$200	$200	$200	$200	$200	$2,400	66.67%
Total	$300	$300	$300	$300	$300	$300	$300	$300	$300	$300	$300	$300	$3,600	

Applying templates

When you save an Excel file as a template, the Template folder is the default location for the template. When you save your templates in this folder, they are available for you to use easily at a later time. To open a workbook based on the template, or **apply** the template, click the File tab, click New, then double-click the My Templates folder under Available Templates. In the New dialog box, click the template you want to use as a basis for your new workbook, then click OK. A file opens with a "1" at the end of the name's file extension. For example, selecting a template named budget.xltx will open a file called budget.xltx1. Then when you save the workbook, the Save As dialog box opens, allowing you to save the new file as an Excel file with the extension .xlsx.

Practice

Concepts Review

For current SAM information, including versions and content details, visit SAM Central (http://www.cengage.com/samcentral). If you have a SAM user profile, you may have access to hands-on instruction, practice, and assessment of the skills covered in this unit. Since various versions of SAM are supported throughout the life of this text, check with your instructor for the correct instructions and URL/Web site for accessing assignments.

FIGURE O-19

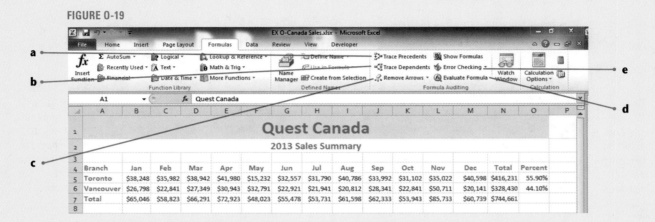

Which element do you click to:

1. Eliminate tracers from a worksheet?
2. Locate cells that reference the active cell?
3. Locate formula errors in a worksheet?
4. Step through a formula in a selected cell?
5. Find cells that may have caused a formula error?

Match each term with the statement that best describes it.

6. Outline symbols
7. [Shift][F9]
8. Template
9. Custom list
10. Comment

a. Note that appears when you place the pointer over a cell
b. Used to hide and display details in grouped data
c. Calculates the worksheet manually
d. A workbook with an .xltx file extension that contains text, formulas, and formatting
e. Entered in a worksheet using the fill handle

Select the best answer from the list of choices.

11. **Which of the following categories of Excel options allows you to change the number of default worksheets in a workbook?**
    - **a.** Proofing
    - **b.** General
    - **c.** Advanced
    - **d.** Formulas

12. **Which of the following categories of Excel options allows you to create Custom Lists?**
    - **a.** Advanced
    - **b.** Add-Ins
    - **c.** Customize
    - **d.** Formulas

13. **The _____ displays the fewest details in grouped data.**
    - **a.** Column Level 1 button
    - **b.** Column Level 2 button
    - **c.** Column Level 3 button
    - **d.** Column Level 4 button

14. **To apply a custom list, you:**
    - **a.** Type the first cell entry and drag the fill handle.
    - **b.** Click the Fill tab in the Edit dialog box.
    - **c.** Press [Shift][F9].
    - **d.** Select the list in the worksheet.

Skills Review

1. **Audit a worksheet.**
    - **a.** Start Excel, open the file EX O-2.xlsx from the drive and folder where you store your Data Files, then save it as **EX O-Camden**.
    - **b.** Select cell B10, then use the Trace Dependents button to locate all the cells that depend on this cell.
    - **c.** Clear the arrows from the worksheet.
    - **d.** Select cell B19, use the Trace Precedents button to find the cells on which that figure is based, then correct the formula in cell B19. (*Hint*: It should be B7–B18.)
    - **e.** Use the Error Checking button to check the worksheet for any other errors. Correct any worksheet errors using the formula bar.

2. **Control worksheet calculations.**
    - **a.** Open the Formulas category of the Excel Options dialog box.
    - **b.** Change the worksheet calculations to manual.
    - **c.** Change the figure in cell B6 to **24,000**.
    - **d.** Recalculate the worksheet manually, using an appropriate key combination or button.
    - **e.** Change the worksheet calculations back to automatic using the Calculation Options button, and save the workbook.

3. **Group worksheet data.**
    - **a.** Group the income information in rows 5 and 6.
    - **b.** Group the expenses information in rows 10 through 17.
    - **c.** Hide the income details in rows 5 and 6.
    - **d.** Hide the expenses details in rows 10 through 17.
    - **e.** Enter your name in the center section of the worksheet footer, then preview the worksheet with the income and expenses detail hidden.
    - **f.** Redisplay the income and expenses details.
    - **g.** Remove the row grouping for the income and expenses details. (*Hint*: With the grouped rows selected, click the Data tab, then click the Ungroup button in the Outline group.)
    - **h.** Save the workbook.

4. **Use cell comments.**
    - **a.** Insert a comment in cell E12 that reads **Does this include newspaper advertising?**.
    - **b.** Click anywhere outside the Comment box to close it.
    - **c.** Display the comment by moving the pointer over cell E12, then check it for accuracy.
    - **d.** Edit the comment in cell E12 to read **Does this include newspaper and magazine advertising?**.

Skills Review (continued)

    e. Preview the worksheet and your comment, with the comment appearing at the end of the sheet.

    f. Save the workbook.

5. Create custom AutoFill lists.

    a. Select the range A4:A19.

    b. Open the Custom Lists dialog box, and import the selected text.

    c. Close the dialog box.

    d. On Sheet2, enter **Income** in cell A1.

    e. Use the fill handle to enter the list through cell A15.

    f. Enter your name in the center section of the Sheet2 footer, then preview the worksheet.

    g. Open the Custom Lists dialog box again, delete the custom list you just created, then save and close the workbook.

6. Customize Excel workbooks.

    a. Open a new workbook, then open the General options of the Excel Options dialog box.

    b. Change the number of sheets in a new workbook to **5**.

    c. Change the default font of a new workbook to 14-point Times New Roman.

    d. Close the workbook and exit Excel.

    e. Start Excel and verify that the new workbook's font is 14-point Times New Roman and that it has five worksheets.

    f. Reset the default number of worksheets to **3** and the default workbook font to 11-point Body Font.

    g. Close the workbook and exit Excel.

7. Customize the Excel screen.

    a. Start Excel, open the EX O-Camden.xlsx workbook from the drive and folder where you store your Data Files, then display Sheet1.

    b. Use the Quick Access Toolbar category of the Excel Options dialog box to add the Print Preview and Print button to the Quick Access toolbar for the EX O-Camden.xlsx workbook.

    c. Use the Customize Ribbon category to add a tab named **Math** to the Ribbon with a group named **Math Tools** containing the buttons Equation and Equation Symbols. (*Hint*: These buttons are in the All Commands list.) Compare your Ribbon to Figure O-20.

    d. Reset the Ribbon.

    e. Verify that the Print Preview button has been added to the Quick Access toolbar, then save the workbook.

FIGURE O-20

8. Create and apply a template.

    a. Delete Sheet2 and Sheet3 from the workbook.

    b. Delete the comment in cell E12.

    c. Delete the income and expense data for all four quarters. Leave the worksheet formulas intact.

    d. Change the fill color for cell A1 to Plum, Accent 3, in the Theme colors. Change the fill for the range B3:G3 and cells A4 and A9 to Dark Purple, Accent 4, Lighter 80%. Change the font color for the worksheet cells in the range A3:G19 to Plum, Accent 3, Darker 25%.

    e. Save the workbook as a template named **EX O-Camden.xltx** in the drive and folder where you store your Data Files.

    f. Close the template, then open a workbook based on the template by double-clicking the template in the folder where you store your Data Files.

    g. Test the template by entering your own data for all four quarters and in every budget category. Adjust the column widths as necessary. Your screen should be similar to Figure O-21.

FIGURE O-21

	A	B	C	D	E	F	G
1		Camden Chowder House					
2							
3		Q1	Q2	Q3	Q4	Total	% of Total
4	Income						
5	Beverages	$11,000	$12,000	$14,000	$12,000	$49,000	30%
6	Chowder	$22,000	$23,000	$36,000	$33,000	$114,000	70%
7	Net Sales	$33,000	$35,000	$50,000	$45,000	$163,000	
8							
9	Expenses						
10	Salaries	$13,000	$14,000	$17,000	$13,000	$57,000	42%
11	Rent	$4,000	$4,000	$4,000	$4,000	$16,000	12%
12	Advertising	$3,000	$3,000	$5,000	$3,000	$14,000	10%
13	Cleaning	$2,100	$2,100	$2,800	$2,100	$9,100	7%
14	Fish	$2,500	$2,700	$3,500	$2,500	$11,200	8%
15	Dairy	$1,200	$1,300	$1,800	$1,200	$5,500	4%
16	Beverages	$4,000	$5,000	$7,000	$4,000	$20,000	15%
17	Paper Products	$550	$550	$850	$550	$2,500	2%
18	Total Expenses	$30,350	$32,650	$41,950	$30,350	$135,300	100%
19	Net Profit	$2,650	$2,350	$8,050	$14,650	$27,700	
20							

Skills Review (continued)

h. Save the workbook as **EX O-Camden1.xlsx** in the folder where you store your Data Files.

i. Preview the worksheet, close the workbook, exit Excel, then submit the workbook to your instructor.

Independent Challenge 1

You are the VP of Human Resources at US Tel, a telecommunications contractor with offices in the east and the west regions of the United States. You are tracking the overtime hours for workers using total and percentage formulas. Before you begin your analysis, you want to check the worksheet for formula errors. Then, you group the first quarter data, add a comment to the worksheet, and create a custom list of the east and west locations and total labels.

a. Start Excel, open the file titled EX O-3.xlsx from the drive and folder where you store your Data Files, then save it as **EX O-Hours**.

b. Audit the worksheet, ignoring warnings that aren't errors and correcting the formula errors in the formula bar.

c. Select cell R5 and use the Trace Precedents button to show the cells used in its formula.

d. Select cell B10 and use the Trace Dependents button to show the cells affected by the value in the cell.

e. Remove all arrows from the worksheet.

f. Group the months Jan, Feb, and March, then use the Outline symbols to hide the first quarter details.

g. Add the comment **This looks low.** to cell P11. Display the comment on the worksheet so it is visible even when you are not hovering over the cell.

h. Create a custom list by importing the range A5:A15. Test the list in cells A1:A11 of Sheet2. Delete the custom list.

Advanced Challenge Exercise

- Select cell S5 on the Overtime sheet, then open the Evaluate Formula dialog box.
- In the Evaluate Formula dialog box, click Evaluate three times to see the process of substituting values for cell addresses in the formula and the results of the formula calculations. Close the Evaluate Formula window.
- With cell S6 selected, open the Watch Window. Click Add Watch to add cell S6 to the Watch Window, and observe its value in the window as you change cell G6 to 35. Close the Watch Window.

i. Change the comment display to show only the comment indicators and the comments when hovering over the cell with the comment.

j. Add your name to the center section of the worksheet footer, preview the worksheet with the comment on a separate page, then save the workbook.

k. Close the workbook, exit Excel, then submit the workbook to your instructor.

Independent Challenge 2

You are the property manager of the Layfayette Collection, a commercial retail property located in St. Louis. One of your responsibilities is to keep track of the property's regular monthly expenses. You have compiled a list of fixed expenses in an Excel workbook. Because the items don't change from month to month, you want to create a custom list including each expense item to save time in preparing similar worksheets in the future. You will also temporarily switch to manual formula calculation, check the total formula, and document the data.

a. Start Excel, open the file titled EX O-4.xlsx from the drive and folder where you store your Data Files, then save it as **EX O-Expenses**.

b. Select the range of cells A4:A15 on the Fixed Expenses sheet, then import the list to create a Custom List.

c. Use the fill handle to insert your list in cells A1:A12 in Sheet2.

d. Add your name to the Sheet2 footer, save the workbook, then preview Sheet2.

e. Delete your custom list, then return to the Fixed Expenses sheet.

f. Switch to manual calculation for formulas. Change the expense for Gas to $9,000.00. Calculate the worksheet formula manually. Turn on automatic calculation again.

Independent Challenge 2 (continued)

g. Add the comment **This may increase.** to cell B4. Display the comment on the worksheet so it is visible even when the mouse pointer is not hovering over the cell.

h. Use the Error Checking dialog box for help in correcting the error in cell B16. Verify that the formula is correctly totaling the expenses in column B.

i. Trace the precedents of cell B16. Compare your worksheet to Figure O-22.

j. Remove the arrow and the comment display from the worksheet, leaving only the indicator displayed. Do not delete the comment from the worksheet cell.

k. Trace the dependents of cell B4. Remove the arrow from the worksheet.

l. Edit the comment in cell B4 to **This may increase next month.**, and add the comment **This seems low.** to cell B10.

m. Use the Next and Previous buttons in the Comments group of the Review tab to move between comments on the worksheet. Delete the comment in cell B10.

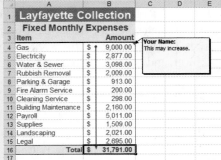
FIGURE O-22

Advanced Challenge Exercise

- Copy the comment in cell B4 and paste it in cell B9. The Comments group on the Review tab has a button named Show Ink. Use online resources to find out how ink is used in Excel.
- Summarize your research findings in cell A20 of the worksheet.

n. Add your name to the center section of the worksheet footer, save the workbook, then preview the Fixed Expenses worksheet with the comment appearing at the end of the sheet.

o. Close the workbook, exit Excel, then submit your workbook to your instructor.

Independent Challenge 3

As the manager of a public radio station you are responsible for the yearly budget. You use Excel to track income and expenses using formulas to total each category and to calculate the net cash flow for the organization. You want to customize your workbooks and settings in Excel so you can work more efficiently. You are also interested in grouping your data and creating a template that you can use to build next year's budget.

a. Start Excel, open the file titled EX O-5.xlsx from the drive and folder where you store your Data Files, then save it as **EX O-Budget**.

b. Add an icon to the Quick Access toolbar for the EX O-Budget.xlsx workbook to preview a worksheet.

c. Add a tab to the Ribbon named Shapes with a group named Shape Tools. Add the buttons Down Arrow, Straight Arrow Connector, and Straight Connector from the Commands Not in the Ribbon list to the new group. Compare your Ribbon and Quick Access toolbar to Figure O-23.

FIGURE O-23

d. Test the new Shape Tools buttons on the Shapes tab by clicking each one and dragging an area on Sheet2 to test the shapes. Rename Sheet2 to **Shapes**, and add your name to the center footer section of the sheet.

e. Test the Print Preview button on the Quick Access toolbar by previewing the Shapes sheet.

f. On the Budget sheet, group rows 4–6 and 9–14, then use the appropriate row-level button to hide the expense and income details, as shown in Figure O-24.

g. Add your name to the center section of the worksheet footer, save the workbook, then use the Print Preview button on the Quick Access toolbar to preview the Budget worksheet.

FIGURE O-24

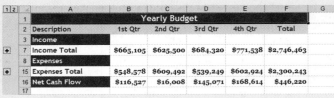

Independent Challenge 3 (continued)

h. Redisplay all rows, using the Outline symbols. Delete the Shapes worksheet and Sheet3. Delete all data in the Budget sheet, leaving the formulas and labels.

i. Save the workbook as a template named **EX O-Budget** in the drive and folder where you store your Data Files. Close the template file, and open a workbook based on the template. Save the workbook as **EX O-New Budget**.

j. Test the template by entering data for the four quarters. Save the workbook, then preview the worksheet using the Print Preview button on the Quick Access toolbar.

k. Customize Excel so that your workbooks will open with four worksheets in Page Layout view and use 12-point Trebuchet MS font.

l. Reset the Ribbon, close your workbook, exit Excel, and then open a new workbook to confirm the new default workbook settings. Reset the default Excel workbook to open with three sheets in Normal view and the 11-point Body Font. Close the new workbook.

Advanced Challenge Exercise

- Open the EX O-Budget.xlsx workbook.
- Create a custom number format that displays currency with negative numbers using a blue font. (*Hint*: Edit one of the formats with a $ that displays negative numbers in a red font.)
- Apply your custom number format to cell B16. Change the first quarter membership amount in cell B4 to **$100,000**, and verify that the value in cell B16 displays using the custom number format. Save then close the workbook.

m. Exit Excel, then submit the EX O-Budget and EX O-New Budget workbooks and the template to your instructor.

Real Life Independent Challenge

This Independent Challenge requires an Internet connection.

Excel offers predesigned templates that you can access from the Web to create your own budgets, maintain your health records, create meeting agendas, put together expense estimates, and plan projects. You can download the templates and create Excel workbooks based on the templates. Then you can add your own data, and customize the worksheet for your purposes.

a. Start Excel, then use the Excel help feature to search for Templates.

b. Review the available templates, and download a template that organizes information you commonly use at home, school, or work.

c. Save the template with the name **EX O-My Template.xltx** in the location where you store your Data Files. If your template was created using an earlier version of Excel, you will be working in compatibility mode. If this is the case, close the template and reopen it.

d. Select a theme, and format the template using the theme colors and fonts.

e. Add your name to the center section of the template's worksheet footer, preview the template worksheet, and change its orientation and scale if necessary to allow a worksheet based on the template to print on one page. Save the template in the drive and folder where you store your Data Files.

f. Close the template, open a workbook based on the template, then save the workbook as **EX O-My Template Example**.

g. Add a button to the workbook's Quick Access toolbar that will help you as you work in the worksheet. Enter your data in the worksheet, save the workbook, then preview the worksheet.

h. Close the workbook, close your browser if necessary, exit Excel, then submit both the workbook and the template to your instructor.

Visual Workshop

Open the Data File EX O-6.xlsx from the drive and folder where you store your Data Files, then save it as **EX O-Garden Supply**. Group the data as shown after removing any errors in the worksheet. Widen columns if necessary to display the worksheet data. Your grouped results should match Figure O-25. (*Hint*: The Outline symbols have been hidden for the worksheet.) The new buttons on the Quick Access toolbar have only been added to the Garden Supply workbook. Add your name to the center section of the worksheet footer, save the workbook, then preview the worksheet. Close the workbook, exit Excel, then submit the workbook to your instructor.

FIGURE O-25

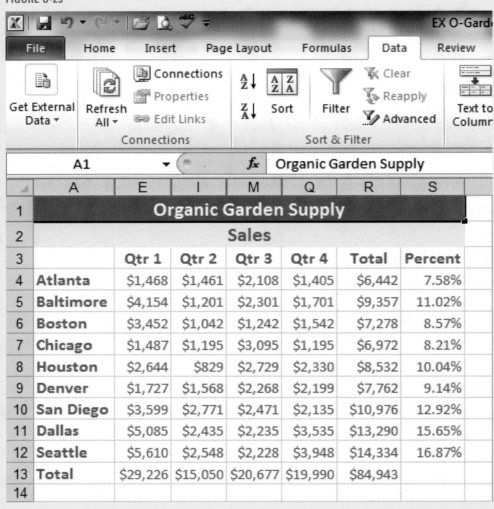

Programming with Excel

All Excel macros are written in a programming language called Visual Basic for Applications, or simply, **VBA**. When you create a macro with the Excel macro recorder, the recorder writes the VBA instructions for you. You can also create an Excel macro by entering VBA instructions manually. The sequence of VBA statements contained in a macro is called a **procedure**. In this unit, you will view and analyze existing VBA code and write VBA code on your own. You learn how to add a conditional statement to a procedure as well as how to prompt the user for information while the macro is running. You also find out how to locate any errors, or bugs, in a macro. Finally, you will combine several macros into one main procedure. Quest's vice president of sales, Kate Morgan, would like to automate some of the division's time-consuming tasks. You help Kate by creating five Excel macros for the sales division.

OBJECTIVES

View VBA code

Analyze VBA code

Write VBA code

Add a conditional statement

Prompt the user for data

Debug a macro

Create a main procedure

Run a main procedure

Viewing VBA Code

Before you can write Excel macro procedures, you must become familiar with the VBA (Visual Basic for Applications) programming language. A common method of learning any programming language is to view existing code. To view VBA code, you open the **Visual Basic Editor**, which contains a Project window, a Properties window, and a Code window. The VBA code for macro procedures appears in the Code window. The first line of a procedure, called the **procedure header**, defines the procedure's type, name, and arguments. **Arguments** are variables used by other procedures that the main procedure might run. An empty set of parentheses after the procedure name means the procedure doesn't have any arguments. Items that appear in blue are **keywords**, which are words Excel recognizes as part of the VBA programming language. **Comments** are notes explaining the code; they are displayed in green, and the remaining code is displayed in black. You use the Visual Basic Editor to view or edit an existing macro as well as to create new ones. Each month, Kate receives text files containing tour sales information from the Quest branches. Kate has already imported the text file for the Miami January sales into a worksheet, but it still needs to be formatted. She asks you to work on a macro to automate the process of formatting the imported information.

STEPS

1. **Start Excel if necessary, click the Developer tab, then click the Macro Security button in the Code group**

   The Trust Center dialog box opens, as shown in Figure P-1. You know the Quest branch files are from a trusted source, so you will allow macros to run in the workbook.

2. **Click the Enable all macros option button if necessary, then click OK**

   You are ready to open a file and view its VBA code. A macro-enabled workbook has the extension .xlsm. Although a workbook containing a macro will open if macros are disabled, they will not function.

3. **Open the file EX P-1.xlsm from the drive and folder where you store your Data Files, save it as EX P-Monthly Sales, then click the Macros button in the Code group**

   The macro dialog box opens with the FormatFile macro procedure in the list box. If you have any macros saved in your Personal Macro workbook, they are also listed in the Macro dialog box.

4. **If it is not already selected click FormatFile, click Edit, then double-click Format in the Modules area of the Project Explorer window**

   The Project Explorer window is shown in Figure P-2. Because the FormatFile procedure is contained in the Format module, clicking Format selects the Format module and displays the FormatFile procedure in the Code window. See Table P-1 to make sure your screen matches the ones shown in this unit.

5. **Make sure both the Visual Basic window and the Code window are maximized to match Figure P-2**

6. **Examine the top three lines of code, which contain comments, and the first line of code beginning with Sub FormatFile( )**

   Notice that the different parts of the procedure appear in various colors. The first two comment lines give the procedure name and tell what the procedure does. The third comment line explains that the keyboard shortcut for this macro procedure is [Ctrl][Shift][F]. The keyword Sub in the procedure header indicates that this is a **Sub procedure**, or a series of Visual Basic statements that perform an action but do not return (create and display) a value. In the next lesson, you will analyze the procedure code to see what each line does.

FIGURE P-1: Macro settings in the Trust Center dialog box

Select to allow macros to run

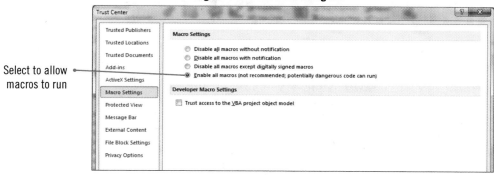

FIGURE P-2: Procedure displayed in the Visual Basic Editor

Procedure header

Project Explorer window

Properties window

Format module

Comments in green

Code window

Keywords in blue

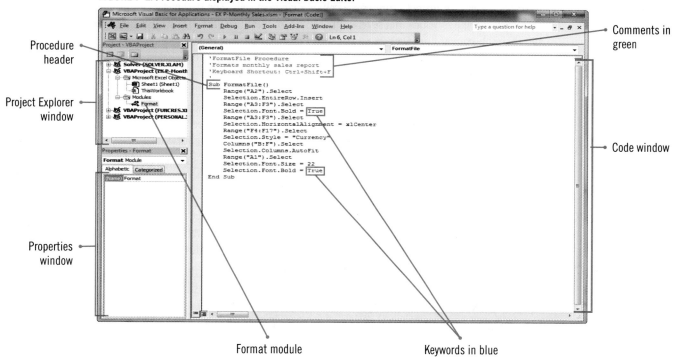

TABLE P-1: Matching your screen to the unit figures

if...	do this...
The Properties window is not displayed	Click the Properties Window button on the toolbar
The Project Explorer window is not displayed	Click the Project Explorer button on the toolbar
You see only the Code window	Click Tools on the menu bar, click Options, click the Docking tab, then make sure the Project Explorer and Properties Window options are selected
You do not see folders in the Explorer window	Click the Toggle Folders button on the Project Explorer window Project toolbar

Understanding the Visual Basic Editor

A **module** is the Visual Basic equivalent of a worksheet. In it, you store macro procedures, just as you store data in worksheets. Modules, in turn, are stored in workbooks (or projects), along with worksheets. A **project** is the collection of all procedures in a workbook. You view and edit modules in the Visual Basic Editor, which is made up of three windows: Project Explorer (also called the Project window), the Code window, and the Properties window. Project Explorer displays a list of all open projects (or workbooks) and the worksheets and modules they contain. To view the procedures stored in a module, you must first select the module in Project Explorer (just as you would select a file in Windows Explorer). The Code window then displays the selected module's procedures. The Properties window displays a list of characteristics (or properties) associated with the module. A newly inserted module has only one property, its name.

Analyzing VBA Code

You can learn a lot about the VBA language simply by analyzing the code generated by the Excel macro recorder. The more VBA code you analyze, the easier it is for you to write your own programming code. Before writing any new procedures, you analyze a previously written procedure that applies formatting to a worksheet. Then you open a worksheet that you want to format and run the macro.

STEPS

1. **With the FormatFile procedure still displayed in the Code window, examine the next four lines of code, beginning with Range("A2").Select**

   Refer to Figure P-3 as you analyze the code in this lesson. Every Excel element, including a range, is considered an **object**. A **range object** represents a cell or a range of cells. The statement Range("A2").Select selects the range object cell A2. Notice that several times in the procedure, a line of code (or **statement**) selects a range, and then subsequent lines act on that selection. The next statement, Selection.EntireRow.Insert, inserts a row above the selection, which is currently cell A2. The next two lines of code select range A3:F3 and apply bold formatting to that selection. In VBA terminology, bold formatting is a value of an object's Bold property. A **property** is an attribute of an object that defines one of the object's characteristics (such as size) or an aspect of its behavior (such as whether it is enabled). To change the characteristics of an object, you change the values of its properties. For example, to apply bold formatting to a selected range, you assign the value True to the range's Bold property. To remove bold formatting, assign the value False.

2. **Examine the remaining lines of code, beginning with the second occurrence of the line Range("A3:F3").Select**

   The next two statements select the range object A3:F3 and center its contents, then the following two statements select the F4:F17 range object and format it as currency. Column objects B through F are then selected, and their widths set to AutoFit. Finally, the range object cell A1 is selected, its font size is changed to 22, and its Bold property is set to True. The last line, End Sub, indicates the end of the Sub procedure and is also referred to as the **procedure footer**.

3. **Click the View Microsoft Excel button 🗷 on the Visual Basic Editor Standard toolbar to return to Excel**

   Because the macro is stored in the EX P-Monthly Sales workbook, Kate can open this workbook and repeatedly use the macro stored there each month after she receives that month's sales data. She wants you to open the workbook containing data for Chicago's January sales and run the macro to format the data. You must leave the EX P-Monthly Sales workbook open to use the macro stored there.

4. **Open the file EX P-2.xlsx from the drive and folder where you store your Data Files, then save it as EX P-January Sales**

   This is the workbook containing the data you want to format.

5. **Press [Ctrl][Shift][F] to run the procedure**

   The FormatFile procedure formats the text, as shown in Figure P-4.

6. **Save the workbook**

   Now that you've successfully viewed and analyzed VBA code and run the macro, you will learn how to write your own code.

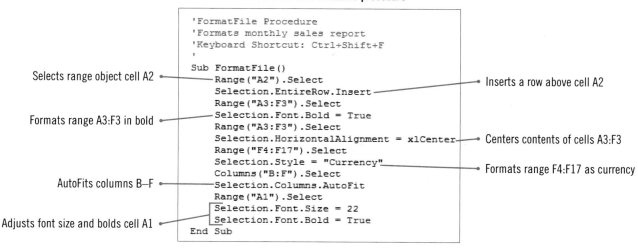

Selects range object cell A2

Formats range A3:F3 in bold

AutoFits columns B–F

Adjusts font size and bolds cell A1

Inserts a row above cell A2

Centers contents of cells A3:F3

Formats range F4:F17 as currency

```
'FormatFile Procedure
'Formats monthly sales report
'Keyboard Shortcut: Ctrl+Shift+F
'
Sub FormatFile()
    Range("A2").Select
    Selection.EntireRow.Insert
    Range("A3:F3").Select
    Selection.Font.Bold = True
    Range("A3:F3").Select
    Selection.HorizontalAlignment = xlCenter
    Range("F4:F17").Select
    Selection.Style = "Currency"
    Columns("B:F").Select
    Selection.Columns.AutoFit
    Range("A1").Select
    Selection.Font.Size = 22
    Selection.Font.Bold = True
End Sub
```

Excel 2010

FIGURE P-4: **Worksheet formatted using the FormatFile procedure**

Formatted title

Row inserted

Formatted column headings

Range formatted as currency

	A	B	C	D	E	F	G
1	**Quest Chicago January Sales**						
2							
3	**Trip Code**	**Depart Date**	**Number of Days**	**Seats Sold**	**Tour**	**Sales**	
4	452R	1/7/2013	30	30	African National Parks	$125,400.00	
5	556J	1/13/2013	14	25	Amazing Amazon	$ 69,875.00	
6	675Y	1/19/2013	14	32	Catalonia Adventure	$100,300.00	
7	446R	1/20/2013	7	18	Yellowstone	$ 46,958.00	
8	251D	1/21/2013	7	10	Costa Rica	$ 28,220.00	
9	335P	1/22/2013	21	33	Corfu Sailing Voyage	$105,270.00	
10	431V	1/25/2013	7	21	Costa Rica Rainforests	$ 54,390.00	
11	215C	1/26/2013	14	19	Silk Road Travels	$ 92,663.00	
12	325B	1/27/2013	10	17	Down Under Exodus	$ 47,600.00	
13	311A	1/29/2013	18	20	Essential India	$102,887.00	
14	422R	1/29/2013	7	24	Exotic Morocco	$ 45,600.00	
15	331E	1/30/2013	12	21	Experience Cambodia	$ 98,557.00	
16	831P	1/30/2013	14	15	Galapagos Adventure	$ 52,698.00	
17	334Q	1/31/2013	18	10	Green Adventures in Ecuador	$ 39,574.00	
18							
19							

Columns widened

Writing VBA Code

To write your own code, you first need to open the Visual Basic Editor and add a module to the workbook. You can then begin entering the procedure code. In the first few lines of a procedure, you typically include comments indicating the name of the procedure, a brief description of the procedure, and shortcut keys, if applicable. When writing Visual Basic code for Excel, you must follow the formatting rules, or **syntax**, of the VBA programming language. A misspelled keyword or variable name causes a procedure to fail. ▰▰▰▰ Kate would like to total the monthly sales. You help her by writing a procedure that automates this routine task.

STEPS

> **TROUBLE**
> If the Code window is empty, verify that the workbook that contains your procedures (EX P-Monthly Sales) is open.

1. **With the January worksheet still displayed, click the Developer tab, then click the Visual Basic button in the Code group**

   Two projects are displayed in the Project Explorer window, EX P-Monthly Sales.xlsm (which contains the FormatFile macro) and EX P-January Sales.xlsx (which contains the monthly data). The FormatFile procedure is again displayed in the Visual Basic Editor. You may have other projects in the Project Explorer window.

2. **Click the Modules folder in the EX P-Monthly Sales.xlsm project**

   You need to store all of the procedures in the EX P-Monthly Sales.xlsm project, which is in the EX P-Monthly Sales.xlsm workbook. By clicking the Modules folder, you have activated the workbook, and the title bar changes from EX P-January Sales to EX P-Monthly Sales.

3. **Click Insert on the Visual Basic Editor menu bar, then click Module**

   A new, blank module with the default name Module1 appears in the EX P-Monthly Sales.xlsm project, under the Format module. You think the property name of the module could be more descriptive.

4. **Click (Name) in the Properties window, then type Total**

   The module name is Total. The module name should not be the same as the procedure name (which will be AddTotal). In the code shown in Figure P-5, comments begin with an apostrophe, and the lines of code under Sub AddTotal( ) have been indented using the Tab key. When you enter the code in the next step, after you type the procedure header Sub AddTotal( ) and press [Enter], the Visual Basic Editor automatically enters End Sub (the procedure footer) in the Code window.

> **TROUBLE**
> As you type, you may see words in drop-down lists. This optional feature is explained in the Clues to Use titled "Entering code using AutoComplete" on the next page. For now, just continue to type.

5. **Click in the Code window, then type the procedure code exactly as shown in Figure P-5, entering your name in the second line, pressing [Tab] to indent text and [Shift][Tab] to move the insertion point to the left**

   The lines that begin with ActiveCell.Formula insert the information enclosed in quotation marks into the active cell. For example, ActiveCell.Formula = "Monthly Total:" inserts the words "Monthly Total:" into cell E18, the active cell. As you type each line, Excel adjusts the spacing.

6. **Compare the procedure code you entered in the Code window with Figure P-5, make any corrections if necessary, then click the Save EX P-Monthly Sales.xlsm button 🖫 on the Visual Basic Editor Standard toolbar**

7. **Click the View Microsoft Excel button 🧾 on the toolbar, click EX P-January Sales.xlsx on the taskbar to activate the workbook if necessary, with the January worksheet displayed click the Developer tab, then click the Macros button in the Code group**

   Macro names have two parts. The first part ('EX P-Monthly Sales.xlsm'!) indicates the workbook where the macro is stored. The second part (AddTotal or FormatFile) is the name of the procedure, taken from the procedure header.

> **TROUBLE**
> If an error message appears, click Debug. Click the Reset button 🔲 on the toolbar, correct the error, then repeat Steps 6–8.

8. **Click 'EX P-MonthlySales.xlsm'!AddTotal to select it if necessary, then click Run**

   The AddTotal procedure inserts and formats the monthly total in cell F18, as shown in Figure P-6.

9. **Save the workbook**

FIGURE P-5: VBA code for the AddTotal procedure

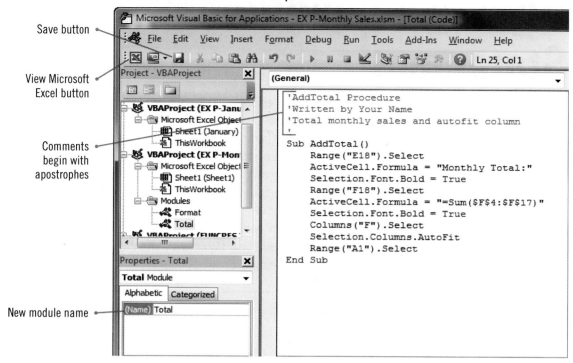

Save button

View Microsoft Excel button

Comments begin with apostrophes

New module name

```
'AddTotal Procedure
'Written by Your Name
'Total monthly sales and autofit column
'
Sub AddTotal()
    Range("E18").Select
    ActiveCell.Formula = "Monthly Total:"
    Selection.Font.Bold = True
    Range("F18").Select
    ActiveCell.Formula = "=Sum($F$4:$F$17)"
    Selection.Font.Bold = True
    Columns("F").Select
    Selection.Columns.AutoFit
    Range("A1").Select
End Sub
```

FIGURE P-6: Worksheet after running the AddTotal procedure

▲	A	B	C	D	E	F	G
1	Quest Chicago January Sales						
2							
3	Trip Code	Depart Date	Number of Days	Seats Sold	Tour	Sales	
4	452R	1/7/2013	30	30	African National Parks	$ 125,400.00	
5	556J	1/13/2013	14	25	Amazing Amazon	$ 69,875.00	
6	675Y	1/19/2013	14	32	Catalonia Adventure	$ 100,300.00	
7	446R	1/20/2013	7	18	Yellowstone	$ 46,958.00	
8	251D	1/21/2013	7	10	Costa Rica	$ 28,220.00	
9	335P	1/22/2013	21	33	Corfu Sailing Voyage	$ 105,270.00	
10	431V	1/25/2013	7	21	Costa Rica Rainforests	$ 54,390.00	
11	215C	1/26/2013	14	19	Silk Road Travels	$ 92,663.00	
12	325B	1/27/2013	10	17	Down Under Exodus	$ 47,600.00	
13	311A	1/29/2013	18	20	Essential India	$ 102,887.00	
14	422R	1/29/2013	7	24	Exotic Morocco	$ 45,600.00	
15	331E	1/30/2013	12	21	Experience Cambodia	$ 98,557.00	
16	831P	1/30/2013	14	15	Galapagos Adventure	$ 52,698.00	
17	334Q	1/31/2013	18	10	Green Adventures in Ecuador	$ 39,574.00	
18					**Monthly Total:**	**$ 1,009,992.00**	
19							

Result of AddTotal procedure

Entering code using AutoComplete

To assist you in entering the VBA code, the Editor uses **AutoComplete**, a list of words that can be used in the macro statement and match what is typed. Typically, the list appears after you press [.] (period). To include a word from the list in the macro statement, select the word in the list, then double-click it or press [Tab].

For example, to enter the Range("E12").Select instruction, type Range("E12"), then press [.] (period). Type s to bring up the words beginning with the letter "s", select the Select command in the list, then press [Tab] to enter the word "Select" in the macro statement.

Adding a Conditional Statement

The formatting macros you entered in the previous lesson could have been created using the macro recorder. However, there are some situations where you cannot use the recorder and must type the VBA macro code. One of these situations is when you want a procedure to take an action based on a certain condition or set of conditions. For example, *if* a salesperson's performance rating is a 5 (top rating), *then* calculate a 10% bonus; otherwise (*else*), there is no bonus. One way of adding this type of conditional statement in Visual Basic is to use an **If...Then...Else statement**. The syntax for this statement is: "If *condition* Then *statements* Else [*else statements*]." The brackets indicate that the Else part of the statement is optional. ⬛⬛⬛⬛ Kate wants the worksheet to point out if the total sales figure meets or misses the $1,000,000 monthly quota. You use Excel to add a conditional statement that indicates this information. You start by returning to the Visual Basic Editor and inserting a new module in the Monthly Sales project.

STEPS

1. **With the January worksheet still displayed, click the Developer tab if necessary, then click the Visual Basic button in the Code group**

2. **Verify that the Total module in the Modules folder of the EX P-Monthly Sales VBAProject is selected in the Project Explorer window, click Insert on the Visual Basic Editor menu bar, then click Module**

   A new, blank module named Module1 is inserted in the EX P-Monthly Sales workbook.

3. **In the Properties window click (Name), then type Sales**

4. **Click in the Code window, then type the code exactly as shown in Figure P-7, entering your name in the second line**

   Notice the green comment lines in the middle of the code. These lines help explain the procedure.

5. **Compare the procedure you entered with Figure P-7, make any corrections if necessary, click the Save EX P-Monthly Sales.xlsm button 🖫 on the Visual Basic Editor toolbar, then click the View Microsoft Excel button 🗷 on the toolbar**

6. **If necessary, click EX P-January Sales.xlsx in the taskbar to display it, with the January worksheet displayed click the Macros button in the Code group, in the Macro dialog box click 'EX P-Monthly Sales.xlsm'!SalesStatus, then click Run**

   The SalesStatus procedure indicates the status "Met Quota", as shown in Figure P-8.

7. **Save the workbook**

FIGURE P-7: **VBA code for the SalesStatus procedure**

```
'SalesStatus Procedure
'Written by Your Name
'Tests whether total sales meets the monthly quota
'
Sub SalesStatus()
    Range("E20").Select
    ActiveCell.Formula = "Sales Status:"
    Selection.Font.Bold = True
    'If the total is less than 1000000 then
    'insert "Missed Quota" in cell F20
    If Range("F18") <= 1000000 Then
        Range("F20").Select
        ActiveCell.Formula = "Missed Quota"
    'otherwise, insert "Met Quota" in cell F20
    Else
        Range("F20").Select
        ActiveCell.Formula = "Met Quota"
    End If
    Range("A1").Select
End Sub
```

If ... Then ... Else statement

FIGURE P-8: **Result of running the SalesStatus procedure**

	A	B	C	D	E	F	G
1	Quest Chicago January Sales						
2							
3	Trip Code	Depart Date	Number of Days	Seats Sold	Tour	Sales	
4	452R	1/7/2013	30	30	African National Parks	$ 125,400.00	
5	556J	1/13/2013	14	25	Amazing Amazon	$ 69,875.00	
6	675Y	1/19/2013	14	32	Catalonia Adventure	$ 100,300.00	
7	446R	1/20/2013	7	18	Yellowstone	$ 46,958.00	
8	251D	1/21/2013	7	10	Costa Rica	$ 28,220.00	
9	335P	1/22/2013	21	33	Corfu Sailing Voyage	$ 105,270.00	
10	431V	1/25/2013	7	21	Costa Rica Rainforests	$ 54,390.00	
11	215C	1/26/2013	14	19	Silk Road Travels	$ 92,663.00	
12	325B	1/27/2013	10	17	Down Under Exodus	$ 47,600.00	
13	311A	1/29/2013	18	20	Essential India	$ 102,887.00	
14	422R	1/29/2013	7	24	Exotic Morocco	$ 45,600.00	
15	331E	1/30/2013	12	21	Experience Cambodia	$ 98,557.00	
16	831P	1/30/2013	14	15	Galapagos Adventure	$ 52,698.00	
17	334Q	1/31/2013	18	10	Green Adventures in Ecuador	$ 39,574.00	
18					Monthly Total:	$ 1,009,992.00	
19							
20					Sales Status:	Met Quota	
21							

Indicates status of monthly total

Excel 2010

Prompting the User for Data

Another situation where you must type, not record, VBA code is when you need to pause a macro to allow user input. You use the VBA InputBox function to display a dialog box that prompts the user for information. A **function** is a predefined procedure that returns (creates and displays) a value; in this case the value returned is the information the user enters. The required elements of an InputBox function are as follows: *object*.InputBox("*prompt*"), where "*prompt*" is the message that appears in the dialog box. For a detailed description of the InputBox function, use the Visual Basic Editor's Help menu. ▰▰▰▰ You decide to create a procedure that will insert the user's name in the left footer area of the worksheet. You use the InputBox function to display a dialog box in which the user can enter his or her name. You also type an intentional error into the procedure code, which you will correct in the next lesson.

STEPS

QUICK TIP
To enlarge your Code window, place the mouse pointer on the left border of the Code window until it turns into ◀▮▶, then drag the border to the left until the Code window is the desired size.

1. **With the January worksheet displayed, click the Developer tab if necessary, click the Visual Basic button in the Code group, verify that the Sales module is selected in the EX P-Monthly Sales VBAProject Modules folder, click Insert on the Visual Basic Editor menu bar, then click Module**

   A new, blank module named Module1 is inserted in the EX P-Monthly Sales workbook.

2. **In the Properties window click (Name), then type Footer**

3. **Click in the Code window, then type the procedure code exactly as shown in Figure P-9 entering your name in the second line**

   Like the SalesStatus procedure, this procedure also contains comments that explain the code. The first part of the code, Dim LeftFooterText As String, **declares**, or defines, LeftFooterText as a text string variable. In Visual Basic, a **variable** is a location in memory in which you can temporarily store one item of information. Dim statements are used to declare variables and must be entered in the following format: Dim *variablename* As *datatype*. The datatype here is "string." In this case, you plan to store the information received from the input box in the temporary memory location called LeftFooterText. Then you can place this text in the left footer area. The remaining statements in the procedure are explained in the comment line directly above each statement. Notice the comment pointing out the error in the procedure code. You will correct this in the next lesson.

4. **Review your code, make any necessary changes, click the Save EX P-MonthlySales.xlsm button 🔲 on the Visual Basic Editor toolbar, then click the View Microsoft Excel button 🗷 on the toolbar**

5. **With the January worksheet displayed, click the Macros button in the Code group, in the Macro dialog box click 'EX P-Monthly Sales.xlsm'!FooterInput, then click Run**

   The procedure begins, and a dialog box generated by the InputBox function opens, prompting you to enter your name, as shown in Figure P-10.

QUICK TIP
If your macro doesn't prompt you for your name, it may contain an error. Return to the Visual Basic Editor, click the Reset button 🔲, correct the error by referring to Figure P-9, then repeat Steps 4 and 5. You'll learn more about how to correct such macro errors in the next lesson.

6. **With the cursor in the text box, type your name, then click OK**

7. **Click the File tab, click Print, then view the worksheet preview**

   Although the customized footer with the date is inserted on the sheet, because of the error your name does *not* appear in the left section of the footer. In the next lesson, you will learn how to step through a procedure's code line by line. This will help you locate the error in the FooterInput procedure.

8. **Click the Home tab, then save the workbook**

   You return to the January worksheet.

```
'FooterInput Procedure
'Written by Your Name
'Customize worksheet footer
'
Sub FooterInput()
    'Declares the LeftFooterText string variable
    Dim LeftFooterText As String
    'Prompts user for left footer text and stores
    'response in LeftFooter Text variable
    LeftFooterText = InputBox("Enter name:")
    'Inserts contents of LeftFooterText into left footer
    '****THERE IS AN ERROR IN THE FOLLOWING LINE****
    Worksheets("January").PageSetup.LeftFooter = LeftFooter
    'Inserts the date in right footer
    Worksheets("January").PageSetup.RightFooter = "&D"
End Sub
```

The phrase Enter name: will appear in a dialog box

Comment points out an error in the next line

FIGURE P-10: **InputBox function's dialog box**

User prompt

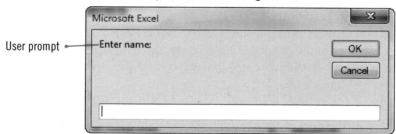

Naming variables

Variable names in VBA must begin with a letter. Letters can be uppercase or lowercase. Variable names cannot include periods or spaces, and they can be up to 255 characters long. Each variable name in a procedure must be unique. Examples of valid and invalid variable names are shown in Table P-2.

TABLE P-2: **Variable names**

valid	invalid
Sales_Department	Sales Department
SalesDepartment	Sales.Department
Quarter1	1stQuarter

Debugging a Macro

When a macro procedure does not run properly, it can be due to an error, referred to as a **bug**, in the code. To assist you in finding the bug(s) in a procedure, the Visual Basic Editor helps you step through the procedure's code, one line at a time. When you locate the error, you can then correct, or **debug**, it. ▰▰▰ You decide to debug the macro procedure to find out why it failed to insert your name in the worksheet footer.

STEPS

1. **With the January worksheet displayed, click the Developer tab if necessary, click the Macros button in the Code group, in the Macro dialog box click 'EX P-Monthly Sales.xlsm'!FooterInput, then click Step Into**

   The Visual Basic Editor opens with the yellow statement selector positioned on the first statement of the procedure, as shown in Figure P-11.

2. **Press [F8] to step to the next statement**

   The statement selector skips over the comments and the line of code beginning with Dim. The Dim statement indicates that the procedure will store your name in a variable named LeftFooterText. Because Dim is a declaration of a variable and not a procedure statement, the statement selector skips it and moves to the line containing the InputBox function.

3. **Press [F8] again, with the cursor in the text box in the Microsoft Excel dialog box type your name, then click OK**

   The Visual Basic Editor opens. The statement selector is now positioned on the statement that reads Worksheets("January").PageSetup.LeftFooter = LeftFooter. This statement should insert your name (which you just typed in the text box) in the left section of the footer. This is the instruction that does not appear to be working correctly.

4. **If necessary scroll right until the end of the LeftFooter instruction is visible, then place the mouse pointer on LeftFooter**

   The value of the LeftFooter variable is displayed as shown in Figure P-12. Rather than containing your name, the variable LeftFooter at the end of this line is empty. This is because the InputBox function assigned your name to the LeftFooterText variable, not to the LeftFooter variable. Before you can correct this bug, you need to turn off the Step Into feature.

5. **Click the Reset button ▣ on the Visual Basic Editor toolbar to turn off the Step Into feature, click at the end of the statement containing the error, then replace the variable LeftFooter with LeftFooterText**

   The revised statement now reads Worksheets("January").PageSetup.LeftFooter = LeftFooterText.

6. **Delete the comment line pointing out the error**

7. **Click the Save EX P-Monthly Sales.xlsm button ▣ on the Visual Basic Editor toolbar, then click the View Microsoft Excel button ▣ on the toolbar**

8. **With the January worksheet displayed click the Macros button in the Code group, in the Macro dialog box click 'EX P-Monthly Sales.xlsm'!FooterInput, click Run to rerun the procedure, when prompted type your name, then click OK**

9. **Click the File tab, click Print, then view the worksheet preview**

   Your name now appears in the left section of the footer.

10. **Click the Home tab, then save the workbook**

FIGURE P-11: **Statement selector positioned on first procedure statement**

Statement selector

```
'FooterInput Procedure
'Written by Your Name
'Customize worksheet footer
'
Sub FooterInput()
    'Declares the LeftFooterText string variable
    Dim LeftFooterText As String
    'Prompts user for left footer text and stores
    'response in LeftFooter Text variable
    LeftFooterText = InputBox("Enter name:")
    'Inserts contents of LeftFooterText into left footer
    '****THERE IS AN ERROR IN THE FOLLOWING LINE****
    Worksheets("January").PageSetup.LeftFooter = LeftFooter
    'Inserts the date in right footer
    Worksheets("January").PageSetup.RightFooter = "&D"
End Sub
```

FIGURE P-12: **Value contained in LeftFooter variable**

```
'FooterInput Procedure
'Written by Your Name
'Customize worksheet footer
'
Sub FooterInput()
    'Declares the LeftFooterText string variable
    Dim LeftFooterText As String
    'Prompts user for left footer text and stores
    'response in LeftFooter Text variable
    LeftFooterText = InputBox("Enter name:")
    'Inserts contents of LeftFooterText into left footer
    '****THERE IS AN ERROR IN THE FOLLOWING LINE****
    Worksheets("January").PageSetup.LeftFooter = LeftFooter
    'Inserts the date in right footer     LeftFooter = Empty
    Worksheets("January").PageSetup.RightFooter = "&D"
End Sub
```

Indicates the LeftFooter variable is empty

Adding security to your macro projects

To add security to your projects, you can add a digital signature to the project. A digital signature guarantees the project hasn't been altered since it was signed. You should sign macros only after they are tested and ready to be distributed. If the code in a digitally signed macro project is changed in any way, its digital signature is removed. To add a digital signature to a Visual Basic project, select the project that you want to sign in the Visual Basic Project Explorer window, click the Tools menu in the Visual Basic Editor, click Digital Signature, click Choose, select the certificate, then click OK twice. When you add a digital signature to a project, the macro project is automatically re-signed whenever it is saved on your computer.

Creating a Main Procedure

When you routinely need to run several macros one after another, you can save time by combining them into one procedure. The resulting procedure, which processes (or runs) multiple procedures in sequence, is referred to as the **main procedure**. To create a main procedure, you type a **Call statement** for each procedure you want to run. The syntax of the Call statement is Call *procedurename*, where *procedurename* is the name of the procedure you want to run. To avoid having to run her macros one after another every month, Kate asks you to create a main procedure that will run (or call) each of the procedures in the EX P-Monthly Sales workbook in sequence.

STEPS

1. **With the January worksheet displayed, click the** Developer tab **if necessary, then click the** Visual Basic button **in the Code group**

2. **Verify that EX P-Monthly Sales is the active project, click** Insert **on the menu bar, then click** Module

   A new, blank module named Module1 is inserted in the EX P-Monthly Sales workbook.

3. **In the Properties window click (Name), then type** MainProc

4. **In the Code window enter the procedure code exactly as shown in Figure P-13, entering your name in the second line**

5. **Compare your main procedure code with Figure P-13, correct any errors if necessary, then click the** Save EX P-Monthly Sales.xlsm button ▣ **on the Visual Basic Editor Standard toolbar**

   To test the new main procedure, you need an unformatted version of the EX P-January Sales worksheet.

6. **Click the** View Microsoft Excel button ▣ **on the toolbar, then save and close the** EX P-January Sales workbook

   The EX P-Monthly Sales workbook remains open.

7. **Open the file** EX P-2.xlsx **from the drive and folder where you store your Data Files, then save it as** EX P-January Sales 2

   In the next lesson, you'll run the main procedure.

FIGURE P-13: **VBA code for the MainProcedure procedure**

```
'MainProcedure Procedure
'Written by Your Name
'Calls sub procedures in sequence
'
Sub MainProcedure()
    Call FormatFile
    Call AddTotal
    Call SalesStatus
    Call FooterInput
End Sub
```

MainProcedure calls each procedure in the order shown

Excel 2010

Writing and documenting VBA code

When you write VBA code in the Visual Basic Editor, you want to make it as readable as possible. This makes it easier for you or your coworkers to edit the code when changes need to be made. The procedure statements should be indented, leaving the procedure name and its End statement easy to spot in the code. This is helpful when a module contains many procedures. It is also good practice to add comments at the beginning of each procedure that describe its purpose and any assumptions made in the procedure, such as the quota amounts. You should also explain each code statement with a comment. You have seen comments inserted into VBA code by beginning the statement with an apostrophe. You can also add comments to the end of a line of VBA code by placing an apostrophe before the comment, as shown in Figure P-14.

FIGURE P-14: **VBA code with comments at the end of statements**

```
'MainProcedure Procedure
'Written by Your Name
'Calls sub procedures in sequence
'
Sub MainProcedure()
    Call FormatFile 'Run FormatFile procedure
    Call AddTotal  'Run AddTotal procedure
    Call SalesStatus  'Run SalesStatus procedure
    Call FooterInput  'Run FooterInput procedure
End Sub
```

Comments at the end of the statements are in green

Running a Main Procedure

Running a main procedure allows you to run several macros in sequence. You can run a main procedure just as you would any other macro procedure. You have finished creating Kate's main procedure, and you are ready to run it. If the main procedure works correctly, it should format the worksheet, insert the sales total, insert a sales status message, and add your name and date to the worksheet footer.

STEPS

TROUBLE

If an error message appears, click Debug, click the Reset button ▦ on the toolbar, then correct your error.

1. **With the January worksheet displayed, click the Developer tab, click the Macros button in the Code group, in the Macro dialog box click 'EX P-Monthly Sales.xlsm'!MainProcedure, click Run, when prompted type your name, then click OK**

   The MainProcedure runs the FormatFile, AddTotal, SalesStatus, and FooterInput procedures in sequence. You can see the results of the FormatFile, AddTotal, and SalesStatus procedures in the worksheet window, as shown in Figure P-16. To view the results of the FooterInput procedure, you need to switch to the Preview window.

2. **Click the File tab, click Print, view the worksheet preview and verify that your name appears in the left footer area and the date appears in the right footer area, then click the Developer tab**

3. **Click the Visual Basic button in the Code group**

   You need to add your name to the Format module.

4. **In the Project Explorer window, double-click the Format module, add a comment line after the procedure name that reads Written by [Your Name], then click the Save EX P-Monthly Sales.xlsm button ▦**

   You want to see the options for printing VBA code.

5. **Click File on the Visual Basic Editor menu bar, then click Print**

   The Print - VBAProject dialog box opens, as shown in Figure P-17. The Current Module is selected which will print each procedure separately. It is faster to print all the procedures in the workbook at one time by clicking the Current Project option button to select it. You can also create a file of the VBA code by selecting the Print to File check box. You do not want to print the modules at this time.

6. **Click Cancel in the Print - VBAProject dialog box**

7. **Click the View Microsoft Excel button ▦ on the toolbar**

8. **Save the EX P-January Sales 2 workbook, then preview the worksheet**

   Compare your formatted worksheet to Figure P-18.

9. **Close the EX P-January Sales 2 workbook, close the EX P-Monthly Sales workbook, then exit Excel**

QUICK TIP

When you complete your work with macros, you should disable macros to prevent macros containing viruses from running on your computer. To disable macros, click the Developer tab, click the Macro Security button in the Code group, click one of the Disable all macros options, then click OK.

Running a macro using a button

You can run a macro by assigning it to a button on your worksheet. Create a button by clicking the Insert tab, clicking the Shapes button in the Illustrations group, choosing a shape, then drawing the shape on the worksheet. After you create the button, right-click it and select Assign Macro to choose the macro the button will run. It is a good idea to label the button with descriptive text. You can also format macro buttons using clip art, photographs, fills, and shadows. You format a button using the buttons on the Drawing Tools Format tab. To add an image to the button, click Fill in the Format Shape dialog box, then click the Picture or texture fill option button. To insert a picture from a file, click Fill in the Format Shape dialog box, click Picture or texture fill, click File, select a picture, then click Insert. To insert a clip art picture, click Clip Art, select a picture, then click OK. Figure P-15 shows a button formatted with clip art.

FIGURE P-15: Formatted macro button

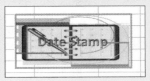

FIGURE P-16: Result of running MainProcedure procedure

Formatted title

Row inserted

	A	B	C	D	E	F	G
1	**Quest Chicago January Sales**						
2							
3	Trip Code	Depart Date	Number of Days	Seats Sold	Tour	Sales	
4	452R	1/7/2013	30	30	African National Parks	$ 125,400.00	
5	556J	1/13/2013	14	25	Amazing Amazon	$ 69,875.00	
6	675Y	1/19/2013	14	32	Catalonia Adventure	$ 100,300.00	
7	446R	1/20/2013	7	18	Yellowstone	$ 46,958.00	
8	251D	1/21/2013	7	10	Costa Rica	$ 28,220.00	
9	335P	1/22/2013	21	33	Corfu Sailing Voyage	$ 105,270.00	
10	431V	1/25/2013	7	21	Costa Rica Rainforests	$ 54,390.00	
11	215C	1/26/2013	14	19	Silk Road Travels	$ 92,663.00	
12	325B	1/27/2013	10	17	Down Under Exodus	$ 47,600.00	
13	311A	1/29/2013	18	20	Essential India	$ 102,887.00	
14	422R	1/29/2013	7	24	Exotic Morocco	$ 45,600.00	
15	331E	1/30/2013	12	21	Experience Cambodia	$ 98,557.00	
16	831P	1/30/2013	14	15	Galapagos Adventure	$ 52,698.00	
17	334Q	1/31/2013	18	10	Green Adventures in Ecuador	$ 39,574.00	
18					Monthly Total:	$ 1,009,992.00	
19							
20					Sales Status:	Met Quota	
21							

Total sales calculated

Sales status message inserted

FIGURE P-17: Printing options for macro procedures

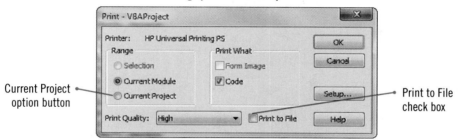

Current Project option button

Print to File check box

FIGURE P-18: Formatted January worksheet

Quest Chicago January Sales

Trip Code	Depart Date	Number of Days	Seats Sold	Tour	Sales
452R	1/7/2013	30	30	African National Parks	$ 125,400.00
556J	1/13/2013	14	25	Amazing Amazon	$ 69,875.00
675Y	1/19/2013	14	32	Catalonia Adventure	$ 100,300.00
446R	1/20/2013	7	18	Yellowstone	$ 46,958.00
251D	1/21/2013	7	10	Costa Rica	$ 28,220.00
335P	1/22/2013	21	33	Corfu Sailing Voyage	$ 105,270.00
431V	1/25/2013	7	21	Costa Rica Rainforests	$ 54,390.00
215C	1/26/2013	14	19	Silk Road Travels	$ 92,663.00
325B	1/27/2013	10	17	Down Under Exodus	$ 47,600.00
311A	1/29/2013	18	20	Essential India	$ 102,887.00
422R	1/29/2013	7	24	Exotic Morocco	$ 45,600.00
331E	1/30/2013	12	21	Experience Cambodia	$ 98,557.00
831P	1/30/2013	14	15	Galapagos Adventure	$ 52,698.00
334Q	1/31/2013	18	10	Green Adventures in Ecuador	$ 39,574.00
				Monthly Total:	$ 1,009,992.00
				Sales Status:	Met Quota

Your Name   2/12/2013

Practice

Concepts Review

FIGURE P-19

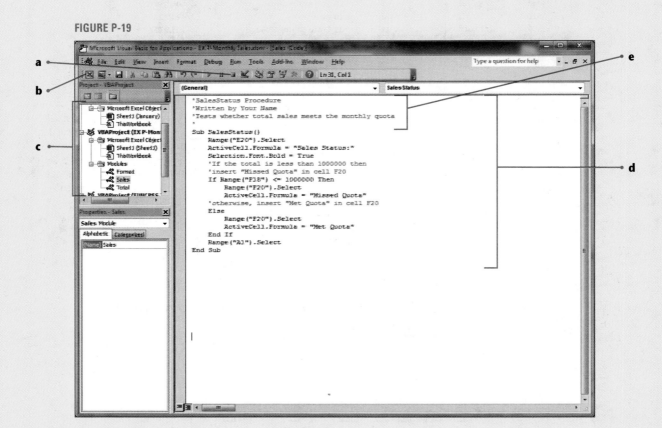

1. Which element points to the Project Explorer window?
2. Which element do you click to return to Excel from the Visual Basic Editor?
3. Which element do you click to turn off the Step Into feature?
4. Which element points to the Code window?
5. Which element points to comments in the VBA code?

Match each term with the statement that best describes it.

6. Function
7. Sub procedure
8. Procedure
9. Keywords
10. Comments

a. Another term for a macro in Visual Basic for Applications (VBA)
b. A procedure that returns a value
c. Words that are recognized as part of the programming language
d. A series of statements that perform an action but don't return a value
e. Descriptive text used to explain parts of a procedure

Select the best answer from the list of choices.

11. A location in memory where you can temporarily store information is a:

  a. Procedure.

  b. Variable.

  c. Sub procedure.

  d. Function.

12. You enter the statements of a macro in:

  a. The Macro dialog box.

  b. Any blank worksheet.

  c. The Code window of the Visual Basic Editor.

  d. The Properties window of the Visual Basic Editor.

13. If your macro doesn't run correctly, you should:

  a. Create an If...Then...Else statement.

  b. Select the macro in the Macro dialog box, click Step Into, then debug the macro.

  c. Click the Project Explorer button.

  d. Click the Properties button.

14. Comments are displayed in _____ in VBA code.

  a. Black

  b. Blue

  c. Green

  d. Red

15. Keywords are displayed in _____ in VBA code.

  a. Blue

  b. Black

  c. Green

  d. Red

Skills Review

1. View and analyze VBA code.

  a. Start Excel, open the file EX P-3.xlsm from the drive and folder where you store your Data Files, enable macros, then save it as **EX P-Home Products**.

  b. Review the unformatted December worksheet.

  c. Open the Visual Basic Editor.

  d. Select the DataFormat module, and review the Format procedure.

  e. Insert comments in the procedure code describing what action you think each line of code will perform. (*Hint*: One of the statements will sort the list by Store #.) Add comment lines to the top of the procedure to describe the purpose of the macro and to enter your name.

  f. Save the macro, return to the worksheet, then run the Format macro.

  g. Compare the results with the code and your comments.

  h. Save the workbook.

2. Write VBA code.

  a. Open the Visual Basic Editor, and insert a new module named **Total** in the EX P-Home Products project.

  b. Enter the code for the SalesTotal procedure exactly as shown in Figure P-20. Enter your name in the second line.

  c. Save the macro.

  d. Return to the December worksheet, and run the SalesTotal macro. Widen column E to view the total in cell E17.

  e. Save the workbook.

FIGURE P-20

```
'SalesTotal Procedure
'Written by Your Name
'Totals December sales
Sub SalesTotal()
    Range("E17").Select
    ActiveCell.Formula = "=SUM($E$3:$E$16)"
    Selection.Font.Bold = True
    With Selection.Borders(xlTop)
        .LineStyle = xlSingle
    End With
    Range("A1").Select
End Sub
```

Skills Review (continued)

3. Add a conditional statement

a. Open the Visual Basic Editor, and insert a new module named **Goal** in the EX P-Home Products project.

b. Enter the SalesGoal procedure exactly as shown in Figure P-21. Enter your name on the second line.

c. Save the macro.

d. Return to the December worksheet, and run the SalesGoal macro. The procedure should enter the message **Missed goal** in cell E18. Save the workbook.

4. Prompt the user for data.

a. Open the Visual Basic Editor, and insert a new module named **Header** in the EX P-Home Products project.

b. Enter the HeaderFooter procedure exactly as shown in Figure P-22. You are entering an error in the procedure that will be corrected in Step 5.

c. Save the macro, then return to the December worksheet, and run the HeaderFooter macro.

d. Preview the December worksheet. Your name should be missing from the left section of the footer.

e. Save the workbook.

5. Debug a macro.

a. Return to the Visual Basic Editor and use the Step Into feature to locate where the error occurred in the HeaderFooter procedure. Use the Reset button to turn off the debugger.

FIGURE P-21

```
'SalesGoal Procedure
'Written by Your Name
'Tests whether sales goal was met
Sub SalesGoal()
    'If the total is >=100000, then insert "Met Goal"
    'in cell E18
    If Range("E17") >= 100000 Then
        Range("E18").Select
        ActiveCell.Formula = "Met goal"
    'otherwise, insert "Missed goal" in cell E18
    Else
        Range("E18").Select
        ActiveCell.Formula = "Missed goal"
    End If
End Sub
```

FIGURE P-22

```
'HeaderFooter Procedure
'Written by Your Name
'Procedure to customize the header and footer
Sub HeaderFooter()
    'Inserts the filename in the header
    Worksheets("December").PageSetup.CenterHeader = "&F"
    'Declares the variable LeftFooterText as a string
    Dim LeftFooterText As String
    'Prompts user for left footer text
    LeftFooter = InputBox("Enter your full name:")
    'Inserts response into left footer
    Worksheets("December").PageSetup.LeftFooter = LeftFooterText
    'Inserts the date into right footer
    Worksheets("December").PageSetup.RightFooter = "&D"
End Sub
```

b. Edit the procedure in the Visual Basic Editor to correct the error. (*Hint*: The error occurs on the line: LeftFooter = InputBox("Enter your full name:"). The variable that will input the response text into the worksheet footer is LeftFooterText. The line should be: LeftFooterText = InputBox("Enter your full name:").)

c. Save the macro, then return to the December worksheet, and run the HeaderFooter macro again.

d. Verify that your name now appears in the left section of the footer, then save the file.

6. Create and run a main procedure.

a. Return to the Visual Basic Editor, insert a new module, then name it **MainProc**.

b. Begin the main procedure by entering comments in the code window that provide the procedure's name (MainProcedure) and explain that its purpose is to run the Format, SalesTotal, SalesGoal, and HeaderFooter procedures. Enter your name in a comment.

c. Enter the procedure header **Sub MainProcedure()**.

d. Enter four Call statements that will run the Format, SalesTotal, SalesGoal, and HeaderFooter procedures in sequence.

e. Save the procedure and return to Excel.

f. Open the file EX P-3.xlsm, then save it as **EX P-Home Products 2**.

g. Run the MainProcedure macro, entering your name when prompted. (*Hint*: In the Macro dialog box, the macro procedures you created will now have EX P-Home Products.xlsm! as part of their names. This is because the macros are stored in the EX P-Home Products workbook, not in the EX P-Home Products 2 workbook.)

FIGURE P-23

	A	B	C	D	E
1	Home Products December Sales				
2	Store #	City	State	Manager	Sales
3	11405	Juno	FL	Clifford	$ 8,745.93
4	19404	Palm Beach	FL	Cloutier	$ 8,656.83
5	29393	Tampa	FL	Nelson	$ 7,654.32
6	29396	Cape Coral	FL	Enos	$ 9,583.66
7	29399	Daytona	FL	DiBenedetto	$ 9,228.33
8	29402	Vero Beach	FL	Guapo	$ 5,534.34
9	29406	Miami	FL	Monroe	$ 4,987.36
10	39394	Naples	FL	Hamm	$ 6,715.68
11	39395	Bonita Springs	FL	Handelmann	$ 4,225.22
12	39397	Clearwater	FL	Erickson	$ 7,594.22
13	39398	Delray Beach	FL	Dever	$ 8,442.90
14	39400	Stuart	FL	Hahn	$ 8,001.34
15	39401	Neptune	FL	Pratt	$ 5,251.22
16	39403	Sanibel	FL	Lo	$ 4,643.93
17					$99,265.28
18					Missed goal
19					

Skills Review (continued)

h. Verify that the macro ran successfully, widen column E to display the calculated total, select cell A1, then compare your worksheet to Figure P-23.

i. Save the EX P-Home Products 2 workbook, preview the December worksheet to check the header and footer, then close the EX P-Home Products 2 workbook.

j. Save the EX P-Home Products workbook, close the workbook, exit Excel, then submit the EX P-Home Products workbook to your instructor.

Independent Challenge 1

You have taken over the management of a small local art museum. The information systems manager asks you to document and test an Excel procedure that the previous manager wrote for the company's accountant. You will first run the macro procedure to see what it does, then add comments to the VBA code to document it. You will also enter data to verify that the formulas in the macro work correctly.

a. Start Excel, open the file EX P-4.xlsm from the drive and folder where you store your Data Files, enable macros, then save it as **EX P-First Quarter**.

b. Run the First macro, noting anything that you think should be mentioned in your documentation.

c. Review the First procedure in the Visual Basic Editor. It is stored in the FirstQtr module.

d. Document the procedure by annotating the printed code, indicating the actions the procedure performs and the objects (ranges) that are affected.

e. Enter your name in a comment line, then save the procedure.

f. Return to the Jan-Mar worksheet, and use Figure P-24 as a guide to enter data in cells B4:D6. The totals will appear as you enter the income data.

g. Format the range B4:D8 using the Accounting Number format with no decimals, as shown in Figure P-24.

h. Check the total income calculations in row 8 to verify that the macro is working correctly.

i. Enter your name in the center section of the Jan-Mar sheet footer, save the workbook, then preview the worksheet.

j. Close the workbook, exit Excel, then submit the workbook to your instructor.

FIGURE P-24

	A	B	C	D
1		January	February	March
2	Income			
3				
4	Donations	$ 1,500	$ 1,200	$ 1,800
5	Fundraisers	$ 2,000	$ 2,500	$ 2,100
6	Grants	$ 20,000	$ 50,000	$ 90,000
7				
8	Total Income	$ 23,500	$ 53,700	$ 93,900
9				

Independent Challenge 2

You work in the Miami branch of Health Place, a nurse recruitment agency. You have three locations where you have monthly quotas for placements. Each month you are required to produce a report stating whether sales quotas were met for the following three medical facilities: Mercy Hospital, Ocean Clinic, and Assisted Home. The quotas for each month are as follows: Mercy Hospital 10, Ocean Clinic 7, and Assisted Home 4. Your sales results this month were 8, 8, and 5, respectively. You decide to create a procedure to automate your monthly task of determining the sales quota status for the placement categories. You would like your assistant to take this task over when you go on vacation next month. Because he has no previous experience with Excel, you decide to create a second procedure that prompts a user with input boxes to enter the actual placement results for the month.

a. Start Excel, open the file EX P-5.xlsm from the drive and folder where you store your Data Files, then save it as **EX P-Placements**.

b. Use the Visual Basic Editor to insert a new module named **Quotas** in the EX P-Placements workbook. Create a procedure in the new module named **PlacementQuota** that determines the quota status for each category and enters Yes or No in the Status column. The VBA code is shown in Figure P-25.

FIGURE P-25

```
Sub PlacementQuota()

    If Range("C4") >= 10 Then
        Range("D4").Select
        ActiveCell.Formula = "Yes"
    Else
        Range("D4").Select
        ActiveCell.Formula = "No"
    End If

    If Range("C5") >= 7 Then
        Range("D5").Select
        ActiveCell.Formula = "Yes"
    Else
        Range("D5").Select
        ActiveCell.Formula = "No"
    End If

    If Range("C6") >= 4 Then
        Range("D6").Select
        ActiveCell.Formula = "Yes"
    Else
        Range("D6").Select
        ActiveCell.Formula = "No"
    End If

End Sub
```

Independent Challenge 2 (continued)

c. Add comments to the PlacementQuota procedure, including the procedure name, your name, and the purpose of the procedure, then save it.

d. Insert a new module named **MonthlyPlacement**. Create a second procedure named **Placement** that prompts a user for placement data for each placement category, enters the input data in the appropriate cells, then calls the PlacementQuota procedure. The VBA code is shown in Figure P-26.

FIGURE P-26

```
Sub Placement()

    Dim Hospital As String
    Hospital = InputBox("Enter Hospital Placements")
    Range("C4").Select
    Selection = Hospital

    Dim Clinic As String
    Clinic = InputBox("Enter Clinic Placements")
    Range("C5").Select
    Selection = Clinic

    Dim Assisted As String
    Assisted = InputBox("Enter Assisted Placements")
    Range("C6").Select
    Selection = Assisted

    Call PlacementQuota

End Sub
```

e. Add a comment noting the procedure name on the first line. Add a comment with your name on the second line. Add a third comment line at the top of the procedure describing its purpose. Enter comments in the code to document the macro actions. Save the procedure.

f. Run the Placement macro, and enter **8** for hospital placement, **8** for clinic placements, and **5** for assisted placements. Correct any errors in the VBA code.

Advanced Challenge Exercise

- Assign a shortcut of **[Ctrl][Shift][S]** to the Placement macro. Insert a line on the worksheet that tells the user to press [Ctrl][Shift][S] to enter placement data.
- Edit the Visual Basic code for the PlacementQuota procedure to reflect a change in quotas to **15** for Hospitals, **8** for Clinics, and **6** for Assisted. Change the worksheet data in the range B4:B6 to display the new quotas.
- Delete the data in cells C4:D6.
- Run the Placement macro using the shortcut key combination entering **12** for hospital placements, **10** for clinic placements, and **5** for assisted placements.

g. Add your name to the center section of the worksheet footer, save the workbook, then preview the worksheet. Close the workbook, exit Excel, then submit your workbook to your instructor.

Independent Challenge 3

You are the marketing director at a car dealership business based in Minneapolis. You have started to advertise using a local magazine, billboards, TV, radio, and local newspapers. Every month you prepare a report with the advertising expenses detailed by source. You decide to create a macro that will format the monthly reports. You add the same footers on every report, so you will create another macro that will add a footer to a document. Finally, you will create a main procedure that calls the macros to format the report and add a footer. You begin by opening a workbook with the January data. You will save the macros you create in this workbook.

a. Start Excel, open the file EX P-6.xlsm from the drive and folder where you store your Data Files, then save it as **EX P-Auto**.

b. Insert a module named **Format**, then create a procedure named **Formatting** that:
- Selects a cell in row 3, and inserts a row in the worksheet above it.
- Selects the cost data in column C, and formats it as currency. (*Hint*: After the row is inserted, this range is C5:C9.)
- Selects cell A1 before ending.

c. Save the Formatting procedure.

d. Insert a module named **Foot**, then create a procedure named **Footer** that:
- Declares a string variable for text that will be placed in the left footer.
- Uses an input box to prompt the user for his or her name, and places the name in the left footer.
- Places the date in the right footer.

e. Save the Footer procedure.

f. Insert a module named **Main**, then create a procedure named MainProc that calls the Footer procedure and the Formatting procedure.

Independent Challenge 3 (continued)

g. Save your work, then run the MainProc procedure. Debug each procedure as necessary. Your worksheet should look like Figure P-27.

h. Document each procedure by inserting a comment line with the procedure name, your name, and a description of the procedure.

FIGURE P-27

	A	B	C
1	Twin Cities Auto		
2	Ad Campaign		
3			
4	Advertising Type	Source	Cost
5	Magazine	Twin Cities Magazine	$ 200.00
6	Newspaper	Tribune	$ 350.00
7	Billboard	Main Street	$ 450.00
8	TV	Local Access Station	$ 50.00
9	Radio	WAQV	$ 500.00
10			

Advanced Challenge Exercise

■ Insert a module named **Total**, then create a procedure named **CostTotal** that does the following:
  - Totals the advertising costs in cells C5:C9, and inserts the total in cell C10.
  - Formats the total as bold, and adds a light purple fill to the total cell. (*Hint*: After a cell is selected, the VBA code Selection.Interior.ColorIndex = 39 will add a purple fill to it.)
  - Selects cell A1.
■ Document the procedure with the procedure name, your name, and a description of the procedure.
■ Run the CostTotal procedure. Widen column C if necessary to display the total.

i. Preview the January worksheet, save the workbook, close the workbook, exit Excel, then submit the workbook to your instructor.

Real Life Independent Challenge

You decide to create a log of your discretionary expenses in an effort to track where you spend your paycheck each week. You will not track essential expenses such as auto expenses, rent/mortgage, groceries, necessary clothing, utilities, and tuition. Rather, your purpose is to identify optional items that may be targeted for reduction in an effort to meet a weekly budget. As part of this log, you record your expenses for each day of the week along with the daily amount spent in each category.

a. Start Excel, open the file EX P-7.xlsm from the drive and folder where you store your Data Files, then save it as **EX P-Expenses**.

b. Expand the modules folder to display the Expenses module. Edit the WeekExpenses procedure to record your expense categories. Record seven or fewer categories, and remember to edit the total cells and the formatting ranges in the procedure.

c. Run the macro and debug the procedure as necessary.

d. Use the worksheet to enter your expenses for each day of the past week, as best you can remember.

e. Save your work.

f. Verify that the totals are correct for each day and each category.

g. Enter your name as a comment in the second line of the procedure, then save the procedure.

h. Enter your name in the center section of the worksheet footer, then preview the worksheet.

Advanced Challenge Exercise

■ Insert a module named **Preview** with a procedure named **PreviewSheetdata** that previews a worksheet. The VBA code is shown in Figure P-28.
■ Save the macro and return to the worksheet.
■ Assign the macro PreviewSheetdata to a button on the worksheet. (*Hint*: Use the Rectangle tool to create the button, label the button **Print Preview**, then right-click one of the button's edges to assign the macro.)
■ Test the button, then close the Print Preview.

FIGURE P-28

```
Sub PreviewSheetdata ()


ActiveSheet.PrintPreview


End Sub
```

i. Save the workbook, close the workbook, exit Excel, then submit the workbook to your instructor.

Visual Workshop

Open the file EX P-8.xlsm from the drive and folder where you store your Data Files, then save it as **EX P-Florist**. Create a macro procedure named **Formatting** in a module named **FormatFile** that will format the worksheet as shown in Figure P-29. (*Hint*: The font size is 12.) Run the macro and debug it as necessary to make the worksheet match Figure P-29. Insert your name in a comment line under the procedure name and in the worksheet footer, then preview the worksheet. Submit the workbook to your instructor.

FIGURE P-29

	A	B	C
1	Portland Florist		
2	Monthly Sales		
3			
4	Flowers	$897.89	
5	Plants	$522.87	
6	Silks	$324.58	
7	Home Décor	$569.88	
8			

Importing and Exporting Data

Access can share data with many other Microsoft Office programs. For example, you can import data from an Excel workbook into an Access database or go the other way and export data from Access to Excel. You may want to merge Access data into a Word document to create a mass mailing. Or you may want to share data from your Access database using Outlook e-mail messages. At Quest Specialty Travel, Jacob Thomas, director of staff development, has asked you to develop an Access database that tracks professional staff continuing education. First you will explore the Access templates for creating a new database. Then you will work with Access tools that allow you to share Access data with other software programs so that each Quest department can have the necessary data in a format they can use.

OBJECTIVES

Use database templates

Use Application Parts

Import data from Excel

Link data

Export data to Excel

Publish data to Word

Merge data with Word

Collect data with Outlook

Using Database Templates

A **database template** is a tool that you use to quickly create a new database based on a particular subject such as assets, contacts, events, or projects. When you install Access 2010 on your computer, Microsoft provides many database templates for you to use. Additional templates are available from Microsoft Office Online, where they are organized by category such as business, personal, and education. Jacob Thomas, director of staff development, asks you to develop a new Access database to track the continuing education of Quest employees. You explore Microsoft database templates to learn more about Access.

STEPS

> **TROUBLE**
> If you don't see the Education folder, use the Search box to search for the Student database.

> **TROUBLE**
> The Browse button looks like a yellow folder on the far-right side of the window, to the right of the database path.

> **QUICK TIP**
> To review the video later, open the Getting Started form.

1. **Start Access 2010**

   As shown in Figure I-1, Microsoft provides many templates to help you create a new database. **Online templates** are available to download from the Microsoft Office Online Web site. Templates change over time as more are added and enhancements to existing templates are provided by Microsoft. The database you want to create should track employees and the continuing education courses they have completed, so you will explore the Education template category.

2. **Click the Education folder, click Student database, click the Browse icon** 🖼, **navigate to the drive and folder where you store your Data Files, click OK, then click Download**

   The template builds a new database named Student database that includes several sample tables, queries, forms, reports, macros, and a module object. You can use or modify these objects to meet your needs. A Getting Started window opens to provide video support for the database.

3. **Close the Access help window, close the Getting Started window, then enable content if prompted and close the Getting Started window again to explore the actual database as shown in Figure I-2**

   The Student List form is automatically opened, and the other objects in the database are presented in the Navigation Pane.

4. **Right-click the Student List form tab, click Close, then double-click the Student Details form in the Navigation Pane**

   Objects created by database templates are rich in functionality and can be modified for your specific needs or analyzed to learn more about Access.

5. **Close the Student Details form, then double-click the Guardian Details form to open it**

   If you wanted to use this database, your next step would be to enter sample data and continue exploring the other objects in the database. Because this database is designed for a traditional school rather than a corporate educational environment, you won't be using it at Quest. However, you can still learn a great deal by exploring the objects that the template created.

6. **Close the Guardian Details form**

FIGURE I-1: Available Templates

Template suggestions

Office.com online templates; the templates displayed in your window may differ

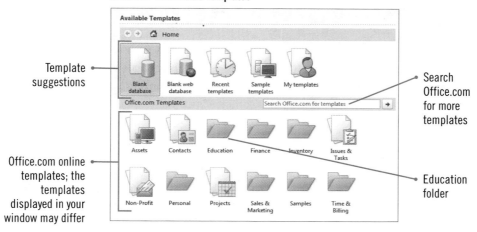

Search Office.com for more templates

Education folder

FIGURE I-2: Student database template

Student List form tab

Student database template created all these objects

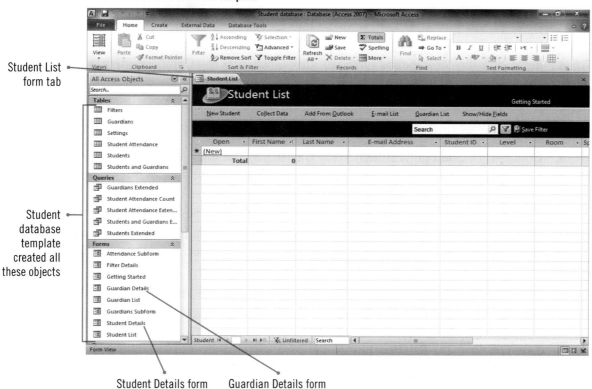

Student Details form   Guardian Details form

Using Application Parts

Application Parts are object templates that create objects such as tables and forms. Application Parts include several **table templates**, tools you can use to quickly create a single table in a database, and **form templates** to help you create forms. As with database templates, Microsoft is constantly updating and improving this part of Access. You continue your study of templates by exploring the Access 2010 Application Parts in the new Students database.

TROUBLE

After you click the Create tab, you might need to enable content and close the Getting Started window.

1. **Click the** Create **tab, then click the** Application Parts **button as shown in Figure I-3, click** Comments, **click the** There is no relationship **option button, then click** Create

   Access creates a new table named Comments that you can modify and relate to the other tables in the database as needed. You also want to explore the form templates.

2. **Close the Getting Started window, close the Student List form, click the** Application Parts **button in the Templates group, click** Msgbox, **close the Getting Started window and the Student List form, click** Yes **if prompted to close all open objects, then double-click the new** MessageBox **form in the Navigation Pane to open it**

   Every time you create a new object using the Application Parts button, the database reopens, which loads the Getting Started and Student List forms. A sample message box form is created with three standard command buttons. To use this form, you would further modify it in Layout View to meet your specific needs.

   Note that some database and Application Parts templates create objects that are compatible with the Web. Web-compatible objects display a small Web symbol in their icon. The Web symbol means that if you published this database to a **Microsoft SharePoint server**, users could access this form using only a Web browser such as Internet Explorer, Safari, or Firefox.

3. **Right-click the** MessageBox **form tab, click** Close, **click the** Database Tools **tab, then click the** Relationships **button**

   When you use a database or table template, you need to check the Relationships window to make sure the tables participate in a meaningful relational database. The Student database template did not create relationships between the tables. You'll connect four of the main tables.

4. **Double-click** Guardians, Students and Guardians, Students, **and** Student Attendance, **click** Close, **then resize the** Guardians **and** Students **field lists to view as many fields as possible**

   With the four field lists for the main tables in the database positioned in the Relationships window so that you can see all of the fields, you will build the one-to-many relationships between the tables.

5. **Drag the** ID **field from the Guardians table to the** GuardianID **field in the Students and Guardians table, click the** Enforce Referential Integrity **check box, then click** Create

TROUBLE

Be sure to use the exact fields shown in Figure I-4 to create the relationships. If you make a mistake, right-click the relationship, click Delete, and try again.

6. **Create the other two relationships as shown in Figure I-4**

   Note that in this database, the linking fields do not have the same name in both the "one" and "many" tables. Also recall that referential integrity helps prevent orphan records—records in the "many" table that don't have a matching record in the "one" table.

7. **Save and close the Relationships window, continue studying the tables and other objects of the Student database as desired, then close the database and exit Access 2010**

   Access database templates and Application Parts provide powerful tools to build databases and objects quickly. Templates are also an exciting way to learn more about Access features and possibilities.

FIGURE I-3: Application Parts list

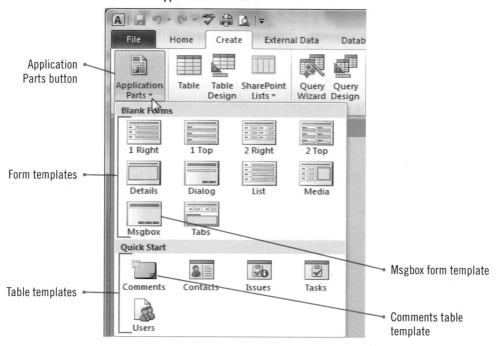

Application Parts button

Form templates

Table templates

Msgbox form template

Comments table template

FIGURE I-4: Major relationships for the Student database

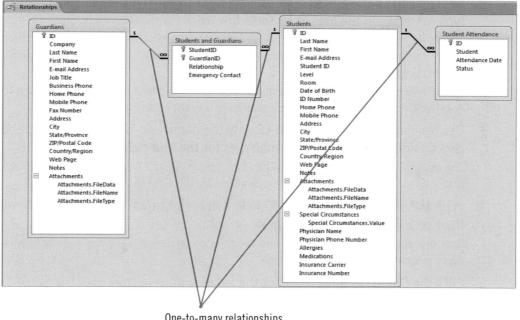

One-to-many relationships

Referential integrity cascade options

When connecting tables in one-to-many relationships, apply referential integrity whenever possible. This feature prevents orphan records from being created in the database and lets you select cascade options. **Cascade Update Related Fields** means that if a value in the primary key field (the field on the "one" side of a one-to-many relationship) is modified, all values in the foreign key field (the field on the "many" side of a one-to-many relationship) are automatically updated as well. **Cascade Delete Related Records** means that if a record in the "one" side of a one-to-many relationship is deleted, all related records in the "many" table are also deleted. Because both of these options automatically change or delete data in the "many" table behind the scenes, they should be used carefully. Often these features are not employed as standard options, but are used temporarily to correct a problem in the database.

Importing Data from Excel

Importing enables you to quickly copy data from an external file into an Access database. You can import data from many sources such as another Access database, Excel spreadsheet, SharePoint site, Outlook e-mail, or text files in an HTML, XML, or delimited text file format. A **delimited text file** stores one record on each line. Field values are separated by a common character, the **delimiter**, such as a comma, tab, or dash. A **CSV (comma-separated values)** file is a common example of a delimited text file. An **XML file** is a text file containing **Extensible Markup Language (XML)** tags that identify field names and data. One of the most common file formats from which to import data into an Access database is **Microsoft Excel**, the spreadsheet program in the Microsoft Office suite.  Jacob Thomas gives you an Excel spreadsheet that contains a list of supplemental materials used for various courses, and asks you to import the information in the new internal training database.

STEPS

1. **Start Access, open the Education-I.accdb database from the drive and folder where you store your Data Files, enable content if prompted, click the External Data tab, click the Excel button in the Import & Link group, click the Browse button, navigate to the drive and folder where you store your Data Files, double-click CourseMaterials.xlsx, then click OK**

   The **Import Spreadsheet Wizard** dialog box opens, as shown in Figure I-5, guiding you through the steps of importing Excel data into an Access database.

2. **Click Next, click the First Row Contains Column Headings check box, click Next, click Next to accept the default field options, click Next to allow Access to add a primary key field, type Materials in the Import to Table box, click Finish, then click Close**

   To save the import steps so that they can be easily repeated, click the Save import steps check box on the last step of the import process. You run a saved import process by using the **Saved Imports** button on the External Data tab.

   You review the imported records and relate the Materials table to the Courses table in a one-to-many relationship. One course can be related to many records in the Materials table.

3. **Double-click the Materials table to view the datasheet, right-click the Materials tab, then click Design View to view the data types for the four fields**

   The Materials table contains four fields and 45 records. The ID field is the primary key field for this table. CourseID will be used as the foreign key field to relate this table to the Courses table.

4. **Type MaterialID to replace the ID field name, right-click the Materials tab, click Close, then click Yes to save the changes**

   Now that you've examined the data and design of the Materials table, you're ready to relate it in a one-to-many relationship with the Courses table.

5. **Click the Database Tools tab, click the Relationships button, click the Show Table button, double-click Materials, click Close, drag the CourseID field in the Courses table to the CourseID field in the Materials table, click the Enforce Referential Integrity check box, then click Create**

   The final Relationships window is shown in Figure I-6. One employee record is related to many enrollments. One course record is related to many enrollments and also to many materials.

6. **Click the Close button, then click Yes to save the changes to the database relationships**

FIGURE I-5: Import Spreadsheet Wizard

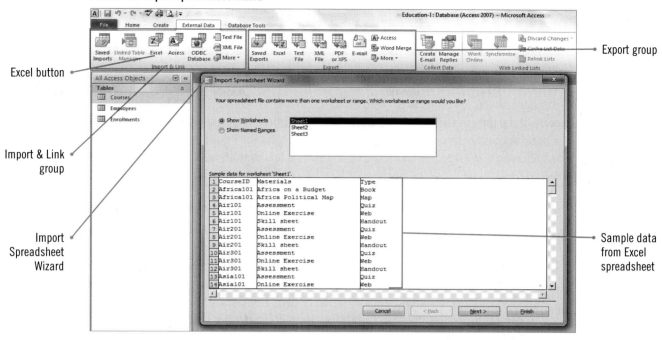

Excel button

Import & Link group

Import Spreadsheet Wizard

Export group

Sample data from Excel spreadsheet

FIGURE I-6: Relationships window with imported Materials table

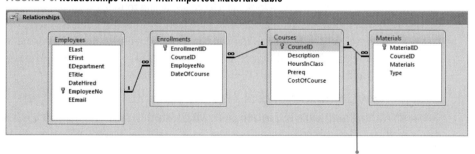

One-to-many relationship between Courses and Materials tables with referential integrity enforced

Access 2010

Linking Data

Linking connects an Access database to data in an external file such as another Access database, Excel spreadsheet, text file, HTML file, XML file, or other data sources that support **ODBC (open database connectivity)** standards. Linking is different from importing in that linked data is not copied into the database. If you link, data is only stored and updated in the original file. Importing, in contrast, makes a copy of the data in the Access database.  Jacob Thomas has created a small spreadsheet with information about the departments at Quest. He wants to use the information in the Education-I database while maintaining it in Excel. He asks you to help create a link to this Excel file from the Education-I database.

STEPS

1. **Click the External Data tab, then click the Excel button in the Import & Link group**

   The Get External Data - Excel Spreadsheet dialog box opens, as shown in Figure I-7. This dialog box allows you to choose whether you want to import, append, or link to the data source.

2. **Click Browse, navigate to the drive and folder where you store your Data Files, double-click DepartmentData.xlsx, click the Link to the data source by creating a linked table option button, click OK, click Next to accept the default range selection, click Next to accept the default column headings, type Departments as the linked table name, click Finish, then click OK**

   The **Link Spreadsheet Wizard** guides you through the process of linking to a spreadsheet. The linked Departments table appears in the Navigation Pane with a linking Excel icon, as shown in Figure I-8. Like any other table, in order for the linked table to work with the rest of a database, a one-to-many relationship between it and another table should be created.

3. **Click the Database Tools tab, click the Relationships button, click the Show Table button, double-click Departments, then click Close**

   The Dept field in the Departments table is used to create a one-to-many relationship with the EDepartment field in the Employees table. One department may be related to many employees.

4. **Drag the Departments field list near the Employees table, drag the Dept field in the Departments table to the EDepartment field in the Employees table, then click Create in the Edit Relationships dialog box**

   Your Relationships window should look like Figure I-9. A one-to-many relationship is established between the Departments and Employees tables, but because referential integrity is not enforced, the one and many symbols do not appear on the link line. You cannot establish referential integrity when one of the tables is a linked table. Now that the linked Departments table is related to the rest of the database, it can participate in queries, forms, and reports that select fields from multiple tables.

5. **Click the Close button, then click Yes when prompted to save changes**

   You work with a linked table just as you work with any other table. The data in a linked table can be edited through either the source program (in this case, Excel) or in the Access database, even though the data is only physically stored in the original source file.

FIGURE I-7: **Get External Data – Excel Spreadsheet dialog box**

Your path
might differ

Import

Append

Link

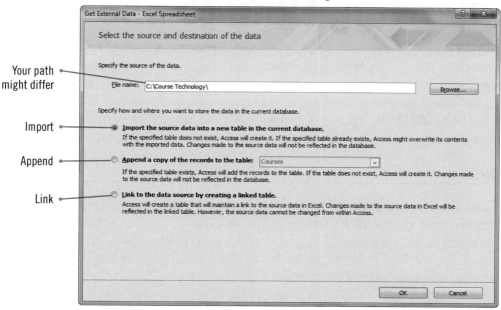

FIGURE I-8: **Departments table is linked from Excel**

Linked Departments
table

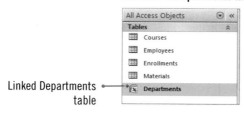

FIGURE I-9: **Relationships window with linked Departments table**

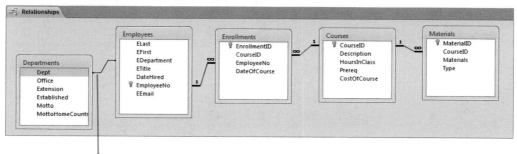

One-to-many relationship
between Departments and
Employees tables without
referential integrity enforced

Access 2010

Exporting Data to Excel

Exporting is a way to copy Access information to another database, spreadsheet, or file format. Exporting is the opposite of importing. You can export data from an Access database to other file types, such as those used by Excel or Word, and in several general file formats including text, HTML, and XML. Given the popularity of analyzing numeric data in Excel, it is common to export Access data to an Excel spreadsheet for further analysis. ▓▓▒▒▓▓ The Finance Department asks you to export some Access data to an Excel spreadsheet so they can use Excel to analyze how increases in the cost of the courses would affect departments. You can gather the fields needed in an Access query, then export the query to an Excel spreadsheet.

STEPS

1. **Click the Create tab, click the Query Design button, double-click Employees, double-click Enrollments, double-click Courses, then click Close**

   The fields you want to export to Excel—EDepartment and CostOfCourse—are in the Employees and Courses tables. You also need to include the Enrollments table in this query because it provides the connection between the Employees and Courses tables.

2. **Double-click EDepartment in the Employees field list, double-click CostOfCourse in the Courses field list, click the Sort cell for the EDepartment field, click the Sort cell list arrow, click Ascending, then click the View button ▦ to display the query datasheet**

   The resulting datasheet has 403 records. You want to summarize the costs by department before exporting this to Excel.

3. **Click the View button ◤ to return to Design View, click the Totals button in the Show/Hide group, click Group By for the CostOfCourse field, click the Group By list arrow, click Sum, click ▦ to display the query datasheet, then widen the SumOfCostOfCourse column as shown in Figure I-10**

   Save the query with a meaningful name to prepare to export it to Excel.

4. **Click the Save button ▦ on the Quick Access toolbar, type DepartmentCosts, click OK, right-click the DepartmentCosts tab, then click Close**

   Before you start an export process, be sure to select the object you want to export in the Navigation Pane.

5. **Click the DepartmentCosts query in the Navigation Pane (if it is not already selected), click the External Data tab, click the Excel button in the Export group, click Browse, navigate to the drive and folder where you store your Data Files, click Save, click OK, then click Close**

   The data in the DepartmentCosts query has now been exported to an Excel spreadsheet file named DepartmentCosts and saved in the drive and folder where you store your Data Files. As with imports, you can save and then repeat the export process by saving the export steps when prompted by the last dialog box in the Export Wizard. Run the saved export process using the **Saved Exports** button on the External Data tab or by assigning the export process to an Outlook task.

   Access can work with data in a wide variety of file formats. Other file formats that Access can import from, link with, and export to are listed in Table I-1.

FIGURE I-10: New query selects and summarizes data to be exported to Excel

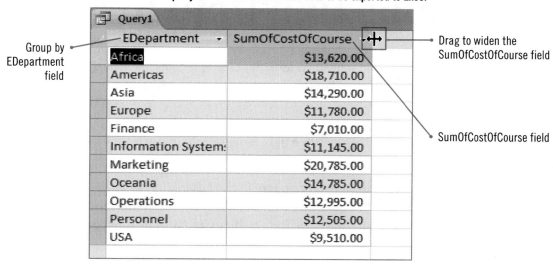

Group by EDepartment field

Drag to widen the SumOfCostOfCourse field

SumOfCostOfCourse field

TABLE I-1: File formats that Access can link to, import, and export

file format	import	link	export
Access	Yes	Yes	Yes
Excel	Yes	Yes	Yes
Word	No	No	Yes
SharePoint site	Yes	Yes	Yes
E-mail file attachments	No	No	Yes
Outlook folder	Yes	Yes	No
ODBC database (such as SQL Server)	Yes	Yes	Yes
dBASE	Yes	Yes	Yes
HTML document	Yes	Yes	Yes
PDF or XPS file	No	No	Yes
Text file (delimited or fixed width)	Yes	Yes	Yes
XML file	Yes	No	Yes

Publishing Data to Word

Microsoft Word, the word-processing program in the Microsoft Office suite, is a premier program for entering, editing, and formatting text. You can easily export data from an Access table, query, form, or report into a Word document. This is helpful when you want to use Word's superior text-editing features to combine the information in a Word document with Access data. ⬛⬛⬛ You have been asked to write a memo to the management committee describing departmental costs for continuing education. You export an Access query with this data to a Word document where you finish the memo.

STEPS

1. **Click the DepartmentCosts query in the Navigation Pane (if it is not already selected), click the External Data tab, click the More button in the Export group, click Word, click Browse, navigate to the drive and folder where you store your Data Files, click Save, click OK, then click Close**

   The data in the DepartmentCosts query is exported as an **RTF (Rich Text Format)** file, which can be opened and edited in Word.

2. **Start Word, then open DepartmentCosts.rtf from the drive and folder where you store your Data Files**

   Currently, the document contains only a table of information, the data you exported from the DepartmentCosts query. Use Word to add the memo information.

3. **Press [Enter], then type the following text, pressing [Tab] after typing each colon:**

   To: Management Committee

   From: Your Name

   Re: Analysis of Continuing Education Courses

   Date: Today's date

   The following information shows the overall cost for continuing education subtotaled by department. The information shows that the Americas and Marketing departments are the highest consumers of continuing education.

4. **Proofread your document, which should now look like Figure I-11, then preview and print it**

   The **word wrap** feature in Word determines when a line of text extends into the right margin of the page and automatically forces the text to the next line without you needing to press [Enter]. This allows you to enter and edit large paragraphs of text in Word very efficiently.

5. **Save and close the document, then exit Word**

   In addition to exporting data, Table I-2 lists other techniques you can use to copy Access data to other applications.

FIGURE I-11: Final Word document

To: Management Committee

From: Student Name

Re: Analysis of Continuing Education Courses

Date: Today's date

The following information shows the overall cost for continuing education subtotaled by department.
The information shows that the Americas and Marketing Departments are the highest consumers of
continuing education.

EDepartment	SumOfCostOfCourse
Africa	$13,620.00
Americas	$18,710.00
Asia	$14,290.00
Europe	$11,780.00
Finance	$7,010.00
Information Systems	$11,145.00
Marketing	$20,785.00
Oceania	$14,785.00
Operations	$12,995.00
Personnel	$12,505.00
USA	$9,510.00

TABLE I-2: Techniques to copy Access data to other applications

technique	button or menu option	description
Drag and drop	Resize Access window so that the target location (Word or Excel, for example) can also be seen on the screen	With both windows visible, drag the Access table, query, form, or report object icon from the Access window to the target (Excel or Word) window
Export	Use the buttons on the Export section of the External Data tab	Copy information from an Access object into a different file format
Office Clipboard	Copy and Paste	Click the Copy button to copy selected data to the Office Clipboard (the Office Clipboard can hold multiple items); open a Word document or Excel spreadsheet, click where you want to paste the data, then click the Paste button

Merging Data with Word

Another way to export Access data is to merge it to a Word document as the data source for a mail-merge process. In a **mail merge**, data from an Access table or query is combined into a Word form letter, label, or envelope to create mass mailing documents. Jacob Thomas wants to send Quest employees a letter announcing two new continuing education courses. You merge Access data to a Word document to customize a letter to each employee.

STEPS

1. **Click the Employees table in the Navigation Pane, click the External Data tab, then click the Word Merge button in the Export group**

   The **Microsoft Word Mail Merge Wizard** dialog box opens asking whether you want to link to an existing document or create a new one.

2. **Click the Create a new document and then link the data to it option button, click OK, then maximize the Word window**

   Word starts and opens the **Mail Merge task pane**, which steps you through the mail-merge process. Before you merge the Access data with the Word document, you must create the **main document**, the Word document that contains the standard text for each letter in the mail-merge process.

TROUBLE

The "Next" links are at the bottom of the Mail Merge task pane.

3. **Type the standard text shown in Figure I-12, click the Next: Starting document link in the bottom of the Mail Merge task pane, click the Next: Select recipients link to use the current document, click the Next: Write your letter link to use the existing list of names, press [Tab] after To: in the letter, then click the Insert Merge Field button in the Write & Insert Fields group on the Mailings tab**

   The Insert Merge Field dialog box lists all of the fields in the original data source, the Employees table. You use the Insert Merge Field dialog box to insert **merge fields**, codes that are replaced with the values in the field that the code represents when the mail merge is processed.

TROUBLE

You cannot type the merge codes directly into the document. You must use the Insert Merge Field dialog box.

4. **Double-click EFirst, double-click ELast, click Close, click between the EFirst and ELast codes, then press [Spacebar] to insert a space between the codes as shown in Figure I-13**

   With the main document and merge fields inserted, you are ready to complete the mail merge.

5. **Click the Next: Preview your letters link in the Mail Merge task pane, click the Next: Complete the merge link to complete the merge, click the Edit individual letters link to view the letters on the screen, then click OK to complete the merge**

   The mail-merge process combines the EFirst and ELast field values from the Employees table with the main document, creating a 24-page document as shown in the Word status bar. Each page is a customized letter for each record in the Employees table. The first page is a letter to Ron Dawson. "Ron" is the field value for the EFirst field in the first record in the Employees table, and "Dawson" is the field value for the ELast field.

6. **Press [Page Down] several times to view several pages of the final merged document, then close the merged document, Letters1, without saving it**

   You generally don't need to save the final, large merged document. Saving the one-page main document, however, is a good idea in case you need to repeat the merge process.

TROUBLE

The main document may display the data from the first record in the Access employees table, Ron Dawson, instead of the merge codes.

7. **Click the Save button 💾 on the Quick Access toolbar, navigate to the drive and folder where you store your Data Files, enter Employees in the File name text box, click Save, then close Word**

FIGURE I-12: Creating the main document in Word

Mailings tab

Insert Merge Field button

Standard text

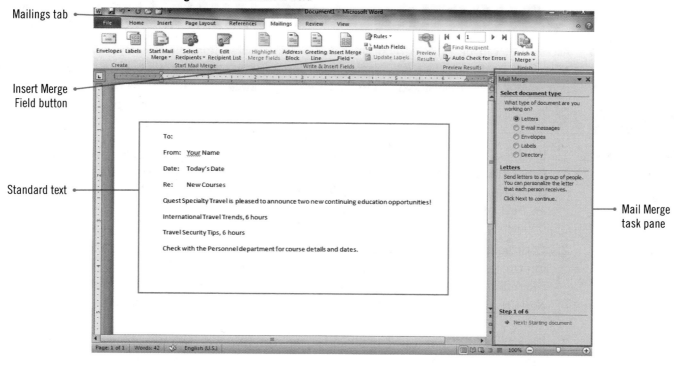

Mail Merge task pane

FIGURE I-13: Inserting merge fields

EFirst merge code

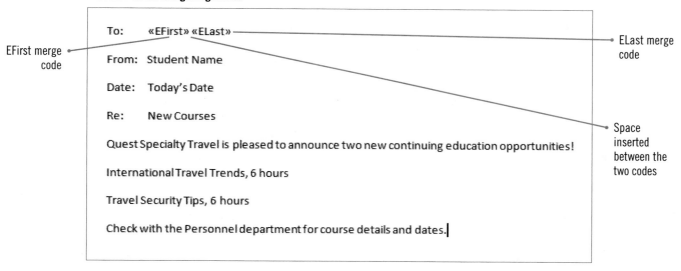

ELast merge code

Space inserted between the two codes

Collecting Data with Outlook

Access data can be collected and entered into the database from e-mail messages using Outlook. **Microsoft Outlook** is the e-mail program in Microsoft Office, a fast electronic method to share information. Jacob Thomas asks you to make sure all employee information in the Education database is up to date. You will distribute this information and collect updates using Outlook e-mail messages.

STEPS

1. **Double-click the Employees table in the Navigation Pane, tab to the EE-mail field, enter your Outlook e-mail address, close the Employees table, click the External Data tab, click the Create E-mail button in the Collect Data group, then read the steps in the wizard**

   An **Outlook data collection wizard** helps you through the steps of collecting Access data through Outlook e-mail.

2. **Click Next, click Next to accept an HTML form message, click the Update existing information option button, click Next, click the Select All Fields button >> , click Next, click the Automatically process replies and add data to Employees check box, then click Next**

   Now that you've specified how to send and process the e-mail, the wizard asks about the recipients' e-mail addresses.

3. **Click Next to accept the EE-mail field in the current table, click Next to accept the default subject and introduction text, click Next to create the e-mail messages, click Next to see the e-mail addresses that are selected, click the Select All check box to clear it, click the check box for the e-mail address you entered in Step 1, then click Send**

   To view the e-mail that has been sent, you would open Outlook and display the Sent Items folder. The e-mail message includes the employee data for the first record in the Employees table as shown in Figure I-14.

4. **Complete the Outlook portion of this lesson by starting Outlook, double-click the e-mail message in your Inbox that you sent from Access in Step 1 to open it, click Reply, enter your name in the ELast and EFirst fields, then click Send**

   If you cannot complete the Outlook portion of this lesson, you can still review the settings on your e-mail data collection processes using the Manage Replies button.

5. **Return to the Education-I database, then click the Manage Replies button in the Collect Data group**

   The Manage Data Collection Messages dialog box opens in Access to provide details of the data collection process as shown in Figure I-15. In Outlook, a folder named **Access Data Collection Replies** collects and helps you manage the e-mails initiated by Access and responses to them.

6. **Click Close to close the Manage Data Collection Messages dialog box, and if you completed the task to update the record via an Outlook e-mail in Step 4, double-click the Employees table to review the first record**

   If you completed all of the steps, you used Access to send an e-mail that contained Access data from the first record of the Employees table. You used Outlook to respond to that e-mail, editing both the EFirst and ELast fields. You then returned to Access, opened the Employees table, and made sure that the edits you made to the first record in the Employees table in an Outlook e-mail message were automatically applied in the Access database, as shown in Figure I-16.

7. **Close the Employees table, close the Education-I.accdb database, then close Access 2010 and Outlook**

FIGURE I-14: Reviewing e-mails sent in Outlook

Reply button

E-mail address of sender

E-mail address of recipient

ELast field

EFirst field

In this exercise, your e-mail address appears for both sender and recipient

Data for Ron Dawson, first record in Employees table

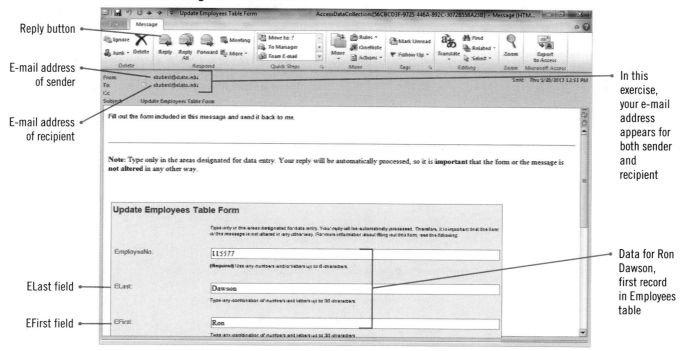

FIGURE I-15: Manage Data Collection Messages dialog box

Manage Replies button

Create E-mail button

Each e-mail sent is identified in this list

E-mail management options

Fields in message

Responses are processed automatically

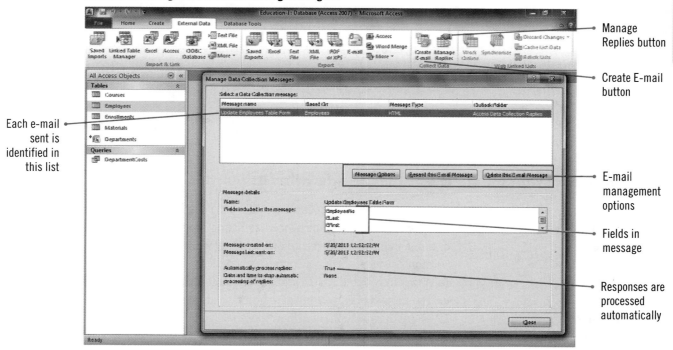

FIGURE I-16: Employees table updates

ELast	EFirst	EDepartment	ETitle	DateHired	EmployeeNo	EEmail
StudentLast	StudentFirst	Marketing	Vice President	2/15/2000	11-55-77	student@state.edu
Lane	Keisha	Operations	Vice President	3/22/2000	13-47-88	klane@quest.com
Wong	Grace	Finance	Vice President	8/20/2002	17-34-22	gwong@quest.com
Ramirez	Juan	Personnel	Director	8/6/2003	22-33-44	jramirez@quest.com
Owen	Gail	Africa	Tour Developer	1/3/2007	23-45-67	gowen@quest.com

Practice

For current SAM information, including versions and content details, visit SAM Central (http://www.cengage.com/samcentral). If you have a SAM user profile, you may have access to hands-on instruction, practice, and assessment of the skills covered in this unit. Since various versions of SAM are supported throughout the life of this text, check with your instructor for the correct instructions and URL/Web site for accessing assignments.

Concepts Review

Identify each element of the database window shown in Figure I-17.

FIGURE I-17

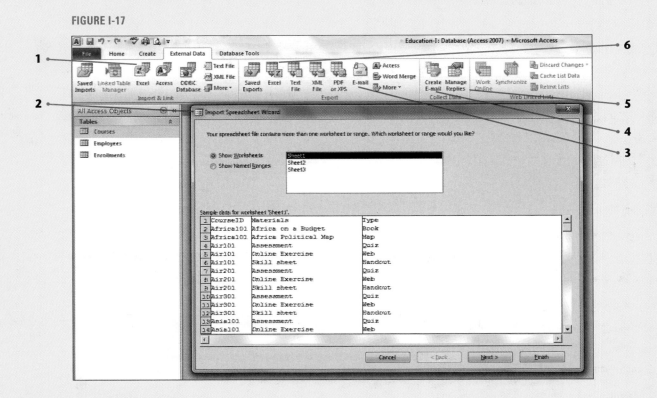

Match each term with the statement that best describes its function.

7. **Exporting**

8. **Main document**

9. **Linking**

10. **Delimited text file**

11. **Mail merge**

12. **Importing**

13. **Database template**

14. **Table template**

a. A tool used to quickly create a single table within an existing database

b. A file used to determine how a letter and Access data will be combined

c. A file that stores one record on each line, with the field values separated by a common character such as a comma, tab, or dash

d. A way to copy Access information to another database, spreadsheet, or file format

e. The process of converting data from an external source into an Access database

f. A way to connect to data in an external source without copying it

g. A tool used to quickly create a new database based on a particular subject such as assets, contacts, events, or projects

h. To combine data from an Access table or query into a Word form letter, label, or envelope to create mass mailing documents

Select the best answer from the list of choices.

15. Which of the following is *not* true about database templates?

   a. Microsoft provides online templates in areas such as business and personal database applications.

   b. They create multiple database objects.

   c. They analyze the data on your computer and suggest database applications.

   d. They cover a wide range of subjects including assets, contacts, events, or projects.

16. Which of the following is *not* true of exporting?

   a. Access data can be exported into Excel.

   b. Access data can be exported to Word.

   c. Exporting retains a link between the original and target data files.

   d. Exporting creates a copy of data.

17. Which of the following is *not* a file format that Access can import?

   a. Excel

   b. Access

   c. HTML

   d. Word

18. Which of the following software products would most likely be used to help electronically merge Access data to a list of e-mail addresses?

   a. Word

   b. Access

   c. Outlook

   d. Excel

19. Which is *not* true about enforcing referential integrity?

   a. It is required for all one-to-many relationships.

   b. It prevents records from being deleted in the "one" side of a one-to-many relationship that have matching records on the "many" side.

   c. It prevents records from being created in the "many" side of a one-to-many relationship that do not have a matching record on the "one" side.

   d. It prevents orphan records.

20. Which of the following is *not* true about linking?

   a. Linking copies data from one data file to another.

   b. Access can link to data in an HTML file.

   c. Access can link to data in an Excel spreadsheet.

   d. You can edit linked data in Access.

21. How does an imported table differ from a table created in Access?

   a. They do not differ.

   b. The imported table is merely a link to the original source data.

   c. There is no data in an imported table.

   d. The imported table displays an imported table icon.

Skills Review

1. **Use database templates.**
   a. Start Access 2010 and use the Assets database template within Office.com to build a new Access database with the name **Assets-I**. Save the new database in the drive and folder where you store your Data Files. (*Hint*: This step requires that you are connected to the Internet to download online templates.)
   b. Click the New User link in the Login dialog box, enter your e-mail and full name, click Save & Close, click your name, then click Login.
   c. In the Main form, click all of the tabs—Current Assets, Retired Assets, Users, Report Center, and Getting Started—to explore the database.
   d. Right-click the Main form tab, then click Close.
   e. Expand the Navigation Pane, then explore several other tables, queries, forms, and reports to familiarize yourself with the database created by the Assets template. Note that each of the objects in this database displays the Web-compatible icon, showing that if this database were published to a Microsoft SharePoint server, users could access each object using a browser such as Internet Explorer, Safari, or Firefox.
   f. Close all objects but leave the new Assets-I.accdb database open.

2. **Use Application Parts.**
   a. Use the Issues table template in Application Parts to create a new table in the Assets-I.accdb database named Issues.
   b. Creating a new table with the Application Parts automatically closes and reopens the database, so you are presented with the initial Login dialog box each time you use Application Parts. When prompted with the Login dialog box, click your name and then click Login.
   c. Click Next to accept the relationship of one Assets record to many Issues records, then click Create to accept the other default options on the relationship.
   d. Note that the new Issues table also sports the Web-compatible icon. Double-click the Issues table to open and study it in Datasheet View.
   e. Close all open objects, then use the Application Parts feature to create a new Dialog form.
   f. When prompted with the Login dialog box, click your name and click Login.
   g. Double-click the new Web-compatible Dialog form in the Navigation Pane to view it.
   h. Return to the Main form, then explore the links in the Help Videos and Get more help sections as desired.
   i. Close all open objects, then close the Assets-I.accdb database.

3. **Import data from Excel.**
   a. Open the Machinery-I.accdb database from the drive and folder where you store your Data Files. Enable content if prompted.
   b. Import the MachineryEmp.xlsx spreadsheet, which contains employee information, from the drive and folder where you store your Data Files to a new table in the current database, using the Import Spreadsheet Wizard to import the data. Make sure that the first row is specified as the column headings.
   c. Choose the EmployeeNo field as the primary key, and import the data to a table named **Employees**. Do not save the import steps.
   d. In Table Design View for the Employees table, change the Data Type of the EmployeeNo field to Number. Save the table and click Yes when prompted. The EmployeeNo field values are from 1 to 6. No data will be lost. Close the Employees table.

4. **Link data from Excel.**
   a. Link to the Vendors.xlsx Excel file stored on the drive and folder where you store your Data Files.
   b. In the Link Spreadsheet Wizard, specify that the first row contains column headings.
   c. Name the linked table **Vendors**.

Skills Review (continued)

d. Open the Relationships window, and display all five field lists in the window. Link the tables together with one-to-many relationships, as shown in Figure I-18. Be sure to enforce referential integrity on all relationships except for the relationship between Products and the linked Vendors table.

e. Save and close the Relationships window.

5. Export data to Excel.

a. Open the Products table to view the datasheet, then close it.

b. Export the Products table data to an Excel spreadsheet named **Products.xlsx**. Save the spreadsheet to the drive and folder where you store your Data Files. Do not save the export steps.

FIGURE I-18

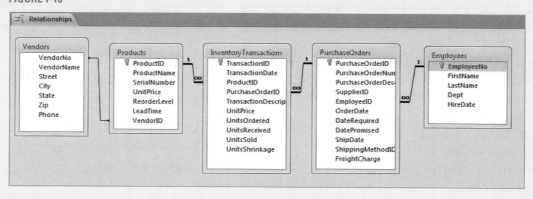

6. Publish data to Word.

a. In the Machinery-I.accdb database, export the Products table to a Word document named **Products.rtf**. Save the Products.rtf file in the drive and folder where you store your Data Files. Do not save the export steps.

b. Start Word, open the Products.rtf document from the drive and folder where you store your Data Files. Press [Enter] twice, press [Ctrl][Home] to return to the top of the document, then type the following text:

INTERNAL MEMO

From:	**Your Name**
To:	**Sales Staff**
Date:	**Today's date**

Do not forget to mention the long lead times on the Back Hoe, Thatcher, and Biodegrader to customers. We usually do not keep these items in stock.

c. Proofread the document, then save and print it. Close the document, then exit Word.

7. Merge data with Word.

a. In the Machinery-I.accdb database, merge the data from the Employees table to a Word document.

b. Use the "Create a new document and then link the data to it" option in the Microsoft Word Mail Merge Wizard dialog box. In the Word document, enter the following text as the main document for the mail merge.

Date:	**Today's date**
To:	
From:	**Your Name**
Re:	**CPR Training**

The annual CPR Training session will be held on Friday, February 26, 2013. Please sign up for this important event in the lunchroom. Friends and family over 18 years old are also welcome.

c. To the right of **To:**, press [Tab] to position the insertion point at the location for the first merge field.

d. Click the Next links at the bottom of the Mail Merge task pane to move to Step 4 of 6, click the Insert Merge Field button, then use the Insert Merge Field dialog box to add the FirstName and LastName fields to the main document.

e. Close the Insert Merge Field dialog box, and insert a space between the <<FirstName>> and <<LastName>> merge codes.

f. Complete the mail-merge process to merge all records in the Employees table to the letter.

Skills Review (continued)

g. Print the last page of the merged document if required by your instructor (the letter to Don Balch), then close the six-page final merged document without saving changes.

h. Save the main document with the name **CPR.docx**, then exit Word.

8. **Collect data with Outlook.**

(*Note:* Steps 8a–8h require that you have a valid Outlook e-mail address to both send and receive e-mail, and Outlook 2010 or later installed and configured on the computer you are using. If not, read but do not perform the following steps.)

a. In the Machinery-I database, click the Products table in the Navigation Pane, then click the Create E-mail button on the External Data tab.

b. Choose HTML Form, choose to Collect new information only, select all fields from the Products form, and choose to automatically process replies and add data to Products.

c. Choose to Enter the e-mail addresses in Microsoft Outlook, accept the default Subject and Introduction text, and click Create.

d. Enter your Outlook e-mail address, and click Send.

e. Open Outlook, double-click the new message that you sent yourself through Access, click Reply, and enter a new record using the form as follows:

Product Name: **Wood Chipper**

Serial Number: **12345**

Unit Price: **99.95**

Reorder Level: **10**

Lead Time: **20**

VendorID: **1**

f. When you have the e-mail form filled out, click Send.

g. Return to the Machinery-I.accdb database and open the Products table to make sure that the new record for the Wood Chipper was automatically added to the database. Note that the time required to update the database varies between systems so you may have to wait a few seconds before the new record is entered.

h. Once you have confirmed that the Products table has been successfully updated, close the Machinery-I.accdb database and exit Access 2010 and Outlook.

Independent Challenge 1

As the manager of a women's college basketball team, you have created a database called Basketball-I that tracks the players, games, and player statistics. You want to link to an Excel file that contains information on the player's course load. You also want to export a report to a Word document in order to add a paragraph of descriptive text.

a. Open the database Basketball-I.accdb from the drive and folder where you store your Data Files. Enable content if prompted.

b. In the Relationships window, connect the Games and Stats tables with a one-to-many relationship based on the common GameNo field. Connect the Players and Stats tables with a one-to-many relationship based on the common PlayerNo field. Be sure to enforce referential integrity on both relationships. Save and close the Relationships window.

c. Export the Player Statistics report to Word with the name **Player Statistics.rtf**. Save the Player Statistics.rtf document in the drive and folder where you store your Data Files. Do not save the export steps.

d. Start Word and open the Player Statistics.rtf document.

e. Press [Enter] three times to enter three blank lines at the top of the document, then press [Ctrl][Home] to position the insertion point at the top of the document.

f. Type your name on the first line of the document, enter today's date as the second line, then write a sentence or two that explains the Player Statistics data that follows. Save, print, and close the Player Statistics document.

g. Exit Word. Close the Basketball-I.accdb database, then exit Access.

Independent Challenge 2

As the manager of a women's college basketball team, you have created a database called Basketball-I that tracks the players, games, and player statistics. The 2013-2014 basketball schedule has been provided to you as an Excel spreadsheet file. You will import that data and append it to the current Games table.

a. Open the database Basketball-I.accdb from the drive and folder where you store your Data Files. Enable content if prompted.

b. If the relationships haven't already been established in this database, create relationships as described in Step b of Independent Challenge 1.

c. Open the Games table to observe the datasheet. It currently contains 22 records with scores for the 2012-2013 basketball season.

d. Start Excel and open the 2013-2014Schedule.xlsx file from the drive and folder where you store your Data Files. Note that it contains 22 rows of data indicating the opponent, mascot, home or away status, and date of the games for the 2013-2014 season. You have been told that the data will import more precisely if it is identified with the same field names as have already been established in the Games table in Access, so you'll insert those field names as a header row in the Excel spreadsheet.

e. Click anywhere in row 1 of the 2013-2014Schedule.xlsx spreadsheet, click the Insert button in the Cells group, and click Insert Sheet Rows to insert a new blank row.

f. In the new blank row 1, enter the field names that correspond to the field names in the Games table for the same data above each column: **Opponent**, **Mascot**, **Home-Away**, and **GameDate**. Be careful to enter the names precisely as shown.

g. Save and close the 2013-2014Schedule.xlsx spreadsheet, exit Excel, and return to the Basketball-I.accdb database.

h. Close the Games table, click the External Data tab, click the Excel button on the Import & Link group, browse for the 2013-2014Schedule.xlsx spreadsheet in your data files, and choose the Append a copy of the records to the table option button. Be sure that Games is selected as the table to use for the append process.

i. Follow the steps of the Import Spreadsheet Wizard process through completion (do not save the import steps), then open the Games table. It should contain the original 22 records for the 2012-2013 season plus 22 more from the 2013-2014Schedule.xlsx spreadsheet with default values of 0 for both the HomeScore and OpponentScore fields.

j. Change the Opponent value in the first record to your last name's College, then print the first page of the Games table if requested by your instructor.

k. Save and close the Games table, close the Basketball-I.accdb database, then exit Access.

Independent Challenge 3

You have been asked by a small private school to build a database to track library books. You decide to explore Microsoft database templates to see if there is a tool that could help you get started.

a. Create a new database using the Lending library database template from the Personal category of online templates. Enable content if prompted. Name the database **Lending library.accdb**, and store it in the drive and folder where you store your Data Files.

b. Read and then close the Access Help window. Enable content, if prompted, then close the Asset List form.

Independent Challenge 3 (continued)

c. Review the Relationships window. Rearrange the field lists as shown in Figure I-19, then print the Relationships report. Save the report with the default name, **Relationships for Lending library**, then close it.

FIGURE I-19

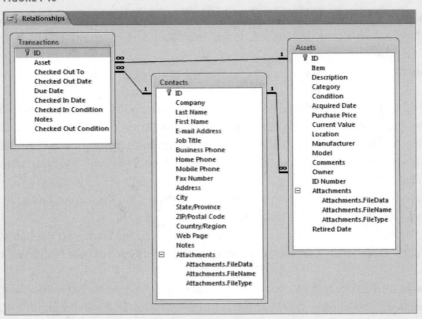

d. Save and close the Relationships window.

e. Expand the Contacts group in the Navigation Pane, double-click the Contact Details form to open it, then enter your name in the First Name and Last Name text boxes. Enter fictional but reasonable data for each field, but do not enter anything for the Notes field. Close the Contacts Details form.

Advanced Challenge Exercise

- Click the Lending library title bar in the Navigation Pane, then choose Object Type.
- In Design View of the Assets table, select the Category field, then delete the existing entry in the Default Value property.
- For the Category field, change the Row Source property on the Lookup tab to **Book;Movie;Music**.
- Select the Location field, then change the Row Source property on the Lookup tab to **East;Midwest;West**.
- Save the table, then display it in Datasheet View and test the lookup properties for the Category and Location fields.
- Save and close the Assets table, and explore the other forms and reports created by the Lending Library database template as desired.

f. Close the Lending library.accdb database, then exit Access.

Real Life Independent Challenge

This Independent Challenge requires an Internet connection.

Learning common phrases in a variety of foreign languages is extremely valuable if you travel or interact with people from other countries. As a volunteer with the foreign student exchange program at your college, you have created a database that documents the primary and secondary languages used by foreign countries. The database also includes a table of common words and phrases that you can use to practice basic conversation skills.

a. Open the Languages-I.accdb database from the drive and folder where you store your Data Files. Enable content if prompted.

Real Life Independent Challenge (continued)

b. Open the datasheets for each of the three tables to familiarize yourself with the fields and records. The Primary and Secondary fields in the Countries table represent the primary and secondary languages for that country. Close the datasheets for each of the three tables.

c. Open the Relationships window, and create a one-to-many relationship between the Languages and Countries table using the LanguageID field in the Languages table and the Primary field in the Countries table. Enforce referential integrity on the relationship.

d. Create a one-to-many relationship between the Languages and Countries tables using the LanguageID field in the Languages table and the Secondary field in the Countries table. Click No when prompted to edit the existing relationship, and enforce referential integrity on the new relationship. The field list for the Languages table will appear twice in the Relationships window with Languages_1 as the title for the second field list as shown in Figure I-20. The Words table is used for reference and does not have a direct relationship to the other tables.

e. Create a Relationships report, then display it in Design View.

f. Add a label to the Report Header section with your name, change the font color of the new label to black, then save the report with the name **Relationships for Language-I**.

g. Print the report if requested by your instructor, and close it.

h. Save and close the Relationships window.

i. Connect to the Internet and go to www.ask.com, www.about.com, or any search engine. Your goal is to find a Web site that translates English to other languages, and to print the home page of that Web site.

j. Add a new field to the Words table with a new language that isn't already represented. Use the Web site to translate the existing three words into the new language. Add three new words or phrases to the Words table, making sure that the translation is made in all of the represented languages: English, French, Spanish, German, Italian, Portuguese, Polish, and the new language you added.

k. Print the updated datasheet for the Words table, close the Words table, close the Languages-I.accdb database, then exit Access.

FIGURE I-20

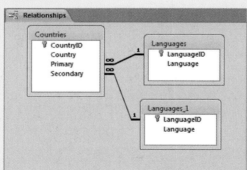

Visual Workshop

Start Access and open the Basketball-I.accdb database from the drive and folder where you store your Data Files. Enable content if prompted. Merge the information from the Players table to a form letter. The first page of the merged document is shown in Figure I-21. Notice that the player's first and last names have been merged to the first line and that the player's first name is merged a second time in the first sentence of the letter. Be very careful to correctly add spaces as needed around the merge fields. Print the last page of the merged document if requested by your instructor, close the 13-page final merged document without saving it, save the main document as **Champs.docx**, then close it.

FIGURE I-21

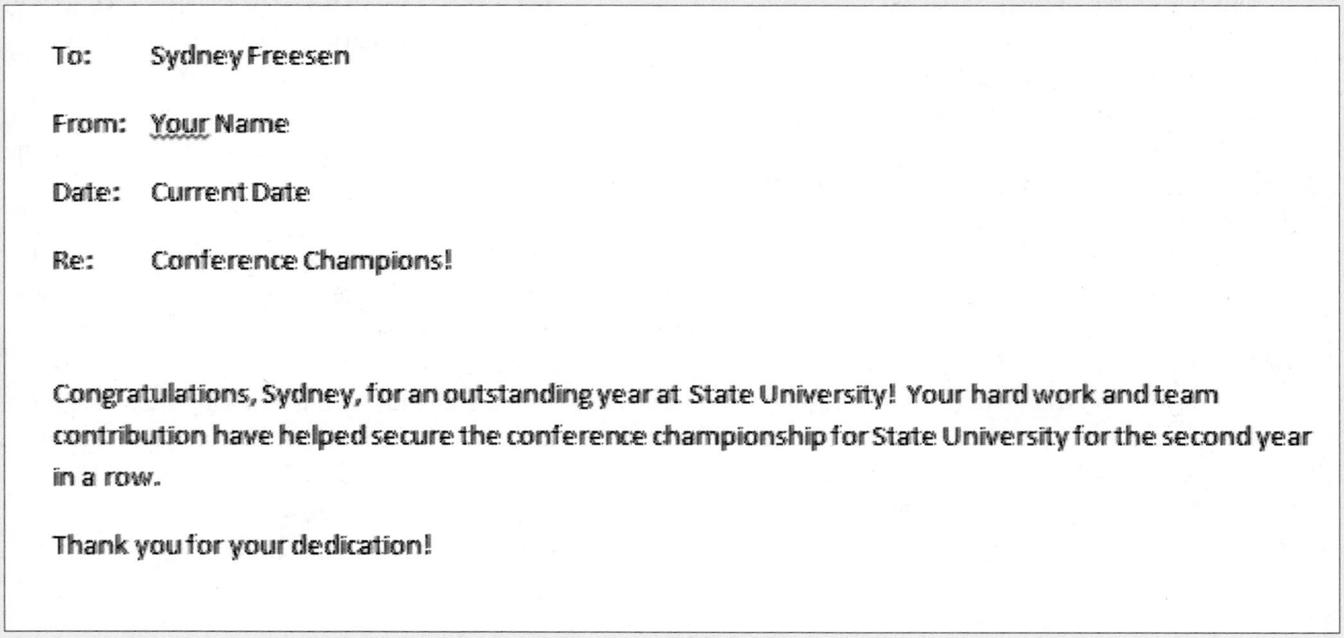

To: Sydney Freesen

From: Your Name

Date: Current Date

Re: Conference Champions!

Congratulations, Sydney, for an outstanding year at State University! Your hard work and team contribution have helped secure the conference championship for State University for the second year in a row.

Thank you for your dedication!

Importing and Exporting Data

Analyzing Database Design Using Northwind

Files You Will Need:

Northwind.mdb
Education-J.accdb
Basketball-J.accdb
RealEstate-J.accdb
JobSearch-J.accdb
QuestDives-J.accdb

Over time, hundreds of hours are often spent designing and modifying Access database files as users discover new ways to analyze and apply the data. One of the best ways to teach yourself advanced database skills is to study a well-developed database. Microsoft provides a fully developed database example called **Northwind**, which illustrates many advanced database techniques that you can apply to your own development needs.  You work with Jacob Thomas, director of staff development at Quest Specialty Travel, to examine the Microsoft Northwind database and determine what features and techniques could be applied to improve the Education database.

OBJECTIVES

Normalize data

Analyze relationships

Evaluate tables

Improve fields

Use subqueries

Modify joins

Analyze forms

Analyze reports

Normalizing Data

Normalizing data means to structure it for a relational database. A normalized database reduces inaccurate and redundant data, decreases storage requirements, improves database speed and performance, and simplifies overall database maintenance. It also helps you create accurate queries, forms, and reports. ▄▄▄▄ Jacob Thomas asks you to study the Northwind database to learn techniques you could use to improve the Education-J database.

1. **Start Access, open the Northwind.mdb database from the drive and folder where you store your Data Files, enable content if prompted, then click OK if the Welcome to Northwind Traders window opens**

   Northwind.mdb, a database in the Access 2000 file format, was provided by Microsoft with Access 2000, Access 2002, and Access 2003 to help you learn about relational databases and Access. Access 2010 can open and work with an Access database in a 2000 or 2002-2003 file format.

2. **Double-click the Categories table in the Navigation Pane, press [Tab] to move from one field to another, note the number of records in the Current Record box, close the datasheet, then open, observe, and close each of the seven other tables**

   A clue that data might need to be better normalized is repeating data in any field. The tables of the Northwind database contain few fields with unnecessary repeating data. You look for repeating data in the fields of the Education-J database.

3. **Start a second session of Access, then open the Education-J.accdb database from the drive and folder where you store your Data Files, enabling content if prompted**

4. **Double-click the Employees table in the Navigation Pane**

   The Department and Title fields both contain repeating data. You decide to further normalize the Department data by creating a Departments table that uses a one-to-many relationship to the Employees table.

5. **Close the Employees datasheet, click the Create tab, click the Table Design button in the Tables group, type Department as the field name, press [Tab], click the Primary Key button in the Tools group, save the table with the name Departments, then close it**

6. **Double-click the new Departments table in the Navigation Pane, then enter the values shown in Figure J-1**

7. **Save and close the Departments datasheet, right-click the Employees table in the Navigation Pane, then click Design View**

   You can use the Lookup Wizard to establish the Department field in the Employees table as the foreign key field linked to the Department field in the Departments table.

8. **Click the Department field in the Data Type column, click the list arrow in the Text Data Type cell, click Lookup Wizard, click Next to look up values in a table, click Table: Departments, click Next, double-click Department as the selected field, click Next, click the first sort arrow, click Department, click Next, click Next, click Finish, then click Yes**

9. **Click the View button 🔳 to switch to Datasheet View, click any record in the Department field, then click the field list arrow as shown in Figure J-2**

   The Departments and Employees tables are now linked in a one-to-many relationship, which provides the valid Department choices for the Department field in the Employees table. Now data entry for that field will be faster, more consistent, and more accurate.

FIGURE J-1: Departments datasheet

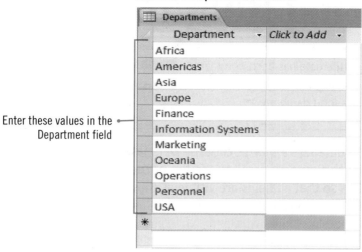

Enter these values in the Department field

Department	▾	Click to Add	▾
Africa			
Americas			
Asia			
Europe			
Finance			
Information Systems			
Marketing			
Oceania			
Operations			
Personnel			
USA			

FIGURE J-2: Department field of the Employees datasheet

Last ▾	First ▾	Department ▾	Title ▾	DateHired ▾	EmployeeN(▾	Click to Add ▾
⊞ Dawson	Ron	Marketing	Vice President	2/15/2000	11-55-77	
⊞ Lane	Keisha	Operations	Vice President	3/22/2000	13-47-88	
⊞ Wong	Grace	Finance	Vice President	8/20/2002	17-34-22	
⊞ Ramirez	Juan	Africa	Director	8/6/2003	22-33-44	
⊞ Owen	Gail	Americas	Tour Developer	1/3/2007	23-45-67	
⊞ Latsky	Ellen	Asia	Tour Developer	7/1/2004	32-10-68	
⊞ Hoppengarth	Wim	Europe	Tour Developer	1/1/2005	33-38-37	
⊞ McDonald	Nancy	Finance	Tour Developer	9/23/2007	33-44-09	
⊞ Opazo	Derek	Information System	Tour Developer	4/8/2003	34-58-99	
⊞ Long	Jessica	Marketing	Marketing Manager	3/1/2004	34-78-13	
⊞ Rock	Mark	Oceania	Tour Developer	2/25/2007	42-42-42	
⊞ Rice	Julia	Operations	Staff Development Manage	1/10/2001	45-99-11	
⊞ Arnold	Martha	Personnel	Staff Assistant	3/1/2006	55-11-22	
⊞ Hosta	Boyd	USA / Africa	Staff Assistant	8/16/2005	55-66-77	

Click the Department list arrow to display the values in the Department field

Understanding third normal form

The process of normalization can be broken down into degrees, which include **first normal form (1NF)**, a single two-dimensional table with rows and columns; **second normal form (2NF)**, where redundant data in the original table is extracted, placed in a new table, and related to the original table; and **third normal form (3NF)**, where calculated fields (also called derived fields) such as totals or taxes are removed. In an Access database, calculated fields can be created "on the fly" using a query, which means that the information in the calculation is automatically produced and is always accurate based on the latest updates to the database. Strive to create databases that adhere to the rules of third normal form.

Analyzing Relationships

The relationships between tables determine the health and effectiveness of a database. The Relationships window shows how well the data has been normalized.  You study the Relationships window of the Northwind database to see if you can apply the techniques used with the relationships of Northwind to the relationships of the Education-J database.

STEPS

QUICK TIP

Move field lists by dragging their title bars.

1. **In the Northwind database window, click the Database Tools tab, click the Relationships button, maximize the window, scroll to the top of the window as needed, then resize and move the field lists so that all fields are visible as shown in Figure J-3**

   Notice that all of the relationships between the tables are one-to-many relationships with referential integrity enforced. Recall that referential integrity helps prevent orphan records—records in the "many" (child) table that do not link to a matching record in the "one" (parent) table.

2. **Switch to the Education-J database window, close the Employees datasheet, click the Database Tools tab, click the Relationships button, then click All Relationships**

   The Lookup Wizard created a one-to-many relationship between the Departments and Employees tables using the common Department field, but you still need to add referential integrity to the relationship. Recall that you may enforce referential integrity on a relationship if orphan records do not exist in the "many" table.

TROUBLE

If you could not enforce referential integrity, that means you made a data-entry error in the Departments table. Open the Departments table in Datasheet View, edit your data to match Figure J-1, then redo Step 3.

3. **Double-click the link line between the Departments and Employees tables, click the Enforce Referential Integrity check box, click OK, then drag the title bars of the field lists to look like Figure J-4**

   Most relationships between tables are "one-to-many." **One-to-one relationships** are rare and occur when the primary key field of the first table is related to the primary key field of a second table. In other words, one record in the first table is related to one and only one record in the second table. An example of when a one-to-one relationship would be appropriate is when you want to separate sensitive information such as emergency contact information from an employee table that stores basic demographic data. One employee record would be linked to one record stored in the emergency contacts table.

4. **Click the Save button 🖫 on the Quick Access toolbar, close the Education-J database, then switch to the Northwind database window**

   A **many-to-many relationship** cannot be created directly between two tables in Access. However, two tables have a many-to-many relationship when they are both related to the same intermediate table, called the **junction table**, with one-to-many relationships. Note that the Employees and Shippers tables have a many-to-many relationship, as do the Employees and Customers tables in the Northwind database. In each case, the Orders table is the junction table.

   Also note that the Order Details table has a **multifield primary key** that consists of the OrderID and ProductID fields. In other words, an OrderID value can be listed multiple times in the Order Details table, and a ProductID value can be listed multiple times in the Order Details table. But the combination of a particular OrderID value plus a ProductID value should be unique for each record.

FIGURE J-3: Northwind.mdb relationships

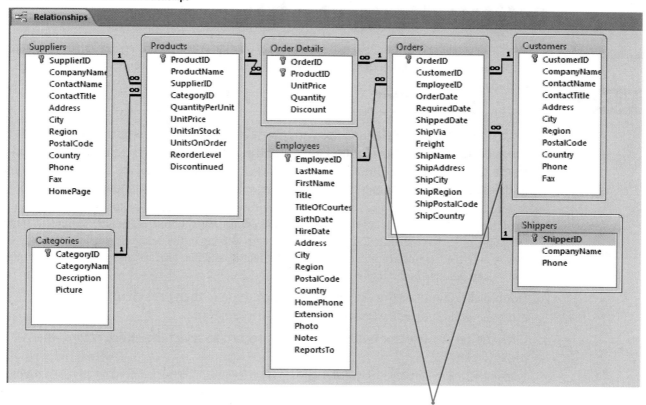

All relationships in the Northwind database
have referential integrity enforced

FIGURE J-4: Education-J.accdb relationships

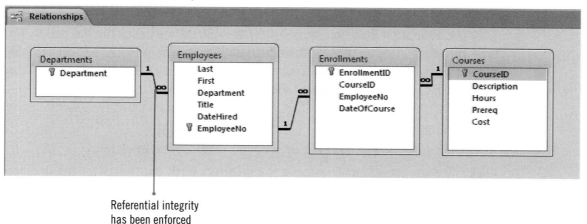

Referential integrity
has been enforced

Evaluating Tables

Access offers several table features that make analyzing existing data and producing results, such as datasheet subtotals, much easier and faster. ▓▓▓▓ You review the tables of the Northwind database to analyze data and to study table properties.

STEPS

1. **Close the Northwind Relationships window, save the layout if prompted, double-click the Products table in the Navigation Pane, click the Totals button in the Records group on the Home tab, scroll to the Units In Stock field, click the Total cell for the Units In Stock field at the end of the datasheet, click the list arrow, then click Sum as shown in Figure J-5**

   A subtotal of the units in stock, 3119, appears in the Total cell for the Units In Stock field. As shown in the Totals list, a numeric field allows you to calculate the Average, Sum, Count, Maximum, Minimum, Standard Deviation, or Variance statistic for the field. If you were working in the Total cell of a Text field, you could choose only the Count statistic. Notice that the Current Record box displays the word "Totals" to indicate that you are working in the Total row.

2. **Double-click Totals in the Current Record box, type 6, then press [Enter]**

   Access moves the focus to the Units In Stock field of the sixth record.

3. **Click the record selector button of the sixth record to select the entire record, then press [Delete]**

   Working with a well-defined relational database with referential integrity enforced on all relationships, you are prevented from deleting a record in a "one" (parent) table if the record is related to many records in a "many" (child) table. In this case, the sixth record in the Products table is related to several records in the Order Details table, and therefore it cannot be deleted. Next, you examine table properties.

4. **Click OK, close the Products table, click Yes to save changes to the layout, right-click the Employees table, click Design View, then click the Property Sheet button in the Show/Hide group to open the Property Sheet**

   The Property Sheet for a table controls characteristics for the entire table object, such as an expanded description of the table, default view, and validation rules that use more than one field. In this case, you can prevent data-entry errors by specifying that the HireDate field value is greater than the BirthDate field value. Because two fields are used in the Validation Rule expression, you should enter the rule in the table Property Sheet instead of in the Validation Rule property of an individual field.

5. **Click the Validation Rule box, type [HireDate]>[BirthDate], click the Validation Text box, type Hire date must be greater than birth date as shown in Figure J-6, click the Save button 🖫 on the Quick Access toolbar, click Yes, then click the View button 🔲 on the Design tab to switch to Datasheet View**

   Test the new table validation rule by entering a birth date greater than the hire date for the first record.

6. **Tab to the Birth Date field, type 5/5/2010, then press [↓]**

   A dialog box opens, displaying the text entered in the Validation Text property.

7. **Click OK, then press [Esc] to remove the incorrect birth date entry for the first record**

FIGURE J-5: Products datasheet with Total row

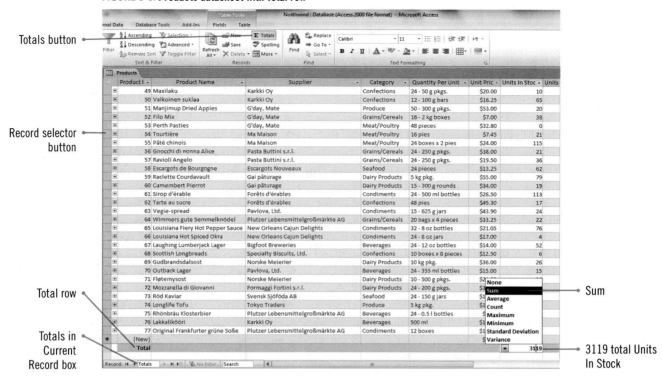

FIGURE J-6: Property Sheet for Employees table

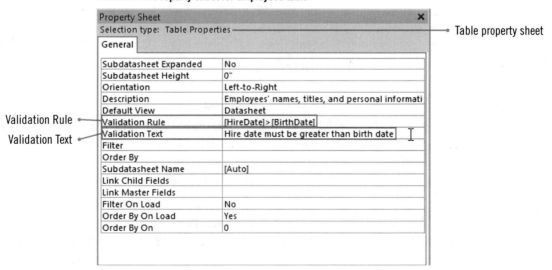

Improving Fields

To improve and enhance database functionality, the Northwind database also employs several useful field properties, such as Caption, Allow Zero Length, and Index.  You review the Northwind database to study how lesser-used field properties have been implemented in the Employees table.

1. **Click the View button 🔲 to switch to Design View, close the Property Sheet, click the EmployeeID field, then press [↓] to move through the fields of the Employees table while observing the Caption property in the Field Properties pane**

    The Northwind database uses the Caption property on all fields that consist of two words, such as HireDate, to separate the words with a space, as in Hire Date. The **Caption** property text is displayed as the default field name at the top of the field column in datasheets as well as in labels that describe fields on forms and reports.

2. **Select Reports To in the Caption property of the ReportsTo field, then type Manager**

    The Caption property doesn't have to match the field name. Use the Caption property any time you want to clarify or better describe a field for the users, but prefer not to change the actual field name.

3. **Click the HireDate field, then change the Indexed property to Yes (Duplicates OK)**

    An **index** keeps track of the order of the values in the indexed field as data is being entered and edited. Therefore, if you often sort on a field, the Index property should be set to Yes so that Access can sort and present the data faster. The Index property improves database performance when a field is often used for sorting because it creates the index for the sort order as data is being entered, rather than building the index from scratch when the field is used for sorting. Fields that are not often used for sort orders should have their Index property set to No because creating and maintaining indexes is a productivity drain on the database. You can sort on any field at any time, whether the Index property is set to Yes or No.

4. **Click the HomePhone field and examine the Allow Zero Length property**

    Currently, the **Allow Zero Length** property is set to No, meaning zero-length strings ("") are not allowed. A zero-length string is an *intentional* "nothing" entry (as opposed to a **null** entry, which also means that the field contains nothing, but doesn't indicate intent). Zero-length strings are valuable when you want to show that the "nothing" entry is on purpose. For example, some employees might intentionally *not* want to provide a home phone number. In those instances, a zero-length string entry is appropriate. Note that you query for zero-length strings using "" criteria, whereas you query for null values using the operator **Is Null**.

    QUICK TIP
    A description of the current property is displayed in the lower-right corner of Table Design View.

5. **Double-click the Allow Zero Length property to switch the choice from No to Yes as shown in Figure J-7**

    With the field changes in place, you test them in Datasheet View.

6. **Click the View button 📇 to switch to Datasheet View, click Yes to save the table, tab to the Home Phone field, enter "" (two quotation marks without a space), tab to the Extension field, enter "", then press [Tab]**

    An error message appears, as shown in Figure J-8, indicating that you cannot enter a zero-length string in the Extension field.

7. **Click OK to acknowledge the error message, press [Esc], press [Tab] three more times to observe the Manager caption for the ReportsTo field, then close the Employees table**

FIGURE J-7: Changing field properties in the Employees table

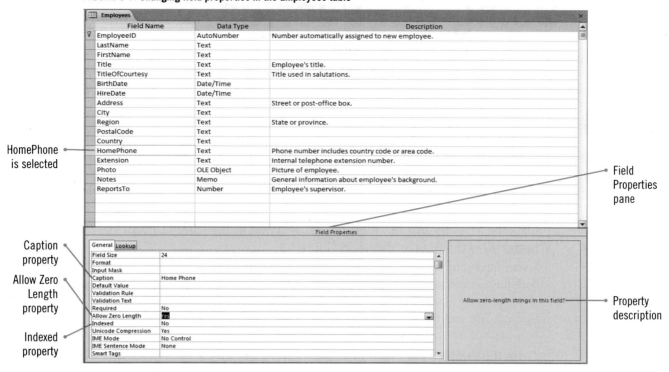

HomePhone is selected

Field Properties pane

Caption property

Allow Zero Length property

Indexed property

Property description

FIGURE J-8: Testing field properties in the Employees table

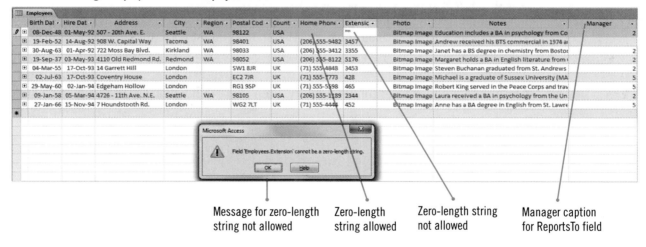

Message for zero-length string not allowed

Zero-length string allowed

Zero-length string not allowed

Manager caption for ReportsTo field

Using Memo fields

Use Memo fields when you need to store more than 256 characters in a field, which is the maximum Field Size value for a Text field. Fields that store comments, reviews, notes, or other ongoing conversational information are good candidates for the Memo data type.

Set the **Append Only** property to Yes to allow users to add data to a Memo field, but not to change or remove existing data. The Append Only property is available for Memo fields in Access 2007 databases created in Access 2007 or Access 2010.

Using Subqueries

The Northwind database contains several interesting queries that demonstrate advanced query techniques, such as grouping on more than one field, using functions in calculated fields, and developing subqueries, which you might not have studied yet. ██████ You work in the Northwind database to study how to use advanced query techniques, including subqueries.

STEPS

1. **Double-click the Product Sales for 1995 query to view the datasheet**

   This query summarizes product sales by product name for the year 1995. The datasheet includes 77 records, and each record represents one product name. The third column summarizes product sales for the product name. To analyze the construction of the query, switch to Design View.

2. **Click the View button ▨, then resize the panes in the Query Design View window to better view the data as shown in Figure J-9**

   Several interesting techniques have been used in the construction of this query. The records are grouped by both the CategoryName and the ProductName fields. A calculated field, ProductSales, is computed by first multiplying the UnitPrice field from the Order Details table by the Quantity field, then subtracting the Discount. The result of this calculation is subtotaled using the Sum function. In addition, the ShippedDate field contains criteria so that only those sales between the dates of 1/1/1995 and 12/31/1995 are selected.

3. **Close the Product Sales for 1995 query, saving changes if prompted, then double-click the Category Sales for 1995 query in the Navigation Pane to open the query datasheet**

   This query contains only eight records because the sales are summarized (grouped) by the Category field and there are only eight unique categories. The CategorySales field summarizes total sales by category. To see how this query was constructed, switch to Design View.

4. **Click ▨ to switch to Design View, then resize the field list and the panes in the Query Design View window to display all of the fields**

   Note that the field list for the query is based on the Product Sales for 1995 query, as shown in Figure J-10. When a query is based on another query's field list, the field list is called a **subquery**. In this case, the Category Sales for 1995 query used the Product Sales for 1995 as its subquery to avoid having to re-create the long ProductSales calculated field.

5. **Close the Category Sales for 1995 query, then click No if you are asked to save changes**

Analyzing Database Design Using Northwind

FIGURE J-9: Design View of the Product Sales for 1995 query

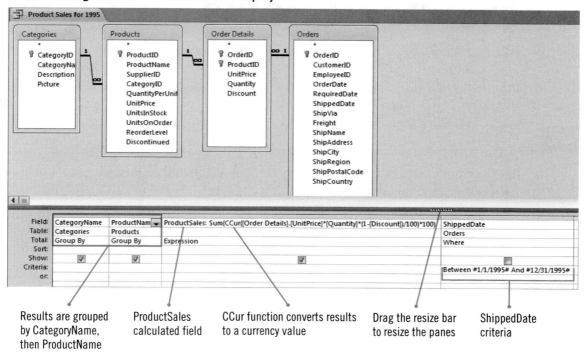

Results are grouped by CategoryName, then ProductName

ProductSales calculated field

CCur function converts results to a currency value

Drag the resize bar to resize the panes

ShippedDate criteria

FIGURE J-10: Using the Product Sales for 1995 query as a subquery

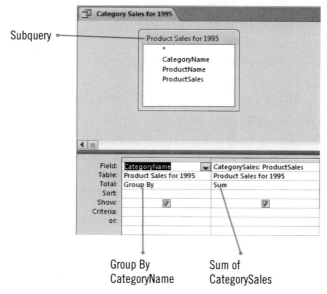

Subquery

Group By CategoryName

Sum of CategorySales

Modifying Joins

When you create a query based on multiple tables, only records that have matching data in each of the field lists present in the query are selected. This is due to the default **inner join** operation applied to the one-to-many relationship between two tables. Other join types are described in Table J-1. They help select records that do not have a match in a related table. You use the Northwind database and modify the join operation to find records in the Customers table that do not have a matching record in the Orders table.

STEPS

1. **Click the Create tab, click the Query Design button in the Queries group, double-click Customers, double-click Orders, then click Close**

2. **Double-click the CompanyName in the Customers table, double-click the OrderDate in the Orders table, double-click Freight in the Orders table, then click the View button 🔳 to view the datasheet**

   This query selects 830 records using the default inner join between the tables. An inner join means that records are selected only if a matching value is present in both tables. Therefore, any records in the Customers table that did not have a related record in the Orders table would not be selected. You modify the join operation to find those customers.

3. **Click the View button 🔳 to switch to Design View, then double-click the middle of the one-to-many relationship line between the tables to open the Join Properties dialog box shown in Figure J-11**

   The Join Properties dialog box provides information regarding how the two tables are joined and also allows you to change from the default inner join (option 1) to a left outer join (2) or right outer join (3).

QUICK TIP
Use SQL View of a query to view the SQL for an inner, left, or right join.

4. **Click the 2 option button, click OK, then resize the field lists so that you can see all the fields as shown in Figure J-12**

   The arrow pointing to the Orders table indicates that the join line has been modified to be a left outer join. With join operations, "left" always refers to the "one" table of a one-to-many relationship regardless of where the table is physically positioned in Query Design View.

5. **Click 🔳 to view the datasheet**

   The datasheet now shows 832 records, two more than when an inner join operation was used. To find the two new records quickly, use Is Null criteria.

6. **Click 🔳 to return to Design View, click the Criteria cell for the OrderDate field, type Is Null, then click 🔳 to view the datasheet again**

   The datasheet now only shows two records as shown in Figure J-13, the two customers who do not have any matching order records. Left outer joins are very useful for finding records on the "one" side of a relationship (parent records) that do not have matching records on the "many" side (child records).

   When referential integrity is enforced on a relationship before data is entered, it is impossible to create records on the "many" side of a relationship that do not have matching records on the "one" side (orphan records). Therefore, a right outer join operation is very useful to help find orphan records in a poorly designed database, but a right outer join operation would not be useful in the Northwind database because referential integrity has been applied on all relationships since the tables were created.

7. **Save the query as CustomersWithoutOrders, then close the query and the Northwind.mdb database**

FIGURE J-11: **Join Properties dialog box**

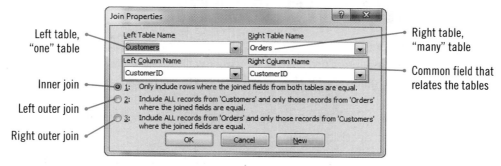

Left table, "one" table — Left Table Name: Customers; Left Column Name: CustomerID

Right table, "many" table — Right Table Name: Orders; Right Column Name: CustomerID

Common field that relates the tables

Inner join — 1: Only include rows where the joined fields from both tables are equal.

Left outer join — 2: Include ALL records from 'Customers' and only those records from 'Orders' where the joined fields are equal.

Right outer join — 3: Include ALL records from 'Orders' and only those records from 'Customers' where the joined fields are equal.

FIGURE J-12: **Left outer join line**

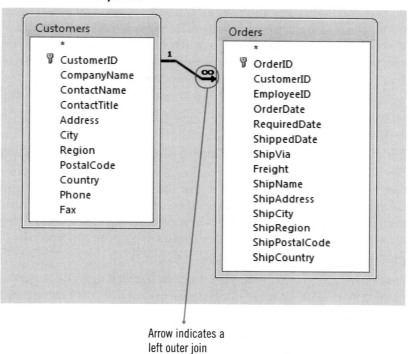

Arrow indicates a left outer join

FIGURE J-13: **Customers without orders**

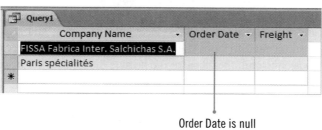

Order Date is null

TABLE J-1: **Join operations**

join operation	description
inner	Default join; selects records from two related tables in a query that have matching values in a field common to both tables
left outer	Selects all the records from the left table (the "one" table in a one-to-many relationship) even if the "one" table doesn't have matching records in the related "many" table
right outer	Selects all the records from the right table (the "many" table in a one-to-many relationship) even if the "many" table doesn't have matching records in the related "one" table

Analyzing Forms

Database developers create forms to provide a fast and easy-to-use interface for database users. In a fully developed database, users generally do not work with individual objects or the Navigation Pane. Rather, they use forms to guide all of their activities. The Northwind database provides several examples of sophisticated forms used to easily navigate and work with the data in the underlying database. You examine Northwind forms to gain an understanding of how well-designed forms could be applied to the databases at Quest Specialty Travel.

STEPS

TROUBLE

If you click the "Don't show this screen again" check box on the Startup form, you will not see the splash screen when you open the Northwind database.

1. **Reopen the** Northwind.mdb **database**

   When the Northwind database opens, a splash screen appears as shown in Figure J-14. A **splash screen** is a special form used to announce information. To create a splash screen, you create a new form in Form Design View with the labels, graphics, and command buttons desired, plus you set the **Border Style** property of the form to None. You also set the following form properties to No: **Record Selectors**, **Navigation Buttons**, **Scroll Bars** (Neither), **Control Box**, **Min Max Buttons** (None).

   To automatically load the splash screen when the database opens, set the **Display Form option** in the Current Database category of the Options dialog box to the name of the form you want to open when the database starts. In this case, the name of the splash screen form is Startup.

2. **Click OK, then double-click the** Main Switchboard form **in the Navigation Pane**

   The Main Switchboard form opens as shown in Figure J-15. A **switchboard** is a special form used to help users navigate throughout the rest of the database. A switchboard contains command buttons to give users fast and easy access to the database objects they use. A switchboard form is created in Form Design View using many of the same form properties used to create a splash screen. Also note that the Record Source property for the splash screen and switchboard forms is not used because neither form is used for data entry.

3. **Click the** Orders command button

   The Orders form opens for the first of 830 orders. This form shows the attractiveness and sophistication of a well-developed form. You modify the first order to learn about the form's capabilities.

4. **Click the** Bill To: combo box arrow, **click** Around the Horn, **click the** Salesperson combo box arrow, **click** King, Robert, **click the** Spegesild list arrow **(the first product in the order), click** Steeleye Stout, **press** [Tab], **type** 20 **for the Quantity value, press** [Tab], **enter** 50% **for the Discount value, then press** [Tab]

   The first order in the Orders form should look like Figure J-16. The Orders form is a traditional Access form in that it is used to enter and edit data. The form uses combo boxes and calculations (in the extended price, subtotal, and total text boxes) to make data entry fast, easy, and accurate. Also notice the Print Invoice command button used to print the current record, the current invoice. Well-designed forms contain a command button to print the *current* record because the regular Print button will print *all* records (in this case, all 830 orders).

5. **Right-click the** Orders tab, **then click** Close

   Northwind contains many other forms you can explore later to learn more about form design and construction.

FIGURE J-14: Northwind splash screen form, Startup

Welcome to Northwind Traders, a sample database you can use to learn about Microsoft Access. You can experiment with the data stored in Northwind, and use the forms, reports, and other database objects as models for your own database.

All the objects in Northwind are available from the Database window, which will be displayed when you click OK. In the Database window, you can display descriptions of the objects by clicking Details on the View menu.

☐ Don't show this screen again.   OK

The names of companies, products, people, characters, and/or data mentioned herein are fictitious and are in no way intended to represent any real individual, company, product, or event, unless otherwise noted.

FIGURE J-15: Northwind switchboard form, Main Switchboard

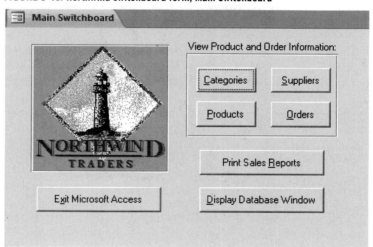

Main Switchboard

View Product and Order Information:

Categories   Suppliers

Products   Orders

Print Sales Reports

Exit Microsoft Access   Display Database Window

FIGURE J-16: Northwind Orders form

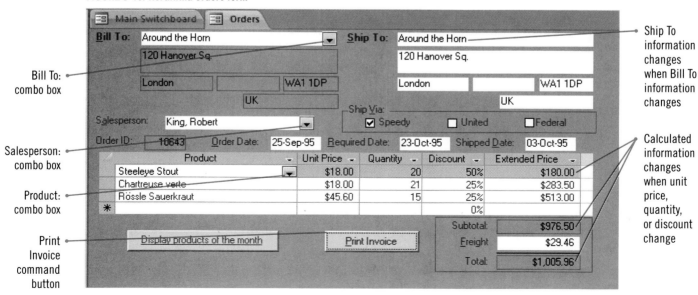

Bill To: combo box

Salesperson: combo box

Product: combo box

Print Invoice command button

Ship To information changes when Bill To information changes

Calculated information changes when unit price, quantity, or discount change

Main Switchboard   Orders

Bill To: Around the Horn
120 Hanover Sq.
London   WA1 1DP
UK

Ship To: Around the Horn
120 Hanover Sq.
London   WA1 1DP
UK

Salesperson: King, Robert

Ship Via: ☑ Speedy   ☐ United   ☐ Federal

Order ID: 10643   Order Date: 25-Sep-95   Required Date: 23-Oct-95   Shipped Date: 03-Oct-95

Product	Unit Price	Quantity	Discount	Extended Price
Steeleye Stout	$18.00	20	50%	$180.00
Chartreuse verte	$18.00	21	25%	$283.50
Rössle Sauerkraut	$45.60	15	25%	$513.00
*			0%	

Display products of the month   Print Invoice

Subtotal:	$976.50
Freight:	$29.46
Total:	$1,005.96

Analyzing Reports

In a fully developed database, the database designer creates reports for the printed information needs of the users. In a well-designed database, the user can select what data they want the report to display by making choices in a dialog box or by using parameter criteria in a query on which the report is based.  You study some reports in the Northwind database to gain new ideas and skills.

STEPS

1. **Click the Print Sales Reports command button on the Main Switchboard form**

   A form, the Sales Reports dialog box shown in Figure J-17, opens. A **dialog box** is a type of form used to make choices to modify the contents of another query, form, or report. In this case, the selections you make in the Sales Reports dialog box will help you create a specific report.

   > **QUICK TIP**
   > The Record Source property of a report identifies the record-set (table or query) on which the report is based.

2. **Click the Sales by Category option button to enable the Category list box**

   In a well-designed form, controls are often enabled and disabled based on choices the user makes. In this case, the Category list box is enabled only if the Sales by Category option button is selected. You will learn how to modify a form to respond to user interaction when you work with Visual Basic for Applications (VBA.)

3. **Click the Employee Sales by Country option button, click Preview, type 1/1/1995 in the Beginning Date text box, click OK, type 12/31/1995 in the Ending Date text box, click OK, then click the report to display it at 100% zoom, if necessary**

   The Employee Sales by Country report opens in Print Preview, as shown in Figure J-18. It is based on the Employee Sales by Country query, which contains parameter criteria that prompted you for the beginning and ending dates to select the desired data for this report.

   The Employee Sales by Country report presents several advanced report techniques including a calculated date expression in the Report Header section, multiple grouping levels, and a watermark effect. The watermark effect is achieved by specifying the desired watermark image, in this case Confidential.bmp, in the report's **Picture** property.

4. **Right-click the Employee Sales by Category report tab, click Close All, then close the Northwind.mdb database and exit Access**

   The Northwind.mdb database provides many sample objects from which you can learn a great deal. Microsoft provided this database so you can analyze several objects and techniques, and apply what you learn to your own Access databases.

FIGURE J-17: Sales Reports dialog box

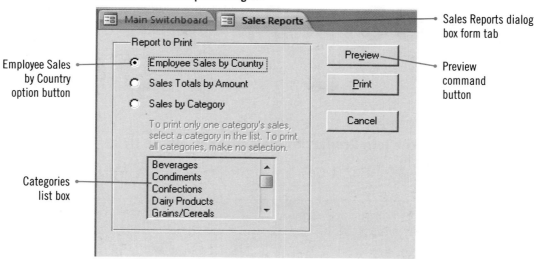

Sales Reports dialog box form tab

Employee Sales by Country option button

Preview command button

Categories list box

FIGURE J-18: Employee Sales by Country report

Expression based on date criteria

Records are grouped by country and salesperson

Confidential watermark

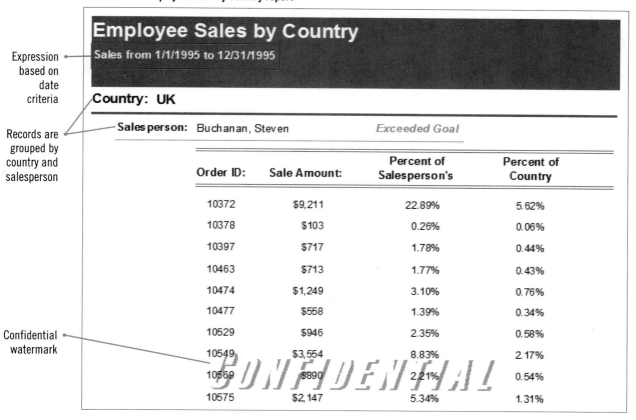

Employee Sales by Country

Sales from 1/1/1995 to 12/31/1995

Country: UK

Salesperson: Buchanan, Steven — *Exceeded Goal*

Order ID:	Sale Amount:	Percent of Salesperson's	Percent of Country
10372	$9,211	22.89%	5.62%
10378	$103	0.26%	0.06%
10397	$717	1.78%	0.44%
10463	$713	1.77%	0.43%
10474	$1,249	3.10%	0.76%
10477	$558	1.39%	0.34%
10529	$946	2.35%	0.58%
10549	$3,554	8.83%	2.17%
10569	$890	2.21%	0.54%
10575	$2,147	5.34%	1.31%

Practice

Concepts Review

For current SAM information, including versions and content details, visit SAM Central (http://www.cengage.com/samcentral). If you have a SAM user profile, you may have access to hands-on instruction, practice, and assessment of the skills covered in this unit. Since various versions of SAM are supported throughout the life of this text, check with your instructor for the correct instructions and URL/Web site for accessing assignments.

Identify each element of the Join Properties dialog box in Figure J-19.

FIGURE J-19

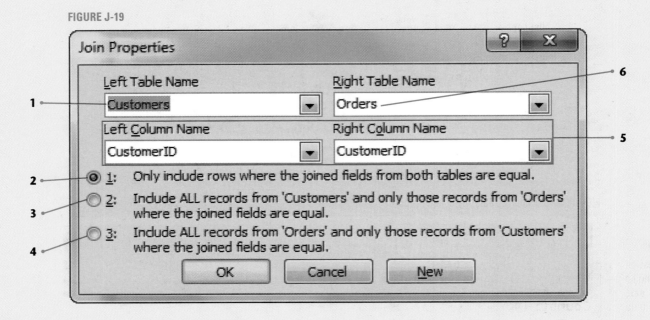

Match each term with the statement that best describes its function.

7. **Normalization**
8. **Caption**
9. **Index**
10. **Subquery**
11. **Zero-length string**

a. An *intentional* "nothing" entry
b. Displayed as the default field name at the top of the field column in datasheets as well as in labels that describe fields on forms and reports
c. Keeps track of the order of the values in the indexed field as data is entered and edited
d. Created when a query is based on another query's field list
e. The process of structuring data into a well-formed relational database

Select the best answer from the list of choices.

12. Which of the following is *not* a benefit of a well-designed relational database?
   a. Reduces redundant data
   b. Improves reporting flexibility
   c. Is easier to create than a single-table database
   d. Has lower overall storage requirements

13. First normal form can be described as:
   a. Any collection of data in any form.
   b. A single two-dimensional table with rows and columns.
   c. A series of queries and subqueries.
   d. A well-functioning, fully developed relational database.

14. Which of the following activities occurs during the creation of second normal form?
   a. Calculated fields are removed from tables.
   b. Additional calculated fields are added to tables.
   c. Redundant data is removed from one table, and relationships are created.
   d. One-to-one relationships are examined and eliminated.

15. Which of the following activities occurs during the creation of third normal form?
   a. Calculated fields are removed from tables.
   b. Additional calculated fields are added to tables.
   c. Redundant data is removed from one table, and relationships are created.
   d. One-to-one relationships are examined and eliminated.

16. One-to-one relationships occur when:
   a. The foreign key field of the first table is related to the primary key field of a second table.
   b. The foreign key field of the first table is related to the foreign key field of a second table.
   c. The primary key field of the first table is related to the foreign key field of a second table.
   d. The primary key field of the first table is related to the primary key field of a second table.

17. A multifield primary key consists of:
   a. One field.
   b. An AutoNumber field.
   c. A primary key field that also serves as a foreign key field.
   d. Two or more fields.

18. Which of the following is *not* true for the Caption property?
   a. It is the default field name at the top of the field column in datasheets.
   b. The value of the Caption property is the default label that describes a field on a report.
   c. The value of the Caption property is the default label that describes a field on a form.
   d. It is used instead of the field name when you build expressions.

19. Which of the following fields would most likely be used for an index?
   a. MiddleName
   b. ApartmentNumber
   c. LastName
   d. FirstName

20. Which of the following phrases best describes the need for both null values and zero-length strings?
   a. They represent two different conditions.
   b. Having two different choices for "nothing" clarifies data entry.
   c. Null values speed up calculations.
   d. They look different on a query datasheet.

Skills Review

1. Normalize data.

  a. Start Access, open the Education-J.accdb database from the drive and folder where you store your Data Files, and enable content if prompted.

  b. Double-click the Employees table to view its datasheet. Notice the repeated data in the Title field. Close the Employees datasheet. You will build a lookup table to better manage the values in the Title field.

  c. Click the Create tab, click Table Design, then create a table with one field, **TitleName**. Give it a Text data type, and set it as the primary key field.

  d. Save the table with the name **Titles**, and enter the data in the datasheet shown in Figure J-20. Be very careful to type the data exactly as shown. Save and close the Titles table when you are finished.

FIGURE J-20

Titles	
TitleName	
Director	
Marketing Manager	
President	
Staff Assistant	
Staff Development Manager	
Tour Developer	
Vice President	

  e. Open the Employees table in Design View, click the Title field, then choose Lookup Wizard using the Data Type list arrow.

  f. Choose the "I want the lookup column to look up the values…" option, click Next, choose Table: Titles, select the TitleName field for the list and specify an ascending sort order on the TitleName field, accept the column widths, accept the Title label, click the Enable Data Integrity check box, finish the Lookup Wizard, then click Yes to save the table. (If you were unable to enforce referential integrity, it means you've made a data-entry error in the Titles table. Open the Titles table in Datasheet View, and check your data against the values in Figure J-20, then redo Step f.)

  g. Close Table Design View for the Employees table, open the Relationships window, click the All Relationships button, then drag the title bar of the field lists to match Figure J-21.

FIGURE J-21

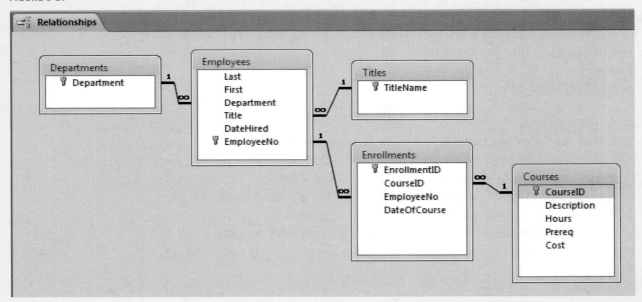

  h. Save and close the Relationships window, then close the Education-J.accdb database.

Skills Review (continued)

2. Analyze relationships.

a. Open the Northwind.mdb database from the drive and folder where you store your Data Files, and enable content if prompted.

b. Click OK to close the splash screen, click the Database Tools tab, then click the Relationships button.

c. It is easy to see that all of the relationships are one-to-many relationships with referential enforced due to the presence of the "1" and "infinity" symbols. When two parent tables both have a one-to-many relationship with the same child table, they are said to have a many-to-many relationship with each other. This database has five many-to-many relationships. Use the following table to identify the tables involved. One many-to-many relationship is provided as an example.

Table 1	Junction Table	Table 2
Employees	Orders	Customers

d. If requested by your instructor, create a Relationships report. Use landscape orientation so that the report is only one page long, and insert your name as a label in the Report Header using black text and a 12-point font size. Save and close the report using the default name, **Relationships for Northwind**.

e. Save and close the Relationships window.

3. Evaluate tables.

a. Open the datasheet for the Order Details table.

b. Tab to the Quantity field, then click the Totals button to open the Total row at the end of the datasheet.

c. Use the Total row to find the Sum of the Quantity field, 51335, which represents the total quantity of products sold for this database.

d. Save and close the Order Details table.

4. Improve fields.

a. Open the Products table in Design View.

b. Change the Caption property for the Unit Price field to **Retail Price**.

c. At the end of the field list, add a new field named **StandardQuantity** with a Number data type and a Caption property of **Standard Quantity**.

d. At the end of the field list, add a new field named **UnitOfMeasure** with a Text data type and a Caption property of **Unit of Measure**.

e. Save the table, then display it in Datasheet View.

f. Enter the correct information into the new Standard Quantity and Unit of Measure fields for the first two records. (Base this on the information currently provided in the Quantity Per Unit field; for example, 10 is the Standard Quantity for the first record, and boxes × 20 bags is the Unit of Measure.)

g. Explain the benefits of separating quantities from their units of measure. (*Hint*: Think about how you find, filter, sort, and calculate data.) If these benefits were significant to your company, you would want to convert the rest of the data from the Quantity Per Unit field to the new Standard Quantity and Unit of Measure fields, too. Once all of the new data was in place, you could delete the original Quantity Per Unit field.

h. Close the Products table datasheet.

Skills Review (continued)

5. Use subqueries.

a. Click the Create tab, then click the Query Design button.

b. Double-click Orders, Order Details, and Products, then click Close.

c. Double-click the OrderDate field in the Orders table, the Quantity and UnitPrice fields in the Order Details table, and the ProductName field in the Products table.

d. In the fifth column, enter the following calculated field:

GrossRevenue:[Quantity]*[Products].[UnitPrice]

Because the UnitPrice field is given the same name in two tables present in this query, you use [TableName].[FieldName] syntax to specify which table supplies these fields.

e. Save the query with the name **GrossRevenue**, then close it.

f. Click the Create tab, then click the Query Design button.

g. Click the Queries tab in the Show Table dialog box, double-click GrossRevenue, then click Close.

h. Double-click the Product Name and GrossRevenue fields, then click the Totals button.

i. Change Group By in the GrossRevenue field to Sum.

j. Open the Property Sheet for the GrossRevenue field, change the Format property to Currency, change the Caption property to **Total Gross Revenue**, then view the resulting datasheet.

k. Save the query with the name **GrossRevenueByProduct**, then close it.

6. Modify joins.

a. Open the Suppliers table in Datasheet View, and enter a record using your own last name as the company name. Enter realistic but fictitious data for the rest of the record, then close the Suppliers table.

b. Click the Create tab, click the Query Design button, double-click Suppliers, double-click Products, then click Close.

c. Double-click CompanyName from the Suppliers table, and ProductName from the Products table. Add an ascending sort order for both fields, then view the datasheet. Note that there are 77 records in the datasheet.

d. Return to Query Design View, then change the join properties to option 2, which will select all Suppliers records even if they don't have matching data in the Products table.

e. View the datasheet, and note it now contains 78 records.

f. Return to Query Design View, and add **Is Null** criteria to the ProductName field.

g. View the datasheet noting that the only supplier without matching product records is the one you entered in Step a. That tells you that every other supplier in the database is related to at least one record in the Products table.

h. Save the query with the name **SuppliersWithoutProducts**, then close it.

7. Analyze forms.

a. Open the Customer Orders form in Form View.

b. Notice that this form contains customer information in the main form and in two subforms. The first subform is for order information, and the second subform shows order details. Navigate to the fourth record, which shows the orders for the company named Around the Horn.

c. Click the Order ID value 10383 in the upper subform, and notice that the order details automatically change in the lower subform as you move from order to order.

d. Explore the form by moving through customer and order records, then ask yourself this question: How would this form be used? As navigation, information, data entry, or as a dialog box that specifies criteria for a query, form, or report?

e. After you're done exploring the Customer Orders form, close it.

8. Analyze reports.

a. Double-click the Sales by Year report.

b. The Sales by Year Dialog form appears. Enter **1/1/95** in the Enter beginning date text box, enter **6/30/95** in the Enter ending date text box, then click OK.

c. The Sales by Year report for the first two quarters of 1995 appears, indicating that 186 orders were shipped during this period. A subreport is used in the ShippedDate Header section to provide summary information for the entire report before the Detail section prints.

d. Close the Sales by Year report, close the Northwind database, and exit Access.

Independent Challenge 1

As the manager of a basketball team, you have created an Access database called Basketball-J.accdb to track players, games, and statistics. You have recently learned how to create lookup tables to better control the values of a field that contain repeated data and to apply your new skills to your database.

a. Start Access, open the Basketball-J.accdb database from the drive and folder where you store your Data Files, and enable content if prompted.

b. Double-click the Players table to view its datasheet. Notice the repeated data in the Position and HomeState fields. You will build lookup tables to better describe and manage the values in those fields. Close the Players datasheet.

c. Click the Create tab, click Table Design, then create a two-field database with the field names **PositionDescription** and **PositionID**. Both fields should have a Text data type. Set PositionID as the primary key field. Save the table with the name **Positions**, and enter the data in the datasheet shown in Figure J-22. Save and close the Positions table.

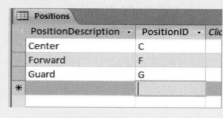

d. Open the Players table in Design View, click the Position field, then choose Lookup Wizard using the Data Type list arrow.

e. Choose the "I want the lookup column to look up the values..." option, choose Table: Positions, choose both fields, choose PositionDescription for an ascending sort order, do not hide the key column, choose PositionID as the field that uniquely identifies the row, accept the Position label, click the Enable Data Integrity check box, finish the Lookup Wizard, then click Yes to save the table. Close the Players table.

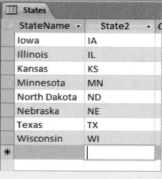

f. Repeat Step c creating a **States** table instead of a Positions table using the field names and data shown in Figure J-23. Make the State2 field the primary key field, then close the States table.

g. Repeat Step d by using the Lookup Wizard with the HomeState field in the Player table to look up data in the States table. Choose both fields, sort in ascending order by the StateName field, do not hide the key column, choose State2 as the field that uniquely identifies the row, accept the HomeState label, click the Enable Data Integrity check box, finish the Lookup Wizard, then click Yes to save the table. Close the Players table.

h. Open the Relationships window, click the All Relationships button to make sure you're viewing all relationships. The final Relationships window should look like Figure J-24.

i. Create a Relationships report with the default name **Relationships for Basketball-J**. If requested by your instructor, print the report, then close it.

j. Save and close the Relationships window, close the Basketball-J.accdb database, then exit Access.

FIGURE J-22

Positions

PositionDescription	PositionID
Center	C
Forward	F
Guard	G

FIGURE J-23

States

StateName	State2
Iowa	IA
Illinois	IL
Kansas	KS
Minnesota	MN
North Dakota	ND
Nebraska	NE
Texas	TX
Wisconsin	WI

FIGURE J-24

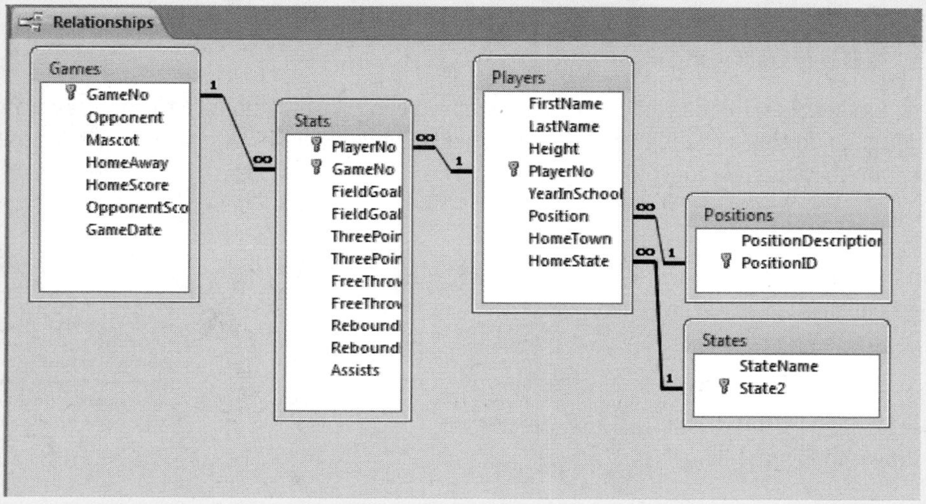

Independent Challenge 2

You have been asked to create a query that displays employees as well as their manager in the same datasheet. Because each employee, regardless of title and rank, is entered as a record in the Employees table, you know that you will need to relate each record in the Employees table to another record in the same table to show the employee–manager relationship. You will work in the Northwind database to learn how to join a table to itself in order to answer this challenge.

a. Start Access, open the Northwind.mdb database from the drive and folder where you store your Data Files, enable content if prompted, and click OK if prompted with the splash screen.

b. Click the Create tab, click the Query Design button, double-click Employees, double-click Employees table a second time, click Close, right-click the Employees_1 field list, click Properties, select Employees_1 in the Alias text box, type **Managers**, press [Enter], then close the Property Sheet. The Employees table relates to itself through the EmployeeID and ReportsTo fields because each employee record reports to another employee whose EmployeeID value has been entered in the ReportsTo field.

c. Resize the panes and the field lists so that you can see all fields, then drag the EmployeeID field in the Managers field list to the ReportsTo field in the Employees field list. In other words, one Manager can be related to many employees.

d. Double-click the LastName field, then double-click the FirstName field in the Managers field list.

e. Double-click the LastName field, then double-click the FirstName field in the Employees field list.

f. Add an ascending sort order on both LastName fields as shown in Figure J-25.

g. Display the query datasheet, then widen each column to display all data. The datasheet shows that three employees report to Buchanan and five report to Fuller.

h. Save the query as **ManagerList**, close the query, then close the Northwind database and exit Access.

FIGURE J-25

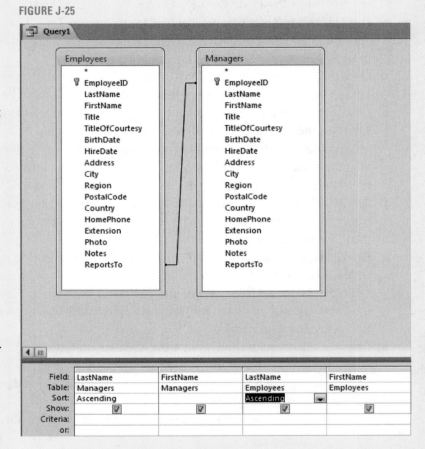

Independent Challenge 3

As the manager of a regional real estate information system, you've been asked to enhance the database to keep track of offers for each real estate listing. To do this you will need to create a new table to track the offers, and relate it to the rest of the database in an appropriate one-to-many relationship.

a. Start Access, open the RealEstate-J.accdb database from the drive and folder where you store your Data Files, and enable content if prompted.

b. Create a table named **Offers** with the fields, data types, descriptions, and primary key shown in Figure J-26.

FIGURE J-26

Field Name	Data Type	
OfferID	AutoNumber	primary key field
ListingNo	Number	foreign key field to Listings table
OfferDate	Date/Time	date of offer
OfferAmount	Currency	dollar value of the offer
Buyer	Text	last name or company name of entity making the offer
Accepted	Yes/No	was offer accepted? yes or no
DateAccepted	Date/Time	date the offer was accepted

Independent Challenge 3 (continued)

Advanced Challenge Exercise

- Use the Lookup Wizard on the ListingNo field in the Offers table to connect the Offers table to the Listings table. Select all the fields from the Listings table, sort in ascending order on the Type, Area, and SqFt fields, hide the key column, store the value in the ListingNo field, accept the ListingNo label for the lookup field, enable data integrity, and finish the wizard. Save the table when prompted.
- In Table Design View, on the Lookup tab for the ListingNo field, change the value for the Column Heads property from No to Yes.
- In Table Design View, on the Lookup tab for the ListingNo field, change the value for the List Rows property from 16 to **100**.
- Save the table, click Yes when asked to check the data, then display it in Datasheet View.
- Enter the record shown in the first row of Figure J-27, using the new combo box for the ListingNo field as shown.

FIGURE J-27

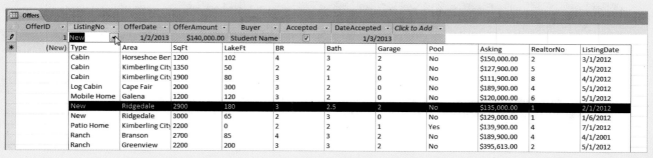

OfferID	ListingNo	OfferDate	OfferAmount	Buyer	Accepted	DateAccepted	Click to Add
1	New	1/2/2013	$140,000.00	Student Name	✓	1/3/2013	
(New)							

Type	Area	SqFt	LakeFt	BR	Bath	Garage	Pool	Asking	RealtorNo	ListingDate
Cabin	Horseshoe Ber	1200	102	4	3	2	No	$150,000.00	2	3/1/2012
Cabin	Kimberling City	1350	50	2	2	2	No	$127,900.00	5	1/5/2012
Cabin	Kimberling City	1900	80	3	1	0	No	$111,900.00	8	4/1/2012
Log Cabin	Cape Fair	2000	300	3	2	0	No	$189,900.00	4	5/1/2012
Mobile Home	Galena	1200	120	3	2	0	No	$120,000.00	6	5/1/2012
New	Ridgedale	2900	180	3	2.5	2	No	$135,000.00	1	2/1/2012
New	Ridgedale	3000	65	2	3	0	No	$129,000.00	1	1/6/2012
Patio Home	Kimberling City	2200	0	2	2	1	Yes	$139,900.00	4	7/1/2012
Ranch	Branson	2700	85	4	3	2	No	$189,900.00	4	4/1/2001
Ranch	Greenview	2200	200	3	3	2	No	$395,613.00	2	5/1/2012

c. Close the Offers table, close the RealEstate-J.accdb database, then exit Access.

Real Life Independent Challenge

An Access database can help record and track your job search efforts. In this exercise, you will work with a database that tracks employers and job positions to better normalize and present the data.

a. Start Access, open the JobSearch-J.accdb database from the drive and folder where you store your Data Files, and enable content if prompted.

b. Open both the Employers and Positions tables in Datasheet View to review the data. One employer may offer many positions, so the tables are related by the common EmployerID field. You decide to add Lookup properties to the EmployerID field in the Positions table to better identify each employer in this view.

c. Close both table datasheets, open the Relationships window, right-click the join line between the Employers and Positions tables, then click Delete. Click Yes to confirm you want to delete the relationship. Before you can start the Lookup Wizard on the EmployerID field in the Positions table, all existing relationships must be deleted.

d. Close the Relationships window, then open the Positions table in Design View.

e. Start the Lookup Wizard for the EmployerID field to lookup values in the Employers table. Select all fields, sort in ascending order on the CompanyName field, hide the key column, select EmployerID if asked to select the field containing the value you want to store, use the EmployerID label, enable data integrity, finish the wizard, then save the table.

f. Display the Positions table in Datasheet View, then test the new Lookup properties on the EmployerID field by changing the EmployerID for both of the "Professor" positions to **JCCC**.

g. Close the Positions table, then start a new query in Query Design View. Add both the Employers and Positions tables.

h. Add the CompanyName field from the Employers table, and the Title and CareerArea fields from the Positions table.

i. Modify the join line to include all records from Employers, then view the datasheet.

j. Save the query with the name **EmployerPositions**, then close it.

k. Close the JobSearch-J.accdb database, then exit Access.

Visual Workshop

Start Access, open the QuestDives-J.accdb database from the drive and folder where you store your Data Files, and enable content if prompted. Add Lookup properties to the DiveMasterID field of the DiveTrips table to achieve the result shown in Figure J-28, which looks up every value from the DiveMasters table for the lookup list and sorts the information on the LName field. First you'll have to delete the existing relationship between the DiveMasters and DiveTrips tables. You'll also want to modify the Lookup properties of the DiveMasterID field so that Column Heads is set to Yes and List Rows is set to 100. Also, be sure that referential integrity is enforced on the final relationship between the DiveMasters and DiveTrips tables.

FIGURE J-28

ID	DiveMasterID	Location	City	State/Province	Country	TripStartDate	Lodging
1	Chow	Great Barrier Reef	Cairns		Australia	5/14/2012	Royal Palm
2						2/7/2013	Travel 6 Inn
3						10/7/2013	Marriott Sands
4						12/30/2012	Fairwind
5						4/30/2011	Fairwind
6						12/16/2012	Fairwind
7						4/26/2013	Sun Breeze
8						4/25/2013	Sun Breeze
9						10/2/2012	Pink Flamingo
10						6/20/2013	Sea Star
11						10/3/2012	Pink Flamingo
12	Stedo	South Shore	Kralendijk		Bonaire	6/21/2013	Sea Star
13	Randal	South Shore	Kralendijk		Bonaire	3/30/2013	Sea Star
14	Randal	South Shore	Kralendijk		Bonaire	5/19/2012	Pink Flamingo
15	Zenk	South Shore	Kralendijk		Bonaire	10/20/2011	Sea Star

Lookup list (overlay):

Name	Address	City	State/Provin	Postal Code	Phone Number
Barnes	333 Elm Avenu	New York City	NY	15875	1117777890
Chow	111 Maple Stre	Filmont	NM	77881	7779110101
Crone	12345 100th Str	Long Beach	CA	90222	9997711234
Fillmore	444 Lincoln Wa	Ft. Dodge	IA	50111	5558887777
Franklin	555 Perry Stree	Key Largo	FL	29922	3338884545
Hend	222 Oak Street	Erie	PA	34567	3332342344
Randal	600 Lenexa Roa	Hartford	CT	12345	2227060500
Stedo	789 Jackson Str	Dallas	TX	68686	6662234343
Tomi	12344 99th Stre	Branson	MO	55880	4448877788
Zenk	128 Main Stree	Green River	FL	24242	3332827799

Analyzing Database Design Using Northwind

Creating Advanced Queries

Queries are database objects that answer questions about the data. The most common query is the **Select query**, which selects fields and records that match specific criteria and displays them in a datasheet. Select queries, including all of their variations such as summary, crosstab, top values, and parameter queries, constitute the majority of queries you will create. Another very powerful type of query is the action query. Unlike Select queries that only *select* data, an **action query** *changes* all of the selected records when it is run. Access provides four types of action queries: Delete, Update, Append, and Make Table.  You use advanced query techniques to help Jacob Thomas handle the requests for information about data stored in the Education database.

OBJECTIVES

Query for top values

Create a parameter query

Modify query properties

Create a Make Table query

Create an Append query

Create a Delete query

Create an Update query

Specify join properties

Find unmatched records

Querying for Top Values

After you enter a large number of records into a database, you want to select only the most significant records by choosing a subset of the highest or lowest values from a sorted query. Use the **Top Values** feature in Query Design View to specify a number or percentage of sorted records that you want to display in the query's datasheet. Employee attendance at continuing education classes has grown at Quest Specialty Travel. To help plan future classes, Jacob Thomas wants a listing of the top five classes, sorted in descending order by the number of attendees for each class. You can create a summary query to find and sort the total number of attendees for each class, then use the Top Values feature to find the five most attended classes.

DETAILS

1. **Start Access, open the Education-K.accdb database, enable content if prompted, click the Create tab, then click the Query Design button in the Queries group**

   You need fields from both the Enrollments and Courses tables.

> **TROUBLE**
> If you add a table's field list to Query Design View twice by mistake, click the title bar of the extra field list, then press [Delete].

2. **Double-click Enrollments, double-click Courses, then click Close in the Show Table dialog box**

   Query Design View displays the field lists of the two related tables in the upper pane of the query window.

3. **Double-click EnrollmentID in the Enrollments field list, double-click Description in the Courses field list, then click the View button to switch to Datasheet View**

   The datasheet shows 443 total records. You want to know how many people took each course, so you need to group the records by the Description field and count the EnrollmentID field.

4. **Click the View button to switch to Query Design View, click the Totals button in the Show/Hide group, click Group By for the EnrollmentID field, click the Group By list arrow, then click Count**

   Sorting is required in order to find the top values.

> **QUICK TIP**
> Click the Datasheet View button as you design a query to view the datasheet at that point in development.

5. **Click the EnrollmentID field Sort cell, click the EnrollmentID field Sort list arrow, then click Descending**

   Your screen should look like Figure K-1. Choosing a descending sort order lists the courses with the highest count value (the most attended courses) at the top of the datasheet.

6. **Click the Top Values list arrow in the Query Setup group**

   The number or percentage specified in the Top Values list box determines which records the query returns, starting with the first record on the sorted datasheet. This is why you *must sort* your records before you use the Top Values feature. See Table K-1 for more information on Top Values options.

7. **Click 5, click to display the resulting datasheet, then widen the first column to show the complete field name**

   Your screen should look like Figure K-2. The datasheet shows the six most attended continuing education courses. The query selected the top six, rather than top five courses because there was a tie for fifth place. Both the USA Hiking Tours I and USA Biking Tours II courses had 18 attendees.

8. **Click the Save button on the Quick Access toolbar, type TopCourses, click OK, then close the datasheet**

   As with all queries, if you enter additional enrollment records into this database, the count statistics in the TopCourses query are automatically updated.

FIGURE K-1: Designing a summary query for top values

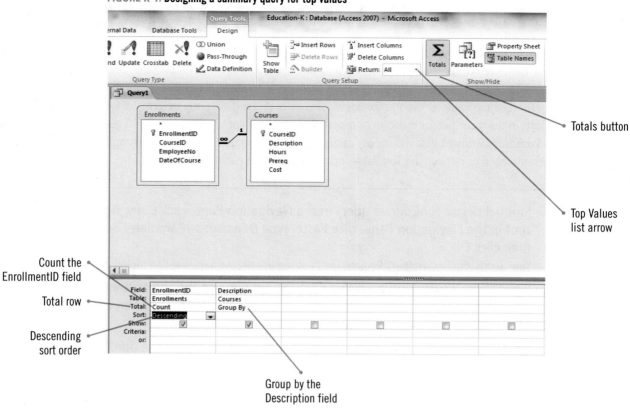

Totals button

Top Values list arrow

Count the EnrollmentID field

Total row

Descending sort order

Group by the Description field

FIGURE K-2: Top Values datasheet

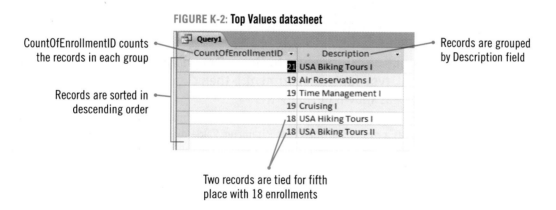

CountOfEnrollmentID counts the records in each group

Records are grouped by Description field

Records are sorted in descending order

Two records are tied for fifth place with 18 enrollments

TABLE K-1: Top Values options

action	displays
Click 5, 25, or 100 from the Top Values list	Top 5, 25, or 100 records
Enter a number, such as 10, in the Top Values text box	Top 10, or whatever value is entered, records
Click 5% or 25% from the Top Values list	Top 5 percent or 25 percent of records
Enter a percentage, such as 10%, in the Top Values text box	Top 10%, or whatever percentage is entered, of records
Click All	All records

Access 2010

Creating a Parameter Query

A **parameter query** displays a dialog box that prompts you for field criteria. Your entry in the dialog box determines which records appear on the final datasheet, just as if you had entered that criteria directly in the query design grid. You can also build a form or report based on a parameter query. When you open the form or report, the parameter dialog box opens. The entry in the dialog box determines which records the query selects in the recordset for the form or report. You want to create a query to display the courses for an individual department that you specify each time you run the query. To do so, you copy the TopCourses query then modify it to remove the Top Values option and include parameter prompts.

STEPS

1. **Right-click the TopCourses query in the Navigation Pane, click Copy, right-click a blank spot in the Navigation Pane, click Paste, type DepartmentParameter as the Query Name, then click OK**

   You modify the DepartmentParameter query to remove the top values and to include the parameter prompt.

2. **Right-click DepartmentParameter, click Design View on the shortcut menu, click the Show Table button in the Query Setup group, double-click Employees, then click Close**

   The Employees table contains the Department field needed for this query.

3. **Drag the title bar of the Courses field list to the left, then drag the title bar of the Enrollments field list to the right so that the relationship lines do not cross behind a field list**

   You are not required to rearrange the field lists of a query, but doing so can help clarify the relationships between them.

4. **Double-click the Department field in the Employees field list, click the Top Values list arrow in the Query Setup group, click All, then click the View button 🖩 to display the datasheet**

   The query now counts the EnrollmentID field for records grouped by Description as well as Department. Because you only want to query for one department at a time, however, you need to add parameter criteria to the Department field.

QUICK TIP
To enter a long crite-rion, right-click the Criteria cell, then click Zoom.

5. **Click the View button 🖾 to return to Query Design View, click the Department field Criteria cell, type [Enter department:], then click 🖩 to display the Enter Parameter Value dialog box as shown in Figure K-3**

   In Query Design View, you must enter parameter criteria within [square brackets]. The parameter criterion you enter appears as a prompt in the Enter Parameter Value dialog box. The entry you make in the Enter Parameter Value box is used as the final criterion for the field that contains the parameter criterion. You can combine logical operators such as greater than (>) or less than (<) as well as wildcard characters such as an asterisk (*) with parameter criteria to create flexible search options. See Table K-2 for more examples of parameter criteria.

QUICK TIP
Query criteria are not case sensitive, so "marketing", "Marketing", and "MARKETING" all yield the same results.

6. **Type Marketing in the Enter department: text box, then click OK**

   Only those records with "Marketing" in the Department field are displayed, a portion of which are shown in Figure K-4. The records are still sorted in descending order by the CountOfEnrollmentID field, and they are grouped by the Description field.

7. **Save and close the DepartmentParameter query**

FIGURE K-3: Using parameter criteria for the Department field

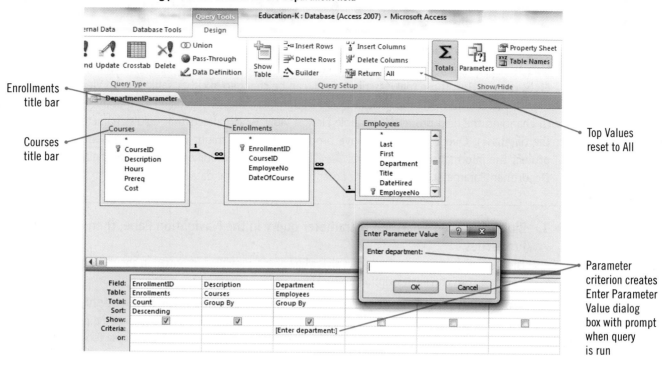

Enrollments title bar

Courses title bar

Top Values reset to All

Parameter criterion creates Enter Parameter Value dialog box with prompt when query is run

FIGURE K-4: Datasheet for parameter query when Department equals Marketing

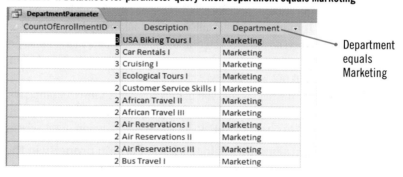

Department equals Marketing

TABLE K-2: Examples of parameter criteria

field data type	parameter criteria	description
Date/Time	>=[Enter start date:]	Searches for dates on or after the entered date
Date/Time	>=[Enter start date:] and <=[Enter end date:]	Prompts you for two date entries and searches for dates on or after the first date and on or before the second date
Text	Like [Enter the first character of the last name:] & "*"	Searches for any name that begins with the entered character
Text	Like "*" & [Enter any character(s) to search by:] & "*"	Searches for words that contain the entered characters anywhere in the field

Modifying Query Properties

Properties are characteristics that define the appearance and behavior of items in the database such as objects, fields, sections, and controls. You can view the properties for an item by opening its Property Sheet. **Field properties**, those that describe a field, can be changed in either Table Design View or Query Design View. If you change field properties in Query Design View, they are modified for that query only (as opposed to changing the field properties in Table Design View, which affects that field's characteristics throughout the database). Query objects also have properties that you might want to modify to better describe or protect the information they provide. You want to modify the query and field properties of the DepartmentParameter query to better describe and present the data.

STEPS

1. **Right-click the DepartmentParameter query in the Navigation Pane, then click Object Properties**
    The DepartmentParameter Properties dialog box opens, providing information about the query and a text box where you can enter a description for the query.

2. **Type Counts enrollments per course description, prompts for Department, then click OK**
    The **Description** property allows you to better document the purpose or author of a query. The Description property also appears on **Database Documenter** reports, a feature on the Database Tools tab that helps you create reports with information about the database.

TROUBLE
The title bar of the Property Sheet always indicates which item's properties are shown. If it shows anything other than "Query Properties," click a blank spot beside the field lists to display query properties.

3. **Right-click the DepartmentParameter query in the Navigation Pane, click Design View on the shortcut menu, then click the Property Sheet button in the Show/Hide group**
    The Property Sheet opens, as shown in Figure K-5. View the Property Sheet for the query in Query Design View to see a complete list of the query's properties including the Description property that you modified earlier. The **Recordset Type** property determines if and how records displayed by a query are locked and has two common choices: Snapshot and Dynaset. **Snapshot** locks the recordset (which prevents it from being updated). **Dynaset** is the default value and allows updates to data. Because a summary query's datasheet summarizes several records, you cannot update the data in a summary query regardless of the Recordset Type property value. For regular Select queries, you can specify Snapshot in the Recordset Type property to give users read (but not write) access to that datasheet.

    To change the field name, you modify the field's **Caption** property in the Property Sheet for field properties. When you click a property in a Property Sheet, a short description of the property appears in the status bar. Press [F1] to open Access Help for a longer description of the selected property.

4. **Click the EnrollmentID field, click the Caption property in the Property Sheet, type Total Enrollment, click the View button ▦, type Marketing as the parameter value, then click OK**
    The Total Enrollment Caption clarifies the first column of data as shown in Figure K-6.

5. **Save and close the DepartmentParameter query**

FIGURE K-5: **Query Property Sheet**

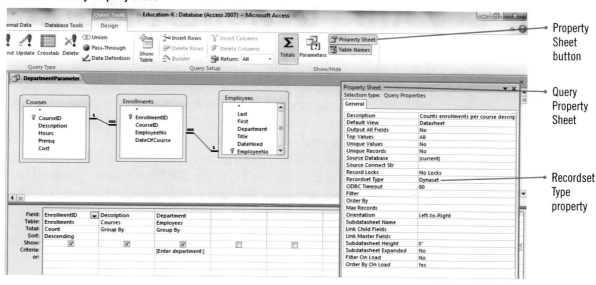

Property Sheet button

Query Property Sheet

Recordset Type property

FIGURE K-6: **Final DepartmentParameter datasheet**

Total Enrollment Caption

Total Enrollment	Description	Department
3	USA Biking Tours I	Marketing
3	Car Rentals I	Marketing
3	Cruising I	Marketing
3	Ecological Tours I	Marketing
2	Customer Service Skills I	Marketing
2	African Travel II	Marketing
2	African Travel III	Marketing
2	Air Reservations I	Marketing
2	Air Reservations II	Marketing
2	Air Reservations III	Marketing
2	Bus Travel I	Marketing

Creating a Make Table Query

An **action query** *changes* many records in one process. The four types of action queries are Delete, Update, Append, and Make Table. For an action query to complete its action, you run the action query using the Run button in Query Design View. Because you cannot undo an action query, it is always a good idea to create a backup of the database before running the query. See Table K-3 for more information on action queries. A **Make Table query** creates a new table of data for the selected datasheet. The Make Table query works like an export feature in that it creates a copy of the selected data and pastes it into a new table in a database specified by the query. The location of the new table can be the current database or another Access database. Sometimes a Make Table query is used to back up data. ▰▰▱▱▱ You decide to use a Make Table query to archive the first quarter's records for the year 2012 that are currently stored in the Enrollments table.

STEPS

1. **Click the Create tab, click the Query Design button, double-click Enrollments in the Show Table dialog box, click Close, then close the Property Sheet if it is open**

2. **Double-click the * (asterisk) at the top of the Enrollments field list**

   Adding the asterisk to the query design grid includes in the grid all of the fields in that table. Later, if you add new fields to the Enrollments table, they are also added to this query.

QUICK TIP
Access automatically adds pound signs (#) around the date criteria in a date field.

3. **Double-click the DateOfCourse field to add it to the second column of the query grid, click the DateOfCourse field Criteria cell, type >=1/1/2012 and <=3/31/2012, click the DateOfCourse field Show check box to uncheck it, then use the resize pointer ↔ to widen the DateOfCourse column to view the entire Criteria entry as shown in Figure K-7**

   Before changing this query into a Make Table query, it is always a good idea to view the selected data.

4. **Click the View button ▦ to switch to Datasheet View, click any entry in the DateOfCourse field, then click the Descending button in the Sort & Filter group**

   Sorting the records in descending order based on the values in the DateOfCourse field allows you to confirm that no records after the first quarter of 2012 appear in the datasheet.

5. **Click the View button ◩ to return to Design View, click the Make Table button in the Query Type group, type ArchiveEnrollments in the Table Name text box, then click OK**

   The Make Table query is ready, but the new table has not yet been created. Action queries do not change data until you click the Run button. All action query icons include an exclamation point to remind you that they *change* data when you run them. To prevent running an action query accidentally, use the Datasheet View button to *view* the selected records, and use the Run button only when you want to run the action.

6. **Click the Run button in the Results group, click Yes when prompted that you are about to paste 180 rows, then save the query with the name MakeArchiveEnrollments and close it**

   When you run an action query, Access prompts you with an "Are you sure?" message before actually updating the data. The Undo button cannot undo changes made by action queries.

QUICK TIP
Double-clicking an action query in the Navigation Pane runs the query.

7. **Double-click the ArchiveEnrollments table in the Navigation Pane to view the new table's datasheet**

   All 180 records are pasted into the new table, as shown in Figure K-8.

8. **Close the ArchiveEnrollments table**

FIGURE K-7: Setting up a Make Table query

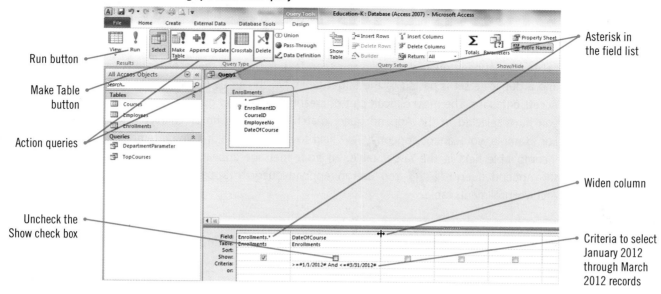

Run button

Make Table button

Action queries

Uncheck the Show check box

Asterisk in the field list

Widen column

Criteria to select January 2012 through March 2012 records

FIGURE K-8: ArchiveEnrollments table

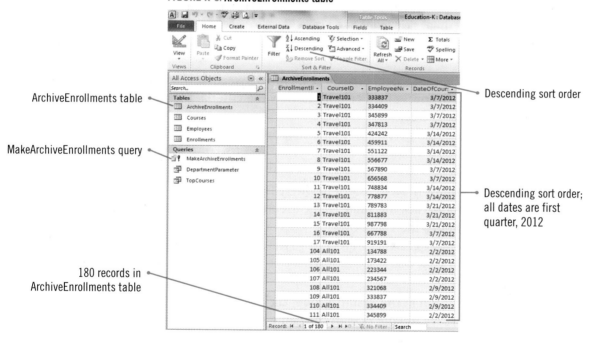

ArchiveEnrollments table

MakeArchiveEnrollments query

180 records in ArchiveEnrollments table

Descending sort order

Descending sort order; all dates are first quarter, 2012

TABLE K-3: Action queries

action query	query icon	description	example
Delete	✖!	Deletes a group of records from one or more tables	Remove products that are discontinued or for which there are no orders
Update	✎!	Makes global changes to a group of records in one or more tables	Raise prices by 10 percent for all products
Append	✦!	Adds a group of records from one or more tables to the end of another table	Append the employee address table from one division of the company to the address table from another division of the company
Make Table	▦!	Creates a new table from data in one or more tables	Export records to another Access database or make a backup copy of a table

Creating an Append Query

An **Append query** adds selected records to an existing table. The existing table is called the **target table**. The Append query works like an export feature because the records are copied from one location and a duplicate set is pasted to the target table, which can be in the current database or in any other Access database. The most difficult part of creating an Append query is making sure that all of the fields you have selected in the Append query match fields with similar characteristics in the target table. For example, you cannot append a Text field to a Number field. If you attempt to append a field to an incompatible field in the target table, an error message appears allowing you to cancel and correct the Append query. You use an Append query to append the records in April 2012 to the ArchiveEnrollments table.

STEPS

1. **Click the Create tab, click the Query Design button, double-click Enrollments in the Show Table dialog box, then click Close**

2. **Double-click the title bar in the Enrollments table's field list, then drag the highlighted fields to the first column of the query design grid**

    Double-clicking the title bar of the field list selects all of the fields, allowing you to add them to the query grid very quickly. To successfully append records to a table, you need to identify how each field in the query is connected to an existing field in the target table. Therefore, the technique of adding all of the fields to the query grid by using the asterisk does not work when you append records, because using the asterisk doesn't list each field in a separate column in the query grid.

3. **Click the DateOfCourse field Criteria cell, type Between 4/1/12 and 4/30/12, use ✛ to widen the DateOfCourse field column to view the criteria, then click the View button ▦ to display the datasheet**

    The datasheet should show 111 records with an April date in the DateOfCourse field. **Between...and** criteria select all records between the two dates, including the two dates. Between...and operators work the same way as the >= and <= operators.

4. **Click the View button ◹ to return to Query Design View, click the Append button in the Query Type group, click the Table Name list arrow in the Append dialog box, click ArchiveEnrollments, then click OK**

    The **Append To row** appears in the query design grid as shown in Figure K-9 to show how the fields in the query match fields in the target table, ArchiveEnrollments. You can now click the Run button to append the selected records to the table.

5. **Click the Run button in the Results group, click Yes to confirm that you want to append 111 rows, then save the query with the name AppendArchiveEnrollments and close it**

6. **Double-click the ArchiveEnrollments table in the Navigation Pane, click any entry in the DateOfCourse field, then click the Descending button**

    The 111 April records are appended to the ArchiveEnrollments table, which previously had 180 records and now has a new total of 291 records, as shown in Figure K-10.

7. **Save and close the ArchiveEnrollments table**

FIGURE K-9: Creating an Append query

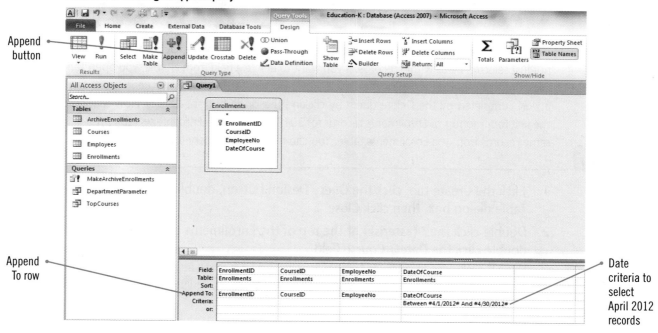

Append button

Append To row

Date criteria to select April 2012 records

FIGURE K-10: ArchiveEnrollments table with appended records

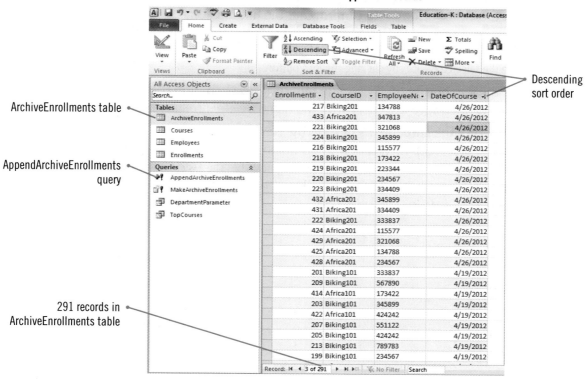

ArchiveEnrollments table

AppendArchiveEnrollments query

291 records in ArchiveEnrollments table

Descending sort order

1900 versus 2000 dates

If you type only two digits of a date, Access assumes that the digits 00 through 29 are for the years 2000 through 2029. If you type 30 through 99, Access assumes the years refer to 1930 through 1999.

If you want to specify years outside these ranges, you must type all four digits of the year.

Creating a Delete Query

A **Delete query** deletes a group of records from one or more tables. Delete queries delete entire records, not just selected fields within records. If you want to delete a field from a table, you open Table Design View, click the field name, then click the Delete Rows button. As in all action queries, you cannot reverse the action completed by the Delete query by clicking the Undo button. Now that you have archived the first four months of Enrollments records for 2012 in the ArchiveEnrollments table, you want to delete the same records from the Enrollments table. You can use a Delete query to accomplish this task.

STEPS

1. **Click the Create tab, click the Query Design button, double-click Enrollments in the Show Table dialog box, then click Close**

2. **Double-click the * (asterisk) at the top of the Enrollments table's field list, then double-click the DateOfCourse field**

   Using the asterisk adds all fields from the Enrollments table to the first column of the query design grid. You add the DateOfCourse field to the second column of the query design grid so you can enter limiting criteria for this field.

3. **Click the DateOfCourse field Criteria cell, type Between 1/1/12 and 4/30/12, then use ✛ to widen the DateOfCourse field column to view the criteria**

   Before you run a Delete query, check the selected records to make sure that you have selected the same 291 records that you previously added to the ArchiveEnrollments table.

4. **Click the View button 📧 to confirm that the datasheet has 291 records, click the View button 📐 to return to Design View, then click the Delete button in the Query Type group**

   Your screen should look like Figure K-11. The **Delete row** now appears in the query design grid. You can delete the selected records by clicking the Run button.

5. **Click the Run button on the Design tab, click Yes to confirm that you want to delete 291 rows, then save the query with the name DeleteEnrollments and close it**

6. **Double-click the Enrollments table in the Navigation Pane, click any entry in the DateOfCourse field, then click the Ascending button in the Sort & Filter group**

   The records should start in May, as shown in Figure K-12. The Delete query deleted all records from the Enrollments table with dates between 1/1/2010 and 4/30/2010.

7. **Save and close the Enrollments table**

FIGURE K-11: Creating a Delete query

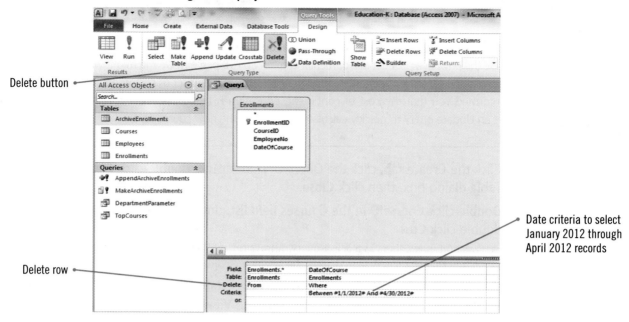

Delete button

Delete row

Date criteria to select January 2012 through April 2012 records

FIGURE K-12: Final Enrollments table after deleting 291 records

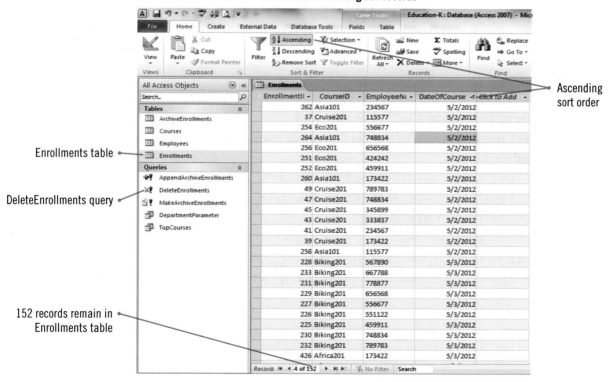

Enrollments table

DeleteEnrollments query

152 records remain in Enrollments table

Ascending sort order

Reviewing referential integrity

Recall that you can establish, or enforce, **referential integrity** between two tables when joining tables in the Relationships window. Referential integrity applies a set of rules to the relationship that ensures that no orphaned records currently exist, are added to, or are created in the database. A table has an **orphan record** when information in the foreign key field of the "many" table doesn't have a matching entry in the primary key field of the "one" table. The term "orphan" comes from the analogy that the "one" table contains **parent records**, and the "many" table contains **child records**. Referential integrity means that a Delete query would not be able to delete records in the "one" (parent) table that has related records in the "many" (child) table.

Creating an Update Query

An **Update query** is a type of action query that updates the values in a field. For example, you might want to increase the price of a product in a particular category by 10 percent. Or you might want to update information such as assigned sales representative, region, or territory for a subset of customers. ▰▰ Jacob Thomas has just informed you that the cost of continuing education is being increased by $20 for each class. You can create an Update query to quickly calculate and update the new course costs.

STEPS

1. **Click the Create tab, click the Query Design button, double-click Courses in the Show Table dialog box, then click Close**

2. **Double-click CourseID in the Courses field list, double-click Description, then double-click Cost**

   Every action query starts as a Select query. Always review the datasheet of the Select query before initiating any action that changes data to double-check which records are affected.

3. **Click the View button ▦ to display the query datasheet, note that the values in all three of the Africa courses are $450, then click the View button ▨ to return to Design View**

   After selecting the records you want to update and reviewing the values in the Cost field, you're ready to change this Select query into an Update query.

4. **Click the Update button in the Query Type group**

   The **Update To row** appears in the query design grid. To update the values in the Cost field by $20, you need to enter the appropriate expression in the Update To cell for the Cost field to add $20 to the current Cost field value.

   TROUBLE
   Be sure to enter the expression for the Cost field, not for the CourseID or Description fields.

5. **Click the Update To cell for the Cost field, then type 20+[Cost]**

   Your screen should look like Figure K-13. The expression adds 20 to the current value of the Cost field, but the Cost field is not updated until you run the query.

6. **Click the Run button in the Results group, then click Yes to confirm that you want to update 32 rows**

   To view the records, change this query back into a Select query, then view the datasheet.

7. **Click the Select button in the Query Type group, then click ▦ to display the query datasheet as shown in Figure K-14**

   The Africa records have been updated from $450 to $470. All other Cost values have increased by $20 as well.

8. **Click ▨ to return to Design View, click the Update button in the Query Type group to switch this query back to an Update query, save the query with the name UpdateCost, then close it**

   Often, you do not need to save action queries, because after the data has been updated, you generally won't use the same query again. Keep in mind that if you double-click an action query from the Navigation Pane, you run the query (as opposed to double-clicking a Select query, which opens its datasheet).

FIGURE K-13: **Setting up an Update query**

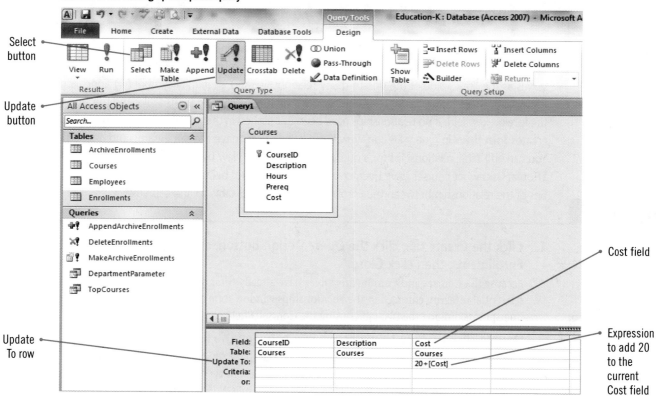

FIGURE K-14: **Updated Cost values**

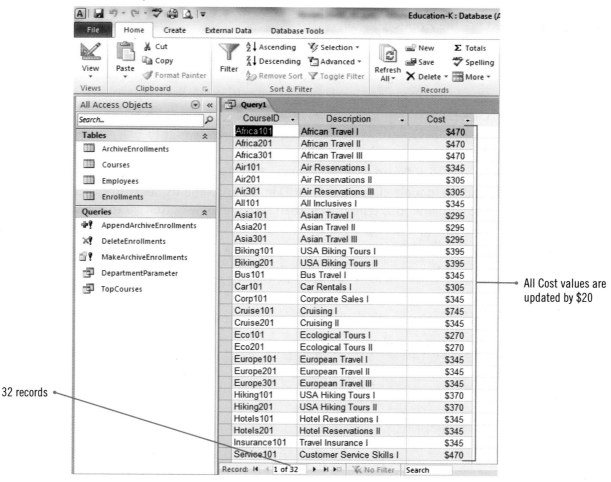

Specifying Join Properties

When you use the Relationships window to define table relationships, the tables are joined in the same way in Query Design View. If referential integrity is enforced on a relationship, a "1" appears next to the field that serves as the "one" side of the one-to-many relationship, and an infinity symbol (∞) appears next to the field that serves as the "many" side. The "one" field is the primary key field for its table, and the "many" field is called the foreign key field. If no relationships have been established in the Relationships window, Access automatically creates **join lines** in Query Design View if the linking fields have the same name and data type in two tables. You can edit table relationships for a query in Query Design View by double-clicking the join line. Jacob Thomas asks what courses have been created that have never been attended. You can modify the join properties of the relationship between the Enrollments and Courses table to find this answer.

STEPS

1. **Click the Create tab, click the Query Design button, double-click Courses, double-click Enrollments, then click Close**

   Because the Courses and Enrollments tables have already been related with a one-to-many relationship with referential integrity enforced in the Relationships window (one course can have many enrollments), the join line appears, linking the two tables using the CourseID field common to both.

   > **TROUBLE**
   > Double-click the middle portion of the join line, not the "one" or "many" symbols, to open the Join Properties dialog box.

2. **Double-click the one-to-many join line between the field lists**

   The Join Properties dialog box opens and displays the characteristics for the join, as shown in Figure K-15. The dialog box shows that option 1 is selected, the default join type, which means that the query displays only records where joined fields from *both* tables are equal. In **SQL (Structured Query Language)**, this is called an **inner join**. This means that if the Courses table has any records for which there are no matching Enrollments records, those courses do not appear in the resulting datasheet.

   > **QUICK TIP**
   > To view the Relationships window from within Query Design View, right-click to the right of the field lists, then click Relationships.

3. **Click the 2 option button**

   By choosing option 2, you are specifying that you want to see *all* of the records in the Courses table (the "one," or parent table), even if the Enrollments table (the "many," or child table) does not contain matching records. In SQL, this is called a **left join**. Option 3 selects all records in the Enrollments (the "many," or child table) even if there are no matches in the Courses table. In SQL, this is called a **right join**.

4. **Click OK**

   The join line's appearance changes, as shown in Figure K-16. With the join property set, you add fields to the query grid.

5. **Double-click CourseID in the Courses field list, double-click Description in the Courses field list, double-click EnrollmentID in the Enrollments field list, click the Criteria cell for the EnrollmentID, type Is Null, then click the View button to display the datasheet**

   The query finds 17 courses that currently have no matching records in the Enrollments table, as shown in Figure K-17. These courses contain a null (nothing) value in the EnrollmentID field. Changing the join property between the tables to include *all* records from the Courses table selects these records because the default join type, the inner join, requires a matching record in both tables to display a record in the resulting datasheet.

6. **Save the query with the name CoursesWithoutEnrollments, then close it**

Null and zero-length string values

The term **null** describes a field value that does not exist because it has never been entered. In a datasheet, null values look the same as a zero-length string value but have a different purpose. A **zero-length string** value is a *deliberate* entry that contains no characters. You enter a zero-length string by typing two quotation marks ("") with no space between them. A null value, on the other hand, indicates *unknown* data. By using null and zero-length string values appropriately, you can later query for the records that match one or the other condition. To query for zero-length string values, enter two quotation marks ("") as the criterion. To query for null values, use **Is Null** as the criterion. To query for another value other than a null value, use **Is Not Null** as the criterion.

FIGURE K-15: **Join Properties dialog box**

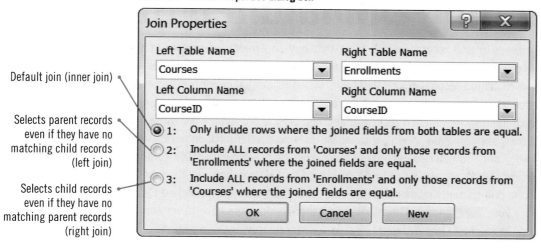

Default join (inner join)

Selects parent records even if they have no matching child records (left join)

Selects child records even if they have no matching parent records (right join)

FIGURE K-16: **Left join symbol**

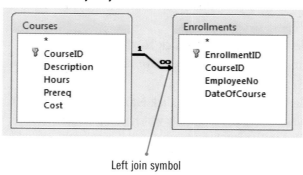

Left join symbol

FIGURE K-17: **Courses with no matching enrollments**

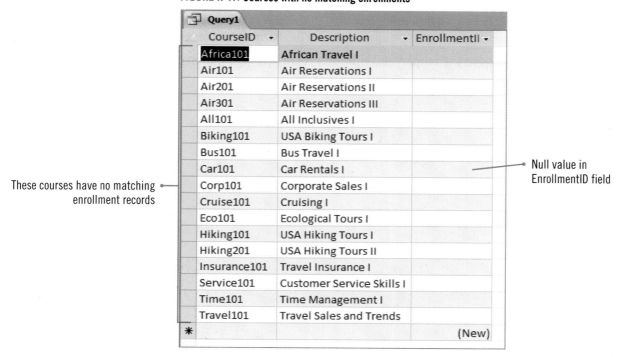

These courses have no matching enrollment records

Null value in EnrollmentID field

Finding Unmatched Records

Another way to find records in one table that have no matching records in another is to use the **Find Unmatched Query Wizard**. A **find unmatched query** is a query that finds records in one table that do not have matching records in a related table. When referential integrity is enforced on a relationship before you enter data into a database, orphan records cannot be created. Therefore, with referential integrity enforced, the only unmatched records that could exist in a database are those in the "one" (parent) table. Sometimes, though, you inherit a database in which referential integrity was not imposed from the beginning, and unmatched records already exist in the "many" table (orphans). You could use your knowledge of join properties and null criteria to find unmatched records in either the "one" or "many" tables of a one-to-many relationship. Or you could use the Find Unmatched Query Wizard to structure the query for you. ■■■ Jacob Thomas wonders if any employees have never enrolled in a class. You can use the Find Unmatched Query Wizard to create a query to answer this question.

STEPS

1. **Click the Create tab, click the Query Wizard button, click Find Unmatched Query Wizard, then click OK**

   The Find Unmatched Query Wizard starts, prompting you to select the table or query that may contain no related records.

2. **Click Table: Employees, then click Next**

   You want to find which employees have no enrollments, so you select the Enrollments table as the related table.

3. **Click Table: Enrollments, then click Next**

   The next question asks you to identify which field is common to both tables. Because the Employees table is already related to the Enrollments table in the Relationships window via the common EmployeeNo field, those fields are already selected as the matching fields, as shown in Figure K-18.

4. **Click Next**

   Now you must select the fields from the Employees table that you want to display in the query datasheet.

5. **Click the Select All Fields button** `>>`

6. **Click Next, type EmployeesWithoutEnrollments, then click Finish**

   The final datasheet is shown in Figure K-19. One employee who was recently hired has not yet enrolled in any class. To complete any further study or to modify this query, you could work in Query Design View.

7. **Save and close the EmployeesWithoutEnrollments query, then close the Education-K.accdb database**

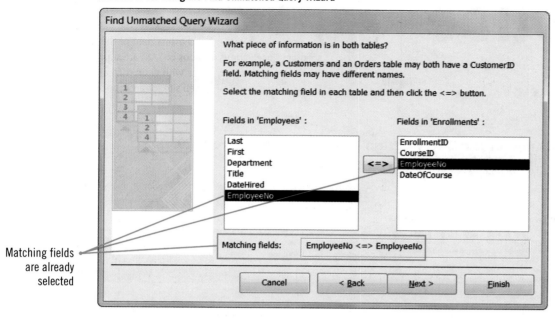

Matching fields are already selected

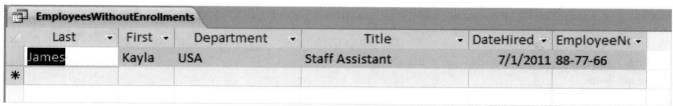

EmployeesWithoutEnrollments

Last	First	Department	Title	DateHired	EmployeeNo
James	Kayla	USA	Staff Assistant	7/1/2011	88-77-66

Find Duplicates Query Wizard

The Find Duplicates Query Wizard is another query wizard that is only available from the New Query dialog box. As you would suspect, the **Find Duplicates Query Wizard** helps you find duplicate values in a field, which can assist in finding and correcting potential data entry errors. For example, if you suspect that the same customer has been entered with two different names in your Customers table, you could use the Find Duplicates Query Wizard to find records with duplicate values in the Street or Phone field. After you isolated the records with the same values in a field, you could then edit incorrect data and delete redundant records.

Access 2010

Practice

Concepts Review

For current SAM information, including versions and content details, visit SAM Central (http://www.cengage.com/samcentral). If you have a SAM user profile, you may have access to hands-on instruction, practice, and assessment of the skills covered in this unit. Since various versions of SAM are supported throughout the life of this text, check with your instructor for the correct instructions and URL/Web site for accessing assignments.

Identify each element of the Query Design View shown in Figure K-20.

FIGURE K-20

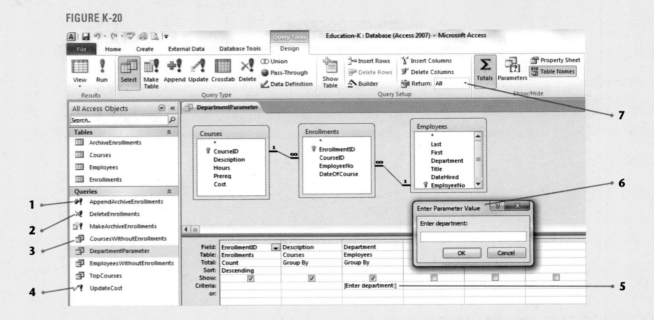

Match each term with the statement that best describes its function.

8. **Null**
9. **Top Values query**
10. **Inner join**
11. **Action query**
12. **Properties**
13. **Parameter**

a. Characteristics that define the appearance and behavior of items within the database

b. Displays only a number or percentage of records from a sorted query

c. Displays a dialog box prompting you for criteria

d. Means that the query displays only records where joined fields from both tables are equal

e. Makes changes to data

f. A field value that does not exist

Select the best answer from the list of choices.

14. **Which join type selects all records from the "one" (parent) table?**
    a. Inner
    b. Central
    c. Left
    d. Right

15. **Which of the following is a valid parameter criterion entry in the query design grid?**
    a. >=[Type minimum value here:]
    b. >=(Type minimum value here:)
    c. >=Type minimum value here:
    d. >={Type minimum value here: }

16. **You *cannot* use the Top Values feature to:**
    a. Select the bottom 10 percent of records.
    b. Display a subset of records.
    c. Show the top 30 records.
    d. Update a field's value by 5 percent.

17. **Which of the following is *not* an action query?**
    a. Union query
    b. Make table query
    c. Delete query
    d. Append query

18. **Which of the following precautions should you take before running a Delete query?**
    a. Check the resulting datasheet to make sure the query selects the right records.
    b. Have a current backup of the database.
    c. Understand the relationships between the records you are about to delete in the database.
    d. All of the above.

19. **When querying tables in a one-to-many relationship with referential integrity enforced, which records appear (by default) on the resulting datasheet?**
    a. All records from both tables will appear at all times.
    b. All records from the "one" table, and only those with matching values from the "many" side.
    c. Only those with matching values in both tables.
    d. All records from the "many" table, and only those with nonmatching values from the "one" side.

Skills Review

1. **Query for top values.**
   a. Start Access, then open the Seminar-K.accdb database from the drive and folder where you store your Data Files. Enable content if prompted.
   b. Create a new query in Query Design View with the EventName field from the Events table and the RegistrationFee field from the Registration table.
   c. Add the RegistrationFee field a second time, then click the Totals button. In the Total row of the query grid, Group By the EventName field, Sum the first RegistrationFee field, then Count the second RegistrationFee field.
   d. Sort in descending order by the summed RegistrationFee field.
   e. Enter **3** in the Top Values list box to display the top three seminars in the datasheet, then view the datasheet.
   f. Save the query as **Top3Revenue**, then close the datasheet.

2. **Create a parameter query.**
   a. Create a new query in Query Design View with the AttendeeLastName field from the Attendees table, the RegistrationDate field from the Registration table, and the EventName field from the Events table.
   b. Add the parameter criteria **Between [Enter Start Date:] and [Enter End Date:]** in the Criteria cell for the RegistrationDate field.
   c. Specify an ascending sort order on the RegistrationDate field.
   d. Click the Datasheet View button, then enter **5/1/13** as the start date and **5/31/13** as the end date to find everyone who has attended a seminar in May 2013. You should view five records.
   e. Save the query as **RegistrationDateParameter**, then close it.

3. **Modify query properties.**
   a. Right-click the RegistrationDateParameter query in the Navigation Pane, click Object Properties, then add the following description: **Prompts for a starting and ending registration date. Created by Your Name.**

Skills Review (continued)

b. Close the RegistrationDateParameter Properties dialog box, then open the RegistrationDateParameter query in Query Design View.

c. Right-click the RegistrationDate field, then click Properties on the shortcut menu to open the Property Sheet for the Field Properties. Enter **Date of Registration** for the Caption property, change the Format property to Medium Date, then close the Property Sheet.

d. View the datasheet for records between **5/1/13** and **5/31/13**, then widen the fields as needed to view the caption and the Medium Date format applied to the RegistrationDate field.

e. Change Skorija to your last name, then print the RegistrationDateParameter datasheet if requested by your instructor.

f. Save and close the RegistrationDateParameter query.

4. **Create a Make Table query.**

a. Create a new query in Query Design View, and select all the fields from the Registration table by double-clicking the Registration field list's title bar and dragging the selected fields to the query design grid.

b. Enter **<=3/31/2013** in the Criteria cell for the RegistrationDate field to find those records in which the RegistrationDate is on or before 3/31/2013.

c. View the datasheet. It should display 23 records.

d. In Query Design View, change the query into a Make Table query that creates a new table in the current database. Give the new table the name **BackupRegistration**.

e. Run the query to paste 23 rows into the BackupRegistration table.

f. Save the Make Table query with the name **MakeBackupRegistration**, then close it.

g. Open the BackupRegistration table, view the 23 records to confirm that the Make Table query worked correctly, then close the table.

5. **Create an Append query.**

a. Create a new query in Query Design View, and select all the fields from the Registration table by double-clicking the Registration field list's title bar and dragging the selected fields to the query design grid.

b. Enter **>=4/1/13 and <=4/30/13** in the Criteria cell for the RegistrationDate field to find those records in which the RegistrationDate is in April 2013.

c. View the datasheet, which should display one record.

d. In Query Design View, change the query into an Append query that appends records to the BackupRegistration table.

e. Run the query to append the row into the BackupRegistration table.

f. Save the Append query with the name **AppendBackupRegistration**, then close it.

g. Open the BackupRegistration table to confirm that it now contains the additional April record for a total of 24 records, then close the table.

6. **Create a Delete query.**

a. Create a new query in Query Design View, and select all the fields from the Registration table by double-clicking the Registration field list's title bar and dragging the selected fields to the query design grid.

b. Enter **<5/1/2013** in the Criteria cell for the RegistrationDate field to find those records in which the RegistrationDate is before May 1, 2013.

c. View the datasheet, which should display 24 records, the same 24 records you added to the BackupRegistration table.

d. In Query Design View, change the query into a Delete query.

e. Run the query to delete 24 records from the Registration table.

f. Save the query with the name **DeleteRegistration** then close it.

g. Open the Registration table in Datasheet View to confirm that it contains only five records, all with RegistrationDate values greater than or equal to 5/1/2013, then close the table.

7. **Create an Update query.**

a. Create a query in Query Design View, and select all the fields from the Registration table by double-clicking the Registration field list's title bar and dragging the selected fields to the query design grid.

b. Sort the records in descending order on the RegistrationFee field, then view the datasheet, which should display five records. Note the values in the RegistrationFee field.

Skills Review (continued)

   c. In Query Design View, change the query to an Update query, then enter **[RegistrationFee]*2** in the RegistrationFee field Update To cell to double the RegistrationFee value in each record.

   d. Run the query to update the five records.

   e. Save the query with the name **UpdateRegistrationFee**, then close it.

   f. Open the Registration table to confirm that the RegistrationFee for the five records has doubled, then close it.

8. Specify join properties.

   a. Create a new query in Query Design View with the following fields: AttendeeFirstName and AttendeeLastName from the Attendees table, and EventID and RegistrationFee from the Registration table.

   b. Double-click the join line between the Attendees and Registration tables to open the Join Properties dialog box. Click the 2 option button to include *all* records from Attendees and only those records from Registration where the joined fields are equal.

   c. View the datasheet, add your own first and last name as the last record, but do not enter anything in the EventID or RegistrationFee fields for your record.

   d. In Query Design View, add **Is Null** criteria to either field from the Registration table to select only those names who have never registered for an event.

   e. Save this query as **PeopleWithoutRegistrations**, then view, print (if requested by your instructor), and close the query.

9. Find unmatched queries.

   a. Start the Find Unmatched Query Wizard.

   b. Select the Events table, and then the Registration table to indicate that you want to view the Events records that have no related records in the Registration table.

   c. Specify that the two tables are related by the EventID field.

   d. Select all of the fields from the Events table in the query results.

   e. Name the query **EventsWithoutRegistrations**, then view the results. Change one of the entries in the Location field to **Your Name College**, as shown in Figure K-21.

   f. Print the EventsWithoutRegistrations query, then close the query, close the Seminar-K.accdb database, and exit Access.

FIGURE K-21

Independent Challenge 1

As the manager of a college women's basketball team, you want to create several queries using the Basketball-K database.

a. Start Access, then open the Basketball-K.accdb database from the drive and folder where you store your Data Files. Enable content if prompted.

b. Create a query in Query Design View with the FirstName and LastName fields from the Players table, the FG (field goal), 3P (three pointer), and FT (free throw) fields from the Stats table, and the Opponent and GameDate fields from the Games table.

c. Enter **Between [Enter start date:] and [Enter end date:]** in the Criteria cell for the GameDate field.

d. View the datasheet for all of the records between **12/1/2012** and **12/31/2012**. It should display 18 records.

e. Save the query with the name **StatsParameter**, change Lindsey Swift's name to your own, then print the datasheet if requested by your instructor.

f. In Query Design View of the StatsParameter query, insert a new calculated field named **TotalPoints** between the FT and Opponent field with the expression **TotalPoints:[FG]*2+[3P]*3+[FT]**, then sort the records in descending order on the TotalPoints field.

g. Apply the 25% Top Values option, and view the datasheet for all of the records between **12/1/2012** and **12/31/2012**. It should display five records.

h. Use the Save Object As feature to save the revised query as **StatsParameterTopValues**. Print the datasheet if requested by your instructor, then close it.

i. Create a new query in Query Design View with the Opponent, Mascot, HomeScore, and OpponentScore fields from the Games table, then add a new calculated field as the last field with the following field name and expression: **WinRatio:[HomeScore]/[OpponentScore]**.

j. View the datasheet to make sure that the WinRatio field calculates properly, and widen all columns as necessary to see all of the data. Because the home score is generally greater than the opponent score, most values are greater than 1.

Advanced Challenge Exercise

- In Query Design View, change the Format property of the WinRatio field to Percent and the Decimal Places property to 0.
- View the datasheet, a portion of which is shown in Figure K-22.

k. Save the query as **WinPercentage**, change the first opponent's name (Iowa) and mascot to your own name and a mascot of your choice, print the WinPercentage datasheet if requested by your instructor, and close the WinPercentage query.

l. Close the Basketball-K.accdb database, then exit Access.

FIGURE K-22

Opponent	Mascot	HomeScore	OpponentScore	WinRatio
Iowa	Hawkeyes	81	65	125%
Creighton	Bluejays	106	60	177%
Northern Illinois	Huskies	65	60	108%
Louisiana Tech	Red Raiders	69	89	78%
Drake	Bulldogs	80	60	133%
Northern Iowa	Panthers	38	73	52%
Buffalo	Bulls	50	55	91%
Oklahoma	Sooners	53	60	88%
Texas	Longhorns	57	60	95%
Kansas	Jayhawks	74	58	128%
Colorado	Buffaloes	90	84	107%
Texas A&M	Aggies	77	60	128%

Creating Advanced Queries

Independent Challenge 2

As the manager of a college women's basketball team, you want to enhance the Basketball-K database by creating several action queries.

a. Start Access, then open the Basketball-K.accdb database from the drive and folder where you store your Data Files. Enable content if prompted.

b. Create a new query in Query Design View, and select all the fields from the Stats table by double-clicking the field list's title bar and dragging the selected fields to the query design grid.

c. Add criteria to find all of the records with the GameNo field equal to **1**, **2**, or **3**, then view the datasheet. It should display 26 records.

d. In Query Design View, change the query to a Make Table query to paste the records into a table in the current database called **Stats123**.

e. Run the query to paste the 26 rows, save the query with the name **MakeStatsBackup**, then close it.

f. Open the datasheet for the Stats123 table to confirm that it contains 26 records, then close it.

g. In Query Design View, create another new query that includes all of the fields from the Stats table by double-clicking the field list's title bar and dragging the selected fields to the query design grid.

h. Add criteria to find all of the statistics for those records with the GameNo field equal to **4** or **5**, then view the datasheet. It should display 12 records.

i. In Query Design View, change the query to an Append query to append the records to the Stats123 table.

j. Run the query to append the 12 rows, save it with the name **AppendStatsBackup**, then close it.

k. Right-click the Stats123 table in the Navigation Pane, click Rename, then edit the name to **Stats12345**.

l. Open the Stats12345 table to make sure it contains 38 records, print it if requested by your instructor, then close the Stats12345 table.

m. Close the Basketball-K.accdb database, then exit Access.

Independent Challenge 3

As the manager of a college women's basketball team, you want to query the Basketball-K database to find specific information about each player.

    a. Start Access, then open the Basketball-K.accdb database from the drive and folder where you store your Data Files. Enable content if prompted.

    b. Create a query in Query Design View using the Players and Stats tables. Resize the field lists to view all of the fields in each table.

    c. Double-click the join line to open the Join Properties dialog box, then change the join properties to option 2 to include *all* records from Players and only those from Stats where the joined fields are equal.

    d. Add the FirstName and LastName fields from the Players table and the Assists field from the Stats table.

    e. Type **Is Null** in the Criteria cell for the Assists field, as shown in Figure K-23, then view the datasheet to find those players who have never recorded an Assist value in the Stats table. It should display one record.

    f. Change the last name to your own last name.

    g. Print the datasheet if requested by your instructor, save the query as **NoAssists**, then close the query.

    h. Close Basketball-K.accdb, then exit Access.

FIGURE K-23

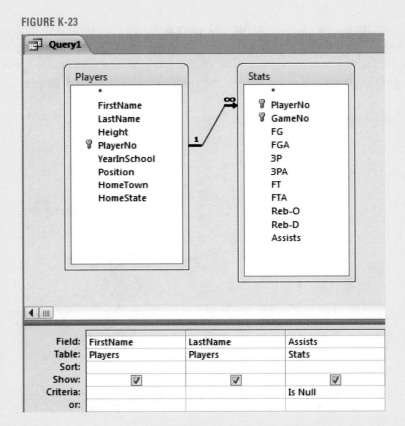

Creating Advanced Queries

Real Life Independent Challenge

This Independent Challenge requires an Internet connection.

One way to use Access to support your personal interests is to track the activities of a club or hobby. For example, suppose you belong to a culinary club that specializes in cooking with chocolate. The club collects information on international chocolate factories and museums and asks you to help build a database to organize the information.

a. Start Access, then open the Chocolate-K.accdb database from the drive and folder where you store your Data Files. Enable content if prompted.

b. Open the Countries table, then add two more country records, allowing the CountryID field to automatically increment because it is an AutoNumber data type. Close the Countries table.

c. Create a query in Query Design View with the Country field from the Countries table, and the PlaceName, City, and State fields from the ChocolatePlaces query.

d. Name the query **PlacesOfInterest**, double-click the join line between the Countries and ChocolatePlaces tables, then choose the 2 option that includes *all* records from the Countries table.

e. Save and view the PlacesOfInterest query. Expand each column to show all of the data.

f. Print the PlacesOfInterest query if requested by your instructor, then close it.

Advanced Challenge Exercise

■ Using the Internet, research a chocolate-related place of interest (a factory or museum) for one of the countries you entered in Step b.

■ Open the Countries table, and use the Subdatasheet for the country you selected to enter the data for the chocolate-related place of interest. Enter **F** for factory or **M** for museum in the FactoryorMuseum field.

■ Close the Countries table, and open the PlacesOfInterest query in Design View. Modify the link line to option 1, so that records that have a match in both tables are selected.

■ Save and open the PlacesOfInterest query in Datasheet View as shown in Figure K-24, and print the resulting datasheet if requested by your instructor. Note that the last record will show the unique data you entered.

g. Close Chocolate-K.accdb, then exit Access.

FIGURE K-24

PlacesOfInterest

Country	PlaceName	City	State
Germany	Lindt factory	Aachen	
Germany	Imhoff Stollwerk Chocolate Museum	Cologne	
Switzerland	Lindt factory	Kilchberg	
Switzerland	Museum del Cioccolato Alprose	Caslano	Canton Ticino
Switzerland	Nestle	Broc	Canton Fribourg
France	Lindt Factory	Oloron	
France	Atelier Musee du Chocolat, Biarritz	Biarritz	
Italy	Lindt Factory	Induno	
Italy	Lindt Factory	Luserna	
Italy	Museo Storico della Perugina	Perugia	
Italy	Museo del Cioccolato Antia Norba	Norma	Latina Province
Austria	Lindt Factory	Gloggnitz	
USA	Lindt Factory	San Leandro	CA
USA	Lindt Factory	Stratham	NH
Belgium	Musee du Cacao et du Chocolat	Brussels	
Great Britian	Cadbury World	Bourneville	
Japan	Shiroi Koibito Park	Sapporo	

Visual Workshop

As the manager of a college women's basketball team, you want to create a query from the Basketball-K.accdb database with the fields from the Players, Stats, and Games tables as shown. The query is a parameter query that prompts the user for a start and end date using the GameDate field from the Games table. Figure K-25 shows the datasheet where the start date of **11/13/2012** and end date of **11/16/2012** are used. Also note that the records are sorted in ascending order first by GameDate, and then by LastName. Save and name the query **Rebounds**, then print the datasheet if requested by your instructor. Be sure to change one player's name to your own if you haven't previously done this to identify your printout.

FIGURE K-25

Rebounds

GameDate	FirstName	LastName	Reb-O	Reb-D	TotalRebounds
11/13/2012	Kristen	Czyenski	2	2	4
11/13/2012	Denise	Franco	2	3	5
11/13/2012	Theresa	Grant	1	3	4
11/13/2012	Megan	Hile	1	2	3
11/13/2012	Amy	Hodel	5	3	8
11/13/2012	Ellyse	Howard	1	2	3
11/13/2012	Jamie	Johnson	0	1	1
11/13/2012	Student First	Student Last	1	2	3
11/13/2012	Morgan	Tyler	4	6	10
11/16/2012	Kristen	Czyenski	3	2	5
11/16/2012	Denise	Franco	5	3	8
11/16/2012	Sydney	Freesen	2	3	5
11/16/2012	Theresa	Grant	3	3	6
11/16/2012	Megan	Hile	1	5	6
11/16/2012	Amy	Hodel	1	4	5
11/16/2012	Ellyse	Howard	3	3	6
11/16/2012	Sandy	Robins	0	1	1
11/16/2012	Student First	Student Last	2	2	4
11/16/2012	Morgan	Tyler	3	6	9
11/16/2012	Abbey	Walker	2	4	6

Creating Advanced Queries

Creating Advanced Reports

In this unit you will learn techniques to make sure that the data in your reports are logical and clear using advanced formatting, grouping, and print layout features. You will also learn how to graphically display data in a variety of chart types such as pie, bar, and line charts. Jacob Thomas, coordinator of training at Quest Specialty Travel, wants to enhance existing reports to more professionally and clearly present the information in the Education-L database.

OBJECTIVES

Apply advanced formatting

Control layout

Set advanced print layout

Create charts

Modify charts

Apply chart types

Create multicolumn reports

Use domain functions

Applying Advanced Formatting

Each control on a report has formatting properties such as Text Align, Width, and Format that you can modify using the Ribbon or Property Sheet. For example, the **Format property** provides several ways to format dates (19-Jun-13, 6/19/2013, or Friday, June 19, 2013), and numbers can be formatted as Currency ($77.25), Percent (52%), or Standard (890).  You review the Departmental Summary Report to identify and correct formatting problems.

1. **Start Access, open the Education-L.accdb database from the drive and folder where you store your Data Files, enable content if prompted, double-click DeptSummary in the Navigation Pane, then scroll so your screen looks like Figure L-1**

   Some of the information is not displayed correctly and subtotals are not formatted properly.

2. **Right-click the report, click Design View, click the Department label in the Page Header section, click the ⊞ symbol to the left of the Department label to select the grouped controls, click the Arrange tab, then click the Remove Layout button in the Table group**

   Often, Access Form and Report Wizards will group controls together, which helps you work with them as a group in Layout View. Ungrouping controls allows you to work with them individually. With the controls ungrouped, you build an expression to calculate the entire employee name in one text box.

   > **TROUBLE**
   > Be sure to include a space after the comma to separate the parts of the name.

3. **Click a blank spot on the report to remove the selection, click the First label in the Page Header section, press [Delete], click the EFirst text box in the EmployeeNo Header section, press [Delete], double-click the border of the Last label to open its Property Sheet, modify the Caption property on the Format tab to Name, click the ELast text box in the EmployeeNo Header section to select it, use ↔ to drag the right edge of the ELast text box to about the 3.5" mark on the horizontal ruler to widen it, then modify the Control Source property of ELast to =[ELast]&", "&[EFirst]**

   The name expression requires less horizontal space and looks professional. Now widen the date controls.

   > **TROUBLE**
   > Drag the title bar of the Property Sheet to move it as needed.

4. **Click the Date label in the Page Header section, press and hold [Shift], click the DateOfCourse text box in the Detail section, release [Shift], use ↔ to drag the left edge of the controls to about the 3.5" mark on the horizontal ruler to widen them, click the Home tab, then click the Center button in the Text Formatting group twice**

   You also want to change the subtotal values so that they align directly under the columns they represent (Hours or Cost). In addition, you want all Cost values to be formatted as currency (with dollar signs).

   > **TROUBLE**
   > If Currency isn't available for the Format property, click another property then try again.

5. **Click the 7.75" mark on the horizontal ruler to select all controls in the Cost column (see Figure L-2), click the Align Text Right button twice, click the Arrange tab, click the Align button, click Right, press and hold [Shift], click the Cost label in the Page Header section to deselect it, release [Shift], click the Format tab in the Property Sheet, click the Format list arrow, click Currency, click the Decimal Places list arrow, then click 0**

   With the Cost column formatted properly, you work on the Hours column.

6. **Click the 7" mark on the horizontal ruler to select all controls in the Hours column, click the Arrange tab, click the Align button, click Right, click the Home tab, click the Align Text Right button twice, press and hold [Shift], click the Hours label in the Page Header section, release [Shift], click the Format list arrow in the Property Sheet, click Standard, click the Decimal Places list arrow, then click 0**

7. **Right-click the DeptSummary report tab, click Report View, scroll to match Figure L-3, then save and close the report**

FIGURE L-1: Reviewing problems with the Departmental Summary Report

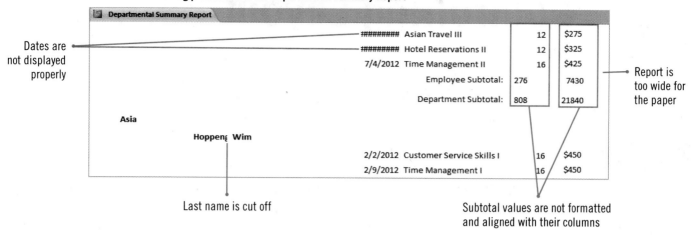

Dates are not displayed properly

Last name is cut off

Report is too wide for the paper

Subtotal values are not formatted and aligned with their columns

FIGURE L-2: Formatting and aligning controls in Report Design View

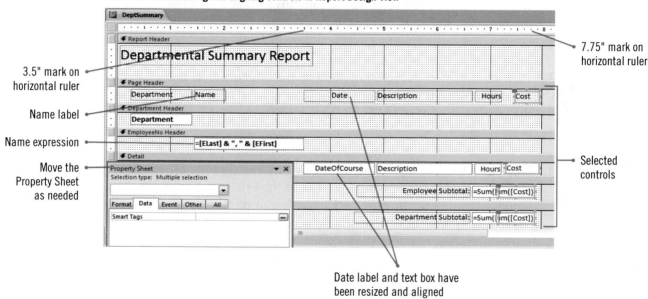

3.5" mark on horizontal ruler

Name label

Name expression

Move the Property Sheet as needed

7.75" mark on horizontal ruler

Selected controls

Date label and text box have been resized and aligned

FIGURE L-3: Reviewing the Departmental Summary Report

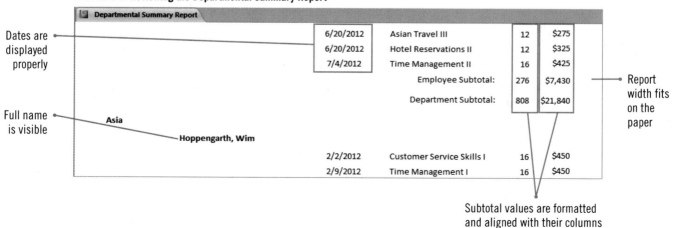

Dates are displayed properly

Full name is visible

Report width fits on the paper

Subtotal values are formatted and aligned with their columns

Access 2010

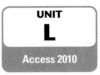
Controlling Layout

Layout in Access forms and reports refers to connecting controls as a set so that when you move or resize them in Layout or Design View, the action you take on one control applies to all controls in the group. When you create a report using the Report button or Report Wizard, many of the controls are automatically grouped together in a layout. To productively work in Report Design View, you may need to remove the layout of existing controls or group controls in new layouts for your own purposes. ▆▆▆▆▆ Jacob Thomas asks you to create a new employee listing report.

STEPS

1. **Click the Employees table in the Navigation Pane, click the Create tab, click the Report button, then close the Property Sheet if it is open**

   The Report button creates a report on the selected table or query and displays it in Layout View. Controls that are grouped together in the same layout can be resized easily in Layout View.

2. **Click Dawson in the ELast column, use ↔ to drag the right edge of the column to the left, click Ron in the EFirst column, use ↔ to drag the right edge of the column to the left, and continue resizing the columns so that they all fit within the right border of the report as shown in Figure L-4**

   Controls in the same layout move to provide space for the control you are moving. You move the EFirst column to the first column of the report.

3. **Click Ron in the EFirst column, point to the middle of the text box and use ↖ to drag the column to the left of Dawson in the ELast column, click the EFirst label, use ↖ to drag the label to the left of the ELast label, click the blank column placeholder, then press [Delete]**

   To individually move controls, you must remove the layout in Design View.

   TROUBLE

   The ⊞ might be superimposed on the ELast label.

4. **Right-click the Employees tab, click Design View, click the EFirst label to select it, click the ⊞ symbol in the upper-left corner of the EFirst label, click the Arrange tab, click the Remove Layout button, then click a blank spot on the report to deselect the controls**

   You open a Department Header section and move the Department text box to that section.

5. **Click the Design tab, click the Group & Sort button to open the Group, Sort, and Total pane, click the Add a group button, click Department, right-click the Department text box in the Detail section, click Cut, right-click the Department Header section, then click Paste**

   With the Department Header section in place, you make a few more modifications to the report to finish it.

6. **Click the Department label in the Page Header section, press [Delete], move the Page expression in the Page Footer section to the left, then drag the right edge of the report as far left as possible as shown in Figure L-5**

   For now, you decide to connect the ELast and EFirst controls together in a layout so they can be moved and resized as a group.

7. **Click the EFirst label in the Page Header section, press and hold [Shift], click the EFirst text box in the Detail section, click the ELast label in the Page Header section, click the ELast text box in the Detail section, release [Shift], click the Arrange tab, click the Tabular button in the Table group, then drag the four controls to the right to fill the blank space**

   See Table L-1 for more information on layouts you can apply to a group of selected controls. You might also notice other formatting embellishments you would like to make at a later time, but for now, save, preview, and close the report.

8. **Click the Save button 🖫 on the Quick Access toolbar, click OK to accept Employees as the report name, right-click the Employees report tab, click Print Preview to review the Employees report, then close it**

   Advanced sizing, moving, formatting, and aligning skills are at the heart of report design.

FIGURE L-4: Resizing controls in the same layout in Report Layout View

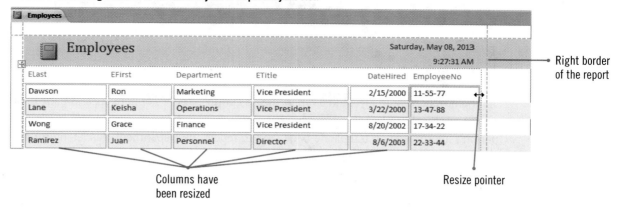

Right border of the report

Columns have been resized

Resize pointer

FIGURE L-5: Working with individual controls in Report Design View

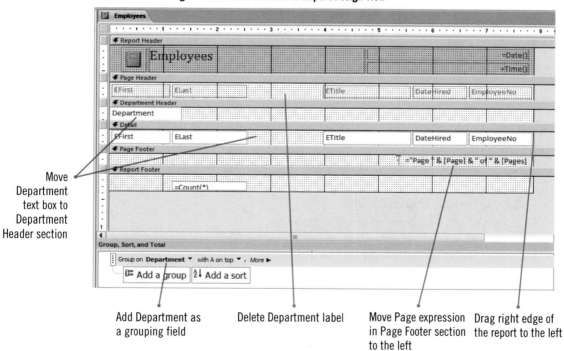

Move Department text box to Department Header section

Add Department as a grouping field

Delete Department label

Move Page expression in Page Footer section to the left

Drag right edge of the report to the left

TABLE L-1: Layouts

layout	description
Stacked	Labels are positioned to the left of the text box; most often used in forms
Tabular	Labels are positioned across the top in the Page Header section forming columns of data with text boxes positioned in the Detail section; most often used in reports

Creating Advanced Reports

Setting Advanced Print Layout

Setting advanced print layout in a report means controlling print options such as page breaks, margins, or printing only selected pages. ▄▄▄▄ In the Departmental Summary Report, Jacob asks you to print each person's information on a separate page, and to repeat the Department Header information at the top of each page.

1. **Right-click the DeptSummary report in the Navigation Pane, click Design View, double-click the Department Header section bar to open its Property Sheet, double-click the Repeat Section property to change the property from No to Yes, then double-click the Force New Page property to change the property from None to Before Section as shown in Figure L-6**

   The controls in the Department Header section will now repeat at the top of every page.

2. **Click the EmployeeNo Header section bar, click the Force New Page property list arrow, then click Before Section**

   Access will format the report with a page break before each EmployeeNo Header. This means each employee's records will start printing at the top of a new page.

3. **Right-click the DeptSummary report tab, click Print Preview, click the One Page button in the Zoom group, then use the navigation buttons to move through the pages of the report**

   Previewing multiple pages helps you make sure that the department name repeats at the top of every page, that each new department starts on a new page, and that each employee starts on a new page.

4. **Navigate to page 2, then click the top of the page if you need to zoom in as shown in Figure L-7**

   To print only page 2 of the report, you use the Print dialog box.

> **QUICK TIP**
> If you want your name to be on the report, enter it as a label in the Page Footer section.

5. **Click the Print button on the Print Preview tab, click the From box, enter 2, click the To box, enter 2, then click OK**

   Only page 2 of a 24-page report is sent to the printer.

6. **Save and close the DeptSummary report**

FIGURE L-6: Working with section properties in Report Design View

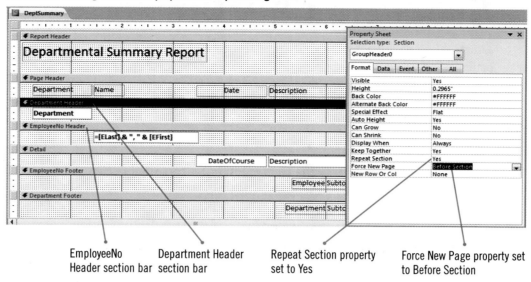

EmployeeNo Header section bar

Department Header section bar

Repeat Section property set to Yes

Force New Page property set to Before Section

FIGURE L-7: Previewing the final Departmental Summary Report

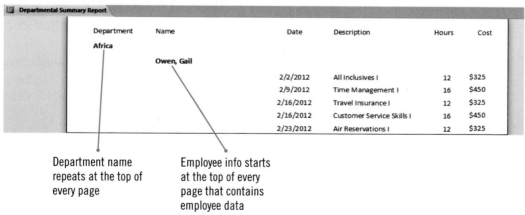

Department name repeats at the top of every page

Employee info starts at the top of every page that contains employee data

Creating Charts

Charts, also called graphs, are visual representations of numeric data that help users see comparisons, patterns, and trends in data. Charts can be inserted on a form or report. Access provides a **Chart Wizard** that helps you create the chart. Common **chart types** that determine the presentation of data on the chart such as column, pie, and line are described in Table L-2. 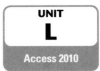 Jacob wants you to create a chart of the total number of course registrations by department.

STEPS

1. **Click the Create tab, click the Query Design button, double-click Employees, double-click Enrollments, click Close, then close the Property Sheet if it is open**

   The first step in creating a chart is to select the data that the chart will graph.

2. **Double-click Department in the Employees field list, double-click EnrollmentID in the Enrollments field list, save the query with the name DepartmentEnrollments, then close it**

   You build a chart on a report from this query. Charts can be added to forms or reports.

3. **Click the Create tab, click the Report Design button, click the More button ⊟ in the Controls group, click the Chart button ⅏ in the Controls group, then click in the Detail section of the report as shown in Figure L-8**

   The Chart Wizard starts by asking which table or query holds the fields you want to add to the chart, and then asks you to select a chart type.

4. **Click the Queries option button, click Next to choose the DepartmentEnrollments query, click the Select All Fields button ⏩, click Next, click Next to accept Column Chart, then drag the EnrollmentID field from the Series area to the Data area as shown in Figure L-9**

   The **Data area** determines what data the chart graphs. If you drag a Number or Currency field to the Data area, the Chart Wizard automatically sums the values in the field. For Text or AutoNumber fields (such as EnrollmentID), the Chart Wizard automatically counts the values in that field.

5. **Click Next, type Department Enrollment Totals as the chart title, click Finish, use ⬉ to drag the lower-right corner of the chart to fill the Detail section, right-click the Report1 tab, then click Print Preview**

   When charts are displayed in Design View or Layout View, they appear as a generic Microsoft chart placeholder. The chart should look similar to Figure L-10. The chart is beginning to take shape, but some of the labels on the x-axis may not have room to display all of their text depending on the size of the chart. You'll enhance this chart in the next lesson.

TABLE L-2: Common chart types

chart type	chart icon	used to show most commonly	example
Column		Comparisons of values (vertical bars)	Each vertical bar represents the annual sales for a different product for the year 2013
Bar		Comparisons of values (horizontal bars)	Each horizontal bar represents the annual sales for a different product for the year 2013
Line		Trends over time	Each point on the line represents monthly sales for one product for the year 2013
Pie		Parts of a whole	Each slice represents total quarterly sales for a company for the year 2013
Area		Cumulative totals	Each section represents monthly sales by representative, stacked to show the cumulative total sales effort for the year 2013

FIGURE L-8: Inserting a chart on a report

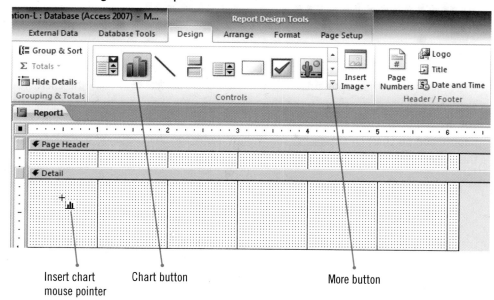

Insert chart mouse pointer

Chart button

More button

FIGURE L-9: Choosing the chart areas

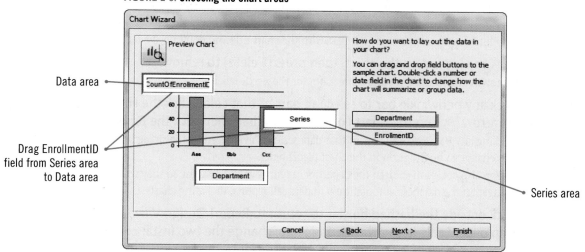

Data area

Drag EnrollmentID field from Series area to Data area

Series area

FIGURE L-10: Department Enrollment Totals column chart

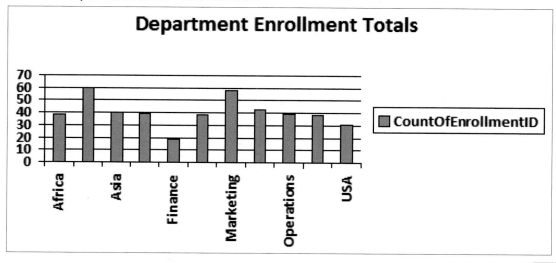

Modifying Charts

You modify charts in Design View of the form or report that contains the chart. Modifying a chart is challenging because Design View doesn't always show you the actual chart values, but instead, displays a chart placeholder that represents the embedded chart object. To modify the chart, you modify the chart elements and chart areas within the chart placeholder. To view the changes as they apply to the real data you are charting, return to either Form View for a form or Print Preview for a report. See Table L-3 for more information on chart areas. ▓▓▓▓ You want to resize the chart, change the color of the bars, and remove the legend to better display the values on the x-axis.

STEPS

1. **Right-click the report, click Design View, then close the Group, Sort, and Total pane if it is open**

   To make changes to chart elements, you open the chart in edit mode by double-clicking it. Use **edit mode** to select and modify individual chart elements such as the title, legend, bars, or axes. If you double-click the edge of the chart placeholder, you open the Property Sheet for the chart instead of opening the chart itself in edit mode.

2. **Double-click the chart**

   The hashed border of the chart placeholder control indicates that the chart is in edit mode, as shown in Figure L-11. The Chart Standard and Chart Formatting toolbars also appear when the chart is in edit mode. They may appear on one row instead of stacked. Given there is only one series of bars that count the enrollments, you can describe the data with the chart title and don't need a legend.

   > **TROUBLE**
   > If you make a mistake, use the Undo button 🔄 on the Chart Standard toolbar.

3. **Click the legend on the chart, then press [Delete] to remove it**

   Removing the legend provides more room for the x-axis labels.

   > **TROUBLE**
   > If you can't see the Fill Color button on the Formatting toolbar, drag the left edge of the toolbars to position them on two rows to show all buttons.

4. **Click any periwinkle bar to select all bars of that color, click the Fill Color button list arrow 🖌 ▾ on the Chart Formatting toolbar, then click the Bright Green box**

   Clicking any bar selects all bars in that data series as evidenced by the sizing handle in each of the bars. The bars change to bright green in the chart placeholder.

   You also decide to shorten the department names in the database so they will better fit on the x-axis. Data changed in the database automatically updates all reports, including charts, that are based on that data.

5. **Click outside the hashed border to return to Report Design View, double-click the Employees table in the Navigation Pane, change the two instances of Information Systems to IS in the Department field, then close the Employees table**

   Preview the updated chart.

   > **TROUBLE**
   > If you are prompted that the report width is greater than the page width, return to Report Design View and resize the chart and right edge of the report to fit within a width of 8".

6. **Save the report as DepartmentChart, then display it in Print Preview**

   The final chart is shown in Figure L-12.

Creating Advanced Reports

FIGURE L-11: **Editing a chart placeholder**

Chart Standard toolbar
Chart Formatting toolbar

Hashed border indicates
the chart is being edited

Click outside the chart
to return to Design View

Datasheet

Legend

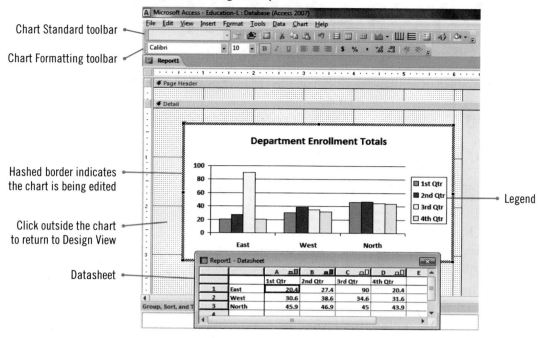

FIGURE L-12: **Final Department Enrollment Totals column chart**

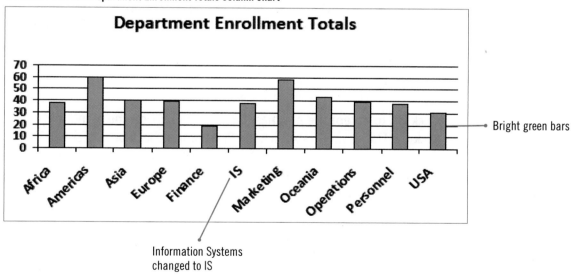

Bright green bars

Information Systems
changed to IS

TABLE L-3: **Chart areas**

chart area	description
Data	Determines what field the bars (lines, wedges, etc.) on the chart represent
Axis	The x-axis (horizontal axis) and y-axis (vertical axis) on the chart
Series	Displays the legend when multiple series of data are graphed

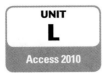

Applying Chart Types

The Chart Wizard provides 20 different chart types to choose from. While column charts are the most popular, you can also use line, area, and pie charts to effectively show some types of data. Three-dimensional effects can be used to enhance the chart, but those effects can also make it difficult to compare the sizes of bars, lines, and wedges, so choose a three-dimensional effect only if it does not detract from the point of the chart. ▆▆▉▉▉ You change the existing column chart to other chart types and subtypes to see how the data is presented.

STEPS

1. **Right-click the chart, click Design View, then double-click the chart placeholder**
   You must open the chart in edit mode to change the chart type.

2. **Click Chart on the menu bar, then click Chart Type**
   The Chart Type dialog box opens as shown in Figure L-13. All major chart types plus many chart subtypes are displayed. A button is available to preview any choice before applying that chart subtype.

3. **Click the Clustered column with a 3-D visual effect button (second row, first column in the Chart sub-type area), click and hold the Press and Hold to View Sample button, click the 3-D Column button (third row, first column in the Chart sub-type area), then click and hold the Press and Hold to View Sample button**
   A Sample box opens, presenting a rough idea of what the final chart will look like. While 3-D charts appear more interesting than 2-D chart types, the samples do not show the data more clearly, so you decide to preview other 2-D chart types.

4. **Click the Bar Chart type in the Chart type list, click and hold the Press and Hold to View Sample button, click the Line Chart type in the Chart type list, click and hold the Press and Hold to View Sample button, click the Pie Chart type in the Chart type list, click and hold the Press and Hold to View Sample button, click the Default formatting check box, then click and hold the Press and Hold to View Sample button**
   Because this chart only has one set of values that represent 100% of all enrollments, the data fits a pie chart. Other chart options help you enhance pie charts.

5. **Click OK to accept the pie chart type, click Chart on the menu bar, click Chart Options, click the Data Labels tab, click the Percentage check box, click the Titles tab, click the Chart title box, type Enrollment % by Dept, click the Legend tab, make sure the Show legend check box is selected, then click OK**
   With the modifications made to change the chart into a pie chart, you view it in Print Preview to see the final result.

6. **Click outside the hashed border to return to Report Design View, then display the report in Print Preview**
   The same departmental data, expressed as a pie chart, is shown in Figure L-14. The title of the chart is Enrollment % by Dept, but the name of the report is still DepartmentChart.

7. **Save and close the DepartmentChart report**

FIGURE L-13: Chart Type dialog box

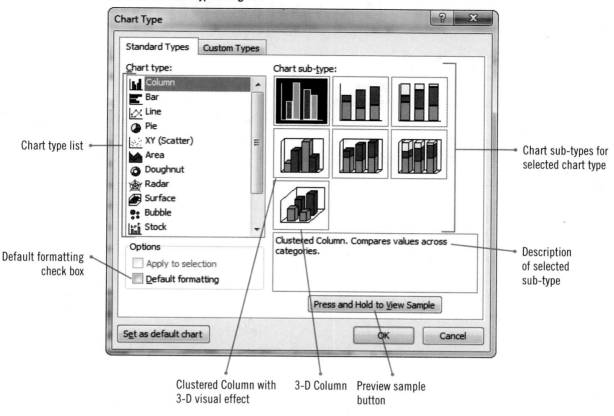

Chart type list

Default formatting check box

Chart sub-types for selected chart type

Description of selected sub-type

Clustered Column with 3-D visual effect   3-D Column   Preview sample button

FIGURE L-14: Department Enrollment Totals pie chart

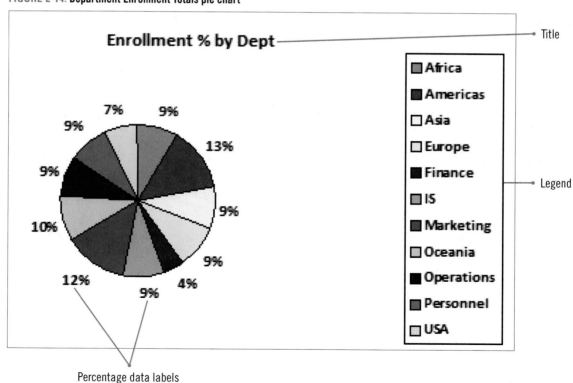

Title

Legend

Percentage data labels

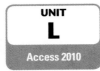
Creating Multicolumn Reports

A **multicolumn report** repeats information in more than one column on the page. To create multiple columns, you use options in the Page Setup dialog box. Samantha asks you to create a report that shows employee names sorted in ascending order for each course. A report with only a few fields is a good candidate for a multicolumn report.

STEPS

1. **Click the Create tab, click the Report Wizard button, click the Tables/Queries list arrow, click Table:Courses, double-click Description, click the Tables/Queries list arrow, click Table: Employees, double-click EFirst, double-click ELast, click Next, click Next to view the data by Courses, click Next to bypass adding any more grouping levels, click the first sort list arrow, click ELast, click Next, click Stepped, click Landscape, click Next, type Attendance List for the title, click Finish, then click the Last Page button** ▶│

    The initial report is displayed in Print Preview as a 19- or 20-page report (or twice that long if the report is too wide, which causes twice as many pages). This report would work well as a multicolumn report because only three fields are involved. You also decide to combine the names into a single expression with the employee's full name. First, delete the existing EFirst and ELast controls.

2. **Right-click the report, click Design View, click the ELast label, press [Delete], click the EFirst label, press [Delete], click the ELast text box, press [Delete], click the EFirst text box, press [Delete], click the Page expression text box in the Page Footer section, press [Delete], then drag the right edge of the report as far to the left as possible**

    You add a new text box to the Detail section with an expression that contains both the first and last names.

3. **Click the Text Box button** ⓐⓑⓒ **in the Controls group, click at about the 1" mark of the Detail section to insert a new text box control, then delete the accompanying label**

4. **Click the Unbound text box to select it, click Unbound, type =[ELast]&", "&[EFirst], press [Enter], widen the new control to about 2" wide, right-click the Attendance List report tab, then click Print Preview**

    With the information clearly presented in a single, narrow column, you're ready to specify that the report print multiple columns.

5. **Click the Page Setup button, click the Columns tab, click the Number of Columns box, type 3, then click the Down, then Across option button as shown in Figure L-15**

    The content of the report is now set to print in three newspaper-style columns.

6. **Click OK**

    The final Attendance List report is shown in Figure L-16. By specifying that the report is three columns wide, the number of pages in the report is significantly reduced.

7. **Save and close the Attendance List report**

FIGURE L-15: Page Setup dialog box

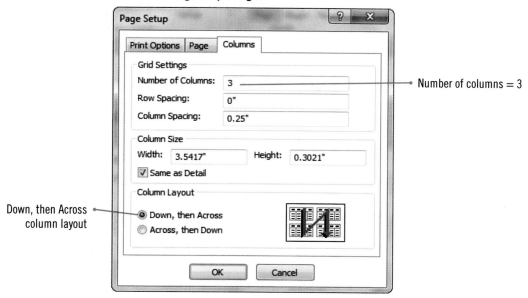

Number of columns = 3

Down, then Across column layout

FIGURE L-16: Attendance List report in three columns

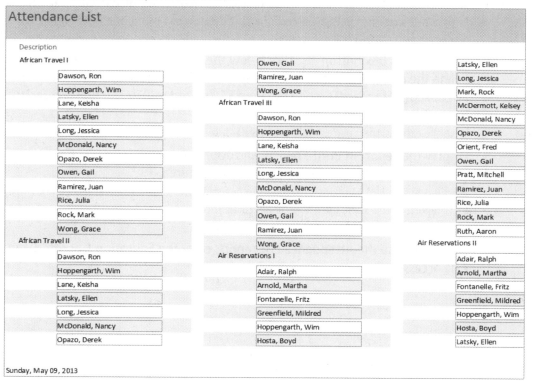

Using Domain Functions

Domain functions, also called domain aggregate functions, are used in an expression to calculate a value based on a field that is not included in the Record Source property for the form or report. Domain functions start with a "D" for "domain" such as DSum, DAvg, or DCount, and perform the same calculation as their Sum, Avg, and Count counterparts. Domain functions have two required arguments: the field that is used for the calculation and the domain name. The **domain** is the table or query that contains the field used in the calculation. A third optional argument allows you to select given records based on criteria you specify. ▓▓▓▓ Jacob asks you to add a standard disclaimer to the bottom of every report. This is an excellent opportunity to use the DLookup function.

STEPS

1. **Click the Create tab, click the Table Design button, then build a new table with the fields, data types, primary key field, and table name shown in Figure L-17**

   With the Disclaimers table established, you add two records of standard text used at Quest Specialty Travel.

   > **TROUBLE**
   > Widen the StandardText column as needed to view all text.

2. **Save the Disclaimers table, click the View button 🔲, then enter the two records shown in Figure L-18**

   The first disclaimer is used with any report that contains employee information. The second is to be added to all internal reports that do not contain employee information. With the data in place, you're ready to use the DLookup function on a report to insert standard text.

3. **Save and close the Disclaimers table, right-click the Attendance List report in the Navigation Pane, click Design View, then use ✛ to drag the top of the Report Footer section down to expand the Page Footer section to about twice its current size**

   With added space in the Page Footer for a new control, you can now add a text box to return the correct disclaimer using the DLookup function.

4. **Click the Text Box button 🔲, click below the Now() text box in the Page Footer section, delete the label, click the text box to select it, click Unbound, type the expression =DLookup("[StandardText]","Disclaimers", "[StandardID]=1"), press [Enter], then widen the text box to about 3"**

   With the expression in place, you'll preview it.

   > **TROUBLE**
   > If you see an #Error message in the Page Footer, return to Report Design View and double-check your expression.

5. **Display the report in Print Preview and zoom and scroll to the Page Footer to view the result of the DLookup function as shown in Figure L-19**

   By entering standard company disclaimers in one table, the same disclaimer text can be consistently added to each report. If the standard text is changed in the Disclaimers table, all reports would be automatically updated as well.

   > **QUICK TIP**
   > If you want your name to be on the report when you print it, enter your name as a label in the Page Footer section.

6. **Save and close the Attendance List report, close the Education-L.accdb database, then exit Access**

FIGURE L-17: New Disclaimers table

Name the table
Disclaimers •---•

Primary key field •---•

	Field Name	Data Type
🔑	StandardID	AutoNumber
	StandardText	Text

Disclaimers

FIGURE L-18: Records in the Disclaimers table

Disclaimers

StandardID	StandardText	Click to Add
1	Confidential - Quest Specialty Travel	
2	For internal use only - Quest Specialty Travel	
* (New)		

FIGURE L-19: Standard disclaimer in Report Footer section

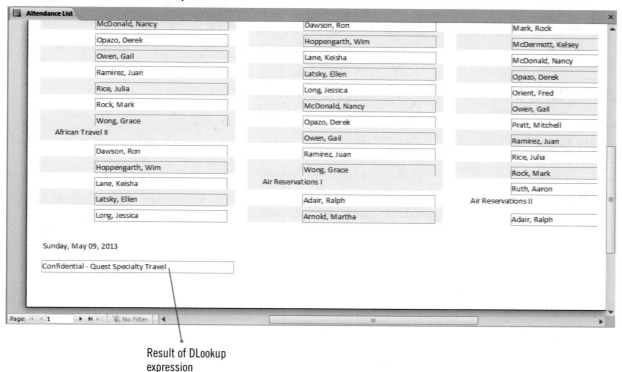

Result of DLookup
expression

Practice

Concepts Review

For current SAM information, including versions and content details, visit SAM Central (http://www.cengage.com/samcentral). If you have a SAM user profile, you may have access to hands-on instruction, practice, and assessment of the skills covered in this unit. Since various versions of SAM are supported throughout the life of this text, check with your instructor for the correct instructions and URL/Web site for accessing assignments.

Identify each element of the Report Design View shown in Figure L-20.

FIGURE L-20

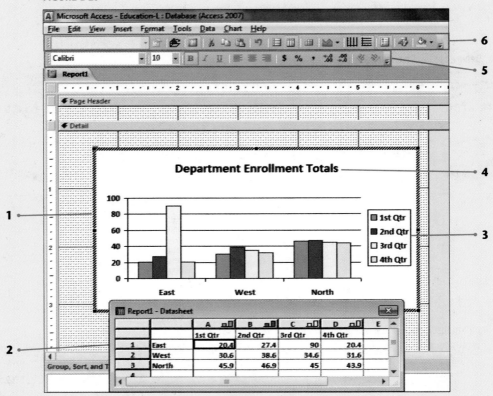

Match each term with the statement that best describes its function.

7. **Charts**

8. **Domain functions**

9. **Chart types**

10. **Data area**

11. **Edit mode**

a. Visual representations of numeric data

b. Calculate a value based on a field that is not included in the Record Source property for the form or report

c. Used to select and modify individual chart elements such as the title, legend, bars, or axes

d. Determines what data is graphed on the chart

e. Determine the presentation of data on the chart such as column, pie, and line

Select the best answer from the list of choices.

12. **Which button aligns the edges of two or more selected controls?**
    - **a.** Align Text Right button on the Arrange tab
    - **b.** Align button on the Arrange tab
    - **c.** Align Text Right button on the Design tab
    - **d.** Align button on the Design tab

13. **To set a page break before a Group Header section on a report, you would modify the properties of the:**
    - **a.** Report.
    - **b.** Group Header section.
    - **c.** Detail section.
    - **d.** Page Footer section.

14. **Which control layout is common for reports?**
    - **a.** Stacked
    - **b.** Tabular
    - **c.** Datasheet
    - **d.** Gridlines

15. **Which dialog box allows you to specify the number of columns you want to view in a report?**
    - **a.** Print
    - **b.** Columns
    - **c.** Page Setup
    - **d.** Property Sheet

16. **Which type of chart is best to show an upward sales trend over several months?**
    - **a.** Column
    - **b.** Pie
    - **c.** Line
    - **d.** Scatter

17. **Which task can be performed on a chart *without* being in edit mode?**
    - **a.** Modifying the title
    - **b.** Deleting the legend
    - **c.** Changing bar colors
    - **d.** Resizing the chart

18. **Which chart area determines the field that the bars (lines, wedges, etc.) on the chart represent?**
    - **a.** Data
    - **b.** X-axis
    - **c.** Category
    - **d.** Legend

19. **Which chart area is used to identify the legend?**
    - **a.** Data
    - **b.** X-axis
    - **c.** Y-axis
    - **d.** Series

20. **Which chart type is best at showing cumulative totals?**
    - **a.** Column
    - **b.** Area
    - **c.** Bar
    - **d.** Pie

21. **Which chart type is best at showing parts of a whole?**
    - **a.** Column
    - **b.** Area
    - **c.** Bar
    - **d.** Pie

Skills Review

1. **Apply advanced formatting.**
   - **a.** Start Access, then open the RealEstate-L.accdb database from the drive and folder where you store your Data Files. Enable content if prompted.
   - **b.** Preview the AgencyListings report, noting the format for the SqFt and Asking fields.
   - **c.** In Report Design View, change the Format property for the SqFt text box in the Detail section to **Standard** and change the Decimal Places property to **0**.
   - **d.** In Report Design View, change the Format property for the Asking text box in the Detail section to **Currency** and change the Decimal Places property to **0**.
   - **e.** Preview the report to make sure your SqFt values appear with commas, the Asking values appear with dollar signs, and neither shows any digits to the right of the decimal place.

2. **Control layout.**
   - **a.** Open the AgencyListings report in Design View.
   - **b.** Open the Group, Sort, and Total pane, and open the AgencyName Footer section.
   - **c.** Add a text box in the AgencyName Footer under the SqFt text box in the Detail section with the expression **=Sum([SqFt])**. Modify the new label to have the caption **Subtotals:**.

Skills Review (continued)

d. Add a text box in the AgencyName Footer under the Asking text box in the Detail section with the expression **=Sum([Asking])**. Delete the extra label in the AgencyName Footer section.

e. Format the text boxes using the Property Sheet, and align the text boxes under the fields they subtotal so that Print Preview looks similar to Figure L-21.

3. Set advanced print layout.

a. Open the AgencyListings report in Design View.

b. Modify the AgencyName Footer section to force a new page after that section prints.

c. Preview the report to make sure each of the four agencies prints on its own page.

d. Close and save the AgencyListings report.

FIGURE L-21

Marvin and Pam Realtors					
Angelina	555-220-4466				
	9	Ranch	Horseshoe Bend	2,000	$105,000
Duncan	555-228-5577				
	24	Mobile Home	Galena	1,200	$120,000
Welch	555-223-0044				
	22	Cabin	Kimberling City	1,350	$127,900
	23	Two Story	Galena	2,000	$124,900
			Subtotals:	6,550	$477,800

4. Create charts.

a. Open the Inventory query in Query Design View, then add criteria to select only the Ranch (in the Type field) records.

b. Save the query with a new name as **RanchHomes**, then close it.

c. Start a new report in Report Design View.

d. Insert a chart in the Detail section based on the RanchHomes query.

e. Choose the RLast and Asking fields for the chart, choose a Column Chart, then make sure the SumOfAsking field appears in the Data area, and move the RLast field from the Axis to the Series area.

f. Title the chart **Ranch Inventory**, then preview the report to view the chart.

g. Save the report with the name **RanchInventoryReport**.

5. Modify charts.

a. Return to Report Design View, double-click the chart to open it in edit mode, then remove the legend.

b. Double-click the y-axis values to open the Format Axis dialog box, click the Number tab, then choose the Currency format from the Category list, entering **0** for the Decimal places.

c. Change the color of the periwinkle bars to red.

d. Click the By Column button on the Chart Standard toolbar to switch the fields in the x-axis and legend positions.

e. Return to Report Design View, then switch to Print Preview. Resize the chart as necessary so it looks like Figure L-22.

6. Apply chart types.

a. Close the report, then copy and save the report with the name **RanchInventoryReport3D**.

b. Switch to Report Design View, open the chart in edit mode, then change the chart type to a Clustered column with a 3-D visual effect.

c. Switch between Report Design View and Print Preview, resizing the chart as needed so that all of the labels on the x-axis are displayed clearly.

d. Print RanchInventoryReport3D if requested by your instructor, then save and close it.

FIGURE L-22

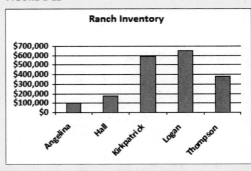

7. Create multicolumn reports.

a. Use the Report Wizard to create a report with the AgencyName field from the Agencies table, the RFirst and RLast fields from the Realtors table, and the Type field from the Listings table. Be sure to select the fields from the table objects.

b. View the data by Listings, add AgencyName as the grouping level, sort the records in ascending order by RLast, use a Stepped layout and a Landscape orientation, and use **Listings** as the report title.

c. In Report Design View, delete the RLast and RFirst labels and text boxes.

Skills Review (continued)

d. Delete the page expression in the Page Footer section, delete the Type label in the Page Header section, and delete the AgencyName label in the Page Header section. Move the Type field in the Detail section to the left to just under the AgencyName text box.

e. Add a new text box to the right of the Type control in the Detail section with the following expression:
=[RLast]&", "&[RFirst]

f. Delete the label for the new text box, then widen the =[RLast]&", "&[RFirst] text box in the Detail section to be about 2" wide. Drag the right edge of the report as far as you can to the left so that the report is approximately 5" wide.

g. Preview the report, and use the Page Setup dialog box to set the Number of Columns setting to **2** and the column layout to Down, then Across. It should look like Figure L-23. If you want your name to appear on the printout, change the name of Tom Hall to your own name in the Realtors table.

h. Save and close the Listings report.

8. Use domain functions.

a. Create a new table named **Legal** with two new fields: **LegalID** with an AutoNumber data type and **LegalText** with a Memo data type. Make LegalID the primary key field.

b. Add one record to the table with the following entry in the LegalText field: **The realtor makes no guarantees with respect to the accuracy of the listing**. Widen the column of the LegalText field as needed. Note the value of the LegalID field for the first record, then save and close the Legal table.

FIGURE L-23

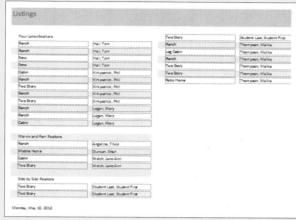

c. Open the ListingReport in Design View, expand the Page Footer section to about 0.5", then use a DLookup function in an expression in a text box in the Page Footer section to look up the LegalText field in the Legal table as follows: **=DLookup("[LegalText]","Legal", "LegalID=1")**. Delete the accompanying label. (Note that the number in the expression must match the value of the LegalID field for the first record that you created in Step b.)

d. Preview the report, then review the Page Footer. Switch back and forth between Report Design View and Print Preview to fix and widen the text box to be about 8" wide so that it clearly displays the entire expression, then save and close the ListingReport.

e. Open the Legal table, and modify the LegalText in the first record to read: The realtor **and agency make** no guarantees with respect to the accuracy of the listing.

f. Preview the ListingReport again to observe the Page Footer, then print the report if requested by your instructor.

g. Close the RealEstate-L.accdb database and exit Access 2010.

Independent Challenge 1

As the manager of a college women's basketball team, you want to enhance a form within the Basketball-L.accdb database to chart the home versus visiting team scores. You will build on your report creation skills to do so.

a. Start Access, then open the database Basketball-L.accdb from the drive and folder where you store your Data Files. Enable content if prompted.

b. Open and then maximize the GameInfo form. Page down through several records as you observe the Home and Visitor scores.

c. Open the form in Form Design View, then insert a chart on the right side of the form based on the Games table. Choose the HomeScore and OpponentScore fields for the chart. Choose a Column Chart type.

d. Add both the HomeScore and OpponentScore fields to the Data area, double-click the SumOfHomeScore field, select None as the summarize option, double-click the SumOfOpponentScore field, then select None as the summarize option.

e. Click Next and choose GameNo as the Form Field and as the Chart Field so that the chart changes from record to record showing the HomeScore versus the OpponentScore in the chart.

Independent Challenge 1 (continued)

f. Title the chart **Scores**, and do not display a legend.

g. Open the form in Form View, and print the record for GameNo 10 as shown in Figure L-24 if requested by your instructor. To insert your name on the printout, add it as a label to the Form Header section.

h. Save the GameInfo form, close it, close the Basketball-L.accdb database, and exit Access 2007.

FIGURE L-24

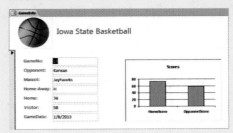

Independent Challenge 2

As the manager of a college women's basketball team, you want to build a report that shows a graph of total points per player per game.

a. Start Access, then open the database Basketball-L.accdb from the drive and folder where you store your Data Files. Enable content if prompted.

b. Open the PlayerStatistics report, and study the structure. Notice that this report has the total points per player you want to graph per game in the last column. Open the PlayerStatistics report in Report Design View.

c. Double-click the far-right text box in the Detail section, and click the Data tab in the Property Sheet to study the Control Source property. The expression =[FT]+([fg]*2)+([3p]*3) adds one-point free throws [FT] to two-point field goals [fg] to three-point three-pointers [3p] to find the player's total contribution to the score. You will calculate the total point value in the underlying query instead of on the report to make it easier to graph.

d. Click the report selector button, then click the Build button for the Record Source property, which currently displays the PlayerStats query. In the first blank column add a new field with the following expression:
TotalPts:[FT]+([fg]*2)+([3p]*3).

e. Save and close the PlayerStats query, then return to Design View for the PlayerStatistics report. Open the Property Sheet for the GameNo Footer section. On the Format tab, change the Force New Page property to After Section.

f. Drag the top of the Page Footer section bar down so the height of the GameNo Footer section is about 3 inches high, then insert a chart just below the existing controls in the GameNo Footer section.

g. In the Chart Wizard, choose the PlayerStats query to create the chart, choose the LastName and TotalPts fields for the chart, and choose the Column Chart type.

h. Use SumOfTotalPts in the Data area and the LastName field in the Axis area (which should be the defaults). Choose <No Field> to link the Report Fields and Chart Fields, and title the chart **Player Total Points**.

i. Widen the chart placeholder and report to be about 6" wide in Report Design View, delete the legend, then save and preview the report. The chart should look like Figure L-25.

j. Save the PlayerStatistics report, add your name as a label to the Report Header section, print the first page, then close the report.

k. Close the Basketball-L.accdb database, and exit Access 2010.

FIGURE L-25

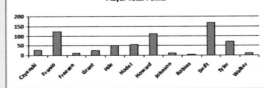

Independent Challenge 3

As the manager of a college women's basketball team, you want to create a multicolumn report from the Basketball-L.accdb database to summarize total points per game per player.

a. Start Access, then open the database Basketball-L.accdb from the drive and folder where you store your Data Files. Enable content if prompted.

b. Open the PlayerStats query in Design View. In the first blank column add a new field with the following expression (if it has not already been added): **TotalPts:[FT]+([fg]*2)+([3p]*3)**.

c. Save and close the PlayerStats query.

d. Create a new report using the Report Wizard from the PlayerStats query with the fields **Opponent**, **GameDate**, **LastName**, and **TotalPts**. View the data by Games, do not add any more grouping levels, then sort the records in descending order by TotalPts.

Creating Advanced Reports

Independent Challenge 3 (continued)

e. Click the Summary Options button, then click the Sum check box for the TotalPts field.

f. Choose a Stepped layout and a Landscape orientation. Title the report **Point Production**, and preview it.

g. In Report Design View delete the long text box with the Summary expression in the GameNo Footer section.

h. Delete the LastName and TotalPts labels from the Page Header section.

i. Delete the page expression in the Page Footer section, then move the TotalPts and LastName text boxes in the Detail section to the left. Move any other text boxes to the left so that no control extends beyond the 4" mark on the horizontal ruler.

j. Drag the right edge of the report to the left, so that it is no wider than 4", then right-align text boxes with the subtotal for total points in the GameNo Footer and the Report Footer sections. Right-align the values within their respective controls as well. Also move and right-align the Sum and Grand Total labels closer to the text boxes they describe.

k. Preview the report, and in the Page Setup dialog box, set the report to **2** columns, and specify that the column layout go down, then across.

Advanced Challenge Exercise

- In Design View, improve the report by adding a horizontal line across the bottom of the GameNo Footer section to separate the records from game to game.
- For the GameNo Footer section, change the New Row or Col property to After Section.
- Add other formatting improvements as desired.

l. Preview the Point Production report. It should structurally look like Figure L-26. Print the first page of the report if requested by your instructor, adding your name as a label to the Report Header section if needed for the printout.

m. Close the Point Production report, close the Basketball-L.accdb database, then exit Access.

FIGURE L-26

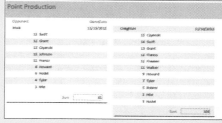

Real Life Independent Challenge

In your quest to become an Access database consultant, you want to know more about the built-in Microsoft Access templates and what you can learn about report design from these samples. In this exercise, you'll explore the reports of the Sales pipeline template.

a. Start Access 2010, then select the Sales Pipeline template from the Sales & Marketing folder. (You may find the Sales Pipeline template in the Samples folder.) Use the Browse button to specify the drive and folder where you store your Data Files, name the database **Sales**, then click Download.

b. Expand the Navigation Pane to review the objects in the database.

c. Briefly open then close each object in the Opportunities, Employees, and Customers navigation sections to study the structure of the available forms and reports. Close all open objects.

d. Open the Employees table in the Supporting Objects section, and enter your name in the Last Name and First Name fields. Enter fictitious but realistic data in the other fields. Close the Employees table.

e. Open the Customers table in the Supporting Objects section, and enter your teacher's name with other fictitious data in the first record. Close the Customers table.

f. Open the Opportunities table in the Supporting Objects section, and add a record with the title **Big Sale** entering appropriate but fictitious values in the fields. Add two more records to the Opportunities table choosing your teacher as the customer, yourself as the employee, but varying the choices in the other fields. Choose fictitious categories (1), (2), and (3) for the Category field. Close the Opportunities datasheet.

g. Open the Forecast Tracking Charts form in the Opportunities section to see how the information is being tracked. Click the Assigned To list arrow, then choose your name. Click each of the four tabs in the lower part of the form to see how the information from the Opportunity records in this database is presented.

h. If requested to print the form, add your name as a label to the Report Header section, print the form, close the Forecast Tracking Charts form, close the Sales.accdb database, and exit Access 2010.

Visual Workshop

As the manager of a college women's basketball team, you need to create a report from the Basketball-L.accdb database that lists information about each game played and subtracts the OpponentScore from the HomeScore field to calculate the number of points by which the game was won or lost in the Win/Loss column. Use the Report Wizard to start the report. Base it on the Games table, and sort the records in ascending order on the GameDate field. Use Report Layout and Design View to move, resize, align, modify, and add controls as necessary to match Figure L-27. If requested to print the report, add your name as a label to the Report Header section before printing.

FIGURE L-27

Iowa State Basketball

Game Date	Opponent	Mascot	Home-Away	Home	Opponent	Win/Loss
11/13/2012	Iowa	Hawkeyes	A	81	65	16
11/16/2012	Creighton	Bluejays	H	106	60	46
11/23/2012	Northern Illinois	Huskies	H	65	60	5
11/30/2012	Louisiana Tech	Red Raiders	A	69	89	-20
12/11/2012	Drake	Bulldogs	H	80	60	20
12/19/2012	Northern Iowa	Panthers	A	38	73	-35
12/29/2012	Buffalo	Bulls	H	50	55	-5
1/1/2013	Oklahoma	Sooners	A	53	60	-7
1/4/2013	Texas	Longhorns	H	57	60	-3

Creating Advanced Reports

Creating Macros

A **macro** is a database object that stores Access actions. **Actions** are the tasks that you want the macro to perform. When you run a macro, you execute the stored set of actions. Access provides over 80 actions from which to choose when creating a macro. Repetitive Access tasks such as printing several reports, or opening and maximizing a form, are good candidates for a macro. Automating routine tasks by using macros builds efficiency, accuracy, and flexibility into your database.  Kayla Green, the network administrator at Quest Specialty Travel, has identified several Access tasks that are repeated on a regular basis. She has asked you to help her automate these processes with macros.

OBJECTIVES

Understand macros

Create a macro

Modify actions and arguments

Assign a macro to a command button

Use If statements

Work with events

Create a data macro

Troubleshoot macros

Understanding Macros

A macro object may contain one or more actions, the tasks that you want Access to perform. Actions are entered in **Macro Design View**, the window in which you build and modify macros. Each action has a specified set of arguments. **Arguments** provide additional information on how to carry out the action. For example, the OpenForm action contains six arguments, including Form Name (identifies which form to open) and View (determines whether the form should be opened in Form View or Design View). After choosing the macro action you want, the associated arguments for the action automatically appear below the macro action. You decide to study the major benefits of using macros, macro terminology, and the components of the Macro Design View before building your first macro.

DETAILS

The major benefits of using macros include:

- Saving time by automating routine tasks
- Increasing accuracy by ensuring that tasks are executed consistently
- Improving the functionality and ease of use of forms by using macros connected to command buttons
- Ensuring data accuracy in forms by using macros to respond to data entry errors
- Automating data transfers such as collecting data from Outlook
- Creating your own customized user interface

Macro terminology:

- A **macro** is an Access object that stores a series of actions to perform one or more tasks.
- Macro Design View is the window in which you create a macro. Figure M-1 shows Macro Design View with an OpenForm action. See Table M-1 for a description of the Macro Design View components.
- Each task that you want the macro to perform is called an **action**.
- Arguments are properties of an action that provide additional information on how the action should execute.
- A **conditional expression** is an expression resulting in either a true or false answer that determines whether a macro action will execute. Conditional expressions are used in If statements.
- An **event** is something that happens to a form, window, toolbar, or control—such as the click of a command button or an entry in a field—that can be used to initiate the execution of a macro.
- A **submacro** is a collection of actions within a macro object that allows you to name and create multiple, separate macros within a single macro object.

FIGURE M-1: Macro Design View with OpenForm action

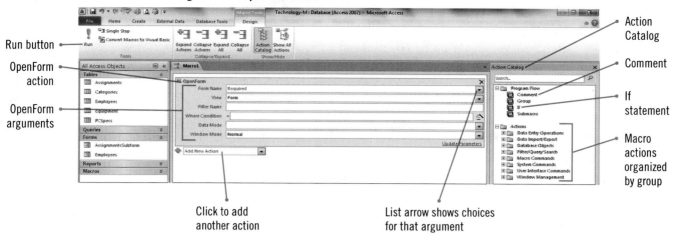

Run button

OpenForm action

OpenForm arguments

Action Catalog

Comment

If statement

Macro actions organized by group

Click to add another action

List arrow shows choices for that argument

TABLE M-1: Macro Design View components

component	description
Action Catalog	Lists all available macro actions organized by category. Use the Search box to narrow the number of macro actions to a particular subject.
If statement	Contains conditional expressions that are evaluated either true or false. If true, the macro action is executed. If false, the macro action is skipped. If statements in Access 2010 may contain Else If and Else clauses.
Comment	Allows you to document the macro with explanatory text.
Arguments	Lists required and optional arguments for the selected action.
Run button	Runs the selected macro.

Creating a Macro

In Access, you create a macro by choosing a series of actions in Macro Design View that accomplishes the job you want to automate. Therefore, to become proficient with Access macros, you must be comfortable with macro actions. Some of the most common actions are listed in Table M-2. When you create a macro in other Microsoft Office products such as Word or Excel, you create Visual Basic for Applications (VBA) statements. In Access, macros do not create VBA code, but after creating a macro, you can convert it to VBA if desired. Kayla observes that users want to open the AllEquipment report from the Employees form, so she asks you to create a macro to help automate this task.

STEPS

1. **Start Access, open the Technology-M.accdb database from the drive and folder where you store your Data Files, enable content if prompted, click the Create tab, then click the Macro button**

   Macro Design View opens, ready for you to choose your first action.

TROUBLE
If you choose the wrong macro action, click the Delete button ✕ in the upper-right corner of the macro action block and try again.

2. **Click the first row's Action list arrow, type op to quickly scroll to the actions that start with the letters "op", then scroll and click OpenReport**

   The OpenReport action is now the first action in the macro, and the arguments that further define the OpenReport action appear in the action block. The **action block** organizes all of the arguments for a current action and is visually highlighted with a rectangle and gray background. You can expand or collapse the action block to view or hide details by clicking the Collapse/Expand button to the left of the action name or the Expand and Collapse buttons on the Design tab in Macro Design View.

   The **OpenReport** action has three required arguments: Report Name, View, and Window Mode. View and Window Mode have default values, but the word "Required" is shown in the Report Name argument indicating that you must select a choice. The Filter Name and Where Condition arguments are optional as indicated by their blank boxes.

3. **Click the Report Name argument list arrow, then click AllEquipment**

   All of the report objects in the Technology-M.accdb database appear in the Report Name argument list, making it easy to choose the report you want.

4. **Click the View argument list arrow, then click Print Preview**

   Your screen should look like Figure M-2. Macros can contain one or many actions. In this case, the macro has only one action.

5. **Click the Save button 🖫 on the Quick Access toolbar, type PreviewAllEquipmentReport in the Macro Name text box, click OK, right-click the PreviewAllEquipmentReport macro tab, then click Close**

   The Navigation Pane lists the PreviewAllEquipmentReport object in the Macros group.

QUICK TIP
To print Macro Design View, click the File tab, click Print, click the Print button, then click OK in the Print Macro Definition dialog box.

6. **Double-click the PreviewAllEquipmentReport macro in the Navigation Pane to run the macro**

   The AllEquipment report opens in Print Preview.

7. **Close the AllEquipment report**

FIGURE M-2: Macro Design View with OpenReport action

Action Collapse/Expand button

Filter Name and Where Condition arguments are optional

Delete button

Argument list arrows help you choose values for that argument

Action block

Print Preview is selected for View argument

AllEquipment is selected for Report Name argument

Report Name argument list arrow

TABLE M-2: Common macro actions

subject area	macro action	description
Data Entry Operations	DeleteRecord	Deletes the current record
	SaveRecord	Saves the current record
Data Import/Export	ImportExportSpreadsheet	Imports or exports the spreadsheet you specify
	ImportExportText	Imports or exports the text file you specify
	EMailDatabaseObject	Sends the specified database object through Outlook with specified e-mail settings
Database Objects	OpenForm	Opens a form in Form View, Design View, Print Preview, or Datasheet View
	OpenQuery	Opens a select or crosstab query in Datasheet View, Design View, or Print Preview; runs an action query
	OpenReport	Opens a report in Design View or Print Preview, or prints the report
	OpenTable	Opens a table in Datasheet View, Design View, or Print Preview
	GoToControl	Moves the focus (where you are currently typing or clicking) to a specific field or control
	GoToRecord	Makes a specified record the current record
	SetValue	Sets the value of a field, control, or property
Filter/Query/Search	ApplyFilter	Restricts the number of records that appear in the resulting form or report by applying limiting criteria
	FindRecord	Finds the first record that meets the criteria
Macro Commands	RunCode	Runs a Visual Basic function (a series of programming statements that do a calculation or comparison and return a value)
	RunMacro	Runs a macro or attaches a macro to a custom menu command
	StopMacro	Stops the currently running macro
System Commands	Beep	Sounds a beep tone through the computer's speaker
	PrintOut	Prints the active object, such as a datasheet, report, form, or module
	SendKeys	Sends keystrokes directly to Microsoft Access or to an active Windows application
User Interface Commands	MessageBox	Displays a message box containing a warning or an informational message
	ShowToolbar	Displays or hides a given toolbar
Window Management	CloseWindow	Closes a window
	MaximizeWindow	Enlarges the active window to fill the Access window

Modifying Actions and Arguments

Macros can contain as many actions as necessary to complete the process that you want to automate. Each action is evaluated in the order in which it appears in Macro Design View, starting at the top. While some macro actions open, close, preview, or export data or objects, others are used only to make the database easier to use. **MessageBox** is a useful macro action because it displays an informational message to the user. 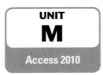 You add a MessageBox action to the PrintAllEquipmentReport macro to display a descriptive message in a dialog box.

STEPS

1. **Right-click the PreviewAllEquipmentReport macro in the Navigation Pane, then click Design View on the shortcut menu**

   The PreviewAllEquipmentReport macro opens in Macro Design View.

2. **Click the Add New Action list arrow, type me to quickly scroll to the actions that start with the letters "me", then click MessageBox**

   Each action has its own arguments that further clarify what the action does.

3. **Click the Message argument text box in the action block, then type Click the Print button to print this report**

   The Message argument determines what text appears in the message box. By default, the Beep argument is set to "Yes" and the Type argument is set to "None".

4. **Click the Type argument list arrow in the action block, then click Information**

   The Type argument determines which icon appears in the dialog box that is created by the MessageBox action.

5. **Click the Title argument text box in the action block, then type To print this report. . .**

   Your screen should look like Figure M-3. The Title argument specifies what text is displayed in the title bar of the resulting dialog box. If you leave the Title argument empty, the title bar of the resulting dialog box displays "Microsoft Access."

6. **Save the macro, then click the Run button in the Tools group**

   If your speakers are turned on, you should hear a beep, then the message box appears, as shown in Figure M-4.

7. **Click OK in the dialog box, close the AllEquipment report, then save and close Macro Design View**

FIGURE M-3: **Adding the MessageBox action**

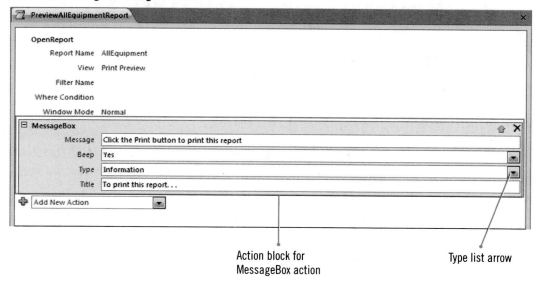

Action block for
MessageBox action

Type list arrow

FIGURE M-4: **Dialog box created by MessageBox action**

Title bar text from
Title argument

Information icon
from Type argument

Message text from
Message argument

Assigning a macro to a key combination

You can assign a key combination such as [Ctrl][L] to a macro by creating a macro with the name **AutoKeys**. Enter the key combination in the Macro Names column for the first action of the associated macro. Any key combination assignments you make in the AutoKeys macro override those that Access has already specified. Therefore, check the Keyboard Shortcuts information in the Microsoft Access Help system to make sure that the AutoKey assignment that you are creating doesn't override an existing Access quick keystroke that may be used for another purpose.

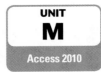

Assigning a Macro to a Command Button

Access provides many ways to run a macro: clicking the Run button in Macro Design View, clicking the Run Macro button from the Database Tools tab, assigning the macro to a command button, or assigning the macro to a Ribbon or shortcut menu command. Assigning a macro to a command button on a form provides a very intuitive way for the user to access the macro's functionality. ▰▰▰▰ You decide to modify the Employees form to include a command button that runs the PreviewAllEquipmentReport macro.

STEPS

QUICK TIP

Be sure the Use Control Wizards button is selected. To find it, click the More button in the Controls group on the Design tab.

1. **Right-click the Employees form in the Navigation Pane, click Design View, expand the Form Footer about 0.5", click the Button button ▤ in the Controls group, then click the left side of the Form Footer section**

   The **Command Button Wizard** starts, presenting you with 28 actions on the right organized in 6 categories on the left. If you wanted the command button to open a report, you would choose the OpenReport action in the Report Operations category. In this case, however, you want to run the PreviewAllEquipmentReport macro, which not only opens a report but also presents a message. The Miscellaneous category contains an action that allows you to run an existing macro.

2. **Click Miscellaneous in the Categories list, click Run Macro in the Actions list as shown in Figure M-5, click Next, click PreviewAllEquipmentReport, click Next, click the Text option button, select Run Macro, type All Equipment Report, then click Next**

   The Command Button Wizard asks you to give the button a meaningful name.

3. **Type cmdAllEquipment, click Finish, then click the Property Sheet button in the Tools group to open the Property Sheet for the command button**

   The new command button that runs a macro has been added to the Employees form in Form Design View. Some developers give all controls three-character prefixes to make the control easier to identify in macros and VBA.

   You work with the Property Sheet to change the text color of the button to differentiate it from the button color as well as to examine how the macro was attached to the command button.

4. **Click the Format tab in the Property Sheet, scroll down and click the Fore Color list arrow, click Text Dark, then click the Event tab in the Property Sheet, noting that the On Click property contains [Embedded Macro]**

   The PreviewAllEquipment macro was attached to the **On Click property** of this command button. In other words, the macro is run when the user clicks the command button. To make sure that the new command button works as intended, you view the form in Form View and test the command button.

5. **Close the Property Sheet, click the View button ▤ to switch to Form View, click the All Equipment Report command button in the Form Footer section, click OK in the message box, then close the AllEquipment report**

   The Employees form with the new command button should look like Figure M-6. It's common to put command buttons in the Form Footer so that users have a consistent location to find them.

6. **Save and close the Employees form**

FIGURE M-5: Adding a command button to run a macro

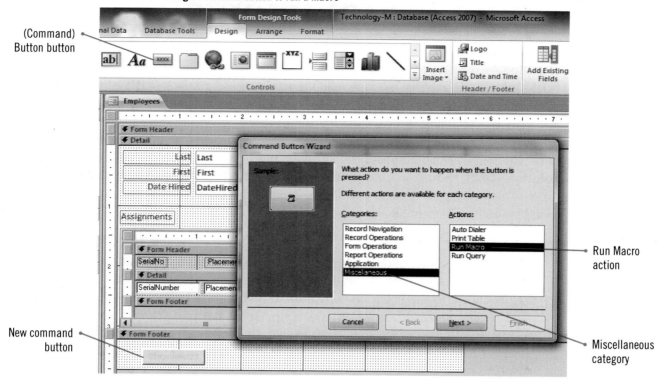

(Command) Button button

Run Macro action

Miscellaneous category

New command button

FIGURE M-6: Employees form with new command button

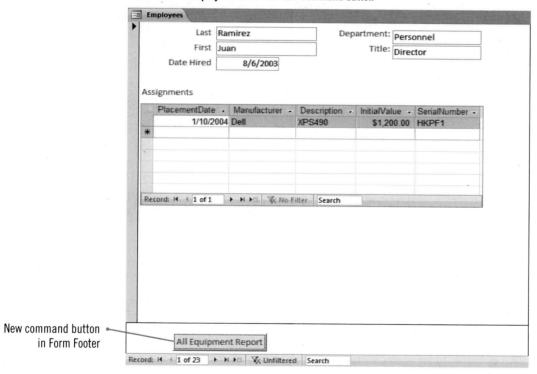

New command button in Form Footer

Using a trusted database and setting up a trusted folder

A **trusted database** allows you to run macros and VBA. By default, a database is not trusted. To trust a database, click the Enable Content button on the Security Warning bar each time you open a database. To permanently trust a database, store the database in a **trusted folder**.

To create a trusted folder, open the Options dialog box from the File tab, click the Trust Center, click the Trust Center Settings button, click the Trusted Locations option, click the Add new location button, then browse for and choose the folder you want to trust.

Using If Statements

An **If statement** allows you to run macro actions based on the result of a conditional expression. A **conditional expression** is an expression such as [Price]>100 or [StateName]="MO" that results in a true or false value. If the condition evaluates true, the actions that follow the If statement are executed. If the condition evaluates false, the macro skips those actions. When building a conditional expression that refers to a value in a control on a form or report, use the following syntax: [Forms]![*formname*]![*controlname*] or [Reports]![*reportname*]![*controlname*]. Separating the object type (Forms or Reports) from the object name and from the control name by using [square brackets] and exclamation points (!) is called **bang notation**. At Quest Specialty Travel, everyone who has been with the company longer than 5 years is eligible to take their old PC equipment home as soon as it has been replaced. You use a conditional macro to help evaluate and present this information in a form.

STEPS

1. **Click the Create tab, click the Macro button, click the Action Catalog button in the Show/Hide group to toggle on the Action Catalog window if it is not already visible, double-click If in the Program Flow area, then type the following in the If box: [Forms]![Employees]![DateHired]<Date()-(5*365)**

   The conditional expression shown in Figure M-7 says, "Check the value in the DateHired control on the Employees form and evaluate true if the value is earlier than 5 years from today. Evaluate false if the value is not earlier than 5 years ago."

QUICK TIP
Macro actions that require a trusted database are not shown unless you click the Show All Actions button in the Show/Hide group.

2. **Click the Add New Action list arrow in the If block, then scroll and click SetProperty**

   The **SetProperty** action has three arguments: Control Name, Property, and Value, which set the control, property, and value of that property.

3. **Click the Control Name argument text box in the Action Arguments pane, type LabelPCProgram, click the Property argument list arrow, click Visible, click the Value Property argument, then type True**

   Your screen should look like Figure M-8. The **Control Name** argument for the label is set to LabelPCProgram, which must match the **Name property** in the Property Sheet of the label that will be modified. The **Property** argument determines what property is being modified for the LabelPCProgram control. In this case, you are modifying the Visible property. The **Value** argument determines the value of the Visible property. For properties such as the Visible property that have only two choices in the Property Sheet, Yes or No, you enter a value of False for No and True for Yes.

4. **Save the macro with the name 5YearsPC, then close Macro Design View**

   Test the macro using the Employees form.

TROUBLE
Be sure Juan Ramirez with a hire date of 8/6/2003 is the current record.

5. **In the Navigation Pane, double-click the Employees form to open it**

   The record for Juan Ramirez, hired 8/6/2003, appears. Given that Juan has worked at Quest much longer than 5 years, you anticipate that the macro will display the label when it is run.

TROUBLE
Be sure the insertion point is in the main form when you run the 5YearsPC macro so it can find all of the controls to which it refers.

6. **Click the Database Tools tab, click the Run Macro button, verify that 5YearsPC is in the Macro Name text box, then click OK**

   After evaluating the HireDate field of this record and determining that this employee has been working at Quest Specialty Travel longer than 5 years, the LabelPCProgram label's Visible property was set to Yes, as shown in Figure M-9. The LabelPCProgram label's **Caption** property is "Eligible for PC Program!".

7. **Navigate through several records and note that the label remains visible for each employee even though the hire date may not be longer than 5 years ago**

   Because the macro only ran once, the label's Visible property remains Yes regardless of the current data in the HireDate field. You need a way to rerun or trigger the macro to evaluate each employee.

8. **Close the Employees form**

FIGURE M-7: Using an If statement to set a control's Visible property

Action Catalog button

Conditional expression

Add New Action list arrow in the If block

Action Catalog

If in the Action Catalog

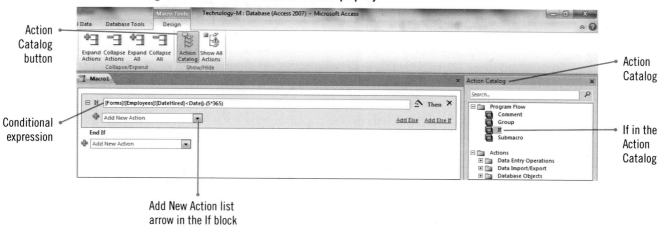

FIGURE M-8: Entering arguments for the SetProperty action

SetProperty action in If block

SetProperty argument values

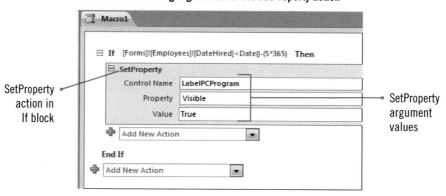

FIGURE M-9: Running the 5YearsPC macro

Run Macro button

Employees form

LabelPCProgram Visible property is set to True (Yes)

HireDate field value is more than 5 years ago

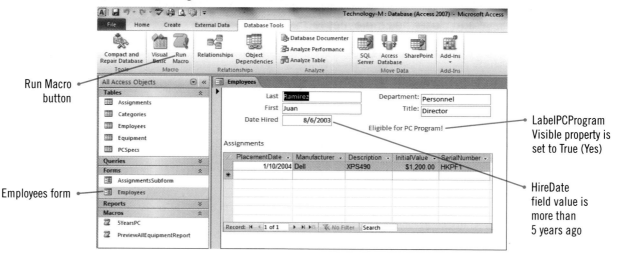

Access 2010

Creating Macros

Working with Events

An **event** is a specific activity that occurs within the database, such as clicking a command button, moving from record to record, editing data, or opening or closing a form. Events can be triggered by the user or by the database itself. By assigning a macro to an appropriate event rather than running the macro from the Database Tools tab or command button, you further automate and improve your database.  You need to modify the 5YearsPC macro so that it evaluates the DateHired field to display or hide the label as you move from record to record.

STEPS

1. **Right-click the 5YearsPC macro in the Navigation Pane, click Design View on the shortcut menu, click anywhere in the If block to activate it, then click the Add Else link in the lower-right corner of the If block**

   The **Else** portion of an If statement allows you to run a different set of macro actions if the conditional expression evaluates False. In this case, you want to set the Value of the Visible property to False if the conditional expression evaluates False (if the HireDate is less than 5 years from today's date) so that the label does not appear if the employee is not eligible for the PC program.

   TROUBLE
   If your screen doesn't match Figure M-10, use the Undo button 🔄 to try again.

2. **Right-click the SetProperty action block, click Copy, right-click the Else block, click Paste, select True in the Value property, then type False as shown in Figure M-10**

   With the second action edited, the macro will now turn the label's Visible property to True (Yes) or False (No), depending on HireDate value. You attach the macro to the event on the form that is triggered each time you move from record to record.

3. **Save and close the 5YearsPC macro, right-click the Employees form in the Navigation Pane, click Design View, then click the Property Sheet button**

   All objects, sections, and controls have a variety of events to which macros can be attached. Most event names are self-explanatory, such as the **On Click** event (which occurs when that item is clicked).

   TROUBLE
   Be sure you are viewing the Property Sheet for the form. If not, click the Form Selector button to select the form.

4. **Click the Event tab in the Property Sheet, click the On Current list arrow, then click 5YearsPC**

   Your screen should look like Figure M-11. The **On Current** event occurs when focus moves from one record to another, therefore the 5YearsPC macro will automatically run each time you move from record to record in the form. Test your new macro by moving through several records in Form View.

5. **Close the Property Sheet, click the View button 🖥 to switch to Form View, then click the Next record button ▶ in the navigation bar for the main form several times while observing the Eligible for PC Program! label**

   For every DateHired value that is earlier than five years before today's date, the Eligible for PC Program! label is visible. If the DateHired is less than five years before today's date, the label is hidden.

6. **Save and close the Employees form**

FIGURE M-10: Adding an Else portion to an If block

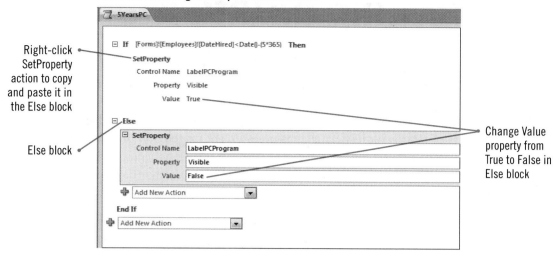

Right-click SetProperty action to copy and paste it in the Else block

Else block

Change Value property from True to False in Else block

FIGURE M-11: Attaching a macro to the On Current event of the form

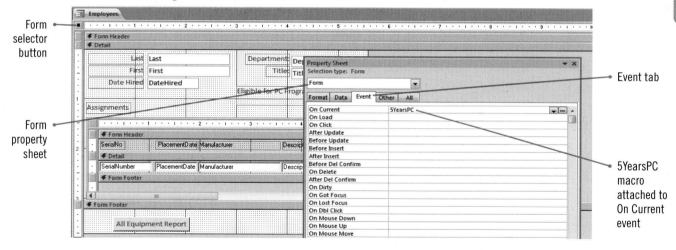

Form selector button

Form property sheet

Event tab

5YearsPC macro attached to On Current event

Creating a Data Macro

A **data macro** allows you to embed macro capabilities directly in a table to add, change, or delete data based on conditions you specify. Data macros are a new feature of Access 2010. Data macros are managed directly from within tables, and do not appear in the Macros group in the Navigation Pane. You most often run a data macro based on a table event, such as modifying data or deleting a record, but you can run a data macro separately as well, similar to how you run a regular macro. Quest Specialty Travel grants 10 days of regular vacation to all employees except for those in the Africa and Asia departments, who receive 15 days due to the extra travel requirements of their positions. Kayla asks you to figure out an automatic way to assign each employee the correct number of vacation days based on their department. A data macro will work well for this task.

STEPS

1. **Double-click the Employees table in the Navigation Pane, then observe the Vacation field throughout the datasheet**

   Currently, the Vacation field contains the value of 10 for each record, or each employee.

2. **Right-click the Employees table tab, click Design View on the shortcut menu, click the Create Data Macros button in the Field, Record & Table Events group, click After Insert, then click the Action Catalog button in the Show/Hide group if the Action Catalog window is not already open**

   In this case, you chose the After Insert event, which is run after a new record is entered. See Table M-3 for more information on table events. Creating a data macro is very similar to creating a regular macro. You add the logic and macro actions needed to complete the task at hand.

   > **QUICK TIP**
   > You can also drag a block or action from the Action Catalog to Macro Design View.

3. **Double-click ForEachRecord in the Action Catalog to add a For Each Record In block, click the For Each Record In list arrow, click Employees in the list, click the Where Condition text box, type [Department]="Africa" or [Department]="Asia", double-click the EditRecord data block in the Action Catalog, double-click the SetField data action in the Action Catalog, click the Name box in the SetField block, type Vacation, click the Value box in the SetField block, then type 15 as shown in Figure M-12**

   The Default value for the Vacation field is set to 10 in Table Design View of the Employees table so all existing records should have a value of 10 in the Vacation field. Test the new data macro by adding a new record.

   > **TROUBLE**
   > Be sure to tab to a completely new record to trigger the data macro attached to the After Insert event.

4. **Click the Close button, click Yes when prompted to save changes, click the View button ⊞ to display the datasheet, click Yes when prompted to save changes, click the New button in the Records group, enter the new record as shown in Figure M-13, except do not enter a Vacation value, then press [Tab] to move to a new record**

   The macro is triggered by the After Insert event of the record, and the Vacation field is automatically updated to 15 for that record and all other records with Asia or Africa in the Department field as shown in Figure M-13.

5. **Right-click the Employees table tab, then click Close on the shortcut menu**

   Data is automatically saved when you move from record to record or close a database object.

FIGURE M-12: Creating a data macro

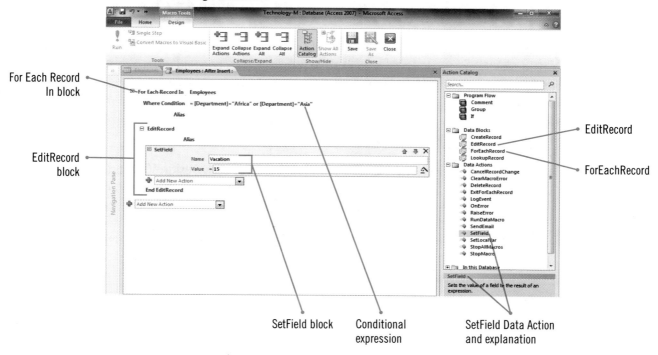

For Each Record In block

EditRecord block

SetField block Conditional expression SetField Data Action and explanation

EditRecord

ForEachRecord

FIGURE M-13: Running a data macro

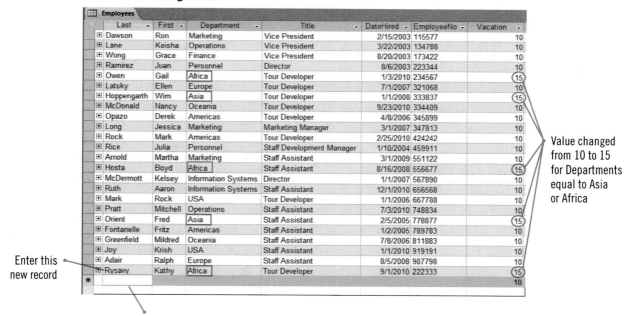

Enter this new record

Value changed from 10 to 15 for Departments equal to Asia or Africa

Tab to a new record to trigger the After Insert event

TABLE M-3: Table events

table event	runs...
After Insert	...after a new record has been inserted into the table
After Update	...after an existing record has been changed
After Delete	...after an existing record has been deleted
Before Delete	...before a record is deleted, to help the user validate or cancel the deletion
Before Change	...before a record is changed, to help the user validate or cancel the edits

Troubleshooting Macros

When macros don't run properly, Access supplies several tools to debug them. **Debugging** means determining why the macro doesn't run correctly. It usually involves breaking down a dysfunctional macro into smaller pieces that can be individually tested. For example, you can **single step** a macro, which means to run it one line (one action) at a time to observe the effect of each specific action in the Macro Single Step dialog box. You use the PreviewAllEquipmentReport to learn debugging techniques.

STEPS

1. **Right-click the PreviewAllEquipmentReport macro, click Design View on the shortcut menu, click the Single Step button in the Tools group, then click the Run button**

   The screen should look like Figure M-14, with the Macro Single Step dialog box open. This dialog box displays information including the macro's name, the action's name, the action arguments, and whether the current action's condition is true. From the Macro Single Step dialog box, you can step into the next macro action, halt execution of the macro, or continue running the macro without single stepping.

2. **Click Step in the Macro Single Step dialog box**

   Stepping into the second action lets the first action run and pauses the macro at the second action. The Macro Single Step dialog box now displays information about the second action.

3. **Click Step**

   The second action, the MessageBox action, is executed, which displays the message box.

4. **Click OK, then close the AllEquipment report**

5. **Click the Design tab, then click the Single Step button to toggle it off**

   Another technique to help troubleshoot macros is to use the built-in prompts and Help system provided by Microsoft Access. For example, you may have questions about how to use the optional Filter Name argument for the OpenReport macro action.

6. **Click the OpenReport action block, point to the Filter Name argument to view the ScreenTip that supplies information about that argument as shown in Figure M-15**

   The redesigned Access 2010 Macro Design View window has been improved with interactive prompts.

7. **Save and close the PreviewAllEquipmentReport macro, close the Technology-M.accdb database, then exit Access**

Creating Macros

FIGURE M-14: Single stepping through a macro

Run button

Single Step button

Information about first action in PreviewAllEquipmentReport macro

Macro Single Step dialog box

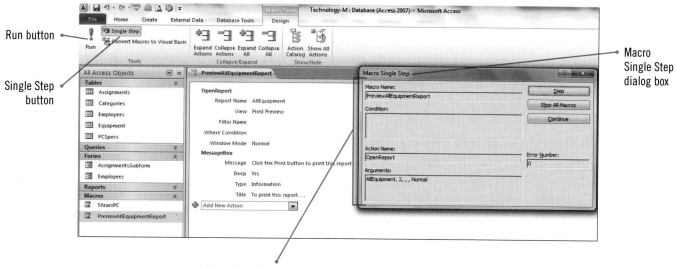

FIGURE M-15: Viewing automatic prompts

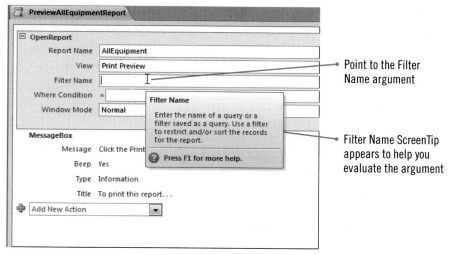

Point to the Filter Name argument

Filter Name ScreenTip appears to help you evaluate the argument

Practice

For current SAM information, including versions and content details, visit SAM Central (http://www.cengage.com/samcentral). If you have a SAM user profile, you may have access to hands-on instruction, practice, and assessment of the skills covered in this unit. Since various versions of SAM are supported throughout the life of this text, check with your instructor for the correct instructions and URL/Web site for accessing assignments.

Concepts Review

Identify each element of Macro Design View shown in Figure M-16.

FIGURE M-16

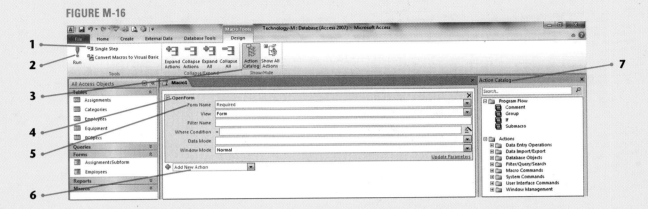

Match each term with the statement that best describes its function.

8. **Action**
9. **Event**
10. **Debugging**
11. **Argument**
12. **Conditional expression**
13. **Macro**

a. Specific action that occurs within the database, such as clicking a button or opening a form
b. Part of an If statement that evaluates as either true or false
c. Individual step that you want the Access macro to perform
d. Access object that stores one or more actions that perform one or more tasks
e. Provides additional information to define how an Access action will perform
f. Determines why a macro doesn't run properly

Select the best answer from the list of choices.

14. **Which of the following is *not* a major benefit of using a macro?**
    a. To make the database more flexible or easy to use
    b. To redesign the relationships among the tables of the database
    c. To ensure consistency in executing routine or complex tasks
    d. To save time by automating routine tasks

15. **Which of the following best describes the process of creating an Access macro?**
    a. Use the single-step recorder to record clicks and keystrokes as you complete a task.
    b. Use the macro recorder to record clicks and keystrokes as you complete a task.
    c. Use the Macro Wizard to determine which tasks are done most frequently.
    d. Open Macro Design View and add actions, arguments, and If statements to accomplish the desired task.

16. **Which of the following would *not* be a way to run a macro?**
    a. Click the Run Macro button on the Database Tools tab.
    b. Assign the macro to a command button on a form.
    c. Assign the macro to an event of a control on a form.
    d. Double-click a macro action within the Macro Design View window.

17. **Which of the following is *not* a reason to run a macro in single-step mode?**
    a. You want to debug a macro that isn't working properly.
    b. You want to run only a few of the actions of a macro.
    c. You want to observe the effect of each macro action individually.
    d. You want to change the arguments of a macro while it runs.

18. **Which of the following is *not* true of conditional expressions in If statements in macros?**
    a. Conditional expressions allow you to skip over actions when the expression evaluates as false.
    b. Conditional expressions give the macro more power and flexibility.
    c. Macro If statements provide for Else and Else If clauses.
    d. More macro actions are available when you are also using conditional expressions.

19. **Which example illustrates the proper syntax to refer to a specific control on a form?**
    a. [Forms] ! [*formname*] ! [*controlname*]
    c. Forms ! formname. controlname
    b. {Forms} ! {*formname*} ! (*controlname*)
    d. (Forms) ! (formname) ! (controlname)

20. **Which event is executed every time you move from record to record in a form?**
    a. Next Record
    c. On Current
    b. New Record
    d. On Move

Skills Review

1. **Understand macros.**
    a. Start Access, then open the Basketball-M.accdb database from the drive and folder where you store your Data Files. Enable content if prompted.
    b. Open the PrintMacroGroup macro in Macro Design View, then record your answers to the following questions on a sheet of paper:
       - What is the name of the first submacro?
       - How many macro actions are in the first submacro?
       - What arguments does the first action in the first submacro contain?
       - What values were chosen for these arguments?
    c. Close Macro Design View for the PrintMacroGroup object.

2. **Create a macro.**
    a. Start a new macro in Macro Design View.
    b. Add the OpenQuery action.
    c. Select PlayerStats as the value for the Query Name argument.
    d. Select Datasheet for the View argument.
    e. Select Edit for the Data Mode argument.
    f. Save the macro with the name **ViewPlayerStats**.
    g. Run the macro to make sure it works, close the PlayerStats query, then close the ViewPlayerStats macro.

3. **Modify actions and arguments.**
    a. Open the ViewPlayerStats macro in Macro Design View.
    b. Add a MessageBox action as the second action of the query.
    c. Type **We had a great season!** for the Message argument.
    d. Select Yes for the Beep argument.
    e. Select Warning! for the Type argument.
    f. Type **Iowa State Cyclones** for the Title argument.
    g. Save the macro, then run it to make sure the MessageBox action works as intended.
    h. Click OK in the dialog box created by the MessageBox action, close the PlayerStats query, then close the ViewPlayerStats macro.
    i. Open the PrintMacroGroup macro object in Design View.
    j. Modify the View argument for the OpenReport object of the PlayerStatistics submacro from Print to Print Preview.
    k. Save and close the PrintMacroGroup macro.

Skills Review (continued)

4. Assign a macro to a command button.

    a. In Design View of the PlayerInformationForm, use the Command Button Wizard to add a command button to the Form Footer that runs the PlayerStatistics submacro in the PrintMacroGroup macro (PrintMacroGroup.PlayerStatistics).

    b. The text on the button should read **View Player Statistics**.

    c. The meaningful name for the button should be **cmdPlayerStatistics**.

    d. Test the command button in Form View, click OK in the message box, then close the PlayerStats report.

    e. Save and close the PlayerInformationForm.

5. Use If statements.

    a. Start a new macro in Macro Design View, and open the Action Catalog window if it is not already open.

    b. Double-click If in the Action Catalog pane to add an If block to the macro.

    c. Enter the following condition in the If box: **[Forms]![GameSummaryForm]![HomeScore]> [OpponentScore]**.

    d. Add the SetProperty action to the If block.

    e. Type **VictoryLabel** in the Control Name box for the SetProperty action.

    f. Select Visible for the Property argument for the SetProperty action.

    g. Enter **True** for the Value argument for the SetProperty action to indicate Yes.

    h. Click the Add Else link in the lower-right corner of the If block.

    i. Copy the existing SetProperty action, then paste it under the Else clause.

    j. Modify the Value property from True to **False** for the second SetProperty action.

    k. Save the macro with the name **VictoryCalculator**, compare it to Figure M-17, make any necessary adjustments, then close Macro Design View.

FIGURE M-17

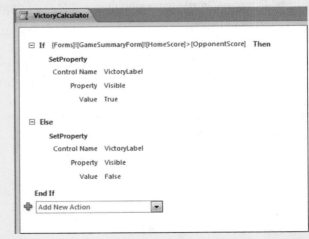

6. Work with events.

    a. Open the GameSummaryForm in Form Design View.

    b. Open the Property Sheet for the form.

    c. Assign the VictoryCalculator macro to the On Current event of the form.

    d. Close the Property Sheet, save the form, then open the GameSummaryForm in Form View.

    e. Navigate through the first four records. The Victory label should be visible for the first three records, but not the fourth.

    f. Add your name as a label in the Form Footer section to identify your printouts, print the third and fourth records if requested by your instructor, then save and close the GameSummaryForm.

7. Create a data macro.

    a. Open the Games table in Table Design View.

    b. Add a field named **RoadWin** with a Yes/No data type and the following Description: **Enter Yes if the Home-Away field is Away and the HomeScore is greater than the OpponentScore**.

    c. Save the Games table and switch to Datasheet View to note that the RoadWin check box is empty (No) for every record.

    d. Switch back to Table Design View, and create a data macro based on the After Insert event.

    e. Insert a ForEachRecord data block, and specify Games for the For Each Record In argument.

    f. The Where Condition should be: **[Home-Away]="A" and [HomeScore]>[OpponentScore]**.

    g. Add an EditRecord data block in the For Each Record In block, and a SetField data action. Be careful to add the EditRecord block *within* the For Each Record Block.

Skills Review (continued)

h. Enter **RoadWin** in the Name argument and **Yes** in the Value argument as shown in Figure M-18.

i. Save and close the data macro, save the Games table and switch to Datasheet View, then test the new data macro by entering a new record in the Games table as follows:

Opponent: **Tulsa**
Mascot: **Hurricanes**
Home-Away: **A**
HomeScore: **100**
OpponentScore: **50**
GameDate: **3/1/2013**

j. Tab to a new record. The six existing records where the Home-Away field is set to "A" and the HomeScore is greater than the OpponentScore should be checked. Close the Games table.

8. Troubleshoot macros.

a. Open the PrintMacroGroup in Macro Design View.

b. Click the Single Step button, then click the Run button.

c. Click Step twice to step through the two actions of the submacro, PlayerStatistics, then click OK in the resulting message box.

d. Close the PlayerStats report.

e. Return to Macro Design View of the PrintMacroGroup macro, and click the Single Step button on the Design tab to toggle off this feature.

f. Save and close the PrintMacroGroup macro, close the Basketball-M.accdb database, then exit Access.

Independent Challenge 1

As the manager of a doctor's clinic, you have created an Access database called Patients-M.accdb to track insurance claim reimbursements. You use macros to help automate the database.

a. Start Access, then open the database Patients-M.accdb from the drive and folder where you store your Data Files. Enable content if prompted.

b. Open Macro Design View of the CPT Form Open macro. (CPT stands for Current Procedural Terminology, which is a code that describes a medical procedure.) If the Single Step button is toggled on, click it to toggle it off.

c. On a separate sheet of paper, identify the macro actions, arguments for each action, and values for each argument.

d. In two or three sentences, explain in your own words what tasks this macro automates.

e. Close the CPT Form Open macro.

f. Open the Claim Entry Form in Form Design View. Maximize the window.

g. In the Form Footer of the Claim Entry Form are several command buttons. Open the Property Sheet of the Add CPT Code button, then click the Event tab.

h. On your paper, write the event to which the CPT Form Open macro is assigned.

i. Open the Claim Entry Form in Form View, then click the Add CPT Code button in the Form Footer.

j. On your paper, write the current record number that is displayed for you.

k. In the CPT Form, find the record for CPT Code 99243. Write down the RBRVS value for this record, then close the CPT form and Claim Entry form. (RBRVS stands for Resource-Based Relative Value System, a measurement of relative value between medical procedures.)

l. Close the Patients-M.accdb database, then exit Access.

Independent Challenge 2

As the manager of a doctor's clinic, you have created an Access database called Patients-M.accdb to track insurance claim reimbursements. You use macros to help automate the database.

a. Start Access, then open the database Patients-M.accdb from the drive and folder where you store your Data Files. Enable content if prompted.

b. Start a new macro in Macro Design View, and open the Action Catalog window if it is not already open.

c. Double-click the Submacro entry in the Program Flow folder to add a submacro block.

d. Type **Preview DOS Denied** as the first macro name, then add the OpenReport macro action.

e. Select Date of Service Report — Denied for the Report Name argument, then select Print Preview for the View argument of the OpenReport action.

f. Double-click the Submacro entry in the Program Flow folder to add another submacro block.

g. Type **Preview DOS Fixed** as a new macro name, then add the OpenReport macro action.

h. Select Date of Service Report - Fixed for the ReportName argument, then select Print Preview for the View argument of the second OpenReport action.

i. Save the macro with the name **Preview Group**, then close Macro Design View.

j. Using the Run Macro button on the Database Tools tab, run the Preview Group.Preview DOS Denied macro to test it, then close Print Preview.

k. Using the Run Macro button on the Database Tools tab, run the Preview Group.Preview DOS Fixed macro to test it, then close Print Preview.

Advanced Challenge Exercise

■ In the Preview Group macro, click the Collapse buttons to the left of the Submacro statements to collapse the two submacro blocks.

■ Create two more submacros, one that previews Monthly Claims Report — Denied and the other that previews Monthly Claims Report - Fixed. Name the two macros **Preview MCR Denied** and **Preview MCR Fixed** as shown in Figure M-19.

■ Save and close the Preview Group macro.

■ In Design View of the Claim Entry Form, add four separate command buttons to the Form Footer of the subform to run the four submacros in Preview Group macro. (The Form Footer of the main form already includes four command buttons, so be sure to add the new command buttons to the subform.) Use the captions and meaningful names of **DOS Denied** and **cmdDOSDenied**; **DOS Fixed** and **cmdDOSFixed**; **MCR Denied** and **cmdMCRDenied**; and **MCR Fixed** and **cmdMCRFixed** to correspond with the four submacros in the Preview Group macro.

■ Change the font color on the new command buttons to black.

■ Select all four new command buttons in the Form Footer section of the subform and use the Size/Space and Align commands on the Arrange tab to precisely size, align, and space the buttons equally in the Form Footer section.

■ Save the Claim Entry Form, switch to Form View as shown in Figure M-20, then test each of the new command buttons to make sure it opens the correct report.

■ Close the Claim Entry Form.

l. Close the Patients-M.accdb database, then exit Access.

FIGURE M-19

FIGURE M-20

Independent Challenge 3

As the manager of a doctor's clinic, you have created an Access database called Patients-M.accdb to track insurance claim reimbursements. You use macros to help automate the database.

a. Start Access, then open the Patients-M.accdb database from the drive and folder where you store your Data Files.

b. Start a new macro in Macro Design View, then add an If statement.

c. Enter the following in the If box: **[Forms]![CPT Form]![RBRVS]=0**.

d. Select the SetProperty action for the first action in the If block.

e. Enter the following arguments for the SetProperty action: Control Name: **ResearchLabel**, Property: **Visible**, and Value: **True**.

f. Click the Add Else link.

g. Select the SetProperty action for the first action of the Else clause.

h. Enter the following arguments for the SetProperty action: Control Name: **ResearchLabel**, Property: **Visible**, and Value: **False**.

i. Save the macro with the name **Research** as shown in Figure M-21, then close Macro Design View.

j. Open the CPT Form in Form Design View, and open the Property Sheet for the form.

k. Assign the Research macro to the On Current event of the form.

l. Close the Property Sheet, save the form, then open the CPT Form in Form View.

m. Use the Next record button to move quickly through all 64 records in the form. Notice that the macro displays Research! only when the RBRVS value is equal to zero.

n. Save and close the CPT Form, then close the Patients-M.accdb database.

FIGURE M-21

Real Life Independent Challenge

This Independent Challenge requires an Internet connection.

Suppose your culinary club is collecting information on international chocolate factories, museums, and stores, and asks you to help build a database to organize the information. You can collect some information on the Web to enter into the database, then tie the forms together with macros attached to command buttons.

a. Open the Chocolate-M.accdb database from the drive and folder where you store your Data Files, enable content if prompted, then open the Countries form in Form View.

b. Click the New (blank) record button for the main form, then type **Poland** in the Country text box.

c. In the subform for the Poland record, enter **Cadbury-Wedel Polska** in the Name field, **F** in the Type field (F for factory), **Praga** in the City field, and **Lodz** in the StateProvince field.

d. Open Macro Design View for a new macro, then add the MaximizeWindow action. Save the macro with the name **Maximize**, then close it.

e. If the Countries form is maximized, restore it, view it in Design View, add the Maximize macro to the On Load event of the Countries form, then open the Countries form in Form View to test it.

f. Save and close the Countries form.

g. Add the Maximize macro to the On Load event of the Places of Interest report, then open the Places of Interest report in Print Preview to test it.

h. Save and close the Places of Interest report.

i. Close the Chocolate-M.accdb database, then exit Access.

Visual Workshop

As the manager of a doctor's clinic, you have created an Access database called Patients-M.accdb to track insurance claim reimbursements. Develop a new macro called **QueryGroup** with the actions and argument values shown in Table M-4 and Figure M-22. Run both macros to test them by using the Run Macro button on the Database Tools tab, and debug the macros if necessary.

TABLE M-4

submacro	action	argument	argument value
Denied	OpenQuery	Query Name	Monthly Query – Denied
		View	Datasheet
		Data Mode	Edit
	MaximizeWindow		
	MessageBox	Message	These claims were denied
		Beep	Yes
		Type	Information
		Title	Denied
Fixed	OpenQuery	Query Name	Monthly Query – Fixed
		View	Datasheet
		Data Mode	Edit
	MaximizeWindow		
	MessageBox	Message	These claims were fixed
		Beep	Yes
		Type	Information
		Title	Fixed

FIGURE M-22

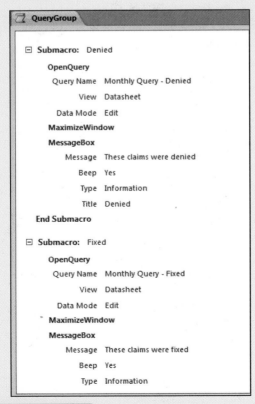

Creating Macros

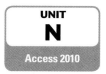

Creating Modules and VBA

Access is a robust and easy-to-use relational database program. Access provides user-friendly tools, such as wizards and Design Views, to help users quickly create reports and forms that previously took programmers hours to build. You may, however, want to automate a task or create a new function that goes beyond the capabilities of the built-in Access tools. Within each program of the Microsoft Office suite, a programming language called **Visual Basic for Applications (VBA)** is provided to help you extend the program's capabilities. In Access, VBA is stored within modules.  You want to learn about VBA and create modules to enhance the capabilities of the Technology-N database for Quest Specialty Travel.

OBJECTIVES

Understand modules and VBA

Compare macros and modules

Create functions

Use If statements

Document procedures

Build class modules

Modify sub procedures

Troubleshoot modules

Understanding Modules and VBA

A **module** is an Access object that stores Visual Basic for Applications (VBA) programming code. VBA is written in the **Visual Basic Editor (VBE)**, shown in Figure N-1. The components and text colors of the VBE are described in Table N-1. An Access database has two kinds of modules. **Standard modules** contain global code that can be executed from anywhere in the database and are displayed as module objects in the Navigation Pane. **Class modules** are stored within the form or report object itself. Class modules contain VBA code used only within that particular form or report. Before working with modules, you ask some questions about VBA.

DETAILS

The following questions and answers introduce the basics of Access modules:

*   **What does a module contain?**

    A module contains VBA programming code organized in procedures. A procedure contains several lines of code, each of which is called a **statement**. Modules can also contain **comments**, text that helps explain and document the code.

*   **What is a procedure?**

    A **procedure** is a series of VBA statements that performs an operation or calculates an answer. VBA has two types of procedures: functions and subs. **Declaration statements** precede procedure statements and help set rules for how the statements in the module are processed.

*   **What is a function?**

    A **function** is a procedure that returns a value. Access supplies many built-in functions such as Sum, Count, Pmt, and Now that can be used in an expression in a query, form, or report to calculate a value. You might want to create a new function, however, to help perform calculations unique to your database. For example, you might create a new function called RetireDate to calculate the date an employee is eligible to retire with full benefits at your company.

*   **What is a sub?**

    A **sub** (also called **sub procedure**) performs a series of VBA statements to manipulate controls and objects. Subs are generally executed when an event occurs, such as when a command button is clicked or a form is opened. Unlike a function, a sub does not return a value and cannot be used in an expression.

*   **What are arguments?**

    Arguments are constants, variables, or expressions passed to a procedure that the procedure needs in order to execute. For example, the full syntax for the Sum function is Sum (*expr*), where *expr* represents the argument for the Sum function, the field that is being summed. In VBA, arguments are declared in the first line of the procedure. They are specified immediately after a procedure's name and are enclosed in parentheses. Multiple arguments are separated by commas.

*   **What is an object?**

    In VBA, an **object** is any item that can be identified or manipulated, including the traditional Access objects (table, query, form, report, macro, and module) as well as other items that have properties such as controls, sections, and existing procedures.

*   **What is a method?**

    A **method** is an action that an object can perform. Procedures are often written to invoke methods in response to user actions. For example, you could invoke the GoToControl method to move the focus to a specific control on a form in response to the user clicking a command button.

FIGURE N-1: Visual Basic Editor window for a standard module

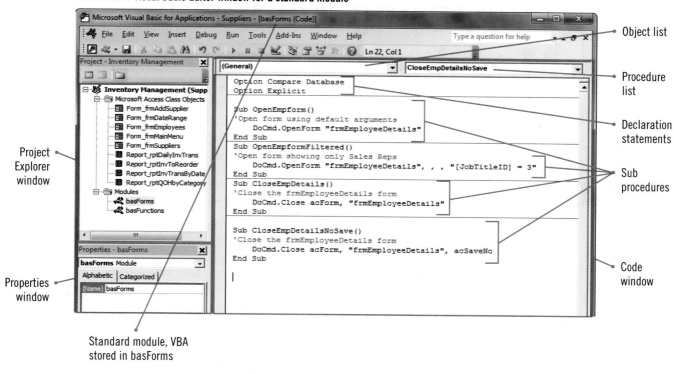

Object list

Procedure list

Declaration statements

Sub procedures

Code window

Project Explorer window

Properties window

Standard module, VBA stored in basForms

TABLE N-1: Components and text colors for the Visual Basic Editor window

component or color	description
Visual Basic Editor, VBE	Comprises the entire Microsoft Visual Basic program window that contains smaller windows, including the Code window and Project Explorer window
Code window	Contains the VBA for the project selected in the Project Explorer window
Project Explorer window	Displays a hierarchical list of the projects in the database; a **project** can be a module object or a form or report object that contains a class module
Declaration statements	Includes statements that apply to every procedure in the module, such as declarations for variables, constants, user-defined data types, and external procedures in a dynamic link library
Object list	In a class module, lists the objects associated with the current form or report
Procedure list	In a standard module, lists the procedures in the module; in a class module, lists events (such as Click or Dblclick)
Blue	Indicates a VBA keyword; blue words are reserved by VBA and are already assigned specific meanings
Black	Indicates normal text; black words are the unique VBA code developed by the user
Red	Indicates syntax error text; a red statement indicates that it will not execute correctly because of a syntax error (perhaps a missing parenthesis or a spelling error)
Green	Indicates comment text; any text after an apostrophe is considered documentation, or a comment, and is therefore ignored in the execution of the procedure

Comparing Macros and Modules

Both macros and modules help run your database more efficiently and effectively. Creating a macro or a module requires some understanding of programming concepts, an ability to follow a process through its steps, and patience. Some tasks can be accomplished by using an Access macro or by writing VBA. Guidelines can help you determine which tool is best for the task. You compare Access macros and modules by asking more questions.

DETAILS

The following questions and answers provide guidelines for using macros and modules:

- **For what types of tasks are macros best suited?**
  Macros are an easy way to handle common, repetitive, and simple tasks such as opening and closing forms, showing and hiding toolbars, and printing reports.

- **Which is easier to create, a macro or a module, and why?**
  Macros are generally easier to create because Macro Design View is more structured than the VBE. The hardest part of creating a macro is choosing the correct macro action. But once the action is selected, the arguments associated with that macro action are displayed, eliminating the need to learn any special programming syntax. To create a module, however, you must know a robust programming language, VBA, as well as the correct **syntax** (rules) for each VBA statement. In a nutshell, macros are simpler to create, but VBA is more powerful.

- **When must I use a macro?**
  You must use macros to make global, shortcut key assignments. **AutoExec** is a special macro name that automatically executes when the database first opens.

- **When must I use a module?**
  You must use modules to create unique functions. Macros cannot create functions. For instance, you might want to create a function called Commission that calculates the appropriate commission on a sale using your company's unique commission formula.

  Access error messages can be confusing to the user. But using VBA procedures, you can detect the error when it occurs and display your own message.

  Although Access 2010 macros have been enhanced to include more powerful If-Then logic, VBA is still more robust in the area of programming flow statements with tools such as nested If statements, Case statements, and multiple looping structures. Some of the most common VBA keywords, including If...Then, are shown in Table N-2. VBA keywords appear blue in the VBE code window.

  VBA code may declare **variables**, which are used to store data that can be used, modified, or displayed during the execution of the procedure.

  VBA may be used in conjunction with SQL (Structured Query Language) to select, update, append, and delete data.

  Class modules, like the one shown in Figure N-2, are stored as part of the form or report object in which they are created. If you develop forms and reports in one database and copy them to another, class module VBA automatically travels with the object that stores it.

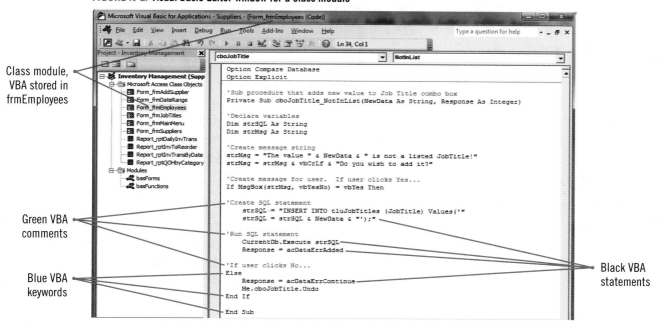

Class module,
VBA stored in
frmEmployees

Green VBA
comments

Blue VBA
keywords

Black VBA
statements

TABLE N-2: Common VBA keywords

statement	explanation
Function	Declares the name and arguments that create a new function procedure
End Function	When defining a new function, the End Function statement is required as the last statement to mark the end of the VBA code that defines the function
Sub	Declares the name for a new Sub procedure; **Private Sub** indicates that the Sub is accessible only to other procedures in the module where it is declared
End Sub	When defining a new sub, the End Sub statement is required as the last statement to mark the end of the VBA code that defines the sub
If...Then	Executes code (the code follows the Then statement) when the value of an expression is true (the expression follows the If statement)
End If	When creating an If...Then statement, the End If statement is required as the last statement
Const	Declares the name and value of a **constant**, an item that retains a constant value throughout the execution of the code
Option Compare Database	A declaration statement that determines the way string values (text) will be sorted
Option Explicit	A declaration statement that specifies that you must explicitly declare all variables used in all procedures; if you attempt to use an undeclared variable name, an error occurs at **compile time**, the period during which source code is translated to executable code
Dim	Declares a **variable**, a named storage location that contains data that can be modified during program execution
On Error GoTo	Upon an error in the execution of a procedure, the On Error GoTo statement specifies the location (the statement) where the procedure should continue
Select Case	Executes one of several groups of statements called a **Case** depending on the value of an expression; use the Select Case statement as an alternative to using **ElseIf** in **If...Then...Else** statements when comparing one expression to several different values
End Select	When defining a new Select Case group of statements, the End Select statement is required as the last statement to mark the end of the VBA code

Creating Functions

Access supplies hundreds of functions such as Sum, Count, IIf, First, Last, Date, and Hour. However, you might want to create a new function to calculate a value based on your company's unique business rules. You would create the new function in a standard module so that it can be used in any query, form, or report throughout the database. ▰▰▱▱ Quest Specialty Travel allows employees to purchase computer equipment when it is replaced. Equipment that is less than a year old will be sold to employees at 75 percent of its initial value, and equipment that is more than a year old will be sold at 50 percent of its initial value. Kayla Green, network administrator, asks you to create a new function called EmpPrice that determines the employee purchase price of replaced computer equipment.

STEPS

QUICK TIP
The Option Explicit statement appears if the Require Variable Declaration option is checked in the VBA Options dialog box. To view the default settings, click Options on the VBA Tools menu.

1. **Start Access, open the Technology-N.accdb database from the drive and folder where you store your Data Files, enable content if prompted, click the Create tab, click the Module button in the Macros & Code group, then maximize the Visual Basic window**

   Access automatically inserts the Option Compare Database declaration statement in the Code window. You will create the new EmpPrice function one step at a time.

2. **Type Function EmpPrice(StartValue), then press [Enter]**

   This statement creates a new function named EmpPrice, and states that it contains one argument, StartValue. VBA automatically adds the **End Function** statement, a required statement to mark the end of the function. Because both Function and End Function are VBA keywords, they are blue. The insertion point is positioned between the statements so that you can further define how the new EmpPrice function will calculate by entering more VBA statements.

3. **Press [Tab], type EmpPrice = StartValue * 0.5, then press [Enter]**

   Your screen should look like Figure N-3. The second statement explains how the EmpPrice function will calculate. The function will return a value that is calculated by multiplying the StartValue by 0.5. It is not necessary to indent statements, but indenting code between matching Function/End Function, Sub/End Sub, or If/End If statements enhances the program's readability. Also, it is not necessary to enter spaces around the equal sign and the asterisk used as a multiplication sign, but when you press [Enter] at the end of a VBA statement, Access automatically adds spaces as appropriate to enhance the readability of the statement.

4. **Click the Save button 🖫 on the Standard toolbar, type basFunctions in the Save As dialog box, click OK, then click the upper Close button ▬▬✕▬ in the upper-right corner of the VBE to close the Visual Basic Editor**

   It is common for VBA programmers to use three-character prefixes to name objects and controls. This makes it easier to identify that object or control in expressions and modules. The prefix **bas** is short for Basic, and applies to global modules. Naming conventions for other objects and controls are listed in Table N-3 and used throughout the Technology-N.accdb database. You can use the new function, EmpPrice, in a query, form, or report.

5. **Click the Queries bar in the Navigation Pane to expand the Queries section if it is collapsed, right-click the qryEmpPricing query in the Navigation Pane, then click Design View on the shortcut menu**

   Now you can use the new EmpPrice function in the query to determine the employee purchase price of replaced computer equipment.

QUICK TIP
Field names used in expressions are not case sensitive, but they must exactly match the spelling of the field name as defined in Table Design View.

6. **Click the blank Field cell to the right of the InitialValue field, type Price:EmpPrice([InitialValue]), then click the View button 🖽 to switch to Datasheet View**

   Your screen should look like Figure N-4. In this query, you created a new field called Price that uses the EmpPrice function. The value in the InitialValue field is used for the StartValue argument of the new EmpPrice function. The InitialValue field is multiplied by 0.5 to create the new Price field.

7. **Save then close the qryEmpPricing query**

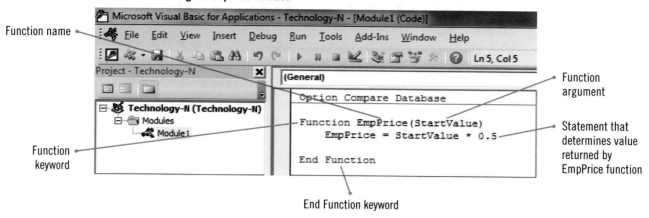

FIGURE N-3: Creating the EmpPrice function

Function name

Function argument

Function keyword

Statement that determines value returned by EmpPrice function

End Function keyword

```
Option Compare Database

Function EmpPrice(StartValue)
    EmpPrice = StartValue * 0.5

End Function
```

FIGURE N-4: Using the EmpPrice function in a query

ELast	Manufacture	Description	PlacementDat	InitialValue	Price
Joy	Micron	Transtrek4000	7/8/2010	$2,000.00	1000
Joy	Micron	Transtrek4000	7/8/2011	$2,000.00	1000
Dawson	Micron	Prosignet403	7/15/2010	$1,800.00	900
Rock	Micron	Prosignet403	7/31/2010	$1,800.00	900
McDermott	Micron	Prosignet403	7/31/2010	$1,800.00	900
Garmin	Micron	Prosignet403	7/31/2010	$1,800.00	900
Rice	Micron	Prosignet403	1/9/2010	$1,700.00	850
Boyd	Micron	Prosignet403	8/14/2010	$1,700.00	850
McDonald	Micron	Prosignet403	8/14/2011	$1,700.00	850
Long	Micron	Prosignet403	8/14/2010	$1,700.00	850
Orient	Compaq	Centuria9099	6/14/2011	$1,500.00	750

Calculated field, Price, uses EmpPrice custom function

TABLE N-3: Three-character prefix naming conventions

object or control type	prefix	example
Table	tbl	tblProducts
Query	qry	qrySalesByRegion
Form	frm	frmProducts
Report	rpt	rptSalesByCategory
Macro	mcr	mcrCloseInventory
Module	bas	basRetirement
Label	lbl	lblFullName
Text Box	txt	txtLastName
Combo box	cbo	cboStates
Command button	cmd	cmdPrint

Using If Statements

If...Then...Else logic allows you to test logical conditions and execute statements only if the conditions are true. If...Then...Else code can be composed of one or several statements, depending on how many conditions you want to test, how many possible answers you want to provide, and what you want the code to do based on the results of the tests. You need to add an If statement to the EmpPrice function to test the age of the equipment, and then calculate the answer based on that age. Right now, the EmpPrice function multiplies the StartValue argument by 50% (0.5). You want to modify the EmpPrice function so that if the equipment is less than one year old, the StartValue is multiplied by 75% (0.75).

STEPS

1. **Scroll down the Navigation Pane, right-click the basFunctions module, then click Design View**

   To determine the age of the equipment, the EmpPrice function needs another argument, the purchase date of the equipment.

2. **Click just before the right parenthesis in the Function statement, type , (a comma), press [Spacebar], type DateValue, then press [↓]**

   Now that you established another argument, you can work with the argument in the definition of the function.

QUICK TIP
Indentation doesn't affect the way the function works, but does make the code easier to read.

3. **Click to the right of the right parenthesis in the Function statement, press [Enter], press [Tab], then type If (Now()–DateValue) >365 Then**

   The expression compares whether today's date, represented by the Access function **Now()**, minus the DateValue argument value is greater than 365 days (1 year). If true, this indicates that the equipment is older than one year.

4. **Indent and type the rest of the statements exactly as shown in Figure N-5**

   The **Else** statement is executed only if the expression is false (if the equipment is less than 365 days old). The **End If** statement is needed to mark the end of the If block of code.

TROUBLE
If a compile or syntax error appears, open the Visual Basic window, check your function against Figure N-5, then correct any errors.

5. **Click the Save button 🖫 on the Standard toolbar, close the Visual Basic window, right-click the qryEmpPricing query in the Navigation Pane, then click Design View on the shortcut menu**

   Now that you've modified the EmpPrice function to include two arguments, you need to modify the calculated Price field expression, too.

6. **Right-click the Price field in the query design grid, click Zoom on the shortcut menu, click between the right square bracket and right parenthesis, then type ,[PlacementDate]**

   Your Zoom dialog box should look like Figure N-6. Both of the arguments used to define the EmpPrice function in the VBA code are replaced with actual field names that contain the data to be analyzed. Field names must be typed exactly as shown and surrounded by square brackets. Commas separate multiple arguments in the function.

7. **Click OK in the Zoom dialog box, then click the View button 🖩 to display the datasheet**

TROUBLE
The new calculated Price field is based on the current date on your computer, so your results may vary.

8. **Click any entry in the PlacementDate field, then click the Ascending button in the Sort & Filter group as shown in Figure N-7**

   The EmpPrice function now calculates one of two different results, depending on the age of the equipment determined by the date in the PlacementDate field.

9. **Save and then close the qryEmpPricing query**

FIGURE N-5: Using an If...Then...Else structure

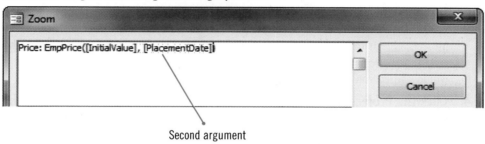

```
                                                          Second
                                                          argument
      Function EmpPrice(StartValue, DateValue)
If ─────── If (Now() - DateValue) > 365 Then ────
               EmpPrice = StartValue * 0.5        ──── Then
Else ──────── Else
               EmpPrice = StartValue * 0.75
End If ────── End If

      End Function
```

FIGURE N-6: Using the Zoom dialog box for long expressions

```
┌─ Zoom ──────────────────────────────────────────────── x ─┐
│                                                            │
│ Price: EmpPrice([InitialValue], [PlacementDate])    ▲   ┌──────┐ │
│                                                     │   │  OK  │ │
│                                                         └──────┘ │
│                                                         ┌──────┐ │
│                                                     ▼   │Cancel│ │
│                                                         └──────┘ │
└────────────────────────────────────────────────────────────┘

                           Second argument
```

FIGURE N-7: Price field is calculated at 50% or 75% based on age of equipment

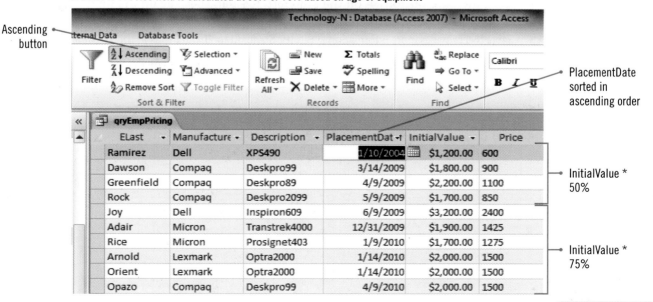

Documenting Procedures

Comment lines are statements in the code that document the code; they do not affect how the code runs. At any time, if you want to read or modify existing code, you can write the modifications much more quickly if the code is properly documented. Comment lines start with an apostrophe and are green in the VBE. ▚▚▚▚ You decide to document the EmpPrice function in the basFunctions module with descriptive comments. This will make it easier for you and others to follow the purpose and logic of the function later.

You can also create comments by starting the statement with the Rem statement (for remark).

Be sure to use an ' (apostrophe) and not a " (quotation mark) to begin the comment line.

1. **Right-click the basFunctions module in the Navigation Pane, then click Design View**
    The Code window for the basFunctions module opens.

2. **Click the blank line between the Option Compare Database and Function statements, press [Enter], type 'This function is called EmpPrice and has two arguments, then press [Enter]**
    As soon as you move to another statement, the comment statement becomes green.

3. **Type 'Created by Your Name on Today's Date, then press [Enter]**
    Your screen should look like Figure N-8. You can also place comments at the end of a line by entering an apostrophe to mark that the next part of the statement is a comment. Closing the Project Explorer window gives you more room for the Code window. (You use the **Project Explorer window** to switch between open projects, objects that can contain VBA code. The **utility project** contains VBA code that helps Access with certain activities such as presenting the Zoom dialog box. It automatically appears in the Project Explorer window when you use the Access features that utilize this code.)

4. **Click the Project Explorer Close button [×], click to the right of Then at the end of the If statement, press [Spacebar], type 'Now() returns today's date, then press [↓]**
    This comment explains that the Now() function is today's date. All comments are green, regardless of whether they are on their own line or at the end of an existing line.

5. **Click to the right of 0.5, press [Spacebar] three times, then type 'If > 1 year, multiply by 50%**

6. **Click to the right of 0.75, press [Spacebar] twice, type 'If < 1 year, multiply by 75%, then press [↓]**
    Your screen should look like Figure N-9. Each comment will turn green as soon as you move to a new statement.

7. **Click the Save button [💾] on the Standard toolbar, click File on the menu bar, click Print if requested by your instructor, then click OK**
    Table N-4 provides more information about the Standard toolbar buttons in the Visual Basic window.

8. **Click File on the menu bar, then click Close and Return to Microsoft Access**

FIGURE N-8: Adding comments

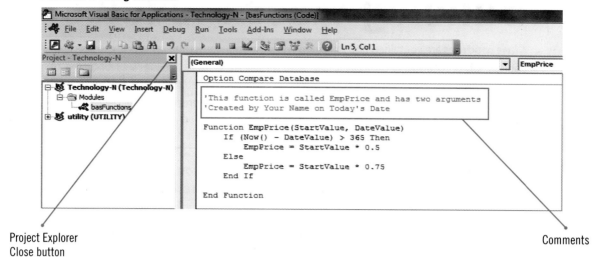

Project Explorer
Close button

Comments

FIGURE N-9: Adding comments at the end of a statement

Insert Module
button

View Microsoft
Access button

Run Sub/
UserForm button

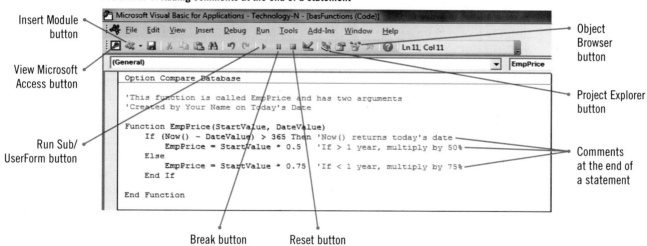

Object
Browser
button

Project Explorer
button

Comments
at the end of
a statement

Break button

Reset button

TABLE N-4: Standard toolbar buttons in the Visual Basic window

button name	button	description
View Microsoft Access		Switches from the active Visual Basic window to the Access window
Insert Module		Opens a new module or class module Code window, or inserts a new procedure in the current Code window
Run Sub/UserForm	▷	Runs the current procedure if the insertion point is in a procedure, or runs the UserForm if it is active
Break	‖	Stops the execution of a program while it's running and switches to break mode, which is the temporary suspension of program execution in which you can examine, debug, reset, step through, or continue program execution
Reset	▪	Resets the procedure
Project Explorer		Displays the Project Explorer, which displays a hierarchical list of the currently open projects (set of modules) and their contents
Object Browser		Displays the Object Browser, which lists the defined modules and procedures as well as available methods, properties, events, constants, and other items that you can use in the code

Creating Modules and VBA

Building Class Modules

Class modules are contained and executed within specific forms and reports. Class modules most commonly contain sub procedures and run in response to an **event**, a specific action that occurs as the result of a user action. Common events include clicking a command button, editing data, or closing a form. ▓▓▓▓ You examine an existing class module to understand and create sub procedures connected to events that occur on the form.

QUICK TIP

frmEmployees has a Caption property of Employees displayed in the form tab.

1. **Double-click the frmEmployees form in the Navigation Pane to open it in Form View, then click the Branch of Service combo box list arrow to review the choices**

   The Branch of Service combo box provides a list of the branches of the armed services. For a choice to make sense, however, an employee would first need to be a veteran. You'll set the Visible property for the Branch of Service combo box to True if the Veteran check box is checked and False if the Veteran check box is not checked.

TROUBLE

If the first line of your procedure is not Private Sub chkVeteran_ AfterUpdate( ), delete the stub, close the VBE, and repeat Step 2.

2. **Right-click the Employees tab, click Design View on the shortcut menu, double-click the edge of the Veteran check box to open its Property Sheet, click the Event tab in the Property Sheet, click the After Update property, click the Build button, click Code Builder, then click OK**

   The class module for the frmEmployees form opens. Because you opened the VBE from within a specific event of a specific control on the form, the **stub**, the first and last lines of the sub procedure, were automatically created. The procedure's name in the first line, chkVeteran_AfterUpdate, contains *both* the name of the control, chkVeteran, as well as the name of the event, AfterUpdate, that triggers this procedure. (Recall that the **Name property** of a control is found on the Other tab in the control's property sheet. The **After Update property** is on the Event tab.) A sub procedure that is triggered by an event is often called an **event handler**.

3. **Enter the statements shown in Figure N-10**

   When you use three-character prefixes for all controls and objects in your database, it increases the meaning and readability of your VBA. In this case, the name of the sub procedure shows that it runs on the AfterUpdate event of the chkVeteran control. (The sub runs when the Veteran check box is checked or unchecked.) The If structure contains VBA that makes the cboBranchOfService control either visible or not visible based on the value of the chkVeteran control. To test the sub procedure, you switch to Form View.

4. **Save the changes and close the VBE, click the View button 📋 to switch to Form View, click the Veteran check box for the first record several times, then navigate through several records**

   By clicking the Veteran check box in the first record, you triggered the procedure that responds to the After Update event of the Veteran check box. However, you also want the procedure to run every time you move from record to record. The **On Current** event of the form is triggered when you navigate through records.

TROUBLE

If the VBA code window appears with a yellow line, it means the code cannot be run successfully. Click the Reset button 🔲, then compare your VBA to Figure N-11.

5. **Right-click the Employees form tab, click Design View on the shortcut menu, click the Form Selector button, click the Event tab in the Property Sheet, click the On Current event property in the Property Sheet, click the Build button, click Code Builder, click OK, then copy or retype the If structure from the chkVeteran_AfterUpdate sub to the Form_ Current sub as shown in Figure N-11**

   By copying the same If structure to a second sub procedure, you've created a second event handler. Now, the cboBrandOfService combo box will either be visible or not based on two different events: updating the chkVeteran check box or moving from record to record. To test the new sub procedure, you switch to Form View.

6. **Save the changes and close the VBE, click 📋 to switch to Form View, then navigate to the fifth record for Gail Owen to test the new procedures**

   Now, as you move from record to record, the Branch of Service combo box should be visible for those employees with the Veteran check box selected, and not visible if the Veteran check box is not selected.

7. **Click the Branch of Service combo box list arrow, click Army as shown in Figure N-12, then save and close the frmEmployees form**

FIGURE N-10: Creating your first sub procedure

```
Private Sub chkVeteran_AfterUpdate()

If chkVeteran.Value = True Then
    cboBranchOfService.Visible = True
Else
    cboBranchOfService.Visible = False
End If

End Sub
```

FIGURE N-11: Copying the If structure to a new event handler

If structure copied from chkVeteran_AfterUpdate sub to Form_Current sub

```
Private Sub chkVeteran_AfterUpdate()

If chkVeteran.Value = True Then
    cboBranchOfService.Visible = True
Else
    cboBranchOfService.Visible = False
End If

End Sub
```

```
Private Sub Form_Current()

If chkVeteran.Value = True Then
    cboBranchOfService.Visible = True
Else
    cboBranchOfService.Visible = False
End If

End Sub
```

FIGURE N-12: Using the Branch of Service combo box when the Veteran check box is selected

frmEmployees form has a Caption property of Employees

Gail Owen record

Veteran check box is selected

cboBranchOfService combo box

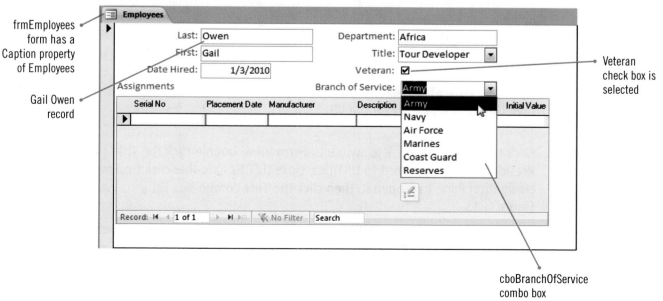

Access 2010

Modifying Sub Procedures

Sub procedures can be triggered on any event identified in the Property Sheet such as **On Got Focus** (when the control gets the focus), **After Update** (after a field is updated), or **On Dbl Click** (when the control is double-clicked). Not all items have the same set of event properties. For example, a text box control has both a Before Update and After Update event property, but neither of these events exists for unbound controls such as a label or command button because those controls are not used to update data. Kayla Green asks if there is a way to easily add new items to the Title combo box. You use VBA sub procedures to handle this request.

STEPS

1. **Right-click the frmEmployees form, click Design View on the shortcut menu, then double-click the edge of the ETitle combo box to open its Property Sheet**

   When entering a new employee, if the desired title is not available on the list, you want to give the user a way to add the new title. You decide to use the double-click event property of the ETitle combo box to open the tblTitles table where you can add the new title.

2. **Click the Event tab in the Property Sheet, click the On Dbl Click text box, click the Build button, click Code Builder, then click OK**

   The class module opens and creates a stub for the new procedure. The name of the new procedure is cboETitle_DblClick indicating that it is an event handler procedure that will run when the cboETitle control is double-clicked. As you type the statement, be sure to watch the screen carefully for IntelliSense programming support.

3. **Type DoCmd.Close, press [Enter], then type DoCmd. (include the period)**

   DoCmd is a VBA object that supports many methods to run common Access commands such as closing windows, opening forms, previewing reports, navigating records, and setting the value of controls. The first DoCmd statement will close the current object, frmEmployees. The second DoCmd statement will open the tblTitles table. As you write a VBA statement, visual aids that are part of **IntelliSense technology** help you complete it. For example, when you press the period (.) after the DoCmd object, a list of available methods appears. Watching the VBA window carefully and taking advantage of all IntelliSense clues as you complete a statement can greatly improve your accuracy and productivity in writing VBA.

4. **Type OpenTab, press [Tab] when OpenTable is highlighted in the IntelliSense list, press [Spacebar], type "tblTitles", then type , (comma)**

   Your sub procedure should look like Figure N-13. IntelliSense helps you fill out the rest of the statement, indicating the order of arguments needed for the method to execute (the current argument is listed in bold), and whether the argument is required or optional (optional arguments are listed in [square brackets]). Optional arguments can be skipped by typing a comma (,). Optional arguments at the end of a statement can be ignored.

5. **Press [Backspace] to delete the unneeded comma, press [↓] as shown in Figure N-14, then save the changes and close the VBE**

   Test the new procedure.

6. **Click the View button 📄 to switch to Form View, double-click the Title combo box, add President as a new record to tblTitles, close tblTitles, double-click frmEmployees in the Navigation Pane to reopen it, then click the Title combo box list arrow as shown in Figure N-15**

   TROUBLE
   Be sure to double-click the combo box and not the Title label.

7. **Click President as the new Title for Ron Dawson, then close frmEmployees**

   VBA is a robust and powerful programming language. It takes years of experience to appreciate the vast number of objects, events, methods, and properties that are available. With only modest programming skills, however, you can create basic sub procedures that greatly help the users enter, find, and analyze information.

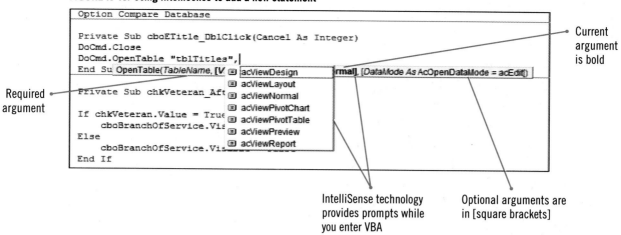

Required argument

Current argument is bold

IntelliSense technology provides prompts while you enter VBA

Optional arguments are in [square brackets]

FIGURE N-14: **Final cboETitle_DblClick sub**

DoCmd statement to close the current object

DoCmd statement to open the tblTitles table

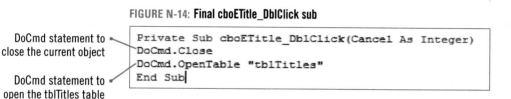

FIGURE N-15: **Updated combo box**

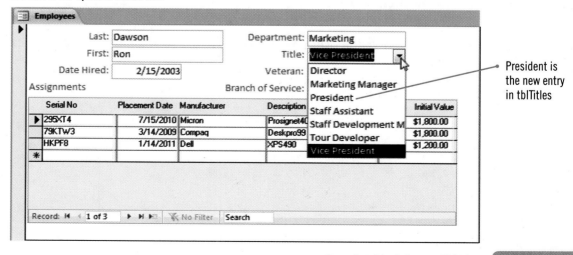

President is the new entry in tblTitles

Access 2010

Troubleshooting Modules

Access provides several techniques to help you **debug** (find and resolve) different types of VBA errors. A **syntax error** occurs immediately as you are writing a VBA statement that cannot be read by the Visual Basic Editor. This is the easiest type of error to identify because your code turns red when the syntax error occurs. **Compile-time errors** occur as a result of incorrectly constructed code and are detected as soon as you run your code or select the Compile option on the Debug menu. For example, you may have forgotten to insert an End If statement to finish an If structure. **Run-time errors** occur as incorrectly constructed code runs and include attempting an illegal operation such as dividing by zero or moving focus to a control that doesn't exist. When you encounter a run-time error, VBA will stop executing your procedure at the statement in which the error occurred and highlight the line with a yellow background in the Visual Basic Editor. **Logic errors** are the most difficult to troubleshoot because they occur when the code runs without obvious problems, but the procedure still doesn't produce the desired result. You study debugging techniques using the basFunctions module.

STEPS

1. **Right-click the basFunctions module in the Navigation Pane, click Design View, click to the right of the End If statement, press the [Spacebar], type your name, then press [↓]**
   Because the End If your name statement cannot be resolved by the Visual Basic Editor, it immediately turns red.

2. **Click OK in the Compile error message box, delete your name, then press [↓]**
   Another VBA debugging tool is to set a **breakpoint**, a bookmark that suspends execution of the procedure at that statement to allow you to examine what is happening.

> **QUICK TIP**
> Click the gray bar to the left of a statement to toggle a breakpoint on and off.

3. **Click in the If statement line, click Debug on the menu bar, then click Toggle Breakpoint**
   Your screen should look like Figure N-16.

4. **Click the View Microsoft Access button 🅰 on the Standard toolbar, then double-click the qryEmpPricing query in the Navigation Pane**
   When the qryEmpPricing query opens, it immediately runs the EmpPrice function. Because you set a breakpoint at the If statement, the statement is highlighted as shown in Figure N-17, indicating that the code has been suspended at that point.

> **QUICK TIP**
> Pointing to an argument in the Code window displays a ScreenTip with the argument's current value.

5. **Click View on the menu bar, click Immediate Window, type ? DateValue, then press [Enter]**
   Your screen should look like Figure N-18. The **Immediate window** is an area where you can determine the value of any argument at the breakpoint.

6. **Click Debug on the menu bar, click Clear All Breakpoints, click the Continue button ▶ on the Standard toolbar to execute the remainder of the function, then save and close the basFunctions module**
   The qryEmpPricing query's datasheet should be visible.

7. **Close the qryEmpPricing datasheet, close the Technology-N.accdb database, then exit Access**

Creating Modules and VBA

FIGURE N-16: **Setting a breakpoint**

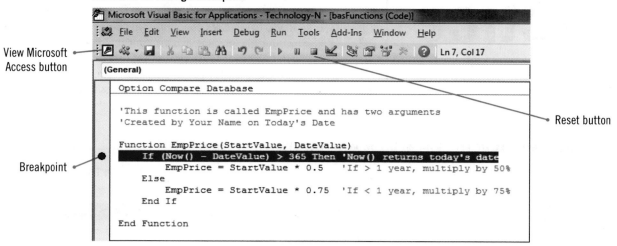

View Microsoft Access button

Reset button

Breakpoint

FIGURE N-17: **Stopping execution at a breakpoint**

```
'This function is called EmpPrice and has two arguments
'Created by Your Name on Today's Date

Function EmpPrice(StartValue, DateValue)
    If (Now() - DateValue) > 365 Then 'Now() returns today's date
        EmpPrice = StartValue * 0.5    'If > 1 year, multiply by 50%
    Else
        EmpPrice = StartValue * 0.75   'If < 1 year, multiply by 75%
    End If

End Function
```

Execution stopped at breakpoint

FIGURE N-18: **Updated combo box**

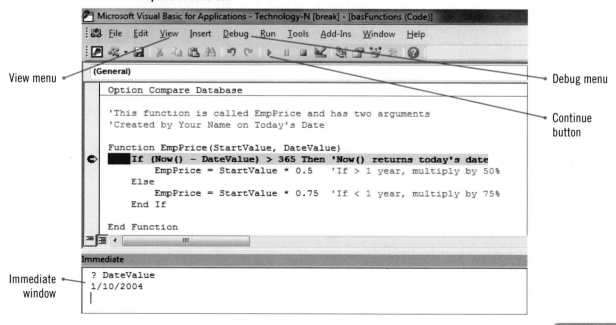

View menu

Debug menu

Continue button

Immediate window

Practice

Concepts Review

Identify each element of the Visual Basic window shown in Figure N-19.

FIGURE N-19

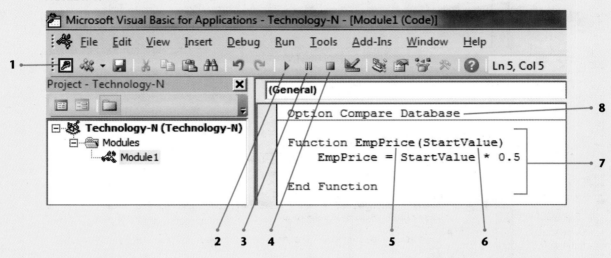

Match each term with the statement that best describes its function.

9. **Visual Basic for Applications (VBA)**

10. **Debugging**

11. **If...Then...Else statement**

12. **Breakpoint**

13. **Function**

14. **Module**

15. **Procedure**

16. **Arguments**

17. **Class modules**

a. Allows you to test a logical condition and execute commands only if the condition is true

b. The programming language used in Access modules

c. A line of code that automatically suspends execution of the procedure

d. A process to find and resolve programming errors

e. A procedure that returns a value

f. Constants, variables, or expressions passed to a procedure to further define how it should execute

g. Stored as part of the form or report object in which they are created

h. The Access object where VBA code is stored

i. A series of VBA statements that perform an operation or calculate a value

Select the best answer from the list of choices.

18. **Which type of procedure returns a value?**
    a. Function
    b. Sub procedure
    c. Sub
    d. Class module

19. **Which of the following is *not* a reason to use modules rather than macros?**
    a. Modules are used to create unique functions.
    b. Modules contain code that can work with other Microsoft Office programs.
    c. Modules are usually easier to write than macros.
    d. Modules can contain procedures that mask error messages.

20. Which of the following is *not* a type of VBA error?

   a. Class action   **c.** Logic

   b. Run time   **d.** Compile time

21. Which of the following is a specific action that occurs on or to an object, and is usually the result of a user action?

   a. Argument   **c.** Function

   b. Event   **d.** Sub

Skills Review

1. Understand modules and VBA.

   a. Start Access, then open the Baseball-N.accdb (not the Basketball-N.accdb) database from the drive and folder where you store your Data Files. Enable content if prompted.

   b. Open the Code window for the basFunctions module.

   c. Record your answers to the following questions on a sheet of paper.

     • What is the name of the function defined in this module?

     • What are the names of the arguments defined in this module?

     • What is the purpose of the If statement?

     • What is the purpose of the End Function statement?

     • Why is the End Function statement in blue?

     • Why are some of the lines indented?

2. Compare macros and modules.

   a. If not already opened, open the Code window for the basFunctions module.

   b. Record your answers to the following questions on a sheet of paper.

     • Why was a module rather than a macro used to create this procedure?

     • Why is VBA generally more difficult to create than a macro?

     • Identify each of the VBA keywords or keyword phrases, and explain the purpose for each.

3. Create functions.

   a. If not already opened, open the Code window for the basFunctions module.

   b. Create a function called **SluggingAverage** below the End Function statement of the BattingAverage function by typing the VBA statements shown in Figure N-20.

FIGURE N-20

```
Function SluggingAverage(SingleValue, DoubleValue, TripleValue, HRValue, AtBatsValue)
    SluggingAverage = (SingleValue + 2 * DoubleValue + 3 * TripleValue + 4 * HRValue) / AtBatsValue
End Function
```

   In baseball, the slugging average is a popular statistic because it accounts for the power of each hit. In the regular batting average, a single, double, triple, and home run are all given the same weight. In the slugging average, each hit is multiplied by the number of bases earned (one for single, 2 for double, 3 for triple, and 4 for home run). A perfect batting average is 1 (any type of a hit each time at bat). A perfect slugging average is 4 (a home run, or 4 bases, each time at bat).

   c. Save the basFunctions module, then close the Visual Basic window.

   d. Use Query Design View to create a new query using the PlayerFName and PlayerLName fields from the tblPlayers table, and the AtBats field from the tblPlayerStats table.

   e. Create a calculated field named **Batting** in the next available column by carefully typing the expression as follows: **Batting: BattingAverage([1Base],[2Base],[3Base],[4Base],[AtBats]).**

   f. Create a second calculated field named **Slugging** in the next available column by carefully typing the expression as follows: **Slugging: SluggingAverage([1Base],[2Base],[3Base],[4Base],[AtBats]).**

   g. View the datasheet, change Louis Gehrig to your first and last name, save the query with the name **qryStats**, then close qryStats.

Skills Review (continued)

4. Use If statements.

a. Open the Code window for the basFunctions module, then modify the function to add the If structure shown in Figure N-21. The If structure prevents the error caused by attempting to divide by zero. The If structure checks to see if the AtBatValue argument is equal to 0. If so, the SluggingAverage function is set to 0. Else, the SluggingAverage function is calculated.

FIGURE N-21

```
Function SluggingAverage(SingleValue, DoubleValue, TripleValue, HRValue, AtBatsValue)
If AtBatsValue = 0 Then
    SluggingAverage = 0
Else
    SluggingAverage = (SingleValue + 2 * DoubleValue + 3 * TripleValue + 4 * HRValue) / AtBatsValue
End If
End Function
```

b. Save the basFunctions module, then close the Visual Basic window.

c. Open the qryStats datasheet, then change the AtBats value to **0** for the first record to test the If statement. Both the Batting and Slugging calculated field should equal 0.

d. Close the datasheet.

5. Document procedures.

a. Open the Code window for the basFunctions module, and add the two statements above each End Function statement as shown in Figure N-22. The statements use the Format function to format the calculation as a number with three digits to the right of the decimal. The comments help clarify the statement.

FIGURE N-22

```
Function BattingAverage(SingleValue, DoubleValue, TripleValue, HRValue, AtBatsValue)
If AtBatsValue = 0 Then
    BattingAverage = 0
Else
    BattingAverage = (SingleValue + DoubleValue + TripleValue + HRValue) / AtBatsValue
End If
'Format the answer as a number with three digits to the right of the decimal point
BattingAverage = Format(BattingAverage, "0.000")
End Function


Function SluggingAverage(SingleValue, DoubleValue, TripleValue, HRValue, AtBatsValue)
If AtBatsValue = 0 Then
    SluggingAverage = 0
Else
    SluggingAverage = (SingleValue + 2 * DoubleValue + 3 * TripleValue + 4 * HRValue) / AtBatsValue
End If
'Format the answer as a number with three digits to the right of the decimal point
SluggingAverage = Format(SluggingAverage, "0.000")
End Function

'Created by (Your Name) on (Today's Date)
```

b. Add a comment at the end of the VBA code that identifies your name and today's date as shown in Figure N-22.

c. Save the changes to the basFunctions module, print the module if requested by your instructor, then close the Visual Basic window.

d. Open the qryStats query datasheet and change the AtBats value to **3** for the first record to observe how the values in the Batting and Slugging calculated fields change and how they are now formatted consistently due to the VBA statements you added to format the values.

e. Print the qryStats datasheet if requested by your instructor, then close it.

6. Build class modules.

a. Open frmPlayerEntry in Form View, then move through several records to observe the data.

b. Switch to Design View, and on the right side of the form, select the Print Current Record button.

Skills Review (continued)

   c. Open the Property Sheet for the button, click the Event tab, click the On Click property, then click the Build button to open the class module.

   d. Add a comment to the last line to show your name and the current date. Save the module, print it if requested by your instructor, then close the Visual Basic window.

7. Modify sub procedures.

   a. Open the frmPlayerEntry form in Form View, move through a couple of records to observe the txtSalary text box (currently blank), then switch to Design View.

   b. The base starting salary in this league is $24,000. You will add a command button with VBA to help enter the correct salary for each player. Use the Button button to add a command button below the txtSalary text box, then cancel the Command Button Wizard if it starts.

   c. Open the Property Sheet for the new command button, then change the Caption property on the Format tab to **Base Salary**. Change the Name property on the Other tab to **cmdBaseSalary**.

   d. On the Event tab of the Property Sheet, click the On Click property, click the Build button, click Code Builder, then click OK. The stub for the new cmdBaseSalary_Click sub is automatically created for you.

   e. Enter the following statement between the Sub and End Sub statements:
     txtSalary.Value = 24000

   f. Save the changes, then close the Visual Basic window.

   g. Close the Property Sheet, then save and open the frmPlayerEntry form in Form View.

   h. Click the Base Salary command button for the first player, move to the second record, then click the Base Salary command button for the second player.

   i. Save, then close the frmPlayerEntry form.

8. Troubleshoot modules.

   a. Open the Code window for the basFunctions module.

   b. Click anywhere in the If AtBatsValue = 0 Then statement in the BattingAverage function.

   c. Click Debug on the menu bar, then click Toggle Breakpoint to set a breakpoint at this statement.

   d. Save the changes, then and close the Visual Basic window and return to Microsoft Access.

   e. Open the qryStats query datasheet. This action will attempt to use the BattingAverage function to calculate the value for the Batting field, which will stop and highlight the statement in the Visual Basic window where you set a breakpoint.

   f. Click View on the menu bar, click Immediate Window (if not already visible), delete any previous entries in the Immediate window, type **?AtBatsValue**, then press [Enter]. At this point in the execution of the VBA, the AtBatsValue should be 3, the value for the first record.

   g. Type **?SingleValue**, then press [Enter]. At this point in the execution of the VBA code, the SingleValue should be 1, the value for the first record.

   h. Click Debug on the menu bar, click Clear All Breakpoints, then click the Continue button on the Standard toolbar. Close the Visual Basic window.

   i. Return to the qryStats query in Datasheet View.

   j. Close the qryStats query, close the Baseball-N.accdb database, then exit Access.

Independent Challenge 1

As the manager of a doctor's clinic, you have created an Access database called Patients-N.accdb to track insurance claim reimbursements and general patient health. You want to modify an existing function within this database.

   a. Start Access, then open the Patients-N.accdb database from the drive and folder where you store your Data Files. Enable content if prompted.

   b. Open the basBodyMassIndex module in Design View, and enter the **Option Explicit** declaration statement just below the existing Option Compare Database statement.

   c. Record your answers to the following questions on a sheet of paper:

     • What is the name of the function in the module?

Independent Challenge 1 (continued)

- What are the function arguments?
- What is the purpose of the Option Explicit declaration statement?

d. Edit the BMI function by adding a comment below the last line of code with your name and today's date.

e. Edit the BMI function by adding a comment above the Function statement with the following information: **'A healthy BMI is in the range of 21-24**.

f. Edit the BMI function by adding an If clause that checks to make sure the height argument is not equal to 0. The final BMI function code should look like Figure N-23.

g. Save the module, print it if requested by your instructor, then close the Visual Basic window.

h. Create a new query that includes the following fields from the tblPatients table: **PtLastName**, **PtFirstName**, **PtHeight**, **PtWeight**.

i. Create a calculated field with the following field name and expression: **BMICalculation: BMI([PTWeight], [PTHeight])**.

FIGURE N-23

```
Option Compare Database
Option Explicit

'A healthy BMI is in the range of 21-24.

Function BMI(weight, height)

If height = 0 Then
    BMI = 0
Else
    BMI = (weight * 0.4536) / (height * 0.0254) ^ 2
End If

End Function

'Student Name and current date
```

j. Save the query as **qryPatientBMI**, view the qryPatientBMI query datasheet, then test the If statement by entering **0** in the PtHeight field for the first record. Press [Tab] to move to the BMICalculation field, which should recalculate to 0.

k. Edit the first record to contain your first and last name, print the datasheet if requested by your instructor, then close the qryPatientBMI query.

l. Close the Patients-N.accdb database, then exit Access.

Independent Challenge 2

As the manager of a doctor's clinic, you have created an Access database called Patients-N.accdb to track insurance claim reimbursements. You want to study the existing sub procedures stored as class modules in the Claim Entry Form.

a. Start Access, then open the Patients-N.accdb database from the drive and folder where you store your Data Files. Enable content if prompted.

b. Open frmClaimEntryForm in Form View, then switch to Design View.

c. Open the Visual Basic window to view this class module, then record your answers to the following questions on a sheet of paper:

- What are the names of the sub procedures in this class module? (*Hint*: Be sure to scroll the window to see the complete contents.)
- What Access functions are used in the PtFirstName_AfterUpdate sub?
- How many arguments do the functions in the PtFirstName_AfterUpdate sub have?
- What do the functions in the PtFirstName_AfterUpdate sub do? (*Hint*: You may have to use the Visual Basic Help system if you are not familiar with the functions.)
- What is the purpose of the On Error command? (*Hint*: Use the Visual Basic Help system if you are not familiar with this command.)

Advanced Challenge Exercise

- Use the Property Sheet of the form to create an event handler procedure based on the On Load property. The statement will be one line using the Maximize method of the VBA DoCmd object, which will maximize the form each time it is loaded.
- Save the changes, close the Visual Basic window and the Claim Entry Form, then open frmClaimEntryForm in Form View to test the new sub.

d. Close the Visual Basic window, save and close frmClaimEntryForm, close the Patients-N.accdb database, then exit Access.

Independent Challenge 3

As the manager of a doctor's clinic, you have created an Access database called Patients-N.accdb to track insurance claim reimbursements that are fixed (paid at a predetermined fixed rate) or denied (not paid by the insurance company). You want to enhance the database with a class module.

a. Start Access, then open the Patients-N.accdb database from the drive and folder where you store your Data Files. Enable content if prompted.

b. Open frmCPT in Form Design View.

c. Use the Command Button Wizard to add a command button in the Form Header section. Choose the Add New Record action from the Record Operations category.

d. Accept **Add Record** as the text on the button, then name the button **cmdAddRecord**.

e. Use the Command Button Wizard to add a command button in the Form Header section to the right of the existing Add Record button. (*Hint*: Move and resize controls as necessary to put two command buttons in the Form Header section.)

f. Choose the Delete Record action from the Record Operations category.

g. Accept Delete Record as the text on the button, and name the button **cmdDeleteRecord**.

h. Size the two buttons to be the same height and width, and align their top edges.

i. Save and view frmCPT in Form View, then click the Add Record command button.

j. Add a new record (it will be record number 65) with a CPTCode value of **999** and an RBRVS value of **1.5**.

k. To make sure that the Delete Record button works, click the record selector for the new record you just entered, click the Delete Record command button, then click Yes to confirm the deletion. Save and close frmCPT.

Advanced Challenge Exercise

- In Design View of the frmCPT form, open the Property Sheet for the Delete Record command button, click the Event tab, then click the Build button beside [Embedded Macro]. The Command Button Wizard created the embedded macro that deletes the current record. You can convert macro objects to VBA code to learn more about VBA. To convert an embedded macro to VBA, you must first copy and paste the embedded macro actions to a new macro object.
- Press [Ctrl][A] to select all macro actions, then press [Ctrl][C] to copy all macro actions to the clipboard.
- Close the macro window, then save and close frmCPT.
- On the Create tab, open Macro Design View, then press [Ctrl][V] to paste the macro actions to the window.
- Click the Convert Macros to Visual Basic button, click Yes when prompted to save the macro, click Convert, then click OK when a dialog box indicates the conversion is finished.
- Save and close all open windows with default names if prompted. Open the Converted Macro-Macro1 VBE window. Add a comment as the last line of code in the Code window with your name and the current date, save the module, print it if requested by your instructor, then close the Visual Basic window.

l. Close the Patients-N.accdb database, then exit Access.

Real Life Independent Challenge

This Independent Challenge requires an Internet connection.

Learning a programming language is sometimes compared to learning a foreign language. Imagine how it would feel to learn a new programming language if English wasn't your primary language, or if you had another type of accessibility challenge. Advances in technology are helping to break down many barriers to those with vision, hearing, mobility, cognitive, and language issues. In this challenge, you explore the Microsoft Web site for resources to address these issues.

a. Go to www.microsoft.com/enable, then print that page. Explore the Web site.

b. After exploring the Web site for products, profiles, demos, and tutorials, write a one- or two-page, double-spaced paper describing five types of accessibility solutions that might make a positive impact on someone you know. Refer to your acquaintances as "my friend," "my cousin," and so forth as appropriate. Do not include real names.

c. Go back to www.microsoft.com/enable, then find the International link to change languages. Write down the languages for which the Microsoft Accessibility Web site is available.

Visual Workshop

As the manager of a college basketball team, you are helping the coach build meaningful statistics to compare the relative value of the players in each game. The coach has stated that one offensive rebound is worth as much to the team as two defensive rebounds, and would like you to use this rule to develop a "rebounding impact statistic" for each game. Open the Basketball-N.accdb (not the Baseball-N.accdb) database, enable content if prompted, and use Figure N-24 to develop a new function. Name the new function **ReboundImpact** in a new module called **basFunctions** to calculate this statistic. Include your name and the current date as a comment in the last row of the function.

FIGURE N-24

```
Function ReboundImpact(OffenseValue As Integer, DefenseValue As Integer) As Integer
     ReboundImpact = (OffenseValue * 2) + DefenseValue
End Function


'Your Name, Current Date
```

Create a query called **qryRebounds** with the fields shown in Figure N-25. Note that the records are sorted in ascending order on GameNo and LastName. The ReboundCalculation field is created using the following expression: **ReboundImpact([Reb-O],[Reb-D])**. Enter your own first and last name instead of Kristen Czyenski, and print the datasheet if requested by your instructor.

FIGURE N-25

GameNo	FirstName	LastName	Reb-O	Reb-D	ReboundCalculation
1	StudentFirst	StudentLast	2	2	6
1	Denise	Franco	2	3	7
1	Theresa	Grant	1	3	5
1	Megan	Hile	1	2	4
1	Amy	Hodel	5	3	13
1	Ellyse	Howard	1	2	4
1	Jamie	Johnson	0	1	1
1	Lindsey	Swift	1	2	4
1	Morgan	Tyler	4	6	14
2	StudentFirst	StudentLast	3	2	8
2	Denise	Franco	5	3	13

UNIT
O

Access 2010

Building a Database Interface

Files You Will Need:

Technology-O.accdb
Basketball-O.accdb
RealEstate-O.accdb
Baltic-O.accdb

As your database grows in size and functionality, the number of objects (especially queries and reports) grows as well. As the database expands in scope and complexity, you need to build a database interface to make it easy to use for yourself and others.  Kayla Green is the network administrator at Quest corporate headquarters. You have helped Kayla develop a database to document Quest computer equipment. The number of objects in the database makes it increasingly difficult to find and organize information. You will use Access tools and create a database interface to manage the growing database and make it easier to navigate for new users.

OBJECTIVES

Work with objects

Group objects

Create a dialog box

Create a pop up form

Create a navigation form

Create a switchboard

Modify a switchboard

Use the Documenter

Working with Objects

You work with objects in the **Navigation Pane**. The Navigation Pane is most commonly organized to show database objects listed by object type (tables, queries, forms, reports, macros, and modules). The Navigation Pane can also organize objects by their table association, created date, modified date, or a custom group. To copy, delete, or rename an object, you right-click it in the Navigation Pane, and then choose the desired option from the shortcut menu. ▓▓▓▓ Kayla Green asks you to make several queries easier to find. You decide to delete, rename, sort, and add descriptions to several queries to meet her request.

STEPS

1. **Start Access, open the Technology-O.accdb database from the drive and folder where you store your Data Files, enable content if prompted, click All Access Objects on the title bar of the Navigation Pane, then click Modified Date in the Navigate To Category section**

   In this case, the filter is still showing all of the objects in order of the most recently modified to the last modified. To further organize them, you can use other sorting and viewing options.

2. **Click All Dates in the Navigation Pane title bar, click Object Type, right-click All Access Objects in the title bar of the Navigation Pane, point to Category, point to Sort By, point to View By, then click Details**

   The **Sort By option** allows you to change the sort order of the objects in the Navigation Pane. The **View By option** changes the way the objects are displayed: with Details, as Icons, or in a List. When viewing the objects by Details, the Navigation Pane displays Date Created and Date Modified information for each table as shown in Figure O-1.

3. **Click the tblPCSpecs table, click the Database Tools tab, click the Object Dependencies button, then click OK if prompted**

   The **Object Dependencies task pane** opens, as shown in Figure O-2. Option buttons allow you to view either the objects that depend on the selected object or objects that the selected object itself depends on.

4. **Click the expand button to the left of the qryAfrica query in the Object Dependencies task pane**

   Expanding the qryAfrica query reveals that the rptAfrica report depends on the qryAfrica query. Another way to organize and manage objects is to check default database options. All default options are stored in the Access Options dialog box.

5. **Click the File tab on the Ribbon, click Options toward the bottom, then click the Current Database category as shown in Figure O-3**

   The Access Options dialog box provides many important default options and techniques to customize Access, which are summarized in Table O-1.

6. **Click the Datasheet category and several others to explore Access Options, then click Cancel to close the Access Options dialog box**

7. **Click the Close button ✖ in the upper-right corner of the Object Dependencies task pane to close it**

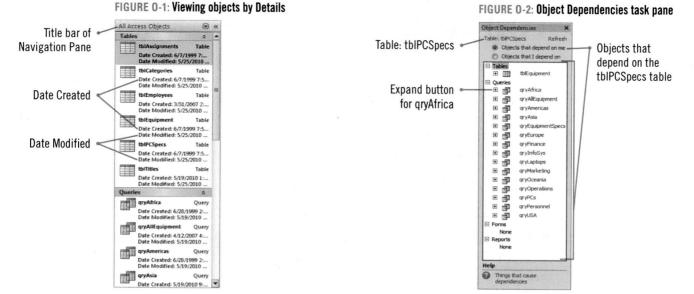

Title bar of Navigation Pane

Date Created

Date Modified

Table: tblPCSpecs

Expand button for qryAfrica

Objects that depend on the tblPCSpecs table

FIGURE O-3: **Access Options dialog box**

Current Database category is selected

Categories

Tabbed Documents option

Compact on Close option

Access 2010

TABLE O-1: **Access options**

category	description
General	Sets default interface, file format, default database folder, and user name options
Current Database	Provides for application changes such as whether the windows are overlapping or tabbed, the database compacts on close, and Layout View is enabled; also provides Navigation Pane, Ribbon, toolbar, and AutoCorrect options
Datasheet	Determines the default gridlines, cell effects, and fonts of datasheets
Object Designers	Determines default Design View settings for tables, queries, forms, and reports; also provides default error-checking options
Proofing	Sets AutoCorrect and Spelling options
Language	Sets Editing, Display, and Help languages
Client Settings	Sets defaults for cursor action when editing, display elements, printing margins, date formatting, and advanced record management options
Customize Ribbon	Provides an easy-to-use interface to modify the buttons and tabs on the Ribbon (new in Access 2010)
Quick Access Toolbar	Provides an easy-to-use interface to modify the buttons on the Quick Access toolbar
Add-ins	Provides a way to manage **add-ins**, software that works with Access to add or enhance functionality
Trust Center	Provides a way to manage trusted publishers, trusted locations, trusted documents, macro settings, and other privacy and security settings

Grouping Objects

Viewing every object in the Navigation Pane can be cumbersome when your database contains many objects. **Groups** are also used to organize objects by subject or purpose. For example, you might create a group for each department so that the forms and reports used by that department are organized together. A group consists of **shortcuts** (pointers) to the objects that belong to that group. You use these shortcuts to open the object without affecting the original location of the object. You can create more than one shortcut to the same object and place it in several groups. You add and display groups in the Navigation Pane. You organize the objects in your database by creating groups for two different departments: Travel and Operations.

1. **Right-click All Access Objects on the Navigation Pane title bar, point to View By, click List to return to the default view, right-click All Access Objects, click Navigation Options, then click Custom Groups**

   The **Favorites** custom group is provided by default, but you can create your own custom groups, too. Objects that have not been placed in a custom group remain in the **Unassigned Objects** group.

   TROUBLE
   If you make a mistake, use the Delete Group or Rename Group buttons to fix it.

2. **Click the Add Group button, type Travel, click the Add Group button, type Operations, then press [Enter] to create two groups as shown in Figure O-4**

   With the new groups in place, you're ready to organize objects within them.

3. **Click OK in the Navigation Options dialog box, right-click All Access Objects on the Navigation Pane title bar, point to Category, click Custom Groups, then scroll to the top of the Navigation Pane**

   Dragging an object to a group icon places a shortcut to that object within the group. A shortcut icon looks different from the actual object because it has a small blue arrow in its lower-left corner.

4. **Drag the qryAfrica query icon in the Navigation Pane to the Travel group, then drag the rptAfrica report icon to the Travel group as shown in Figure O-5**

   You have added shortcut icons representing the qryAfrica query and rptAfrica report in the Travel group. You can open or design an object by accessing it through a shortcut icon.

5. **Double-click the rptAfrica report icon in the Travel group to open the rptAfrica report, then close the report**

   You can create multiple shortcuts to the same object in different groups, and you can rename shortcuts to be more meaningful.

6. **Right-click the rptAfrica report icon in the Travel group, click Rename Shortcut, type Africa report, press [Enter], right-click the qryAfrica query icon in the Travel group, click Rename Shortcut, type Africa query, then press [Enter] to rename the objects as shown in Figure O-6**

   You can make your database interface much easier and faster for others to use by creating custom groups, adding shortcuts to those groups for only the objects that user needs, and then renaming shortcuts to be meaningful to the user.

FIGURE O-4: Creating custom groups in the Navigation Options dialog box

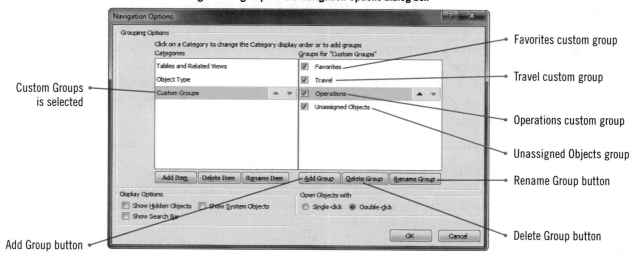

Custom Groups is selected

Favorites custom group

Travel custom group

Operations custom group

Unassigned Objects group

Rename Group button

Delete Group button

Add Group button

FIGURE O-5: Navigation Pane with custom Travel and Operations groups

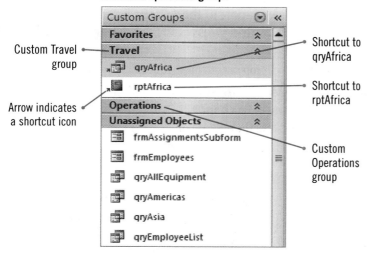

Custom Travel group

Arrow indicates a shortcut icon

Shortcut to qryAfrica

Shortcut to rptAfrica

Custom Operations group

FIGURE O-6: Navigation Pane with renamed shortcuts in custom Travel group

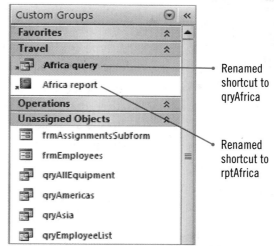

Renamed shortcut to qryAfrica

Renamed shortcut to rptAfrica

Naming objects

Object names can be 64 characters long and can include any combination of letters, numbers, spaces, and special characters, except a period (.), exclamation point (!), accent (`), or brackets ([ ]). It is helpful to keep the names as short, yet as descriptive, as possible. Short names make objects easier to reference in other places in the database, such as in the Record Source property for a form or report. Three-character prefixes such as tbl for table or qry for query provide more meaning when viewed from within an expression, Macro Design View, or a VBA module.

Creating a Dialog Box

A **dialog box** is a form used to display messages or prompt a user for a choice. Creating dialog boxes helps to simplify use of various database objects. For example, you might create a dialog box to give the user access to a list of reports the user needs to preview or print. To make a form look like a dialog box, you modify form properties that affect its appearance and borders. ⬛⬛⬛ You want to create a dialog box to provide an easy way for Quest users to print various reports.

STEPS

1. **Click the Create tab, then click the Form Design button**

   A dialog box form is not bound to an underlying table or query, and therefore it doesn't use the form's Record Source property. You place unbound controls, such as labels and command buttons, on a dialog box to offer the user information and choices.

TROUBLE

Be sure the Use Control Wizards button is selected. To find it, click the More arrow in the Controls group on the Design tab.

2. **Click the Button button in the Controls group, then click in the upper-middle section of the form**

   The **Command Button Wizard** shown in Figure O-7 organizes over 30 of the most common command button actions within six categories.

3. **Click Report Operations in the Categories list, click Preview Report in the Actions list, click Next, click rptAfrica as the report choice, click Next, click the Text option button, press [Tab], type Africa, click Next, type cmdAfrica as the button name, then click Finish**

   The command button appears in Form Design View.

QUICK TIP

Every command button must have a unique name.

4. **Click the Button button, click below the first command button on the form, click Report Operations in the Categories list, click Preview Report in the Actions list, click Next, click rptAmericas, click Next, click the Text option button, press [Tab], type Americas, click Next, type cmdAmericas, then click Finish**

   With the command buttons in place, you modify form properties to make the form look like a dialog box.

TROUBLE

You may need to scroll the Property Sheet to find the Border Style property.

5. **Double-click the Form Selector button to open the form's Property Sheet, click the Format tab, then double-click the Border Style property to change it from Sizable to Dialog**

   The **Border Style** property determines the appearance of the outside border of the form. The **Dialog** option indicates that the form will have a thick border and may not be maximized, minimized, or resized. A dialog box does not need a record selector or navigation buttons, so you want to remove them from this form using the Record Selectors and Navigation Buttons properties.

6. **Double-click the Record Selectors property to change it from Yes to No, then double-click the Navigation Buttons property to change it from Yes to No as shown in Figure O-8**

QUICK TIP

Resize the cmdAfrica button as needed to match Figure O-9.

7. **Close the Property Sheet, save the form with the name frmDialogBox, then click the View button 📄 to switch to Form View as shown in Figure O-9**

   Note that the form has a thin dialog style border, no record selector, and no navigation buttons. Test the command buttons.

8. **Click the Americas command button**

   Clicking the Americas command button displays the Americas report. Given more time, you'd want to add command buttons for all departmental reports to frmDialogBox.

9. **Close the Americas report, then save and close the frmDialogBox form**

Button button

Report
Operations
category

New
Command
button

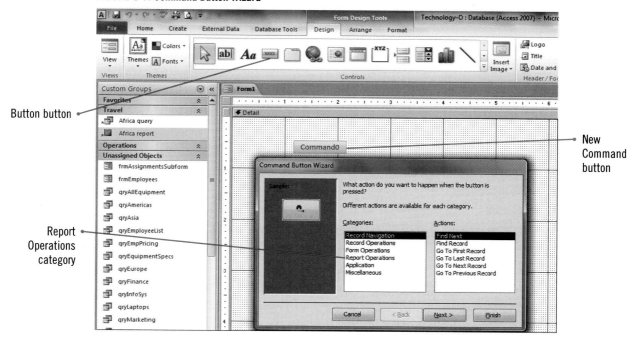

Form Selector button

Two new command
buttons

Border Style property

Record Selectors
property

Navigation Buttons
property

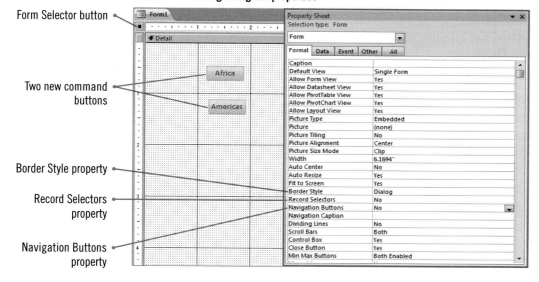

Dialog Border Style

No record selector

No navigation buttons

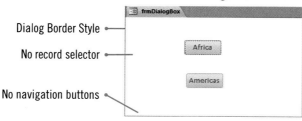

Access 2010

Creating a Pop Up Form

A **pop up form** is a form that stays on top of other open forms, even when another form is active. For example, you might want to create a pop up form to give the user easy access to a reference list of phone numbers or e-mail addresses. You create a pop up form to access employee department information. You add a command button to the frmDialogBox form to open the pop up form.

1. **Click the Create tab, click the Form Design button, click the Property Sheet button, click the Data tab in the Property Sheet, click the Record Source list arrow, then scroll and click tblEmployees**

    You want to add three fields to the pop up form: EFirst, ELast, and EDepartment.

    > **TROUBLE**
    > If the Property Sheet remains open, close it.

2. **Click the Add Existing Fields button to open the Field List, double-click EFirst, double-click ELast, double-click EDepartment, close the Field List, then save the form as frmEmployeePopup**

    You change a regular form into a pop up form by changing its **Pop Up property**.

3. **Double-click the Form Selector button to reopen the Property Sheet for the form, click the Other tab, then double-click the Pop Up property to change it from No to Yes as shown in Figure O-10**

    You add a command button to the right side of the frmDialogBox form to open the frmEmployeePopup form.

4. **Right-click frmDialogBox in the Navigation Pane, click Design View, click the Button button in the Controls group, click to the right of the existing command buttons on the form, click the Form Operations category, click the Open Form action, click Next, click frmEmployeePopup, click Next, click Next to show all of the records, click the Text option button, press [Tab], type Employee Departments, click Next, type cmdEmployee, then click Finish**

    You need to test your pop up form.

5. **Save frmDialogBox, click the View button 🖳 to switch to Form View, click the Employee Departments command button, then save and close frmEmployeePopup**

    Pop up forms are often used to display reference information. If the records were presented as a datasheet, you would be able to see much more information. You make this change by modifying the embedded macro that is triggered on the Employee Departments command button.

6. **Switch to Design View of frmDialogBox, open the Property Sheet for cmdEmployee if it is not already open, click the Event tab, click the Build button ⋯ for the On Click property, click Form in the View argument, click the View list arrow, then click Datasheet as shown in Figure O-11**

    Save and test the updated macro.

    > **QUICK TIP**
    > The rptAmericas report has a Caption property of Americas, which is displayed in the report tab.

7. **Click the Close button ✕, click Yes when prompted to save, close the Property Sheet, click 🖳, click the Employee Departments command button, resize and move the frmEmployeePopup window to the right, then click the Americas command button**

    The frmEmployeePopup form stayed "on top" even though you opened a report, as shown in Figure O-12. Given more time, you'd want to automatically resize and position the pop up form. You set the width of a form using the form's **Width** property. You can set the position of the form using the DoCmd.MoveSize VBA statement triggered by the form's Load property.

8. **Close the frmEmployeePopup form, close the Americas report, then save and close the frmDialogBox form**

FIGURE O-10: Creating a pop up form

Form selector button

Pop Up property

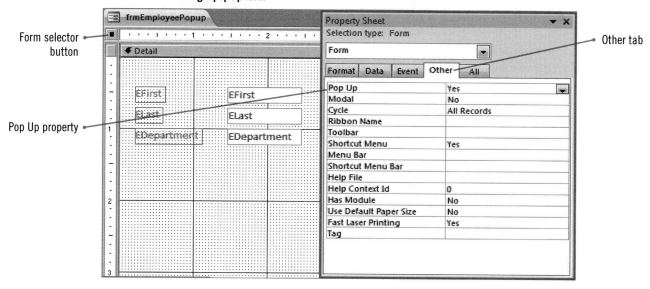

Other tab

FIGURE O-11: Changing the View argument for frmEmployeePopup

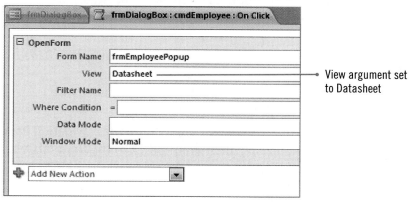

View argument set to Datasheet

FIGURE O-12: Working with a pop up form

The rptAmericas report has a Caption property of Americas

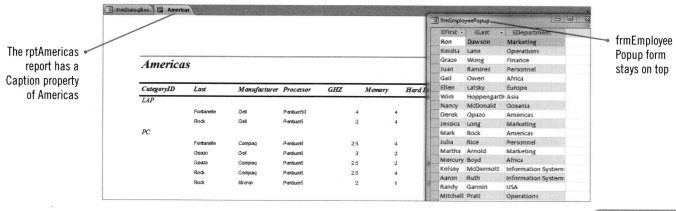

frmEmployee Popup form stays on top

Creating a Navigation Form

A **navigation form** is a special Access form that provides an easy-to-use database interface that is also Web compatible. Being **Web compatible** means that the form can be opened and used with Internet Explorer when the database is published to a SharePoint server. A **SharePoint server** is a special type of Microsoft Web server that allows people to share and collaborate on information using only a browser such as Internet Explorer. Navigation forms can be used with any Access database, however, even if you don't publish it to a SharePoint server. You create a navigation form to easily access forms and reports in the Technology-O database.

STEPS

1. **Click the Create tab, click the Navigation button in the Forms group, click the Horizontal Tabs option, then close the Field List window**

   Horizontal Tabs is a **navigation system style** that determines how the navigation buttons will be displayed on the form. Other navigation system styles include vertical tabs (buttons) on the left or right, or both horizontal and vertical tabs.

   The new navigation form opens in Layout View, ready for you to add the objects that you want to quickly find. To easily access the forms and reports in this database, you change the Navigation Pane to organize the objects by object type.

2. **Click Custom Groups in the Navigation Pane title bar, click Object Type, scroll the Navigation Pane, then click the Expand buttons for the Forms and Reports categories to open those parts of the Navigation Pane if they are not already visible**

   To add objects to the tabs of the new navigation forms, you can type the name of an object in the tab or drag an object to the tab.

3. **Drag the frmEmployees form from the Navigation Pane to the first tab, which displays [Add New]**

   The frmEmployees form is added as the first tab, as shown in Figure O-13, and a new tab with [Add New] is automatically created as well. The second and third tabs will display reports.

4. **Drag the rptAllEquipment report from the Navigation Pane to the second tab, which displays [Add New], then drag rptPCs to the third tab, which also displays [Add New]**

   With the objects in place, you'll rename the tabs to be less technical.

5. **Double-click the frmEmployees tab, edit it to read Employees, double-click the rptAllEquipment tab, edit it to read All Equipment, double-click the rptPCs tab, edit it to read PCs, then click the View button ▦ to display the form in Form View as shown in Figure O-14**

   Test, save, and close the new navigation form.

6. **Click the All Equipment tab, click the Employees tab, click the Save button ▦ on the Quick Access toolbar, type frmNavigation, click OK, then close frmNavigation**

FIGURE O-13: Adding frmEmployees as the first tab of the navigation form

frmEmployees tab

[Add New] tab

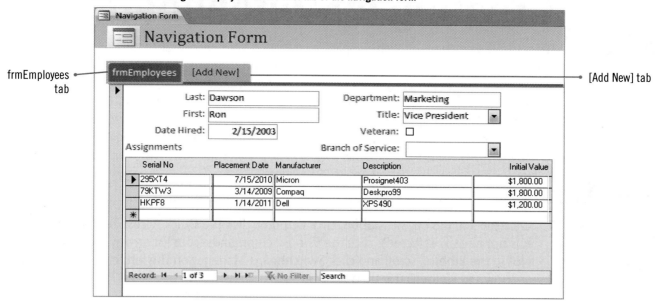

FIGURE O-14: Final navigation form in Form View

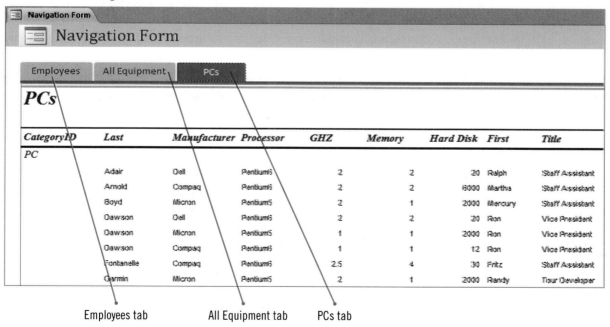

Employees tab

All Equipment tab

PCs tab

Creating a Switchboard

Given the new emphasis on Web-compatible navigation forms, Access 2010 puts less emphasis on older form navigation tools such as the switchboard. A **switchboard** is a special Access form that uses command buttons to provide an easy-to-use and secure database interface, and it was very popular with previous versions of Access. You create and modify switchboards by using an Access tool called the **Switchboard Manager**. ▆▆▆▆▆ Because your employees are already familiar with switchboard forms from older databases, you decide to create a switchboard form to serve as the opening database interface for Technology-O.accdb. Your first challenge is finding the Switchboard Manager functionality, which is no longer provided on the default Access 2010 Ribbon.

STEPS

TROUBLE

If this step is already completed on your computer, skip Step 1 and continue with Step 2.

1. **Click the File tab on the Ribbon, click Options, click the Quick Access Toolbar category (if it is not already selected), click the Choose commands from list arrow, click Commands Not in the Ribbon, scroll and click Switchboard Manager on the left, click the Add button as shown in Figure O-15, then click OK**

   With the Switchboard Manager functionality available on the Quick Access toolbar, you can use it to create a switchboard form.

2. **Click the Switchboard Manager button 🖼 on the Quick Access toolbar, then click Yes when prompted to create a switchboard**

   The Switchboard Manager dialog box opens and presents the options for the first switchboard page. One switchboard page must be designated as the **default switchboard**, which links to additional switchboard pages as needed. Your switchboard page will start with two command buttons.

QUICK TIP

To rename the switchboard, edit "Main Switchboard" in the Switchboard Name text box.

3. **Click Edit, then click New**

   The Edit Switchboard Item dialog box opens, prompting you for three pieces of information: Text (a label on the switchboard form that identifies the corresponding command button), Command (which corresponds to a database action), and Switchboard (an option that changes depending on the command and further defines the command button action).

4. **Type Open Employees Form in the Text text box, click the Command list arrow, click Open Form in Edit Mode, click the Form list arrow, then click frmEmployees**

   The Edit Switchboard Item dialog box should look like Figure O-16. Opening a form in **Edit Mode** allows you to edit records, whereas **Add Mode** only allows you to add new records.

5. **Click OK to add the first command button to the switchboard, click New, type Select Reports in the Text text box, click the Command list arrow, click Open Form in Edit Mode, click the Form list arrow, click frmDialogBox, then click OK**

   The Edit Switchboard Page dialog box has two items. Each entry in this dialog box represents a command button that will appear on the final switchboard.

TROUBLE

To delete a switchboard form and start over, first delete the Switchboard Items table so you can create the switchboard from scratch.

6. **Click Close to close the Edit Switchboard Page dialog box, click Close to close the Switchboard Manager dialog box, then double-click the new Switchboard form in the Navigation Pane**

   The finished switchboard opens in Form View, as shown in Figure O-17. Note that creating a switchboard form using the Switchboard Manager also creates a table called **Switchboard Items**, which contains information the form needs.

7. **Click the Open Employees Form command button on the Switchboard, close the frmEmployees form, click the Select Reports command button, then close the frmDialogBox form**

   Switchboard forms provide a fast and easy way to help users work with only those objects they need in a database. Given more time, you'd want to add more buttons to the switchboard to access more database objects.

Building a Database Interface

FIGURE O-15: Customizing the Quick Access toolbar to include the Switchboard Manager button

Quick Access Toolbar

Switchboard Manager

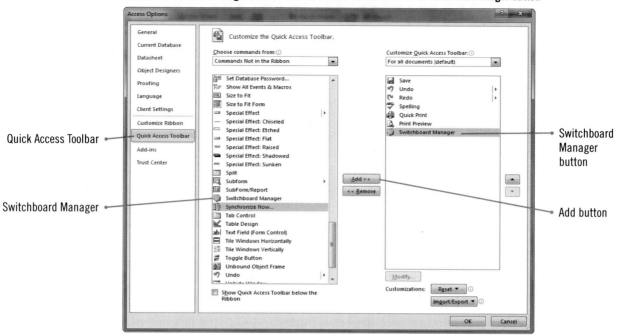

Switchboard Manager button

Add button

FIGURE O-16: Adding an item to a switchboard page

Text

Command

Form

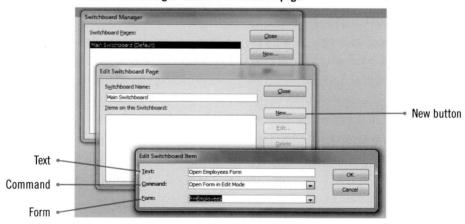

New button

FIGURE O-17: Switchboard form

Command buttons

Labels

Modifying a Switchboard

Always use the Switchboard Manager to add, delete, move, and edit the command buttons and labels on a switchboard form. Use Form Design View to make formatting modifications such as changing form colors, adding clip art, or changing the switchboard title. ▓▓▓▓▓ Kayla Green is pleased with the steps you've taken to make the database easier to use, but she suggests changing the title, colors, and order of the command buttons to improve the switchboard. You use Form Design View to make the formatting changes and the Switchboard Manager to change the order of the buttons.

STEPS

1. **Right-click the** Switchboard tab, **click** Design View, **then click the** teal rectangle **on the left of the Detail section**

   The teal areas on the left and top portion of the Switchboard are rectangles. You can modify their color or shape just as you would modify any drawn object.

2. **Click the** Home tab, **click the Background Color button arrow** 🎨▾, **click the** yellow box **in the last row, click the** teal rectangle **in the Form Header section, click the Background Color button arrow** 🎨▾, **then click the** red box **in the last row**

TROUBLE

Do not delete the existing labels in the Form Header section, as this will cause an error when opening the switchboard.

3. **Click the** Design tab, **click the Label button** Aa, **click the left side of the Form Header section, type** your name, **press [Enter], click the** Home tab, **click the Font Color button arrow** A▾, **then click the** Automatic box **to change the text color to black**

   Your switchboard should look like Figure O-18. You use Form Design View to modify colors, clip art, and labels. Notice that neither the command buttons nor the text describing each command button appears in Form Design View. You use the Switchboard Manager to modify the command buttons on a switchboard.

4. **Save and close the Switchboard form, click the** Switchboard Manager button 🗊 **on the Quick Access toolbar, then click** Edit

   Use the Switchboard Manager to add, delete, or modify the command buttons on the switchboard, including the text labels that describe them.

5. **Click** Select Reports, **click** Edit, **click immediately before Reports in the Text text box, type** Departmental, **press [Spacebar], then click** OK **to change the reference to Select Departmental Reports**

   You can also change the order of the command buttons from the Edit Switchboard Page dialog box.

6. **Click** Move Up **to make Select Departmental Reports the first item in the Switchboard, click** Close, **then click** Close **again**

7. **Double-click the** Switchboard form **in the Navigation Pane to open it in Form View as shown in Figure O-19, save, print it if requested by your instructor, then close the Switchboard form**

FIGURE O-18: Modifying a switchboard in Form Design View

Add your name

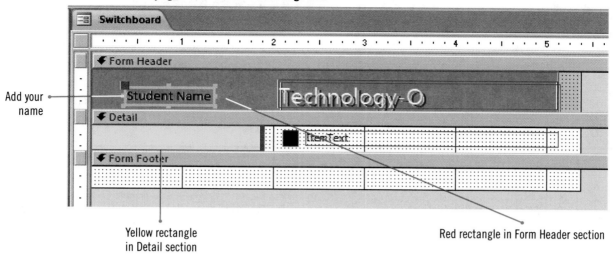

Yellow rectangle
in Detail section

Red rectangle in Form Header section

FIGURE O-19: Final switchboard in Form View

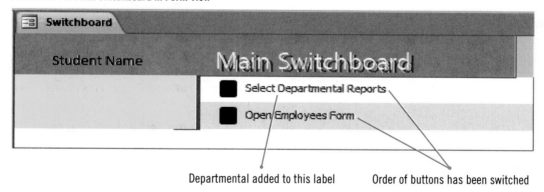

Departmental added to this label

Order of buttons has been switched

Using the Documenter

As your Access database grows, users will naturally request new ways to use the data. Your ability to modify a database depends on your understanding of existing database objects. Access provides an analysis feature called the **Documenter** that creates reports on the properties and relationships among the objects in a database. You use the Documenter to create paper documentation that describes the Technology-O database.

STEPS

1. **Click the Database Tools tab, then click the Database Documenter button**

   The Documenter dialog box opens, displaying tabs for each object type.

2. **Click the Tables tab, then click Options in the Documenter dialog box**

   The Print Table Definition dialog box opens as shown in Figure O-20. This dialog box gives you some control over what type of documentation you will print for the table. The documentation for each object type varies slightly. For example, the documentation on forms and reports also includes information on controls and sections.

3. **Click the Names, Data Types, and Sizes option button in the Include for Fields section, click the Nothing option button in the Include for Indexes section, then click OK**

   You can select or deselect individual objects by clicking the check box to the left of each object, or you can click the Select All button to quickly select all objects of that type.

4. **Click the Select All button to select all of the tables, click the Forms tab, click the Select All button to select all of the forms, click OK, navigate to the second page, click the ⊕ pointer on the report preview to zoom in, then scroll to display the table relationships as shown in Figure O-21**

   The Documenter creates a report for all of the table and form objects in the Technology-O.accdb database. The first page contains information about the first table in the database, the Switchboard Items table. The second page contains information about the second table in the database, tblAssignments.

   QUICK TIP

   Click the More button in the Data group on the Print Preview tab to display the report exporting options.

5. **Click the Last Page button ▶│ in the navigation bar, then click the Previous Page button ◀**

   The last part of the report contains information about the forms in the database. The properties for each control on the form are listed in two columns. Because most form controls have approximately 50 properties, the documentation to describe a form can be quite long. You can print the report or export it to a Word document, but you cannot modify a Documenter report in Report Design View or save it as an object within this database.

6. **Click the Close Print Preview button, then close the Technology-O.accdb database and exit Access**

FIGURE O-20: **Print Table Definition dialog box**

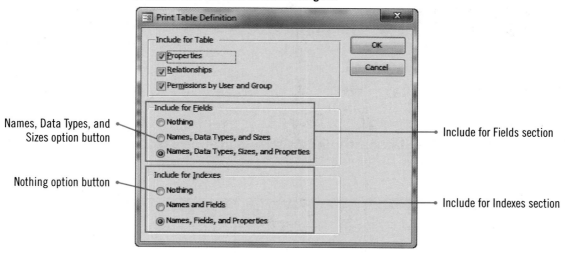

Names, Data Types, and Sizes option button

Nothing option button

Include for Fields section

Include for Indexes section

FIGURE O-21: **Object Definition report**

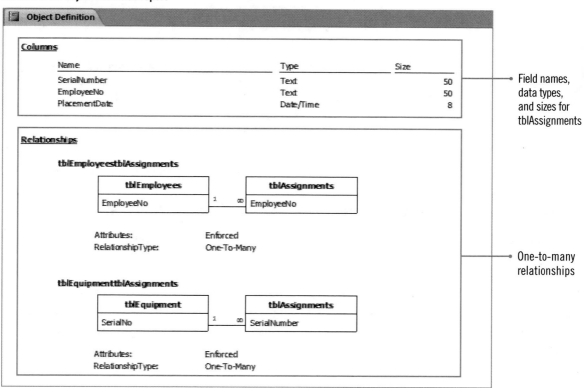

Field names, data types, and sizes for tblAssignments

One-to-many relationships

Practice

For current SAM information, including versions and content details, visit SAM Central (http://www.cengage.com/samcentral). If you have a SAM user profile, you may have access to hands-on instruction, practice, and assessment of the skills covered in this unit. Since various versions of SAM are supported throughout the life of this text, check with your instructor for the correct instructions and URL/Web site for accessing assignments.

Concepts Review

Identify each element of the database window shown in Figure O-22.

FIGURE O-22

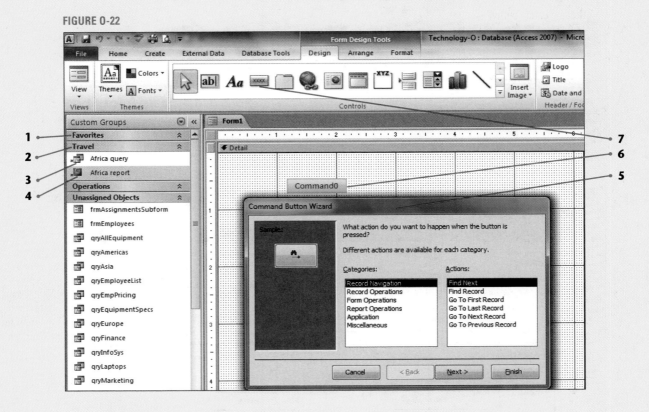

Match each term with the statement that best describes its function.

8. Dialog box

9. Pop up form

10. Switchboard

11. Shortcut

12. Command Button Wizard

13. Documenter

a. Creates reports on the properties and relationships among the objects in your database

b. Pointer to a database object

c. Stays on top of other open forms, even when another form is active

d. Uses command buttons to simplify access to database objects

e. Used to display information or prompt a user for a choice

f. Organizes over 30 of the most common command button actions within six categories

Building a Database Interface

Select the best answer from the following list of choices.

14. **Which View By option do you use to display the date that an object was created?**
    a. Small Icons
    b. Details
    c. List
    d. Date

15. **If you wanted to add a command button to a switchboard, which view or tool would you use?**
    a. Form Design View
    b. Switchboard Analyzer
    c. Report Design View
    d. Switchboard Manager

16. **Which item would *not* help you organize the Access objects that the Human Resources (HR) department most often uses?**
    a. A report that lists all HR employees
    b. A switchboard that provides command buttons to the appropriate HR objects
    c. A dialog box with command buttons that reference the most commonly used HR forms and reports
    d. An HR group with shortcuts to the HR objects

17. **A dialog box is which type of object?**
    a. Form
    b. Report
    c. Table
    d. Macro

18. **A switchboard is which type of object?**
    a. Form
    b. Report
    c. Table
    d. Macro

19. **If you want to change the color of a switchboard, which view or tool do you use?**
    a. Form Design View
    b. Switchboard Documenter
    c. Form View
    d. Switchboard Manager

20. **Which is *not* a valid name for an Access object?**
    a. tblEmployees
    b. E1-E2
    c. Employees table
    d. E1!E2

Skills Review

1. **Work with objects.**
   a. Start Access, open the Basketball-O.accdb database from the drive and folder where you store your Data Files, and enable content if prompted.
   b. Using the Navigation Pane, change the view to Icon.
   c. Show the Object Dependencies for qryPlayerStats.
   d. Switch the Object Dependencies task pane to show Objects that depend on me for qryPlayerStats if it is not already selected.
   e. Close the Object Dependencies task pane.

2. **Group objects.**
   a. Use the Navigation Options dialog box to create a custom group named **Offense** and another named **Defense**.
   b. In the Navigation Pane, change the category grouping to Custom.
   c. Create shortcuts for the qryFieldGoalStats query and the rptPointProduction report in the Offense group.
   d. Rename the qryFieldGoalStats report shortcut in the Offense group to **Field Goal Stats**.
   e. Rename the rptPointProduction report shortcut in the Offense group to **Point Production**.

3. **Create a dialog box.**
   a. Create a new form in Form Design View.
   b. Add a command button to the upper-left corner of the form using the Command Button Wizard. Select Report Operations from the Categories list, select Preview Report from the Actions list, then select the rptPlayerStatistics report.
   c. Type **Preview Player Statistics** as the text for the button, then type **cmdPlayerStats** for the button name.
   d. Add a second command button below the first to preview the rptPointProduction report.
   e. Type **Preview Point Production** as the text for the button, then type **cmdPointProduction** for the button name.

Skills Review (continued)

f. Below the two buttons, add a label to the form with your name.

g. In the Property Sheet for the form, change the Border Style property of the form to Dialog, the Record Selectors property to No, and the Navigation Buttons property to No.

h. Close the Property Sheet, then size the buttons to be the same size and aligned on their left edges.

i. Save the form as **frmTeamReports**.

j. Open the frmTeamReports form in Form View, test the buttons, close the reports, then print the form if requested by your instructor. Your frmTeamReports form should be similar to Figure O-23.

k. Close the frmTeamReports form.

4. **Create a pop up form.**

a. Create a form in Form Design View, change the Record Source for the form to tblPlayers, and add the following fields to the form: FirstName, LastName, and PlayerNo.

b. Save the form with the name **frmPlayerPopup**.

c. Open the Property Sheet for the frmPlayerPopup form, change the Pop Up property on the Other tab to Yes. Change the Width property on the Format tab to 3.

d. Save, then close the frmPlayerPopup form.

FIGURE O-23

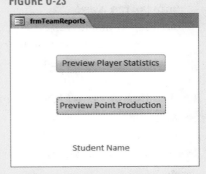

e. Open the frmTeamReports form in Form Design View, then add a command button below your name using the Command Button Wizard.

f. In the Command Button Wizard, select the Form Operations category, the Open Form action, and the frmPlayerPopup form to open. The form should be opened to show all of the records.

g. Type **Open Player Popup** as the text for the button, then name the button **cmdPlayerPopup**.

h. Modify the Embedded Macro on the On Click property of the cmdPlayerPopup button so that the View property is Datasheet.

i. Save the frmTeamReports form, then open it in Form View. Click the Open Player Popup command button to test it. Test the other buttons as well. The frmPlayerPopup form should stay on top of all other forms and reports until you close it.

j. Save then close all open forms and reports.

5. **Create a navigation form.**

a. Create a Navigation form using the Vertical Tabs, Left style.

b. Close the Field List.

c. Add the frmGameInfo form, the frmGameSummaryForm, and the frmPlayerInformationForm to the tabs.

d. Rename the tabs **Game Info**, **Game Summary**, and **Player Information**.

e. Display the form in Form View, then test each tab.

f. Save the form with the name **frmNavigationForms**, then close it.

6. **Create a switchboard.**

a. Start the Switchboard Manager, and click Yes to create a new switchboard.

b. Click Edit to edit the Main Switchboard, then click New to add the first item to it.

c. Type **Select a Team Report** as the Text entry for the first command button, select Open Form in Add Mode for the Command, select frmTeamReports for the Form, then click OK to add the first command button to the switchboard.

d. Click New to add a second item to the switchboard. Type **Open Player Entry Form** as the Text entry, select Open Form in Add Mode for the Command, select frmPlayerInformationForm for the Form, then click OK to add the second command button to the switchboard.

e. Close the Edit Switchboard Page dialog box, then close the Switchboard Manager dialog box. Open the Switchboard form and click both command buttons to make sure they work. Notice that when you open the Player Entry Form in Add Mode (rather than using the Open Form in Edit Mode action within the Switchboard Manager), the navigation buttons indicate that you can only add a new record, and not edit an existing one.

f. Close all open forms, including the Switchboard form.

Skills Review (continued)

7. Modify a switchboard.

   a. Open the Switchboard Manager, then click Edit to edit the Main Switchboard.

   b. Click the Open Player Entry Form item, then click Edit.

   c. Select Open Form in Edit Mode for the Command, select frmPlayerInformationForm for the Form, then click OK.

   d. Move the Open Player Entry Form item above the Select a Team Report item, then close the Edit Switchboard Page and Switchboard Manager dialog boxes.

   e. In Form Design View of the Switchboard form, add a label with your name and another label with the name of your favorite team to the Form Header section of the form. Change the text color to white for both of the labels.

   f. View the modified switchboard in Form View, as shown in Figure O-24, then test the buttons. Notice the difference in the Open Player Entry Form button (the Player Entry Form opens in Edit Mode versus Add Mode).

   g. Save, print (if requested by your instructor), then close the Switchboard form.

FIGURE O-24

8. Use the Documenter.

   a. Use the Database Documenter tool to document all tables and forms in the database.

   b. Print the first two pages and the last two pages of the report.

   c. Close the report created by Documenter without saving it.

   d. Close the Basketball-O.accdb database, then exit Access.

Independent Challenge 1

As the manager of a real estate office, you have created a database to track local real estate agencies, agents, and property listings. You want to create a group to organize the database objects used by the realtors. You also want to document the database's relationships.

   a. Start Access, open the database RealEstate-O.accdb from the drive and folder where you store your Data Files, and enable content if prompted.

   b. In the Navigation Pane, create a custom group named **Realtors**.

   c. View the objects in the Navigation Pane by Custom Groups, then add the following shortcuts to the Realtors group: frmListingsEntryForm, rptRealtorList report, and rptPropertyList report.

   d. Test all of the shortcuts to make sure they open the object they point to, then close all open objects.

   e. Start the Documenter. On the Current Database tab, click the Relationships check box, then click OK.

   f. Print the Documenter's report, then close it. Write your name on the printout.

Advanced Challenge Exercise

   ■ Create a switchboard form with the following four command buttons in the following order:

Text	Command	Form or Report
Open Agency Information Form	**Open Form in Edit Mode**	**frmAgencyInformation**
Open Listings Entry Form	**Open Form in Edit Mode**	**frmListingsEntryForm**
Open Realtor List Report	**Open Report**	**rptRealtorList**
Open Property List Report	**Open Report**	**rptPropertyList**

   ■ Open the Switchboard, and insert a label that reads **Your Name's Real Estate Agency** on the left side of the Form Header section, and change the text color to white.

   ■ Save, print (if requested by your instructor), then close the switchboard form. It should look like Figure O-25.

   g. Close the RealEstate-O.accdb database, then exit Access.

FIGURE O-25

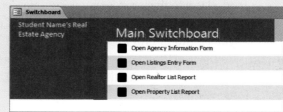

Independent Challenge 2

As the manager of a real estate office, you have created a database to track local real estate agencies, agents, and property listings. You want to create a new dialog box to make it easier to preview the reports within your database.

a. Start Access, then open the database RealEstate-O.accdb from the drive and folder where you store your Data Files. Enable content if prompted.

b. Start a new form in Form Design View.

c. Using the Command Button Wizard, add a command button to the form. Select Report Operations from the Categories list, select Preview Report from the Actions list, then select the rptRealtorList report.

d. Type **Realtor List** as the text for the button, then type **cmdRealtorList** for the button name.

e. Using the Command Button Wizard, add a second command button below the first. Select Report Operations from the Categories list, select Preview Report from the Actions list, then select the rptPropertyList report.

f. Type **Property List** as the text for the button, then type **cmdPropertyList** for the button name.

g. Using the Command Button Wizard, add a third command button below the second. Select Form Operations from the Categories list, and select Close Form from the Actions list.

h. Type **Close** as the text for the button, then type **cmdClose** as the meaningful name for the button.

i. Add a label to the form with your name and any other formatting enhancements you desire.

j. Open the Property Sheet for the form, change the Border Style property to Dialog, the Record Selectors property to No, and the Navigation Buttons property to No.

k. Close the Property Sheet, and then save the form as **frmDialogBox**.

l. Resize all the command buttons to be the same width and aligned on the left edges.

m. Open the frmDialogBox form in Form View, test the buttons, save the form when prompted, then print the form if requested by your instructor. It should look similar to Figure O-26.

n. Close the frmDialogBox form, close the RealEstate-O.accdb database, then exit Access.

FIGURE O-26

Independent Challenge 3

As the manager of a real estate office, you have created a database to track local real estate agencies, agents, and property listings. You want to create a pop up form to provide agent information. You want to add a command button to the frmListingsEntry-Form to open the pop up form.

a. Start Access, then open the database RealEstate-O.accdb from the drive and folder where you store your Data Files. Enable content if prompted.

b. Use the Form Wizard to create a form with the RealtorNo, RealtorFirst, RealtorLast, and RealtorPhone fields from the Realtors table.

c. Use a Tabular layout, and type **Realtor Popup** for the form title.

d. Open the Property Sheet for the form, then change the Pop Up property to Yes.

e. Save, then close the Realtor Popup form. Rename it **frmRealtorPopup** in the Navigation Pane.

f. In Form Design View of frmListingsEntryForm, open the Form Header section about 0.5", then use the Command Button Wizard to create a command button on the right side of the Form Header.

g. Select Form Operations from the Categories list, select Open Form from the Actions list, select the frmRealtorPopup form, then open the form and show all of the records.

h. Type **Realtor Popup** as the text for the button, then type **cmdRealtorPopup** for the button name.

i. Add a label to the left side of the Form Header with your name.

j. Modify the embedded macro in the On Click property of the Realtor Popup command button by changing the View argument from Form to Datasheet.

k. Save the frmListingsEntryForm, open it in Form View, then click the Realtor Popup command button.

l. Move through the records of the frmListingsEntryForm. The frmRealtorPopup form should stay on top of all other forms.

Independent Challenge 3 (continued)

Advanced Challenge Exercise

- Create a second pop up form using the Form Wizard with all of the fields of the Agencies table except for AgencyNo.
- Use a Tabular layout, and title the form **Agency Popup**.
- Change the form's Pop Up property to Yes, then save and close the form. Rename it **frmAgencyPopup** in the Navigation Pane.
- In Design View of the frmListingsEntryForm, add another command button just below the Realtor Popup command button in the Form Header section to open the frmAgencyPopup form and show all of the records.
- Type **Agency Popup** as the text for the button, then type **cmdAgencyPopup** for the button name.
- Move, resize, and align the controls in the Form Header as needed.
- Modify the embedded macro in the On Click property of the Agency Popup command button by changing the View argument from Form to Datasheet.
- Open frmListingsEntryForm in Form View, and test both command buttons.

m. Close any open pop up forms, then print the first record in the frmListingsEntryForm if requested by your instructor.

n. Save and close all open forms, close the RealEstate-O.accdb database, then exit Access.

Real Life Independent Challenge

This Independent Challenge requires an Internet connection.

The larger your database becomes, the more important it is to document it properly so that others can also work with it successfully. Many companies require that you use an adopted set of naming standards when you create new fields, objects, and controls so that other database developers can more readily understand and modify a database they have not created. In this Real Life Independent Challenge, you will search for and report on database naming standards.

a. Connect to the Internet, go to *www.google.com*, *www.bing.com*, or your favorite search engine, then search for Web sites with the key words **Access naming conventions**. You might also try searching for the **Leszynski Naming Convention**, **object naming convention**, or **database naming convention**.

b. Find and print two different reference pages that describe naming conventions for fields, objects, or controls.

c. Find and print two different discussions of the advantages of adopting a common naming convention for all database development for your company.

Advanced Challenge Exercise

- Call two local businesses and contact a programmer in the Information Systems Department who is willing to answer questions about naming conventions. Ask whether their business employs standardized naming conventions in database development. Ask what types of database software they use. Ask what types of challenges they face in database development, maintenance, and standards. Finally, ask what type of advice they have for a future database developer. Be sure to thank them for their time and advice.

d. Write a two-page paper summarizing your findings. If using references or information from articles or interviews, be sure to reference those sources of information properly, in accordance with class instructions.

Visual Workshop

As the manager of a tourism company that promotes travel to European countries, you have created an Access database called Baltic-O.accdb that tracks events at various European cities. Create a switchboard form to give the Baltic-O users an easy-to-use interface, as shown in Figure O-27. All command buttons on the switchboard access a report for the country they reference. Be sure to add your own name as a label to the switchboard, and include any other formatting improvements that you desire.

FIGURE O-27

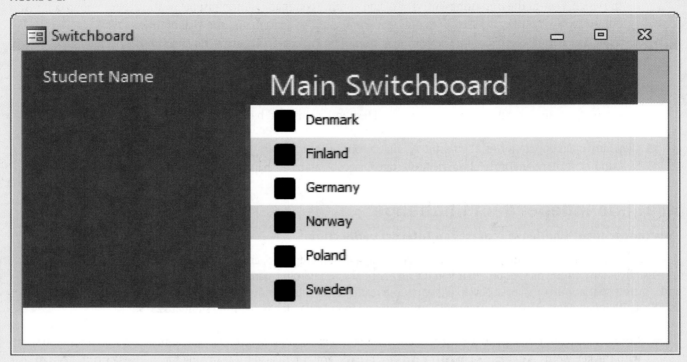

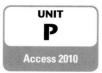

Administering the Database

Access databases are unlike the other Microsoft Office files, such as Word documents or Excel spreadsheets, in that they are typically used by multiple people and for extended periods. Therefore, spending a few hours to secure a database and improve its performance is a good investment. **Database administration** involves making the database faster, easier, more secure, and more reliable. You work with Kayla Green, network administrator at Quest Specialty Travel, to examine several administrative issues such as setting passwords, changing startup options, and analyzing database performance to protect, improve, and enhance the database.

OBJECTIVES

Compact and repair a database

Change startup options

Set a database password

Analyze database performance

Analyze table performance

Back up a database

Convert a database

Split a Database

Compacting and Repairing a Database

Compacting and repairing a database refers to a process that Access 2010 uses to reorganize the parts of a database to eliminate wasted space on the disk storage device, which also helps prevent data integrity problems. You can compact and repair a database at any time, or you can set a database option to automatically compact and repair the database when it is closed. You and Kayla Green decide to compact and repair the Technology database, and then learn about the option to automatically compact and repair the database when it is closed.

STEPS

1. **Start Access, then open the Technology-P.accdb database from the drive and folder where you store your Data Files, enabling content if prompted**

   You can compact and repair the database at any time with an option on the File tab.

2. **Click the File tab on the Ribbon, then click the Compact & Repair Database button**

   The database is closed, the compact and repair process is completed, and the database reopened automatically.

   Compacting and repairing a database can reduce the size of the database by 10, 50, or even 75 percent because the space occupied by deleted objects and deleted data is not reused until the database is compacted. Therefore, it's a good idea to set up a regular schedule to compact and repair a database. You decide to change Access options to automatically compact the database when it is closed.

3. **Click the File tab on the Ribbon, then click Options**

   The Compact on Close feature is in the Current Database category.

4. **Click the Current Database category, then click the Compact on Close check box**

   Your screen should look like Figure P-1. Now, every time the database is closed, Access will also compact and repair it. This helps you keep the database as small and efficient as possible and protects your database from potential corruption. For other database threats and solutions, see Table P-1.

5. **Click OK to close the Access Options dialog box, then click OK when prompted to close and reopen the current database**

FIGURE P-1: Setting the Compact on Close option

Current Database category

Compact on Close

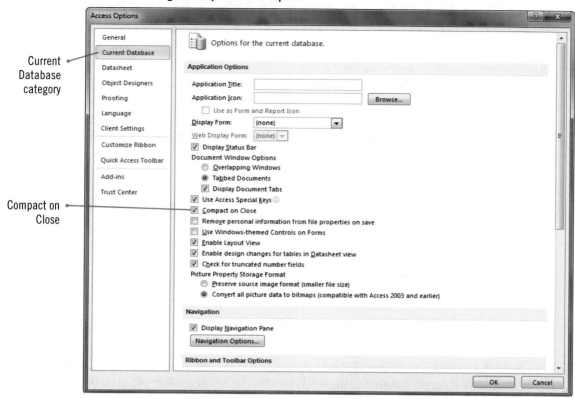

TABLE P-1: Database threats

incident	what can happen	appropriate actions
Virus	Viruses can cause a wide range of harm, from profane messages to corrupted files	Purchase the leading virus-checking software for each machine, and keep it updated
Power outage	Power problems such as construction accidents, **brown-outs** (dips in power often causing lights to dim), and **spikes** (surges in power) can damage the hardware, which may render the computer useless	Purchase a **UPS** (uninterruptible power supply) to maintain constant power to the file server Purchase a **surge protector** (power strip with surge protection) for each user
Theft or intentional damage	Computer thieves or other scoundrels steal or vandalize computer equipment	Place the file server in a room that can be locked after hours Use network drives for user data files, and back them up on a daily basis Use off-site storage for backups Set database passwords and encrypt the database so that files that are stolen cannot be used; use computer locks for equipment that is at risk, especially laptops

Changing Startup Options

Startup options are a series of commands that execute when the database is opened. You manage the default startup options using features in the Current Database category of the Access Options dialog box. More startup options are available through the use of **command-line options**, a special series of characters added to the end of the pathname (for example, C:\My Documents\Quest.accdb /excl), which execute a command when the file is opened. See Table P-2 for information on common startup command-line options. ▰▰▰ You want to view and set database properties and then specify that the frmEmployees form opens when the Technology-P.accdb database is opened.

STEPS

1. **Click the File tab on the Ribbon, click Options, then click Current Database if it is not already selected**

   The Access Options dialog box opens. The startup options are in the Application Options area of the Current Database category.

2. **Click the Application Title text box, then type Quest Specialty Travel**

   The Application Title database property value appears in the title bar instead of the database filename.

3. **Click the Display Form list arrow, then click frmEmployees**

   See Figure P-2. You test the Application Title and Display Form database properties.

4. **Click OK to close the Access Options dialog box, click OK when prompted, close the Technology-P.accdb database, then reopen the Technology-P.accdb database and enable content if prompted**

   The Technology-P.accdb database opens with the new application title, followed by the frmEmployees form, as shown in Figure P-3. If you want to open an Access database and bypass startup options, press and hold [Shift] while the database opens.

5. **Close the frmEmployees form**

TABLE P-2: Startup command-line options

option	effect
/excl	Opens the database for exclusive access
/ro	Opens the database for read-only access
/pwd *password*	Opens the database using the specified *password* (applies to Access 2002–2003 and earlier version databases only)
/repair	Repairs the database (in Access 2000 and 2002, compacting the database also repairs it; if you choose the Compact on Close command, you don't need the /repair option)
/convert *target database*	Converts a previous version of a database to an Access 2000 database with the *target database* name
/x *macro*	Starts Access and runs the specified *macro*
/wrkgrp *workgroup information file*	Starts Access using the specified *workgroup information file* (applies to Access 2002–2003 and earlier version databases only)

FIGURE P-2: Setting the Display Form option

Current Database category

Display Form set to frmEmployees

Application Title entered

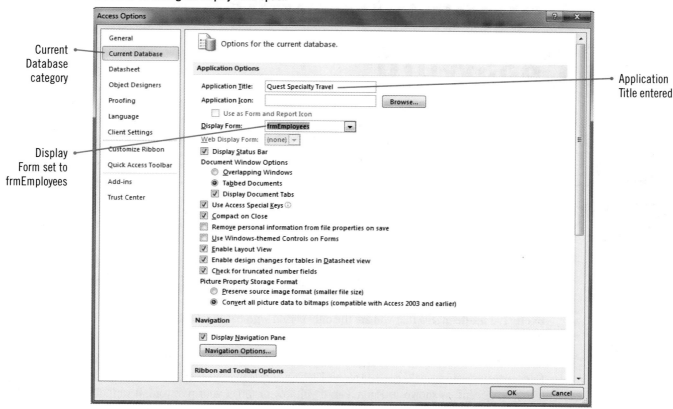

FIGURE P-3: Form and Application Title startup options are in effect

Quest Specialty Travel is the Application Title

frmEmployees opens automatically

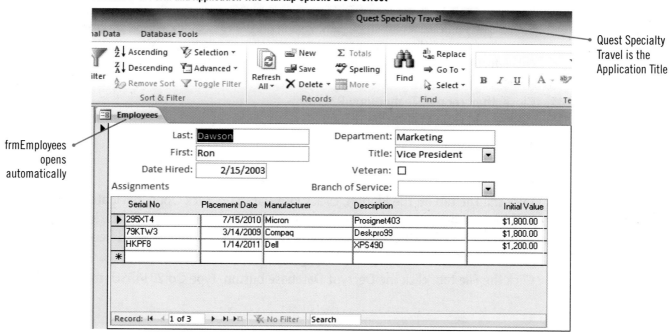

Access 2010

Setting a Database Password

A **password** is a combination of uppercase and lowercase letters, numbers, and symbols that the user must enter to open the database. Setting a database password means that anyone who doesn't know the password cannot open the database. Other ways to secure an Access database are listed in Table P-3. ▟▟▟▟ You apply a database password to the Technology-P.accdb database to secure its data.

STEPS

QUICK TIP
It's always a good idea to back up a database before creating a database password.

1. **Click the File tab on the Ribbon, then click Close Database**

   The Technology-P.accdb database closes, but the Access application window remains open. To set a database password, you must open the database in Exclusive mode.

2. **Click Open, navigate to the drive and folder where you store your Data Files, click Technology-P.accdb, click the Open button arrow, click Open Exclusive, then enable content if prompted**

   Exclusive mode means that you are the only person who has the database open, and others cannot open the file during this time.

3. **Click the File tab on the Ribbon, click Info, then click the Encrypt with Password button**

   Encryption means to make the data in the database unreadable by other software. The Set Database Password dialog box opens, as shown in Figure P-4. If you lose or forget your password, it cannot be recovered. For security reasons, your password does not appear as you type; for each keystroke, an asterisk appears instead. Therefore, you must enter the same password in both the Password and Verify text boxes to make sure you haven't made a typing error. Passwords are case sensitive, so Cyclones and cyclones are different.

QUICK TIP
Check to make sure the Caps Lock light is not on before entering a password.

4. **Type Go!2014!ISU in the Password text box, press [Tab], type Go!2014!ISU in the Verify text box, click OK, then click OK if prompted about row-level security**

   Passwords should be easy to remember, but not as obvious as your name, the word "password," the name of the database, or the name of your company. **Strong passwords** are longer than eight characters and use the entire keyboard including uppercase and lowercase letters, numbers, and symbols. Microsoft provides an online tool to check the strength of your password. Go to www.microsoft.com and search for password checker.

5. **Close, then reopen Technology-P.accdb**

   The Password Required dialog box opens, as shown in Figure P-5.

6. **Type Go!2014!ISU, then click OK**

   The Technology-P.accdb database opens, giving you full access to all of the objects. To remove a password, you must exclusively open a database, just as you did when you set the database password.

7. **Click the File tab on the Ribbon, click Close Database, click Open, navigate to the drive and folder where you store your Data Files, click Technology-P.accdb, click the Open button arrow, click Open Exclusive, type Go!2014!ISU in the Password Required dialog box, then click OK**

8. **Click the File tab, click the Decrypt Database button, type Go!2014!ISU, then click OK**

FIGURE P-4: **Set Database Password dialog box**

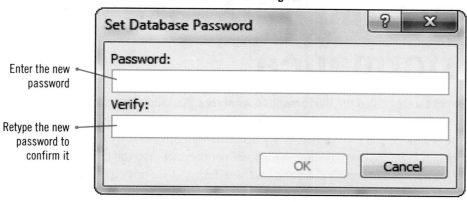

Enter the new password ●

Retype the new password to confirm it ●

FIGURE P-5: **Password Required dialog box**

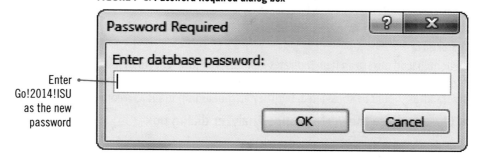

Enter Go!2014!ISU as the new password ●

TABLE P-3: **Methods to secure an Access database**

method	description
Password	Restricts access to the database, and can be set at the database, workgroup, or VBA level
Encryption	Makes the data indecipherable to other programs
Startup options	Hides or disables certain functions when the database is opened
Show/hide objects	Shows or hides objects in the Navigation Pane; a simple way to prevent users from unintentionally deleting objects is to hide them in the database window by checking the Hidden property in the object's Property Sheet
Split a database	Separates the back-end data and the front-end objects (such as forms and reports) into two databases that work together; splitting a database allows you to give each user access to only those front-end objects they need as well as add security measures to the back-end database that contains the data

Analyzing Database Performance

Access provides a tool called the **Performance Analyzer** that studies the structure and size of your database and makes a variety of recommendations on how you can improve its performance. With adequate time and Access skills, you can alleviate many performance bottlenecks by using software tools and additional programming techniques to improve database performance. You can often purchase faster processors and more memory to accomplish the same goal. See Table P-4 for tips on optimizing the performance of your computer. ▓▓▓▓▓ You use the Database Performance Analyzer to see whether Access provides any recommendations on how to easily maintain peak performance of the Technology-P.accdb database.

STEPS

1. **Close frmEmployees, click the Database Tools tab, click the Analyze Performance button in the Analyze group, then click the All Object Types tab**

   The Performance Analyzer dialog box opens, as shown in Figure P-6. You can choose to analyze selected tables, forms, other objects, or the entire database.

2. **Click the Select All button, then click OK**

   The Performance Analyzer examines each object and presents the results in a dialog box, as shown in Figure P-7. The key shows that the analyzer gives four levels of advice regarding performance: recommendations, suggestions, ideas, and items that were fixed.

3. **Click each line in the Analysis Results area, then read each description in the Analysis Notes area**

   The light bulb icon next to an item indicates that this is an idea. The Analysis Notes section of the Performance Analyzer dialog box gives you additional information regarding the specific item. All of the Performance Analyzer's ideas should be considered, but they are not as important as recommendations and suggestions.

4. **Click Close to close the Performance Analyzer dialog box**

TABLE P-4: Tips for optimizing performance

degree of difficulty	tip
Easy	To free memory and other computer resources, close all applications that you don't currently need
Easy	If they can be run safely only when you need them, eliminate memory-resident programs such as complex screen savers, e-mail alert programs, and virus checkers
Easy	If you are the only person using a database, open it in Exclusive mode
Easy	Use the Compact on Close feature to regularly compact and repair your database
Moderate	Add more memory to your computer; once the database is open, memory is generally the single most important determinant of overall performance
Moderate	If others don't need to share the database, load it on your local hard drive instead of the network's file server (but be sure to back up local drives regularly, too)
Moderate	Split the database so that the data is stored on the file server, but other database objects are stored on your local (faster) hard drive
Moderate to difficult	If you are using disk compression software, stop doing so or move the database to an uncompressed drive
Moderate to difficult	Run Performance Analyzer on a regular basis, examining and appropriately acting on each recommendation, suggestion, and idea
Moderate to difficult	Make sure that all PCs are running the latest versions of Windows and Access; this might involve purchasing more software or upgrading hardware to properly support these robust software products

FIGURE P-6: **Performance Analyzer dialog box**

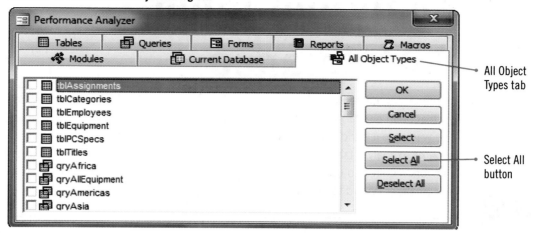

All Object Types tab

Select All button

FIGURE P-7: **Performance Analyzer results**

Analysis Results

Key

Analysis Notes

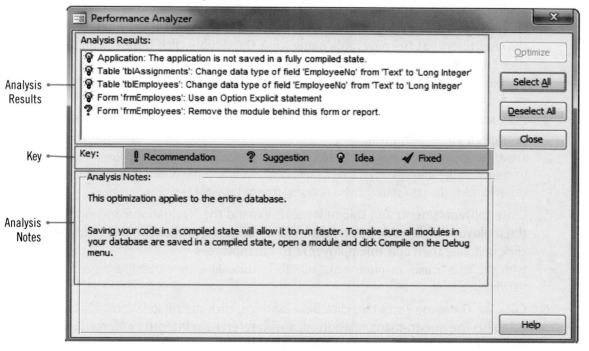

Analyzing Table Performance

Another Access database performance analysis tool, called the **Table Analyzer Wizard**, looks for duplicate information in one table that could be separated and stored in its own table. Storing duplicate data in one table wastes space and causes database accuracy errors, yet it is a very common table design problem. The best time to analyze tables is shortly after you initially build the tables, so that you can minimize the amount of rework required to update other queries, forms, and reports that rely on the table. 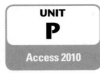 You use the Table Analyzer Wizard to examine the tblEmployees table.

STEPS

1. **Click the Database Tools tab, then click the Analyze Table button**

   The Table Analyzer Wizard starts, as shown in Figure P-8. The first dialog box describes the problems caused by storing duplicate data in one table. The **Show me an example** buttons give you more information by using a common example to explain the problem.

2. **Click Next, read about solving the redundant data problem, click Next, click tblEmployees in the Tables list, click Next, click the No, I want to decide option button, then click Next**

   The Table Analyzer Wizard helps you break repeated information into separate **lookup tables**. For example, the EDepartment field contains a given number of values that could be supplied by a lookup table. By using a lookup table for EDepartment data, users could not enter the same department name two or more ways (HR and Human Resources, for example).

3. **Drag EDepartment from the Table1 field list to a blank spot on the right, type tblDepartments as the new table name, click OK, double-click Table1, type tblEmployees2, click OK, then resize both field lists to see all of the fields**

   See Figure P-9. The wizard prevents you from using the names of existing tables so you do not replace any existing data.

4. **Click Next, click the No, don't create the query option button, click Finish, then click OK if prompted about tiling windows**

   The tblDepartments table is connected in a one-to-many relationship with the tblEmployees2 table using the ID field in tblDepartments and the field captioned Lookup to tblDepartments in tblEmployees2. Your next step is to delete the extra tblEmployees table and rename the new table.

5. **Close tblDepartments and tblEmployees2, expand the Navigation Pane, right-click the tblEmployees table, click Delete, click Yes, click Yes, right-click the tblEmployees2 table, click Rename, then edit tblEmployees2 to tblEmployees**

   With the table names in place, make sure the relationships are established correctly with the new tblEmployees table.

6. **Click the Database Tools tab, click Relationships, click the All Relationships button, then establish the one-to-many relationships with referential integrity enforced with the new tblEmployees table as shown in Figure P-10**

   Any time you change or modify tables, it's important to check the Relationships window to make sure that all relationships are still in place.

7. **Close the Relationships window, then click Yes when prompted to save changes**

FIGURE P-8: Table Analyzer Wizard

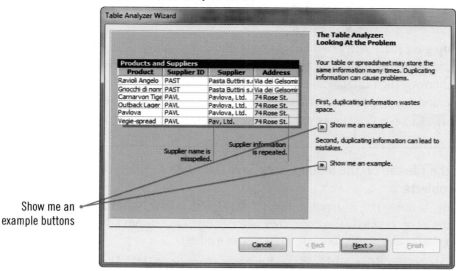

Show me an
example buttons

FIGURE P-9: Creating a lookup table

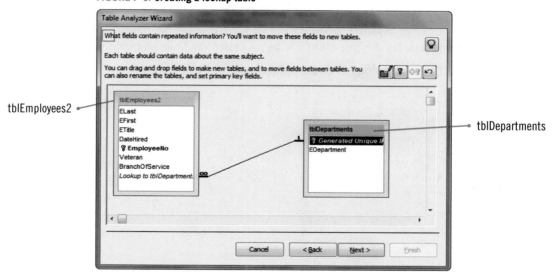

tblEmployees2

tblDepartments

FIGURE P-10: Establishing relationships

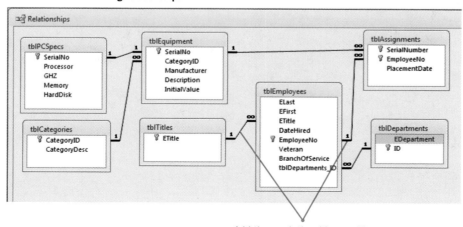

Add these relationships, making
sure to enforce referential integrity

Backing Up a Database

Backing up a database refers to making a copy of it in a secure location. Backups can be saved on an external hard drive, the hard drive of a second computer, or a Web server. Several years ago, portable backup technology such as tape drives or compact discs (CDs) were used. Because most users are familiar with saving and copying files to hard drives, the new technology streamlines the effort of backing up a database. Kayla Green asks you to review the methods of backing up the database.

STEPS

1. **Click the File tab on the Ribbon, click Save Database As, then click Yes to close all open objects**

   The Save As dialog box is shown in Figure P-11. Note that **Save Database As** saves the entire database including all of its objects to a completely new database file. The **Save Object As** option saves only the current object (table, query, form, report, macro, or module).

2. **Navigate to the drive and folder where you store your Data Files, enter Technology-P-Backup in the File name box, then click Save**

   A copy of the Technology-P.accdb database is saved in the location you selected with the name Technology-P-Backup.accdb. Access also automatically closed the Technology-P.accdb database and opened Technology-P-Backup.accdb.

   Another way to make a backup copy of an Access database file, or any file, is to use your Windows skills to copy and paste the database file in a Windows Explorer or Computer window.

3. **Close the Technology-P-Backup database and exit Access**

Administering the Database

Use the Previous Locations list or folder window to navigate to your data files

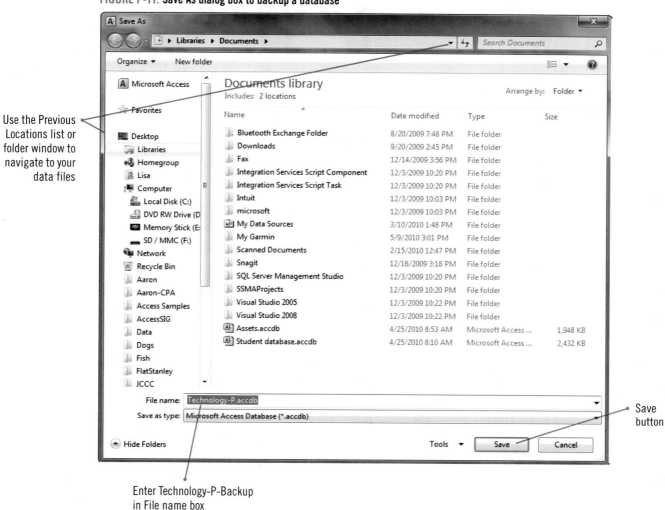

Save button

Enter Technology-P-Backup in File name box

Using portable storage media

Technological advancements continue to make it easier and less expensive to store large files on portable storage devices. A few years ago, 3.5-inch disks with roughly 1 **MB** (megabyte, a million bytes) of storage capacity were common. Today, 3.5-inch disks have been replaced by a variety of inexpensive, high-capacity storage media that work with digital devices such as digital cameras, cell phones, tablet computers, and personal digital assistants (PDAs). **Secure digital (SD) cards** are quarter-sized devices that slip directly into a computer and typically store around 4 **GB** (gigabyte, 4,000 MB).

CompactFlash (CF) cards are slightly larger, about the size of a matchbook, and store more data, around 8 GB. **USB (Universal Serial Bus) drives** (which plug into a computer's USB port), are also popular. USB drives are also called thumb drives, flash drives, and travel drives. USB devices typically store 1 GB to 10 GB of information. Larger still are **external hard drives**, sometimes as small as the size of a cell phone, that store anywhere from 20 to about 400 GB of information and connect to a computer using either a USB or FireWire port.

Converting a Database

When you **convert** a database, you change the file into one that can be opened in another version of Access. In Access 2010, the default file format is Access 2007, but in Access 2003, the default file format for a new database was Access 2000, a file format that could be seamlessly opened in Access 2000, Access 2002 (also called Access XP), or Access 2003. Therefore, Access users must now consider the version of Access they want to create ahead of time because Access 2007 databases work only with Access 2007 and Access 2010. If you want to open an Access 2007 database in Access 2000, 2002, or 2003, you need to convert it to an Access 2000 database first. ▓▓▓▓ The Training Department asks you to convert the Technology-P. accdb database to a version that they can open and use in Access 2000, 2002, or 2003.

STEPS

1. **Start Access, then open the Technology-P.accdb database from the drive and folder where you store your Data Files, enabling content if prompted**

TROUBLE

If you do not see the extensions on the filenames, click Organize on the toolbar, click Folder and search options, click the View tab, then uncheck the Hide file extensions for known file types check box.

2. **Click the File tab on the Ribbon, click Save & Publish, click Access 2000 Database (*.mdb), click the Save As button, then click Yes to close open objects**

   To convert a database, you must make sure that no other users are currently working with it. Because you are the sole user of this database, it is safe to start the conversion process. The Save As dialog box opens, prompting you for the name of the database.

3. **Navigate to the drive and folder where you store your Data Files, then type Technology-P-2000.mdb in the File name text box as shown in Figure P-12**

   Because Access 2000, 2002, and 2003 all work with Access 2000 databases equally well, to allow for maximum backward compatibility you decide to convert this database to an Access 2000 version database. Recall that Access 2007 databases have an **.accdb** file extension, but Access 2000 and 2002–2003 databases have the **.mdb** file extension.

   Also note that you may see two other database extensions, .ldb for older databases and .laccdb for newer databases. The **.ldb** and **.laccdb** files are temporary files that keep track of record-locking information when the database is open. They help coordinate the multiuser capabilities of an Access database so that several people can read and update the same database at the same time.

4. **Click Save, then click OK**

   A copy of the database with the name Technology-P-2000.mdb is saved to the drive and folder you specified and is opened in the Access window. You can open and use Access 2000 and 2002–2003 databases in Access 2010 just as you would open and use an Access 2007 database. Each database version has its advantages, however, which are summarized in Table P-5.

5. **Close the database and exit Access**

FIGURE P-12: **Save As dialog box to convert a database**

Use the Previous Locations list or folder window to navigate to your data files

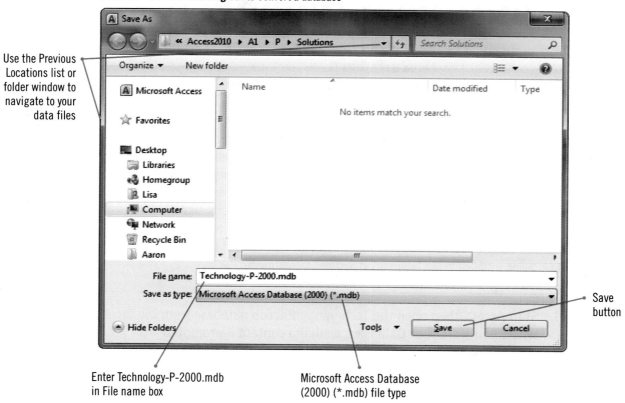

Save button

Enter Technology-P-2000.mdb in File name box

Microsoft Access Database (2000) (*.mdb) file type

TABLE P-5: **Differences between database file formats**

database file format	file extension	Access version(s) that can read this file	benefits
2000	.mdb	2000, 2002, 2003, 2007, and 2010	Most versatile if working in an environment where multiple versions of Access are still in use
2002–2003	.mdb	2002, 2003, 2007, and 2010	Provides some advanced technical advantages for large databases over the Access 2000 file format
2007	.accdb	2007 and 2010	Supports the Attachment data type
			Supports multivalued fields
			Provides excellent integration with SharePoint and Outlook
			Provides more robust encryption

Splitting a Database

As your database grows, more people will want to use it, which creates the need for higher levels of database connectivity. **Local area networks (LANs)** are installed to link multiple PCs so they can share hardware and software resources. After a LAN is installed, a shared database can be moved to a **file server**, a centrally located computer from which every user can access the database via the network. The more users who share the same database, however, the slower it responds. To improve the performance of a database shared among several users, you might want to **split** the database into two files: the **back-end database**, which contains the actual table objects and is stored on the file server, and the **front-end database**, which contains the other database objects (forms and reports, for example), and links to the back-end database tables. You copy the front-end database for as many users as needed because the front-end database must be located on each user's PC. You can also customize the objects contained in each front-end database. Therefore, front-end databases not only improve performance but also add a level of customization and security. ░░░░ You split the Technology-P.accdb database into two databases in preparation for the new LAN being installed in the Information Systems Department.

STEPS

1. **Start Access, then open the Technology-P.accdb database from the drive and folder where you store your Data Files, enabling content if prompted**

2. **Close the frmEmployees form, click the Database Tools tab, click the Access Database button in the Move Data group, read the dialog box, then click Split Database**
    Access suggests the name of Technology-P_be.accdb for the back-end database in the Create Back-end Database dialog box.

3. **Navigate to the drive and folder where you store your Data Files, click Split, then click OK**
    Technology-P.accdb has now become the front-end database, which will contain all of the Access objects except for the tables, as shown in Figure P-13. The tables have been replaced with links to the physical tables in the back-end database.

4. **Point to several linked table icons to read the path to the back-end database, right-click any of the linked table icons, then click Linked Table Manager**
    The Linked Table Manager dialog box opens, as shown in Figure P-14. This allows you to select and manually update tables. This is useful if the path to the back-end database changes and you want to reconnect the front-end and back-end database.

5. **Click Cancel**
    Linked tables work just like regular physical tables, even though the data is physically stored in another database.

6. **Close the Technology-P.accdb database and exit Access**

FIGURE P-13: Front-end database

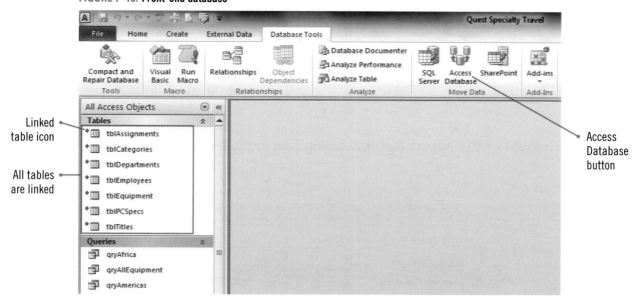

Linked table icon

All tables are linked

Access Database button

FIGURE P-14: Linked Table Manager

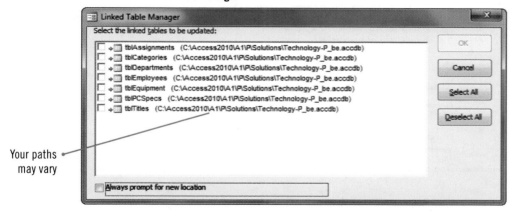

Your paths may vary

Databases and client/server computing

Splitting a database into a front-end and back-end database that work together is an excellent example of client/server computing. **Client/server computing** can be defined as two or more information systems cooperatively processing to solve a problem. In most implementations, the **client** is defined as the user's PC and the **server** is defined as the shared file server, mini computer, or mainframe computer. The server usually handles corporate-wide computing activities such as

data storage and management, security, and connectivity to other networks. Within Access, client computers generally handle those tasks specific to each user, such as storing all of the queries, forms, and reports used by a particular user. Effectively managing a client/server network in which many front-end databases link to a single back-end database is a tremendous task, but the performance and security benefits are worth the effort.

Practice

For current SAM information, including versions and content details, visit SAM Central (http://www.cengage.com/samcentral). If you have a SAM user profile, you may have access to hands-on instruction, practice, and assessment of the skills covered in this unit. Since various versions of SAM are supported throughout the life of this text, check with your instructor for the correct instructions and URL/Web site for accessing assignments.

Concepts Review

Identify each element of the Access Options dialog box in Figure P-15.

FIGURE P-15

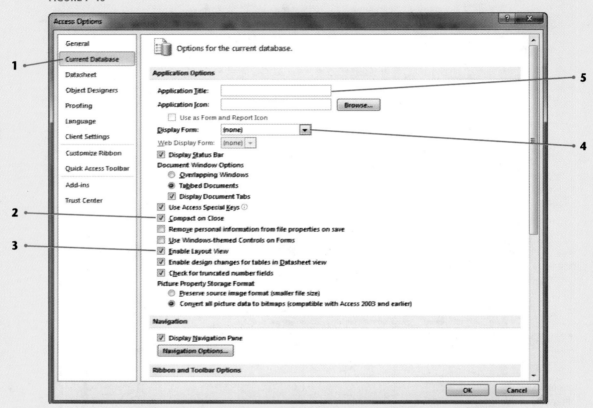

Match each term with the statement that best describes its function.

6. **Table Analyzer Wizard**
7. **Back-end database**
8. **Encrypting**
9. **Database Performance Analyzer**
10. **Exclusive mode**

a. Scrambles data so that it is indecipherable when opened by another program
b. Studies the structure and size of your database, and makes a variety of recommendations on how you can improve its speed
c. Contains database tables
d. Looks for duplicate information in one table that should be separated and stored in its own table
e. Means that no other users can have access to the database file while it's open

Select the best answer from the list of choices.

11. **Changing a database file so that a previous version of Access can open it is called:**
    a. Splitting.
    b. Analyzing.
    c. Converting.
    d. Encrypting.

12. **Which is *not* a strong password?**
    a. 1234$College=6789
    b. password
    c. 5Matthew14?
    d. Lip44Balm*!

13. **Power outages can be caused by which of the following?**
    a. Surges
    b. Spikes
    c. Construction accidents
    d. All of the above

14. **Which character precedes a command-line option?**
    a. ^
    b. /
    c. @
    d. !

Skills Review

1. Compact and repair a database.

a. Start Access, open the Basketball-P.accdb database from the drive and folder where you store your Data Files, and enable content if prompted.

b. Compact and repair the database using an option on the File tab.

c. Open the Access Options dialog box, and check the Compact on Close option in the Current Database category.

2. Change startup options.

a. Open the Access Options dialog box.

b. Type **Iowa State Cyclones** in the Application Title text box, click the Display Form list arrow, click the frmGameInfo form, then apply the changes.

c. Close the Basketball-P.accdb database, then reopen it to check the startup options. Notice the change in the Access title bar.

d. Close the frmGameInfo form that automatically opened when the database was opened.

e. Close the Basketball-P.accdb database.

3. Set a database password.

a. Open the Basketball-P.accdb database in Exclusive mode.

b. Set the database password to **b*i*g*1*2**. (*Hint*: Check to make sure the Caps Lock light is not on because passwords are case sensitive.) Click OK if prompted.

c. Close the Basketball-P.accdb database, but leave Access open.

d. Reopen the Basketball-P.accdb database to test the password. Close the Basketball-P.accdb database.

e. Reopen the Basketball-P.accdb database in Exclusive mode. Type **b*i*g*1*2** as the password.

f. Unset the database password.

g. Close the frmGameInfo form.

4. Analyze database performance.

a. On the Database Tools tab, click the Analyze Performance button.

b. On the All Object Types tab, select all objects, then click OK.

c. Read each of the ideas and descriptions, then close the Performance Analyzer.

5. Analyze table performance.

a. On the Database Tools tab, click the Analyze Table button.

b. Step through the wizard, choosing the tblPlayers table to analyze. Choose the No, I want to decide option button when prompted.

c. Drag the Position field from Table1 to a blank spot in the Table Analyzer Wizard dialog box to create a new lookup table named **tblPositions**.

d. Rename Table1 to **tblPlayers2** so that the Table Analyzer Wizard dialog box looks like Figure P-16.

FIGURE P-16

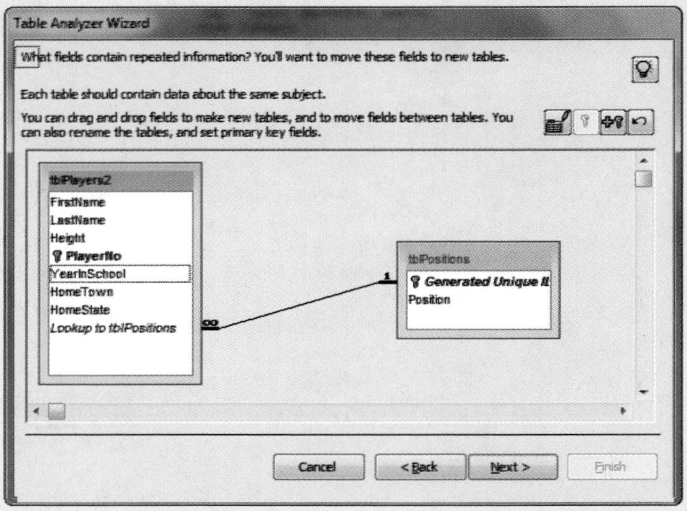

Skills Review (continued)

    e. Move through the rest of the Table Analyzer Wizard, do not make any corrections, do not create a query, click Finish, then click OK if prompted at the end.

    f. Close the tblPositions and tblPlayers2 tables.

    g. Delete the tblPlayers table, then rename tblPlayers2 to **tblPlayers**.

    h. Open the Relationships window, click the All Relationships button, then connect the tblPlayers table to the tblStats table using the common PlayerNo field. Be sure to enforce referential integrity.

    i. Save and close the Relationships window.

6. Back up a database.

    a. Click the File tab, click Save Database As, click Yes to have Access close all open objects if prompted, then save the database backup with the name **Basketball-P-Backup.accdb** in the drive and folder where you store your Data Files.

    b. Close the Basketball-P-Backup.accdb database.

7. Convert a database.

    a. Start Access, open the Basketball-P.accdb database from the drive and folder where you store your Data Files, and enable content if prompted.

    b. Close frmGameInfo.

    c. Click the File tab, click Save & Publish, and save the database backup as an Access 2000 database with the name **Basketball-P-2000.mdb** in the drive and folder where you store your Data Files.

    d. Close the Basketball-P-2000.mdb database and exit Access 2010.

8. Split a database.

    a. Start Access, open the Basketball-P.accdb database from the drive and folder where you store your Data Files, and enable content if prompted.

    b. Close frmGameInfo.

    c. On the Database Tools tab, click the Access Database button and split the database.

    d. Name the backend database **Basketball-P_be.accdb**, and save it in the drive and folder where you store your Data Files.

    e. Close the Basketball-P.accdb database and exit Access.

Independent Challenge 1

As the manager of a doctor's clinic, you have created an Access database called Patients-P.accdb to track insurance claims. You want to set a database password and encrypt the database, as well as set options to automatically compact the database when it is closed.

    a. Start Access. Open Patients-P.accdb in Exclusive mode from the drive and folder where you store your Data Files. Enable content if prompted.

    b. Encrypt the database with a password.

    c. Enter **4-your-health** in the Password text box and the Verify text box, then click OK.

    d. Close the Patients-P.accdb database, but leave Access running.

    e. Reopen the Patients-P.accdb database, enter **4-your-health** as the password, then click OK.

    f. In the Access Options dialog box, check the Compact on Close option.

    g. Close the database and Access.

Independent Challenge 2

As the manager of a doctor's clinic, you have created an Access database called Patients-P.accdb to track insurance claims. You want to analyze database performance.

a. Open the Patients-P.accdb database from the drive and folder where you store your Data Files, and enable content if prompted.
b. Enter **4-your-health** as the password if prompted.
c. Use the Performance Analyzer tool on the Database Tools tab to analyze all objects.
d. Click each item in the Performance Analyzer results window, and record the idea on another sheet of paper.

Advanced Challenge Exercise

ACE

- Implement each of the ideas in the Performance Analyzer results window. Apply each suggestion to the database.
- Note that the data type of the Diag1 field in the tblClaimLineItems table will be changed to Number with a Double Field Size property.
- Eventually you end up with only one suggestion: to save the application as an MDE file. To implement this suggestion, use the Make ACCDE button after you click Save & Publish on the File tab.

e. Close the Patients-P.accde database, then close Access.

Independent Challenge 3

As the manager of a community service club, you have created an Access database called Membership-P.accdb to track community service hours. You want to convert the database to an Access 2007 database and analyze table performance.

a. Start Access, then open the database Membership-P.accdb from the drive and folder where you store your Data Files.
b. Analyze table performance for the Members table. Let the wizard decide how to split the tables.
c. Rename Table1 as **Members2**, and rename Table2 as **ZipCodes**.
d. Click Next when prompted about the bold fields, do not make any corrections, and do not create a query. Click Finish, then click OK if prompted.
e. Close the Members2 and ZipCodes tables.
f. Delete the Members table, and rename the Members2 table to **Members**.
g. In the Relationships window, click the All Relationships button.
h. Link the Status and Members tables using the common StatusNo field. Enforce referential integrity on the relationship. The Relationships window should look like Figure P-17.
i. Save and close the Relationships window.
j. Close the Membership-P.accdb database, then exit Access.

FIGURE P-17

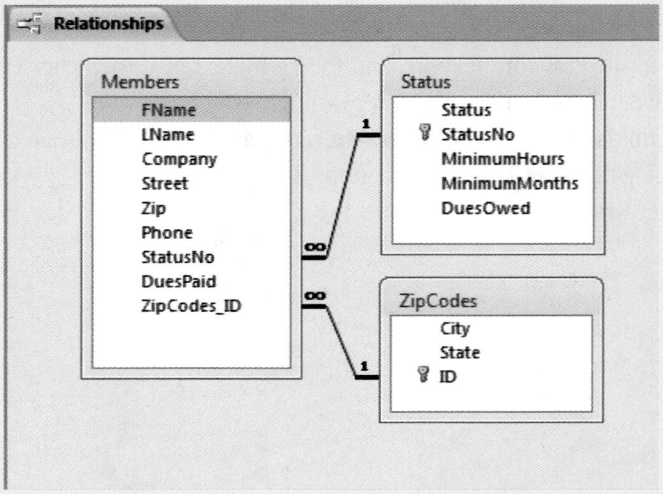

Relationships
Members
FName
LName
Company
Street
Zip
Phone
StatusNo
DuesPaid
ZipCodes_ID
Status
Status
StatusNo
MinimumHours
MinimumMonths
DuesOwed
ZipCodes
City
State
ID
1
∞
∞
1

Real Life Independent Challenge

Microsoft provides extra information, templates, files, and ideas at a Web site called Tools on the Web. You have been given an opportunity to intern with an Access consultant and are considering this type of work for your career. As such, you know that you need to be familiar with all of the resources on the Web that Microsoft provides to help you work with Access. In this exercise, you'll explore the Tools on the Web services.

a. Start Access, but do not open any databases.

b. Click the Microsoft Access Help button.

c. Click the Videos link to open a page similar to the one shown in Figure P-18.

d. Choose three of the videos to watch.

e. In a Word document, write one paragraph for each of the videos summarizing the topic and new concepts and techniques that you learned.

f. Close Access and any open Access Help windows.

FIGURE P-18

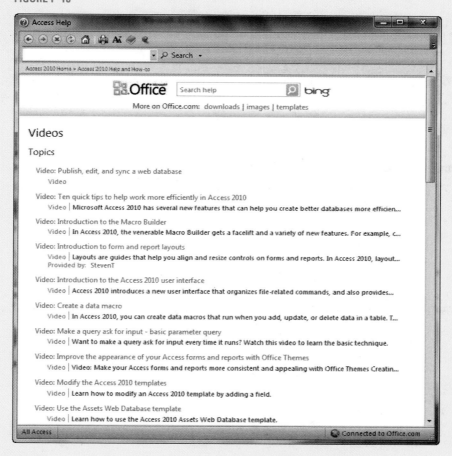

Visual Workshop

As the manager of a music store, you have created an Access database called MusicStore-P.accdb that tracks musical instrument rentals to schoolchildren. Use the Performance Analyzer to generate the results shown in Figure P-19 by analyzing all object types. Save the database as an MDE file, but do not implement the other ideas. In a Word document, explain why implementing the last three ideas might not be appropriate.

FIGURE P-19

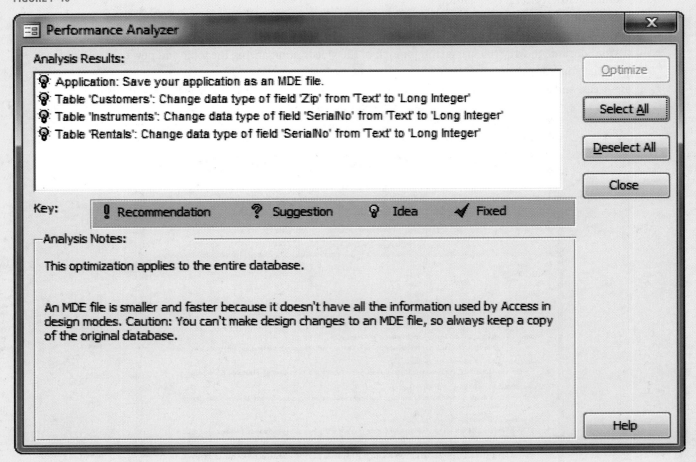

Working with Windows Live and Office Web Apps

If the computer you are using has an active Internet connection, you can go to the Microsoft Windows Live Web site and access a wide variety of services and Web applications. For example, you can check your e-mail through Windows Live, network with your friends and coworkers, and use SkyDrive to store and share files. From SkyDrive, you can also use Office Web Apps to create and edit Word, PowerPoint, Excel, and OneNote files, even when you are using a computer that does not have Office 2010 installed. ▓▓▓ You work in the Vancouver branch of Quest Specialty Travel. Your supervisor, Mary Lou Jacobs, asks you to explore Windows Live and learn how she can use SkyDrive and Office Web Apps to work with her files online.

(*Note*: SkyDrive and Office Web Apps are dynamic Web pages, and might change over time, including the way they are organized and how commands are performed. The steps and figures in this appendix were accurate at the time this book was published.)

OBJECTIVES

Explore how to work online from Windows Live
Obtain a Windows Live ID and sign in to Windows Live
Upload files to Windows Live
Work with the PowerPoint Web App
Create folders and organize files on SkyDrive
Add people to your network and share files
Work with the Excel Web App

Exploring How to Work Online from Windows Live

You can use your Web browser to upload your files to Windows Live from any computer connected to the Internet. You can work on the files right in your Web browser using Office Web Apps and share your files with people in your Windows Live network.  You review the concepts and services related to working online from Windows Live.

DETAILS

- **What is Windows Live?**

  Windows Live is a collection of services and Web applications that you can use to help you be more productive both personally and professionally. For example, you can use Windows Live to send and receive e-mail, to chat with friends via instant messaging, to share photos, to create a blog, and to store and edit files using SkyDrive. Table WEB-1 describes the services available on Windows Live. Windows Live is a free service that you sign up for. When you sign up, you receive a Windows Live ID, which you use to sign in to Windows Live. When you work with files on Windows Live, you are cloud computing.

- **What is Cloud Computing?**

  The term **cloud computing** refers to the process of working with files online in a Web browser. When you save files to SkyDrive on Windows Live, you are saving your files to an online location. SkyDrive is like having a personal hard drive in the cloud.

- **What is SkyDrive?**

  SkyDrive is an online storage and file sharing service. With a Windows Live account, you receive access to your own SkyDrive, which is your personal storage area on the Internet. On your SkyDrive, you are given space to store up to 25 GB of data online. Each file can be a maximum size of 50 MB. You can also use SkyDrive to access Office Web Apps, which you use to create and edit files created in Word, OneNote, PowerPoint, and Excel online in your Web browser.

- **Why use Windows Live and SkyDrive?**

  On Windows Live, you use SkyDrive to access additional storage for your files. You don't have to worry about backing up your files to a memory stick or other storage device that could be lost or damaged. Another advantage of storing your files on SkyDrive is that you can access your files from any computer that has an active Internet connection. Figure WEB-1 shows the SkyDrive Web page that appears when accessed from a Windows Live account. From SkyDrive, you can also access Office Web Apps.

- **What are Office Web Apps?**

  Office Web Apps are versions of Microsoft Word, Excel, PowerPoint, and OneNote that you can access online from your SkyDrive. An Office Web App does not include all of the features and functions included with the full Office version of its associated application. However, you can use the Office Web App from any computer that is connected to the Internet, even if Microsoft Office 2010 is not installed on that computer.

- **How do SkyDrive and Office Web Apps work together?**

  You can create a file in Office 2010 using Word, Excel, PowerPoint, or OneNote and then upload the file to your SkyDrive. You can then open the Office file saved to SkyDrive and edit it using your Web browser and the corresponding Office Web App. Figure WEB-2 shows a PowerPoint presentation open in the PowerPoint Web App. You can also use an Office Web App to create a new file, which is saved automatically to SkyDrive while you work. In addition, you can download a file created with an Office Web App and continue to work with the file in the full version of the corresponding Office application: Word, Excel, PowerPoint, or OneNote. Finally, you can create a SkyDrive network that consists of the people you want to be able to view your folders and files on your SkyDrive. You can give people permission to view and edit your files using any computer with an active Internet connection and a Web browser.

FIGURE WEB-1: SkyDrive on Windows Live

Browser window

SkyDrive - Windows Live tab

By default, one folder is available on SkyDrive; you can create additional folders

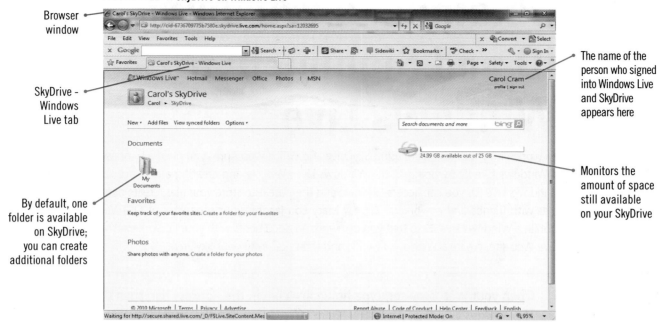

The name of the person who signed into Windows Live and SkyDrive appears here

Monitors the amount of space still available on your SkyDrive

FIGURE WEB-2: PowerPoint presentation open in the PowerPoint Web App

Browser window

Ribbon available in PowerPoint Web App

The presentation in PowerPoint Web App maintains the same look and feel as the same presentation in the desktop version of PowerPoint

Name of PowerPoint presentation open in PowerPoint Web App

TABLE WEB-1: Services available via Windows Live

service	description
E-mail	Send and receive e-mail using a Hotmail account
Instant Messaging	Use Messenger to chat with friends, share photos, and play games
SkyDrive	Store files, work on files using Office Web Apps, and share files with people in your network
Photos	Upload and share photos with friends
People	Develop a network of friends and coworkers, then use the network to distribute information and stay in touch
Downloads	Access a variety of free programs available for download to a PC
Mobile Device	Access applications for a mobile device: text messaging, using Hotmail, networking, and sharing photos

Obtaining a Windows Live ID and Signing In to Windows Live

To work with your files online using SkyDrive and Office Web Apps, you need a Windows Live ID. You obtain a Windows Live ID by going to the Windows Live Web site and creating a new account. Once you have a Windows Live ID, you can access SkyDrive and then use it to store your files, create new files, and share your files with friends and coworkers. ▓▓▓▓ Mary Lou Jacobs, your supervisor at QST Vancouver, asks you to obtain a Windows Live ID so that you can work on documents with your coworkers. You go to the Windows Live Web site, create a Windows Live ID, and then sign in to your SkyDrive.

STEPS

QUICK TIP

If you already have a Windows Live ID, go to the next lesson and sign in as directed using your account.

1. **Open your Web browser, type home.live.com in the Address bar, then press [Enter]**

   The Windows Live home page opens. From this page, you can create a Windows Live account and receive your Windows Live ID.

2. **Click the Sign up button** *(Note: You may see a Sign up link instead of a button)*

   The Create your Windows Live ID page opens.

3. **Click the Or use your own e-mail address link under the Check availability button or if you are already using Hotmail, Messenger, or Xbox LIVE, click the Sign in now link in the Information statement near the top of the page**

4. **Enter the information required, as shown in Figure WEB-3**

   If you wish, you can sign up for a Windows Live e-mail address such as yourname@live.com so that you can also access the Windows Live e-mail services.

TROUBLE

The code can be difficult to read. If you receive an error message, enter the new code that appears.

5. **Enter the code shown at the bottom of your screen, then click the I accept button**

   The Windows Live home page opens. The name you entered when you signed up for your Windows Live ID appears in the top right corner of the window to indicate that you are signed in to Windows Live. From the Windows Live home page, you can access all the services and applications offered by Windows Live. See the Verifying your Windows Live ID box for information on finalizing your account set up.

6. **Point to Windows Live, as shown in Figure WEB-4**

   A list of options appears. SkyDrive is one of the options you can access directly from Windows Live.

TROUBLE

Click I accept if you are asked to review and accept the Windows Live Service Agreement and Privacy Statement.

7. **Click SkyDrive**

   The SkyDrive page opens. Your name appears in the top right corner, and the amount of space available is shown on the right side of the SkyDrive page. The amount of space available is monitored, as indicated by the gauge that fills with color as space is used. Using SkyDrive, you can add files to the existing folder and you can create new folders.

8. **Click sign out in the top right corner under your name, then exit the Web browser**

   You are signed out of your Windows Live account. You can sign in again directly from the Windows Live page in your browser or from within a file created with PowerPoint, Excel, Word, or OneNote.

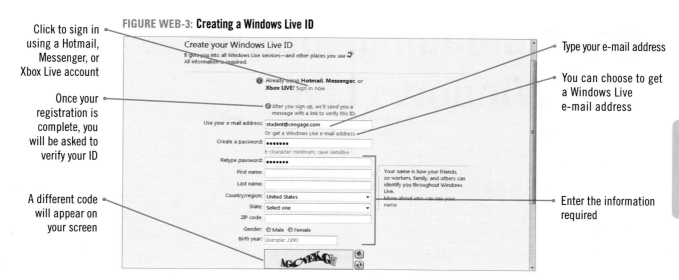

Click to sign in using a Hotmail, Messenger, or Xbox Live account

Once your registration is complete, you will be asked to verify your ID

A different code will appear on your screen

Type your e-mail address

You can choose to get a Windows Live e-mail address

Enter the information required

Web Apps

FIGURE WEB-4: **Selecting SkyDrive**

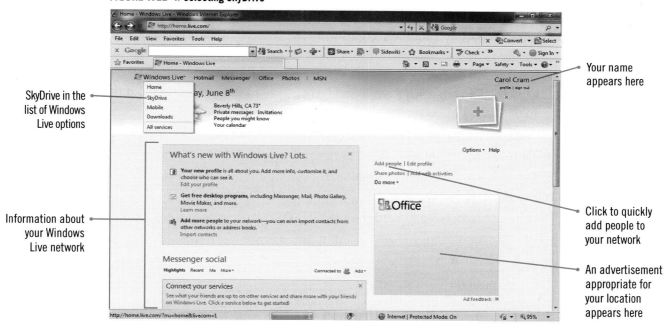

SkyDrive in the list of Windows Live options

Information about your Windows Live network

Your name appears here

Click to quickly add people to your network

An advertisement appropriate for your location appears here

Verifying your Windows Live ID

As soon as you accept the Windows Live terms, an e-mail is sent to the e-mail address you supplied when you created your Windows Live ID. Open your e-mail program, and then open the e-mail from Microsoft with the Subject line: Confirm your e-mail address for Windows Live. Follow the simple, step-by-step instructions in the e-mail to confirm your Windows Live ID. When the confirmation is complete, you will be asked to sign in to Windows Live, using your e-mail address and password. Once signed in, you will see your Windows Live Account page.

Uploading Files to Windows Live

Once you have created your Windows Live ID, you can sign in to Windows Live directly from Word, PowerPoint, Excel, or OneNote and start saving and uploading files. You upload files to your SkyDrive so you can share the files with other people, access the files from another computer, or use SkyDrive's additional storage. ▨▨▨▨ You open a PowerPoint presentation, access your Windows Live account from Backstage view, and save a file to SkyDrive on Windows Live. You also create a new folder called Cengage directly from Backstage view and add a file to it.

STEPS

1. **Start PowerPoint, open the file WEB-1.pptx from the drive and folder where you store your Data Files, then save the file as WEB-QST Vancouver Presentation**

2. **Click the File tab, then click Save & Send**
   The Save & Send options available in PowerPoint are listed in Backstage view, as shown in Figure WEB-5.

3. **Click Save to Web**

QUICK TIP
Skip this step if the computer you are using signs you in automatically.

4. **Click Sign In, type your e-mail address, press [Tab], type your password, then click OK**
   The My Documents folder on your SkyDrive appears in the Save to Windows Live SkyDrive information area.

5. **Click Save As, wait a few seconds for the Save As dialog box to appear, then click Save**
   The file is saved to the My Documents folder on the SkyDrive that is associated with your Windows Live account. You can also create a new folder and upload files directly to SkyDrive from your hard drive.

6. **Click the File tab, click Save & Send, click Save to Web, then sign in if the My Documents folder does not automatically appear in Backstage view**

7. **Click the New Folder button in the Save to Windows Live SkyDrive pane, then sign in to Windows Live if directed**

8. **Type Cengage as the folder name, click Next, then click Add files**

9. **Click select documents from your computer, then navigate to the location on your computer where you saved the file WEB-QST Vancouver Presentation in Step 1**

10. **Click WEB-QST Vancouver Presentation.pptx to select it, then click Open**
    You can continue to add more files; however, you have no more files to upload at this time.

11. **Click Continue**
    In a few moments, the PowerPoint presentation is uploaded to your SkyDrive, as shown in Figure WEB-6. You can simply store the file on SkyDrive or you can choose to work on the presentation using the PowerPoint Web App.

12. **Click the PowerPoint icon 🄿 on your taskbar to return to PowerPoint, then close the presentation and exit PowerPoint**

FIGURE WEB-5: Save & Send options in Backstage view

PowerPoint file

Save & Send area
in Backstage view

Save to Web
option

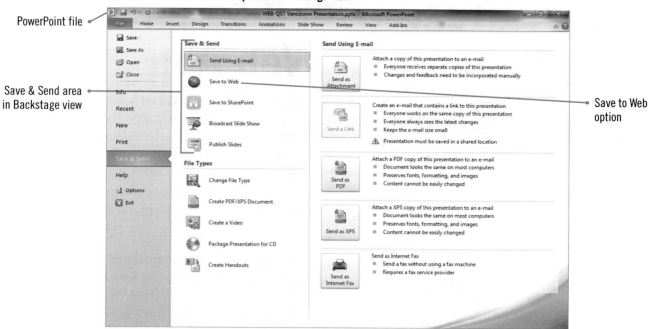

FIGURE WEB-6: File uploaded to the Cengage folder on Windows Live

Browser
window

Path to file

Current folder
menu bar

Uploaded file

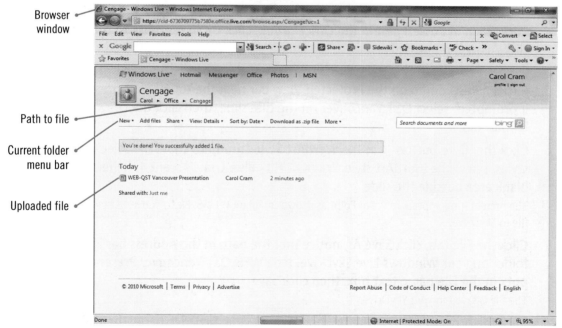

Working with the PowerPoint Web App

Once you have uploaded a file to SkyDrive on Windows Live, you can work on it using its corresponding Office Web App. **Office Web Apps** provide you with the tools you need to view documents online and to edit them right in your browser. You do not need to have Office programs installed on the computer you use to access SkyDrive and Office Web Apps. From SkyDrive, you can also open the document directly in the full Office application (for example, PowerPoint) if the application is installed on the computer you are using. ▓▓▓▓ You use the PowerPoint Web App to make some edits to the PowerPoint presentation. You then open the presentation in PowerPoint and use the full version to make additional edits.

STEPS

1. **Click the WEB-QST Vancouver Presentation file in the Cengage folder on SkyDrive**

   The presentation opens in your browser window. A menu is available, which includes the options you have for working with the file.

2. **Click Edit in Browser, then if a message appears related to installing the Sign-in Assistant, click the Close button ✖ to the far right of the message**

   In a few moments, the PowerPoint presentation opens in the PowerPoint Web App, as shown in Figure WEB-7. Table WEB-2 lists the commands you can perform using the PowerPoint Web App.

3. **Enter your name where indicated on Slide 1, click Slide 3 (New Tours) in the Slides pane, then click Delete Slide in the Slides group**

   The slide is removed from the presentation. You decide to open the file in the full version of PowerPoint on your computer so you can apply WordArt to the slide title. You work with the file in the full version of PowerPoint when you want to use functions, such as WordArt, that are not available on the PowerPoint Web App.

4. **Click Open in PowerPoint in the Office group, click OK in response to the message, then click Allow if requested**

   In a few moments, the revised version of the PowerPoint slide opens in PowerPoint on your computer.

5. **Click Enable Editing on the Protected View bar near the top of your presentation window if prompted, select QST Vancouver on the title slide, then click the Drawing Tools Format tab**

6. **Click the More button ▾ in the WordArt Styles group to show the selection of WordArt styles, select the WordArt style Gradient Fill - Blue-Gray, Accent 4, Reflection, then click a blank area outside the slide**

   The presentation appears in PowerPoint as shown in Figure WEB-8. Next, you save the revised version of the file to SkyDrive.

7. **Click the File tab, click Save As, notice that the path in the Address bar is to the Cengage folder on your Windows Live SkyDrive, type WEB-QST Vancouver Presentation_Revised. pptx in the File name text box, then click Save**

   The file is saved to your SkyDrive.

8. **Click the browser icon on the taskbar to open your SkyDrive page, then click Office next to your name in the SkyDrive path, view a list of recent documents, then click Cengage in the list to the left of the recent documents list to open the Cengage folder**

   Two PowerPoint files now appear in the Cengage folder.

9. **Exit the Web browser and close all tabs if prompted, then exit PowerPoint**

FIGURE WEB-7: Presentation opened in the PowerPoint Web App from Windows Live

Browser window

Name of Web App

PowerPoint Web App Ribbon

URL is the file location

FIGURE WEB-8: Revised PowerPoint presentation

PowerPoint title bar

PowerPoint Ribbon

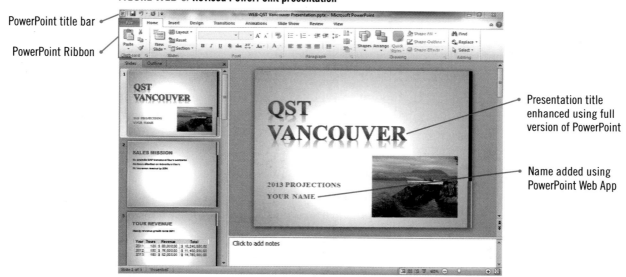

Presentation title enhanced using full version of PowerPoint

Name added using PowerPoint Web App

TABLE WEB-2: Commands on the PowerPoint Web App

tab	commands available
File	• Open in PowerPoint: select to open the file in PowerPoint on your computer • Where's the Save Button?: when you click this option, a message appears telling you that you do not need to save your presentation when you are working on it with PowerPoint Web App. The presentation is saved automatically as you work. • Print • Share • Properties • Give Feedback • Privacy • Terms of Use • Close
Home	• Clipboard group: Cut, Copy, Paste • Slides group: Add a New Slide, Delete a Slide, Duplicate a Slide, and Hide a Slide • Font group: Work with text: change the font, style, color, and size of selected text • Paragraph group: Work with paragraphs: add bullets and numbers, indent text, align text • Office group: Open the file in PowerPoint on your computer
Insert	• Insert a Picture • Insert a SmartArt diagram • Insert a link such as a link to another file on SkyDrive or to a Web page
View	• Editing view (the default) • Reading view • Slide Show view • Notes view

Creating Folders and Organizing Files on SkyDrive

As you have learned, you can sign in to SkyDrive directly from the Office applications PowerPoint, Excel, Word, and OneNote, or you can access SkyDrive directly through your Web browser. This option is useful when you are away from the computer on which you normally work or when you are using a computer that does not have Office applications installed. You can go to SkyDrive, create and organize folders, and then create or open files to work on with Office Web Apps. ▰▰▰ You access SkyDrive from your Web browser, create a new folder called Illustrated, and delete one of the PowerPoint files from the My Documents folder.

STEPS

TROUBLE
Go to Step 3 if you are already signed in.

TROUBLE
Type your Windows Live ID (your e-mail) and password, then click Sign in if prompted to do so.

1. **Open your Web browser, type home.live.com in the Address bar, then press [Enter]**
   The Windows Live home page opens. From here, you can sign in to your Windows Live account and then access SkyDrive.

2. **Sign into Windows Live as directed**
   You are signed in to your Windows Live page. From this page, you can take advantage of the many applications available on Windows Live, including SkyDrive.

3. **Point to Windows Live, then click SkyDrive**
   SkyDrive opens.

4. **Click Cengage, then point to WEB-QST Vancouver Presentation.pptx**
   A menu of options for working with the file, including a Delete button to the far right, appears to the right of the filename.

5. **Click the Delete button ☒, then click OK**
   The file is removed from the Cengage folder on your SkyDrive. You still have a copy of the file on your computer.

6. **Point to Windows Live, then click SkyDrive**
   Your SkyDrive screen with the current selection of folders available on your SkyDrive opens, as shown in Figure WEB-9.

7. **Click New, click Folder, type Illustrated, click Next, click Office in the path under Add documents to Illustrated at the top of the window, then click View all in the list under Personal**
   You are returned to your list of folders, where you see the new Illustrated folder.

8. **Click Cengage, point to WEB-QST Vancouver Presentation_Revised.pptx, click More, click Move, then click the Illustrated folder**

9. **Click Move this file into Illustrated, as shown in Figure WEB-10**
   The file is moved to the Illustrated folder.

FIGURE WEB-9: Folders on your SkyDrive

Current location

Folders currently available

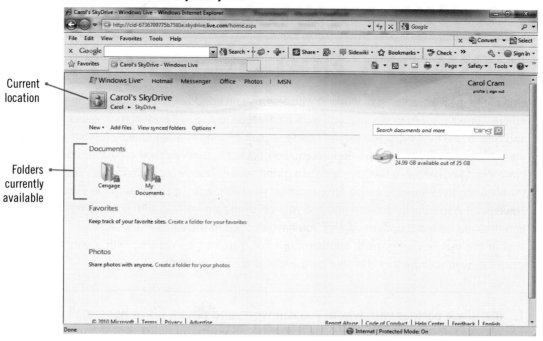

FIGURE WEB-10: Moving a file to the Illustrated folder

Click to move file to this location

Be sure to rename a file before moving it if you are moving it to a location where another copy of the same file exists

Name of file to be moved

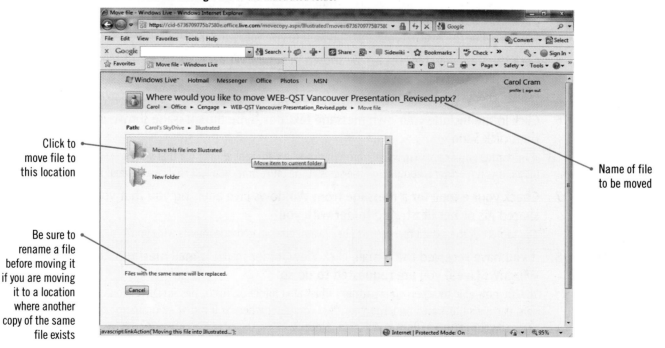

Adding People to Your Network and Sharing Files

One of the great advantages of working with SkyDrive on Windows Live is that you can share your files with others. Suppose, for example, that you want a colleague to review a presentation you created in PowerPoint and then add a new slide. You can, of course, e-mail the presentation directly to your colleague, who can then make changes and e-mail the presentation back. Alternatively, you can save time by uploading the PowerPoint file directly to SkyDrive and then giving your colleague access to the file. Your colleague can edit the file using the PowerPoint Web App, and then you can check the updated file on SkyDrive, also using the PowerPoint Web App. In this way, you and your colleague are working with just one version of the presentation that you both can update. ▓▓▓ You have decided to share files in the Illustrated folder that you created in the previous lesson with another individual. You start by working with a partner so that you can share files with your partner and your partner can share files with you.

STEPS

TROUBLE
If you cannot find a partner, read the steps so you understand how the process works.

1. **Identify a partner with whom you can work, and obtain his or her e-mail address; you can choose someone in your class or someone on your e-mail list, but it should be someone who will be completing these steps when you are**

2. **From the Illustrated folder, click Share**

3. **Click Edit permissions**

   The Edit permissions page opens. On this page, you can select the individual with whom you would like to share the contents of the Illustrated folder.

4. **Click in the Enter a name or an e-mail address text box, type the e-mail address of your partner, then press [Tab]**

   You can define the level of access that you want to give your partner.

5. **Click the Can view files list arrow shown in Figure WEB-11, click Can add, edit details, and delete files, then click Save**

   You can choose to send a notification to each individual when you grant permission to access your files.

TROUBLE
If you do not receive a message from Windows Live, your partner has not yet completed the steps to share the Illustrated folder.

6. **Click in the Include your own message text box, type the message shown in Figure WEB-12, then click Send**

   Your partner will receive a message from Windows Live advising him or her that you have shared your Illustrated folder. If your partner is completing the steps at the same time, you will receive an e-mail from your partner.

7. **Check your e-mail for a message from Windows Live advising you that your partner has shared his or her Illustrated folder with you**

   The subject of the e-mail message will be "[Name] has shared documents with you."

QUICK TIP
You will know you are on your partner's SkyDrive because you will see your partner's first name at the beginning of the SkyDrive path.

8. **If you have received the e-mail, click View folder in the e-mail message, then sign in to Windows Live if you are requested to do so**

   You are now able to access your partner's Illustrated folder on his or her SkyDrive. You can download files in your partner's Illustrated folder to your own computer where you can work on them and then upload them again to your partner's Illustrated shared folder.

9. **Exit the browser**

FIGURE WEB-11: Editing folder permissions

Folder permissions will be changed for the Illustrated folder

Click to select network permission options

Type email address to continue to add people

Person whose permission status will change

Click to select person from list of contacts

Click to select permission option

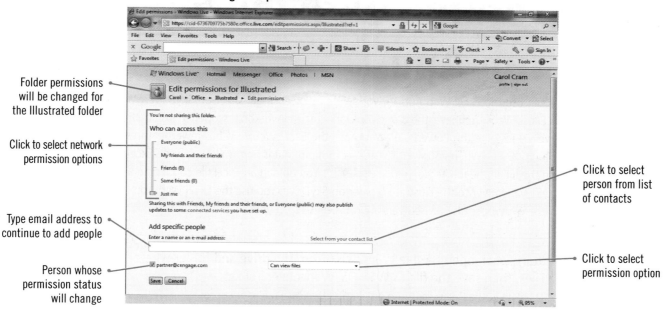

FIGURE WEB-12: Entering a message to notify a person that file sharing permission has been granted

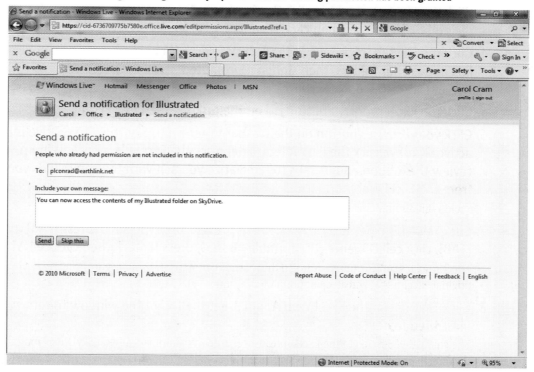

Sharing files on SkyDrive

When you share a folder with other people, the people with whom you share a folder can download the file to their computers and then make changes using the full version of the corresponding Office application.

Once these changes are made, each individual can then upload the file to SkyDrive and into a folder shared with you and others. In this way, you can create a network of people with whom you share your files.

Working with the Excel Web App

You can use the Excel Web App to work with an Excel spreadsheet on SkyDrive. Workbooks opened using the Excel Web App have the same look and feel as workbooks opened using the full version of Excel. However, just like the PowerPoint Web App, the Excel Web App has fewer features available than the full version of Excel. When you want to use a command that is not available on the Excel Web App, you need to open the file in the full version of Excel. ⬛⬛⬛⬛ You upload an Excel file containing a list of the tours offered by QST Vancouver to the Illustrated folder on SkyDrive. You use the Excel Web App to make some changes, and then you open the revised version in Excel 2010 on your computer.

1. **Start Excel, open the file WEB-2.xlsx from the drive and folder where you store your Data Files, then save the file as WEB-QST Vancouver Tours**

   The data in the Excel file is formatted using the Excel table function.

If prompted, sign in to your Windows Live account as directed.

2. **Click the File tab, click Save & Send, then click Save to Web**

   In a few moments, you should see three folders to which you can save spreadsheets. My Documents and Cengage are personal folder that contains files that only you can access. Illustrated is a shared folder that contains files you can share with others in your network. The Illustrated folder is shared with your partner.

3. **Click the Illustrated folder, click the Save As button, wait a few seconds for the Save As dialog box to appear, then click Save**

Alternately, you can open your Web browser and go to Windows Live to sign in to SkyDrive.

4. **Click the File tab, click Save & Send, click Save to Web, click the Windows Live SkyDrive link above your folders, then sign in if prompted**

   Windows Live opens to your SkyDrive.

5. **Click the Excel program button 🖼 on the taskbar, then exit Excel**

6. **Click your browser button on the taskbar to return to SkyDrive if SkyDrive is not the active window, click the Illustrated folder, click the Excel file, click Edit in Browser, then review the Ribbon and its tabs to familiarize yourself with the commands you can access from the Excel Web App**

   Table WEB-3 summarizes the commands that are available.

7. **Click cell A12, type Gulf Islands Sailing, press [TAB], type 3000, press [TAB], type 10, press [TAB], click cell D3, enter the formula =B3*C3, press [Enter], then click cell A1**

   The formula is copied automatically to the remaining rows as shown in Figure WEB-13 because the data in the original Excel file was created and formatted as an Excel table.

8. **Click SkyDrive in the Excel Web App path at the top of the window to return to the Illustrated folder**

   The changes you made to the Excel spreadsheet are saved automatically on SkyDrive. You can download the file directly to your computer from SkyDrive.

9. **Point to the Excel file, click More, click Download, click Save, navigate to the location where you save the files for this book, name the file WEB-QST Vancouver Tours_Updated, click Save, then click Close in the Download complete dialog box**

   The updated version of the spreadsheet is saved on your computer and on SkyDrive.

10. **Exit the Web browser**

FIGURE WEB-13: Updated table in the Excel Web App

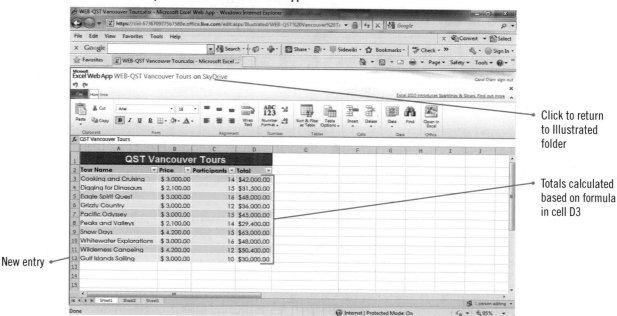

Click to return to Illustrated folder

Totals calculated based on formula in cell D3

New entry

TABLE WEB-3: Commands on the Excel Web App

tab	commands available
File	• Open in Excel: select to open the file in Excel on your computer • Where's the Save Button?: when you click this option, a message appears telling you that you do not need to save your spreadsheet when you are working in it with Excel Web App; the spreadsheet is saved automatically as you work • Save As • Share • Download a Snapshot: a snapshot contains only the values and the formatting; you cannot modify a snapshot • Download a Copy: the file can be opened and edited in the full version of Excel • Give Feedback • Privacy Statement • Terms of Use • Close
Home	• Clipboard group: Cut, Copy, Paste • Font group: change the font, style, color, and size of selected labels and values, as well as border styles and fill colors • Alignment group: change vertical and horizontal alignment and turn on the Wrap Text feature • Number group: change the number format and increase or decrease decimal places • Tables: sort and filter data in a table and modify Table Options • Cells: insert and delete cells • Data: refresh data and find labels or values • Office: open the file in Excel on your computer
Insert	• Insert a Table • Insert a Hyperlink to a Web page

Exploring other Office Web Apps

Two other Office Web Apps are Word and OneNote. You can share files on SkyDrive directly from Word or from OneNote using the same method you used to share files from PowerPoint and Excel. After you upload a Word or OneNote file to SkyDrive, you can work with it in its corresponding Office Web App. To familiarize yourself with the commands available in an Office Web App, open the file and then review the commands on each tab on the Ribbon. If you want to perform a task that is not available in the Office Web App, open the file in the full version of the application.

In addition to working with uploaded files, you can create files from new on SkyDrive. Simply sign in to SkyDrive and open a folder. With a folder open, click New and then select the Web App you want to use to create the new file.

Windows Live and Microsoft Office Web Apps Quick Reference

To Do This	Go Here
Access Windows Live	From the Web browser, type **home.live.com**, then click Sign In
Access SkyDrive on Windows Live	From the Windows Live home page, point to Windows Live, then click SkyDrive
Save to Windows Live from Word, PowerPoint, or Excel	File tab | Save & Send | Save to Web | Select a folder | Save As
Create a New Folder from Backstage view	File tab | Save & Send | Save to Web | New Folder button
Edit a File with a Web App	From SkyDrive, click the file, then click Edit in Browser
Open a File in a desktop version of the application from a Web App: Word, Excel, PowerPoint	Click Open in [Application] in the Office group in each Office Web App
Share files on Windows Live	From SkyDrive, click the folder containing the files to share, click Share on the menu bar, click Edit permissions, enter the e-mail address of the person to share files with, click the Can view files list arrow, click Can add, edit details, and delete files, then click Save

Glossary

Access Data Collection Replies A folder that collects and helps you manage the e-mails initiated by Access and responses to them.

Action Each task that you want a macro to perform.

Action block In Macro Design View, the area of the window that organizes all of the arguments for a current action.

Action query A query that changes all of the selected records when it is run. Access provides four types of action queries: delete, update, append, and make table.

Add Mode When creating a switchboard, an option you can specify so that users can only add new records to an object, such as a form.

Add-in An extra program, such as Solver and the Analysis ToolPak, that provides optional features. To activate an add-in, click the File tab, click Options, click Add-Ins, then select or deselect add-ins from the list.

After Update A property that specifies an action to perform after an object is updated.

Allow Zero Length A field property that does not allow zero-length strings (""), which are intentional "nothing" entries, such as a blank Phone Number field for an employee who does not provide a home phone number.

Alternative text (Alt Text) A text description of a picture or any non-text object that is read by a screen reader for people who are visually impaired.

Append Only A field property available for Memo fields in Access 2007 databases. When enabled, the property allows users to add data to a Memo field, but not change or remove existing data.

Append query A query that adds selected records to an existing table, and works like an export feature because the records are copied from one location and a duplicate set is pasted within the target table.

Append To row When creating an Append query, a row that appears in the query design grid to show how the fields in the query match fields in the target table.

Application Part An object template that creates objects such as tables and forms.

Apply (a template) To open a document based on an Excel template.

Argument Information necessary for a formula or function to calculate an answer. Also part of a macro that provides additional information on how to carry out an action. In VBA, a constant, variable, or expression passed to a procedure that the procedure needs in order to execute. *See also* Main procedure.

ASCII file A text file that contains data but no formatting; instead of being divided into columns, ASCII file data are separated, or delimited, by tabs or commas.

Attributes Styling characteristics such as bold, italic, and underlining that you can apply to change the way text and numbers look in a worksheet or chart. In XML, the components that provide information about the document's elements.

Auditing An Excel feature that helps track errors and check worksheet logic.

AutoComplete In the Visual Basic for Applications (VBA) programming language, a list of words that appears as you enter code; helps you automatically enter elements with the correct syntax.

AutoExec A special macro name that automatically executes when a database opens.

AutoKeys A macro designed to be assigned a key combination (such as [Ctrl][L]).

Back up (verb) To create a duplicate copy of a database that is stored in a secure location.

Back-end database Part of a split database that contains the actual table objects and is stored on a file server.

Backsolving A problem-solving method in which you specify a solution and then find the input value that produces the answer you want; sometimes described as a what-if analysis in reverse. In Excel, the Goal Seek feature performs backsolving.

Bang notation A format that separates the object type from an object name and from a control name by using [square brackets] and exclamation points (!).

Between...and Criteria that selects all records between the two dates, including the two dates. Between...and criteria work the same way as the >= and <= operators.

Bibliography A list of sources that you consulted or cited while creating a document.

Bookmark Text that identifies a location, such as the beginning of a paragraph or a selection of text in a document.

Border Style A form property that determines the appearance of the outside border of the form.

Breakpoint A VBA debugging tool that works like a bookmark to suspend execution of the procedure at that statement so you can examine what is happening.

Brown-out A power problem caused by a dip in power, often making the lights dim.

Bug In programming, an error that causes a procedure to run incorrectly.

Building Block Gallery content control A reusable piece of formatted content or a document part that is stored in a gallery. The Building Block Gallery content control often contains text and objects, such as pictures and SmartArt graphics, into which users can enter content when completing a form.

Caption A field property that determines the default field name at the top of the field column in datasheets as well as in labels that describe fields on forms and reports.

Cascade Delete Related Records A relationship option that means that if a record in the "one" side of a one-to-many relationship is deleted, all related records in the "many" table are also deleted.

Cascade Update Related Fields A relationship option that means that if a value in the primary key field (the field on the "one" side of a one-to-many relationship) is modified, all values in the foreign key field (the field on the "many" side of a one-to-many relationship) are automatically updated as well.

Case In VBA, a programming structure that executes one of several groups of statements depending on the value of an expression.

Category axis Horizontal axis in a chart, usually containing the names of data categories; in a 2-dimensional chart, also known as the x-axis.

Cell comments Notes you've written about a workbook that appear when you place the pointer over a cell.

Change history A worksheet containing a list of changes made to a shared workbook.

Changing cells In what-if analysis, cells that contain the values that change in order to produce multiple sets of results.

Character style A named set of character format settings that can be applied to text to format it all at once; you use a character style to apply format settings only to select text within a paragraph.

Chart A visual representation of numeric data that helps users see comparisons, patterns, and trends in data. Also called a graph.

Chart type A category of chart layouts that determines the presentation of data on the chart such as column, pie, and line.

Chart Wizard A wizard that guides you through the steps of creating a chart in Access.

Check Box content control A content control that inserts a check box. You click a Check Box content control to insert a symbol, such as an "X" or a check mark.

Check Box form field control A legacy tool that inserts a check box, similar to a Check Box content control, but that is inserted using the Legacy Tools command in the Controls group on the Developer tab.

Child record A record contained in the "many" table in a one-to-many relationship.

Citation A parenthetical reference in the document text that gives credit to the source for a quotation or other information used in a document.

Class module An Access module that is contained and executed within specific forms and reports.

Client In client/server computing, the user's PC.

Client/server computing Two or more information systems cooperatively processing to solve a problem.

Cloud computing When data, applications, and resources are stored on servers accessed over the Internet or a company's internal network rather than on users' computers.

Code *See* Program code.

Code window In the Visual Basic Editor, the window that displays the procedures for the project selected in the Project Explorer window, written in the Visual Basic programming language.

Combo Box content control One of the two Drop-Down content controls. To use a Combo Box content control, you select an item from a list of choices or type in a new item.

Comma-separated values (CSV) A text file where fields are delimited, or separated, by commas.

Command Button Wizard A wizard that organizes over 30 of the most common command button actions within six categories.

Command-line option A special series of characters added to the end of the path to the file (for example, C:\My Documents\Quest. accdb /excl), and execute a special command when the file is opened.

Comment (Word) An embedded a note or annotation that an author or a reviewer adds to a document; appears in a comment balloon, usually to the right of the document text. (VBA) In a Visual Basic procedure, a note that explains the purpose of the macro or procedure; it is preceded by a single apostrophe and appears in green. *See also* Cell comments.

Comment line In VBA, a statement in the code that documents the code; it does not affect how the code runs.

Compact and repair To reorganize the pieces of the database to eliminate wasted space on the disk storage device, which also helps prevent data integrity problems.

Compact Flash (CF) card A card about the size of a matchbook that you can plug into your computer to store data.

Compatible The capability of different programs to work together and exchange data.

Compile time The period during which source code is translated to executable code.

Compile-time error In VBA, an error that occurs as a result of incorrectly constructed code and is detected as soon as you run your code or select the Compile option on the Debug menu.

Conditional expression An expression resulting in either a true or false answer that determines whether a macro action will execute.

Constant In VBA, an object that retains a constant value throughout the execution of the code.

Constraints Limitations or restrictions on input data in what-if analysis.

Control A placeholder that the form developer inserts in a form; it is used to contain the data associated with the label.

Control Box A form property that determines whether a control box (which provides access to menu commands that let you close or minimize a form, for example) are displayed in a form.

Control Name A property that specifies the name of a control on a form or report.

Convert To change the database file into one that can be opened in another version of Access.

Crop To trim away part of a graphic. The act of making a picture smaller by taking away parts of the top, bottom, and sides.

Cross-reference Text that electronically refers the reader to another part of the document; you click a cross-reference to move directly to a specific location in the document.

CSV *See* Comma-separated values.

Custom chart type A specially formatted Excel chart.

Cycle layout A SmartArt graphic used to represent a continuing sequence of stages, tasks, or events in a circular flow. Variations include Block Cycle, Segmented Cycle, and Gear.

Data area When creating a chart, the area in the Chart Wizard that determines what data the chart graphs.

Data label Descriptive text that appears above a data marker in a chart.

Data macro A type of macro that allows you to embed macro capabilities directly in a table to add, change, or delete data based on conditions you specify.

Data Picker content control A content control that provides you with a calendar you can use to select a specific date.

Data series A column or row in a datasheet. Also, the selected range in a worksheet that Excel converts into a chart.

Data source (Excel) Worksheet data used to create a chart or a PivotTable. (Word) In mail merge, the file with the unique data for individual people or items; the data merged with a main document to produce multiple versions.

Data table A range of cells that shows the resulting values when one or more input values are varied in a formula; when one input value is changed, the table is called a one-input data table, and when two input values are changed, it is called a two-input data table. In a chart, it is a grid containing the chart data.

Data validation A feature that allows you to specify what data is allowable (valid) for a range of cells.

Database An organized collection of related information. In Excel, a database is called a table.

Database administration The task of making a database faster, easier, more secure, and more reliable.

Database Documenter A feature on the Database Tools tab that helps you create reports containing information about the database.

Database program An application, such as Microsoft Access, that lets you manage large amounts of data organized in tables.

Database table A set of data organized using columns and rows that is created in a database program.

Database template A tool that can be used to quickly create a new database based on a particular subject such as assets, contacts, events, or projects.

Debug In programming, to find and correct a coding error that causes a macro or program to run incorrectly.

Declaration statement A type of VBA statement that precedes procedure statements and helps set rules for how the statements in the module are processed.

Declare In the Visual Basic programming language, to assign a type, such as numeric or text, to a variable.

Default In a program window or dialog box, a value that is already set by the program; you can change the default to any valid value.

Default switchboard The switchboard page designated as the one to contain links to additional switchboard pages.

Delete query A query that deletes a group of records from one or more tables.

Delete row When creating a Delete query, a row that appears in the query design grid to specify criteria for deleting records.

Delimited text file A text file that typically stores one record on each line, with the field values separated by a common character such as a comma, tab, or dash.

Delimiter A separator such as a tab, space, comma, or semicolon between elements in imported data.

Dependent cell A cell, usually containing a formula, whose value changes depending on the values in the input cells. For example, a payment formula or function that depends on an input cell containing changing interest rates is a dependent cell.

Description A query property that allows you to better document the purpose or author of a query.

Destination file The file to which data is copied.

Destination program In a data exchange, the program that will receive the data.

Dialog A Border Style option that indicates a form will have a thick border and cannot be maximized, minimized, or resized.

Dialog box In Access, a special form used to display information or prompt a user for a choice. In Windows, a type of window in which you specify how you want to complete an operation.

Digital signature An electronic stamp attached to a document to authenticate the document.

Dim A VBA keyword that declares a variable.

Display Form option An option in the Access Options dialog box where you can specify a form to display when a database opens.

DoCmd A VBA object that supports many methods to run common Access commands such as closing windows, opening forms, previewing reports, navigating records, and setting the value of controls.

Document To make notes about basic worksheet assumptions, complex formulas, or questionable data. In a macro, to insert comments that explain the Visual Basic code.

Documenter An Access analysis feature that creates reports on the properties and relationships among the objects in a database.

Domain The recordset (table or query) that contains the field used in a domain function calculation.

Domain function A function used to display a calculation on a form or report using a field that is not included in the Record Source property for the form or report. Also called domain aggregate function.

Drawing canvas An area upon which you can create or modify graphics, such as the shapes that make up a clip art picture.

Drop-Down Form Field content control A content control that provides users with a list of choices. Two drop-down content controls are available: the Drop-Down List content control and the Combo Box content control.

Drop-Down List content control One of the two Drop-Down content controls. To use a Drop-Down List content control, you select an item from a list of choices.

Dynaset A query property that allows updates to data in a recordset.

Edit mode When working with Access records, the mode in which Access assumes you are trying to edit a particular field, so keystrokes such as [Ctrl][End], [Ctrl][Home], [↑], and [↓] move the insertion point within the field. When working with charts, a mode that lets you select and modify individual chart elements such as the title, legend, bars, or axes. When creating a switchboard, an option you can specify so that users can open an object, such as a form, for editing records.

Element An XML component that defines the document content.

Else The part of an If statement that allows you to run a different set of actions if the conditional expression evaluates False.

ElseIf In VBA, a keyword that executes a statement depending on the value of an expression.

Embed To insert a copy of data into a destination document; you can double-click the embedded object to modify it using the tools of the source program.

Embedded chart A chart displayed as an object in a worksheet.

Embedded object An object contained in a source file and inserted into a destination file; an embedded object becomes part of the destination file and is no longer linked to the source file.

Encryption To make the data in the database unreadable by tools other than opening the Access database itself, which is protected by a password.

End Function In VBA, a required statement to mark the end of the code that defines the new function.

End If In VBA, a statement needed to mark the end of the If block of code.

End Select When defining a new Select Case group of VBA statements, the End Select statement is required as the last statement to mark the end of the VBA code.

End Sub When defining a new sub in VBA, the End Sub statement is required as the last statement to mark the end of the VBA code that defines the sub.

Endnote Text that provides additional information or acknowledges sources for text in a document and that appears at the end of a document.

Event A specific activity that happens in a database, such as the click of a command button or an entry in a field, that can be used to initiate the execution of a macro.

Event handler A procedure that is triggered by an event. Also called an event procedure.

Exclusive mode A mode indicating that you are the only person who has the database open, and others cannot open the file during this time.

Export To copy Access information to another database, spreadsheet, or file format.

Extensible Markup Language (XML) A programming language in which data can be placed in text files and structured so that most programs can read the data. *See also* XML.

External hard drive A device that plugs into a computer and stores more data than a typical USB drive, anywhere from 20 to 200 GB of information, and connects to a computer using either a USB or FireWire port.

Favorites A custom group for the Navigation Pane that is provided by default.

Field In a table (an Excel database or a PivotTable), a column that describes a characteristic about records, such as first name or city.

Figure Any object such as a chart, a picture, an equation, or an embedded object to which a caption can be added.

File server A centrally located computer from which every user can access the database by using the network.

Find unmatched query A type of query that finds records in one table that do not have matching records in a related table.

First normal form (1NF) The first degree of normalization, in which a table has rows and columns with no repeating groups.

Footnote Text that provides additional information or acknowledges sources for text in a document and that appears at the bottom of the page on which the note reference mark appears.

Form A structured document with spaces reserved for entering information.

Form template A file that contains the structure of a form. You create new forms from a form template. Changes made to new forms based on a form template, such as changing labels, do not affect the structure of the form template file.

Front-end database Part of a split database that contains the database objects other than tables (forms, reports, so forth), and links to the back-end database tables.

Function A special, predefined formula that provides a shortcut for a commonly used or complex calculation, such as SUM (for calculating a sum) or FV (for calculating the future value of an investment). In the Visual Basic for Applications (VBA) programming language, a predefined procedure that returns a value, such as the InputBox function that prompts the user to enter information.

Gigabyte (GB or G) One billion bytes (or one thousand megabytes).

Goal cell In backsolving, a cell containing a formula in which you can substitute values to find a specific value, or goal.

Goal Seek A problem-solving method in which you specify a solution and then find the input value that produces the answer you want; sometimes described as a what-if analysis in reverse; also called backsolving.

Group (noun) In the Navigation Pane, a custom category that organizes the objects that belong to that category. On the Ribbon, a set of related commands on a tab.

Hierarchy layout A SmartArt graphic used to show hierarchical information or reporting relationships within a company or organization. Variations include Organization Chart, Table Hierarchy, and Horizontal Hierarchy.

If statement A statement in a macro that allows you to run macro actions based on the result of a conditional expression.

If...Then In VBA, a logical structure that executes code (the code follows the Then statement) when the value of an expression is true (the expression follows the If statement).

If...Then...Else In VBA, a logical structure that allows you to test logical conditions and execute statements only if the conditions are true. If...Then...Else code can be composed of one or several statements, depending on how many conditions you want to test, how many possible answers you want to provide, and what you want the code to do based on the results of the tests.

If...Then...Else statement In the Visual Basic programming language, a conditional statement that directs Excel to perform specified actions under certain conditions; its syntax is "If *condition* Then *statements* Else [*elsestatements*]."

Immediate window In the Visual Basic Editor, a pane where you can determine the value of any argument at the breakpoint.

Import To quickly convert data from an external file into an Access database. You can import data from one Access database to another— or from many other data sources such as files created by Excel, SharePoint, Outlook, dBase, and Paradox or text files in an HTML, XML, or delimited text file format.

Import Spreadsheet Wizard A wizard that guides you through the steps of importing a spreadsheet into an Access database.

Index (Access) A field property that keeps track of the order of the values in the indexed field as data is being entered and edited. Therefore, if you often sort on a field, the Index property should be set to Yes as this theoretically speeds up the presentation of the sorted data later (because the index has already been created).

Index (Word) Text, usually appearing at the end of a document, that lists terms and topics in a document that you have marked for inclusion in the index, along with the pages on which they appear.

Inner join A type of relationship in which a query displays only records where joined fields from both tables are equal. This means that if a parent table has any records for which there are no matching records in the child table, those records do not appear in the resulting datasheet.

Input cells Spreadsheet cells that contain data instead of formulas and that act as input to a what-if analysis; input values often change to produce different results. Examples include interest rates, prices, or other data.

Input values In a data table, the variable values that are substituted in the table's formula to obtain varying results, such as interest rates.

Integration A process in which data is exchanged among Excel and other Windows programs; can include pasting, importing, exporting, embedding, and linking.

IntelliSense technology In VBA, visual aids that appear as you write a VBA statement to help you complete it.

Keyword Terms added to a workbook's Document Properties that help locate the file in a search. (Macros) In a macro procedure, a word that is recognized as part of the Visual Basic programming language.

.accdb The file extension for a temporary file that keeps track of record-locking information when a .accdb database is open. It helps coordinate the multiuser capabilities of an Access database so that several people can read and update the same database at the same time.

.ldb The file extension for a temporary file that keeps track of record-locking information when a .mdb database is open. It helps coordinate the multiuser capabilities of an Access database so that several people can read and update the same database at the same time.

Label (form) A word or phrase such as "Date" or "Location" that tells you the kind of information required for a given area in a form.

Layout The general arrangement in which a form displays the fields in the underlying recordset. Layout types include Columnar, Tabular, Datasheet, Chart, and PivotTable. Columnar is most popular for a form, and Datasheet is most popular for a subform. In Access forms and reports, layout also refers to connecting controls as a set so that when you move or resize them in Layout or Design View, the action you take on one control applies to all controls in the group.

Left join A type of relationship in which a query displays all of the records in the parent table, even if the child table does not contain matching records.

Legacy Tools controls Form controls used when the form designer requires more control over the type of content entered into the form than is available with content controls. Legacy Tools controls include Text form field controls and Check Box form field controls.

Linear trendline In an Excel chart, a straight line representing an overall trend in a data series.

Link (Access) To connect an Access database to data in an external file such as another Access, dBase, or Paradox database; an Excel or other type of spreadsheet; a text file; an HTML file; or an XML file. (Excel) The dynamic referencing of data in the same or in other workbooks, so that when data in the other location is changed, the references in the current location are automatically updated. (Windows) Text or an image that you click to display another location, such as a Help topic, a Web site, or a device.

Link Spreadsheet Wizard A wizard that guides you through the steps of linking to a spreadsheet.

Linked object An object created in a source file and inserted into a destination file that maintains a connection between the two files; changes made to the data in the source file are reflected in the destination file.

Linked style A named set of format settings that are applied either to characters within a paragraph or to the entire paragraph, depending on whether the entire paragraph or specific text is selected.

List layout A SmartArt graphic used to show information that is non-sequential. Variations include Vertical Bullet List, Stacked List, Horizontal Picture List, and Trapezoid List.

List style A named set of format settings, such as indent and outline numbering, that you can apply to a list to format it all at once.

Local area network (LAN) A type of network installed to link multiple PCs together so they can share hardware and software resources.

Logic error In VBA, an error that occurs when the code runs without obvious problems, but the procedure still doesn't produce the desired result.

Lookup table A table that contains one record for each field value.

Macro A named set of instructions, written in the Visual Basic programming language, that performs tasks automatically in a specified order.

Macro Design View An Access window in which you build and modify macros.

Mail merge A way to export Microsoft Office Access data by merging it to a Word document as the data source for a mail merge process, in which data from an Access table or query is combined into a Word form letter, label, or envelope to create mass mailing documents.

Mail Merge task pane A tool in Microsoft Office Word that steps you through creating a mail merge.

Main document In a mail merge, the document used to determine how the letter and Access data are combined. This is the standard text that will be consistent for each letter created in the mail merge process.

Main procedure A macro procedure containing several macros that run sequentially.

Make table query A query that creates a new table of data based on the recordset defined by the query. The make table query works like an export feature in that it creates a copy of the selected data and pastes it into a new table in a database specified by the query.

Manage Styles dialog box A dialog box used to change options for working with styles (for example, rename and delete styles) and to copy styles between documents.

Manual calculation An option that turns off automatic calculation of worksheet formulas, allowing you to selectively determine if and when you want Excel to perform calculations.

Map An XML schema that is attached to a workbook.

Map an XML element A process in which XML element names are placed on an Excel worksheet in specific locations.

Matrix layout A SmartArt graphic used to show the relationship of components to a whole in quadrants. The three variations include Basic Matrix, Titled Matrix, and Grid Matrix.

Megabyte (MB or M) One million bytes (or one thousand kilobytes).

Merge field A code in the main document of a mail merge that is replaced with the values in the field that the code represents when the mail merge is processed.

MessageBox A macro action that displays an informational message to the user.

Method An action that an object can perform. Procedures are often written to invoke methods in response to user actions.

Microsoft Excel The spreadsheet program in the Microsoft Office suite.

Microsoft Outlook The e-mail program in Microsoft Office, a fast electronic method to share information.

Microsoft SharePoint server A server computer that runs Microsoft SharePoint, software that allows an organization to host Web pages on an intranet.

Microsoft Word The word-processing program in the Microsoft Office suite.

Microsoft Word Mail Merge Wizard A wizard that guides you through the steps of preparing to merge Access data with a Word document.

Min Max Buttons A form property that determines whether Minimize and Maximize buttons are displayed in a form.

Mode In dialog boxes, a state that offers a limited set of possible choices.

Model A worksheet used to produce a what-if analysis that acts as the basis for multiple outcomes.

Modeless Describes dialog boxes that, when opened, allow you to select other elements on a chart or worksheet to change the dialog box options and format, or otherwise alter the selected elements.

Module In Visual Basic, a module is stored in a workbook and contains macro procedures.

Mouse pointer A small arrow or other symbol on the screen that you move by manipulating the pointing device; also called a pointer.

Multicolumn report A report that repeats the same information in more than one column across the page.

Multifield primary key A primary key that is composed of two or more fields. For example, an OrderID value can be listed multiple times in the Order Details table, and a ProductID value can be listed multiple times in the Order Details table. But the combination of a particular OrderID value plus a ProductID value should be unique for each record.

Navigation Buttons A form property that determines whether a navigation bar is displayed in a form. Navigation buttons are also buttons in the lower-left corner of a datasheet or form that allow you to quickly navigate between the records in the underlying object as well as add a new record.

Navigation form A special Access form that provides an easy-to-use database interface that is also Web compatible.

Navigation pane A pane showing the headings and subheadings as entries that you can click to move directly to a specific heading anywhere in a document. The Navigation pane opens along the left side of the document window.

Navigation system style In a navigation form, a style that determines how the navigation buttons will be displayed on the form.

Normal style The paragraph style that is used by default to format text typed in a blank Word document.

Normal template The template that is loaded automatically when a new document is created in Word.

Normalize To structure data for a relational database.

Northwind.mdb A fully developed database example in the Access 2000 file format that illustrates many advanced database techniques you can apply to your own development needs.

Note reference mark A mark (such as a letter or a number) that appears next to text to indicate that additional information is offered in a footnote or endnote.

Now() An Access function that displays today's date.

Null A field value that means that a value has not been entered for the field.

Object (Access) A table, query, form, report, macro, or module in a database. In VBA, any item that can be identified or manipulated, including the traditional Access objects (table, query, form, report, macro, module) as well as other items that have properties such as controls, sections, and existing procedures.

Object (Excel) A chart or graphic image not located in a specific cell; contains resizing handles when selected and can be moved to any location. In object linking and embedding (OLE), the text, spreadsheet data, tables, or video and sound clips to be exchanged between another document or program.

Object Linking and Embedding (OLE) A Microsoft Windows technology that allows you to transfer data from one document and program to another using embedding or linking.

Object list In a VBA class module, lists the objects associated with the current form or report.

Objective See Target cell.

ODBC See Open database connectivity.

Office Web App Versions of the Microsoft Office applications with limited functionality that are available online from Windows Live SkyDrive. Users can view documents online and then edit them in the browser using a selection of functions. Office Web Apps are available for Word, PowerPoint, Excel, and One Note.

OLE See Object Linking and Embedding.

On Click An event that occurs when an item is clicked.

On Current An event that occurs when focus moves from one record to another.

On Dbl Click An Access event that is triggered by a double-click.

On Error GoTo Upon an error in the execution of a procedure, the On Error GoTo statement specifies the location (the statement) where the procedure should continue.

On Got Focus An Access event that is triggered when a specified control gets the focus.

One-input data table A range of cells that shows resulting values when one input value in a formula is changed.

One-to-one relationship A relationship in which the primary key field of the first table is related to the primary key field of a second table. In other words, one record in the first table can be related to one and only one record in the second table.

Online template A database template available to download from the Microsoft Office Online Web site.

Open database connectivity (ODBC) A collection of standards that govern how Access connects to other sources of data.

Open Type Feature A font design element such as ligatures, number spacing options, number form options, and stylistic sets, that can be applied to fonts that use Open Type Features. Not all fonts use Open Type Features.

OpenReport A macro action that opens a specified report.

Option Compare Database A VBA declaration statement that determines the way string values (text) will be sorted.

Option Explicit A VBA declaration statement that specifies that you must explicitly declare all variables used in all procedures; if you attempt to use an undeclared variable name, an error occurs at compile time.

Outline symbols In outline view, the buttons that, when clicked, change the amount of detail in the outlined worksheet.

Outlook Data Collection Wizard A wizard that guides you through the steps of collecting Access data through Outlook e-mail.

Output values In a data table, the calculated results that appear in the body of the table.

Page border A graphical line or series of small graphics that encloses one or more pages of a document.

Paragraph style A named set of paragraph and character format settings that can be applied to a paragraph to format it all at once.

Parameter query A query that displays a dialog box to prompt users for field criteria. The entry in the dialog box determines which records appear on the final datasheet, similar to criteria entered directly in the query design grid.

Parent record A record contained in the "one" table in a one-to-many relationship.

Password A special sequence of numbers and letters known only to selected users, that users can create to control who can access the files in their user account area; helps keep users' computer information secure.

PDF (Portable Document Format) A file format used so a document is accessible to people who do not have Word installed on their computers. Also used for documents that can be posted directly to a Web site.

Performance Analyzer An Access tool that studies the structure and size of your database and makes a variety of recommendations on how you can improve its performance.

Personal macro workbook A workbook that can contain macros that are available to any open workbook. By default, the personal macro workbook is hidden.

Picture A form and report property that determines which image is displayed in the form or report (if any).

Picture content control A content control used in forms that provides a placeholder for a picture; you can insert a picture in a Picture content control in a form.

Picture layout A SmartArt graphic used to convey or emphasize content by using pictures. Variations include Picture Accent list, Continuous Picture list, and Vertical Picture list.

PivotChart report An Excel feature that lets you summarize worksheet data in the form of a chart in which you can rearrange, or "pivot," parts of the chart structure to explore new data relationships.

PivotTable Interactive table format that lets you summarize worksheet data.

PivotTable Field List A window containing fields that can be used to create or modify a PivotTable.

PivotTable Report An Excel feature that allows you to summarize worksheet data in the form of a table in which you can rearrange, or "pivot," parts of the table structure to explore new data relationships; also called a PivotTable.

Plain Text content control A form control used when you do not need formatting applied to text when users complete a form and enter text in the form control. You can also specify that a style be applied to text entered in a Plain Text content control when form users enter text in the form.

Plot The Excel process that converts numerical information into data points on a chart.

Plot area In a chart, the area inside the horizontal and vertical axes.

Point (n.) The unit of measurement for text characters and the space between paragraphs and characters; 1/72 of an inch.

Pop up form A form that stays on top of other open forms, even when another form is active.

Populate The process of importing an XML file and filling the mapped elements on the worksheet with data from the XML file. Also the process of adding data or fields to a table, PivotTable, or a worksheet.

Portrait orientation Page orientation in which the page is taller than it is wide.

Presentation graphics program A program such as Microsoft PowerPoint that you can use to create slide show presentations.

Primary key The field in a database that contains unique information for each record.

Private Sub A statement that indicates a sub procedure is accessible only to other procedures in the module where it is declared.

Procedure A series of VBA statements that performs an operation or calculates an answer. VBA has two types of procedures: functions and subs.

Procedure footer In Visual Basic, the last line of a Sub procedure.

Procedure header The first line in a Visual Basic procedure, it defines the procedure type, name, and arguments.

Procedure list In a VBA standard module, lists the procedures in the module; in a class module, lists events (such as Click or Dblclick).

Process layout A SmartArt graphic used to show a progression or sequential steps in a task. Variations include Accent Process, Basic Timeline, Chevron List, and Basic Bending Process.

Program code Macro instructions, written in the Visual Basic for Applications (VBA) programming language.

Project In the Visual Basic Editor, the equivalent of a workbook; a project contains Visual Basic modules.

Project Explorer In the Visual Basic Editor, a window that lists all open projects (or workbooks) and the worksheets and modules they contain.

Project Explorer window In the Visual Basic Editor, a window you use to switch between open projects, objects that can contain VBA code.

Properties window In the Visual Basic Editor, the window that displays a list of characteristics, or properties, associated with a module.

Property In Access, a characteristic that defines the appearance and behavior of items in the database such as objects, fields, sections, and controls. You can view the properties for an item by opening its Property Sheet. In a macro, an argument that determines what property is being modified. In Visual Basic, an attribute of an object that describes its character or behavior. In Windows, a characteristic or setting of a file, folder, or other item, such as its size or the date it was created.

Pyramid layout A SmartArt graphic used to show proportional, interconnected, or hierarchical relationships with the largest components at the bottom narrowing up or at the top narrowing down. Variations include Basic Pyramid, Inverted Pyramid, Pyramid List, and Segmented Pyramid.

Quick Style A set of format settings that can be applied to text or an object to format it quickly and easily; Quick Styles appear in galleries. *See also* Style.

Quick Style set A group of paragraph and character styles that share common fonts, colors, and formats, and are designed to be used together in a document to give it a cohesive look.

Range object In Visual Basic, an object that represents a cell or a range of cells.

Record Selectors A form property that determines whether record selectors are displayed in a form.

Recordset Type A property that determines if and how records displayed by a query are locked.

Refresh To update a PivotTable so it reflects changes to the underlying data.

Regression analysis A way of representing data with a mathematically-calculated trendline showing the overall trend represented by the data.

Relationship layout A SmartArt graphic used to compare or show relationships between two ideas. Variations include Balance, Funnel, Radial, Stacked Venn, and Target.

Report filter A feature that allows you to specify the ranges you want summarized in a PivotTable.

Reveal Formatting task pane A pane that shows in a list all the formatting applied to selected text, including Font, Paragraph, and Section formatting.

Reviewing pane Used to view comments entered into a document; appears to the left of the document window.

Rich Text content control A form control used when you want the content entered in the Rich Text content control by a user to be formatted with specific font and paragraph formats. You can also specify that a style be applied to text when form users enter text in the Rich Text content control.

Rich Text Format (RTF) A file format used to limit the file size of a document and to share the document with people who do not have Word installed on their computers. Certain formats, such as text effects, are removed when a Word document is saved in RTF file format.

Right join A type of relationship in which a query selects all records in the child table even if there are no matches in the parent table.

RTF *See* Rich Text Format.

Run To play, as a macro.

Run-time error In VBA, an error that occurs as incorrectly constructed code runs and includes attempting an illegal operation such as dividing by zero or moving focus to a control that doesn't exist. When you encounter a run-time error, VBA will stop executing your procedure at the statement in which the error occurred and highlight the line with a yellow background in the Visual Basic Editor.

Saved Exports An option provided in Microsoft Access that lets you save export steps.

Saved Imports An option provided in Microsoft Access that lets you quickly repeat the import process by saving the import steps.

Screenshot Used to take a snapshot of another active window. The snapshot image is inserted into the current document as a graphic object that you can size and position.

Scenario A set of values you use to forecast results; the Excel Scenario Manager lets you store and manage different scenarios.

Scenario summary An Excel table that compiles data from various scenarios so that you can view the scenario results next to each other for easy comparison.

Schema In an XML document, a list of the fields, called elements or attributes, and their characteristics.

Scroll Bars A form property that determines whether vertical, horizontal, or both scroll bars are displayed in a form.

Second normal form (2NF) The second degree of normalization, in which redundant data from an original table is extracted, placed in a new table, and related to the original table.

Secure digital (SD) card A small device that slips directly into a computer, and typically stores around 256 MB.

Select Case In VBA, executes one of several groups of Case statements depending on the value of an expression.

Server In client/server computing, the shared file server, mini, or mainframe computer. The server usually handles corporate-wide computing activities such as data storage and management, security, and connectivity to other networks.

SetProperty A macro action that allows you to manipulate the property value of any control on a form.

Share *See* Shared workbook.

Shared workbook An Excel workbook that several users can open and modify.

SharePoint server *See* Microsoft SharePoint server.

Shortcut In Access, a pointer to the actual database object that is identified as a shortcut by the small black arrow in the lower-left corner of the icon. You double-click a shortcut icon to open that object. In Windows, a link that gives you quick access to a particular folder, file, or Web site.

Show me an example A button that gives you more information on the subject at hand by using a common example to explain the issue.

Single step To run a macro one line (action) at a time to observe the effect of each specific action in the Macro Single Step dialog box.

Slicer A graphic object used to filter a PivotTable.

SmartArt graphic A diagram, list, organizational chart, or other graphic created using the SmartArt command and used to provide a visual representation of data. Eight layout categories of SmartArt graphics are available in Word: List, Picture, Process, Cycle, Hierarchy, Relationship, Matrix, and Pyramid.

Snapshot A query property that locks the recordset (which prevents it from being updated).

Source file The file in which data is originally created and saved.

Source program In a data exchange, the program used to create the data you are embedding or linking.

Spike A surge in power, which can cause damage to the hardware, and can render the computer useless.

Splash screen A special form used to announce information.

Standard module A type of Access module that contains global code that can be executed from anywhere in the database. Standard modules are displayed as module objects in the Navigation Pane.

Startup option One of a series of commands that execute when the database is opened.

Statement A single line of code within a VBA procedure.

Strong password A password that is difficult to guess and that helps to protect your workbooks from security threats; has at least 14 characters that are a mix of upper- and lowercase letters, numbers, and special characters.

Stub In the Visual Basic window, the first and last lines of an event handler procedure.

Style A named collection of character and paragraph formats that are stored together and can be applied to text to format it quickly. *See also* Quick Style.

Style Inspector Shows the Paragraph and Text level formatting applied to selected text; used to reset paragraph and text formatting to the default formats and to clear formatting.

Styles Gallery Location where all the styles associated with a Quick Style set are stored; you access the Style Gallery by clicking the More button in the Styles group on the Home tab.

Styles task pane Contains all the styles available to the current document and the buttons to access the Style Inspector, the Reveal Formatting task pane, and the Manage Styles dialog box.

Sub (sub procedure) A procedure that performs a series of VBA statements, but does not return a value and cannot be used in an expression like a function procedure. You use subs to manipulate controls and objects. They are generally executed when an event occurs, such as when a command button is clicked or a form is opened.

Subentry Text included under a main entry in an index.

Submacro A collection of actions within a macro object that allows you to name and create multiple, separate macros within a single macro object.

Subquery A query based on another query's field list.

Summary function In a PivotTable, a function that determines the type of calculation applied to the PivotTable data, such as SUM or COUNT.

Surge protector A power strip with surge protection.

Switchboard A special Access form that uses command buttons to provide an easy-to-use and secure database interface.

Switchboard Items A table that contains information the Switchboard form needs.

Switchboard Manager An Access tool that help you create and modify switchboards.

Syntax In the Visual Basic programming language, the formatting rules that must be followed so that the macro will run correctly.

Syntax error In VBA, an error that occurs immediately as you are writing a VBA statement that cannot be read by the Visual Basic Editor.

Table Analyzer Wizard An Access tool that looks for duplicate information in one table that should be separated and stored in its own table.

Table style A named set of table format settings that can be applied to a table to format it all at once. The Table style includes settings for both the table grid and the table text.

Table of Figures A list of all the figures used in a document.

Table template A tool you can use to quickly create a single table within an existing database by providing a set of fields that describe a particular subject, such as contacts or tasks, which can be used or modified to meet your needs.

Target cell In what-if analysis (specifically, in Excel Solver), the cell containing the formula; also called objective.

Target table The table to which an append query adds records.

Template (Excel) A predesigned, formatted file that serves as the basis for a new workbook; Excel template files have the file extension .xltx. (Word) A formatted document that contains placeholder text you can replace with new text. A file that contains the basic structure of a document including headers and footers, styles, and graphic elements.

Text effect Formatting that applies a visual effect to text, such as a shadow, glow, outline, or reflection.

Text file *See* ASCII file.

Text Form Field control A Legacy Tool used when the form developer requires more control over how the content control is configured than is possible when using a Rich Text content control or a Plain Text content control. A Text Form Field control is inserted using the Legacy Tools command in the Controls group on the Developer tab.

Third normal form (3NF) The third degree of normalization, in which calculated fields (also called derived fields) such as totals or taxes are removed. Strive to create databases that adhere to the rules of third normal form.

Thumbnail Smaller version of a page that appears in the Navigation pane when you select the Browse pages in your document tab on the Navigation pane.

Toggle A button with two settings, on and off.

Top Values A feature in Query Design View that lets you specify a number or percentage of sorted records that you want to display in the query's datasheet.

Tracer arrows In Excel worksheet auditing, arrows that point from cells that might have caused an error to the active cell containing an error.

Track To identify and keep a record of who makes which changes to a workbook.

Trendline A series of data points on a line that shows data values that represent the general direction of the data.

Trusted database A database that allows you to run macros and VBA.

Trusted folder A folder specified as a trusted location for storing files.

Two-input data table A range of cells that shows resulting values when two input values in a formula are changed.

Unassigned Objects A group for Navigation Pane objects that have not been assigned to a custom group.

Update query A type of action query that updates the values in a field.

Update To row When creating an Update query, a row that appears in the query design grid to specify criteria or an expression for updating records.

UPS (Uninterruptible Power Supply) A device that provides constant power to other devices, including computers.

USB (Universal Serial Bus) drive A device that plugs into a computer's USB port to store data. USB drives are also called thumb drives, flash drives, and travel drives. USB devices typically store 1 GB to 10 GB of information.

User template Any template created by the user.

Utility project A VBA project containing code that helps Access with certain activities such as presenting the Zoom dialog box. It automatically appears in the Project Explorer window when you use the Access features that use this code.

Validate A process in which an XML schema makes sure the XML data follows the rules outlined in the schema.

Validation *See* Data Validation.

Value In a macro, an argument determines the value of a property or field.

Value axis In a chart, the axis that contains numerical values; in a 2-dimensional chart, also known as the y-axis.

Variable In the Visual Basic programming language, an area in memory in which you can temporarily store an item of information; variables are often declared in Dim statements such as *DimNameAsString*. In an Excel scenario or what-if analysis, a changing input value, such as price or interest rate, that affects a calculated result.

VBA *See* Visual Basic for Applications.

VBE *See* Visual Basic Editor.

Virus Destructive software that can damage your computer files.

Visual Basic Editor (VBE) Comprises the entire Microsoft Visual Basic program window that contains smaller windows, including the Code window and Project Explorer window.

Visual Basic for Applications (VBA) A programming language provided with each program of the Microsoft Office suite to help you extend the program's capabilities. In Access, VBA is stored within modules.

Watermark A picture or other type of graphics object that appears lightly shaded behind text in a document.

Web compatible An object that can be opened and used with Internet Explorer when the database is published to a SharePoint server.

Web query An Excel feature that lets you obtain data from a Web, Internet, or intranet site and places it in an Excel workbook for analysis.

What-if analysis A decision-making tool in which data is changed and formulas are recalculated in order to predict various possible outcomes.

Width property A form property that determines the width of a form.

Windows Live A collection of services and Web applications that people can access through a login. Windows Live services include access to e-mail and instant messaging, storage of files on SkyDrive, sharing and storage of photos, networking with people, downloading software, and interfacing with a mobile device.

Word wrap A feature in word processing programs that determines when a line of text extends into the right margin of the page and automatically forces the text to the next line without you needing to press Enter.

WordArt Specially formatted text, created using the WordArt button on the Drawing toolbar.

Workgroup Template A template created for distribution to others.

Works cited A list of sources that you cited while creating a document.

Wrap point A point on a drawn object that you can click and drag to alter the shape of the object.

XE (Index Entry) Field code inserted next to text marked for inclusion in an index.

XML Acronym that stands for eXtensible Markup Language, which is a language used to structure, store, and send information.

XML file A text file containing XML tags that identify field names and data. *See also* Extensible Markup Language (XML)

Zero-length string A deliberate entry that contains no characters. You enter a zero-length string by typing two quotation marks ("") with no space between them.

Index